HOW TO PAY ZERO TAXES

SEVENTEENTH EDITION

Jeff A. Schnepper

McGraw-Hill

New York San Francisco Washington, D.C. Auckland Bogotá Caracas Lisbon London Madrid Mexico City Milan Montreal New Delhi San Juan Singapore Sydney Tokyo Toronto

McGraw-Hill

A Division of The ***McGraw-Hill*** *Companies*

1 2 3 4 5 6 7 8 9 0 DOC/DOC 9 0 9 8 7 6 5 4 3 2 1 0 9

ISBN 0-07-135246-5

The editing supervisor for this book was Fred Dahl and the production supervisor was Tina Cameron. This book was set in Baskerville by Inkwell Publishing Services.

Printed and bound by R.R. Donnelly & Sons Company.

This book is printed on recycled, acid-free paper containing a minimum of 50% recycled, de-inked fiber.

This book is dedicated to my mogul, Barbara, who taught me how to love, and to my children, Brandy, Joshua, and Allison, who gave me three more reasons why.

If I had the choice of doing it all over again, I would begin by loving you again.

Contents

Preface

"Our income tax system is overly complex. It distorts investment decisions and encourages people to put money into schemes to reduce their tax bills instead of into enterprises to create jobs and help our economy grow."

BILL BRADLEY, New Jersey senator (1984)

Question: Who said, "The hardest thing in the world to understand is the income tax"?

Answer: Albert Einstein, who also said, when confronted with a Form 1040 Personal Income Tax Return, "I am a mathematician, not a philosopher."

"The words of such an act as the Income Tax... merely dance before my eyes in a meaningless procession: cross-reference, exception upon exception—couched in abstract terms that offer no handle to seize hold of—leave in my mind only a confused sense of some vitally important, but successfully concealed, purport, which it is my duty to extract, but which is within my power, if at all, only after the most inordinate expenditure of time. I know that these monsters are the result of fabulous industry and ingenuity, plugging up this hole and casting out the net, against all possible evasion; yet at times I cannot help recalling a saying of William James about certain passages of Hegel: that they were, no doubt,

written with a passion of rationality; but that one cannot help wondering whether to the reader they have any significance save that the words are strung together with syntactical correctness…"

Judge Learned Hand, The Thomas Walter Swan, 57 Yale L.J. 167, 169 [1947].

According to the IRS, if you itemized your deductions and had some investment income, it took you more than 22 hours to do last year's tax return. That's three hours longer than the year before.

Our tax code now stands at more than 1.5 million words (before any 1999 changes) and climbing thanks to 1,260 changes enacted by congress and signed by the President in 1997 and 1998 alone. IRS Commissioner Rossotti said in April, 1999, that in the last 12 years, there have been about 9,500 tax code changes.

For last year's filing season, the IRS had to develop 11 new forms and revise 177 others. So much for tax simplification … .

The Republican Congress published its Christmas wish list even though President Clinton told them Santa wasn't coming this year. Possibly, he was in New York trying to establish residency for a Senate run. In any case … .

Here we go again! Fortunately, the 1999 changes were small in comparison to the year before. 1999 marks the 33rd of the last 36 years in which we have had tax law changes. 1998 was a great year for taxes. We got an IRS that finally confessed to lying about the lack of all of those revenue quotas and a Chairman of The House Ways and Means Committee who, after threatening to overload the tax code with minutia in an attempt to sink it of its own weight, finally saw the light and suggested that his "reforms" of the past year may have been a bit complicated. The Tax Reconciliation Act of 1997 proved the adage that the only difference between death and taxes is that death doesn't become more complicated every time Congress meets. In 1986, we had been presented with what Congress called "tax simplification." Our rates were to be flattened, our taxes reduced, and our computations simplified. Congress has spent the last decade reversing that process.

House Republicans, having failed to get a majority to pull the income tax out by its roots, have joined their Democratic colleagues in loading up its branches in the hopes that it would fall of its own weight. The 1998 Reform Act had something for everyone, and this 2000 edition of *How to Pay Zero Taxes* will detail these new tax law changes in Chapter 14, "The Internal Revenue Service Restructuring and Reform Act of 1998." It will also continue to explain the changes made in 1999, the hidden secrets of our tax code, and how you can take advantage of them to keep more of your hard-earned dollars.

According to the Tax Foundation, the United States passed a depressing milestone back in fiscal 1995. Total tax collections exceeded $2 trillion for the first time. That's a two and 12 zeros.

It is April 15, 2000 and the IRS is after your money again. To protect your hard-earned dollars, first turn to the new 2000 edition of *How to Pay Zero Taxes.*

Tax Freedom Day, Selected Years, 1930–1998

Year	Tax Freedom Day
1930	February 13
1940	March 8
1950	April 3
1960	April 17
1970	April 28
1975	April 28
1980	May 1
1981	May 4
1982	May 3
1983	April 30
1984	April 28
1985	May 1
1986	May 1
1987	May 4
1988[a]	May 3
1989	May 4
1990	May 3
1991	May 3
1992	May 3
1993	May 3
1994	May 5
1995	May 6
1996	May 7
1997	May 9
1998	May 10
1999	May 11

It contains all of the new laws, rules, regulations, and court cases to legally minimize your tax outlay. Remember, your objective should be to pay all of the taxes that are due, but not one penny more than the law requires. The law, however, is complicated, convoluted, and constantly changing. The new edition of *How to Pay Zero Taxes* is your guide through the minefield of these changes.

Over a decade ago, on October 22, 1986, former President Reagan signed a sweeping revision of the tax code that touched the lives of all American taxpayers. The text of the Tax Reform Act of 1986 bulks ten inches and weighs more than thirty-three pounds; it details changes in 2,704,000 subsections of the tax code, which cost the Internal Revenue Service an estimated $106,485,000 in fiscal year 1988 to implement. The act dramatically cut tax rates and pays for this decline by eliminating or reducing a vast array of tax breaks. The American tax structure for 1999 is vastly different from that in the past, and will be different again in 2000. Moreover, the fiscal 1988 budget, signed into law on December 22, 1987, included the Revenue Act of 1987, which effected a two-year $23 billion tax hike—a fact unknown to most Americans. This act was followed, in 1988, by additional tax changes contained in the Medicare Catastrophic Loss Protection Act, the Family Support Act, and the Technical and Miscellaneous Revenue Act of 1988 (TAMRA). Tax law changes followed in each year, including 1998's Reconciliation Act which contained 117,972 words itself! The laws and regulations that make up the income tax code increased from 744,000 words in 1955 to 5.6 million words by 1994. (That's when I gave up counting and tried to get a life.) The new laws discussed above and passed in 1998 add to the complexity. The applicable provisions of these acts, 1999 changes, and their impact on your taxes will be covered in this 2000 edition of *How to Pay Zero Taxes.*

It has been claimed that the only difference between death and taxes is that death, on occasion, is allegedly painless. That claim is not completely accurate. Remember, death doesn't get worse every time Congress meets. If the average middle-income taxpayer's 1999 salary, starting from January 1, went to pay taxes, it would have taken until May 11 to meet all the federal, state, and local payments due. By comparison, this "Tax Freedom Day" in 1940 was March 8; and in 1930, it was February 13. It will take 129 days or two hours and fifty-one minutes of each eight hours' earnings by the average middle-income taxpayer to produce one person's share of the 1999 tax bill.[1]

Let's put that in perspective. On average, Americans now spend more time working to pay their taxes than they spend working to provide for food, clothing, and shelter combined!

The federal tax burden has risen a staggering 45% since 1992—rising to $6,690 per person from $4,625. Add in state and local taxes and the total U.S. tax burden in 1998 was $9,881 per person.

According to the Tax Foundation, tax compliance costs are an estimated $250 billion each year. With almost 600 different tax forms to deal with, Americans spend some 5.4 billion hours filling out IRS paperwork.

The combination of taxes and inflation has been likened to a plague of locusts on a field of wheat. Yet there are several individuals earning millions

1. In 1930 it was 57 seconds!

of dollars who pay little or no taxes and many more who earn hundreds of thousands of dollars each year whose tax bill is just as small. In 1982, there were 117 individuals who earned over $1 million and owed the IRS nothing. In 1983, 29,800 taxpayers with incomes of more than $250,000 paid less than 5 percent in income taxes, including 3,170 people who earned more than $1 million. In 1986, 612 couples and individuals with incomes exceeding $200,000 paid zero taxes on their 1985 incomes. For returns filed in 1992 for 1991, 1,131 showed zero U.S. tax owed! For returns filed in 1993 for 1992, 1,799 showed zero U.S. tax owed, for returns filed in 1994 for 1993, 1,950 paid no tax, and for returns filed in 1995 for 1994 1,137 paid no tax! For 1995 and 1996 tax years, filed in 1996 and 1997, 998 and 1,044 returns with incomes over $200,000 paid zero taxes. These people are able to avoid paying taxes by the use of sophisticated tax strategies devised by high-priced and very professional tax planners, who guide their clients along the cracks in the federal tax code.

Many of those cracks have been put there intentionally by Congress as economic and social incentives. For example, to encourage capital spending and to support the U.S. auto industry, a combination of provisions in the tax code allows a knowledgeable average taxpayer to buy a $6,000 car at a net cash cost of only $2,478 (see page 232). If that car is run only 60,000 miles in its first three years, the net cash outlay for the car can be reduced to less than *zero!* In effect, the taxpayer gets a free car; more important, his costless acquisition is completely legal. Exactly how to do this will be explained later in the book.

As the examples indicate, what Congress has created is a financial mechanism whereby certain actions substitute for tax payments. Rather than taking the taxpayers' money in taxes and then paying it out in direct support for certain activities, Congress has indirectly accomplished the same goal by granting taxpayers some credits and deductions if they make expenditures in certain defined areas. *How to Pay Zero Taxes* will expose these areas and detail how you, a now enlightened reader, can structure your transactions to benefit optimally from these completely legal strategies and techniques.

You first will learn how our tax system works and how the structure of the system provides opportunities to save money on your income tax. The crucial difference between tax deductions and tax credits will be explained, and the internal IRS chart detailing the average amount deducted for each tax bracket for each category of itemized deductions will be revealed.

You then will be transported into the nether world of tax shelters and shown what to look for and what to avoid. The section on tax shelter strategies

2. Gregory v. Helvering, 35-1, USTC Par. 9043, 293 U.S. 463, 469 (1935).

is followed by the fun part of the book—how to take tax deductions for your personal expenses and hobbies. Here you will be shown how to turn your normal living expenses into tax deductions. We all must pay housing and food costs, but *How to Pay Zero Taxes* will show you how to structure these costs to reduce your taxes. We all enjoy vacations—*How to Pay Zero Taxes* will show you how the federal government could pay part of their costs. If you have a hobby—stamp collecting, auto racing, etc.—*How to Pay Zero Taxes* will demonstrate how you can get the Internal Revenue Service to help finance it by converting it into a legitimate business.

Finally, *How to Pay Zero Taxes* will detail and explain those more sophisticated legal 1999 and 2000 tax techniques and instruments that have been developed for shifting income, deferring taxes, and avoiding payment completely. These techniques all have been court tested and approved. Most important, *How to Pay Zero Taxes* will not simply explain and document these tax savings strategies but will show you examples, provide you with guidelines and tax cases to support your deductions, and take you step by step through the creation of these money-saving instruments for your own use. Its objective is not merely to reveal and educate but to demonstrate and guide as well.

Taxpayers who can afford expensive professional tax planning don't pay high taxes. The goal of *How to Pay Zero Taxes* is to provide that planning and those techniques to middle-income taxpayers who are unknowingly overpaying. Supreme Court Justice Sutherland once remarked, "The legal right of a taxpayer to decrease his taxes or to altogether avoid them by means which the law permits cannot be doubted."[2] *How to Pay Zero Taxes* is dedicated to that ideal.

ACKNOWLEDGMENTS

I wish to thank Nancie Crook, Barbara Thomassian, Pat Berenson, Pat Forcey, Ronnie Smith, and Anne McVay, without whom this book could not have been written, and the U.S. Congress and the IRS, without whom it need not have been written.

I also want to thank Sayes B. Block and Paul Malagoli for their encouragement and professional guidance; Sandi Walker, April Napolitano, Anne Rigney, Susan Barry, and Philip Ruppel for their typing and editorial assistance; and Sri Haran, CPA, Robert Doyle, Steve Leimberg, Jeff Kelvin, Joel Petchon, John McFadden, Kenn Tacchino, Bill Rotella, George Hasenberg, Frank Kesselman, John Oxley, Stephen D. Leightman, Al Blum, and Ron Campbell for their professional assistance; and Simba T.C. Schnepper and Fred T.C. Schnepper, who give me reason to paws.

Dedicated to the Memory of
Frisco T.D. Schnepper

CHAPTER 1

Is It Legal?

"Taxation must not take from individuals what rightfully belongs to individuals."

HENRY GEORGE

"The purpose of the IRS is to collect the proper amount of tax revenue at the least cost to the public, and in a manner that warrants the highest degree of public confidence in our integrity, efficiency, and fairness. To achieve that purpose, we will: Encourage and achieve the highest degree of voluntary compliance in accordance with the tax laws and regulations; Advise the public of their rights and responsibilities; Determine the extent of compliance and the causes of noncompliance; Do all things needed for the proper administration and enforcement of the tax laws; Continually search and implement new, more efficient and effective ways of accomplishing our Mission" (IRS statement of organization and functions, 39 Fed. Reg. 11,572, 1974).

It has been said that "the Internal Revenue Code is a remarkable essay in sustained obscurity … a conspiracy and restraint of understanding" (*All State Fire Insurance Company* [Ct. Cl.], 80-1 USTC-, 45 AFTR 2d, 80-1096).

When the modern income tax law was introduced in 1913, only one American in 271 was affected; the taxable incomes of the great majority did not exceed the exempt amount of $3,000 for individuals, $4,000 for couples. Those who were affected paid at the rate of 1 percent on taxable income up to $20,000 and, at most, 6 percent on income over that amount. The average tax rate for the 437,036 individual tax returns filed in 1916 was 2.75%. In 1999, over 228 million returns were filed and the IRS processed over two billion pieces of paper—which, if placed side by side, would stretch over 200 miles.

You pay too much in taxes, and it costs too much for you to do your tax returns. Here are a few "for instances."

- Let's talk about complexity. *Before* the 1998 and 1999 tax changes, the Internal Revenue Code was 9,471 pages long and contained 1.3 million words. The epic book *War and Peace*, has 1,444 pages and half as many words—660,000. The tax regulations *then* took up 91,824 pages and consisted of 5.75 million words while the Bible contains 1,291 pages and 774,746 words.

- The tax foundation has projected 1998 tax collections to be $2.7 trillion, a 5.7% increase over 1997 and a 58.4% increase over the 1990 level.

According to Daniel J. Mitchell of the Heritage Foundation:

- The IRS and the government spent $13,700,000,000 to enforce and oversee the tax code.

- There were 31 pages of fine print instructions for filling out the "easy" 1040 EZ tax form.

- The paperwork received by the IRS would circle the globe 36 times.

- The IRS sends out 10,000,000 correction notices each year. 5,000,000 of them are wrong!

- The IRS has lost 6,400 computer tapes and cartridges.

- 6,400,000 taxpayers had to visit IRS customer service centers to get answers to their tax questions in 1996. Another 99,000,000 called the IRS hotline.

- In 1997, 56% of calls to the IRS were unanswered.

- 6,000,000 calls were unanswered in January–February 1998 alone!

IRS Estimates of Time Required to Complete 1998 Tax Forms

The time needed to complete and file Form 1040 and its schedules will vary depending on individual circumstances. The estimated average times are:

Form	Recordkeeping	Learning about the Law or the Form	Preparing the Form	Copying, Assembling, and Sending the Form to the IRS	Totals
Form 1040	3 hr., 34 min.	2 hr., 25 min.	4 hr., 55 min.	40 min.	11 hr., 34 min.
Sch. A	2 hr., 32 min.	26 min.	1 hr., 10 min.	20 min.	4 hr., 28 min.
Sch. B	33 min.	8 min.	11 min.	20 min.	1 hr., 12 min.
Sch. C	6 hr., 26 min.	1 hr., 11 min.	2 hr., 6 min.	35 min.	10 hr., 18 min.
Sch. C-EZ	46 min.	4 min.	34 min.	20 min.	1 hr., 44 min.
Sch. D	1 hr., 11 min.	2 hr., 18 min.	2 hr., 37 min.	35 min.	6 hr., 41 min.
Sch. D-1	13 min.	1 min.	11 min.	35 min.	1 hr.
Sch. E	2 hr., 52 min.	1 hr., 7 min.	1 hr., 16 min.	35 min.	5 hr., 50 min.
Sch. EIC	—	2 min.	5 min.	20 min.	27 min.
Sch. F:					
Cash Method	4 hr., 2 min.	36 min.	1 hr., 14 min.	20 min.	6 hr., 12 min.
Accrual Method	4 hr., 22 min.	25 min.	1 hr., 19 min.	20 min.	6 hr., 26 min.
Sch. H	46 min.	30 min.	48 min.	35 min.	2 hr., 39 min.
Sch. J	20 min.	8 min.	1 hr., 8 min.	20 min.	1 hr., 56 min.
Sch. R	20 min.	15 min.	20 min.	35 min.	1 hr., 30 min.
Sch. SE:					
Short	20 min.	13 min.	11 min.	14 min.	58 min.
Long	26 min.	22 min.	34 min.	20 min.	1 hr., 42 min.

- In 1998, *Money* magazine asked 46 different tax *experts* to compute a family's 1997 tax liability. All 46 got it wrong! (I was not asked.)
- Between 1981 and 1997, 11,410 tax code subsections were changed.
- The average federal tax bill for individuals for fiscal year 1996 was projected to rise to $5,225, an increase of 4.4 percent over the fiscal 1995 level of $5,006, according to a report released by the Tax Foundation August 7, 1996.
- The Tax Foundation estimates that in 1994 businesses spent more than 3.6 billion hours, and individuals spent more than 1.8 billion hours, in preparing tax returns. That equates to approximately three million people working full time 12 months a year just to comply with the tax laws! The total annual cost of tax compliance is $192 billion—an amount equivalent to General Motors' entire output for 1994.
- Total tax burdens for U.S. families in 1996 was expected to range from 32 percent of income to 45 percent, according to a recent Tax Foundation analysis. Conducted by economist Arthur P. Hall, the study compared the tax burdens of four hypothetical families at different income levels (each family has two children).

  The study concluded that:

  - A family earning $25,000 annually would pay 32 percent of its income in taxes;
  - A family making $50,000 per year would owe 36.6 percent to federal, state, and local governments;
  - A family earning $100,000 each year would pay 41.5 percent of that income in taxes; and
  - A family making $200,000 would owe taxes of 44.5 percent.
  - In 1948, the average American family with children paid 3 percent of its income to the federal government in income and payroll taxes.
- According to the Tax Foundation, U.S. families spent more on taxes than they did on food, clothing, and shelter combined.
- Complying with the federal tax system costs Americans over $200 billion a year.

- According to University of Michigan economist Joel B. Slemrod, it took a household an average of 21 hours, 42 minutes, to do federal and state tax returns, at an average cost of $231 in personal time plus $44 in fees for professional aid. Contrast that with the IRS estimate of an average of 9 hours, 54 minutes, to complete a basic Form 1040 in the same year. Then try to recall how long it took you to complete last year's return.

- Even using the minimal IRS computations, assuming 2,040 hours in a work year and a total burden for all taxpayers of 5.3 billion hours (based on a 1994 IRS study), filling out IRS forms would occupy 2.6 million Americans on a full-time basis.

Time is money, and these dollars come out of your pocket and drain your ability to save and invest, while inflation compounds your financial concerns by draining your ability just to keep even.

Even if your earnings can keep even with inflation, you still lose. For example, assume you have a taxable income for 1999 of $62,450 and pay $14,139 in taxes. You have $48, 311 left to spend. With both inflation and a raise of 8 percent, you will now earn $ 67,446 and pay $15,688 in taxes, leaving you $51,758 to spend. But due to inflation, this $51,758 is worth only $47,924. In real dollars, the progressive nature of your tax structure and the purchasing power decay caused by inflation have together decreased your real buying power by $48, 311 minus $47,924 = $387 on a $4,496 increase in earnings! The impact of state and social security taxes further magnifies your financial dilemma.

In order to stay even with inflation, you needed to double your income between 1969 and 1979. But after paying the higher taxes expected from the considerably higher bracket that doubled income would place you in, you ended up way behind. A study by a major accounting firm found that between 1972 and 1979, executives whose compensation rose by as much as 104 percent suffered zero after-tax increases in income.

According to the Tax Foundation, the average family—one earner, employed full time, married, with two dependent children—had $2,010 less purchasing power in 1987 than 10 years before. Measured in constant 1987 dollars, that family's real income after direct federal taxes had gone up $1,242, or 5.6 percent, since 1981. But during the previous four years, the family's purchasing power actually declined by $3,252 in 1987 dollars.

In a 1995 report, the Tax Foundation found that the typical American family's income, after taxes and inflation, lags behind the level attained five years ago. A 1996 report stated that the tax burden of a two-income family, in inflation adjusted dollars, was "the highest ever."

The 1995 report points out that the average two-income family earned $53,354 in 1994 but was left with only $34,728 to spend on food, housing, and other items after taxes were paid. Of course, even though the two-income family's earnings have risen from $36,879 in 1980, much of that difference has been eroded because of taxes and inflation.

Actually, according to the Foundation, in a 1994 report, a 93% rise in pretax income to 1994 had almost been matched by a 90% rise in total taxes plus a 73% rise in the general price level.

"The after-inflation, after-tax income of the typical family has risen only 15% since 1980 with no increase during the last five years."

Moreover, between 1984 and 1994, the average American's total tax bill rose faster than almost all other personal expenditures, according to a Tax Foundation analysis.

Per capita federal, state, and local taxes rose to $7,927 in 1994 from $6,586 in 1984, a 20 percent increase, the foundation said. All figures and percentage changes were expressed in constant 1994 dollars.

By comparison, spending on housing rose 16 percent; on appliances, 14 percent; on furniture, 9 percent; on automobiles, 3 percent; and on food, 1 percent, the foundation said. Expenditures on utilities declined by 4 percent. Only recreation spending outpaced taxes, rising 35 percent.

U.S. workers spend almost half the calendar year working for the government, according to the Americans for Tax Reform Foundation. The organization has designated June 25 its annual "Cost of Government Day for 1998."

According to Americans for Tax Reform, on June 25 the average American worker will have earned enough in gross income to pay off all of his or her direct and hidden taxes.

What can you do? One simple answer is to try to reduce your taxes, and the rest of this book will tell you how to do so. Some of the techniques found in this book are the result of mixing complicated and convoluted tax code sections, but all of them are completely legal. Some are legal not because Congress intended them to be there but because both Congress and the Internal Revenue Service were lax in their homework and the tax code language allowing them is there. While Congress writes the tax law, that law is read and interpreted by the courts. Quite often the Internal Revenue Service and the courts differ in their interpretations of various code sections and their applications—the courts *always* win. Even if a tax effect is contrary to original congressional intent, the courts must and do support the language of the code. Such effects are the law and can be changed or eliminated only by congressional action. Until such action is taken, it is fully within the legal rights of the American taxpayer to use such code combinations to reduce, minimize, or even completely eliminate taxes. Each individual must pay taxes, but not one penny more than the law requires. If you want to make voluntary contributions to our federal Treasury, you have bought the wrong book.

On the other hand, most of the techniques detailed here have been intended by Congress. In many cases, legally reducing your income tax liability is both good for you and good for America. Certain kinds of receipts are intentionally excluded from gross income for tax purposes in order to achieve some economic or social objective. These provisions are frequently referred to as "tax incentives" and are specifically designed to encourage certain types of activity. Tax incentives have the same impact on the federal budget as direct expenditures because they represent revenues not collected by the federal government. These special tax provisions, therefore, have been labeled "tax expenditures" or "tax aids" by the Treasury Department.

These expenditures are revenue losses arising from provisions of the tax code that give special or selective tax relief to certain groups of taxpayers. These provisions either encourage some desired activity or provide special aid to certain taxpayers. For example, the federal government seeks to encourage certain forms of investment. Thus business investment is encouraged by the accelerated rather than straight-line depreciation. This tax advantage has been legislated so that business will have additional capital to be able to expand. Tax advantaged investment helps create new businesses and new jobs. These new jobs produce more paychecks and these additional paychecks produce more taxes. In the long run, if everything works as it should, everyone wins.

Alternatively, other tax expenditure provisions have been adopted as "relief provisions" to ease "tax hardships" or to "simplify tax computations." For example, the elderly and the blind receive special financial benefits through a deduction called the "additional amount." The other tax benefits for the aged—the retirement income credit and the potential exclusion of social security annuity payments from taxable income—also fall into this "personal or tax hardship" category.

These revenue losses are called tax "expenditures" because they are payments or expenditures by the federal government made through a reduction of taxes rather than a direct grant. Just as a forgiveness of debt is equivalent to a payment, so a remission of tax liability is equivalent to an expenditure.

According to the Congressional Budget Office, in 1980 a total of 92 provisions were considered tax expenditures. These were estimated to cost $206 billion in fiscal year 1981, based on laws in effect at the start of 1980. As of 1987, tax expenditures had grown to a list of more than 100 provisions, and were projected to reach a total of over $321 billion in the 1988 fiscal year. Tax subsidies for 1999 were forecast by the Joint Committee on Taxation in December, 1998, to exceed $491.8 billion for individuals alone!

The financial benefits offered by tax expenditure provisions resemble those available through entitlement programs on the spending side of the budget. A tax expenditure provision can provide special tax relief in any of the following ways:

- *Special exclusions, exemptions, and deductions,* which reduce taxable income and thus result in a smaller tax liability. For example, tax-exempt municipal bond interest or the exclusion from taxable income of employee discounts or dependent care assistance programs.
- *Preferential rates,* which reduce liabilities by applying lower rates to all or part of the taxpayer's income. For example, the special reduced maximum tax rate on long-term capital gain income.
- *Special credits,* which are subtracted from the tax liability rather than from the income on which the taxes are figured. For example, the earned income tax credit.
- *Deferrals of tax,* which generally result from allowing deductions that (according to standard accounting principles) are properly attributable to a future year. For example, accelerated depreciation allowances: The taxpayer, paying later rather than now, in effect receives an interest-free loan of the deferred liability.

Tax spending and direct spending are alternative methods of providing federal subsidies. Nearly any tax expenditure could be recast as a spending program, just as most spending programs could be replaced by tax expenditures. Thus, the choice between tax spending and direct spending is essentially a choice between alternative administrative mechanisms. Once it has been decided that a particular subsidy is worth providing, the question of the best method of providing that subsidy arises. In designing or evaluating any subsidy program, however, the following criteria have been applied:

- *Cost and efficiency.* How much does the program cost? How well targeted is the program—that is, does it reach those and only those it is intended to reach? Does it provide the incentive or benefit it was designed to offer? Does it achieve its goal at the least cost?

- *Fairness and equity.* Is the subsidy benefit fairly distributed?
- *Ease of administration.* How much does the program cost to administer? How quickly can the benefits be distributed? Can the benefits be distributed to those and only those for whom they are intended?
- *Budget visibility and control.* Is each program subject to periodic review by the Congress? Are its costs subject to control by the Congress?

In reality, though, many of these expenditures are the result of pressures applied by special interest groups seeking relief provisions for their own constituencies. For example, why is there an additional "standard deduction" amount for the blind and not for the deaf? The answer, I suggest, may have more to do with the political and lobbying power of the two groups than with any inherent difference between the hardships.

These special provisions also arise out of the political needs of our individual representatives in Congress. These are off-budget expenditures that show up as a reduction of revenues rather than as an increase in congressional spending. In effect they allow our representatives to increase our federal fiscal deficit, to spend more tax money, without appearing to do so. Arguments are made that these tax incentives are simple and involve far less government supervision and detail than direct expenditures. It has also been argued that these incentives encourage the private sector to participate in social programs and promote private decision making rather than government-centered decision making.

Whether these asserted virtues of tax incentives are in fact valid or whether their defects outweigh their claimed advantages is not the subject of this book. The fact that they do exist is critical. In order to minimize or to eliminate your taxes completely, you must first accept the fact that the techniques to be detailed in this book are both legal and, for the most part, specifically intended by Congress. That they have not been publicized or made widely known by the Internal Revenue Service is not surprising. Despite publicity releases and continuous claims to the contrary, the Internal Revenue Service is a revenue collector. While the professed goal is a fair administration of the tax law, the service's job is to collect your tax money. No Internal Revenue agent ever received or ever shall receive a raise or promotion by suggesting to a taxpayer how to arrange a financial situation to reduce or eliminate taxes. To discover those techniques, you either have to pay thousands of dollars to a professional tax practitioner, attorney, or accountant—or you can turn to the next chapter.

CHAPTER 2

How Our Tax System Works

"Kings ought to shear, not skin their sheep."

English poet ROBERT HERRICK shortly after the execution of Charles I, who had imposed numerous burdensome taxes on his subjects

"The greater the number of statutes, the greater the number of thieves and brigands."

LAO-TZU

Now that you understand the legal foundation for our tax sheltering and eliminating techniques, it remains necessary first to uncomplicate our federal income tax structure so that you can see where each shelter technique fits into the whole picture. You pay taxes on your taxable income. Your taxable income is your gross income less certain deductions. It is necessary, therefore, to define your "gross" income.

Gross income means *all* income, from whatever source derived, including (but not limited to) the following items:

Compensation for services, including fees, commissions, and similar items
Gross income derived from business
Gains derived from dealings in property
Interest
Rent
Royalties
Dividends
Alimony and separate maintenance payments
Annuities
Income from life insurance and endowment contracts
Pensions
Income from discharge of indebtedness
Distributive share of partnership income
Income in respect of a decedent
Income from an interest in an estate or trust
Unemployment compensation

Income has been defined by the Supreme Court as "undeniable accession to wealth, clearly realized, over which the taxpayers have complete dominion" (348 U.S., 426 [1985]). Everything you receive for personal services must be included in your gross income. This includes many so-called "fringe benefits" as well as wages, salaries, commissions, tips, and fees. You must report income in any form other than cash at the fair market value of the goods or services received.

Amounts withheld from your pay for income and social security taxes or savings bonds are considered received by you and must be included in your income in the year they were withheld. The same generally is true of amounts withheld for insurance and union dues.

If your employer uses your wages to pay your debt, or if wages are *attached* or *garnished,* the full amount is still considered received by you and must be included in your income. The same is true of fines or penalties withheld from your pay.

Vacation allowances paid to you from a vacation fund are wages and are also included in your income. Severance pay as well is taxable. A lump-sum payment for cancellation of your employment contract is income in the year you receive it.

Rewards and bonuses paid to you for outstanding work are income. These include such prizes as an all-expenses-paid vacation trip for meeting a sales goal and even prizes won on a TV quiz show. If a prize or award is in goods or services, you must include its fair market value in income. However, if your employer merely promises to pay you a bonus or award at some future time, it is not taxable until you receive it or it is made available to you.

If you buy property from your employer at a reduced price, you must normally include in your income as extra pay the excess of the property's fair market value over what you paid for it. If you receive a cash allowance from your employer for meals or lodging, you must include that cash allowance in your income. All tips you receive are also subject to federal income tax; they are not tax-free gifts. You must include in gross income the cash tips you receive directly from customers and the tips from charge customers that are paid to you by your employer.

Any interest that you receive or that is credited to your bank account is taxable income unless it is specifically exempt from tax. This is true even if that interest has not been entered in your bank book—it *has* been credited to you on the books of your bank. Certain distributions commonly referred to as dividends must be included in gross income as interest. You must report as interest the so-called "dividends" on deposits, withdrawals, or share accounts in:

Cooperative banks
Credit unions
Domestic building and loan associations
Federal savings and loan associations
Mutual savings banks

In addition, the fair market value of gifts or services received for making long-term deposits or opening accounts in savings institutions is interest and must be reported as income in the year received.

Amounts you receive as rental income must also be included in your gross income. Rental income includes not only the amount you receive for the occupancy of real estate or for the use of personal property but other amounts as well. For example, advance rent must be included in your rental income in the year you receive it regardless of the period covered or the accounting method used. Payments for the cancellation of a lease or the reduction in the principal of a mortgage (even on your home) if paid before due should also be included as income. So, too, are payments made directly by a tenant for any of *your* expenses. For example, if your tenant pays your heating bill in lieu of partial rent, that amount must be included as rental income.

You must also include in your gross income all fees for your services. Examples of these fees are payments you receive for services as:

A corporate director
An executor or administrator of an estate
A notary public
A member of a jury
An election precinct official
An accountant
An attorney
A medical practitioner

Income received in the form of property or services must be included in income at its fair market value on the dates received. If you receive the services of another in return for your services, and you both have definitely agreed ahead of time as to the value of the services, that value will be accepted as the fair market value unless the value can be shown to be otherwise. An exchange of property or services for your property or services is called bartering and should be included in your gross income.

Finally, dividends, capital gain distributions, and all gains on the sale of property also are included in your gross income. Dividends are distributions paid to you by a corporation. You also may receive dividends through a partnership, an estate, a trust, or an association that is taxable as a corporation.

When all of your gains, all of your "accessions to wealth, clearly realized, over which you have dominion," are added together, you arrive at your gross income amount. From this amount you next subtract your allowable deductions to arrive at your taxable income. Your tax is based on that taxable income. Therefore, in order to reduce or eliminate your tax, there are four possible avenues of attack:

1. You can reduce or minimize your gross income figure by converting income that normally would be included in gross income into certain forms of

income that can be excluded from the gross. This means that amount of income will never even enter into the tax computation picture.

2. You can arrange your activities so that certain personal expenditures that you would normally make will be allowable as deductions, thus reducing both your gross income and your taxable income.
3. You can take advantage of special credits that the tax code allows as dollar-for-dollar offsets to your final tax liability.
4. You can reduce or eliminate your tax by attacking the progressivity of our tax rates structure through the allocation of family income to different family members and entities.

Chapter 8 discusses how this fourth very special and very sophisticated tax planning technique works.

The following chapters will take you through these tax sheltering and elimination approaches.

CHAPTER 3

Exclusions—Tax-Free Money

"Thank God we don't get all the government we pay for."

WILL ROGERS

"When men get in the habit of helping themselves to the property of others, they cannot easily be cured of it." The history of our tax code, in economic terms, mirrors the course of most addictions: advancing dependence, diminished returns, and deteriorating health of the afflicted.

A 1909 EDITORIAL OPPOSING THE VERY FIRST INCOME TAX
The New York Times

In their infinite wisdom, Congress and the courts have decided that some income should not be taxed—that is, it should not even enter into the tax computation picture. The tax code and relevant case law therefore have provided that certain items received by you may be excluded from gross income for any one of the following four reasons:

1. The item may be excluded for constitutional reasons. For example, it has been argued that certain interest on state and municipal bonds is not subject to federal taxation because of the fear that "the power to tax is the power to destroy." Such interest, therefore, is constitutionally exempt from federal taxation.

2. The item received may not be true income but rather a return of cost. For example, when you lend money and then later collect it, the receipt of that money collected is merely a return of your original loan. Alternatively, when you sell property, part of the proceeds of the sale represents a return of your cost, and therefore only the excess of the proceeds over your original cost for that property represents true income.

3. Congress has from time to time seen fit to relieve certain items from taxation for equitable or other reasons. Each exclusion has its own legislative history and reason for enactment. Some exclusions are intended as a form of indirect welfare payments, as when certain injury or sickness payments are excluded from income. Other exclusions prevent double taxation of income or provide incentives for socially desirable activities. For example, scholarships for tuition may be excluded from the income of the recipient. Alternatively, other exclusions have been enacted by Congress to rectify the effects of judicially imposed decisions. For example, the value of improvements to property made by a lessee has been excluded from the lessor's income upon the termination of the lease in reaction to a Supreme Court decision that such value was taxable income.

4. Certain items have been excluded from gross income on the basis of administrative discretion and efficiency. For example, if you buy property from your employer at a reduced price, you normally must include in your income as extra pay the excess of the property's fair market value over what you paid for it. But if such employee discounts are generally available and are not part of negotiated compensation, the dis-

counts are not generally included in your gross income. This is because of the administrative difficulty the Internal Revenue Service would have in identifying and valuing such discounts. Other employee fringe benefits, such as free parking or nonbusiness use of your employer's facilities, would also be excluded from your gross income for the same reasons.

This chapter will detail those items that are not taxable and explain how you can use the availability of these items to reduce your income tax.

A Alternatives to "Earned Income"

The most important thing that you as a taxpayer can do to reduce your taxes to zero is to convert fully taxable income into excludable income. An exclusion is something that is not included in gross income. It is the best kind of revenue to receive. If you are in the 31 percent tax bracket (single, taxable income over $62,450), each dollar you convert to excludable income is the equivalent of getting a raise of 31 percent! Therefore, in negotiating compensation, you as an employee-taxpayer should examine the following forms of nontaxable remuneration for services rendered as alternatives to fully taxable cash income.

1 Hospitalization Premiums (Sec. 106)

Hospitalization premiums, including premiums for supplementary medical insurance (Medicare) paid by your employer, or your former employer if you are retired, are excludable from your income. However, if you have the choice when you retire either to receive continued coverage under your employer's group medical insurance plan or to receive a lump-sum payment and you choose the lump-sum payment, you must include the amount of the payment in your gross income at the time you make the choice to receive it. If you choose continued coverage, or if you qualify for itemization of deductions, you may deduct the amount you include in your income as a medical insurance premium.

For example, if you normally would purchase hospitalization insurance costing $500 a year, and you are in the 31 percent tax bracket, you would require pretax earnings of $725 in order to make that purchase. Of that $725, 31 percent or $225 would go to paying your taxes. In other words, having your employer pay the hospitalization premiums ($500) for you is the equivalent of receiving compensation of $725 from your employer and then paying your own hospitalization premiums. The savings of $225 to your employer can come back to you in *additional* alternative compensation.

2 Group Life Insurance Premiums (Sec. 79)

Group term life insurance coverage of $50,000 or less provided to you by your employer is excludable from your income. This rule applies even if you make an irrevocable assignment of your rights in the policy to another person who agrees to pay your part, if any, of the insurance premiums.

Group term life insurance is term life insurance protection (insurance for a fixed period of time) provided under a master policy or a group of individual policies. The policies must be life insurance contracts and form part of a plan of group insurance arranged for by an employer for all employees. The life insurance protection in a policy of permanent insurance (for example, a whole-life policy) is *not* term life insurance protection.

You are not taxed on the cost of group term life insurance protection of *more* than $50,000 if:

a) the coverage is provided after you have retired and are disabled;

b) your employer is the beneficiary of the policy for the entire period the insurance is in force during the tax year; *or*

c) the only beneficiary of the amount over $50,000 is a qualified charitable organization for the entire period the insurance is in force during the tax year. You do not make a deductible charitable contribution by naming a charitable organization as the beneficiary of your policy.

Where the policy provides only term insurance of $50,000 or less, the payment of premiums by your employer does not create any taxable income for you as an employee. The cost of insurance protection in excess of $50,000 paid by your employer is includable in your gross income according to the following tables.

Table I

Uniform premiums for $1,000 of group term life insurance protection before July 1, 1999 (Annual cost per $1,000 of protection) [(Reg. 1.79–3)]

Age	Amount Included in Income
Under 30	$ .96
30–34	$ 1.08
35–39	$ 1.32
40–44	$ 2.04
45–49	$ 3.48
50–54	$ 5.76
55–59	$ 9.00
60–64	$14.04
65–69	$25.20
70 and older	$45.12

For example, assume you are 47 years old, hired July 1, 1999, and your employer carries a group policy that provides you with $60,000 of term life insurance. You therefore must include only $9.00 ($1.80 × 10 divided by 6 months out of 12) in your income for your employer's payment of premiums. The rest of the premium paid for you is tax-free income. For 2000, you work the whole year and the amount is $18.00. Furthermore, any amount contributed by you toward the purchase of such group term life insurance serves to reduce the amount of gross income that you realize. Had you contributed $9.00 in 1999 toward the purchase of the insurance, you would have had zero included in your income.

If two or more employers provide you with group term life insurance coverage, you must figure the amount of income from this source. Moreover, the cost of group term life insurance provided to you is the cost of life insurance provided to you during the tax year, regardless of when your employers pay the premiums.

Table II

Uniform premiums for $1,000 of group term life insurance protection as of July 1, 1999 (Annual cost per $1,000 of protection)

Age	Amount Included in Income
Under 25	$ .60
25–29	$ .72
30–34	$ .96
35–39	$ 1.08
40–44	$ 1.20
45–49	$ 1.80
50–54	$ 2.76
55–59	$ 5.16
60–64	$ 7.92
65–69	$15.24
70 and above	$24.72

For example, assume you are 51 years old and work for two employers in 2000. Both employers provide group term life insurance coverage for you. Your coverage with the first employer is $35,000 and with the second is $45,000. You pay premiums of $50 a year under the second employer's group plan. The amount to be included in your gross income is figured as follows:

First employer coverage	$35,000
Second employer coverage	+45,000
Total coverage	80,000
Minus exclusion	–50,000
Excess amount	30,000
Multiply cost per thousand, age 51 (from table)	×2.76
Cost of excess insurance for tax year	82.80
Minus premiums paid by you	–50.00
Amount included in income	$32.80

The cost of employer-provided group term life insurance must now be included in wages for FICA tax purposes to the extent that it is includable for income tax purposes. However, if you need life insurance, the use of this technique provides that insurance at either a tax-reduced or completely tax-free cost.

3 Group Legal Services Plans (Sec. 120)

Amounts paid by your employer for a qualified group legal services plan and the value of the benefits you receive under such a plan can no longer be excluded from your income. This exclusion expired July 1, 1992.

4 Accident and Health Plans (Sec. 105)

Although you realize no taxable income from the benefits of an accident and health policy on which you pay your own premiums, it may be more tax advantageous to have these policies paid by your employer. The general rule is that any benefits received by you as an employee under such policies are includable in your gross income.

There are, however, certain exceptions permitting you to exclude specific benefits that would otherwise be taxable under the general rule:

1. You may exclude benefits received directly or indirectly as reimbursement for medical expenses incurred for yourself, your spouse, or your dependents. If you deducted such medical expenses in a prior year, however, the reimbursement for these expenses must be included in the current year's income.
2. You may exclude benefits received for the permanent loss or the loss of the use of a member or function of the body, or a permanent disfiguration of yourself or your spouse or dependents, so long as the benefits are not related to absence from work.

The value of the exclusion of accident and health benefits can be shown by the following example:

Assume you lost a leg in an automobile accident that was unrelated to your work and you collected $10,000 from an insurance policy carried by your employer. If the payments were computed with reference to the nature of the injury and were not related to the time period that you were absent from work, then the entire $10,000 would be excluded from your income. Furthermore, if you incurred $3,000 in medical expenses that were covered under an employer-sponsored hospitalization plan, those payments would also be excluded from your income.

5 Employee Death Benefits (Sec. 101)

Amounts received as death benefits by your family or by your estate may be excluded up to an aggregate amount of $5,000, whether paid directly or indirectly by your employer.

This exclusion may not be claimed for accrued salary, unused leave, or compensation for past services. Furthermore, it may be claimed for a nonforfeitable amount you had the right to receive before your death *only* if it is received as a lump-sum distribution from a qualified plan or under an annuity contract purchased by an employer that is a tax-exempt organization.

The Small Business Job Protection Act of 1996 repealed this exclusion for decedents dying after August 20, 1996.

6 Merchandise Distributed to Employees on Holidays

Merchandise distributed to you as an employee on holidays, such as Christmas or New Year's Day, is excludable from your income if it is not of substantial value and is given for substantially noncompensatory reasons.

A turkey, for example, or similar merchandise given to you by your employer on a holiday therefore will not be includable in your taxable income. Unfortunately, this does not apply to cash distributions such as bonuses.

7 "Expenses of Your Employer"

The law does not tax reimbursement expenses that are true reimbursements for expenses of your employer rather than income amounts truly compensatory in nature.

Under this category are such items as reimbursements for cab fares and the payment of supper money. Rather than being excludable on the basis of statutory or constitutional language, these items are truly nontaxable as the result of Internal Revenue Service recognition of the impossible administrative verification problems in auditing such expenses. For whatever reasons, therefore, they are nontaxable.

If you as an employee can arrange with your employer to work from 11:00 A.M. to 7:00 P.M. rather than from 9:00 A.M. to 5:00 P.M. and she agrees to provide you with supper money, these personal supper expenses therefore can be converted into nontaxable income. In effect, no matter what bracket you are in, you have arranged for the Internal Revenue Service to buy you dinner.

8 Meals and Lodgings (Sec. 119)

The value of meals and lodgings provided to you, your spouse, and your dependents without charge by your employer is not taxable income if the following three criteria are met:

1. The meals or lodgings are provided at your employer's place of business.
2. The meals or lodgings are provided for the convenience of your employer.
3. In the case of lodging (but not meals), you must accept the lodging at your employer's place of business as a condition of your employment. This means that you must accept the lodging to carry out the duties of your job properly, for example, if you must be available for duty at all times.

Lodging includes the cost of heat, electricity, gas, water, sewerage service, and similar items that are necessary to make lodging habitable.

With reference to meals, you may exclude from income the value of meals provided to you during working hours so that you can be available for emergency calls, or because the nature of your employer's business restricts you to a short meal period. For example, if you are the only receptionist at your place of work, you must be available "at all times." If your employer provides you with lunch every day, that lunch is not includable in your income. Furthermore, the Supreme Court has ruled that such lunches do not constitute "wages" for social security taxes. They are truly *tax-free* (see TAM 9829001 where meals provided by a casino to its food service and security employees were excluded from their income and *Boyd Gaming Corp. v. Commissioner,* 9th Cir., No. 98-70123, 5/12/99 where 100% of the expenses of a casino's employee cafeteria were deductible as *de minimus fringe* benefits.)

However, if you receive a cash allowance from your employer for meals or lodging, you must include the cash allowance in your income. The solution, therefore, is to have your employer provide the food, not the dollars. The net effect is the same to you but the net cost is substantially less.

Situations in which meals and lodging are furnished for the convenience of the employer normally include the following:

- A waitress is required to eat her meals on the premises during the busy lunch and breakfast hours.
- A worker is employed at a construction site in a remote part of Alaska. The employer must furnish meals and lodging due to the inaccessibility of other facilities.
- A bank furnishes meals on the premises to limit the time tellers are away during the busy hours.
- A hospital provides a free cafeteria for its staff. The hospital's business purpose in providing the meals is to induce employees to stay on the premises in case an emergency arises. These meals are not includable in the income of the staff, even though staff members are *not* required to eat on the premises.

The 1998 Reform Act now provides that *all* meals furnished to employees at the employers place of business shall be treated as "for the convenience of the employer" if more than half of such meals are furnished for the convenience of the employer.

This technique should be used extensively when married couples run their own businesses or professions. For example, assume the situation where one spouse performs the services and the other runs the office. That second spouse needs to be available "at all times" to answer the phone, receive clients, etc., and therefore any meals provided to that spouse would be deductible by the business as an expense but not includable as income to the recipient. The spouse must truly be employed and must be required to be on the business premises during lunchtime or the deduction will be disallowed as a sham (*Weidmann,* 89-1 USTC ¶9197 [DC N.Y., 1989]). In effect, what we have done again is to convert a personal expense—a meal—into nontaxable compensation. Again, the Internal Revenue Service is put into the position of helping to pay for your dinner.

9 Employee Discounts

You need not include as taxable income the discounts or privileges of relatively small value that you, as an employee, receive, where such discounts are given primarily to provide good employee relations and do not take on the character of additional compensation. This exclusion includes the usual courtesy discounts allowed to employees in many retail stores. But the value of discounts beyond a mere courtesy discount would be taxable income to you. Furthermore, if you buy property from your employer at less than fair market value, the amount of that discount is income.

For example, if you pay $2,000 for one of your employer's company cars that has a fair market value of $6,000, you are considered to have earned $4,000 of income on the transaction.

10 Workers' Compensation (Sec. 104)

Workers' compensation received for sickness or injury is fully exempt from tax. If you turn over your workers' compensation payments to your employer, and all or part of your regular salary continues to be paid, the excess of the salary payments over the amount of workers' compensation is taxable income.

For example, assume you are hurt on the job and are out of work for six weeks. Your employer continues to pay your salary of $200 a week, or $1,200 for the time you are absent. You also receive $75 a week, or a total of $450, in workers' compensation. Under your employment contract, you turn over all your workers' compensation to your employer. The $75 a week is fully excludable from your income and the balance is taxable income.

11 "Cafeteria" Plans (Sec. 125)

Employer contributions under a written "cafeteria" plan, or "flexible benefit plan," permitting you as a participant to select between taxable and nontaxable benefits, are excludable from your income to the extent that you choose nontaxable benefits.

Nontaxable benefits include group life insurance (up to $50,000 coverage), disability benefits, and accident and health benefits to the extent that such benefits are excludable from gross income.

Such employer contributions may be excluded if the following conditions are satisfied:

- Participation in the cafeteria plan must be restricted to employees.
- The same service requirement must apply to all participants.
- The participant chooses nontaxable benefits.
- The plan's eligibility requirements do not discriminate in favor of "highly compensated individuals."
- Employer contributions and employee benefits do not favor "highly compensated participants."

12 Dependent Care Assistance Program (Sec. 129)

For tax years after 1981, the value of the dependent care assistance that an employer provides to employees under a dependent care assistance program is not generally includable in the employee's gross income. However, if payments for child care expenses are made to someone who is a child of the employee under age 19 or who qualifies for a dependency exemption for the employee, the payments are not excludable. If the child is not under age 19 and is not claimed as a dependent, such payments *do* qualify (*Langlois,* T.C.M. 1988–415).

The value of dependent care assistance that you may exclude from your pay is limited. If you are an employee who is not married at the end of the tax year, the limit is equivalent to your earned income for that year. For married employees the limit is the lesser of: (a) the employee's earned income for the tax year; or (b) the employee's spouse's earned income for the tax year. The Tax Reform Act of 1986 put a $5,000 cap on dependent care expenses. Moreover, the Family Support Act of 1988 provides that any amount excluded under a dependent care assistance program reduces the amount of expenses otherwise eligible for the child care credit.

A dependent care assistance program is a plan written by the employer for the exclusive benefit of the employees and that meets the following requirements:

1. *Eligibility.* The program must benefit employees who qualify under a classification set up by the employer, and the Secretary of the Treasury must find it nondiscriminatory in favor of employees who are officers, owners, or highly compensated, or who are dependents of these employees. However, the employer does not have to include in this program employees who are covered by what the Secretary of Labor considers to be a collective bargaining agreement between employee representatives and one or more employers if there is evidence that the dependent care benefits were the subject of good faith bargaining between the representatives and the employer.

2. *Limitation on principal shareholders or owners.* Not more than 25 percent of the amounts paid or incurred by an employer for the dependent care assistance during the year may be for individuals who are shareholders or owners (or their spouses or dependents) each of whom—on any day of the year—owns more than 5 percent of the stock or of the capital or profit interest in the employer.

3. *Funding.* An employer is not required to fund a dependent care assistance program.

4. *Notification of availability.* An employer must provide all eligible employees with a reasonable notification of the availability and terms of the dependent care assistance program.

5. *Notification to participants.* The plan will give each employee, by January 31, a written statement showing the amounts paid for the expenses incurred by the employer in providing dependent care assistance to the employee during the calendar year.

13 Employer Educational Assistance (Sec. 127)

This provision excludes from an employee's gross income employer-provided educational assistance, regardless of whether or not the education is job-related. The exclusion, scheduled to expire, was restored retroactively by the Small Business Job Protection Act of 1996 and the Tax Relief Act of 1997 and now expires for courses beginning after May 31, 2000. The extension does not apply to any payment for graduate-level courses (except for those taken in 1995 and those beginning prior to July 1, 1996) taken by an individual pursuing a program leading to an advanced academic or professional degree and is generally not available for any education involving sports, games, or hobbies. Employers are not required to withhold on educational assistance payments, but the exclusion is limited to $5,250 per individual per calendar year. Arguably, educational expenses that would be deductible by an employee as trade or business expenses if they had been paid by the employee are not subject to this $5,250 cap. Moreover, every employer who maintains an educational assistance program must file a return showing the number of employees eligible to participate in the program; the number participating; the total cost of the program; the employer's name, address, and taxpayer identification number; and the type of business in which the employer is engaged.

14 Employee Awards (Sec. 274)

Under prior law, an employee award such as emblematic jewelry or an engraved plaque awarded an employee for job performance, which was not excludable as a scientific or other achievement award, was generally excludable from gross income if it qualified as a gift. If the employee award was includable in the employee's income, the employer was entitled to a deduction for the award as a business expense. If the award was excludable as a gift, the employer's deduction was limited to a maximum of $25 for the cost of gifts to any one employee in any one tax year.

If a gift of tangible personal property was awarded to an employee for length of service, safety achievement, or productivity, the deduction ceiling was raised from $25 to $400. If a length of service, safety, or productivity award was a *qualified plan award,* the ceiling on the employer's deduction was $1,600, provided that the average cost of all awards provided under the plan for qualified awards did not exceed $400. A qualified plan award was one awarded (a) under a permanent written program of the employer which (b) does not discriminate in favor of officers, shareholders, or highly compensated employees.

The Tax Reform Act of 1986 changed these rules. That law states specifically that employee awards will *not* be excludable from the employee's income as gifts. Since such awards will no longer be treated as gifts (and are therefore fully includable as income to the employee), the limitations described on employer deductions for business gifts will no longer apply. The entire amount of the award (assuming ordinary, necessary, and reasonable tests are met) will be deductible.

Employee awards generally will be includable in the income of the employee and will be deductible by the employer, subject to two limited exceptions. One exception applies to awards that are qualified plan awards.

The definition of a qualified plan award under new law is essentially the same as under prior law: one awarded (a) under a permanent written program of the employer which (b) does not discriminate in favor of officers, shareholders, or highly compensated employees. If an award is a qualified plan award, the award is excludable by the employee *and* deductible by the employer only to the extent that the cost to the employer of all such awards made to the employee during the taxable year (whether or not qualified plan awards) does not exceed $1,600. The $400 average cost limitation described for qualified plan awards has been retained: that is, awards will not be considered qualified plan awards unless the average cost limitation is met.

The second exception applies to certain awards that are not qualified plan awards. If the award is not a qualified plan award (for example, if it is awarded under an informal plan or in a discriminatory fashion), the award will be excludable by the employee *and* deductible by the employer only to the extent that the cost of all such awards that are not qualified plan awards provided to the employee during the taxable year does not exceed $400.

Under new law if the cost to the employer of the qualified plan award exceeds the limits just described, then the employee must include in income the *greater* of (a) the excess of the cost of the award over the amount allowable as a deduction (but not more than the award's value), or (b) the excess of the value of the award over the amount allowable as a deduction. If the employer's cost is *not* over the applicable limit, the employee may exclude the award regardless of its value.

Example: If an employer gave an employee one qualified plan award that cost the employer $2,000 and had a value of $1,900, the employee would have to include $400 (cost minus $1,600 limitation) in income. If the award cost $2,000 and had a value of $2,200, the employee would have to include $600 in income (its value minus the $1,600 limitation).

Furthermore, to be excludable under *either* of the exceptions just described, an award must be an *employee achievement award.* Only awards that are length of service awards or safety achievement awards will qualify as employee achievement awards. Professional, administrative, managerial, and clerical employees do not qualify for safety achievement awards for tax purposes. A significant change in the 1986 law is that awards for productivity will no longer qualify for an exclusion. Awards for productivity will simply be treated as compensation.

Also, the 1986 law specifically states that employee achievement awards must be tangible personal property (not cash, securities, or life insurance). To the extent employee awards are excludable from income, they are also exempt from the social security and other employer withholding taxes.

Under the 1986 law there will no longer be any need to make the subjective determination as to whether the employee award is a gift. No employee awards will be treated as gifts for income tax purposes.

However, the 1986 law creates a double whammy with respect to employee achievement awards that are in excess of the applicable limits. They are not deductible by the employer and must be included in the gross income of the employee. Because of this double whammy, beginning in 1987 employers had to keep employee achievement awards for length of service and safety achievement within the applicable dollar amount limitations.

Example: An insurance company has a program of employee achievement awards provided to employees for length of service achievement, but the arrangement discriminates in favor of highly compensated employees. The company provides a top executive with a videocassette recorder that cost the company $600. The VCR has a value of $700. The cost of the video cassette recorder is deductible by the employer only to the extent of $400. Since the VCR's cost to the employer is more than $400, the executive must include the excess of its $700 value over the employer's $400 deductible portion in gross income. The reportable amount would be $300.

The 1986 law does make it easier to plan employee achievement award programs since the interest of the employer corresponds with the interest of the employee; that is, the employer receives a deduction under the same circumstances that the employee receives an exclusion. The 1986 law is less favorable with respect to employee awards in that the exclusion is not available for awards given for productivity of the employee.

The 1986 law does not change the rules for fringe benefits which are *de minimis* under Sec. 132(e). Under these rules employees may exclude from income employee awards that are of nominal value, such as holiday turkeys or employee picnics. However, the Senate Finance Committee's Report on the Tax Reform Act states that certain employee awards for length of service "such as a gold watch" may be treated under the *de minimis* provision! The rationale appears to be that such an award is the functional equivalent of several smaller gifts made over the course of many years of service. Or perhaps the committee has been too busy in recent years to follow the price of gold.

15 Miscellaneous Fringe Benefits

An employer can give discount fare cards, passes, or tokens to an employee who takes public transportation to work. If the subsidy provided is not worth more than $65 a month ($100 per month after December 31, 2001) to an employee, it is considered to be a *de minimis* fringe benefit (EE 42-91). The employer can deduct it, but you, as an employee, received it tax-free (Regulation Section 1.132-6T[d][1]). Note, however, that if the employer supplies you with more than $65 a month toward the public transportation commute, only the amount in excess of $65 is taxable as compensation income (Notice 94-3) (Rev. Proc. 97-57).

Employer-provided free parking, up to a maximum value of $170 per month, is also excludable from income.

B Donative Items

16 Gifts, Bequests, and Inheritances (Sec. 102)

If you receive money or property by bequest, devise, or inheritance, that receipt does not constitute taxable income to you. (Any income produced by that money or property while in your hands, though, is taxable in the usual fashion.)

Only money and property received from a decedent or as a bona fide gift fall under this rule. For a transfer to constitute a gift, there must be a motive of "detached and disinterested generosity." The exclusion, though, applies only to the donee.

Here you must be careful. For purposes of taxation, a simple assignment of income is ineffective. For example, if you make a gift of salary receivable from your employer to your child, even though that check goes directly to your child, that income is still taxable to you. You were the one who earned it and therefore are the one who is taxed on that earning. Your child, however, will exclude the "gift" and not be taxed on its value.

But once property is conveyed, the impact of taxation does shift to the donee. Thus for example, if you are in the 31 percent bracket and own a bond yielding $700 in interest, you must pay taxes of $217, leaving you only $483 of after-tax disposable income. Alternatively, if you transfer that bond to your child and allow your child to receive the income, the first $700 of interest to that child will be completely tax-free. In terms of net family disposable income, the total amount available will be increased by $217.

The advantages of interfamily income allocation will be discussed extensively later in the book. The important thing to recognize under this section is that the transfer of the bond to your child is not at all a taxable transaction—that is, your child will not be taxed on the value of the bonds received. This exclusion of gifts from the gross income of the recipient constitutes the foundation of the income allocation strategies and techniques to be discussed later.

17 Scholarships and Fellowships (Sec. 117)

Under prior law, if you received a scholarship or fellowship grant, you could exclude that amount from your gross income, subject to certain limits, depending upon whether you are a degree candidate. To qualify for this exclusion, the payment had to be made for your education and training. The payment did not qualify, however, if it was made to pay you either for past, present, or future services, or for studies or research conducted mostly for the grantor's benefit.

A scholarship generally means an amount paid for the benefit of a student at an educational organization, to aid in the student's pursuit of studies. An educational organization is any organization that normally maintains a regular faculty and curriculum and has a regularly organized body of students in attendance at the place where its educational activities are carried on. A fellowship is the same as a scholarship, but the individual receiving aid does not have to be enrolled at an educational institution, and research is usually the aim.

Under current law, the exclusion will be limited to scholarships or fellowship grants to individuals who are degree candidates at educational institutions that maintain a regular faculty and curriculum and have a regularly enrolled body of students. There will no longer be an exclusion available to nondegree candidates or for scholarships granted by organizations other than qualified educational institutions. In addition, the exclusion will be available only with respect to payments that are actually used for tuition, enrollment fees, books, supplies, and other equipment required for courses of instruction. Payments for teaching, research, or other services rendered to the institution by a degree candidate will no longer qualify for the exclusion.

The exclusion does apply to *qualified tuition reductions*. A qualified tuition reduction is a tuition reduction for the employees, spouses, and dependent children of employees of educational institutions for studies below the graduate level, under a plan that does not discriminate in favor of officers, owners, or highly compensated employees of the institution.

It is important to remember that this provision does not have a retroactive effect: that is, it does not apply to scholarships and fellowships granted before August 17, 1986.

For those awards, amounts received for expenses under a scholarship or fellowship grant, such as travel (including meals and lodging while traveling and an allowance for the travel expenses of your family), research, clerical help, or equipment, may continue to be excluded from your gross income. You may exclude these amounts without limit if you are a degree candidate. If you are not a degree candidate, you may exclude from your gross income the amount you receive as a scholarship or fellowship, including the value of services, room, and board provided to you, up to $300 times the number of months for which you receive amounts under the grant during the year. For example, if you receive $500 a month for six months, you will include $1,200 and receive $300 × 6 or $1,800 tax-free.

If you are *not* a degree candidate, such grants awarded prior to August 17, 1986, must be from one of the following to be excludable:

- The United States or one of its agencies; a U.S. state, territory, possession, or political subdivision, including the District of Columbia.
- A nonprofit organization exempt from federal income tax and operated exclusively for religious, charitable, scientific, literary, or educational purposes, testing for public safety, preventing cruelty to children or animals, or fostering national or international amateur sports competition.
- A foreign government.
- An international organization or an educational and cultural foundation or commission under the Mutual Educational and Cultural Exchange Act of 1961.

If you are not a degree candidate, the period for which you may exclude amounts you receive as scholarships or fellowship grants is limited to 36 months during your lifetime, which do not need to be consecutive. After they are over, you must include in your gross income all amounts you receive under your grant, including amounts for expenses, and the value of services, meals, and lodging given to you.

You are not a degree candidate if your studies merely allow you to practice a profession but do not lead to a degree. For example, if you are a registered nurse who receives a grant from a charity to take training leading to certification as a psychiatric nurse, these studies for certification do not make you a candidate for a degree.

Amounts paid to help you in pursuing your studies or research are not excludable if the studies or the research is mostly for the benefit of the grantor. However, if the main purpose is to further your education and training, and the amounts are not payment for services, they would be excludable. This is true even if you must give progress reports to the grantor, or if the results of your studies or research may slightly benefit the grantor.

Payments for your past, present, or future services are not excludable, *but* there is a very important exception that must be kept in mind: If you work for pay for a research project, you generally must include that pay in income. Your pay is not a scholarship or fellowship grant merely because the research can be used for credit toward a degree. However, if similar services are required of all candidates for the degree, as a reasonable condition for it, you may exclude the pay from your gross income.

Your pay for services over and above those specifically needed for the degree must be included in your gross income. Interns, resident physicians, and registered nurses in training in a hospital therefore must include their pay in gross income. But tuition and work payments given to you under a work study program are considered scholarships if your college, under its educational philosophy, requires all students to take part in a work program. These payments, therefore, are excludable from your income. Alternatively, payments you receive for service *not* required by the work program must be included in your income. Furthermore, amounts paid by your employer to you when you are on educational leave also are not excludable.

The following example will demonstrate the value of the potential exclusion of scholarships and fellowship grants from your income: In a contest sponsored by a business firm, you receive a scholarship award of $5,000 that you can use only for tuition, books, and supplies when enrolled as a candidate for a degree at a certain college. You do not include any of the $5,000 award in your gross income if:

a) you are not employed by the firm at the time of the award;

b) you are not being paid for services you provided for the firm in the past; *and*

c) you are not required to provide future services for the firm.

If you are in the 31 percent bracket and desire to enroll as a candidate for a degree, you would have had to earn $7,246 before tax in order to have $5,000 after tax to pay for the college tuition and fees. The enormous financial advantage of the exclusion of scholarships and fellowships from taxable income thus becomes very clear. Remember, however, that the same after-tax effect can be achieved if your employer establishes an employee education assistance plan as discussed earlier.

18 Prizes and Awards (Sec. 74)

Prior to 1987, prizes and awards received in recognition of past accomplishments—in religious, charitable, scientific, artistic, educational, literary, or civic fields—were excludable income if the winners were chosen without action on their part and were not expected to perform any future services. For example, if you received a Pulitzer or Nobel Prize or any other award and were selected for your past work, this award was not includable in your income. Under the current law, the exclusion for scientific and other achievement awards is repealed. The only exception to the repeal is when the recipient assigns the award to a governmental unit or charitable organization.

The provision in the new law which permits you to exclude the value of the prize or award if you assign it to the government or a charity is of limited benefit. Under prior law an excludable award could be contributed to charity and the recipient contributor could take a deduction for the contribution. Under new law you may exclude the prize or award if you contribute it to a charitable organization, but your contribution is disallowed. The end result is that you have simply given away what you received and have no extra income and no deduction. In effect, this is no different from your having included the prize or award in gross income and then taken a charitable deduction for contributing it.

In addition, if you win a prize in a lucky number drawing, a television or radio quiz program, a beauty contest, or some other event, that prize is taxable. So, too, are awards or bonuses given to you as an employee for your good work or for suggestions. These are not instances where the winners have been chosen without action on their part and are not expected to perform any future services.

Taxable prizes and awards in goods and services must be included in your income at their fair market value to you. This is very important. It is not the general fair market value but rather the fair market value of that prize *to you*. If you already have two attaché cases and win a third on a quiz show, the value of that third attaché case *to you* may be negligible. It clearly would not be its full retail selling price. However, when sold, the amount received for such prizes or awards is normally deemed to be equal to their fair market value. If, for example, you receive an award of a car that retails for $10,000 and immediately sell that car to a third party for $8,000, the amount to be included in your income would be the $8,000 figure rather than the $10,000 figure.

Be careful here. A bargain sale to a relative may be considered part sale, part gift. If you sold that $10,000 car to your brother for $5,000, the Internal Revenue Service might successfully argue that you received income of $10,000 and made a gift of the $5,000 difference to your brother. One technique that has been used to avoid this is to sell the car for $5,000 to an independent third party, who could turn around and resell the car to your brother for the same $5,000. Watch the structuring of such three-party transactions. There must be no prearranged agreement for the third party to resell to your brother, and that third party must be truly independent. Otherwise, if the Internal Revenue Service catches on, it will collapse the two transactions, deem the first sale to be a sham, and successfully establish the true nature of the gift to your brother.

C Investors

19 Interest on State and Municipal Obligations (Sec. 103)

You can exclude from gross income all interest earned on obligations of a state, territory, municipality, or any political subdivision, except in the case of arbitrage bonds issued after October 9, 1969.

An *arbitrage bond* is an obligation, the proceeds of which are reasonably expected to be used to acquire other securities or obligations that are expected over the term of the issue to yield a materially higher rate of return. This exception prohibits state and local governments from issuing bonds at a low interest rate because of their tax-exempt nature and using the proceeds to buy federal or industrial bonds returning a higher yield. Since the state or local government does not pay an income tax on the difference, this exception prevents the federal government from becoming an unintended source for financing state and local government operations.

If you are in a sufficiently high tax bracket, the advantages of purchasing a state or municipal bond can be substantial. If you are in a 31 percent bracket, a 6fi percent yield on a municipal obligation is the equivalent of a 9.42 percent yield on a nonexempt security. Moreover, the risk factor on a state or municipal obligation will normally be far lower than that on an industrial security.

The higher the tax bracket, the greater the attraction of a tax-exempt security. The following table shows the tax-exempt equivalent yield to a taxable investment at various marginal tax rates:

If Your Marginal Tax Rate Is:	And Your Tax-exempt Investment Yields					
	4%	5%	6%	6.5%	7%	7.5%
	It Is the Equivalent of a Taxable Investment Yielding:					
15%	4.71	5.88	7.06	7.65	8.24	8.82
28%	5.56	6.94	8.33	9.03	9.72	10.42
31%	5.80	7.25	8.70	9.42	10.14	10.87
36%	6.25	7.81	9.38	10.16	10.94	11.72
39.6%	6.62	8.28	9.93	10.76	11.59	12.42

D Benefits for the Elderly

20 Public Assistance Payments

Benefit payments from a general welfare fund in the interest of the general public, such as payments to aid the indigent or the blind, or payments to crime victims, are excludable from your gross income. These welfare payments have been excluded by the Internal Revenue Service, because the IRS sees them in the nature of gifts.[1]

1. Rev. Rul. 71-425, 1971–2 CB 76.

21 Social Security and Other Retirement Benefits

Social security benefits under the federal social security programs are not taxable. Social security benefits received from foreign countries, however, are taxable unless they are specifically exempt by treaty.

Basic railroad retirement benefits are also not taxable. Railroad retirement lump-sum payments, commonly known as either the insurance lump-sum payment or the residual payment, are excluded from your gross income as well.

The Internal Revenue Service tax code does not specifically exclude social security benefits, but these benefits have been declared not subject to tax by the Internal Revenue Commissioner.[2] According to the Internal Revenue Service, these payments are in part a return of the after-tax contributions made by the individual and in part a welfare or annuity payment from the government. These welfare payments have been viewed by the Internal Revenue Service as essentially in the nature of gifts.[3]

Moreover, basic Medicare benefits received under the Social Security Act are also excluded from gross income since they are considered social security payments. So also are supplementary benefits covering costs of doctors' services and other items not covered under basic Medicare, as they are in the nature of medical insurance payments.

Note, however, that since January 1, 1984, part of your Social Security benefits have been subject to tax if your income exceeded a specified level determined by formula. There are three factors used in determining how much of your Social Security benefits, if any, will be included in taxable income: (1) your *income,* defined as your adjusted gross income for federal income tax plus any tax-exempt interest, plus any foreign source income you receive during the year; (2) your *half-benefit,* defined as half the Social Security income you (and, if you're married and filing jointly, your spouse) receive during the year; and (3) your *base amount,* which is $25,000 for a single taxpayer, $32,000 for a married couple filing jointly, and zero for a married couple filing separately (unless they have lived apart for the entire tax year, in which case they qualify for the $25,000 base amount).

The amount of Social Security income to be reported, if any, will be 50 percent of the amount by which (1) your income plus (2) your half-benefit exceeds

2. Rev. Rul. 70-217, 1970-1 CB 12.
3. Rev. Rul. 71-425, 1971-1 CB 76.

(3) your base amount. However, in no event will more than your half-benefit be reported as taxable income.

For example, assume a married couple filing jointly has an adjusted gross income of $20,000 plus tax-exempt interest of $8,000. They therefore have *income* of $28,000. If they have Social Security income of $12,000 they will report $1,000 of that benefit as taxable income as follows:

Income	$28,000
Half-benefit	+$6,000
Total	$34,000
Base Amount	–$32,000
Difference	$2,000
50% of difference	$1,000
Taxable S.S. benefit	$1,000

Effective after December 31, 1993, the Omnibus Reconciliation Act of 1993 created a second tier of Social Security benefit inclusion in gross income. Prior law now applies to *income* up to $34,000 for unmarried individuals and $44,000 for married individuals filing joint returns. For taxpayers with *income* above these amounts, the amount included in income shall be the *lesser* of:

1. 85 percent of your total Social Security benefit, or
2. the sum of:

   a) the smaller of (i) the amount included under prior law; or (ii) $4,500 (if unmarried) or $6,000 (if married filing jointly)[4]

   plus

   b) 85 percent of the excess of your *income* over the new applicable second tier threshold amounts ($34,000 and $44,000).

Now that social security payments may be taxable, recipients should find out whether their benefits are included as part of their adjusted gross income under the income tax laws of the states where they reside. Eleven states have, in the past,

4. These amounts equal 50 percent of the difference between the prior and new thresholds: i.e., 50 percent of $34,000 – $25,000 = $4,500; 50 percent of $44,000 – $32,000 = $6,000.

exempted from their income taxes social security benefits now included in federal adjusted gross income: Delaware, Hawaii, Idaho, Indiana, Maine, New Mexico, New York, South Carolina, Virginia, West Virginia, and Wisconsin. Minnesota has provided an exclusion from federal adjusted gross income for social security benefits in a portion of the calculation of the maximum income exclusion for pensions and retirement benefits. Other states, such as New Jersey, specifically exempt Social Security from taxation. Check your own state rules.

22 Retirement Annuities (Sec. 72)

An annuity is a type of investment that requires you to pay a fixed amount in exchange for the right to receive periodic payments for your life or for some definite period. If the annuity payments are based on your life, or the life of another individual, the amounts of such payments are determined through the use of standard mortality tables.

When you receive the income from this annuity, part of what you are receiving represents a recovery of your initial investment. This recovery amount is fully excluded from income. The Internal Revenue Service provides tables with which you can compute your exclusion ratio. This exclusion ratio remains the same and continues to be applied to annuity payments even if you outlive your life expectancy.

For example, assume you have made principal payments into an annuity of \$60,000 in return for payment of \$500 per month for life. Also assume that the tables show that your life expectancy is 15 years from the annuity starting date. Your investment in the contract is \$60,000 and your expected return is \$6,000 per year times 15 years, or \$90,000. You would exclude two-thirds of each payment (\$6,000 × ⅔) or a total of \$4,000 yearly. That \$4,000 is a nontaxable return of capital; the remaining \$2,000 is taxable income.

In IRS Notice 88-18, the IRS came up with an easier way for some retirees to compute how much of their pension or annuity payments are tax free. Under this IRS safe-harbor method, the expected number of monthly annuity payments is based on your age at the annuity's starting date, rather than on the life expectancy tables contained in Regulation Section 1.72-9. The same number is used for a single-life annuity or a joint and survivor annuity.

IRS Table V—One Life
Life Expectancies

Age	Years Remaining	Age	Years Remaining	Age	Years
			Remaining		
5	76.6	42	40.6	79	10.0
6	75.6	43	39.6	80	9.5
7	74.7	44	38.7	81	8.9
8	73.7	45	37.7	82	8.4
9	72.7	46	36.8	83	7.9
10	71.7	47	35.9	84	7.4
11	70.7	48	34.0	85	6.9
12	69.7	49	34.0	86	6.5
13	68.8	50	33.1	87	6.1
14	67.8	51	32.2	88	5.7
15	66.8	52	31.3	89	5.3
16	65.8	53	30.4	90	5.0
17	64.8	54	29.5	91	4.7
18	63.9	55	28.6	92	4.4
19	62.9	56	27.7	93	4.1
20	61.9	57	26.8	94	3.9
21	60.9	58	25.9	95	3.7
22	59.9	59	25.0	96	3.4
23	59.0	60	24.2	97	3.2
24	58.0	61	23.3	98	3.0
25	57.0	62	22.5	99	2.8
26	56.0	63	21.6	100	2.7
27	55.1	64	20.8	101	2.5
28	54.1	65	20.0	102	2.3
29	53.1	66	19.2	103	2.1
30	52.2	67	18.4	104	1.9
31	51.2	68	17.6	105	1.8
32	50.2	69	16.6	106	1.6
33	49.3	70	16.0	107	1.4
34	48.3	71	15.3	108	1.3
35	47.3	72	14.6	109	1.1
36	46.4	73	13.9	110	1.0
37	45.4	74	13.2	111	.9
38	44.4	75	12.5	112	.8
39	43.5	76	11.9	113	.7
40	42.5	77	11.2	114	.6
41	41.5	78	10.6	115	.5

Age of Distributee	Number of Payments
55 and under	300
56 to 60	260
61 to 65	240
66 to 70	170
71 and over	120

For example, if you begin receiving payments at age 65, you would divide your total investment by 240 to find out how much of each payment is tax free.

The Small Business Job Protection Act of 1996 provides that basis recovery on payments from qualified plan annuities generally will be determined under a method similar to the prior law simplified alternative method provided by the IRS above. The portion of each annuity payment that represents a return of basis is equal to the employee's total basis as of the annuity starting date, divided by the number of anticipated payments under the following table:

Age	Number of Payments
Not more than 55	360
56 to 60	310
61 to 65	260
66 to 70	210
More than 70	160

This provision is effective with respect to annuity starting dates beginning 90 days after the date of enactment (August 20, 1996). Therefore, if your annuity starting date is after November 18, 1996, you must use this new simplified method.

For annuity starting dates beginning after November 18, 1996, but before January 1, 1997, the total number of monthly annuity payments expected to be received is based on the primary annuitant's age at the annuity starting date. The same expected number of payments applies to an annuitant whether he or she is receiving a single life annuity or a joint-and-survivor annuity.

For annuity starting dates after December 31, 1997, the table used to determine the expected number of payments depends on whether payments are based on the life of more than one individual.

For joint and survivor annuities, the total number of monthly annuity payments expected to be received is based on the combined ages of the annuities at the starting date, IRS said. For annuities that are not based on life expectancies, the expected number of payments is the number of monthly annuity payments under the contract (Notice 98-2).

Whichever method you use, once you have received your investment back, your exclusion ratio expires. Although the total tax-free recoupment is the same with both methods, using the optional second method may reclaim your investment faster. For example, under a joint and survivor annuity, payments continue until the death of the second beneficiary. Since two beneficiaries have a longer life expectancy, and therefore more payments over which to recover the investment, using the regular IRS method results in a smaller portion of each payment coming back tax-free. With the optional method, it is irrelevant whether or not the joint and survivor annuity is elected.

The IRS optional second method could have been used for payments from annuities that began distributions after July 1, 1986. If you began receiving payments before then, you must use the old method. New retirees will now use the new method as per the 1996 law.

23 Sale of Your Home (Sec. 121)

You may exclude from your gross income some or all of your gain from the sale or exchange of your main home, if you meet certain ownership and use tests at the time of the sale or exchange.

Prior to May 7, 1997, you could have expected to exclude from your gross income $125,000 (the maximum allowable) of gain on the sale or exchange of your main home *if:*

a) you are age 55 or older before the date of the sale or exchange;

b) you owned and lived in the property sold or exchanged as your main home for at least three years out of the five-year period ending on the date of the sale or exchange; *and*

c) you or your spouse have never excluded gain on the sale or exchange of a home after July 20, 1981.

All three tests must be met by one taxpayer. For example, you may be age 55, and your younger spouse may have owned and lived alone in the property for the required three-year period, but because you are not one taxpayer, you cannot take the exclusion.

THE AGE TEST

You must reach age 55 before the date the home is sold to qualify for the $125,000 exclusion. You do not meet the age 55 test if you sell the property during the year in which you will be 55 but before you actually become 55.[5] The key tax-saving technique here is that if you plan to sell or exchange your home, do not do so until your 55th birthday.

THE THREE-YEAR TEST

The required three years of ownership and use during the five-year period ending on the date of the sale or exchange does not have to be continuous. You meet the test if you can show that you owned and lived in the property as your main home for either 36 full months or 1,095 days (365 times 3) during the five-year period. Short temporary absences for vacations or other seasonal absences (even if you rent out the property during these absences) are counted as periods of use.

A taxpayer who is physically or mentally incapable of self-care may qualify for this exclusion if he or she owned and used the residence for at least one year during the five-year period. In computing whether the three-year test has been met, such a taxpayer will be treated as if he or she used the residence for any period during which he or she owned the property and resided in a facility licensed by a state or political subdivision to care for such an individual.

If your previous home was destroyed or condemned, you may use the time that you owned and lived in that home to meet the ownership and use tests, but only if some part of any gain realized on your previous home was reinvested in the new home. Otherwise, you must have owned and lived in the same home.

THE MAIN HOME TEST

Your main home is the place of your principal residence. It is the home in which you live for most of the year—your permanent address, as opposed to a vacation home. Lot size does not count. In *Bogley*, CA-4, 263 F. 2d, 746, the court ruled that a home plus 13 acres constituted this taxpayer's main home.

---

5. Rev. Rul. 68-210, 1968-1 CB 61.

THE ONE-TIME EXCLUSION TEST

You can exclude gain for sales or exchanges made after July 20, 1981 only once in a lifetime. If you or your spouse choose to exclude gain from a sale or exchange, neither of you can do so again. If you each owned separate homes before your marriage, you may exclude the gain on the sale of one of them but not both. If you exclude once and then your spouse dies, or if you divorce and remarry, you are likewise prohibited from excluding in the future. However, you may revoke an earlier decision to exclude gain.

You may make or revoke the choice to exclude gain for a particular sale or exchange at any time before the *latest* of the following dates:

- Three years from the due date of the tax return for the year of the sale.
- Three years from the date the return was filed.
- Two years from the date the tax was paid.

Once you are beyond these allotted periods, your decision is irrevocable. Furthermore, if you are married at the time you sell or exchange your main home, you may not choose to exclude the gain unless your spouse joins you in making the choice. Joint choices and revocations are needed even if:

a) you and your spouse own separate homes;

b) you and your spouse file separate returns; *or*

c) your spouse does not own an interest in the home to be sold and has not lived in it for the required period before the sale or exchange.

If your spouse dies after the sale or exchange but before making the choice to exclude the gain, the deceased's personal representative (for example, an estate administrator or executor) must join with you in making the choice. You, as the surviving spouse, are considered the personal representative of the deceased only if no one else has been appointed.

This exclusion of the first $125,000 in gain provided substantial planning opportunities. For example, assume you want to give your $200,000 home to your two children but do not want to pay a gift tax on the transfer. One technique that is available to accomplish this is to sell them the home on an installment basis. If the gain you realize is not greater than $125,000 on the sale, no gain is taxable to you. You can then have your children pay you the $200,000 purchase price over ten years at $20,000 per year. But you and your spouse can make nontaxable gifts of $20,000 per year to each child ($40,000 a year for the two children) without any income or gift tax consequences. (Note: Both of you must elect to file a split gift return.) Each year, therefore, you exchange checks for the amount due on the sale of your house and you still have $20,000 of tax-free potential gifts available.

Furthermore, using the installment sales technique, any gain in excess of $125,000 is taxable ratably over the ten-year period. So, for example, if the net *gain* is $135,000, only $1,000 per year is included over the ten-year period.

In effect, what you accomplish is a gift of your appreciated house to your children with little if any income or gift tax consequences.

Alternatively, if the house is actually sold, you have $125,000 in tax-free gain without any requirements to reinvest that gain. In either case, smart tax planning and knowledge make you a winner.

These rules were all changed by the Tax Relief Act of 1997. *After May 6, 1997* joint filers can exclude, as often as every two years, as much as $500,000 ($250,000 for single filers) in gain on the sale of a principal residence occupied for two of the five years prior to sale. See Chapter 13 for details of this new exclusion. There is no age requirement for this exclusion.

24 Buying Your Own Home—Twice!—The Schnepper Bootstrap

If you sold your principal home at a profit prior to May 7, 1997, that gain can be sheltered from tax if it is reinvested in a new home within two years. *Problem:* What if you have a new home but cannot find a buyer for your old home within the two-year period? In Letter Ruling 8350084, just before the two-year tax period was up, a taxpayer sold his old home to his own personal corporation. The IRS ruled that it was OK! So long as the sale was legitimate, there was no current tax.

This technique can be used to have your cake and eat it, too. Suppose that you want to move to a new home but do not want to give up the low interest rate mortgage on your old home. Furthermore, suppose that you want to rent your old home at a substantial positive cash flow because of a low mortgage debt service (monthly interest and principal). What you can do is set up an S corporation, sell the old home to that corporation at the high appreciated fair market value, then have that corporation rent the home to an outside tenant. Because you bought a new home within the two-year period, you will recognize no gain on the sale to your corporation. Even though Section 1239 will require that any recognized gain on the sale of the property to the S corporation (a related party) be treated as ordinary income, Section 1034 will generally postpone recognition of that gain so long as the cost of the new residence is equal to or greater than the old residence's adjusted sales price. Moreover, the S corporation will now be able to take *greater* depreciation deductions on the rental property because it bought that property at *appreciated* fair market value. Your tax benefit? Because this is an S corporation, all income and deductions—including the higher depreciation deductions—are now passed through to you and included on your own tax return.[6] Note that the advantage of this strategy has been eliminated by the Tax Relief Act of 1997 for sales after May 6, 1997.

E Miscellaneous Individual Exclusions

25 Carpool Receipts

If you form a carpool to carry passengers to and from work, the amounts received from these passengers are not included in your income. These amounts are considered reimbursement for transportation expenses incurred.

Although your cost of commuting back and forth to work has been subject to continually increasing costs as energy prices have risen, commuting costs are neither deductible nor normally excludable from income. But establishing a carpool can help you defray these expenses without incurring additional taxable income.

Therefore, what you should do is establish a carpool in which the passengers pay you amounts sufficient to cover the cost of your repairs, gasoline, and similar items used in connection with operating your car to and from work. In doing so, you convert personal nondeductible expenses into excludable income.

For example, if it has been costing you $100 a month to commute in the past, you have had to earn $145 (at the 31-percent tax bracket) in order to have the funds to pay for your commute. With a carpool arrangement in which your expenses are reimbursed, it costs you nothing. The establishment of a carpool, therefore, gives you an extra $145 in after-tax disposable income.

6. See also Letter Ruling 8646036, wherein the Internal Revenue Service sanctioned a tax-free exchange of houses between shareholders (a married couple) and their 100-percent-owned S corporation. Moreover, the application of Section 1239 (treating gain on a sale or exchange of property that is depreciable by the transferee between shareholders and the controlled corporation as ordinary income) is deferred until the shareholders sell the newly acquired residence.
See also Letter Ruling 9625035 allowing deferral on a sale to a wholly-owned corporation.

26 Damages (Sec. 104)

Damages received in settlement of a lawsuit or awarded by a court are normally excluded from income under the return of capital doctrine. Theoretically, damages awarded for personal wrong committed against you (for instance, breach of promise to marry, invasion of privacy, libel, slander, alienation of affection) replace the personal capital destroyed by these wrongful acts.[7] Defamation awards are also excludable.[8] Amounts received as damages for personal injury are excludable under both this doctrine and specific congressional mandate.[9] However, damages received as a substitute for income are generally taxable, since they represent a restoration of lost wages or profits that would have been taxable upon receipt.

However, back pay and liquidated damages recovered under the Age Discrimination in Employment Act are not excludable from income.[10] These rules were modified by the Small Business Job Protection Act of 1996.

Under prior law, gross income did not include any damages received (whether by suit or agreement and whether as lump sums or as periodic payments) on account of personal injury or sickness. The exclusion from gross income of damages received on account of personal injury or sickness specifically does not apply to punitive damages received in connection with a case not involving physical injury or sickness. Courts have differed as to whether the exclusion applies to punitive damages received in connection with a case involving a physical injury or physical sickness. Certain states provide that, in the case of claims under a wrongful death statute, only punitive damages may be awarded.

Courts have interpreted the exclusion from gross income of damages received on account of personal injury or sickness broadly in some cases to cover awards for personal injury that do not relate to a physical injury or sickness. For example, some courts have held that the exclusion applies to damages in cases involving certain forms of employment discrimination and injury to reputation where there is no physical injury or sickness. The damages received in these cases generally consist of back pay and other awards intended to compensate the claimant for lost wages or lost profits. The Supreme Court recent-

7. Rev. Rul. 74-77, 1971-1 CB 33.
8. *Threlkeld,* 87 T.C. No. 76.
9. Internal Revenue Section 104(a) (2).
10. *Comm. v. Schleier,* US Sup Ct, No. 94-500, 6/14/95.

ly held that damages received based on a claim under the Age Discrimination in Employment Act could not be excluded from income.

The 1996 law provides that the exclusion from gross income does not apply to any *punitive* damages received on account of personal injury or sickness whether or not related to a physical injury or physical sickness. Prior law continues to apply to punitive damages received in a wrongful death action if the applicable state law (as in effect on September 13, 1995 without regard to subsequent modification) provides, or has been construed to provide by a court decision issued on or before such date, that only punitive damages may be awarded in a wrongful death action.

The 1996 law also provides that the exclusion from gross income only applies to damages received on account of personal physical injury or physical sickness. If an action has its origin in a physical injury or physical sickness, then all damages (other than punitive damages) that flow therefrom are treated as payments received on account of physical injury or physical sickness whether or not the recipient of the damage is the injured party. For example, damages (other than punitive damages) received by an individual on account of a claim for loss of consortium due to the physical injury or physical sickness of such individual's spouse are and will be excludable from gross income. In addition, damages (other than punitive damages) received on account of a wrongful death continue to be excludable from taxable income as under prior law.

The 1996 law specifically provides that emotional distress is not considered a physical injury or physical sickness. Thus, the exclusion from gross income does not apply to any damages received (other than for medical expenses as discussed below) based on a claim of employment discrimination or injury to reputation accompanied by a claim of emotional distress. Because all damages received on account of physical injury or physical sickness are excludable from gross income, the exclusion from gross income applies to any damages received based on a claim of emotional distress that is attributable to a physical injury or physical sickness. However, the exclusion from gross income only applies to the amount of damages received that is not in excess of the amount paid for medical care attributable to emotional stress.

The above provisions generally are effective with respect to amounts received after the date of enactment (August 20, 1996). The provisions do not apply to amounts received under a written binding agreement, court decree, or mediation award in effect on or issued on or before September 13, 1995.

Amounts received to compensate for damages to property or to the good will of a business are also excludable up to the amount of the adjusted basis of the assets. Only receipts in excess of this basis will be taxable. For example, if your car, which cost you $500, is completely destroyed in an accident and you receive $600 as compensation for damages, the first $500 is nontaxable as a return of your capital; you include in your gross income only the $100 excess over your basis.

The difference between the taxable and excludable nature of alternative damages awarded provides an opportunity for sophisticated tax planning. For example, in arranging an out-of-court settlement of a suit involving personal injury and loss of income, you should be aware that damages from personal injury suits are excluded from income but the proportion representing loss of income is fully taxable. Therefore, negotiate for a maximum allocation to the personal injury portion of the settlement.

In fact, it may be more advantageous to take less, totally, if the tax-free portion is increased. Assume you are in the 31 percent bracket and are offered $10,000 for personal injury and $20,000 for loss of income. That leaves you with $23,800 after taxes. A settlement of $20,000 for personal injury and $7,500 for loss of income would give you $25,175, or $1,375 more after taxes. At the same time, it saves the payer $2,500. In such a case, everybody wins—except the Internal Revenue Service.

27 Divorce and Separation Arrangements (Sec. 71)

Prior to July 18, 1984, alimony and support payments were taxable to the recipient spouse only if:

a) the payments qualified as periodic payments *and*

b) the payments were received under a decree of divorce or separate maintenance; *or*

c) the payments were received under a written separation agreement (provided the husband and wife were not living together and did not file a joint return.)[11]

---

11. A married couple living in the same house are not separated and living apart as a *matter of law.* See *Hertsch,* T. C. Memo 1982-109 Par. 57,684; also see *Washington,* 77 T.C. No. 44; but for a contrary decision in the 8th Circuit, see *Sydnes* 78-2 U.S.T.C. Par. 9487, 42 AFTR 2d 78-5143.

Alimony and support payments are termed periodic payments when no fixed total sum is established or when the cessation of payments is contingent upon the occurrence of some event, such as the death or remarriage of the divorced spouse or change in economic status of either spouse.

If you are the recipient spouse, you should be aware that lump-sum settlements are not taxed. Furthermore, where a fixed total sum is set and is payable in installments, the income is not taxable unless the sum is payable over a period of more than ten years.

For arrangements prior to 1984, if a lump-sum settlement is payable in installments of more than ten years, payments in each year up to 10 percent of the principal sum will qualify as periodic payments and be taxable to you. Ordinary periodic payments are taxable when received, whether received in advance or arrears. Under this same rule, the 10 percent limitation applies to advance payments but not to delinquent installment payments. For example, if under a decree of divorce you are to receive a total payment of $13,000 in thirteen annual installments, each payment regularly received will be taxable as a periodic alimony payment. But if your spouse becomes delinquent in one year and pays $2,000 in the following year, the $2,000 is taxable when received. However, if your spouse pays $1,000 as a regular annual payment and pays an additional $1,000 in advance, the taxable amount will be only $1,300 (10 percent of the principal sum).

The Tax Reform Act of 1984 made several significant changes in domestic relations taxation. Under prior law, gain generally was recognized on transfers of property in exchange for the release of marital claims. The Reform Act provides that transfers of property between spouses that are incident to divorce will generally be nontaxable, carryover basis transactions. This means that your spouse, who takes property from you incident to divorce, will have the same basis in that property that you had.

This provision of the Act applies to transfers after the date of the enactment (July 18, 1984), but not to transfers pursuant to instruments in effect on that date unless both parties elect to have the provisions apply. You and your spouse may, in addition, elect to have the provisions apply just to all transfers after December 31, 1983.

Moreover, the rules for taxation of *alimony* have been changed significantly for agreements executed after 1984. The section on alimony starting on page 87 details these provisions.

If the alimony is taxable to the recipient under the above rules, that same amount can be used by the payer as a deduction from adjusted gross income, even if you do not itemize deductions. Child-support payments are never deductible nor are they ever included in the gross income of the recipient. The amount of child support included in the payments should be clearly designated as such by the decree or written separation agreement. Note, however, that a payment, even one clearly delineated as alimony, will not be considered or treated as alimony if the payment is reduced (a) on the happening of a contingency relating to a child of the payer or (b) at a time that can clearly be associated with such a contingency. For this purpose, a contingency relates to a child of the payer if it depends upon any event relating to that child, regardless of whether such event is certain or likely to occur. Events that relate to a child of the payer include the following: the child's attaining a specified age or income level, dying, marrying, leaving school, leaving the spouse's household, or gaining employment.

There are two situations in which payments that would otherwise qualify as alimony or separate maintenance payments will be treated as arising out of a contingency relating to a child of the payer. The first situation is when the payments are to be reduced not more than six months before or after the date that the child is to attain the age of 18, 21, or local age of majority. The second situation is when the payments are to be reduced on two or more occasions that occur not more than one year before or after a different child of the payer spouse attains a certain age between the ages of 18 and 24, inclusive. The certain age referred to in the preceding sentence must be the same for each child, but need not be a whole number of years.

The presumption in the two situations that payments are to be reduced at a time clearly associated with the happening of a contingency relating to a child of the payer may be rebutted by showing that the time at which the payments are to be reduced was determined independently of any contingencies relating to the children of the payer. The presumption in the first situation will be rebutted conclusively if the reduction is a complete cessation of alimony or separate maintenance payments during the sixth post-separation year or upon the expiration of a 72-month period. The presumption may also be rebutted in other circumstances, for example, by showing that alimony payments are to be made for a period customarily provided in the local jurisdiction, such as a period equal to one-half of the duration of the marriage.

For example, assume husband and wife are divorced on July 1, 1985, when their children—daughter (born July 15, 1970) and son (born September 23, 1972)—are 14 and 12, respectively. Under the divorce decree, husband is to make alimony payments to wife of $2,000 per month. Such payments are to be reduced to $1,500 per month on January 1, 1991, and to $1,000 per month on January 1, 1995. On January 1, 1991, the date of the first reduction in payments, daughter will be 20 years, 5 months, and 17 days old. On January 1, 1995, the date of the second reduction in payments, son will be 22 years, 3 months, and 9 days old. Each of the reductions in payments is to occur not more than one year before or after a different child of husband attains the age of 21 years and 4 months. Actually, the reductions are to occur not more than one year before or after daughter and son attain any of the ages of 21 years, 3 months, and 9 days through 21 years, 5 months, and 17 days. Accordingly, the reductions will be presumed to clearly be associated with the happening of the contingency relating to daughter and son. Unless this presumption is rebutted, payments under the divorce decree equal to the sum of the reductions ($1,000 per month) will be treated as fixed for the support of the children of husband and therefore will not qualify as alimony or separate maintenance payments.

Where payments constituting both alimony and child support are made but constitute less than the required amount each year, the payments are considered first to cover child support, with any excess deemed to be alimony.

The excludability of lump-sum alimony and child-support payments provides another avenue for sophisticated tax planning and negotiation. Remember, if the alimony payments are excludable, they are not deductible to the payer. The person making the alimony payments would clearly favor a divorce settlement that includes provisions for deductible alimony payments. On the other hand, the recipient would prefer that the payments do not qualify as includable income. If the payer is in a higher tax bracket than the recipient, both parties may benefit, after taxes, by increasing the payments and constructing them so that they qualify after taxes as "periodic."

For example, assume a husband and wife with no children are in the process of reaching a divorce agreement. If the wife is in a 15 percent tax bracket and the husband is in a 28 percent tax bracket, then $10,000 shifted from property settlement to alimony would produce a net savings of $1,300 [$10,000 × (28 percent minus 15 percent)]. Here again, the husband could pay the wife's taxes and share the $1,300 net savings, and both parties would still be ahead on an after-tax basis.

The same kind of planning can be used with child support. If the recipient is in a higher bracket than the payer, it is a good idea to negotiate for an increase in the amount designated as child support (excludable/nondeductible) in exchange for a reduction in periodic alimony payments (includable/deductible). If the payer is in a higher bracket, increase the amount of includable/deductible alimony in exchange for a reduction in child support.

28 Life Insurance (Sec. 101)

Life insurance proceeds paid to you because of the death of the insured are not taxable unless the policy was purchased by you or transferred to you for a price. This is true even if the proceeds are paid under an accident or health insurance policy or an endowment contract.

If the death benefits are paid to you in a lump sum rather than at regular intervals, they are included in your gross income only if they are more than the amount originally specified as payable at the time of the insured person's death. If the benefit payable at death was not specified, you include the benefit payments in income when they are more than the present value of the payments at the time of death.

If you receive life insurance proceeds in regular installments, you may exclude part of each installment from your income. To determine the excludable part, you must divide the amount held by the insurance company (generally, the total lump sum, the principal, payable at the death of the insured party) by the number of installments that are to be paid. Anything over this excludable part must be included as interest income.

There was one special exception: If insurance proceeds were payable to you after the death of your spouse, and you received the proceeds in installments, you could have excluded up to $1,000 a year of the interest included in the installments in addition to the part of each installment that was excludable as a recovery of the lump sum payable at death. Even if you remarried, you could have continued to take the exclusion. This provision, however, was repealed by the Tax Reform Act of 1986, effective for deaths occurring after the date of enactment (October 22, 1986).

Under current law, if you leave the proceeds from life insurance on deposit with an insurance company under an agreement to pay interest only, the interest paid to you is taxable.

The Health Insurance Portability and Accountability Act of 1996 amended the above rules.

The new law generally excludes "qualified accelerated death benefits" from income. If a contract meets the definition of a life insurance contract, gross income does not include insurance proceeds that are paid pursuant to the contract by reason of the death of the insured. However, recently many chronically or terminally ill individuals with short life expectancies have sold or assigned their life insurance policies to qualified viatical-settlement providers.

These companies typically buy policies from people with life-threatening illnesses for a percentage of the policy's face value. Under prior law, recipients of viatical payments would owe federal income taxes on those payments. The new law excludes these payments from income effective for amounts received after December 31, 1996.

There is an exception to the general rule that life insurance proceeds are excluded from income. This exception is applicable to a life insurance contract that has been transferred for a fee to another individual, who assumes ownership rights. Upon receipt of the proceeds, that individual must include as income the difference between the proceeds and the amount he or she paid for the contract, plus any premiums paid. For example, assume person A owns an insurance policy in the face amount of $10,000 upon the life of person B and subsequently sells the policy to you for $2,000. When B dies, you receive the proceeds of $10,000. The amount that you can exclude from gross income is limited to $2,000 plus any premiums you paid after the transfer.

There are, however, four exceptions to this rule. These are transfers to:

A partner of the insured
A partnership in which the insured is a partner
A corporation in which the insured is an officer or shareholder
A transferee whose basis in the policy is determined by reference to the transferor's basis

This last item translates into a basic exception for policies that are transferred as part of a tax-free exchange—for example, a transfer of insurance policies to a corporation by its controlling shareholders in exchange for the corporation's stock or securities.

One technique that has been suggested in order to qualify for the previous second exception is the creation of a partnership between shareholders wherein that partnership would lease equipment to the co-owned corporation. Such a structure would avoid the transfer-for-value limitation that would normally be held to transfers between shareholders. In this case, the transfer is not merely between shareholders but between partners.

29 Qualified State Tuition (§529) Programs

Current law provides tax exempt status to "Qualified State Tuition Programs." These are programs established by a state or a state agency under which you can (1) purchase tuition credits or certificates for the payment of education expenses or (2) make contributions into an account established to pay qualified education expenses.

The interest or other earnings from such accounts comes out tax free! Several states (e.g., New York) have programs where you don't even have to go to school in that state to qualify. Don't miss this tax free way to finance your kid's college expenses.

Call toll free at 877-277-6496 or check www.collegesavings.org for more information.

F Schedule of Excludable Items

Accident and health insurance premiums paid by your employer
Accident and health proceeds (under insurance purchased by you or under an employee-supported plan) not attributable to a previous medical expense deduction
Annuities (cost excluded over life expectancies)
Awards for noncompetitive achievements (if contributed)
Bequests and devises
Carpool receipts for transportation of fellow employees
Child-support payments received
Contributions paid by your employer to accident and health plans and to sickness and disability funds under sick-benefit laws
Damages for physical personal injuries or sickness
Dependent care, employer-provided services
Disability payments other than for loss of wages
Disability payments under employer-financed accident and health plans
Endowment policy proceeds until cost is recovered
Fellowship and scholarship grants (limited)
Gain on sale of personal residence
Gifts
Group term life insurance premiums—if coverage is $50,000 or less or if employees' contribution premiums exceed the cost of coverage over $50,000
Health insurance proceeds not attributable to medical expense deductions in prior years
Inheritances
Interest on bonds of the state, city, or other political subdivision

Life insurance proceeds paid on the death of the insured under the terms of the contract, unless paid to a transferee
Medical care payments under employer-financed accident and health plans
Merchandise distributed to employees on holidays
Nobel Prize, Pulitzer Prize, and similar awards (if contributed)
Principal residences—up to $500,000
Qualified State Tuition (§529) Plans
Railroad passes to employees and their families
Sickness and injury benefits equivalent to workers' compensation
Social Security and disability benefits (limited)
Supper money paid by employer
Tuition paid by employer (limited)
Viatical payments
Welfare payments

CHAPTER 4

Credits—Dollar-for-Dollar Tax Reductions

"Taxing is an easy business."

EDMUND BURKE
Thoughts on the Cause of the Present Discontent
1770

"It will be of little avail to the people that the laws are made by men of their own choice if the laws be so voluminous that they cannot be read, or so incoherent that they cannot be understood."

The Federalist Papers

A *credit* is a dollar-for-dollar reduction in your tax; it is the best kind of expense to have. If you are in the 31 percent tax bracket, a deduction of $100 saves you $31 in tax, but a credit of $100 saves you $100 in tax. A credit, therefore, is a payment that counts in full as an offset to your tax liability. Because every dollar of credit is really an additional dollar in your pocket, it is imperative that you recognize those situations where credits are available and that you always claim them on your tax return. A lost or forgotten credit is money thrown away in tax dollars.

There are several areas in which potential credits are available. I shall examine each in turn and discuss the ways you can best take advantage of them. But first I want to detail two significant cash-saving techniques: estimating taxes and withholding exemptions.

A Estimated Tax and Withholding Exemptions

Significant savings can be realized by minimizing the amount of estimated tax payments or of taxes withheld from your income before they are actually due. You must pay estimated tax if your estimated total tax liability is more than $1,000 and you meet certain conditions (see below), but you still can minimize these payments. You should pay as little estimated tax as possible and therefore have the use and availability of these tax funds for as long as legally possible.

You need to pay estimated tax if your estimated tax liability is more than $1,000 and:

1. your expected gross income includes more than $500 in income not subject to withholding; or
2. your expected gross income is more than:
   - a) $20,000 if you are single, a head of household, or surviving spouse; *or*
   - b) $20,000 if you are married and might file a joint declaration, and your spouse has not received wages; *or*
   - c) $10,000 if you are married and might file a joint declaration, and both you and your spouse have received wages; *or*
   - d) $5,000 if you are married and might not file a joint declaration.

Estimated tax normally is paid in quarterly installments. You need *not file* a declaration of estimated tax after 1982 but payments must still be made. There is a penalty, which cannot be deducted as interest, of about 8 percent (this rate changes every 3 months) per year for underpaying the estimated tax—unless the total of all payments ("including withholding") made by the due date of each quarter is at least as much as the smallest of the following figures:

- The amount that you would have paid if the estimated tax were the same as the previous year's tax liability, provided the preceding taxable year was a year of 12 months and you filed a return.
- The amount you would have paid if the estimated tax were 90 percent of the tax on your income up to the month in which the installment date falls. For this purpose, the income is *annualized* (computed at an annual rate), based upon taxable income before exemptions, if deductions are itemized, and the alternative minimum tax if applicable.

The first exception is most advantageous when your current year's income is greater than that of the prior year. The last exception is most useful if the greater part of income is received in the later part of the year. In all cases the objective is to pay no more now than is required. Remember, while you may have to pay the tax on April 15, you will have had the use of the money and the interest earned on it during that interim period.

A special rule for taxable years after 1991 provided that the 100% safe harbor is not available if you have modified adjusted gross income in the current year that exceeds your preceding year's adjusted gross income by more than $40,000 ($20,000 if you are married filing separately) and have modified adjusted gross income in the current year in excess of $75,000 ($37,500 if married filing separately). These rules were changed by the Omnibus Reconciliation Act of 1993 for years beginning after December 31, 1993. If your preceding year's adjusted gross income is $150,000 or less, the 100 percent prior year safe harbor is still available. The present year 90 percent rule is also always available. However, if your preceding year's adjusted gross income exceeded $150,000, the 100 percent safe harbor is changed to 110 percent of the preceding year's tax liability.

The rules were changed again for those with an adjusted gross income in excess of $150,000 when the prior year's estimated tax safe harbor was changed to 100 percent for 1998, 105 percent for 1999, 106 percent for 2000 and 2001, and 112 percent for 2002.

This same pay-as-you-go aspect of the federal income tax system requires your employers to withhold income tax on compensation (salaries, wages, tips) paid to you as their employee. The amount of tax withheld by your employer depends upon the amount of salary or wages paid to you and the information you furnish on the W-4 form (the Employee's Withholding Allowance Certificate) that you file with your employer. If you had no income tax liability for the past year and expect to have no tax liability for the current year, you may claim exemption from withholding of income tax. If you are exempt, your employer will not withhold federal income tax from your wages. To claim exemption from withholding, you still must give your employer a completed W-4 form. On it you need to write "exempt" and no withholding will be taken from your wages.

The money-saving technique recommended here is the same as that with the estimated tax. The objective is to minimize the amount of withholding taken out of each paycheck so that you will have the use and interest on the money until the final tax payment is due. For 1999 returns, there is no penalty on underwithholding as long as the total amount withheld for the year is equal to either 90 percent of your final tax liability or 100/105 percent of your last year's tax liability, whichever is smaller.

Unfortunately, most Americans do not underwithhold; they actually *overwithhold.* In 1981, 70 million Americans—fully 80 percent of the taxpayers affected by withholding—had too much money taken from their paychecks. While the Internal Revenue Service eventually returns all excess funds, the taxpayer loses the interest that the money would have generated during the time that it is in the hands of the government. In periods of high inflation, this is no insignificant loss, especially when one considers that the overwithholding averaged $1,326 per refund in 1998. According to William C. Wood of James Madison University, there were, as of July 8, 1998, 77,220,000 refunds for a total of $102,412 billion for the 1998 filing season. That's a lot of interest-free money!

How then can you eliminate overwithholding—even better, how can you begin underwithholding? The first step is to get a W-4 form from your employer and see how many allowances you are currently claiming. Each allowance that you claim will reduce the amount that is withheld from your income.

Allowances are available for the following:

- You get an automatic allowance for each exemption you can claim on your tax return—for yourself, your spouse, and your dependents.
- You get a special withholding allowance if you are single and have only one employer, or if you are married and have only one employer and your spouse is not employed.
- You get additional withholding allowances for the estimated tax credits you expect to take. If you expect to take the earned income credit, credit for child and dependent care expenses, or credit for the elderly, these credits may lower your tax and therefore make you eligible for additional allowances.

- You get additional withholding allowances for employee business expenses, moving expenses, and if you qualify for the additional standard deduction for the aged or the blind.
- You get additional withholding allowances for estimated net losses from your business or profession, from capital losses, from losses on rental property, and from losses from farming expenses.
- You can get a special withholding allowance for potential contributions to an IRA.
- You can get additional withholding allowances if you expect to itemize your deductions and/or pay alimony during the year. (Section 3402 (F))

You can use creative accounting especially in these last areas. The key is expected, not actual, deductions, contributions, and losses. Additional allowances can always be claimed under the *expectation* of making charitable contributions, incurring higher medical expenses, or borrowing money and incurring an increase in interest expense. Additional withholding allowances are permitted for anticipated tax credits as well. But be careful not to go overboard: If your total withholdings equal 100/105 percent of last year's taxes or 90 percent of this year's taxes, you are immune from any penalties or interest (see page 63). Under Reg. Sec. 31. 3420 (i)-2, employers must accede to an employee's request that withholding exemptions be increased. Note that if you have more than ten withholding exemptions, your employer must notify the IRS of the fact.

The advantages of reducing your withholdings can be significant. For example, if you earn $20,000 a year and are single, one additional allowance that you claim reduces the withholding taken from your salary by about $30 per month. That adds up to $360 a year. With five additional allowances, you have the use and interest on $1,500 every year.

You may file a new W-4 form at any time if you wish to change your withholding allowances for any reason. This gives you yet another opportunity for tax savings. Some sophisticated, tax-knowledgeable individuals significantly underwithhold on their income for the first eleven months of the year, file amended W-4 forms and then significantly overwithhold in the final taxable month. A cooperative employer may even withhold your full final month's wages so that your total yearly withholding meets the 90 percent or 100 percent tests detailed above and you can avoid the penalty for underwithholding. In the meantime, you have had the use of and interest on the underwithheld amount. Sadly, the Internal Revenue Service does not pay any interest on any amount overwithheld. In effect, overwithholding is nothing more than granting an interest-free loan to the Internal Revenue Service. Better that the interest is in your pocket.

B Credits

The remainder of this chapter discusses specific credits that can be taken to reduce your taxes due. Please take advantage of them.

30 The Earned Income Credit (Sec. 32)

Certain eligible low-income workers are entitled to claim a refundable credit on their income tax returns. The amount of the credit an eligible individual may claim depends upon whether the individual has one, more than one, or no qualifying children and is determined by multiplying the credit rate by the taxpayer's earned income up to an earned income amount. The maximum amount of the credit is the product of the credit rate and the earned income amount. For taxpayers with earned income (or adjusted gross income [AGI], if greater) in excess of the beginning of the phaseout range, the maximum credit amount is reduced by the phaseout rate multiplied by the amount of earned income (or AGI, if greater) in excess of the beginning of the phaseout range. For taxpayers with earned income (or AGI, if greater) in excess of the end of the phaseout range, no credit is allowed.

The parameters for the credit depend upon the number of qualifying children the individual claims. For 1999, the parameters are given in the following table:

	Two or More Qualifying Children	One Qualifying Child	No Qualifying Children
Credit rate (in percent)	40.00	34.00	7.65
Earned income amount	$9,540	$6,800	$4,530
Maximum credit	$3,816	$2,312	$347
Phaseout begins	$12,460	$12,460	$5,670
Phaseout rate (in percent)	21.06	15.98	7.65
Phaseout ends	$30,580	$26,928	$10,200

For years after 1999, the credit rates and the phaseout rates will be the same as in the preceding table. The earned income amount and the beginning of the phaseout range are indexed for inflation; because the end of the phaseout range depends on those amounts as well as the phaseout rate and the credit rate, the end of the phaseout range will also increase if there is inflation.

In order to claim the credit, an individual must either have a qualifying child or meet other requirements. A qualifying child must meet a relationship test, an age test, an identification test, and a residence test. In order to claim the credit without a qualifying child, an individual must not be a dependent and must be over age 24 and under age 65.

To satisfy the identification test, individuals must include on their tax return the name and age of each qualifying child. Individuals must also provide a taxpayer identification number (TIN) for all qualifying children. An individual's TIN is generally that individual's social security number.

The Personal Responsibility and Work Opportunity Reconciliation Act of 1996 amended the above rules.

Individuals are not eligible for the credit if they do not include their taxpayer identification number and their spouse's taxpayer identification number on their tax return. If an individual fails to provide a correct taxpayer identification number, such an omission will be treated as a mathematical or clerical error under the new law and the taxpayer must be given an explanation of the asserted error and a period of 60 days to request that the IRS abate its assessment.

A second change relates to the disqualified income test for the earned income credit itself. Under prior law, an individual would not be eligible for the earned income credit if the aggregate amount of "disqualified income" of that taxpayer for the taxable year exceeded $2,350. This threshold was not indexed. Disqualified income was the sum of:

1. Interest (taxable and tax exempt).
2. Dividends.
3. Net rent and royalty income.

Under the new law, the following items are added to the definition of disqualified income: Capital gain net income and net passive income that is not self-employment income.

Moreover, the threshold above which an individual is not eligible for the credit is reduced from $2,350 to $2,200 and that threshold is indexed for inflation after 1996 ($2,350 for 1999).

In addition, the 1996 law modifies the definition of adjusted gross income used for phasing out the earned income credit by disregarding certain losses. The losses disregarded are:

1. Net capital losses.
2. Net losses from trusts and estates.
3. Net losses from nonbusiness rents and royalties.
4. 50% of the net losses from businesses, computed separately with respect to sole proprietorships (other than in farming), sole proprietorships in farming, and other businesses.

For purposes of (4) above, amounts attributable to a business that consist of the performance of services by the taxpayer as an employee are not taken into account.

The Tax Relief Act of 1997 made several modifications to the earned income credit rule. It added compliance provisions, denies eligibility for prior acts of recklessness, requires recertification where the credit was denied in the past, and creates a due diligence requirement for paid preparers.

For the purpose of the EIC phaseout, you must now include in adjusted gross income any nontaxable distribution of IRAs, pensions, annuities, and tax-exempt interest, and an addback of 75 percent of business losses. However, the 1997 law provides that workfare payments do *not* qualify as earned income for purposes of the earned income credit.

The Internal Revenue Service (IRS) is required to provide notice to taxpayers with qualifying children who receive a refund on account of the EITC that the credit may be available on an advance payment basis. To prevent taxpayers from incurring an unexpectedly large tax liability due to receipt of the EITC on an advance payment basis, the amount of advance payment allowable in a taxable year is limited to 60 percent of the maximum credit available to a taxpayer with one qualifying child. After providing these notices to taxpayers for two taxable years, the Secretary of the Treasury is directed to study the effect of the notice program on utilization of the advance payment mechanism. Based on the results of this study, the Secretary may recommend modifications to the notice program to the Committee on Ways and Means and the Committee on Finance.

The earned income credit represents dollars in your pocket, but it must be claimed to be received. In effect, it is a form of negative income tax—that is, a refundable credit for taxpayers who do not even have a tax liability. If you are eligible, you may elect to receive advance payments of the earned income credit from your employer rather than from the Internal Revenue Service next year when you file your tax return. To make this election, you must file a certificate of eligibility with your employer and file a tax return for the year the income is earned. Again, the tax advantage here is the use of the money during the year and the potential interest that could be earned on it. If you think that you may be eligible for the earned income credit, immediately speak to your employer and file a certificate of eligibility. Not doing so would be another instance of making an interest-free loan to the Internal Revenue Service.

31 Excess Social Security Tax

If you work for two or more employers during the tax year, too much social security tax may be withheld from your wages. You may claim this excess amount as a credit against your income tax. The tax consists of two parts: (1) old-age, survivor, and disability insurance (OASDI) and (2) medicare hospital insurance (HI). For 1998 the rate on OASDI is 6.20 percent (12.4 percent if self-employed), and on HI it is 1.45 percent (2.90 percent if self-employed).

Your social security tax obligation is computed each year by applying a fixed rate to your wages. There is, however, a maximum wage base (which is subject to change) to which this tax may be applied. For example, in 1999, all wages in excess of $72,600 will not be subject to OASDI social security tax. There is no cap on HI. Therefore, if you work for two employers, earning $72,600 from each, both employers will take the maximum OASDI (6.20 percent × $72,600, or $4,501.20) from your wages. But because you are only liable for a maximum payment of $4,501.20, you can have a credit against your income tax for the additional $4,501.20 subtracted from your wages. This is money you should get back. Even if you owe no taxes, excess social security payments will be refunded to you.

32 The Child and Dependent Care Credit

Congress has attempted to ease the tax burden of those citizens who must pay for dependent care while earning a living by allowing a child care credit. If, in order to work, you incur expenses in connection with the care of certain dependents, you are permitted a credit for those expenses. This credit, unlike the earned income credit or excess social security payments, cannot reduce your tax liability below zero—that is, it is not refundable.

To qualify for this credit:

1. Your child and dependent care expenses must be incurred to allow you to work, full-time or part-time, whether for others or in your own business or partnership. "Work" even includes actively looking for work. Furthermore, your spouse is considered to have worked if he or she:

   a) was a full-time student for five months during the tax year; *or*

   b) is physically or mentally unable to function without supervision or aid.

   This rule applies to only one spouse for any one month.

2. You must have income from work during the year. Unpaid volunteer work or work for a nominal salary does not qualify.

3. You must maintain a home in which you and one or more qualifying persons live. This means that you (and your spouse, if you are married) pay more than half the cost of maintaining your principal residence. If you are married, you and your spouse must live together.

Upkeep expenses normally include property taxes, mortgage interest, rent, utility charges, home repairs, insurance on the home, and food costs. Excluded from upkeep are payments for clothing, education, medical treatment, vacations, life insurance, transportation, mortgage principle, or the purchase, improvement, or replacement of property. For example, the cost of replacing a water heater is not considered upkeep, but the cost of repairing a water heater can be included.

A qualifying person is:

a) your dependent under age 13 for whom you may claim a personal exemption;

b) your dependent (or any person you could have claimed as a dependent if that person had not earned gross income of $2,750 or more) who is physically or mentally not able to care for himself or herself; *or*

c) your spouse, if physically or mentally unable to care for himself or herself.

The physical or mental incapacity must be disabling. People who are not able to dress, clean, or feed themselves because of physical or mental problems or who require constant attention to prevent them from injuring themselves or others qualify.

Qualification is determined on a daily basis when the disability lasts for less than a calendar month. For example, if a dependent or spouse for whom you paid work-related expenses no longer qualifies on September 16, you may include in your computation all work-related expenses through September 15.

33 Child Care Credits for Children of Divorced or Separated Parents

Expenses for the care of children of divorced or separated parents are also allowed for the child care credit under certain conditions. If you are divorced, legally separated under a decree of divorce or separate maintenance, or separated under a written separation agreement, and you have custody of your child for a longer time during the calendar year than the other parent, your child qualifies if certain conditions are met.

To qualify, *all* these criteria must be met:

1. The child must be under age 13 or unable to care for himself or herself.
2. The child must be in the custody of one or both of the parents for more than half the year.
3. One or both of the parents must provide more than half of the child's support during the year.
4. You must normally file a joint return if you are married. If you are legally separated from your spouse under a decree of divorce or separate maintenance, you are not considered married but can still file for the child care credit. The credit may be claimed on a separate return. If you are married and file a separate return, you will not be considered married if:
   - **a)** your home is the home of a qualifying person for more than half the tax year; *and*
   - **b)** you pay more than half the cost of keeping up your home for the tax year; *and*
   - **c)** your spouse does not live in your home for the last six months of the year.

5. You must pay someone other than your spouse or a person you can claim as a dependent for the child's care. You may count payments made to relatives who are not your dependents, even if they live in your home.

Only work-related expenses qualify for the child or dependent care credit, and your expenses must be for the well-being and protection of a qualifying person. Expenses are considered to be work-related if they allow you (and your spouse, if married) to work, not if you incur them while you are working. However, whether the purpose of the expenses is to allow you to work depends upon the facts. Work-related expenses may include the following:

HOME EXPENSES

This covers the cost of ordinary services done in and around your home that are necessary to maintain the well-being and protection of a qualifying person. The services of a housekeeper, maid, or cook usually are considered necessary to run your home if performed at least partly for the benefit of the qualifying person. Payments for the services of a chauffeur or gardener are not included. The expense of food, clothing, education, or entertainment for the qualifying person is not included.

CHILD CARE EXPENSES

These expenses are not limited to services performed in your home. You may include expenses for nursery school or day care for preschool children, or even summer camp (*ZOLTAN* 79 T.C. 1982) if these expenses allow you to work. The Revenue Act of 1987 excludes overnight camp expenses, but summer day camp expenses are still allowable. Amounts you pay for food, clothing, or schooling are not child care expenses. However, if a nursery school or day care center provides these as part of its service, the entire cost is treated as child care. Schooling in the first grade or higher is not treated as part of child care. Neither is the cost of getting your child to and from the center, whether by bus, subway, taxi, or private car, unless the cost is included in the tuition and is not billed separately (IRS Letter Ruling 8303037).

DISABLED SPOUSE OR DEPENDENT CARE EXPENSES

Expenditures for out-of-home, noninstitutional care of a disabled spouse or dependent who regularly spends at least eight hours a day in your home are eligible for the credit. Under prior law, services outside the home qualified only if they involved the care of a child under 13 years of age.

Meals and lodging provided for housekeepers may be added to your child care expenses, and also any added expenses for lodging your housekeeper. For example, if you have moved to an apartment with an extra bedroom for a housekeeper, you may include the added rent and utility expenses for this bedroom.

The *child care credit,* whether for married, divorced, or separated parents, provides a significant opportunity for effective tax planning. For example, if you have an elderly parent whom you wish to help support, money that you give for food may result in a gift tax liability for you. But if you have this parent baby-sit for your children so that you can work, not only will you avoid a potential gift tax penalty on the money you pay that parent, but you will also receive an income tax credit. Furthermore, if that parent eats at your home while providing child care services, you will receive a tax credit for the value of the food eaten—and the value of that food will *not* be taxable income to your parent.

For example, assume you have your mother provide child care to your son so that you may work, and your mother eats $100 worth of food per week. Even if you pay her nothing in dollars, her income tax is unaffected, your gift tax is unaffected, but your income tax will be reduced by a $20–$30 credit for each week she qualifies.

There are limits on the amount of work-related expenses you may use to figure your credit. These are the earned income limit and the dollar limit.

1. *The earned income limit.* If you are single at the end of your tax year, the amount of work-related expenses that you may use to figure your credit may not be more than your earned income for the tax year. If you are married at the end of your tax year, the amount of work-related expenses may not be more than your earned income or the earned income of your spouse, whichever is *less.*

   If you are married and, for any month, your spouse is either a full-time student or not able to provide self-maintenance, your spouse is considered to have an earned income of $200 a month (if there is one qualifying person in your home) or $400 a month (if there are two or more qualifying persons in your home). That disabled spouse is counted as a qualifying person, along with a dependent child. This rule applies to only one spouse for any one month.

   Earned income is all wages, salaries, tips, other employee compensation, fees for professional services, and net earnings from self-employment. It is reduced by any net loss in earnings from self-employment. It does not include pensions, annuities, or payments for your services that were distributions of earnings and profits, other than a reasonable amount for your work for a corporation. In addition, it does not include amounts received under accident or health plans that are not included in your gross income.

2. *The dollar limit.* The child and dependent care credit is computed on a three-tier basis. First, if you have an adjusted gross income of $10,000 or less, you are entitled to a credit equal to 30 percent of your work-related expenses. Then, the credit is reduced by 1 percentage point for each $2,000 of adjusted gross income (or fraction thereof) above $10,000. Finally, if you have an adjusted gross income of over $28,000, the credit is equal to 20 percent of the work-related expenses you paid during your tax year.

The maximum amount of work-related expenses to which you can apply the credit is $2,400 for one qualifying child or dependent, or $4,800 if more than one is involved. Thus, the maximum credit for one qualifying individual ranges from $720, if your income is below $10,000 ($2,400 × .30), to $480 if your income exceeds $28,000 ($2,400 × .20). Similarly, the maximum credit for two or more qualified individuals ranges from $1,440 to $960.

The following table outlines maximum credits available under the current rule:

		Maximum Credit	
Adjusted Gross Income	**Applicable Percentage**	**One Qualifying Individual**	**Two or More Qualifying Individuals**
Up to $10,000	30%	$720	$1,440
10,001–12,000	29%	696	1,392
12,001–14,000	28%	672	1,344
14,001–16,000	27%	648	1,296
16,001–18,000	26%	624	1,248
18,001–20,000	25%	600	1,200
20,001–22,000	24%	576	1,152
22,001–24,000	23%	552	1,104
24,001–26,000	22%	528	1,056
26,001–28,000	21%	504	1,008
28,001 and over	20%	480	960

This chart has been reproduced with permission from Economic Recovery Tax Act of 1981, published and copyrighted by Commerce Clearing House, Inc., 4025 W. Peterson Avenue, Chicago, Illinois 60646.

These figures are yearly limits. You use the $2,400 limit if you had one qualifying person at *any time* during the year. You use $4,800 if you had more than one at *any time* during the year. It is not based on the length of time during the year that your dependent qualified. However, include only the expenses you had for a qualifying person *during the time the person is qualified.* For example, if your child turned 13 in April, you are eligible for the entire $2,400 limit, but only the expenses you had before your child's 13th birthday can be used. If you had expenses of less than $2,400 during that time, only the smaller amount can be used.

The following example shows you how the child care credit is computed. Assume you are a widow and that you maintain a home for yourself and your two preschool children, whom you claim as dependents. You had an earned income of $28,000 for the year and you incurred work-related expenses of $4,000 (for a housekeeper to care for your children in your home) and $1,200 (for child care at a nursery school).

Your credit is computed as follows:

1. In-home child care expenses	$4,000
2. Plus outside child care expenses	+1,200
3. Total work-related expenses	$5,200
4. Maximum allowable expenses for two qualifying children	4,800
5. Multiply by credit rate	× .20
6. Amount of credit	$ 960

Alternatively, assume you are married and have two children. You have an earned income of $28,000, and your spouse was a full-time student from January 2 through May 31 only. If you paid a housekeeper $450 a month from January 2 to May 31 (a total of $2,250) to look after your children, prepare meals, and do housework as time allowed, your credit is figured in this way:

1. Total work-related expenses	$2,250
2. Your earned income	28,000
3. Income considered earned by your spouse ($400/month for five months)	2,000
4. Multiply by credit rate	× .20
5. Allowable credit	$ 400

Remember: Work-related expenses cannot exceed either the $2,400 (for one child)/$4,800 (for two or more) limit *or* your own or your spouse's earned income, and you must use the smaller earned income in your computations.

Note that the Family Support Act of 1988 amended previous rules. For tax years beginning after 1988, a child of the taxpayer is a qualified individual only if the child is under age 13 (rather than 15, as under prior law). Moreover, the dollar amount of expenses eligible for the credit is reduced, dollar for dollar, by the amount of expenses excludable under a dependent care assistance program provided by an employer. In addition, effective for returns whose due date is after 1989, the taxpayer must identify with name, address, and taxpayer identification number (social security number) each person or each institution providing the child care.

A special planning technique is available for taxpayers in the 15% bracket who normally don't qualify for the child care credit. Hire and pay your spouse. Because no payroll taxes are owed on payments to a spouse *who is a household employee,* the income would be taxed at a 15% rate but be subject to a 20% credit. That's a 5% bonus in your pocket!

34 Credit for the Elderly or Permanently and Totally Disabled

To compensate for tax exclusions offered to recipients of social security benefits, this tax credit is offered to those taxpayers who are not covered by social security and spend their retirement years living off past savings and investments. In this way, the credit attempts to help place all elderly taxpayers on a par.

Prior law provided that individuals aged 65 or over, or under 65 with income from a public retirement system, were eligible for a credit equal to 15 percent of the base amount. *Beginning in 1984,* the law increased the base amounts and limits the credit for those under age 65 to individuals with a permanent and total disability who received disability income from public or private employers on account of that disability. You are considered permanently and totally disabled if (1) you are not able to engage in any "substantial gainful activity" because of your physical or mental condition, and (2) your condition has lasted or can be expected to last continuously for 12 months or more, or lead to your death.

"Substantial gainful activity" usually refers to paid work that requires the performance of significant duties over a reasonable period of time. Nonproductive make-work activities will not be treated as "substantial gainful activity." However, if you work full-time or part-time at your employer's convenience for at least the minimum wage, you will usually be treated as engaging in substantial gainful activity. If you do a type of work as a volunteer that is generally done for pay, you may be considered to have a gainful activity even though you receive no "gain."

Disability income is the total taxable amount you are paid under your employer's accident or health plan or pension plan for the time you are absent from work because of your disability and that is included in your income as wages (or payments in lieu of wages). For purposes of the credit, disability income does not include any amount you receive from your employer's pension plan after you reach your employer's mandatory retirement age.

If you are claiming disability, you must have a physician certify that you are permanently and totally disabled and you must attach that certification to your return. If the certification states your condition will not improve, you will not have to file certifications in subsequent years. The change in base amounts is as follows:

Description	Prior Law	New Law
Married with one spouse eligible or unmarried	$2,500	$5,000
Married, joint return, both spouses eligible	$3,750	$7,500
Married, filing separately	$1,875	$3,750

These base amounts *are reduced,* however, by the following:

- Pensions or annuities received under Social Security, Railroad Retirement, and certain other pensions, disability benefits received, and annuities otherwise excluded from gross income; *and*
- One-half of adjusted gross income over:
  $ 7,500—single return
  $10,000—married, joint return
  $ 5,000—married, separate return

In the case of an individual under age 65, the base amount is limited in any event to the amount of his or her disability income. Note that under the Social Security Amendments in 1983, for a married disabled individual filing jointly, one spouse eligible, all disability income will be taxable and no tax credit will be available if adjusted gross income is $20,000 or more.

There are few tax planning strategies that can be employed with the retirement income credit except to note its existence and the fact that it must be claimed to be received. Any failure to recognize or to claim it represents little more than cutting a hole in your wallet and allowing your tax dollars to float freely in the wind.

35 Credit for Interest Paid on Mortgage Credit Certificates

State and eligible local governments are authorized to issue tax-exempt qualified mortgage bonds under Code Section 103A to provide financing for the purchase of a principal residence of a taxpayer. The governmental entity can elect to issue revocable mortgage credit certificates (MCCs) under a qualified mortgage credit certificate program to certain home buyers instead of issuing qualified mortgage bonds.

A qualifying home buyer is one who receives an MCC then arranges financing through conventional sources to acquire a personal residence without the use of tax-exempt obligations. Such indebtedness must be incurred before the close of the second calendar year following the calendar year for which the governmental entity makes the election, and only one MCC may be in effect for any residence at any given time.

An MCC entitles the home buyer-taxpayer to a nonrefundable personal credit for the applicable percentage of interest paid during any tax year during which the certificate is in effect. An MCC is in effect for interest attributable to the period beginning on the date the certificate is issued until either (a) it is revoked by the issuing authorities or (b) the taxpayer sells the residence or it ceases to be the taxpayer's personal residence.

No credit is allowed for any interest paid or accrued to a related person. The certificate credit rate specified in the MCC may range from 10 percent through 50 percent. *Certified indebtedness amount* means the amount of indebtedness specified in the MCC that (a) is incurred by the taxpayer to provide financing on the taxpayer's principal residence and (b) is issued to the taxpayer for the acquisition, qualified rehabilitation, or qualified home improvement of the taxpayer's principal residence. However, if the certificate rate exceeds 20 percent, the maximum credit is limited to $2,000. For example, if you receive a 50 percent MCC and pay $5,000 in mortgage interest, the amount of credit is limited to $2,000, and the remaining $3,000

($5,000 interest paid less $2,000 credit) may be claimed as an itemized interest deduction.

The MCC program must be established by a state or eligible local government entity for a calendar year for which it is authorized to issue qualified mortgage bonds. The Omnibus Budget Reconciliation Act of 1993 modified and retroactively and *permanently* reinstated the program.

C Special Credits

In the past, Congress provided a number of tax incentives to encourage employment or investment in research.

36 Work Opportunity Credit (Formerly Targeted Jobs Tax Credit) (Sec. 51)

Prior to July 1, 1992, the targeted jobs tax credit was available to employers on an elective basis for hiring individuals from several targeted groups. The targeted groups consist of individuals who are either recipients of payments under means-tested transfer programs, economically disadvantaged, or disabled.

The credit generally is equal to 40 percent of up to $6,000 of qualified first-year wages paid to a member of a targeted group.

Effective for individuals who begin work after June 30, 1992 and before December 31, 1994, the 1993 act extended the credit for 30 months to December 31, 1994.

The Small Business Job Protection Act of 1996 amended the above rules.

The new law replaces the targeted jobs credit with a "work opportunity tax credit." The new credit is available on an elective basis for employers hiring individuals from one or more of eight targeted groups. The credit generally is equal to 40 percent of qualified first year wages up to $6,000. The maximum credit is $2,400.

No credit is allowed for wages paid unless the eligible individual is employed by the employer for at least 120 hours in the first year of employment. The credit applies to employees who start work after September 30, 1996 and before (as per a 1998 change) June 30, 1999.

37 Welfare to Work Credit (Sec. 51)

This is a credit of 35 percent of the first $10,000 of eligible wages paid to recipients of long-term family assistance in the first year of employment and 50 percent of the first $10,000 of eligible wages paid in the second year of employment. This credit applies to wages paid for work done before July 1, 1999.

38 Research Tax Credit (Sec. 41)

Prior to July 1, 1995, a research tax credit equal to 20% of the amount by which a taxpayer's qualified research expenditures for a taxable year exceeded its base amount for that year was allowed. The research tax credit expired and does not apply to amounts paid or incurred after June 30, 1995.

A 20% research tax credit also applied to the *excess* of (1) 100% of corporate cash expenditures (including grants or contributions) paid for basic research conducted by universities (and certain nonprofit scientific research organizations) *over* (2) the sum of (a) the greater of two minimum basic research floors and (b) an amount reflecting any decrease in nonresearch giving to universities by the corporation as compared to such giving during a fixed base period, as adjusted for inflation. This separate credit computation was commonly referred to as "the university basic research credit."

The Small Business Job Protection Act of 1996 extended the research tax credit for eleven months—i.e., for the period July 1, 1996 through May 31, 1997, and the Taxpayer Relief Act of 1997 extended its credit again to June 30, 1998. In 1998, it was again extended to June 30, 1999.

39 Orphan Drug Tax Credit

Prior to January 1, 1995, a 50% nonrefundable tax credit was allowed for qualified clinical testing expenses incurred in testing of certain drugs for rare diseases or conditions generally referred to as "orphan drugs." The Small Business Job Protection Act of 1996 extends the orphan drug tax credit for eleven months, i.e., for the period July 1, 1996 through May 31, 1997. The Tax Relief Act of 1997 expanded it permanently.

40 Adoption Assistance

Prior law did not provide a tax credit for adoption expenses nor did it provide an exclusion from gross income for employer-provided adoption assistance. The Federal Adoption Assistance Program provides financial assistance for the adoption of certain special needs children. Specifically, the program provides assistance for adoption expenses for those special needs children receiving federally assisted adoption assistance payments as well as special needs children in private and state funded programs. The maximum federal reimbursement is $1,000 per special needs child. Reimbursable expenses include those nonrecurring costs directly associated with the adoption process such as legal costs, social services review, and transportation costs.

The Small Business Job Protection Act of 1996 provides taxpayers with a maximum nonrefundable credit against income tax liability of $5,000 per child ($6,000 in the case of special needs adoptions) paid or incurred by the taxpayer. Any unused adoption credit may be carried forward by the taxpayer for up to five years. Qualified adoption expenses are reasonable and necessary adoption fees, court costs, attorney's fees, and other expenses that are directly related to the legal adoption of an "eligible child."

In the case of an international adoption, the credit is not available unless the adoption is finalized. An "eligible child" is an individual (1) who has not attained age 18 as of the time of the adoption, or (2) who is physically or mentally incapable of caring for himself or herself. No credit is allowed for expenses incurred (1) in violation of state or federal law, (2) in carrying out any surrogate parenting arrangement, or (3) in connection with the adoption of a child of the taxpayer's spouse. The credit is phased out ratably for taxpayers with modified adjusted gross income above $75,000, and is fully phased out at $115,000 of modified adjusted gross income.

Note that the credit for non-special-needs adoptions will not be available for expenses paid or incurred after December 31, 2001. Moreover, special needs foreign adoptions are limited to a maximum credit of $5,000 (rather than $6,000) for qualified adoption expenses until December 31, 2001, at which time the credit for special needs foreign adoptions is also repealed. The credit for special needs domestic adoptions ($6,000) is permanent.

With respect to the exclusion from income, under the new law a maximum exclusion of $5,000 ($6,000 in the case of special needs adoptions) is available for specified certain adoption expenses provided by an employer. The limit is a per-child limit, not an annual limitation. The exclusion is phased out ratably for taxpayers with modified adjusted gross income above $75,000 and is fully phased out at $115,000 of modified adjusted gross income. No credit is allowed for adoption expenses paid or reimbursed under an adoption assistance program.

Note that the exclusion is not available for expenses paid or incurred after December 31, 2001 and that special needs foreign adoptions are limited to a maximum exclusion of $5,000 (rather than $6,000) for qualified adoption expenses until December 31, 2001 at which time the exclusion is repealed.

41 Hope Scholarship Credit

The Tax Relief Act of 1997 created this new credit for qualified tuition and fees paid during the *first* two years of post-secondary or certificate education after 1997.

The credit is equal to:

100% of the first $1,000 in tuition and fees	$1,000
50% of the next $1,000 in tuition and fees	500
for a maximum Hope Credit of	$1,500

This credit is phased out between adjusted gross income of $40,000 to $50,000 for singles, and $80,000 to $100,000 for joint returns.

42 Lifetime Learning Credit

The Tax Relief Act of 1997 created this credit for tuition and fees up to $5,000 ($10,000 after December 31, 2001) for undergraduate OR *graduate* level and professional degree courses paid after June 30, 1998.

The maximum credit is 20% of up to $5,000 of qualified tuition and fees or $1,000. It is a per family, not per child (as is the Hope Scholarship Credit), credit.

43 Child Tax Credit

Present law provides a $500 ($400 for 1998) tax credit for each qualifying child under the age of 17. A qualifying child is one you can claim as a dependent and who is either your issue, stepchild, or an eligible foster child. It is non-refundable for less than three children but may be partially refundable for three or more children.

The credit is phased out on a joint return earning more than $110,000 and for singles earning more than $75,000. For every $1,000 or part thereof earned, the credit is reduced by $50. For a joint return earning more than $119,000, the credit is eliminated completely.

44 District of Columbia—First Time Homebuyer

First time homebuyers of a principal residence in the District of Columbia may be eligible for a tax credit of up to $5,000 of the amount of the purchase price.

The credit is available for property purchased between August 4, 1997 and before January 1, 2001. It is phased out on a joint return with adjusted gross income of between $110,000–$130,000 ($70,000 to $90,000 for others).

Author's Note: While some of the preceding credits may not be available for current tax years, if you qualified in a prior year, you can amend the prior year's return and claim any past credit you missed. Returns can be amended up to three years after their due date.

CHAPTER 5

"Above the Line" Deductions

"Take it off. Take it all off...."

GYPSY ROSE LEE

INCOME TAX RATES

Year	Maximum Individual Rate	Year	Maximum Individual Rate
1914	7%	1954	91
1916	15	1964	77
1917	67	1970	70
1918	77	1981	50
1920	65	1987	38.5
1921	50	1988	28/33
1924	40	1989	28/33
1926	25	1990	28/33
1934	63	1991	31
1936	79	1992	31
1941	81	1993	36/39.6
1942	88	1994	36/39.6
1944	94	1995	39.6
1945	91	1996	39.6
1951	92	1997	39.6
		1998	39.6
		1999	39.6

Our tax system is founded on a multistep computation. You begin with gross income. This is all income, all accession to wealth, clearly realized, over which you have dominion, less those items defined earlier as tax exclusions. From gross income you then subtract a certain category of expenses called by tax practitioners adjustments or *"above the line" deductions.* A deduction is a reduction of your taxable income—the income base on which your tax is imposed. *"Above the line" deductions* include trade and business deductions, alimony, reimbursed expenses of employees, IRA, Keogh, and SEP deductions, and employee business expenses of performing artists.

Gross income less adjustments (*"above the line" deductions*) gives your adjusted gross income. From adjusted gross income, you then subtract the greater of your itemized deductions (*"below the line" deductions*) or your standard deduction. The standard deduction is basically similar to the old zero bracket amount. It is different from the zero bracket amount in that it is a deduction from adjusted gross income and not a tax bracket.

Unlike pre-1987 law, if you itemize your deductions you will not be required to reduce your itemized deductions by the amount of the standard deduction (zero bracket amount). Instead, you will deduct 100 percent of your itemized deductions and not take the standard deduction. Therefore, you will only itemize deductions if they exceed the amount of your standard deduction.

For taxable years beginning in 1999, the standard deduction amounts are as follows:

Married taxpayers filing jointly	$7,200
Heads of households	6,350
Single taxpayers	4,300
Married taxpayers filing separately	3,660

Prior to 1987, an additional personal exemption was available if you were 65 or older or blind. (For 1999 tax returns, a taxpayer is deemed to be 65 or older if his or her 65th birthday falls on January 1, 2000, or earlier; one is legally blind if one's central visual acuity does not exceed 20/200 in the better eye with corrective lenses, or if the diameter of one's visual field subtends an angle of 20 degrees or less. This additional personal exemption has been replaced by an increased standard deduction called "the additional amount." If you or your spouse qualified for the age or blindness exemptions under prior law, you will qualify for these additional amounts. The additional amounts are as follows:

1. $1,050 for individuals who are not married and not filing as surviving spouses.
2. $850 for all other taxpayers.

These additional amounts, if available, will be added to the regular standard deduction and treated in the same way as the standard deduction. However, any taxpayer who is the dependent of another taxpayer for purposes of the dependency exemption will have a limited standard deduction. Such a taxpayer's standard deduction will be the greater of either $700 or that individual's earned income plus $250 up to the amount of the regular standard deduction.

Your tax computation continues with a subtraction for your personal exemptions, leaving a figure called your taxable income. Your tax is based on your taxable income. For the taxable year 1999, the amount of the personal exemption is $2,750. For taxable years beginning in a calendar year after 1989, there is an inflation adjustment to the exemption amount. This inflation adjustment will be based on the consumer price index for all urban consumers issued by the U.S. Department of Labor.

In summary, the process appears as follows:

Gross Income
– Adjustments ("above the line" deductions)

Adjusted Gross Income
– Itemized ("below the line") Deductions or Standard Deduction

---

(Subtotal)
– Personal Exemptions

Taxable Income

To reduce your tax you must reduce your taxable income. One of the most important things to do, therefore, is to recognize and claim all available deductions. The chart that follows shows the value of every dollar of deductions in terms of dollars saved for each taxpayer classification.

Note that the higher your taxable income, the more valuable the dollar amount of deductions. This is the result of our progressive tax structure. I will use this structure later to show you how you could reduce your taxes by shifting income from the 39.6 percent bracket (where you keep only 60.4¢ from each additional dollar you earn) to the 15 percent bracket (where you keep 85¢ from

TABLE 1. Dollar Values of Deductions Claimed, 1998

Single			Married Filing Joint Returns and Qualifying Widows and Widowers			Married Filing Separate Returns			Head of Household		
Taxable Income		Value of Each Dollar of Deductions	Taxable Income		Value of Each Dollar of Deductions	Taxable Income		Value of Each Dollar of Deductions	Taxable Income		Value of Each Dollar of Deductions
Over	But not Over		Over	But not Over		Over	But not Over		Over	But not Over	
$ 0	$ 25,750	15¢	$ 0	$ 43,050	15¢	$ 0	$ 21,525	15¢	$ 0	$ 34,550	15¢
25,750	62,450	28¢	43,050	104,050	28¢	21,525	52,025	28¢	34,550	89,150	28¢
62,450	130,250	31¢	104,050	158,550	31¢	52,025	79,275	31¢	89,150	144,400	31¢
130,250	283,150	36¢	158,550	283,150	36¢	79,275	141,575	36¢	144,400	283,150	36¢
283,150		39.6¢	283,150		39.6¢	141,525		39.6¢	283,150		39.6¢

each additional dollar you earn). But first you must recognize and understand the concept of tax-deductible expenses. To do that, you must understand the basic difference between deductions *for* adjusted gross income ("above the line" deductions) and deductions *from* adjusted gross income ("below the line" deductions).

A Deductions for Adjusted Gross Income

There are several categories of deductions for adjusted gross income that you must be aware of to minimize your taxes. We will take each in turn:

45 Trade and Business Deductions

All "ordinary and necessary expenses" paid or incurred by you during your taxable year in carrying on any trade or business are allowed as "above the line" deductions.

Here it is very important to understand that the words "ordinary and necessary" are words of art. For an expense to be deductible, it need not be absolutely necessary in the sense that you cannot conduct your trade without incurring such an expense. The courts have interpreted the words "ordinary and necessary" to mean "reasonable and customary," and this interpretation has been accepted by the Internal Revenue Service. Therefore, any expenses that you might incur in your business that are reasonable and customary for that business, even if not in any sense necessary, are deductible.

This provides you with an excellent opportunity to convert what would normally be nondeductible personal expenses into deductible business expenses. For example, assume that you have your own trade or business in New York and want to take a vacation in Miami. Alternatively, you could live in Miami and want to vacation in California. Almost all businesses have professional associations or trade groups who conduct seminars or hold meetings in resort areas. If you could schedule your vacation in these areas at the same time as the professional meeting and attend that professional meeting, your travel expenses, subject to the limits discussed in Chapter 8, would be converted from personal expenses into allowable, deductible business expenses. While attendance at these conventions or trade shows might not be necessary to your business, it would be reasonable and customary. Later in the book I will discuss more of these extensive tax advantages for those who own their own businesses.

46 Employee Business Expenses of Actors and Other Performing Artists

Employee business expenses of actors and other performing artists are deductible in arriving at adjusted gross income. In order to qualify, the performing artist must have performed services in the performing arts as an employee for at least two employers during the year. For this purpose, a nominal employer, i.e., one from whom less than $200 was received for the performance of such services during the year, is excluded.

Moreover, the allowable expenses in connection with the performance of the services must be more than 10 percent of the taxpayer's gross income from the services, and the individual's adjusted gross income for the year, before deducting these expenses, cannot be more than $16,000.

A performing artist who is married at the end of the taxable year must file a joint return with his/her spouse to qualify for the above the line deduction unless both husband and wife live apart at all times during the year. In the case of a joint return, the two-employer requirement as well as the requirement that the expenses be more than 10 percent of gross income are applied separately with respect to each spouse. However, the $16,000 adjusted gross income test is applied to the combined adjusted gross income of both spouses. In effect, such performing artists are allowed the deductions as if they were independent contractors rather than employees.

Such deductions would be allowable "above the line" and would include all "ordinary and necessary" expenses incurred by you during your taxable year. These expenses are detailed in the section on Miscellaneous Trade and Business Deductions on page 224.

47 Employee Business Expenses

Under prior rules, if an employer reimburses an employee (1) for expenses by the employee in connection with the performance of services as an employee and (2) pursuant to a "reimbursement or other expense allowance arrangement," the amount reimbursed generally is includable in the employee's gross income and is deductible in full by the employee as an adjustment to gross income. On the other hand, unreimbursed employee business expenses can be deducted only as miscellaneous itemized deductions and thus are subject to the 2 percent adjusted gross income floor on such deductions.

In Rev. Rul. 77-350, the Internal Revenue Service held that, in certain circumstances, an employee could claim an "above the line" deduction for certain expenses incurred pursuant to "nonaccountable plans." These are arrangements under which the employee is not required to substantiate the expenses covered by the arrangement to the person providing the reimbursement, or the employee has the right to retain amounts in excess of the substantiated expenses covered under the arrangement. Congress became concerned that the 2 percent floor could be circumvented by restructuring the form of an employee's compensation so that the salary amount is decreased but the employee receives an equivalent nonaccountable expense allowance.

To prevent this, effective for tax years beginning after 1988, employee business expenses paid or incurred under nonaccountable plans are deductible by an employee *only* as an itemized deduction subject to the 2 percent floor. Otherwise allowable employee business expenses are deductible above the line as reimbursed expenses *only* if they were incurred pursuant to a reimbursement or other expense allowance arrangement that *requires* the employee to substantiate expenses covered by the arrangement to the person providing the reimbursement. An employee who receives a per diem or other fixed allowance from an employer will be considered as substantiating the amount of expenses covered by the arrangement up to amounts that have been specified by the IRS.

48 Alimony

Certain payments that constitute "alimony" may be taken as above the line deductions by the payer. Such "alimony" payments may be made from husband to wife or from wife to husband. For illustration purposes, I will refer to payments coming from husband to wife.

The Internal Revenue Service tax code provides that periodic payments received by a wife in discharge of her husband's obligation of support arising out of the marital or family relationship are deductible if any one of the following situations is true:

1. The payments are made in discharge of a legal obligation incurred under a court order, decree of divorce, or legal separation, where the spouses are either divorced or legally separated.
2. The payments are made under a written separation agreement where the spouses are separated, living apart, *and* do not file a joint return.
3. The payments are made under a court order or decree for the spouse's support or maintenance where the spouses are separated, living apart, *and* do not file a joint return.

PRE-TAX REFORM ACT OF 1984 LAW

Such payments are deductible by the husband and would therefore also be included in the wife's income. If any of the payments are fixed, in terms of a total amount of money or of payment for the support of minor children, they will not be deemed alimony and will neither be taxed to the wife nor deductible by the husband. Prior to the Tax Reform Act of 1984, to qualify as child support payments rather than periodic alimony, the amounts must have been designated specifically as child support and not left to determination by inference or conjecture. Any amounts paid will be applied first to child support if such amounts are less than the total required to be paid. To be child support, though, the payments must be used for the support of minor children of the payer, the age of majority to be determined by applicable state law.

Periodic alimony payments will be deductible by the payer as an above the line deduction for adjusted gross income. In order to be deductible, the payments must be periodic rather than installment payments of a principal sum. Whether the payments are made at regular intervals is irrelevant; the key is whether they are periodic or principal sum payments, and the distinction between these two is whether there is a total amount to be paid that can be computed with certainty. If this is the case, the payments are *not* periodic. If the payments are contingent on death, remarriage of the wife, or a change in the economic status of either spouse, they *are* deemed to be periodic. This contingency may be a result of the decree or the separation agreement, or may be imposed by local law.

There is an exception to this general rule: If the principal amount payable under the terms of the divorce or separation decree is to be paid over more than ten years from the date of the decree, then the payments *will* be considered periodic, but only the portion that equals 10 percent of the principal amount. For example, in a settlement of $300,000 to be paid over fifteen years, with a first payment of $40,000, the recipient must include as gross income $30,000; the remainder is excludable. This limitation does not apply to late payments, but it does apply to advance payments. Late payments are treated as if they were made on time, and since both parties are deemed to be cash-basis taxpayers, these payments will be deductible when paid.

A payer may establish a trust or use an existing trust to discharge an obligation created by the decree of separation or divorce. All periodic payments from this kind of trust will be taxable to the recipient. Payments made by the trust will not be deductible by the payer, but an amount of the trust income that is equal to what is paid to the recipient will be excludable from the payer's gross income. An equal inclusion and deduction therefore result.

Other payments may or may not be deductible as "periodic alimony." Payments for medical or dental insurance or direct medical or dental expenses for the spouse, even though made at irregular intervals, would be periodic. If the parties hold property jointly, any payments made that equal the recipient's interest in the property will be deductible by the payer—except where there is a right of survivorship. In that case, the payer will get a deduction only if the recipient is personally liable on the underlying debt or realizes an ascertainable increase in the value of the property that would be received as a survivor. No payments that are allocatable to the payer's interest in the property can be deducted by the payer or included in the recipient's income.

If the recipient resides in the home, utility expenses and repairs will be deductible regardless of ownership because the recipient is receiving a direct economic benefit. Capital expenditures must be capitalized rather than deducted. Periodic payments of life insurance premiums will also constitute deductible alimony payments if the recipient receives an economic benefit and is the absolute owner. Premium payments are not deductible if the policy is merely a security device, or if the recipient interest is contingent upon not remarrying or upon surviving the payer or the children who are the primary beneficiaries of the policy. In these cases, no present economic benefit to the recipient is ascertainable.

Property settlements, moreover, will not constitute periodic alimony. The intent of the parties, as determined by all of the facts and circumstances, will be the controlling factor here, rather than the label used. Property settlements *not* made out of the marital or family obligation of support will therefore be neither deductible nor includable. You should be aware, though, that if appreciated property is transferred in exchange for your spouse's inchoate marital rights, you will realize a gain equal to the full fair market value of the property less your cost or other basis. The character of the gain will be determined by the nature of the property you transfer. The spouse receiving the property will have a stepped-up basis and realize no gain. The amount realized there is deemed to be equal to what is exchanged.

If the property exchanged has depreciated in value, **never** make the transfer until the marriage has been dissolved. Otherwise, the loss will not be recognized. An alternative route to avoid this tax trap would be to sell the property to a third party and give the proceeds to your spouse. Be aware, though, that the rules do *not* apply in a community property state where all divisions are considered to be partitions of jointly owned property. There, taxable income will not be realized unless the division is clearly unequal in value.

POST-TAX REFORM ACT OF 1984 LAW

The Tax Reform Act of 1984 made significant changes both to the alimony rules and to property transfers incident to a divorce. With reference to property transfers incident to a divorce, the transfer will be treated in the same manner as a gift and therefore no capital gain or loss will be recognized for tax purposes. This rules applies to all transfers made after the date of enactment of the Act, or if both parties elect, to both transfers made between December 31, 1983 and the date of enactment as well as to transfers made after the date of enactment pursuant to instruments in effect before that date.

With reference to the rules governing alimony, the 1984 Act requires that alimony be paid in cash and terminate at the death of the payee spouse, that the parties may not be members of the same household at the time the payment is made, and that no amount will be deductible as alimony to the extent the payment is contingent on the status of a child (for example, if the payment terminates when a child marries, dies, or reaches maturity). Furthermore, under the 1984 Act, if payments in any year exceed $10,000, no part of such payments will be deductible unless the agreement provides that the payments be made for at least six years (unless the spouse dies or the payee spouse remarries), and a decline in excess of $10,000 in payments between any two successive years will cause a recapture of the excess amount. The effective date of the rules was January 1, 1985 for divorce or separation agreements executed on or after that date. The provisions apply to divorce or separation agreements executed before January 1, 1985 but modified on or after such date if the modification expressly provides that these provisions will apply.

The Tax Reform Act of 1986, however, amended the six-year rule. Under the new law, amounts that are considered "excess alimony payments" will be included in taxable income of the payer in the *third* postseparation year. This inclusion will eliminate the benefit of the previous deduction for such payments. The payee will also be permitted a deduction corresponding to the amount includable in the payer's income in that third year.

Excess alimony payments are determined as follows:

- For the first postseparation year the excess alimony payment is that amount that exceeds the average of alimony payments in the second and third years plus $15,000. The excess alimony payment for the second year is that amount that exceeds the payment in the third year by more than $15,000. For example, a divorce agreement provides that the husband will pay his former wife alimony over a three-year period as follows:

1st year	$35,000
2nd year	10,000
3rd year	20,000

- To calculate the excess alimony payment for the first year, the average of the second- and third-year payments must be computed. This average is $15,000 ([$10,000 + $20,000] ÷ 2). The excess alimony payment for the first year is therefore $5,000 ($35,000 – [$15,000 + $15,000]). In the third year the husband will have to include the $5,000 excess alimony payment in income, and the ex-wife will receive a corresponding deduction of $5,000.

  The formula is as follows:

$$\text{Excess payments} = \text{alimony paid in 1st year} - \left[\$15{,}000 + \frac{\text{alimony paid in 2nd year} - \text{excess payments in 2nd year} + \text{alimony paid in 3rd year}}{2}\right]$$

- To complete the computation, the second-year excess amount must be determined first.

  The excess payment for the second postseparation year is the excess of the second-year alimony paid over the sum of third-year alimony paid plus $15,000; i.e.,

$$\text{Excess payment} = \text{alimony paid in 2nd year} - \left(\text{alimony paid in 3rd year} + \$15{,}000\right)$$

- If alimony consists of one payment of $30,000 in the first postseparation year, and no alimony is paid thereafter, the amount recaptured is $15,000:

$$\$30{,}000 - \left[\$15{,}000 + \frac{(0 - 0) + 0}{2}\right]$$

- If alimony paid in the first postseparation year is $50,000, in the second is $25,000, and in the third is zero, the second-year excess payment is $10,000:

$$\$25{,}000 - (0 + \$15{,}000)$$

- The first-year excess payment is $27,500:

$$\$50{,}000 - \left[\$15{,}000 + \frac{(\$25{,}000 - \$10{,}000) + 0}{2}\right]$$

- The recapture amount is $37,500, the sum of the first- and second-year excess payments. If $25,000 had also been paid in the third year, the recapture amount would be $10,000, the amount of the first-year excess payment, as there is no second-year excess payment:

$$\$50{,}000 - \left[\$15{,}000 + \frac{(\$25{,}000 - 0) + \$25{,}000}{2}\right]$$

The objective is to allow alimony payments as deductible if they are made in as few as three years. However, if the first payment is made in December 1994, the second in January 1995, and the third in January 1996, the alimony will be deductible even though the payments are in fact spread over only 13 or 14 months.

Moreover, recapture is not required if alimony ceases when death or remarriage occurs before the end of the third postseparation year. Payments under temporary support agreements are also excluded from the recapture rules. In addition, the 1986 Act clarified that payments will not be disqualified from being treated as alimony simply because the divorce or separation agreement does not specifically state that the payments will terminate at the death of the recipient and, finally, that payments contingent on the fluctuating earnings of a business or property or from employment will also not result in recapture, if the obligation to pay extends for at least three years. These 1986 amendments apply to divorce or separation instruments executed after December 31, 1986, and divorce or separation instruments executed before that date if modified on or after such date to expressly state that the new provisions will apply.

The Tax Reform Act of 1984 also changed the rules with respect to which divorced parent receives the dependency exemption for a child. Beginning in 1985, the custodial parent is entitled to the exemption unless:

1. the custodial parent releases the exemption for the year, by written declaration on Form 8332, to the noncustodial parent. This form must be signed by the custodial parent and attached to the noncustodial parent's return.

2. a decree of divorce or separate maintenance or a written agreement was executed before 1985, under which the custodial parent released the exemption to the noncustodial parent. In this event, the noncustodial parent can claim the exemption if he or she provides at least $600 annually for the child's support. However, the parties can expressly modify the document to render this exception inapplicable.

3. a multiple support agreement is in effect.

Note also that under the 1984 Act, support by a remarried parent's new spouse is considered support furnished by that parent, and children of divorced parents are treated as *both* parents' dependents for medical deduction purposes. Hence, a parent can deduct medical expenses paid for a child even though the other parent gets the dependency exemption for that child.

Furthermore, a custodial parent who releases a dependency exemption will be considered as retaining that exemption when determining marital and head of household status, the earned income credit, and the child and dependent care credit. If otherwise eligible, such a parent could still qualify for unmarried and head of household status and those credits. For example, to claim head of household status, an individual must maintain a household as his or her home, which is also the principal place of abode for more than half a year for his or her unmarried children (or their unmarried descendants), married children (or their unmarried descendants) if they are dependents (including "would-be dependents"), or other dependents. The status is also available, as before, if a household is maintained for a taxpayer's dependent parents for a full year.

Several additional tax planning strategies present themselves based upon the rules. If a separation rather than a divorce is desired, you should be aware that while a *decree* of separate maintenance will prevent the filing of a joint return, mere physical separation will not. Physical separation, though, combined with a written separation agreement, will make any periodic payments "alimony," and deductible as such. Therefore, your first tax consideration must be to weigh the benefits of a joint return against an alimony deduction. Depending upon the marginal tax brackets of each party, a limited amount of shifting the tax burden may also occur here. Trade-offs, in terms of higher receipts in exchange for the filing of a joint return, may also be made by sophisticated and aware taxpayers.

You must carefully consider the character of any payments to be made—that is, whether they are for child support or alimony. Child support is neither includable nor deductible. Here again a certain amount of tax shifting is possible. If any payment for child support is not specifically designated as such, it potentially may be taxed or deducted as alimony. If the recipient is in a lower tax bracket than the payer, any increase in "alimony" from child support will be taxable at a lower marginal rate and deductible at the payer's higher marginal rate. Because of this tax savings, the payer can afford to pay a larger amount of "child support," enough to offset the recipient's increased tax burden, plus a little more.

For example, assume that a husband-payer has a marginal tax bracket of 31 percent and his recipient-wife has a marginal tax bracket of 15 percent. The husband plans to pay periodic alimony of $10,000 and child support of $10,000 per year. The wife has agreed. This agreement would cost the husband $16,900 per year:

Child support (no deduction)	$10,000
Alimony [$10,000 × (1 – .31)]	+6,900
	$16,900

The wife would keep $18,500 per year:

Child support (no inclusion)	$10,000
Alimony [$10,000 × 1 – .15]	+8,500
	$18,500

If the husband converted the whole $20,000 to alimony, it would cost him only $13,800:

Alimony [$20,000 × (1 – .31)] = $13,800

He therefore would save $3,100 over the original agreement. The wife would now have:

Alimony [$20,000 × (1 – .85)] = $17,000

which is a loss of $1,500. But this loss could be offset by the $3,100 saved by the husband. All he would have to do is increase the alimony payments to $22,500:

Cost to husband [$22,500 × (1 – .31)] = $15,525

Wife keeps [$22,500 × (1 – .15)] = $19,125

The result of this plan is that the husband would save $1,375 ($16,900 – $15,525) over the first plan. The wife's position would also be better—by $625 ($19,125 – $18,500)!

Another tax planning strategy involves post-1984 separations. If a husband transfers stock that has appreciated in value from $10,000 to $100,000, the 1984 law relieves him of the tax on the gain and gives it to his wife instead. This presents another alternative strategy for shifting income from a high bracket taxpayer (husband) to a lower bracket taxpayer (wife). To offset this incidence of taxation, the recipient wife should again negotiate an increased payout to absorb, or reduce, the husband's net tax savings on the transfer of appreciated, rather than nonappreciated, property.

49 Interest on Qualified Education Loans

Interest paid on qualified education loans is deductible above the line for payments made during the first 60 months in which payments are required.

The maximum amount of this deduction was $1,000 for 1998, is $1,500 for 1999, $2,000 for the year 2000, and $2,500 for tax years 2001 and after.

The deduction is phased out for taxpayers with modified adjusted gross income between $40,000 and $55,000 for single filers, and between $60,000 and $75,000 for joint returns.

You must be legally obligated to make the payments (sign the note) and you can't be claimed as a dependent if you want to qualify for this deduction.

50 Retirement Plan Payments

With any degree of inflation, it is important that you carefully provide for sufficient retirement funds. The same significant consideration must also be given to sheltering current income from the painful bite of our progressive tax system. The above the line deduction for retirement plan payments allows you to satisfy both of these needs.

If you are self-employed, which includes being an owner or a partner of an unincorporated business, you may provide for your retirement by setting up either a Keogh plan (H.R. 10 Plan) or an individual retirement plan, as described below. Under the Self-Employed Individual's Tax Retirement Act of 1962 (also called the Keogh Act and H.R. 10), you are permitted to put a portion of your yearly earned income, on a tax-deferred basis, into a fund that can earn tax-free income until it starts paying out at retirement.

You are eligible for an individual retirement account (IRA) if you or your spouse are employed, self-employed, or even covered by a corporate pension plan. You may not have an IRA in addition to a Keogh plan.

Under both an IRA and a Keogh plan, a portion of your income is sheltered from current taxation; there is no tax on the earnings of the fund until postretirement distribution; there is no tax on income contributed to the fund until postretirement distribution; and qualified contributions made by employers to provide employees with retirement benefits are deductible by the employers. Both Keogh plans and IRAs allow the self-employed owner of a business to shelter current earned income and allow that income to accumulate and earn currently nontaxable income until postretirement distribution.

The primary difference between a Keogh plan and an IRA is the amount of earnings that may be sheltered. Under an IRA, as much as 100 percent of compensation—up to a limit of $2,000 a year—may be put aside, and that amount, subject to the limits detailed below, is deductible. If you have a nonemployed spouse, the contribution maximum increases to $4,000. With a

Keogh plan, the contribution limits are 25[1] percent of earned income or $30,000, whichever is less. (Defined benefit plans allow an amount computed to yield a maximum annual benefit of $130,000 for 1999.) A special type of IRA called a Simplified Pension Plan will also allow contributions—the lesser of $30,000 or 15 percent of earned income. The major constraint for both the Simplified Pension Plan and the Keogh plan is that in both cases the owner (considered an employee as well under certain plans) may be forced to make contributions for other employees as well; however, these contributions will be deductible. The ultimate decision as to whether to establish an IRA or Keogh plan or both should be made on the basis of which has the greatest cash savings after tax.

If you are an employer, you may set up an individual retirement account for yourself without setting up a similar one for your employees. With a Keogh plan you must cover your employees.

IRA PLAN[2]

There are several advantages to an IRA. An IRA allows the owner of a business to shelter personal earned income for retirement *without* the requirement to make contributions for employees. As a taxpayer eligible for an IRA, you would be allowed to contribute for a nonemployed spouse and the contribution maximum would increase ($2,000 each for years after 1996). The purpose of this is to provide retirement income for nonemployed homemakers. Contributions are deposited into separate accounts for you and your nonemployed spouse or into one account with subaccounts for each. No one account, however, may have attributed to it more than $2,000 in contributions per year. In case of divorce, the homemaker keeps his or her share of the money. Of course, if both spouses are employed and are eligible, each can set aside 100 percent of earnings, up to $2,000 each year, in separate IRAs.

The tax deduction for the IRA contribution is available as an above the line deduction. Taxes on both contributions to and earnings of the account may be deferred until the funds are withdrawn as retirement benefits. At that time you may be in a lower tax bracket than previously and may qualify for retirement income credits. At age 65 you are entitled to the additional standard deduction. So during the period you receive your IRA funds, you may be

1. For owner-employees only, this is 25 percent of income after the Keogh deduction. This really equals 20 percent of pre-Keogh earned income.
2. Note that for tax years beginning after 1997, the Tax Relief Act of 1997 created new IRAs and modified the phaseout rules for old IRAs. The details can be found in Chapter 13.

paying a smaller percentage of your income for taxes than you did in earlier years. Benefits from IRA plans can be drawn without penalty anytime after reaching age $59^1/_2$. Distribution must begin no later than April 1st in the year following the year you attain age $70^1/_2$. This rule has been modified by the Small Business Protection Act of 1996.

The 1996 law modified the rule that requires all participants in qualified plans to commence distributions by age $70^1/_2$ without regard to whether the participant is still employed by the employer and generally replaces it with the rule in effect prior to the Tax Reform Act of 1986. Under the 1996 law, distributions are generally required to begin by April 1 of the calendar year following the later of first, the calendar year in which the employee attains age $70^1/_2$ or the calendar year in which the employee retires. However, in the case of a 5% owner of the employer, distributions are required to begin at no later than April 1 of the calendar year following the year in which the 5% owner attains age $70^1/_2$.

In addition, in the case of an employee (other than a 5% owner) who retires in a calendar year after attaining age $70^1/_2$, the 1996 law requires the employee's accrued benefit to be actuarially increased to take into account the period after age $70^1/_2$ in which the employee was not receiving benefits under the plan. Thus, under the 1996 law, the employee's accrued benefit is required to reflect the value of benefits that the employee would have received if the employee had retired at age $70^1/_2$ and had begun receiving benefits at that time. However, this actuarial adjustment rule does not apply in the case of a defined contribution plan.

Earnings eligible for IRA contributions include wages, salaries, or professional fees and other amounts received for personal services actually rendered, including (but not limited to) commissions paid to sales personnel, compensation for services on the basis of a percentage of profits, commissions on insurance premiums, tips, and bonuses. All contributions must be made in cash. No deductions are allowable for contributions of property.

If you receive payment from an IRA before you reach age $59^1/_2$ or before you become disabled, the payment will be considered a premature distribution. That amount received is included in your gross income in the tax year of receipt. In addition, your income tax liability for that year will be increased by an amount equal to 10 percent of the premature distribution includable in gross income. This penalty can be avoided by withdrawing substantially equal annual amounts over your life expectancy, until age $59^1/_2$ or for five years, whichever comes later. For example, if you are 58, you must make withdrawals through age 63. However, if you are age 45, you must continue making withdrawals through age $59^1/_2$. Once you finish making the *required withdrawals* they may be modified or stopped.

As discussed above, amounts withdrawn from an individual retirement arrangement (IRA) are includable in income (except to the extent of any nondeductible contributions). In addition, a 10% additional tax applies to withdrawals from IRAs made before age $59^1/_2$ and unless the withdrawal is made on account of death or disability or is made in the form of annuity payments.

A similar additional tax applies to early withdrawals from employer-sponsored tax qualified pension plans. However, the 10% additional tax does not apply to withdrawals from such plans to the extent used for medical expenses that exceed 7.5% of adjusted gross income.

The Small Business Job Protection Act of 1996 extends the exception to the 10% tax for medical expenses in excess of 7.5% of adjusted gross income to withdrawals from IRAs. In addition, it provides that the 10% additional tax does not apply to withdrawals for medical insurance (without regard to the 7.5% of adjusted gross income) if the individual (including a self-employed individual) has received unemployment compensation under federal or state law for at least 12 weeks, and the withdrawal is made in the year such unemployment compensation is received or the following year. If a self-employed individual is not eligible for unemployment compensation under applicable law, he or she is treated as having received unemployment compensation for at least 12 weeks if the individual would have received unemployment compensation but for the fact the individual was self-employed.

The Taxpayer Relief Act of 1997 extended the exception to the 10% penalty to *first time home purchases* and *qualified higher education expenses.*

A first-time home buyer is an individual (and/or spouse) who has had no present ownership interest in a primary residence during the two-year period ending on the date of acquisition (see below) of the principal residence. A first-time home buyer under these rules does not necessarily mean a person buying a home for the first time. For example, individuals could be buying their fifth home yet qualify as "first-time" home buyers if they have had no ownership interest in a primary residence for the past two years.

A Date of acquisition is the date when a binding contract to purchase a principal residence is executed or the date when construction or reconstruction of a principal residence begins.

Qualified acquisition cost is the cost of acquiring, constructing or reconstructing a residence.

The amount withdrawn for the purchase of a principal residence is required to be used within 120 days of the date of withdrawal. You are limited to a $10,000 lifetime withdrawal. Even though withdrawals made from traditional IRAs for first-time home purchases are penalty-free, they may be subject to regular income taxes. (Withdrawals from a Roth IRA, discussed below, can be both penalty *and* tax free if the five year requirement is met).

The 1997 tax law also allows you to make penalty-free withdrawals from traditional IRAs for higher education expenses, such as tuition at an eligible postsecondary education institution, room and board, fees, books, supplies, and equipment required for enrollment or attendance. Expenses for graduate-level courses also are covered. You can use your IRA distribution to pay for these expenses incurred by you, your spouse, your children, your spouse's children, your grandchildren, or your spouse's grandchildren. Please note that this type of withdrawal is not an income-tax-free distribution.

SUMMARY OF PREMATURE DISTRIBUTION RULES

Many taxpayers mistakenly fail to pay the additional 10% tax due on premature distributions. Premature distributions (sometimes called early withdrawals or early distributions) are subject to an additional 10% tax. The definition of premature distributions are amounts that are withdrawn from traditional Individual Retirement Accounts (IRAs) or annuities before the individual reaches the age of $59^1/_2$.

In certain circumstances, the additional tax does not apply to premature distributions from the IRA or annuity even though they are made prior to reaching the age of $59^1/_2$.

There are exceptions for:

- Certain unemployed individuals to pay health insurance premiums
- Certain medical expenses (beginning after December 31, 1996)
- Disability
- Death
- Annuity distributions
- Qualified higher education expenses (beginning after December 31, 1997)
- Qualified first-time homebuyer (beginning after December 31, 1997 $10,000.00 lifetime limitation)
- IRS levy on IRA (beginning after December 31, 1999)

The additional tax is equal to 10% of the premature distribution that must be included in gross income. The tax is in addition to any regular income tax that is due. It does not include tax-free rollovers. For more information regarding the additional 10% tax, see Publication 590, Individual Retirement Account Arrangements (IRAs) including Roth IRAs and Education IRAs.

Taxable distributions from an individual retirement account are taxed as ordinary income regardless of their source. They are not eligible for capital gains treatment or the special averaging rules that apply to lump-sum distribution from qualified employer plans (which are available only through December 31, 1999).

If you die before receiving the entire interest on your individual retirement account, the remaining interest must be distributed to your beneficiary within five years after death, or be applied to purchase an immediate annuity for the beneficiary payable over the life or for a period not exceeding the life expectancy of that beneficiary. Any annuity contracts so purchased must be distributed immediately to the beneficiary.

Tax deductible contributions to an IRA must be made through:

a) an individual retirement account at a bank, federally insured credit union, or savings and loan association, or with certain applicants, any of whom, under temporary regulations, may act as a trustee or custodian;

b) an individual retirement annuity of a life insurance company;

c) individual retirement bonds purchased from the U.S. government; *or*

d) a trust account established by an employer or employee association.

The following transactions with IRA money are prohibited by law:

1. You cannot borrow money from your IRA.
2. You cannot use money in an IRA as collateral for a loan.
3. You cannot transfer property to an IRA in exchange for money.
4. You can put only cash into an IRA. For example, you cannot put stock that you currently own into an IRA account. You must sell the stock first, put the cash from that sale into your IRA, and then purchase the stock again if you want to have that stock in the IRA account.

While not specifically prohibited, note that an IRA investment in a limited partnership interest where business income is passed through would trigger an IRA tax on "unrelated business income" (IRS Letter Ruling 9703026).

You can, however, invest your IRA funds in real estate—from raw land to rental property. While you can't manage the property, your trustee can hire a third party to do so. Moreover, the property must remain in the IRA trust until distribution at retirement and the property can't be mortgaged.

Moreover, you should note that any stock in an IRA account that is sold loses the capital gains treatment. This means that when you withdraw your money from the IRA, gains cannot be offset by capital losses in excess of $3,000.

Starting with 1987, the Tax Reform Act of 1986 made substantial changes in IRA eligibility. Under the prior law, IRA deduction is retained for returns of taxpayers who meet *either* of the following requirements:

1. The taxpayer is not an active participant in certain specified retirement arrangements for any part of the plan year ending with or within the taxpayer's tax year. Active participation status is determined without regard to whether a taxpayer has a vested right to any benefits under a plan and may depend upon the type of plan in which an individual participates or is eligible to participate. For example, for defined benefit plans, a person who is not excluded under the plan's eligibility provisions for any part of the plan year ending with or within the taxpayer's tax year is an active participant. Therefore, even if you elect not to participate in a plan or fail to make an employee contribution required to accrue a benefit attributable to employer contributions, you nevertheless are an active participant in the plan. For defined contribution plans, a taxpayer is an active participant if employer or employee contributions or forfeitures are required to be allocated to his account for a plan year ending with or within the taxpayer's tax year. According to the IRS, a taxpayer may be an active participant even if a required contribution for the plan year is not actually made. However, unlike defined benefit plans, an individual who does not meet the hours of service requirements of a defined contribution plan is not considered an active participant unless contributions or forfeitures have been allocated to her account. For a married individual filing a joint return, neither the individual taxpayer nor the taxpayer's spouse may be an active participant. Moreover, retirement arrangements not only include traditional qualified plans, annuity plans, and trusts, but also include simplified employee pensions and 401(k) plans. For 401(k) plans however, you are usually not an "actual participant" until pay-ins are made to the plan.)

2. The taxpayer has adjusted gross income that does not exceed the "applicable dollar amount." For a married couple filing jointly, combined income may not exceed the applicable dollar amount. The applicable dollar amount was (a) $25,000 for an individual, (b) $40,000 for a married couple filing a joint return, and (c) $0 for a married couple filing separately.

Active participants whose adjusted gross incomes exceed the applicable dollar amount by no more than $10,000 are still entitled to deduct IRA contributions, but only in a reduced amount calculated according to the following formula provided by the IRS:
Note that for this purpose, adjusted gross income includes social security benefits and passive income or losses, but not IRA contributions.

For example, assume that you and your spouse earn $25,000 and $20,000 in adjusted gross income (total $45,000) and that your spouse is a participant in a qualified pension plan. Your maximum permissible dollar deduction would be $4,000 ($2,000 for you and $2,000 for your spouse). Your maximum deductible IRA, however, would be computed as follows:

$$\frac{\$10{,}000 - \text{excess adjusted gross income}}{\$10{,}000} \times \begin{array}{c}\text{the maximum permissible}\\ \text{dollar deduction defined}\\ \text{as the lesser of 100}\\ \text{percent of compensation}\\ \text{or \$2,000 (\$2,250 for}\\ \text{spousal IRAs)}\end{array} = \begin{array}{c}\text{adjusted dollar}\\ \text{deduction limit}\end{array}$$

Your maximum tax-deductible IRA would therefore be only $2,000. Taxpayers not above the phaseout maximum ($50,000 for a joint return) are permitted a minimum IRA deduction of $200. Moreover, prior to the Tax Reform Act of 1986, a spousal IRA of $250 was allowed only if the spouse had no compensation. Under new law, an individual may elect to be treated as if he or she had no compensation for the taxable year. This means, for an otherwise qualifying couple, the annual deduction contribution was increased from $2,000 to $2,250 ($4,000 for years after 1996 under the Small Business Job Protection Act of 1996).

Maximum IRA		$4,000
Less: Phaseout over $40,000		
($45,000 – 40,000) × $4,000 / $10,000	=	$2,000
Tax-deductible IRA		$2,000

The Taxpayer Relief Act of 1997 changed the rules again. We now have three kinds of IRAs. The first is the current deductible IRA. The 1997 law raises the phaseout income limits on these front-loaded IRAs for those covered by a qualified plan. Under prior law, if your modified adjusted income (for a joint return) was between $40,000 and $50,000, your IRA deduction was reduced and then eliminated (the limits were $25,000–$35,000 for single filers). These phaseout amounts are raised by $10,000 for couples and $5,000 for singles in 1998, and by $1,000 per year through 2002; in 2003 they increase to $40,000 for single filers and $60,000 for joint filers, and by $5,000 per year thereafter. At the end of that time the phaseout limits would have doubled. The phaseout will then be from $80,000–$100,000 for joint returns, and $50,000–$60,000 for single filers. Moreover, the new law allows a nonworking spouse to contribute a fully deductible $2,000, even if the other spouse participates in a qualified retirement plan, with a phaseout between $150,000 and $160,000. The following table summarizes the changes in phaseout rules:

	Joint (in thousands)	**Single (in thousands)**
1997	$40–50	$25–35
1998	50–60	30–40
1999	51–61	31–41
2000	52–62	32–42
2001	53–63	33–43
2002	54–64	34–44
2003	60–70	40–50
2004	65–75	45–55
2005	70–80	50–60
2006	75–85	
2007	80–100	

The new, second kind of IRA is the *Roth IRA*. Here, contributions will not be deductible but, if the IRA is held for at least five years (the five-year period starts on the first day of the year for which a contribution is made or in which the first conversion contribution is made) and the account holder is at least 59.5 years old, then all withdrawals will be tax free! Moreover, more people will be eligible for these accounts because the income limits phase out at from $95,000–$110,000 for single taxpayers and from $150,000–$160,000 for couples.

Holders of either of these two IRAs will be able to make penalty-free withdrawals to make a first-time home purchase, or for college expenses. However, the combined contributions to these two types of accounts is limited to $2,000 per year for each taxpayer, and you cannot withdraw the money for five years. You could roll savings over from a regular IRA in the Roth IRA account but some taxes would be assessed upon the rollover. These taxes will be spread over 4 years, if done in 1998, to minimize the impact of the change. I think it is a reasonable toll charge to avoid all future taxes on the account. After 1998, the four-year spread is not available. Whether you should convert is a function of your age and the expected return on the account. The older you are, the less advantageous the conversion becomes.

The law also created a new *Education IRA*, also called *Education Savings Accounts.* Contributions can be made of up to $500 per child under age 18 into an Education IRA, with an income limit of from between $95,000–$110,000 for singles and $150,000–$160,000 for couples. These IRAs will be nondeductible, but the earnings are tax free. There is no penalty if they are used for educational purposes (including tuition, fees, room and board), regardless of your age. Any unused portion of an Education IRA can be rolled over to another child but, if the children do not attend college, the amounts must be paid out when the last child turns 30. Even if you don't qualify because of income limits, your parents may qualify to set up an account for their grandchildren. With an education IRA, the donor doesn't even have to be related to the beneficiary!

Table 2, from Steve Leightman of A.G. Edwards, on pages 111–112 compares the traditional and the Roth IRA. The table on page 113 calculates your deductibility/eligibility for the traditional and Roth IRA.

Since 1987, *nondeductible* contributions to an IRA may be made up to the maximum deduction, reduced by any deductible contributions. Therefore, even if your contribution deduction is reduced under the adjusted gross income limitation, you can contribute the difference without deducting it. The earnings on such contributions are not taxed until distribution. Any nondeductible contribution must be indicated on your tax return for the contribution year.

If nondeductible contributions are made, withdrawals from IRAs must be divided between taxable and nontaxable segments. The Tax Reform Act of 1986 uses an averaging approach to accomplish this task. For purposes of the

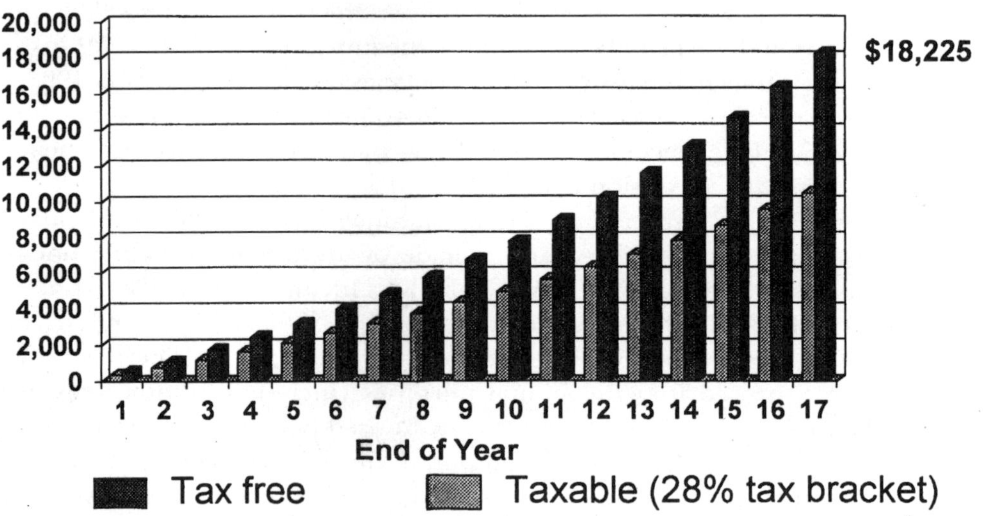

computations, all of a taxpayer's IRAs are considered to be one single IRA and all withdrawals made during the year are added together and considered as one withdrawal. The percentage of an IRA withdrawal treated as a return of a nondeductible contribution, and therefore not taxable, is represented by a ratio whose numerator is the sum of all nondeductible contributions made to any of the taxpayer's IRAs and whose denominator is the sum of the balances in the taxpayer's IRAs at the end of the tax year plus withdrawals made during the year.

Tables 3 to 6, on pages 114–115, developed by Jerrold J. Stern of the Graduate School of Business, Indiana University, show break-even points at various tax and interest rates for deductible IRA contributions and nondeductible IRA contributions. Note that the tables include a 10 percent penalty on withdrawals prior to age 59. Where the taxable percentage of the principal is zero, the tables assume that tax and penalty are paid only on the interest earned, and

TABLE 2. Comparison of Traditional and Roth IRA

		Traditional IRA	Roth IRA (Effective Jan. 1, 1998)
CONTRIBUTIONS	**Maximum**	$2,000 per year of W-2 or Schedule G earnings up to age 70fi. $2,000 maximum combined contribution into traditional or Roth IRA per individual, per year. Contribution is not limited by adjusted gross income (AGI)	$2,000 per year of W-2 or Schedule G earnings (contributions allowed after age 70fi). Contributions amount is limited if AGI is between: • $95,000 and $110,000 for individual returns • $150,000 and $160,000 for joint returns $2,000 maximum combined contribution into Roth IRA or traditional IRA per individual, per year.
	Provisions Above AGI Limits	Nondeductible contributions allowed above AGI limits (up to $2,000 maximum) when participating in employer retirement plan.	Cannot participate if AGI exceeds stated limits (see "Maximum" subsection above).
	Tax Deductibility	When covered by an employer's retirement plan, tax-deductible if AGI is less than: • $51,000 for individual returns • $51,000 for joint returns Partially deductible if covered by an employer's retirement plan and if AGI is between: • $31,000 and $41,000 for individual returns • $51,000 and $61,000 for joint returns *A spouse not covered by an employer-sponsored retirement plan may fully deduct an IRA contribution if joint AGI is less than $150,000 and partially deduct a contribution when joint AGI falls between $150,000 and $160,000.*	Contributions are not tax deductible
ACCUMULATIONS	**Interest, Dividends and Capital Gains**	Grow tax deferred until withdrawn.	Grow tax-deferred and distributed income tax free as long as you abide by withdrawal rules (see "Distributions" section below).
	Suitable Investments	CDs; common and preferred stocks; unit investment trusts; government, corporate, and mortgage-backed bonds; mutual funds; private money managers.	CDs; common and preferred stocks; unit investment trusts; government, corporate and mortgage-backed bonds; mutual funds; private money managers.

DISTRIBUTIONS	**When Allowed**	After reaching age 59fi.	May withdraw up to original contribution amount at any time (may not apply to converted balances).
	Taxation	Withdrawals after age 59fi taxed at ordinary income tax rates.	Withdrawal of earnings after age 59fi are income-tax-free as long as investments have been in the account for five consecutive years. Before age 59fi and meeting the five-consecutive-year requirement, earnings may be withdrawn income-tax-free if one of the following qualifications is met: • Death. • Disability. • First-time home purchase up to $10,000 (once-in-a-lifetime use).
	When Penalty Applies	10% IRS penalty (in addition to ordinary income tax rates) applies to taxable withdrawals before reaching age 59fi (unless certain exceptions apply or withdrawal qualifies as "special purpose;" see conditions described below).	10% IRS penalty (in addition to ordinary income tax rates) applies to investment earnings withdrawn before reaching age 59fi regardless of the five-year investment period (unless certain exceptions apply as described below or withdrawal qualifies as "special purpose," also described below).
	Exceptions to 10% IRS Penalty	• First-time home purchase up to $10,000 (once-in-a-lifetime use). • Qualified higher education expenses. • Death. • Disability. • Substantially equal payments (annuitization). • Medical expenses exceeding 7.5% of AGI. • Health insurance premiums when receiving unemployment compensation for longer than 12 months.	• First-time home purchase up to $10,000 (once-in-a-lifetime use). • Qualified higher education expenses. • Death. • Disability. • Substantially equal payments (annuitization). • Medical expenses exceeding 7.5% of AGI. • Health insurance premiums when receiving unemployment compensation for longer than 12 months.
ROLLOVERS/CONVERSIONS	**Mandatory Distributions**	Required minimum payments must begin by age 70fi.	No required minimum payments at any time.
	Qualifications	In 1998, taxpayers with less than $100,000 AGI may roll over traditional IRA balances to a Roth IRA. Subject to ordinary income tax that may be spread over the four subsequent tax years. After 1998, taxpayers with less than $100,000 AGI who roll over traditional IRA balances to a Roth IRA will incur ordinary income taxes on amounts rolled over and taxes may be due in the year the rollover occurs. Rollovers must follow the 60-day rules.	Taxpayers may roll over a Roth IRA to another Roth IRA without incurring income or penalty taxes. Rollovers must follow the 60-day rules. Rollovers from a qualified retirement plan are not allowed into a Roth IRA.

Roadmap to IRA Eligibility

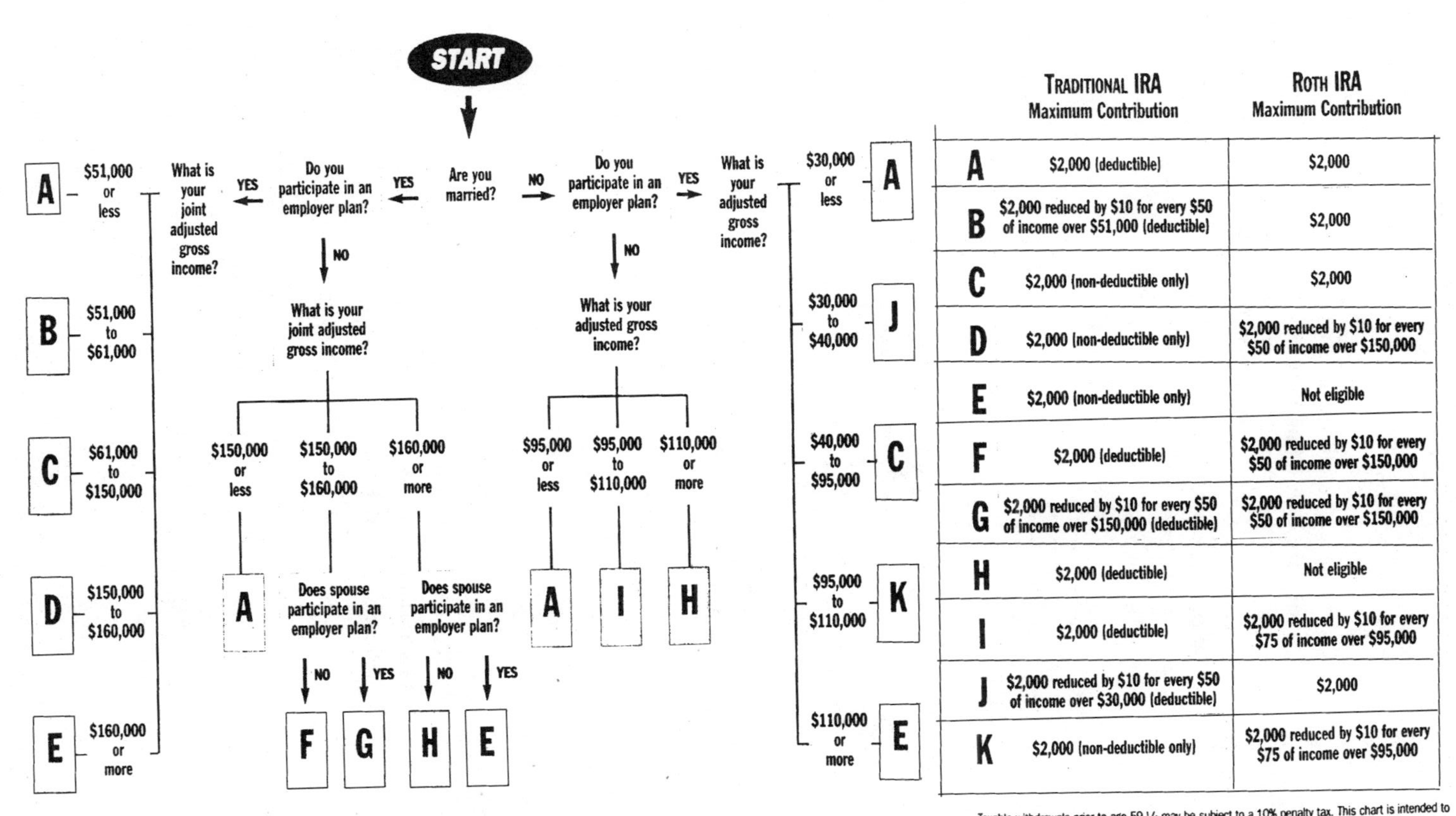

This road map applies only to single taxpayers or married taxpayers filing jointly. Married taxpayers filing separately should not use it.

	Traditional IRA Maximum Contribution	Roth IRA Maximum Contribution
A	$2,000 (deductible)	$2,000
B	$2,000 reduced by $10 for every $50 of income over $51,000 (deductible)	$2,000
C	$2,000 (non-deductible only)	$2,000
D	$2,000 (non-deductible only)	$2,000 reduced by $10 for every $50 of income over $150,000
E	$2,000 (non-deductible only)	Not eligible
F	$2,000 (deductible)	$2,000 reduced by $10 for every $50 of income over $150,000
G	$2,000 reduced by $10 for every $50 of income over $150,000 (deductible)	$2,000 reduced by $10 for every $50 of income over $150,000
H	$2,000 (deductible)	Not eligible
I	$2,000 (deductible)	$2,000 reduced by $10 for every $75 of income over $95,000
J	$2,000 reduced by $10 for every $50 of income over $30,000 (deductible)	$2,000
K	$2,000 (non-deductible only)	$2,000 reduced by $10 for every $75 of income over $95,000

Taxable withdrawals prior to age 59 1/2 may be subject to a 10% penalty tax. This chart is intended to give you a general summary of the IRA contribution rules; you should consult your tax adviser about your individual situation.

TABLE 3. Years before Break-Even: Deductible IRA Contributions

Interest Rates	Marginal Tax Rates 15%	28%	33%
4%	22	14	13
6	15	10	9
8	12	8	7
10	10	6	6
12	8	5	5

TABLE 4. Years before Break-Even: Nondeductible IRA Contributions, Taxable Percentage of Principal = 0%

Interest Rates	Marginal Tax Rates 15%	28%	33%
4%	37	26	24
6	25	18	17
8	20	14	13
10	16	11	11
12	14	10	9

TABLE 5. Years before Break-Even: Nondeductible IRA Contributions, Taxable Percentage of Principal = 100%

Interest Rates	Marginal Tax Rates 15%	28%	33%
4%	50	45	44
6	34	30	30
8	26	23	23
10	21	19	19
12	18	16	16

TABLE 6. Years before Break-Even: Nondeductible IRA Contributions, Taxable Percentage of Principal = 50%

	Marginal Tax Rates		
Interest Rates	**15%**	**28%**	**33%**
4%	45	38	38
6	31	26	26
8	24	20	20
10	19	17	16
12	17	14	14

Calculating Deductibility of Your Traditional IRA Contribution*

	1999 Single	Joint
AGI Limit	$41,000	$61,000
Your modified AGI	– ______	– ______
AGI limit less your modified AGI	______	______
Divide remainder by†	$10,000	$10,000
Percentage of your contribution eligible	______%	______%
Multiply by $2,000	× 2,000	× $2,000
Amount you can deduct	$______	______

Calculating Eligibility for a Roth IRA Contribution*

	1999 Single	Joint
AGI Limit	$110,000	$160,000
Your modified AGI	– ______	– ______
AGI limit less your modified AGI	______	______
Divide remainder by†	$15,000	$10,000
Percentage of your contribution eligible	______%	______%
Multiply by $2,000	× 2,000	× $2,000
Amount you can contribute	$______	______

*Maximum combined contribution may not exceed $2,000 per individual, per year.
†These numbers are determined by the range between minimum and maximum AGI for partially deductible contributions to the traditional IRA and for eligible contributions to the Roth IRA.

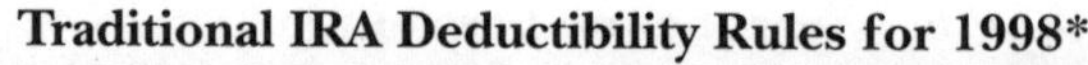

Traditional IRA Deductibility Rules for 1998*

NO — **Are you or your spouse covered by a retirement plan at work?** — **YES**

NO: *IRA contribution 100% deductible*

YES: **What is your adjusted gross income? (AGI)**

Single individual covered by retirement plan at work

Less than $31,000
IRA contribution 100% deductible

Between $31,000 and $41,000
IRA contribution partially deductible

More than $41,000
IRA contribution nondeductible

Married couple filing jointly, both covered by retirement plan at work

Less than $51,000
Both spouses' IRA contributions 100% deductible

Between $51,000 and $61,000
Both spouses' IRA contributions partially deductible

More than $61,000
Both spouses' IRA contributions nondeductible

Married couple filing jointly, one spouse covered by retirement plan at work

Less than $51,000
Both spouses' IRA contributions 100% deductible

Between $51,000 and $61,000
— Noncovered spouse's IRA contribution 100% deductible
— Covered spouse's IRA contribution partially deductible

$61,000 to $150,000
— Noncovered spouse's IRA contribution 100% deductible
— Covered spouse's IRA contribution nondeductible

$150,000 to $160,000
— Noncovered spouse's IRA contribution partially deductible
— Covered spouse's IRA contribution nondeductible

More than $160,000
— Both spouse's IRA contributions nondeductible

* *The income limits for deductibility will rise each year for unmarried individuals through 2004 and for married individuals through 2007.*

that the principal contribution (for example, $2,000) withdrawn is received tax-free.

Remember that if a taxpayer and spouse have joint income in excess of $50,000 and if even one spouse is covered by a retirement plan, joint return deductions for payments to individual retirement accounts are phased out. In IRS Notice 87-16 the IRS held that if separate returns were filed, an IRA deduction could be taken by the spouse who was not in a retirement plan. For some couples that deduction might outweigh the tax cost of separate returns. However, the staff of Congress's Joint Tax Committee has reported that an IRA was not meant to be deductible on a separate return unless a couple "did not live together at any time during the taxable year." This contradicts the prior IRS holding and eliminates this avenue of tax deductibility.

Certain investments are off limits to IRA holders. They include investments in collectibles, such as rare books; rugs; artworks; metals, such as gold, silver, and platinum; antiques; stamps; coins; alcoholic beverages; and any other forms of tangible personal property. In addition, life insurance, as opposed to annuities offered by life insurance companies, is also off limits to IRA investors. Under the Tax Reform Act of 1986, however, you may invest in gold and silver coins issued by the United States. This provision is effective for coins acquired after 1986.

The deadline for making contributions to an IRA is April 15, the date for filing the taxpayer's return. Taxpayers who establish an individual retirement account or annuity are required to file Form 5239, Return for Individual Retirement Savings Arrangements, with their income tax return only if they owe IRA penalty taxes (for instance, on excess contributions, premature distributions, or the failure to distribute at age $70^1/_2$).

In private ruling 8527082 the IRS affirmed that you may deduct interest paid on money borrowed to put into an IRA. Note, however, that the Tax Reform Act of 1986 makes interest potentially nondeductible as "consumer interest" over a five-year phaseout period. Moreover, the IRS has ruled that the separate payment by an IRA beneficiary or trustee of administration fees for the IRA will not reduce the amount the beneficiary would otherwise be entitled to treat as a deductible contribution to the IRA, and is deductible as an expense incurred for the production or collection of income (Rev. Rul. 84-146). However, no separate deduction is allowed for brokers' commissions paid by IRAs or even qualified plans. Brokers' commissions are not recurring administrator or overhead expenses, such as trustee or actuary fees, incurred in connection with the maintenance of the trust or plan. Brokers' commissions rather are intrinsic to the value of a trust's assets—buying commissions are a part of the cost of the securities purchased and selling commissions are an offset against the sales price. Therefore, the Internal Revenue Service has ruled that contributions to reimburse for brokers' commissions are not deductible (Rev. Rul. 86-142, 1986-48 I.R.B. 4).

SIMPLIFIED PENSION PLANS

Under a normal IRA, your deduction is limited to the lesser of 100 percent of earned income or $2,000 ($4,000 for years after 1996 in the case of spousal IRAs) for contributions made. Under the Simplified Pension Plan, the exclusion limitation for all contributions to this type of IRA is the lesser of $30,000 or 15 percent of compensation. In the case of a self-employed individual or owner-employee in a noncorporate plan, "compensation" is defined to mean net earnings from self-employment, less excludable contributions to the plan made on his or her own behalf. This effectively reduces the self-employed maximum contribution percentage from 15 to 13.04 percent. Moreover, if an employer maintains another qualified plan, the maximum amount that can be contributed to that plan for any employee is reduced by all amounts contributed to the SEP. There is a 25 percent limitation on deductible contributions to more than one qualified plan. [Internal Revenue Code Section 404(h)(3)]

The intent of this type of plan is to establish a simpler mechanism by which employers can make employer-deductible contributions to provide employees with retirement benefits. It offers the owner-employee the opportunity to increase the maximum contributions that may be made to a personal plan, but it does so at the cost of requiring contributions for certain other employees as well.

Contributions made to an SEP by the employer or by a self-employed individual are deposited into individual IRAs in the name of the plan member. Employer contributions to an SEP are not includable in an employee's gross income. The employer contribution must be a specified percentage of the employee's total compensation up to $160,000, and the same percentage rate must be used for all employees. That rate may be specified in the plan or set by the employer annually by a written resolution. Unlike profit-sharing plans, an SEP does not require employers to make recurring contributions to the plan to remain qualified.

Under prior law, an employee could contribute the lesser of $2,000 ($2,250 for an employee with a nonworking spouse) or his or her compensation. Any excess contribution by an employee or employer to the employee's account above the yearly deduction limitations may be withdrawn without penalty on or before the earlier of the employee's tax filing date or April 15. Excess contributions left beyond that time are subject to a 6 percent excise tax. Under the Tax Reform Act of 1986, employees may, as of 1989, make elective contributions to their Simplified Employee Pension up to $7,627 per year (indexed) (but only into grandfathered salary reduction SEPs (SARSEPs, see page 120). These elective contributions are wages subject to FICA and FUTA taxes.

The five requirements for the establishment of a Simplified Pension Plan are as follows:

1. The IRA must be maintained solely by the individual employee. This means that all employees, including the owner as an employee, must maintain their own individual IRA accounts.
2. Employer contributions must be made pursuant to a written allocation formula.
3. The program must provide for contributions for each employee who has attained age 21, has performed services for the employer during any part of three of the immediately preceding five calendar years, and receives compensation of at least $400 during the current year (indexed). Employees under collective bargaining agreements and nonresident aliens may be excluded; part-time employees, however, must be covered.
4. Employer contributions must not discriminate in favor of officers, shareholders, or highly compensated employees. Generally, discrimination will not exist if the contributions bear a uniform relationship to the first $160,000 of each employee's total compensation. Employer contributions may be reduced by the amount of the employer's share of the social security tax.
5. No limitations may be imposed by the employer on the employee's right of withdrawal.

Unlike the Keogh plan, an SEP can be set up after the end of the calendar year so long as the contribution is made before April 16 of the year following. Moreover, there are no annual reporting requirements for SEPs, so long as each individual who participates in the plan receives a copy of the plan agreement and a written document from the employer each year informing that individual of the amount of contributions made on his or her behalf by the employer. An employer can create an SEP by using an unmodified Model Form (Form 5305-SEP), which is available from the Internal Revenue Service. An employer who follows the instructions on this two-page form will automatically satisfy IRS reporting and disclosure requirements.

Additional advantages of an SEP include the following:

- Low start-up costs compared to the cost of establishing regular pension or profit sharing plans
- No need to pay contributions to the SEP every year
- Portability of benefits—that is, participants who end their employment can take their benefits with them in the form of Individual Retirement Accounts
- Low administrative costs
- Reduced fiduciary responsibility, because participants choose their own vehicle when they establish an IRA

SARSEP

A salary reduction SEP, known as a SARSEP, is available for firms with 25 or fewer workers. Under a SARSEP, each worker chooses how much he or she wants to set aside through regular payroll deductions up to a maximum of 15% of salary or $10,000 a year, whichever is less.

With a SARSEP, 50% of all eligible employees must participate and no more than 60% of contributions can be made by highly compensated employees. If a firm fails the latter test, called the *top-heavy rule,* the IRS will require the firm to contribute a minimum of 3% of salary into employee accounts.

The amounts put into a SARSEP are not currently taxed and therefore you will get tax-free compounding on your investment until the money is withdrawn.

Unfortunately, effective for tax years beginning after 1986, employers are no longer able to start SARSEPs.

PLANNING WITH IRAs

As noted, the deadline for making IRA contributions is April 15, but what if you don't have the necessary cash at the moment? One possible solution to this problem is to use a rollover IRA for the funds required for the current IRA contribution.

There are no immediate tax consequences when an individual withdraws part or all of his or her interest in an IRA and within 60 days rolls over the amount withdrawn into another IRA. The trustee of the original IRA must be notified that the withdrawal is for a rollover, and no more than one rollover is permitted within a one-year period. Therefore, if you have an IRA account established in an earlier year, you can withdraw $2,000 from it and use it for your subsequent year's contribution. So long as the rollover is completed within 60 days, there is no problem. Only one IRA rollover per year is allowed as nontaxable.

Question: Where do you get the money to roll over your original contribution? *Solution:* It is hoped that you get it with the refund you will get from your tax return as filed with the additional IRA deduction. *Worst case theory:* If you cannot find the $2,000 to roll over within the 60-day period, then you are still entitled to the deduction for the current contribution year, but you have to include the $2,000 withdrawn (with penalty) on your next year's tax return.

Rather than wait for the last minute, you should make your IRA contribution as early as possible. When you delay, you lose not only the tax-free interest for the year but the interest that would have been compounded on it in future years.

The following table shows how much you lose by making a contribution at the last minute. It assumes that $2,000 is placed annually into an IRA earning 10 percent interest, and it shows the interest forfeited after a given number of years when the contributions are regularly made as late as possible (April 15), as opposed to as early as possible (on January 1 of the preceding year).

Number of Years	Interest Lost
5	$ 1,500
10	$ 4,000
15	$ 8,000
20	$ 14,000
30	$ 41,000
40	$112,000

In 1985, the Internal Revenue Service ruled that a jobless widow could add to her own IRA for the year her husband died. The decedent had created a spousal IRA for his unemployed wife in 1982 and 1983. He died on February 23, 1984, after earning over $2,250 but before adding to either IRA for that year. The taxpayer's spouse earned no wages in 1984 but wanted to make and deduct a $2,000 payment from the decedent's 1984 income to her spousal IRA for 1984. In Private Ruling 8527083, the Internal Revenue Service said that she could so long as she had no earned income of her own, filed a joint return, and showed that no 1984 payment was made to the decedent's IRA.

SIMPLE RETIREMENT PLANS

The Small Business Job Protection Act of 1996 creates a simplified retirement plan for small businesses called the Savings Incentive Match Plan for Employees ("SIMPLE") Retirement Plan. A SIMPLE plan can be adopted by employers who employ 100 employees or fewer with at least $5,000 in compensation for the preceding year. Employers who no longer qualify are given a two-year grace period to continue to maintain the plan. A SIMPLE plan can be either an IRA for each employee or part of a qualified cash or deferred arrangement ("401(k)") plan. If established in IRA form, a SIMPLE plan is not subject to the nondiscrimination rules generally applicable to qualified plans (including the top-heavy rules) and simplified reporting requirements apply. Within limits, contributions to a SIMPLE plan are not taxable until withdrawn.

A SIMPLE plan can also be adopted as part of a 401(k) plan. In that case, the plan does not have to satisfy the special nondiscrimination tests applicable to 401(k) plans and is not subjected to the top-heavy rules. The other qualified plan rules continue to apply.

A SIMPLE retirement plan allows employees to make elective contributions to an IRA. Employee contributions have to be expressed as a percentage of the employee's compensation, and cannot exceed $6,000 per year. The $6,000 limit is indexed for inflation in $500 increments.

All contributions to an employee's SIMPLE account have to be fully vested. Contributions to a SIMPLE account generally are deductible by the employer. Early withdrawals from a SIMPLE account generally are subject to the 10% early withdrawal tax applicable to IRAs. However, withdrawals of a contribution during the two-year period beginning on the date the employee first participated in the SIMPLE plan are subject to a 25% early withdrawal tax, rather than 10%. The provisions relating to SIMPLE plans are effective for years beginning after December 31, 1996.

Under prior law, contributions to an IRA could also be made by an employer at the election of an employee under a Salary Reduction Simplified Employee Pension ("SARSEP"). Under SARSEPs, which are not qualified plans, employees could elect to have contributions made to the SARSEP or to receive the contributions in cash. The amount that an employee elected to have contributed to the SARSEP was not currently included in income. Under the 1996 law, SARSEPs are repealed for years beginning after December 31, 1996, unless the SARSEP was established before January 1, 1997. Consequently, an employee is not permitted to establish a SARSEP after December 31, 1996. SARSEPs established before January 1, 1997 can continue to receive contributions under prior law rules, and new employees of the employer who are hired after December 31, 1996 can participate in the SARSEP in accordance with such rules.

KEOGH PLAN

The alternative to an IRA or IRA/SEP is the Keogh plan. Since 1962, self-employed individuals and their employees have been eligible to receive qualified retirement benefits under what is known as an H.R. 10 or Keogh plan. These qualified pension, annuity, profit sharing, or bond purchase plans must meet the following qualifications:

1. They must be in writing.
2. They must be effective within the tax year for which a qualification is sought.
3. They must be established by an owner for the benefit of employees or their beneficiaries. Self-employed individuals will be treated as employees under these plans.
4. They must be funded plans (that is, a trust or custodial account, an insured plan, or a bond purchase plan).
5. They must benefit a stipulated percentage of employees, or alternatively, the owner may establish a classification of employees that is found by the Internal Revenue Service not to discriminate in favor of highly paid employees.
6. They may not discriminate in favor of highly paid employees for contributions or benefits.

7. In the case of a plan that provides contributions or benefits only for owner-employees, contributions made on behalf of any owner-employee may not exceed the amount deductible by the individual. This means that an owner cannot contribute into a personal plan, in an attempt to defer taxes, an amount in excess of what is deductible for employees.

8. When an owner-employee covered under the plan, alone or in conjunction with another employee, controls the trade or business for which the plan is established, any transaction between that owner-employee and the trust-forming part of the plan is prohibited. Transactions between the members of the owner-employee's family and the trust are deemed to be transactions between the owner-employee and the trust. Furthermore, even if the owner-employee does not control the trade or business, a transaction between the trust and that owner-employee is prohibited.

   Generally, a disqualified person who engages in a prohibited transaction by contributing property to the trust is subject to a 5 percent excise tax on the amount involved in the transaction. An additional tax of 100 percent of the amount involved is imposed if the prohibited transaction is not corrected within 90 days from the mailing of a notice of deficiency.

9. A plan that covers an owner-employee must also cover all employees age 21 or older (whether or not U.S. citizens) of the trade or business who have completed 2 or more years of service. A year of service is a 12-month period, beginning on the date of hire, during which an employee has provided at least 500 hours of service (1,000 hours if it is the first year the employee qualifies). In addition, the employees' rights to contributions in their behalf must be 100 percent vested when the contributions are made.

   If eligibility to participate is shortened to one year, employees can be made to wait for a longer time before being able to leave with benefits. A plan can be set up so that an employee with fewer than 5 years of plan participation is not entitled to any benefit whatsoever. This relieves an employer from the expense of paying retirement benefits to all but true long-term employees. Note, however, that if the plan is "top-heavy"—if more than 60 percent of the benefits are for the owners, officers, and more highly paid employees—plan participants' benefits must vest immediately, or 20 percent after 2 years and 20 percent thereafter, with full vesting after 6 years (Section 416 [b][1]).

   The following employees are not required to be covered under a self-employed retirement plan, even though they have completed one or more years of service:

- Employees included in a unit covered by a collective bargaining agreement, if there is evidence that retirement benefits were subject to good faith bargaining between employee representatives and the employer.
- Nonresident alien employees who do not have earned income from a U.S. source.

10. If the employer is a partnership, each partner is considered the employee of that partnership. The partners must mutually consent to the establishment of the plan, which means that one partner cannot establish a plan for individual services to that partnership. But each owner-employee can decide whether to be covered under the plan, so a partner who is an owner-employee can agree to the plan and still not participate in it.

Under a Keogh plan, both the maximum contribution permitted on behalf of owner-employees and the deduction allowed self-employed individuals are the lesser of:

a) $30,000; *or*

b) 25 percent of the earned income from the trade or business for which the plan is established.

Note that a Keogh plan may be structured either as a "money-purchase pension" plan or as a "profit-sharing" plan, or as a combination of both. An owner-employer must reduce his or her compensation base by the contribution made. This effectively translates into a limit for *profit-sharing* plan-based deductions of 13.0435 percent and a limit for *money-purchase pension* or combination *money-purchase pension/profit-sharing* deductions of 20 percent of earned income.

With a money-purchase pension plan, the employer is locked into making the contributions every year, unless granted a limited reprieve. Contributions can be the lesser of 25 percent of compensation or $30,000. Note that the 25 percent figure is reduced to 20 percent for an owner-employer making contributions for himself or herself.

The profit-sharing plan is the simplest type of defined contribution plan. Contributions can be discretionary with respect to both amounts and whether they are made at all. Deductible contributions for nonowner-employers can be as much as 15 percent of compensation, up to $30,000 each year for each participant.

Combination plans typically contribute a fixed 10 percent each year to the money-purchase plan, and, if the cash is available, up to 15 percent to the profit-sharing plan. Note that plan contributions can be reduced to account for an employer's contribution to Social Security made on an employee's behalf. This is known as Social Security integration. Note, however, that if a plan is top-heavy, a minimum 3 percent annual contribution must be made for nonkey employees, and the employer must fund a benefit of at least 2 percent of compensation per year of service for the first 10 years of service. These requirements limit the cost savings sought by Social Security integration.

The contribution maximums were computed under what is known as a *defined contribution plan,* in which the limits are delineated on the basis of how much may be contributed. A self-employed individual may choose instead to establish what is known as a *defined benefit plan,* in which the limits are based on payable benefits. This type of plan permits a self-employed individual to state the retirement benefits desired and contribute amounts necessary to provide those benefits. In addition, a defined benefit plan permits yearly contributions to a plan without regard to profits.

Unlike an SEP or an IRA, lump-sum distributions from a Keogh plan qualify for what is known as the special 5-year forward averaging method (repealed by the Small Business Job Protection Act of 1996, for years after December 31, 1999). The theory behind the name is that the lump-sum payment is separated from the recipient's other taxable income and is taxed as if it had been received evenly over a 5-year period. This method ignores both the taxpayer's other income and the length of time in the plan. It is a significant benefit, which you should be aware of and take advantage of when appropriate.

The chart on page 127, from Steve Lightman of A.G. Edwards, summarizes various retirement plan characteristics.

BENEFITS OF RETIREMENT PLANS

It is almost always financially superior to adopt either an individual retirement account or a Keogh plan rather than have no plan at all. Both the IRA and the Keogh plan allow you to shelter current earnings and allow those earnings to appreciate without making that appreciation currently taxable. There may be an extraordinary situation in which having no plan would be superior. Such a situation would exist if the after-tax cash remaining from funds not invested in an IRA or Keogh plan could be invested in a project

Retirement Plan Comparison

Characteristics	SEP-IRA (*Simplified Employee Pension*)	Profit Sharing (*Defined Contribution*)	Age-Weighted/Cross Tested Profit Sharing (*Defined Contribution*)	Money Purchase (*Defined Contribution*)	Defined Benefit Pension Plan (*Defined Benefit*)	SIMPLE-IRA (*Savings Incentive Match Plan for Employees*)	401(k) Profit Sharing (*Defined Contribution*)	403(b)	457 Plan (*Nonqualified Deferred Compensation*)
Who may use	Corporation, partnership, self-employed, S corporation, nonprofit.	Corporation, partnership, self-employed, S corporation, nonprofit.	Corporation, partnership, self-employed, S corporation, nonprofit.	Corporation, partnership, self-employed, S corporation, nonprofit.	Corporation, partnership, self-employed, S corporation, nonprofit.	Corporation, partnership, self-employed, S corporation, nonprofit and government entities. Business must have 100 or fewer employees and cannot have any other qualified plan.	Corporation, partnership, self-employed, S corporation, nonprofit (excluding government entities).	Organizations qualified under IRC section 501(c)(3), such as schools, churches and hospitals.	State and local governments and nonprofit organizations, such as universities and hospitals. Does not include churches and qualified church-controlled organizations.
Client profile	Best suited for business owners who want simplicity. Ideally suited for companies with more volatile profits and low employee turnover.	Best suited for companies with more volatile profits where employee turnover may be a problem and the desired contribution rate does not exceed 15% of payroll.	The **Age-Weighted** profit sharing plan is best suited for companies that want to favor older employees. The **Cross-Tested** plan is best suited for companies that want to favor particular groups of employees	Best suited for companies with stable yearly profits. May be useful in combination with a profit sharing plan, subject to combined limit of lesser of 25% or $30,000 of compensation.	Best suited for established companies with consistent profits. Benefits companies with key employees age 50 or older.	Best suited for employers who want to encourage employee retirement savings and avoid costly administration. Employer obligation to contribute is relatively small compared with other plan choices.	Best suited for employers that want to minimize employer contributions and encourage employee savings.	Best suited for employers that want to minimize employer contributions and encourage employee savings, particularly plans that will be employee-funded only.	Best suited for employers that want to minimize employer contributions and encourage employee savings.
Deadline for establishing	Tax filing due date, including extensions.	Last day of employer's tax year.	Last day of employer's tax year.	Last day of employer's tax year.	Last day of employer's tax year.	Oct. 1 for contributions in current calendar year. (Plan year must be calendar.)	Last day of employer's fiscal year, but no later than commencement of employee contributions.	Can be established anytime during calendar year.	Last day of employer's tax year.
Deadline for employer contributions	Due date of employer's tax return, including extensions.	Due date of employer's tax return, including extensions.	Due date of employer's tax return, including extensions.	Due date of employer's tax return, including extensions.	Due date of employer's tax return, including extensions.	Due date of employer's tax return, including extensions. Deferrals must be deposited no later than 30 days following month of payroll.	Due date of employer's tax return, including extensions. Deferrals must be deposited no later than 15 days following month of payroll.	Due date of employer's tax return, including extensions.	Due date of employer's tax return, including extensions.
Who must be included	Any employee older than age 21 who has worked for the employer for any part of three of last five plan years. May exclude employees earning less than $400 per year.	Any employee with 1,000 hours of service in two 12-month periods who is at least age 21. Can exclude certain employees.	Any employee with 1,000 hours of service in two 12-month periods who is at least age 21. Can exclude certain employees.	Any employee with 1,000 hours of service in two 12-month periods who is at least age 21. Can exclude certain employees.	Any employee with 1,000 hours of service in two 12-month periods who is at least age 21. Can exclude certain employees.	Any employee who earned $5,000 or more during any two preceding years and is expected to earn $5,000 or more in the current year. For 401(k) SIMPLE, see 401(k) column.	Any employee with 1,000 hours of service within 12 months who is age 21 or older. Can exclude certain employees.	All employees of qualified organizations; some exclusions may be allowed.	Any employee with 1,000 hours of service within 12 months who is age 21 or older. Can exclude certain employees.
Obligation to contribute[1]	Employer makes discretionary contributions and can change or discontinue them each year.	Unless fixed as a percentage of compensation or profits, contributions are at the discretion of the employer and are not dependent on profits.	Unless fixed as a percentage of compensation or profits, contributions are at the discretion of the employer and are not dependent on profits.	Employer must meet minimum funding requirement by making the percentage contribution chosen when the plan was adopted.	Employer must meet minimum funding requirements, dictated by the benefit formula and calculated annually by an actuary.	Employer contribution required. Choice of dollar-for-dollar matching contribution up to 3% of employee's compensation or nonelective, nonmatching contribution of 2% of compensation for all eligible employees.	Contributions come from employee salary reduction, and/or from employer.	Contributions typically come from employee salary reduction. Employer contributions are permitted but may subject the plan to additional reporting/ discrimination requirement.	Employer is not obligated to make contributions. All contributions are voluntary salary reductions.
Maximum annual combined contribution (from the employer and employee) that the employer may deduct	15% of employee's pay (maximum eligible pay per employee is $160,000).	15% of total eligible payroll (maximum eligible pay per employee is $160,000).	15% of total eligible payroll (maximum eligible pay per employee is $160,000).	25% of employee's eligible pay, up to $30,000 (maximum eligible pay per employee is $160,000).	Contribution is not limited (maximum pay per employee to determine benefits is $160,000). Note: Annual benefit from the plan may not exceed the lesser of 100% of participant's compensation or $130,000.	SIMPLE-IRA — $12,000 ($6,000 maximum match up to 3% of pay plus $6,000 deferral). SIMPLE 401(k) — see 401(k) column.	15% of total eligible payroll (maximum eligible pay per employee is $160,000).	25% of employee's eligible pay up to $30,000 (maximum eligible pay per employee is $160,000).	Employee contributions limited to 33 1/3% of includable compensation with a maximum of $8,000. Employee and employer contributions combined are unlimited.
Maximum annual allocation[2] **to employee's account**	15% of employee's gross pay or $30,000, whichever is less.	25% of employee's gross pay or $30,000, whichever is less.	25% of employee's gross pay or $30,000, whichever is less.	25% of employee's gross pay or $30,000, whichever is less.	No individual accounts.	Refer to maximum combined contribution, above.	25% of employee's gross pay or $30,000, whichever is less.	25% of employee's gross pay or $30,000, whichever is less.	$8,000. A limited catch-up provision can be used for any or all of the last three years before normal retirement age
Maximum annual employee contribution	No employee contributions allowed, except in grandfathered SAR-SEPs.	No employee contributions allowed.	No employee contributions allowed.	No employee contributions allowed.	No employee contributions allowed.	$6,000 (adjusted for cost-of-living increases).	Elective contributions up to 25% of net annual compensation,[3] not to exceed $10,000.	Up to 20% of net annual compensation,[3] not to exceed $10,000.[4]	$8,000 (adjusted for cost-of-living increases).
Vesting	Immediate 100% vesting.	Vesting schedules available.	Vesting schedules available.	Vesting schedule available.	Vesting schedules available.	Immediate 100% vesting.	**Employee elective deferrals:** immediate 100% vesting. **Employer contributions:** vesting schedules available.	**Employee elective deferrals:** immediate 100% vesting. **Employer contributions:** vesting schedules available.	**Employee elective deferrals:** immediate 100% vesting. **Employer contributions:** vesting schedules available.
Reporting and disclosure	When plan has been established, employer fills out SEP agreement and gives a copy to the employee when the employee becomes eligible. No additional annual reporting is required.	Full ERISA requirements. IRS Forms 5500, 5500-C, 5500-R or 5500-EZ and applicable schedules must be filed annually.	Full ERISA requirements. IRS Forms 5500, 5500-C, 5500-R or 5500-EZ and applicable schedules must be filed annually.	Full ERISA requirements. IRS Forms 5500, 5500-C, 5500-R or 5500-EZ and applicable schedules must be filed annually.	Full ERISA requirements. IRS Forms 5500, 5500-C, 5500-R or 5500-EZ and applicable schedules must be filed annually.	Minimal for SIMPLE-IRA. Employer must give employees Summary Plan and Contribution Notice no later than Nov. 2 each year. For 401(k) type, see 401(k) column.	Full ERISA requirements. IRS Forms 5500, 5500-C or 5500-R and applicable schedules must be filed annually. Discrimination test applies to deferrals.	If employer makes contributions, IRS Forms 5500, 5500-C or 5500-R must be filed annually.	Under some circumstances, may require full ERISA reporting.

[1] Top-heavy minimums apply when more than 60% of account balances/accrued benefits are attributable to key employees (or for SEP-IRAs, 60% of aggregate contribution for key employees).
[2] Allocation refers to the total of employer-deductible contributions, forfeitures, and any employee salary deferral or voluntary after-tax contribution.
[3] Compensation is amounts shown on W-2 (wages, salaries, bonuses, etc.) and self-employed earned income.
[4] Maximum exclusions, allowances and/or catch-up options may affect individual deferral limits.

whose yield would exceed, after taxes, both the amount that could be earned on the qualified retirement investment and the amount initially lost in taxes.

For example, assume you could put $1,000 in an individual retirement account that would yield 5 percent interest, or $50 a year. For simplicity, assume that your present tax bracket is 20 percent, so that if you do not adopt the individual retirement account, you would have only $800 to invest. But this $800 could be invested in a project yielding 25 percent, or $200 a year. After taxes (at 20 percent) the project would allow you to keep $160 a year. At the end of two years you would therefore have, after taxes, $800 + $160 + $160: $1,120. (The example has been simplified by excluding compound interest on the investment yield.) Under the IRA, you would have only $1,000 + $50 + $50 = $1,100, and that $1,100 would be taxable at a later date, when withdrawn from the individual retirement account. In this case, the decision not to adopt any plan would clearly be superior.

To choose a Keogh plan rather than an IRA, you must answer the following questions:

1. How much money can you afford to surrender the present use of? If not over $2,000 ($4,000 after 1996 if you have an unemployed spouse), choose an IRA.
2. What will be the tax savings on your contributions to each plan?
3. Must you make contributions for your employees?
4. What will be the after-tax cost of those contributions?
5. Compare the net after-tax savings from an individual retirement account compared with a Keogh plan.

For example, assume you are in the 31 percent bracket and are making $200,000 a year. You plan to retire in ten years. You can adopt a Keogh plan, yielding 5 percent. Under the Keogh plan, you would contribute $15,000 at the end of each year.

Under the Keogh plan, you would contribute $150,000 plus earnings on these contributions, for a total untaxed accumulation of $188,668. You would defer $58,487 in taxes.

But with a Keogh plan qualified employees must also be covered. If you have qualified employees, you would have to contribute 7.5 percent of their earnings (as you contribute 7.5 percent of your own earnings) each year. If you have one qualified employee earning $20,000, you would have to contribute an additional $1,500 per year ($20,000 × 7.5 percent), or $15,000 over the ten-year period. If you have four qualified employees, the contributions would rise to $60,000.

But you are in the 31 percent bracket. Therefore, this would involve an after-tax cost to you of only $41,400. But remember, Keogh saving is merely a tax *deferral,* not a savings. Therefore, the real question is whether the $41,400 after-tax outflow can be justified by a deferral of the taxes of $58,487!

Under the Keogh plan you would accumulate $188,668. If you expected to be in the 15 percent bracket after you retire, the difference between your marginal tax today and your postretirement marginal tax would be .16 (31 percent – 15 percent).[3] Therefore, your true net savings on the Keogh plan would be the difference in your tax bracket (.16) times the accumulations under the Keogh plan ($188,668), or a net savings of the present value of $30,187. Thus the determining question is whether the present value of $30,187 is greater than the present value of the after-tax outflow for the contributions you would have to make for your employees.

With a single employee, the cash outflow cost would be the present value of 31 percent of $15,000, or the present value of $4,650. Here the net savings of $30,187 would be greater than the incremental cost of $4,650, and therefore the Keogh adoption would still be superior. If there were four employees, the decision model would compare the present value of $30,187 with the present value of 69 percent of $15,000 × 4, or $41,400. Here the IRA would be financially superior.

Finally, you must consider whether the employee Keogh contributions would merely replace alternative additional compensation that would be paid to the employee in any case. If so, then the Keogh penalty for employee payments must be reduced by this amount.

DISTRIBUTIONS

On July 3, 1992 former President Bush signed the Unemployment Compensation Amendments Act of 1992 primarily to extend unemployment benefits. Nevertheless, you need to be aware of several significant changes to the pension rules relating to rollovers and withholding on distributions from

3. The numbers have been simplified for purposes of this example. You would not be in the 15 percent bracket with a lump-sum distribution of $188,668.

such qualified plans as profit sharing, money purchase, 401(k), defined benefit, and tax-sheltered annuities [403(b) plans]. *The new rules do not apply to IRAs.*

These provisions affect all qualified plans that make lump sum distributions or allow in-service withdrawals. The changes are effective for distributions made after Dec. 31, 1992 (except for a delayed effective date for certain tax-sheltered annuities of state and local governments). The new provisions include:

- *Optional direct transfer of distribution.* Under current law, a participant has 60 days to roll over an eligible distribution from a qualified plan to an IRA or another qualified plan to avoid current taxation. At the time of the distribution, the participant may elect to have federal income taxes withheld or not.

  The 1992 legislation requires a qualified plan sponsor to provide participants who are eligible to receive a rollover distribution the option of making a direct transfer to an IRA or a new employer's qualified plan. However, a qualified plan is not required to accept transfers.

  Even though the participant does not actually receive the money, such a direct trustee-to-trustee transfer is considered a distribution under the new law. Therefore, the spousal consent rules, if applicable, and other beneficiary protection rules will continue to apply.

- *Withholding on nonperiodic distributions.* To encourage plan participants to use this direct transfer option, the 1992 law imposes a *mandatory* 20 percent income tax withholding on any amount distributed to the participant. If a participant wants to avoid withholding on the distribution, the participant needs to instruct the employer to transfer the amount directly to another retirement plan or an IRA. Plan participants can no longer elect out of this withholding.

- *Partial distribution rules repealed.* The 1992 Act also changes the situations in which partial distributions can be rolled into an IRA. Under prior law, partial distributions can only be rolled over when:

  the distribution represents 50 percent or more of the balance to the credit of the employee;

  the distribution is not one of a series of periodic payments;

  the distribution is made because of death, disability, or separation from service;

  the employee elects rollover treatment.

The 1992 rules allow *any part* of the taxable portion of a qualified plan distribution to be rolled over to an IRA, qualified annuity, or another qualified plan unless the distribution is:

one of a series of substantially equal periodic payments made over the life expectancy (or joint life expectancies) of the participant and the designated beneficiary;

one of a series of substantially equal periodic payments made for a specified period of 10 years or more;

required as a result of the mandatory distribution rules at age $70^1/_2$ under section 401(a)(9) of the IRS code;

after-tax employee contributions, which are not eligible for rollover.

TRADITIONAL V. ROTH IRA

Table 2 compares the benefits of the traditional and the Roth IRA. Which should *you* use? That depends on the benefits you want to get and your current and projected tax brackets.

The younger you are, the better the Roth IRA appears. If you start early, the Roth allows more years of tax-free accumulations. The younger you are, presumably, the better the chances you are in a lower bracket, therefore reducing the benefit of its deduction with the traditional IRA.

Alternatively, if you are older and in a higher bracket, the better the traditional IRA looks. Additional elements that must be examined or projected are the yields you expect to earn, whether you want to make contributions after age $70^1/_2$, and the marginal bracket you expect to be in when the dollars are withdrawn.

There are no simple answers. Every brokerage account out there has computer programs that will find you an "answer" based on your assumptions. I have even found different answers with the same input, depending on when the computer assumes the money is invested. Pen your own numbers and relax—your decision is between the better of two strategies, both of which are winners!

CONVERTING A TRADITIONAL IRA TO A ROTH IRA

Should you convert your traditional IRA into a Roth IRA and change from *tax deferral* to *tax free* accumulations? The answer here also depends on a number of factors.

You can roll all or part of a traditional IRA into a Roth IRA at any time, even if you have started to take withdrawals, long as your adjusted gross income doesn't exceed $100,000. However, when you do, you owe income tax on the money you move. If you made the rollover in 1998, you can spread that extra income, and tax, over four years. If you find you exceed the $100,000 limit, you can reverse the transfer up to the due date of your return plus expenses.

Your first consideration should be where you get the money to pay the tax on the rollover. It can't come from the regular IRA or there will be a premature distribution with a penalty because those dollars are not going into the Roth.

Once you have funded your rollover, the considerations are the same as between a traditional and Roth IRA—your age and years to retirement, your bracket now and at retirement, do you want to contribute after age $70^1/_2$, and will this impact on the taxability of your Social Security. (Traditional IRAs require annual distributions which could increase the taxability of your Social Security receipts. You *don't* have to ever take money out of your Roth although your beneficiaries are subject to minimum distribution rules.) The big difference here is the immediate reduction of your wealth from taxes paid on the rollover, reducing your liquidity for future investments. Again, all of the major brokerage and mutual fund houses offer computer programs which will give you an "answer," based on the assumptions you input.

COMPANY STOCK ROLLOVERS

"Never" roll over *company stocks* in your 401(k) into an IRA. If you do, all distributions will be ordinary income.

If you place the stock into a regular brokerage account instead, you will be taxed, at ordinary income rates at *only* the cost basis of that stock.That's the value when your employer put the stock in your account.

The difference between the cost basis and the market value of the stock at the time of distribution, called the "net unrealized appreciation" (NUA), isn't taxed until you sell the stock, and, at that time, at a rate no greater than the 20% maximum long-term capital gains rate.

51 Self-Employment Tax

Beginning in 1990, if you had income from self-employment and you owe self-employment tax, you may deduct one half of that tax above the line. Note that this deduction reduces your income base for Keogh and SEP deductions previously discussed.

52 Health Insurance Deduction for Self-Employeds

For taxable years starting after December 31, 1994, self-employed individuals may deduct 30 percent of payments for health insurance for themselves, their spouses, and their dependents. The amount for 1994 and prior years was 25 percent. This special deduction for health insurance is not subject to the floor of 7.5 percent of adjusted gross income for medical expense deductions.

Current law increases the deduction for health insurance of self-employed individuals as follows: the deduction would be 40 percent in 1997; 45 percent in 1998; 60 percent in 1999 through 2001; 70 percent in 2002; 100 percent in 2003.

Certain limitations apply to this new health insurance deduction. No deduction is allowed to the extent that health insurance payments exceed your earned income for the taxable year. Nor is any deduction allowed for any month for which you are eligible to participate in a subsidized accident and health plan provided by an organization that employs (whether on a full- or part-time basis) either you or your spouse. Moreover, no deduction is allowed unless you provide coverage under one or more accident or health plans for all of your employees, should you have any. Those plans must also satisfy nondiscrimination rules.

This deduction is available even if you do not itemize your deductions. However, this deduction does not reduce your earnings for the computation of self-employment tax. In addition, it is available for partnerships and S corporation owners (Rev. Rul. 91-26).

53 Moving Expenses

Moving expenses incurred if you change job locations or if you start a new job are generally deductible if you meet certain requirements. For moves made after 1993, your new job location must be at least 50 miles from your former job location, you must make your move within one year from the date you start your new job, and you must work full-time for a specified period of time. For moves in 1994 or after, expenses are above the line deductions. (Pre-1994, the mileage was 30 miles and the expenses were itemized deductions).

You may take a moving expense deduction, subject to dollar limits explained later, for the following expenses:

- Travel to your new job location.
- Moving your household goods and personal items.
- House-hunting trips before you move (pre-1994 only).
- Temporary living expenses at the new location (pre-1994 only).
- Expenses incurred in disposing of your former home and acquiring your new one (pre-1994 only).

You may qualify for such deductions whether you are self-employed or an employee. These expenses, though, must be in connection with starting work at a new job location. You will be able to deduct your moving expenses if you meet the requirements of certain tests.

THE DISTANCE TEST

You may now deduct your moving expenses if your new principal job location is at least 50 miles further from your former home than was your former principal job location. In addition, the distance from your new home to your new job location must not be longer than the distance from your old home to the new job location. Your home is your primary residence; it may be a house, apartment, condominium, houseboat, housetrailer, or similar dwelling. It does not include other homes owned or kept up by you or members of your family, or a seasonal home (such as a beach cottage).

The distance between two points is measured by the shortest of the most commonly traveled routes between the points. If your old job was three miles from your former home, your new job must be at least 53 miles from that home. If you did not have an old job location, your new job location must be at least 50 miles from your former home. This does not apply to the location of your *new* home.

For example, assume your old job was three miles from your former home. Your new job is 55 miles from that home. You qualify because the difference (52 miles) is over the minimum of 50 miles. Your new home may be less than 50 miles from your former home, but it must be at least as close to your new job as your former home. If so, you have met the distance test.

			55 miles			
Old Job	3 miles	Old Home	49 miles	New Home	6 miles	New Job

New Job to Old Home	= 55 miles	Old Home to New Job	= 55 miles
Old Home to Old Job	= −3 miles	New Home to New Job	= 6 miles
Qualifying distance	= 52 miles	New Home is at least as close to New Job as Old Home	

Your principal job location is usually the place where you do most of your work and spend most of your time. A new principal job location is a new place where you will work on a permanent or indefinite basis rather than on a temporary basis. However, you may have a principal job location even if there is no one place where you spend a substantial part of your work and time. In this case, use the distance to the place where your work is centered—for example, where you report for work or otherwise have the "base" for your work.

If you work for a number of employers on a short-term basis, or get work under a union hall system (such as in construction and the building trades), use the distance between your home and the union hall.

TIME TEST

To deduct your moving expenses you also must meet one of the following time tests:

1. If you are an employee, you must work full-time at least 39 weeks during the 12-month period following your arrival in the general area of your new job location. You do not have to work for one employer for the 39 weeks; you do not even have to work 39 weeks in a row. But you must work full-time within the same general commuting area. Whether you are employed full-time depends upon the custom for your type of work. For example, a school teacher on a 12-month contract who teaches on a full-time basis for more than six months is considered a full-time employee for the entire 12 months. Any week that you work full-time is used to satisfy the 39 week full-time work test. If the work is seasonal, you are considered to be working full-time during the off-season weeks if your contract or agreement covers

an off-season of less than six months. You are considered to be working during any week you are temporarily absent from work because of illness, strikes, natural disasters, or the like. You are also considered to be a full-time employee during any week you are absent from work for leave or for vacation that is provided for in your work contract or agreement.

2. If you are self-employed, you must work full-time for at least 39 weeks during the first 12 months and a total of 78 weeks during the 24 months after your arrival in the area of your new job location. Whether you perform services full-time during any one week depends upon the custom of your type of work in your area.

Despite these restrictions, you may deduct your moving expenses even if you have not met the time test by the time your return is due. You may do this if you *expect* to work for 39 weeks by the end of the next year, or for 78 weeks by the end of the second year. Furthermore, you do not have to meet the time test at all if any one of the following situations applies:

- You are in the armed forces and your move is due to a permanent change of stations.
- You move to the United States because you retire or are the survivor of a person who dies while living and working outside the United States.
- Your job ends because of disability, transfer for the employer's benefit, or layoff other than for willful misconduct. The time test does not have to be met in case of your death. If you are transferred, you are expected to meet the test at the time you start the job.

THE START OF WORK TEST

In general you must have moving expenses within one year from the time you first report to your job or business at the new location, and the move must be in connection with the start of work at the new location. If you do not move within one year, the expenses are ordinarily not deductible unless you can show that certain circumstances prevented the move within that time period. For example, if your family moved more than a year after you started work at the new location in order to allow your child to complete junior high school in the same school, your allowable moving expenses are deductible.

A move is considered closely related to the start of work if:

a) you are required to live at the new location as a condition of employment; *or*

b) you will spend less time or money commuting from the new home to the new job.

It is important that you understand and recognize all of the possible expenses that are deductible under this category. You can deduct expenses of moving your possessions, traveling to your new home, looking for a new home (pre-1994), living temporarily in a new area (pre-1994), selling and buying a home (pre-1994), or settling and signing a lease (pre-1994).

If you use your car to take yourself, your family, or your things to your new home, or for house hunting, you figure your expenses in either of two ways:

1. You may deduct your actual expenses such as gas, oil, and repairs (but not depreciation) for the use of your car, if you keep an accurate record of each expense.
2. You may deduct 10¢ a mile instead of the actual costs if you can prove the mileage traveled. You may deduct parking fees and tolls you pay in moving no matter which way you figure your expenses.

Not only may you deduct the expenses of moving your own possessions, but you may also deduct the costs for transporting the possessions of the members of your household. This includes the actual cost of transportation or hauling from your former home to your new one. The cost of packing and crating, in-transit storage, and insurance is included. Expenses of storing and insuring household goods and personal effects are in-transit expenses if incurred within 30 consecutive days after your things are moved from your former home and before they are delivered at your new one.

Moving expenses also include the cost of transportation, lodging for yourself and members of your household while traveling to your new home, and 80 percent of the cost of meals while moving (pre-1994). This includes expenses for the day you arrive, and any meals and lodging expenses incurred in your old neighborhood within one day after your former home becomes uninhabitable because your furniture has been moved out. You may deduct expenses for only one trip to your new home for yourself and each member of your household. However, all members do not have to travel together.

Prior to 1994, deductions were allowed as well for premove house-hunting expenses. House-hunting expenses include the cost of transportation, meals, and lodging for yourself and members of your household while traveling to and from the area of your new job and while you are there. You may deduct these expenses only if you begin your trip *after* you get the job in the new area and if you go primarily to look for a new place to live. Your house hunting does not have to be successful to qualify for this deduction. You and members of your household may travel separately. Furthermore, you are not limited in the number of trips you or members of your household may take.

Prior to 1994, you also could deduct the cost of temporary living expenses. These expenses include not only the cost of lodging in the area of your new job but the cost of meals as well.

HOME SALE, PURCHASE, OR LEASE EXPENSES

In addition, pre-1994, home sale, purchase, and lease expenses also were deductible. You therefore could deduct the costs of selling your home or settling your lease in the former area and buying or leasing a home in the new area.

When you sold or exchanged a home, you could deduct real estate commissions, attorney's fees, title fees, escrow fees, points or loan placement charges you were required to pay, state transfer taxes, and similar expenses connected to the sale or exchange. You could not, however, deduct the cost of physical improvements intended to improve the condition or appearance of your former home. When you bought your new home, you could again deduct attorney's fees, escrow fees, appraisal fees, title fees, points and loan placement charges that did not represent payment or prepayment of interest, and similar expenses connected to the purchase. When you lease a new home, you cannot deduct payments or prepayments of rent.

There are certain dollar limits that you must remember. Deductions for the costs of moving household goods and traveling to your new home are not limited to any amount. For premove travel, meals, and lodging expenses, temporary living expenses, and home sale, purchase, or lease expenses, you could not deduct more than $3,000. Deductions for house-hunting trip costs and temporary living expenses together could not be more than $1,500.

If you are a homeowner, you should have claimed the costs of premove house-hunting expenses and temporary living expenses before you claimed the costs of selling and buying your home as moving expenses. However, within the dollar limits you may choose to deduct any combination of these expenses. If you have expenses from selling or buying a home that you cannot deduct as moving expenses because of the $3,000 limit, you should use these expenses to reduce the gain on the sale of your former home or to increase the basis of your new home.

The following items cannot be deducted as moving expenses:

Home improvements to help sell your home
Loss on the sale of your home
Mortgage penalties
Losses from the disposing of memberships and clubs
Any part of the purchase price of your new home
Real estate taxes
Car tax for the state you move to
Driver's license for the state you move to
Refitting carpets and draperies
New security deposits on a new lease
Security deposits on an old lease because the vacated space needed cleaning or redecorating when the lease ended.

However, you may deduct a security deposit that you give up if the lease is broken as a result of the move.

The Omnibus Budget Reconciliation Act of 1993 made several substantial changes in the moving expense deduction—effective for expenses incurred after December 31, 1993. As of 1994, the Act excludes from the definition of moving expenses: (1) the costs related to the sale of (or settlement of an unexpired lease on) the old residence, and the purchase of (or acquisition of a lease on) the new residence in the general location of the new job and (2) the costs of meals consumed while traveling and while living in temporary quarters near the new job. It also contains the following additional modifications:

1. The cost of premove house-hunting trips is excluded from the definition of moving expenses.
2. The cost of temporary living expenses for up to 30 days in the general location of the new job is excluded from the definition of moving expenses.
3. The mileage limit is increased from 35 miles to 50 miles.
4. Moving expenses not paid or reimbursed by the taxpayer's employer are allowable as a deduction in calculating adjusted gross income.

5. Moving expenses paid or reimbursed by the taxpayer's employer are excludable from gross income. *Moving expenses* are now defined as the reasonable costs of

   a) moving household goods and personal effects from the former residence to the new residence; and

   b) traveling (including lodging during the period of travel) from the former residence to the new place of residence.

   Moving expenses do not include any expenses for meals.

EMPLOYER-PAID MOVING EXPENSES

Moving expenses are excludable from gross income and wages for income and employment tax purposes to the extent paid for by the taxpayer's employer (whether directly or through reimbursement). Moving expenses are not excludable if the taxpayer actually deducted the expenses in a prior taxable year. The 1993 law intends that the employer treat moving expenses as excludable unless it has actual knowledge that the employee deducted the expenses in a prior year. The employer has no obligation to determine whether the individual deducted the expenses. Rules similar to the rules relating to accountable plans will apply to reimbursed expenses.

MOVING EXPENSES NOT PAID FOR BY THE EMPLOYER

Moving expenses are deductible in computing adjusted gross income to the extent not paid for by the taxpayer's employer (whether directly or through reimbursement). Allowing such a deduction will treat taxpayers whose expenses are not paid for by their employer in a comparable manner to taxpayers whose moving expenses are paid for by their employer.

TAX STRATEGIES

The availability of the moving expense deduction allows you several very sophisticated tax planning strategies. First, recognize that some expenses in connection with a change in employment involving moving your residence could be considered either as moving expenses or as expenses related to the sale of your old home or purchase of your new residence. Careful identification and documentation of such expenses can result in either a moving expense deduction or an adjustment of the gain from the sale of your former residence. You must carefully weigh the advantages of these alternative adjustments to your tax.

The second strategic tax move may come about if you are considering retirement and a move to a different—warmer—climate. If you make the move in connection with a change in employment and satisfy the 39-week work requirement, you get a deduction for your moving expenses. The tax effect of this deduction will, in effect, increase your compensation for the 39 weeks of work and perhaps make it worthwhile to postpone your actual retirement. Note that included in the definition of moving expenses are all of your "personal effects." See, for example, *John R. Fogg*, 89 T.C. No. 27 (decided in 1988), wherein a marine officer's moving expense deduction included the cost of moving his boat.

Finally, you should recognize that the deductibility of your moving expenses is in effect a tax subsidy of those expenses. So, for example, if you think it may be too expensive to hire a moving company, your decision to save money by moving your household goods yourself may be modified by considering the tax effect of the deduction for moving expenses. Moving company charges of $3,000 actually would represent a cash outflow of only $2,070 if you are single and have taxable income at the $62,450 level or above ($3,000 × .31 = $930 in tax savings).

CHAPTER 6

"Below the Line" Deductions

"I am proud to be paying taxes in the United States. The only thing is—I could be just as proud for half the money."

ARTHUR GODFREY

Under the Tax Reform Act of 1986, you are not required to reduce your itemized, or "below the line," deductions by the amount of the standard deduction (zero bracket amount). Instead, you deduct 100 percent of your itemized deductions and do not take the standard deduction. Therefore, you itemize deductions only if they exceed the amount of your standard deduction.

For 1999 the standard deduction amounts are as follows:

If your filing status is:	**Your Standard Deduction Is:**
Single	$ 4,300
Married, filing jointly, or a qualifying widow or widower	$ 7,200
Married, filing separately	$ 3,600
Head of household	$ 6,350

The minimum income levels for filing a tax return are:

Single	$ 7,050
Single, age 65 or older	$ 8,100
Married, filing jointly	$12,700
Married, filing jointly, one spouse age 65 or older	$13,550
Married, filing jointly, both spouses age 65 or older	$14,400

In addition, the personal tax exemption is $2,750 for 1999 and the added standard deduction for the aged or blind is $850 each on a joint return and $1,050 for a single.

A The Importance of Filing Status

Your filing status is determined on the last day of each year. This affords you another opportunity for sophisticated tax planning. The rates for married individuals, filing either jointly *or* separately, are much lower than those for single, unmarried taxpayers. For example, for 1999, on taxable income of $62,450, a single person pays a marginal tax rate of 31 percent and a total tax of $14,139. On the other hand, a married taxpayer with a spouse who has no income would pay a marginal rate of only 28 percent and a total tax of

$11,890. If you are planning a New Year's wedding, advancing it only a few days to Christmas would therefore save you $2,249—enough to pay for your honeymoon.

Alternatively, if both married partners work, there is, in effect, a tax on the marriage. In 1999, two individuals earning $25,750 in taxable income would each pay $3,863 in taxes for a total outlay of $7,726. If they got married before the year-end, their total income would be $51,500, and they would have filed either a joint return or a return as married, filing separately—either way mandating a total tax payment of $8,824, $1,098 more than what they would have paid had they remained unmarried!

Marriage Penalties and Bonuses on Income Tax

An April 1999 Treasury Department study shows that nearly as many couples receive a "marriage bonus" as pay a "marriage penalty." In most cases, the average bonus is greater than the average penalty.

1999 Adjusted Gross Income	Percent of Couples Penalized	Average Penalty	Percent of Couples Who Get a Bonus	Average Bonus	Percent Getting Neither
$0–15,000	7.4%	$302	33.4%	$418	59.2%
$15,001–30,000	40.2%	$607	49.5%	$528	10.3%
$30,001–40,000	52.5%	$792	45.7%	$662	1.8%
$40,001–50,000	57.3%	$578	40.0%	$952	2.7%
$50,001–60,000	48.8%	$535	44.3%	$1,299	6.9%
$60,001–75,000	50.6%	$798	41.4%	$1,537	8.0%
$75,001–100,000	64.9%	$1,384	34.4%	$1,960	0.7%
$100,001–200,000	65.0%	$1,926	34.9%	$2,580	0.1%
$200,001 and more	48.5%	$5,688	50.0%	$3,428	1.5%

Source: Treasury Department

This extraordinary penalty on marriage is the result of previous congressional actions that attempted to correct apparent inequities in the old tax structure. Prior to 1948, husbands and wives in community property states could each claim half of their household income for tax purposes even if only one of them actually earned all of the income. The law of the individual state attributed half of the income ("property") to the other spouse. For example, if only the husband worked, earning $30,000, both he and his wife would have reported $15,000 in income. Given our progressive tax rate, where each additional dollar earned is taxed at a higher rate, this was a substantial advantage. In 1948, the federal income tax code was amended to allow this benefit to all married taxpayers—including those in non-community property states. This was done by doubling the income brackets for married taxpayers associated with each rate. For example, if the first $500 of income was taxed at 11 percent for a single person, the first $1,000 of income for married couples would have also been taxed at 11 percent.

While those who were married rejoiced, single taxpayers making the same income as married couples were subject to much higher tax rates. In 1970, for example, single taxpayers could have been liable for as much as 42 percent more in taxes than a married couple earning an equivalent income. In response to this harsh inequity, Congress in 1971 changed the rates for single taxpayers to reduce this differential to a 20 percent maximum. The Tax Reform Act of 1986 reduced the differential even further. However, according to the Congressional Budget Office, 21 million couples filing jointly in 1996 suffered the marriage penalty averaging around $1,400 each! According to Senator Hutchison of Texas, that $1,400 marriage penalty number was still valid in March of 1999.

The tax penalty on marriage when both husband and wife work is compounded by the standard deduction. A married couple is allowed a total of $7,200 of nontaxable income. Two single workers get $4,300 each for a total of $8,600. By getting married, an additional $1,400 becomes taxable—and at the highest rates!

Moreover, high-income earners who marry will also lose write-offs for personal exemptions faster than their single counterparts. Under the Tax Reform Act of 1986, the 1999 exemption of $2,750 is phased out for singles with taxable incomes above $126,600, but the phase-out for a married couple starts at $189,950, 75 percent of the income amount for two single persons.

Marriage may also wipe out potential IRA deductions. If two taxpayers with incomes of $30,000 each marry and either is covered by an employer plan, neither could write off an IRA contribution. They would lose $4,000 in deductions and pay as much as $1,120 more in total tax.

According to a study by the National Bureau of Economic Research, Inc., for 1994, 52 percent of U.S. couples paid a marriage tax averaging about $2,244. For certain very high-income families, it can exceed $10,000 annually!

Love and Taxes: Some Winners, Some Losers

The Marriage Penalty
20.9 million couples experienced a tax penalty as a result of their married status in 1996.

	Single		Married	
	Income	**Tax**	**Income**	**Tax**
Man	$24,000	$2,580	$24,000	—
Woman	$24,000	$2,580	$24,000	—
Total	$48,000	$5,160	$48,000	$5,370
Penalty: $210				

The Marriage Bonus
25.3 million married couples experienced a tax bonus as a result of their married status in 1996.

	Single		Married	
	Income	**Tax**	**Income**	**Tax**
Man	$48,000	$8,332	$48,000	—
Woman	None	None	None	—
Total	$48,000	$8,332	$48,000	$5,370
Bonus: $2,962				

Source: Congressional Budget Office.

Because your marital status for the entire year is based upon your status as of December 31, many individuals have been advised to fly to a Caribbean divorce haven, such as the Dominican Republic, for a quickie divorce before the year ends and to remarry in January. The tax savings can often more than offset the cost of legal fees and the Caribbean "vacation."

The Internal Revenue Service has reacted to this situation, declaring: "If you obtain a foreign divorce for the sole purpose of enabling you and your spouse to qualify as unmarried individuals eligible to file separate returns, and if you then remarry each other early in the next tax year, you and your spouse must file as married individuals."

This response has been tested in the Tax Court with interesting results. The Tax Court has ruled that it will not recognize such "quickie divorces" solely on the basis of the fact that the state in which the taxpayers are domiciled will not recognize such divorces. (The Fourth Circuit Court of Appeals ruled in 1981 that there may be a sham even if your state does recognize the divorce [668 F 2d.

1238]. This ruling is not universally accepted—see *Wake Forest Law Review,* Volume 18, pages 881–901, 1982). But many states *do* recognize such divorces; by implication, therefore, if you reside in such a state, a "quickie" divorce and a remarriage could save you substantial tax dollars. Your divorce, though, must be real, with significant economic consequences—for example, loss of rights under a will—and not merely a sham. (See *Felt Estate v. Commissioner,* T.C. Memo 1987-465, September 16, 1987, in which a divorce decree obtained by a husband in the Dominican Republic was recognized for federal income tax purposes.)

In cases where divorces or legal separations would be either impractical or unwanted, you could at least make a substantial initial tax savings by postponing your original Christmas wedding until New Year's. This several days' wait may be worth several thousand tax dollars.

Being single may also be an advantage in qualifying for excess itemized deductions. For example, assume your spouse has total below the line deductions of $7,200. As you are married and don't exceed the amount of the joint standard deduction, none of these deductions is allowable.

Filing separately may sometimes help, but a husband and wife filing separate returns must use the same method of claiming deductions: If one itemizes, the other must itemize as well. This could result in a situation in which one spouse who itemizes has an allowable itemized deduction in excess of the standard deduction by, say, $2,000, but the other spouse who has no itemized deductions would have to *add* $2,000 to the gross income (e.g., subtract $2,000 from $0 in deductions)!

This may be profitable if the spouse who has itemized deductions is in a higher tax bracket. For example, if one is in the 31 percent bracket and the other is in the 15 percent bracket, the first would save $620 ($2,000 × .31) at a cost to the second of only $300 ($2,000 × .15), or a net gain of $320.

However, this advantage may be dissipated by the greater advantage of the married tax schedule over the potentially more costly schedule for married filing separately. For example, filing jointly, a husband with a taxable income of $60,000 and a wife with $50,000 would pay $25,382 in taxes on a total income of $110,000. Filing separately, the husband would owe $14,241 and the wife $11,202, a total of $25,443 and a net *loss* of $61! Note that as the rates are condensed, the potential net loss is reduced.

The usual instance in which filing separately is advantageous is when substantial excess itemized deductions can be picked up. For example, as you will see later, medical expenses must be reduced by 7.5 percent of your adjusted gross income before they can be included in your itemized deduction computation. Assume one spouse has $3,000 in medical expenses and an adjusted gross income of $10,000, while the other spouse has no medical expenses and an adjusted gross income of $50,000. Filing separately would require a reduction of only $750 (7.5 percent of $10,000) rather than $4,500 (7.5 percent of $60,000)—a net additional itemized deduction of $2,250. In this case, depending upon the other itemized deductions and specific credits available to each spouse, it might pay to file separately. In any case, if you are married and both parties earn income, it is always to your advantage to prepare your return each way to see which provides the lower tax.

B Tax Planning with Itemized Deductions

There are a number of general strategies that should be implemented when planning for your itemized deductions. The most important of these is the timing of your deductions. Many deductions can be shifted from one year to the next.

You might want to implement such shifting if your itemized deductions are close to the standard deduction amount. Your aim should be to bunch your deductions for expenses so that they exceed the full value of your standard deduction amount. For example, assume that you have itemized deductions of $7,200 each year, of which $3,000 can be accelerated or deferred. With a standard deduction amount of $7,200, none of these deductions would be allowed as excess. What you do, therefore, is to time the expenses you can control so as to itemize deductions of $10,200 in the alternate years ($7,200 + $3,000). This strategy allows you an extra deduction of $3,000 every second year ($10,200 – $7,200), and if you are in the 31 percent bracket, it saves you $930 in taxes each time.

For you to be able to claim all of your available itemized deductions and to time them appropriately, we must examine and dissect each one in turn.

54 Medical Expenses

You may deduct certain medical and dental expenses not only for yourself but for your spouse and your dependents as well. Medical expenses are payments that you make for the diagnosis, cure, relief, treatment, or prevention of disease. They also include payments for treatment affecting any part or function of the body. Expenses for transportation for needed medical care are included in medical expenses. Payments for insurance that provide medical care for you, your spouse, and your dependents are also included in medical expenses.

The following list shows those items that are generally deductible as medical expenses:

- Fees for doctors, surgeons, dentists, ophthalmologists, optometrists, chiropractors, osteopaths, chiropodists, podiatrists, psychiatrists, psychologists, and Christian Science practitioners.
- Fees for hospital services, therapy, nursing services (including nurses' meals while on duty), ambulance hire, and laboratory, surgical, obstetrics, diagnostic, dental, and X-ray services.
- Meals and lodging provided by a hospital during medical treatment, and meals and lodging provided by a center during treatment for alcoholism or drug addiction.
- Medical and hospital insurance premiums.
- Special equipment such as motorized wheelchairs, hand controls on a car, and special telephones for the deaf.
- Special items, including false teeth, artificial limbs, eyeglasses, hearing aids, crutches, and guide dogs for the blind or deaf.
- Transportation for needed medical care.
- Insulin and prescription medicines and drugs, including special foods and drinks your doctor prescribes specifically for the treatment of an illness, and pills, birth control items, and vitamins and iron your doctor prescribes.
- Under certain conditions, medical deductions may be allowed for boarding school expenses. In Letter Ruling 8447014, the IRS ruled that a psychiatrically oriented boarding school is a special school. Thus, the taxpayer was able to deduct, as a medical expense, tuition as well as transportation expenses to and from the school.
- The cost of special school programs for children with Attention Deficit Hyperactivity Disorder (P.L.R. 9852015).
- The cost of programs and prescriptions to help you stop smoking (but not over the counter patches and gums) (Rev. Pub. 99-28).
- Radical keratotomy surgery to correct vision is deductible (Ltr. Rul. 9625049) but, so far, even medically prescribed marijuana, even in a state where it is legal, is not (Rev. Rul. 97-9).

There are certain limitations on the amount you may deduct. You may deduct only that part of your medical and dental expenses that is more than 7.5

percent of your adjusted gross income. Drug expenses, which include *only* prescription drugs and insulin, are included in this 7.5 percent pool.

As of 1983, the separate deduction for one-half of medical insurance premiums up to $150 was eliminated. All medical insurance premiums are included in the 7.5 percent pool.

Medical care includes a wide array of services. It includes payments for a legal abortion as well as payments for an operation legally performed to make a person unable to have children. It no longer includes payments for cosmetic surgery, such as a face-lift, but does cover charges for medical care that are included in the tuition fee of a college or private school, as long as the breakdown of the charges is included in the bill given by the school.

Payments for acupuncture and payments to a treatment center for drug addicts or alcoholics, including meals and lodging provided by the center during the treatment, are also deductible. So too are payments for surgical, hospital, laboratory, and transportation expenses by an actual or possible donor of a kidney or other body organ.

Wages for an attendant who provides nursing services and any out-of-pocket amounts you pay for the attendant's meals are also deductible. Divide the food expense among the household members to find the cost of the attendant's food. If you had to pay additional out-of-pocket amounts for household upkeep because of the attendant, this extra amount you paid is deductible as well. This includes items such as extra rent you paid because you moved to a larger apartment to provide space for the attendant, or the extra cost of utilities for the attendant. If the attendant also provided personal and household services, costs for these must be separated from costs for the nursing, since only the amount spent for nursing services is allowable as a deduction. Remember, though, that even the part of the social security (FICA) tax you pay for a worker who provides medical care is deductible.

You may also deduct payments for psychiatric care mainly for relieving a mental illness or defect. You may include the cost of supporting a mentally ill dependent at a specially equipped medical center where the dependent receives medical care, as well as your transportation expenses for regular visits that are recommended as part of that dependent's treatment.

MEDICAL INSURANCE PREMIUMS

Medical insurance premiums are deductible within the limits described earlier. The premiums you pay for medical insurance are for medical care, whether the insurance company pays the provider of the care (hospital, doctor, etc.) directly or reimburses you for payments you've made. Medical insurance premiums you pay may be included in your medical expenses if the premiums are for:

a) policies that pay for hospitalization, surgical fees, and other medical expenses;

b) policies that pay only for prescription drugs;

c) policies that replace lost or damaged contact lenses;

d) the medical part in policies that provide more than one type of payment, if the medical charge is reasonable and is stated separately in the insurance contract or is given to you in a separate statement;

e) membership in an association furnishing cooperative, "free choice" medical service, or group hospitalization clinical care;

f) Medicare B, supplementary medical insurance for the aged (check the information you receive from the Social Security Administration to find out your premium rate and the amount of your deduction);

g) Medicare A, the part of social security that covers basic Medicare (you may deduct premiums you voluntarily pay for Medicare A coverage if you are 65 or older and are not entitled to social security benefits; Medicare A premiums are not deductible if they are paid as part of your social security tax); *or*

h) prepaid insurance premiums you pay before you are 65 for medical care coverage—for yourself, your spouse, or dependents—after you are 65. These are deductible when paid if they are paid in equal installments yearly or more often. The payments must be made for ten years or more; if paid until you reach 65, the payments must be made for a minimum of five years.

You may not deduct premiums paid for life insurance policies or for policies providing repayment for loss of earnings or for the accidental loss of limb, life, sight, etc. Nor can you deduct premiums for a policy that guarantees a specified amount each week (for a specified number of weeks) if you are hospitalized for sickness or injury.

LONG-TERM CARE INSURANCE AND SERVICES

Prior to 1996, the Internal Revenue Code did not provide explicit rules relating to the tax treatment of long-term care insurance contracts or long-term care services. Beginning in 1997, the Health Insurance Portability and Accountability Act of 1996 provides that qualified long-term care insurance premiums will count toward itemized medical expenses and, to the extent that such expenses exceed 7.5% of adjusted gross income, a tax deduction will be available.

There is a cap on the amount of premium that can be applied to the medical expense deduction. The limit varies by attained age as follows:

Attained Age at the End of the Tax Year	1999 Maximum Deduction
Not more than 40	$ 210
More than 40 but not more than 50	$ 400
More than 50 but not more than 60	$ 800
More than 60 but not more than 70	$2,120
More than 70	$2,660

For taxable years beginning after 1997, these dollar limits have been indexed for increases in the medical care component of the Consumer Price Index. Moreover, long-term care insurance premiums will now qualify for the self-employed health insurance deduction.

HOSPITAL MEALS AND LODGING

Meals and lodging are also deductible if they are furnished by a hospital or similar institution as a necessary part of medical care and if the main reason for your being in the hospital is to receive that medical care. The cost of your meals or lodging while you are away from home for medical treatment, or for the relief of a specific condition, however, is not deductible if you are not at a hospital or similar institution, even if the trip is made on the advice of your doctor. Under the Tax Reform Act of 1984, a deduction of up to $50 per day per individual for lodging expenses, but not for meals, for the patient and certain accompanying individuals away from home to receive outpatient care at hospitals or certain outpatient clinics is allowed. For example, treatment in an outpatient clinic, such as the Mayo Clinic, that provides substantially similar services to those provided by a hospital would qualify. Moreover, although food costs are not deductible, presumably if they are included in the cost of the lodging, no allocation is necessary and the full cost will be deductible subject to the $50 per day per person limit. (See Letter Ruling 8516025.)

Alternatively, if an individual is in a nursing home or a home for the aged because of a physical condition, and the main reason for being there is to get medical care, the entire cost, including meals *and* lodging, may be included as a deductible medical expense.

TRANSPORTATION EXPENSES

Transportation payments necessary for medical care also qualify as a deductible medical expense. Assume that you have been ill with a bad heart condition and you live in an area that has extremely cold winters, which makes your condition worse. Your doctor advises you to spend the winter in a warmer place, and you and your family spend the winter in a rented house in Florida. The trip is made for a specific medical reason, and although none of your expenses for food and lodging while on your way to Florida or during your stay there are deductible, your share of the transportation expenses between your home and Florida *is* deductible.

Transportation expenses include the following:

- Amounts paid for bus, taxi, train, or plane fare, or for ambulance hire.
- Out-of-pocket expenses for your car, such as gas and oil. You may not deduct any part of general repair or maintenance expenses. If you do not wish to deduct your actual expenses, you may use the *standard rate* of 10¢ a mile for each mile you use your car for medical reasons, and add to that any parking fees and tolls that you pay.
- Transportation expenses of a parent who must accompany a child needing medical care.
- Transportation expenses of a nurse familiar with injections, medications, and other treatments required by a patient who is traveling to get medical care but cannot travel alone.

CARE FOR THE HANDICAPPED

Special care may be needed for handicapped individuals. You may include the following payments for this care in your deductible medical expenses:

1. Payments to a special school for mentally or physically handicapped individuals, if the main reason for going is the school's means for relieving the handicap. The cost of sending a blind child to school to learn braille, or a deaf child to learn lip reading, is a medical expense. If you pay for remedial language training to correct a condition caused by a birth defect of the brain, you may deduct these payments as medical expenses.

   Tuition or tutoring expenses you pay on your doctor's advice for a child who has severe learning disabilities caused by a nervous system disorder are also medical expenses. So too are the costs of meals, lodging, and ordinary education supplied by the special school, but only if the main reason for the child's attendance is the availability of medical care.

2. The cost of keeping a mentally retarded individual, at the advice of a psychiatrist, in a specially chosen home that is not the home of a relative; for example, a "halfway" house to help in the adjustment from life in a mental hospital to community living.

3. Payments to a nonprofessional individual for giving "patterning" exercises (coordinated physical manipulation of the individual's limbs to imitate crawling and other normal movements) to a mentally retarded child.

4. Advance payments to a private institution for the lifetime care, treatment, and training of your physically and mentally handicapped dependent in the event that you die or become unable to care for your dependent. The payments must be required as a condition for the institution's future acceptance of your dependent and cannot be refundable.

5. Expenses paid for the care of your invalid spouse in your home. Only amounts spent for care to relieve your spouse's illness are deductible. The cost of household services, such as cooking and cleaning, is not deductible as a medical expense but may be eligible for the credit for household and dependent care expenses.

SPECIAL MEDICAL EQUIPMENT

Moreover, you may also deduct payments for special items and equipment. This includes payments for:

1. False teeth, artificial limbs, eyeglasses, hearing aids, and crutches, or the cost and care of guide dogs for the blind and deaf. Such expenses are medical, not business, even if you use the dog in carrying on your business.
2. The part of the cost of braille books and magazines that is more than the price for regular books and magazines.
3. The cost and repair of special telephone equipment that enables a deaf person to communicate over a regular telephone.
4. Amounts paid for oxygen equipment and oxygen to relieve problems in breathing due to a medical condition.
5. The cost of special attachments, such as a motorized wheelchair or autoette or special hand controls that are installed in a car for the use of a physically handicapped driver.
6. The amount you pay for a special design of a car to hold a wheelchair, as well as the cost of operating and keeping up an autoette or wheelchair used mainly for the relief of sickness or disability.
7. The cost of removing lead-based paints from walls, woodwork, etc., in your home to prevent a child who has lead poisoning (or who has had lead poisoning) from eating the paint. This must be on the advice of a doctor, and it must be determined that the paint contains lead. The areas covered with lead-based paint have to be in poor repair (peeling or cracking) or within the child's reach. The cost of painting the scraped area is not a deductible medical expense.

Payments for special equipment installed in a home, or similar improvements made for medical reasons, may be deductible even if they are capital improvements. If these expenses are for permanent improvements that increase the value of the property, only the amount in excess of the increase in value may be deducted as a medical expense. For example, assume you have a heart ailment, and on your doctor's advice you install an elevator in your home so that you will not need to climb stairs. The elevator costs $1,000. According to competent appraisals, the elevator increases the value of your home by $700. The $300 difference is a medical expense. If the elevator did not increase the value of your home, the whole cost would have been a medical expense.

If a capital expense qualifies as a medical expense, any amount paid for operation or upkeep also qualifies as a medical expense, as long as the medical reason for the capital expense still exists. These expenses are deductible even if none or only part of the original expense was deductible.

Amounts paid by a handicapped individual to buy and install special plumbing fixtures in a rented house are also deductible medical expenses. For example, assume you are handicapped with arthritis and a bad heart condition. You cannot climb stairs or get into a bathtub. On your doctor's advice, you install a bathroom with a shower stall on the first floor of your two-story rented house. The landlord does not pay any of the cost of buying or installing the special plumbing and does not lower your rent. The whole amount you pay for this bathroom is a deductible medical expense. A medical expense deduction is also available for the cost of special equipment used to display subtitles on the television set of a hearing impaired individual (Rev. Rul. 80-340).

In 1987, the IRS released a list of thirteen such deductible home improvements. If these improvements are made to accommodate yourself or a family member with a physical handicap, they count in full toward the 7.5 percent deduction floor (Rev. Rul. Section 7-106, I.R.B. 1987-43).

The improvements on the IRS list are the following:

1. Constructing entrance or exit ramps to the home
2. Widening doorways and entrances or exits to the home
3. Widening or otherwise modifying halls and interior doorways
4. Installing railings, support bars, or other modifications to bathrooms
5. Lowering or making other modifications to kitchen cabinets and equipment
6. Altering the location of or otherwise modifying electrical outlets and fixtures
7. Installing porch lifts or other forms of lifts (this does not include elevators, as they may increase the value of the home)
8. Modifying fire alarms, smoke detectors, and other warning systems

9. Modifying stairs
10. Adding handrails and grab bars, whether or not in bathrooms
11. Modifying hardware on doors
12. Modifying areas in front of entrance and exit doorways
13. Grading of ground to provide access to the home

Note that just because an improvement is not on the list, this does not necessarily mean that such an improvement is not a fully deductible expense.

COMPUTING YOUR MEDICAL EXPENSES

Computing your medical expenses is a simple process. Your allowable drugs, your medical insurance premiums, plus all of your other medical expenses, are reduced by 7.5 percent of your adjusted gross income. Taxpayers and dependents 65 or older, as well as younger persons, are subject to this 7.5 percent limitation.

If you and your spouse live in a community property state and file separate returns, any amount you paid for medical expenses out of community funds is divided equally. Each of you may deduct half of the expenses. If medical expenses are paid out of the separate funds of one spouse, only the spouse who paid the medical expenses may deduct them.

If you and your spouse do not live in a community property state and you file separate returns, each of you may deduct only the medical expenses you actually paid. Any medical expenses paid out of a joint checking account in which you and your spouse have the same interest are considered to have been paid equally by each of you, unless you can show otherwise. Furthermore, you must reduce your total medical expenses for the year by the total reimbursements (repayments) you receive from insurance or other sources for those expenses during the year. This includes payments you receive from Medicare A and Medicare B. The reimbursement may be paid directly to you or to the doctor or hospital.

The actual computation of your medical expense deduction can be demonstrated by the following example. Assume you and your spouse paid the following medical expenses:

a) \$595.60 for hospital insurance, \$80.40 for medical and surgical insurance, \$125 for allowable medicines and drugs, \$237.86 for hospital bills, \$39 for doctor bills, and \$20 for transportation;

b) $200 for doctors and $75 for medicines and allowable drugs for your spouse's dependent mother;

c) $350 for doctors and $100 for medicines for your sister, whom you claim as your dependent.

The hospital and doctor expenses cited have already been reduced by repayment from your insurance company. Your adjusted gross income is $20,374.33. The deductible amount is computed as follows:

Medicines and drugs	
You and spouse	$ 125.00
Spouse's mother	75.00
Sister	+100.00
Total medicines and drugs	$ 300.00
Insurance:	
Hospitalization	$ 595.60
Medical and surgical	+ 80.40
Total insurance	$ 676.00
Other medical expenses:	
You and spouse (doctors)	$ 39.00
Spouse's mother (doctors)	200.00
Sister (doctors)	350.00
You and spouse (hosp.)	237.86
Transportation	+ 20.00
	$ 846.86
Total medical expenses [medicine plus insurance plus other expenses ($300.00 + 676.00 + 846.86)]	$1,822.86
Minus 7.5 percent exclusion ($20,374.33 × .075)	−1,528.07
Total deduction	$ 294.79

Not only must you reduce your total medical expenses by the total reimbursements you have received from insurance and other sources for those expenses, but if you receive payment under an accident insurance contract, you must also reduce your medical expenses by that part of the payment set aside for hospitalization and medical care. However, you need not reduce medical expenses by any repayments you have received for loss of earnings or damages for personal injury. But you must also reduce medical expenses by that amount received in settlement of a damage suit for personal injuries that has been set aside for future medical expenses. Medical expenses paid this year and in future years because of these injuries must be reduced until the amount received in settlement has been completely used. Any amount you pay after that may be deductible.

Even if you fail to file a claim under an insurance policy that would have covered your medical expenses, those expenses that you pay are still deductible (*Weaver*, TCM 1984-634).

If you are reimbursed for medical expenses you deducted in an earlier year, you must report as income the amount of the reimbursement that is equal to or less than the amount you previously deducted as medical expenses. For example, assume you had an adjusted gross income in year A of $10,000, and during that year you paid medical insurance premiums of $200 and incurred medical expenses of $800. No amount was included for medicine and drugs. You deducted $250, figured as follows:

Medical expenses	$ 800
Plus insurance	+200
Total medical expenses	$1,000
Minus 7.5 percent of adjusted gross income	–750
Total deduction	$ 250

In year B you collected $200 under your insurance policy as reimbursement for part of your year A medical expenses. If you had collected in year A, your deduction for medical expenses would have been only $50, figured as follows:

Medical expenses	$ 800
Plus insurance	+200
Total medical expenses	$1,000
Minus insurance reimbursements	–200
Balance	$ 800
Minus 7.5 percent of adjusted gross income	–750
Total deduction	$ 50

Since the $200 reimbursement is less than the $250 deduction, you should include $200 in income in year B.

If you did not deduct a medical expense in the year you paid it, either because you did not itemize deductions or because your medical expenses were not more than the 7.5 percent limitation, you should not include in income the reimbursement for this expense that you received in a later year. For example, assume in year C you paid $150 for medical insurance premiums and $400 for medical expenses, but you could not deduct the $550 because it was under the 7.5 percent limitation. If in year D you were reimbursed for any of the $400 medical expenses, you would also not include the reimbursement in your gross income because you received no tax benefit for it in the earlier year.

There are a number of sophisticated tax planning strategies that you can utilize when claiming medical expense deductions. First, you must recognize that these expenses are deductible only in the year that they are paid. If you charge medical expenses to your credit card, these expenses are deducted in the year the charge is made—it does not matter when you paid the amount charged. But expenses for eyeglasses, dental work, hearing aids, elective surgery, and year-end doctor visits can often be juggled as to the year in which they are actually paid. Since these medical expenses must exceed 7.5 percent of your adjusted gross income before you can begin taking deductions, it may pay to bunch expenses in one year if that will get you over the hump. You currently cannot deduct a mere prepayment of a possible future bill, however. There must be an actual bill or at least an actual scheduling of services.

Medical expense shifting can be demonstrated by the following example. Assume your adjusted gross income is $30,000. Late this year your doctor bills you $2,000. Your other medical expenses amount to only $250. If you can, pay in January of next year. You will get no deduction in this year, anyway (7.5 percent of $30,000 is $2,250), so deferring the expense until next year will give you another chance of exceeding the 7.5 percent floor.

Alternatively, if you have already met your 7.5 percent floor, you should accelerate the payment of your medical expenses. Payments in December of this year will reduce your taxes and increase your cash balance, and the potential earnings on it, for all of next year. If you wait till January to make the payment, the deduction and its attendant tax benefit will be deferred for an additional year (even assuming that you meet the percent limit in the second year).

For example, assume you have exceeded the standard deduction amount and the 7.5 percent floor for deducting medical expenses. Further assume that in mid-December you have a $1,000 doctor bill due in 30 days. If you are in the

31 percent bracket and pay the bill in December, you save $310 in taxes, *and* you have an additional $310 on which you can earn interest throughout the next tax year. If you wait until January to make the payment, you will lose the interest on the saved $310 in taxes and may lose the deduction completely if you cannot both pass the percent floor test and exceed your standard deduction amount for excess itemized deductions. The solution in this case, clearly, is to make the payment on December 31.

MEDICAL SAVINGS ACCOUNTS

Under law prior to the Health Insurance Portability and Accountability Act of 1996, self-employed individuals were entitled to deduct 30% of the amount paid for health insurance for the self-employed individual and his or her spouse or dependents. Any individual who itemized tax deductions could deduct unreimbursed medical expenses (including expenses for medical insurance) paid during the year to the extent that the total of such expenses exceeded 7.5% of the individual's adjusted gross income. Prior law did not contain any special rules for medical savings accounts.

A Medical Savings Account (MSA) is a trust or custodial account created exclusively for the benefit of the account holder and is subject to rules similar to those applicable to individual retirement accounts. Within limits, contributions to a medical savings account are deductible if made by an eligible individual and are excludable if made by an employer of an eligible individual. Moreover, earnings on amounts in a medical savings account are not currently taxable and distributions from a medical savings account for medical expenses will also not be taxable.

Beginning in 1997, Medical Savings Accounts will be available to employees covered under an employer-sponsored high-deductible plan of a small employer and to self-employed individuals. An employer is a small employer if it employed on an average no more than 50 employees during either the preceding or second preceding year. In order for an employee of an eligible employer to be eligible to make medical savings account contributions (or to have the employer contributions made on his or her behalf), the employee must not be covered under any other health plan. In the case of an employee, contributions can be made to a medical savings account either by the individual or by the individual's employer. However, an individual is not eligible to make contributions to a medical savings account for a year if any employer contributions are made to a medical savings account on behalf of the individual for the year.

Similarly, in order to be eligible to make contributions to a Medical Savings account, a self-employed individual must be covered under a high-deductible health plan and no other health plan is allowed (except certain permitted coverages). With both self-employed individuals and employees, Medical Savings Accounts are allowable if the taxpayer has another health plan that provides *only* certain limited permitted coverage for accidents, disability, dental care, vision care, or long-term care. This coverage may be by insurance or otherwise and permitted insurance includes: (1) Medicare supplemental insurance; (2) insurance if substantially all of the coverage provided under such insurance relates to (a) liabilities incurred under Workers' Compensation Law, (b) tort liabilities, (c) liabilities relating to ownership and use of property (e.g., auto insurance), or (d) such other similar liabilities as the Secretary of the Treasury may prescribe by regulations; (3) insurance for a specified disease or illness; and (4) insurance that provides a fixed payment for hospitalization.

Individual contributions to a Medical Savings Account are deductible (within limits) above the line. In addition, employer contributions are excludable within the same limits.

In the case of a self-employed individual, the deduction cannot exceed your earned income from the trade or business with respect to which the high-deductible plan is established. In the case of an employee, the deduction cannot exceed your compensation attributable to the employer sponsoring the high-deductible plan in which you are enrolled.

The maximum annual contribution that can be made to a Medical Savings Account for a year is 65% of the deductible under the high-deductible plan in the case of individual coverage and 75% of the deductible in the case of family coverage. No other dollar limits on the maximum contribution apply. The annual contribution limit is the sum of the limits determined separately for each month, based upon the individual's status and health plan coverage as of the first day of the month.

A high-deductible plan is a health plan with an annual deductible of at least $1,550 and no more than $2,300 in the case of individual coverage and at least $3,050 and no more than $4,600 in the case of family coverage. In addition, the maximum out-of-pocket expenses with respect to allowed cost (including the deductible) must be no more than $3,050 in the case of individual coverage and no more than $5,600 in the case of family coverage. Beginning after 1998, these dollar amounts have been indexed for inflation in $50 increments based on the Consumer Price Index.

Earnings on amounts in a medical savings account are not currently included in income and distributions from a medical savings account for the medical expenses of an individual and his or her spouse or dependents generally are excludable from income.

The Medical Savings Account plan is a trial plan. The number of taxpayers benefiting annually from a Medical Savings Account contribution is limited to a threshold level (generally, 750,000 taxpayers). If it is determined in a year that the threshold level has been exceeded then, in general, for succeeding years during the four-year pilot period, 1997–2000, only those individuals who (1) made a Medical Savings Account contribution or had an employer Medical Savings Account contribution for the year or a preceding year or (2) are employed by a participating employer, would be eligible for a Medical Savings Account contribution.

During 1997–2000, the Department of the Treasury will evaluate Medical Savings Account participation and the reduction in federal revenues due to such participation and make reports of such evaluations to Congress.

TAX STRATEGIES

Sophisticated tax planning also involves knowing how to structure your personal deductions so that they qualify as allowable medical expenses. Many expenditures that do not readily appear to be deductible are allowable as medical expenses. For example, elastic stockings qualify as medical expenses if needed by an infirm or elderly person. In one case, the cost of a sacroiliac belt prescribed by a doctor was deductible, as was the cost of high blood pressure medication and a blood sugar test. In another instance, a deduction was allowed for a device installed to add fluoride to a home water supply at a controlled rate; it was represented that fluoride is a chemical that strengthens the dental enamel as the teeth grow, making them more resistant to decay, and that the only purpose of the installation and use of the device was to prevent tooth decay. Travel to Alcoholics Anonymous meetings, based on medical advice, is a deductible medical expense (Rev. Rul. 63-273).

Deductions have been allowed for extraordinary forms of medical equipment. For example, the costs of oxygen equipment and oxygen to alleviate breathing difficulty *and* of a reclining chair recommended by a doctor for a person with a cardiac condition have qualified as medical deductions. So, too, have special mattresses and certain thicknesses of plywood boards prescribed for an individual who had arthritis of the spine. In one instance, a wig purchased to avoid mental upset to a patient who had lost her hair was deductible!

Super medical deductions can be obtained if your doctor can find an ailment in yourself, your spouse, or your dependents that would require you to have a whirlpool for baths, or central air conditioning to provide you or your dependents with pure, dehumidified air. Even the expense of a swimming pool may be deducted if it is installed because of a physician's recommendation and if that facility in any way alleviates your physical condition (see *Cherry,* TCM 1983-470 and Rev. Rul. 63-273, 1963-2 C.B. 112). If such a swimming pool is used for a specific medical purpose—for example, to provide hydrotherapy—then not only is a deduction allowed for the installation, but a deduction is also allowed for the cost of upkeep, including chemicals, cleaning, water, and utilities. Note, though, that the installation is a capital expenditure and therefore only the excess cost over the added value to your property is deductible. (See Rev. Rul. 83-33 and Letter Ruling 822-1128 and 832-6095.)

One of my own favorite medical deductions is the cost of an overseas trip for medical or dental work. For example, it has been established that the cost of extensive dental work is far less expensive in Europe than in the United States. Therefore, even adding the transportation costs to go to an overseas dentist, your total cash outlay is lower than having such work performed locally. On this basis, such transportation costs have been allowed as deductible medical expenses. One woman consulted three different dermatologists in the United States, but none was able to improve her skin condition. Finally, she was treated successfully as an outpatient in a foreign country. The IRS agreed that her expenses were deductible (Letter Ruling 812-6044).

In 1991, the Tax Court let Alex L. and Earlene Polyak of Trenton, Mich. deduct $1,124 for 1984 transportation to Palm Beach Gardens as essential to her care for heart and lung ailments and arthritis. Her doctors advised her to winter in warmer climates.

Furthermore, amounts paid for "medical care" may be deductible even if they are for purposes that do not have the sanction of the medical profession or even if the payments are made to persons without medical qualifications. For example, amounts paid to such practitioners as psychotherapists are categorized for tax purposes as fees for medical care, even though those who perform the services may not be licensed, certified, or otherwise qualified to perform these services, and even if certification is required by law. In other words, payments to unlicensed practitioners are deductible if the type and quality of their services are not illegal and if such services may be deemed to fall within the parameters of "medical care." In fact, in IRS Letter Ruling 8442018, the Internal Revenue Service allowed as a deductible medical expense electrolysis performed by a nonlicensed technician as "medical care." Remember, "medical care" means any amounts paid for the diagnosis, cure, mitigation, treatment, or prevention of disease or for the purpose of affecting any structure or function of the body. (In Rev. Rul. 82-111, the IRS had ruled that hair removal through electrolysis performed by a state licensed technician was deductible as a medical expense.)

Note that, effective for tax years beginning after December 31, 1990, expenses for unnecessary cosmetic surgery are no longer deductible as "medical care" expenses, except when the surgery is necessary to correct a deformity due directly to a congenital abnormality, a personal injury resulting from an accident or trauma, or a disfiguring disease.

The law further defines cosmetic surgery as any procedure that is directed at improving the patient's appearance and does not meaningfully promote the proper function of the body or prevent or treat illness or disease.

The definition of cosmetic surgery is quite broad and seems to bar the deductibility of many procedures that are not strictly surgical. The biggest question with the coverage of the definition has to do with orthodontic work and other dental procedures that may be considered strictly cosmetic. No IRS guidance has yet come forth to clarify the issue, but I consider this to be more than merely cosmetic, so in the normal situation, I would go for the deduction!

A second category of below the line deductions is the taxes that you pay during your tax year. Such taxes fall under three classifications, which will be discussed separately.

55 Income Taxes

You may deduct some state and local income taxes, including taxes on interest income that is exempt from federal income tax. You may not deduct state and local taxes on any other exempt income. For example, the part of state income tax on a cost-of-living allowance that is exempt from federal income tax is not deductible.

State and local taxes are those imposed by the fifty states or any of their political subdivisions (such as a county or city) and by the District of Columbia. You may deduct state, local, or foreign income taxes withheld from your salary, as well as estimated payments made under a pay-as-you-go-plan of a state or local government. You also may deduct payments made on taxes due but not paid in an earlier year in the year they were actually withheld or paid. In sum, to be deductible the tax must be paid during your tax year. You may deduct only those taxes paid during the calendar year for which you file a return.

If you receive a refund of these taxes in a later year, you must include the return as income in the year you receive it. This would include refunds resulting from taxes that were overwithheld, not figured correctly, or figured again as a result of an amended return. If you did not itemize your deductions in a previous year, you do not have to include the refunds. Furthermore, the amount included in your income is limited to the tax benefit you received in the earlier years. For example, assume you deducted $500 in taxes and received a refund of $100; your total itemized deductions exceeded your standard deduction amount by only $50. The only tax benefit you received, therefore, was the $50 excess itemized deduction. On this basis you need only include $50 of the refund in your income for the subsequent year.

You also may deduct amounts required to be withheld from your wages for certain state disability benefit funds that provide against loss of wages. These payments to the disability fund are deductible as state income taxes. Furthermore, employee contributions to a state fund that provides indemnity coverage for the loss of wages caused by unemployment resulting from business contingencies are also deductible as taxes. Employee contributions to private disability plans, however, are not deductible.

Foreign taxes include those taxes imposed by a foreign country, a U.S. possession, or any of their political subdivisions.

Foreign income taxes that you pay may either be deducted as an itemized deduction or claimed as a credit against your U.S. tax.

56 Real Property Taxes

Real property (real estate) taxes are any state, local, or foreign taxes on real property levied for the general public welfare. Local benefit taxes are deductible if they are for maintenance or repair, or for interest charges related to these benefits. If only a part of the tax is for maintenance, repair, or interest, you must be able to show the amount of that part to claim the deduction. If you cannot determine what part is for maintenance or repair, none of it is deductible.

If you are a tenant shareholder in a cooperative housing corporation, you may deduct the amounts you pay to that corporation that represent your share of the real estate taxes the corporation pays or incurs on the property. If the corporation leases the land and buildings and is required to pay the real estate taxes under the terms of the lease agreement, however, your part of the taxes is not deductible. Moreover, if your landlord increases your rent in the form of a tax surcharge because of increased real estate taxes, you cannot deduct that increase as taxes either.

Real property taxes also do not include trash and garbage collection fees or homeowners association charges you may pay for the recreation, health, safety, and welfare of residents, and for maintaining common areas.

If real estate is sold during the tax year, the real estate taxes must be divided between the buyer and seller. These taxes must be divided according to the number of days in the real property tax year (the period to which the imposed tax relates) that each owns the property. The seller pays the taxes up to the date of the sale, and the buyer pays the taxes beginning with the date of the sale, regardless of the lien dates under local law. If you use the cash method and do not deduct taxes until they are paid, and the buyer of your property is personally liable for the tax, you are considered to have paid your portion of the imposed tax at the time of the sale. This permits you to deduct the portion of the tax to the date of sale even though you did not actually pay for it.

For example, assume that your real property tax year is the calendar year, with payment due on August 1. Your tax on your old home, sold May 5, was $300, and your tax on your new home, bought on May 3, was $200. You are considered to have paid a proportionate share of the real estate taxes on the old home even though you did not actually pay them to the taxing authority. On the other hand, you may claim only the proportionate share of the taxes you paid on your new property even though you paid the entire amount.

Because you held the old property for 125 days (January 1 to May 4, the day before the sale), you are entitled to a deduction of 125/365 of $300, or $102.73. You owned the new home for 243 days (May 3 to December 31, including the date of the purchase), so your taxes on the new home are 243/365 of $200, or $133.15. Your real estate tax deduction is therefore $102.73 + $133.15, or $235.88.

If you and your spouse held property jointly, and you file separate returns, each of you may deduct only the taxes each of you paid on the property.

57 Personal Property Taxes

Some personal property taxes are also deductible, subject to certain requirements:

1. The tax must be based only on the value of the personal property. For example, assume your state charges a yearly motor vehicle registration tax of 1 percent of value plus 40¢ per hundredweight. You pay $28.60 based on the value ($1,500) and weight (3,400 pounds) of your car. You may deduct $15 as a personal property tax, since it is based on the value. The remaining $13.60, based on the weight, is not deductible.

2. The tax must be charged on a yearly basis, even if it is collected more or less often than once a year.

3. The tax must be charged on personal property. A tax is considered charged on personal property even if it is for the exercise of a privilege. A yearly tax based on value qualifies as a personal property tax although it is called a registration fee—that is, for the privilege of registering motor vehicles or using them on the highways.

58 Interest

Some interest payments qualify as below the line deductions. The type of deduction you may take depends on whether the money was borrowed for personal use, for rental or royalty property, or for your business.

Interest payment on a loan for income-producing rental or royalty property, on a business loan, and on farm business loans are "above the line" deductions. Interest of a personal nature, such as home mortgage interest, is a "below the line" deduction; normally, so is interest paid on margin accounts held with your broker. Interest on these accounts is considered paid when the broker is paid, or when the interest becomes available to the broker through your account.

To deduct interest on a debt, you must be legally liable for that debt. No deduction will be allowed for payments you make for someone else if you are not legally liable to make them. Both the lender and the borrower must intend that the loan be repaid.

For example, assume you make a loan to your son, hoping to be repaid when he is able. If no true debtor-credit relationship is created, he is not legally liable to pay the debt and will not be able to deduct any interest paid. Here he should sign a note and make scheduled repayments to insure his interest deduction. Alternatively, if you cosign a note for a loan made by a bank to your son, even if your son is a student, and if both you and your son are jointly liable on the note, you may deduct any interest you pay on the loan in the year you pay it.

You must normally pay the interest before you may deduct it. But if you use the accrual method of accounting, you may deduct interest over the period it accrues regardless of when it is paid. To show how this works, suppose you borrow $1,000 in September, *payable in 90 days* at 12 percent interest. In December you make the payment with a new note for $1,030 due the following March. If you use the cash method of accounting, that $30 is not deductible in the year you give the new note, since you do not actually pay the interest. However, if you pay the $30 and give a new note for $1,000, the interest is deductible. If you are on the accrual method, the $30 is deductible in either case. If you pay interest in advance for a period that goes beyond the end of the tax year, you must spread the interest over the tax years to which it belongs. You may deduct in each year only the interest that belongs to that year.

The following items are generally deductible as interest:

Mortgage interest
"Points," if you are a buyer (see explanation that follows)
Interest on a business loan
Installment plan interest (unless consumer interest)
Investment interest

The following items normally are *not* deductible as interest:

"Points," if you are a seller (potentially deductible by *buyer* under Rev. Proc. 94-27)
Service charges
Credit investigation fees
Loan fees
Interest relating to tax-exempt income
Interest paid to carry single-premium life insurance
Premium on a convertible bond
Interest owed to related taxpayers, unless there is an actual debtor-creditor relationship

Effective Interest Rates on Mortgages with Points

Stated Rate (%)	Points 1	2	3	4	5
Assuming 30-year mortgage held to maturity					
5	5.09	5.18	5.27	5.36	5.46
6	6.09	6.19	6.29	6.29	6.48
7	7.01	7.20	7.30	7.41	7.52
8	8.11	8.21	8.32	8.44	8.55
9	9.22	9.23	9.34	9.46	9.58
10	10.12	10.24	10.37	10.49	10.62
11	11.13	11.26	11.39	11.52	11.66
12	12.13	12.27	12.41	12.55	12.70
Assuming 30-year mortgage paid off in 15th year					
5	5.11	5.22	5.33	5.44	5.56
6	6.11	6.23	6.35	6.46	6.58
7	7.12	7.24	7.36	7.49	7.61
8	8.12	8.21	8.32	8.44	8.55
9	9.13	9.26	9.40	9.53	9.67
10	10.14	10.28	10.42	10.56	10.70
11	11.14	11.29	11.44	11.59	11.74
12	12.15	12.30	12.46	12.61	12.77
Assuming 30-year mortgage paid off in 7th year					
5	5.18	5.36	5.55	5.73	5.92
6	6.18	6.37	6.56	6.75	6.95
7	7.19	7.38	7.57	7.77	7.97
8	8.19	8.39	8.59	8.79	8.99
9	9.20	9.40	9.61	9.81	10.02
10	10.20	10.41	10.62	10.83	11.05
11	11.21	11.42	11.64	11.86	12.08
12	12.22	12.44	12.66	12.88	13.11

Effective Interest Rates on Mortgages with Points ***(Continued)***

Assuming 30-year mortgage paid off in 3rd year					
5	5.37	5.74	6.12	6.50	6.89
6	6.37	6.75	7.13	7.52	7.91
7	7.38	7.76	8.15	8.54	8.93
8	8.38	8.77	9.16	9.56	9.96
9	9.39	9.78	10.18	10.58	10.98
10	10.39	10.79	11.19	11.60	12.01
11	11.40	11.80	12.21	12.62	13.04
12	12.40	12.81	13.22	13.64	14.06

One of the most usual types of personal interest expense is the interest on your mortgage. You may deduct only the interest part of your mortgage payment. If your records do not show the interest paid, get a statement showing that information from the lender who holds your mortgage. If you are a cash method taxpayer, you may deduct the full amount of interest paid during the year. If you are an accrual method taxpayer, you may deduct the amount accrued each year.

A point is equal to 1 percent of the loan amount, so on a $100,000 mortgage each point would cost you $1,000. If you pay off a mortgage over 30 years, each point on a 12 percent loan adds 0.13 percentage points to the interest rate. Thus on a 12 percent loan with 4 points charged, the effective interest rate is 12.52. On a 14 percent, 30-year loan, each point adds 0.15 percentage points. On a 16 percent loan, it is 0.17 percentage points. Keep in mind that these figures apply only if the mortgage is paid off over the full 30-year term. If you sell the property and pay off the loan sooner, the effective interest is higher, since those extra dollars paid up front are spread over fewer years of borrowing.

The term "points" is sometimes used to describe the charges paid by a borrower. They are also called loan origination fees, maximum loan charges, or premium charges. If the payment of any of these charges is solely for the use of money, then it is considered interest.

In one case, the Tax Court allowed a taxpayer to deduct interest he paid on a mortgage on his residence, even though the title to the home was held in the name of his corporation. The Court reasoned that the taxpayer had always treated the home as his own and the mortgage indebtedness therefore was his (*Lang, Jr.*, TCM 1983-318). In *USLU v. Commissioner,* TC Memo 1997–551,

12/16/97, the Tax Court ruled that a person who lived in a house and made all the payments for it could deduct mortgage interest even though legal title and financing was obtained by the person's brother. All the facts established equitable and beneficial ownership of the house.

The amount you pay in points is deductible in full in the year of payment only if it is paid to buy or improve your main home and if the loan is for that home. The charging of points has to be an established business practice in your area. The deduction may not be more than the number of points generally charged in your area. If these conditions are not met, points are treated as prepaid interest. They must be spread over the life of the mortgage, and are considered as paid and deductible over that period. Moreover, in IRS Notice 86-68, May 13, 1986, the Internal Revenue Service ruled that points paid on refinancing a home mortgage are not *currently* deductible. Thus, they could only be deducted over the loan period. For example, assume that $2,400 of points is paid in connection with refinancing a mortgage that is to run for another 20 years (i.e., 240 monthly payments remain to be paid). These points are deductible over the term of the loan, $10 per monthly payment. The IRS reaffirmed this position in Rev. Rul. 87-22, as did the Tax Court in 1988. Points paid in a refinancing, therefore, must be amortized over the life of the loan, unless the money is used to improve the home (*Huntsman*, T.C. 1988, reversed), or unless the refinancing is an integral part of the original purchase of the property.

Points charged for specific services by the lender for the borrower's account (such as a lender's appraisal fee, the cost of preparing the mortgage note or deed of trust, settlement fees, or notary fees) are not interest. Points charged in connection with getting a V.A. loan were not interest until 1992, retroactive to 1991. For example, assume you get a loan from a bank to buy your main home. The loan was insured by the Veterans Administration and you pay the bank a loan origination fee. This fee is 1 percent of the amount of the loan and is charged in addition to the maximum rate of interest permitted. The amount of the 1 percent loan origination fee (one "point") is now interest and may be deducted.

Alternatively, assume you got a loan of $48,000 to buy a $60,000 home. In addition to interest at the rate of 9 percent, you paid the lender a loan processing fee of $1,440 (three "points"). None of the fee was for specific services. The charging of points was an established business practice in the area and the number of points was not more than that generally charged in the area. This loan processing fee to purchase a principal residence is interest and is deductible in full in the year of payment. [See Section 461(g)(2) and *Schubel*, 77 T.C. No. 701 (1981).] [See also *Pacific First Federal Savings and Loan*

Association, 79 T.C. No. 33 where points were found to be interest where the fee was for the use or forebearance of money and bore no relation to the actual cost to underwrite the loan.] It is best to exchange checks with your bank rather than just reduce the amount received on your mortgage. In the past, unless you formally exchanged checks, the Internal Revenue Service argued a lack of "payment." However, in IRS Notice 90-70, the separate check for points was ruled as unnecessary as long as you provide a down payment, escrow deposit, or other closing funds "at least equal to" the points charged. This means points are now deductible even if the lender finances them if your cost payments are at least equal to the points charged. [See also Rev. Proc. 92-12.]

The term "points" is also used to describe loan placement fees that the seller may have to pay to the lender to arrange financing for the buyer. Prior to 1994, you could *not* deduct these amounts as interest. See Revenue Procedure 94-27 below to see if you may qualify now. (However, these charges are a selling expense that reduces the amount realized by the seller.) Furthermore, if you pay off your mortgage early, you may have to pay a penalty. This amount is deductible as interest, as is any amount you pay as a tenant stockholder in a housing cooperative for the interest on the cooperative's debt, or for points required in the year you became a tenant-stockholder.

In Rev. Proc. 87-15, I.R.B. 1987-14, the Internal Revenue Service set forth the method for determining the amount of points allocable to each tax year during the term of an indebtedness in a situation where points charged to a taxpayer in respect of the indebtedness are required to be deducted over the period of indebtedness. Such points may be deductible on an internal rate of return basis—i.e., considering the time value of money with the bulk of the deduction being taken in the earlier years—or, alternatively, as a matter of administrative convenience, the Internal Revenue Service will allow a taxpayer consistently to allocate the points ratably over the indebtedness. For example, if $3,600 in qualified points were paid on a 30-year (360-month) loan, $10 per payment would be allowed as deductible point interest ($3,600 divided into 360 monthly payments).

Note that the points must be paid at the time the indebtedness is incurred. In *Schubel*, 77 T.C. 701 (1981), the Tax Court held that points withheld by a lender from loan proceeds may not be deducted by a borrower in the year the points are withheld, because the withholding did not constitute payment within that tax year. Note IRS Notice 90-70 discussed above.

The above rules were modified by Revenue Procedure 94-27 and IRS News Release 94-28 wherein it was ruled that home *buyers will* be able to deduct *seller*-paid points on mortgages so long as the purchase price of the home is reduced by the amount of the seller's payment. This rule does not apply to improvement (rather than acquisition) loans, or to loans not for your principal residence.

Other payments also constitute interest. When you buy property on the installment plan, you may deduct your interest payments if they are separately stated, or if they can be determined and proved. Finance charges added to your monthly credit card statements also constitute deductible interest, as do one-time charges made on new cash advances and new check and overdraft advances added to your bank credit card account balance. No part of these one-time charges, though, can be a service charge, loan fee, credit investigation fee, or similar charge.

When you buy personal property such as clothing, jewelry, furniture, or appliances on the installment plan using a revolving charge account, there is usually a separately stated finance charge. The total amount of these finance charges was deductible as interest, subject to the consumer interest deduction phaseout discussed below. For example, if you buy a refrigerator for $300 from the American Department Store and charge it to your revolving charge account, there will be no extra charge if you pay the balance within 30 days after you are billed. But if you make installment payments, your account will be charged the finance charge of 1.5 percent on the unpaid balance each month. These finance charges were previously deductible as interest.

Sometimes when you borrow money the interest is subtracted from the face amount of the note and you receive the balance. If you use the cash method, you may deduct the interest only in the year you make payments. Alternatively, if you use the accrual method, you may deduct the interest as it accrues.

For example, assume you sign a note for $1,200 on March 27, agreeing to pay it in 12 equal installments beginning on April 28. The interest is $1,200 × 12 percent = $144 and is subtracted from the face value of the note so that you receive only $1,056. If you use the cash method, the interest is considered to be repaid in 12 installments of $12 each. Your deduction for the first year is $108 ($12 × nine payments). If you miss two payments in the first year and made only seven payments, your deduction is $84. If you use the accrual method, the deduction is determined by prorating interest over the period in which it accrues. You may therefore deduct $108 (9/12 × $144) in the first year and $36 (3/12 × $144) in the following year.

Interest often is "hidden" in other payments, such as in judgments and personal loans. If you make a late payment of taxes, or if you must pay additional taxes at a later date, part of the amount will usually be for interest. This interest is no longer deductible (see personal interest limitations below). Penalties, in addition, are not deductible. Furthermore, you may not deduct interest on any money you borrow to buy tax-exempt securities or to buy a single-premium life insurance endowment or annuity contract. A single-premium contract includes policies on which you pay almost all the premiums within four years from the date you buy the contract; it also includes policies for which you deposit an amount with the insurer for the payment of future premiums. Also, you may not deduct interest on a loan that is used to buy stock if the collateral on the loan is a single-premium annuity contract.

However, according to Rev. Rul. 83-51, the Internal Revenue Service holds that the "contingent interest" portion of a shared appreciation mortgage (SAM) loan used by a cash-basis individual taxpayer to finance the purchase of a personal residence is deductible as interest when paid. The ruling deals with three situations. In each, the taxpayer purchases a home by securing a SAM from a financial institution. The SAM provides for a fixed interest annual rate and "contingent interest" equal to 40 percent of the appreciation in the value of the residence, payable when the SAM terminates. Termination is to occur at the earliest of (1) prepayment of the entire outstanding balance of the SAM, (2) sale of the residence, or (3) ten years from the SAM loan. The taxpayer also has the option to refinance the mortgage balance and contingent interest due at the prevailing interest rate. The SAM agreement provides that it creates no more than a debtor-creditor relationship.

In the first situation provided for under the ruling, the taxpayer sells the residence at a profit and uses a portion of the sales proceeds to pay the remaining SAM principal balance and the contingent interest. In the second situation, the taxpayer prepays the outstanding principal balance and contingent interest with funds not obtained from the SAM lender. In the third situation, the taxpayer refinances the principal balance and contingent interest due on maturity of the SAM by obtaining a conventional thirty-year mortgage from the SAM lender. The Internal Revenue Service holds that in the first and second situations, the taxpayer can deduct the contingent interest in the year the SAM is paid off, on the grounds that interest, to be deductible, need not be computed at a stated rate. All that is required is that a definitely ascertainable sum be paid for the use of borrowed money pursuant to a loan agreement. In the first and second situations, the contingent interest is ascertainable. In the third situation, however, the taxpayer cannot deduct contingent interest, because merely executing a new note does not constitute payment. But payments on the new note to the extent allocable to the contingent interest will be deductible in the year paid. In all three situations, the taxpayer can deduct the fixed interest when paid.

To insure that you have a debtor-creditor relationship and that the SAM does not in substance create an equity arrangement, the SAM agreement should provide, in addition to stating that only a debtor-creditor relationship is intended, that:

a) the mortgage secures only the indebtedness;

b) the mortgagor can sell, transfer, improve, and encumber the property without the mortgagee's consent;

c) the mortgagee is not liable for any decrease in the value of the property; *and*

d) the mortgagor is solely responsible to pay real estate taxes, insurance premiums, and other charges relating to ownership.

LIMITATIONS

There are certain limitations on the amount of interest that you can deduct.

The deduction for investment interest incurred or continued is limited to net investment income to purchase or carry *property held for investment.* Disallowed investment interest can be carried forward indefinitely and allowed to the extent of future net investment income.

Investment income and investment expenses do not include any income or expenses taken into account when computing income or loss from a passive activity, including any interest paid or accrued on debt to acquire or carry an interest in a passive activity. However, it does include portfolio income from passive activities.

DEFINITIONS

Net investment income means the excess of *investment income* over *investment expenses.* Investment income is defined as income from interest, dividends, rents, royalties, short-term capital gains arising from the disposition of investment assets, and certain recapture amounts (but only if the income is not derived from the conduct of a trade or business), except that all gain (not just short-term gain) attributable to the disposition of property held for investment may be included. The Omnibus Budget Reconciliation Act of 1993 complicated the deductibility of investment interest. The Act provides that long-term capital gains qualify as investment income only if the investor volunteers to have them taxed at the same rate as personal income.

The calculations can get complicated. If you have a long-term gain of $50,000 and $50,000 of investment interest, with no other investment interest, with no other investment income, you could effectively avoid the tax on the gain by opting to treat it as ordinary income. The savings would be 28 percent of $50,000 or $14,000 (or $10,000 if you qualified for the 20 percent maximum capital gains tax).

However, if you expect $50,000 in investment income the next year, and you pay the $14,000 in this year, you could carry the deduction forward and potentially save $19,800 in income tax at the 39.6 percent rate in the second year—a net two-year savings of $5,800. Investment expenses are deductible expenses (other than interest) directly connected with the production of investment income. Investment expenses should be considered as those allowed after application of the 2 percent floor for miscellaneous itemized deductions (see page 224). In computing the amount of expenses that exceed the 2 percent floor, expenses that are not investment expenses are disallowed before any investment expenses are disallowed.

Property held for investment includes property that produces interest, dividends, annuities, or royalties plus any interest held by a taxpayer in an activity involving the conduct of a trade or business that is not a passive activity and in which the taxpayer does not materially participate. A passive activity is defined as an activity that involves the conduct of a trade or business in which the taxpayer does not materially participate. The only activity excluded from this definition is a working interest in an oil and gas property that a taxpayer holds directly or through an entity that does not limit the liability of the taxpayer with respect to that activity. However, regulations may be issued that could broaden the class of activities that are excluded under the definition of a passive activity, and the class of activities so excluded would thereby be considered property held for investment.

EXCEPTION FOR PASSIVE LOSSES DURING PHASE-IN OF THE PASSIVE LOSS RULES

Investment income of a taxpayer for any taxable year must be reduced by the amount of any passive activity loss that is allowed for the taxable year because of the phase-in of the passive loss rules. However, passive losses that are permitted under the $25,000 allowance for rental real estate activities in which the taxpayer actively participates do not reduce investment income when computing the investment interest expense limitation.

Example 1: In 1987 an investor had $20,000 of investment income, before taking into account passive losses that were allowable during the phase-in of passive losses. The investor also had $8,000 of passive losses that were allowable after application of the phase-in passive loss rules from passive activities other than rental real estate activities. The investment income for purposes of determining the limitation on investment interest was $12,000 ($20,000 + $8,000).

Example 2: In 1987 an investor had passive losses of $90,000, of which $40,000 was attributable to rental real estate activities in which the investor actively participated. Assuming the investor was entitled to deduct $25,000 of active rental losses under the special $25,000 allowance for rental real estate activities, then 65 percent (the applicable passive loss phase-in percentage for 1987) of the remaining $65,000 of passive activity losses, $42,250, would have been allowed as a deduction in 1987.

Of the deductible $42,250 of allowed passive losses, the portion not attributable to active rental activities reduced the investor's net income under the investment interest limitation for 1987. The portion of the allowable passive loss attributable to rental real estate activities was $9,750 (.65 × $15,000, where the $15,000 is determined by subtracting the $25,000 allowed under the special allowance from the $40,000 of total passive losses attributable to rental real estate activities). Therefore, when determining the amount of investment interest expense that could be deducted for the year, the taxpayer must have reduced investment income by $32,500 (the $42,250 of deductible passive losses minus the $9,750 of deductible passive losses attributable to rental real estate activities).

PHASE-IN OF DISALLOWANCE

The limitation on investment interest was phased in over four years. Taxpayers other than married individuals filing a separate return and trusts could have deducted investment interest equal to net investment income plus investment interest paid or accrued in the taxable year in excess of net investment income in accordance with the following table:

For Taxable Years Beginning in	The Applicable Amount Is:
1987	$6,500
1988	4,000
1989	2,000
1990	1,000
1991	0

Any interest expense that is disallowed because of the investment interest expense limitation and is carried forward may not be deducted under the excess allowances for later taxable years.

In the case of married individuals filing separate returns the excess interest expense allowances given in the table above are cut in half. In the case of trusts no excess interest expense deductions are allowed in any year.

Example 1: In each of the four years after 1987 an investor has $20,000 of investment interest expense in excess of investment income. The investor's allowable deductions in excess of net investment income during the four-year period will be $6,500 in 1987, $4,000 in 1988, $2,000 in 1989, and $1,000 in 1990.

Example 2: In 1987 an investor has $20,000 of investment interest expense in excess of investment income. The investor is allowed to deduct $6,500 in 1987 and carries $13,500 over to 1988. In 1988 the investor has $10,000 more investment income than investment interest expense before taking into account the $13,500 carryover. The investor is allowed to deduct $10,000 of the investment interest expense carryover. The remaining $3,500 of investment interest expense carryover may not be deducted using the remaining $4,000 excess interest allowance for 1988 because that allowance only applies to investment interest expense paid or accrued in 1988, not carryovers from prior years.

THE DISALLOWANCE OF DEDUCTION FOR PERSONAL INTEREST

Taxpayers other than corporations will no longer be allowed to deduct personal interest paid or accrued during the taxable year. Personal interest means any interest other than (1) interest paid or accrued on indebtedness incurred or continued in connection with the conduct of a trade or business, (2) any investment interest, (3) any interest taken into account when computing income or loss from a passive activity of the taxpayer, (4) any qualified residence interest, and (5) interest payable on extensions of time for payment of estate tax on the value of reversionary or remainder interests in property or where an estate consists largely of interests in a closely held business. In other words, virtually all personal or consumer interest (including interest on underpayment or late payment of taxes) that was allowable as a deduction without limit under prior law may no longer be deducted with the exception of qualified residence interest.

The term *qualified residence interest* means any interest that is paid or accrued during the taxable year on indebtedness secured by any property that (at the time such interest is paid or accrued) is a qualified residence of the taxpayer. The term *qualified residence* means the principal residence of the taxpayer and one vacation home.

Note that interest on income tax deficiencies arising from the conduct of a trade or business *is* personal interest (the Tax Court in *Redlark*, 106 T.C. No. 2, 1/11/96, said it *was* deductible as did the District Court in *Allen v. U.S.,* DC ENC, No. 5:96-CV-909-F, 12/1/97, in North Carolina, but it was later reversed by the 4th Cir. Court of Appeals, No. 98-1401 on 4/20/99, while the Eighth Circuit says it *is not, Miller v. U.S.,* No. A3-92-183, 11/5/93, reversed by the Eighth Circuit, No. 94-3225, 9/7/95). However, the Ninth Circuit also reversed *Redlark* on 4/10/98 (CA-9, No. 96-70398) and was supported by *Stecher v. U.S.,* P. Colo., No. 97-WY-1892-AJ, 6/18/98 and *McDonnell v. U.S.,* 6th Cir., No. 98-5383, 5/27/99. Interest on tax deficiencies of partnerships and S corporations must be taken *below* the line (*True v. U.S.,* No. 91-CV-1004-J, 7/30/93)) as opposed to above the line business entity deductions.

LIMITATION ON THE AMOUNT OF INTEREST DEDUCTIBLE AS QUALIFIED RESIDENCE INTEREST

The amount of interest that may be deducted on a debt secured by a qualified residence is limited in the following manner: Interest is deductible only to the extent that the indebtedness does not exceed the lesser of (1) the fair market value of the qualified residence or (2) the taxpayer's basis in the qualified residence (adjusted only by the cost of any improvements to such residence). However, as of August 16, 1986, if the aggregate amount of outstanding indebtedness secured by a qualified residence exceeded the taxpayer's basis in the property at that time, the amount of indebtedness at that time would substitute for the taxpayer's basis in the qualified residence when determining qualified residence interest.

Taxpayers could have deducted interest on debt secured by a qualified residence in excess of the limitation described above if the debt was secured to pay for *qualified medical expenses* or *qualified educational expenses* that were paid or incurred within a reasonable period of time before or after such indebtedness was incurred.

The term *qualified medical expenses* means amounts not compensated for by insurance or otherwise incurred for medical care for the taxpayer, a spouse, or a dependent. The term *qualified educational expenses* means qualified tuition and related expenses of the taxpayer, a spouse, or a dependent for attendance at a normal educational institution.

PHASE-IN OF LIMITATION

The limitation on the deduction of personal interest was phased in over the four years that began in calendar year 1987 and that continued through 1990.

The percentage of personal interest that could have been deducted during the phase-in period is given in the following table:

For Taxable Years Beginning in	The Applicable Percentage Is:
1987	65%
1988	40
1989	20
1990	10
1991	0

The limitation on the deductibility of personal interest may encourage many taxpayers to seek other ways of financing consumer purchases. Two immediate methods of converting what would otherwise be nondeductible personal interest (except as allowed under the phase-in percentages) into deductible interest are (1) to borrow against marginable securities (or property held for investment) or (2) to borrow against a qualified residence. Each of these techniques presents potential problems.

USING HOME EQUITY

Originally, interest paid on debt secured by a home could be deductible only to the extent that the debt does not exceed the lesser of (1) the fair market value of the home or (2) the taxpayer's adjusted basis in the home (or if the debt secured by the home exceeded the basis on August 16, 1986, that amount of debt).

Many homeowners who have owned their homes for many years or who have acquired new homes in recent years after rolling over gains from the sale of a previous home have relatively low bases in their homes. In addition, they may have debt secured by these homes that already exceeds their bases. Consequently, the opportunity to increase interest-deductible borrowing in many cases may be limited. Even in cases where the potential to tap home equity exists, in many cases it may be unwise to risk the loss of a home to finance consumer purchases since circumstances could evolve that preclude repayment of the debt.

However, taxpayers who have sufficient equity in their homes and untapped borrowing capacity under the qualified residence interest rules may wish to finance new consumer purchases or consolidate consumer loans by increasing qualified residence borrowing.

Some homeowners may wish to consider selling their homes, using the 1998 $250,000/$500,000 gain exclusion, and purchasing a new home. The proceeds from the sale of the home could be used to purchase the new home. They would have potential interest-deductible borrowing capacity equal to the cost of their new homes.

The Revenue Act of 1987, signed in December 1987, modified the above rules on home equity indebtedness but introduced further—and more favorable—limitations for home acquisition indebtedness. Indebtedness that was incurred on or before October 13, 1987, and that was secured by a qualified residence on such date or on any date thereafter is classified as acquisition indebtedness. Such debt will not be subject to the new acquisition indebtedness limitation in 1988 or after. Therefore, interest that was associated with indebtedness incurred on or before October 13, 1987, and that exceeded the limitations under the 1986 Tax Reform Act, will not exceed the limitations under the 1987 act. The related interest will be viewed as qualified residence interest for 1988 and thereafter.

Under the latest rules, the aggregate amount treated as acquisition indebtedness for any period cannot exceed $1,000,000 (or $500,000 in the case of a married individual filing a separate return). Also, refinancing of indebtedness after October 13, 1987, is considered acquisition indebtedness, but only to the extent of the refinanced indebtedness. If a qualified residence is refinanced for more than the existing indebtedness, the excess amount may qualify in total, in part, or not at all as acquisition indebtedness.

Home equity indebtedness is *now* defined as any indebtedness (other than acquisition indebtedness) secured by a qualified residence to the extent that the aggregate amount for any period does not exceed the lesser of (1) $100,000 (or $50,000 for a married individual filing separately), or (2) the fair market value of such qualified residence less the amount of acquisition indebtedness with respect to the residence.

Example 1: Assume that you buy a house for $1,000,000 and borrow $800,000 to finance the purchase. You reduce your debt to $600,000 by making payments over several years. In 1988, you refinance and take out a new mortgage for $700,000. Your acquisition debt will still be $600,000. However, if you used $100,000 to substantially improve your home, the $100,000 would be added to acquisition debt.

Example 2: Assume that you bought your home 15 years ago for $50,000. You have completely paid off your mortgage, and the property is now worth $200,000. In 1988, you take out a $120,000 home loan. You use $110,000 to make additions to the home and $10,000 to buy a car. Interest on the entire loan is deductible: $110,000 of the loan is acquisition debt, and the balance qualifies as home equity debt.

Example 3: Assume that you have an unpaid balance of $90,000 on your home, which is valued at $300,000. You obtain a second mortgage of $110,000 and use the proceeds to help your parents buy a home and to buy personal assets. Interest on $100,000 of the new mortgage is deductible as qualified residence interest. Interest on the $10,000 balance is personal interest.

Note that the 1987 limits on acquisition indebtedness make it very important not to overlook many elements of the cost of a house besides the amount paid to the seller. These would include appraisal fees, title search, transfer taxes, survey fees, bank or lender fees, legal fees, mortgage taxes, brokers' commissions (if paid by the buyer), and other nondeductible closing costs. Note that the cost of the home and improvements does not include painting and routine maintenance and repairs. However, it does include additions to the home and improvement or replacement of equipment that is part of the home. Such improvements include landscaping; resurfacing the driveway; installing a swimming pool; constructing a new roof; finishing an attic or basement; replacing or making a major improvement to heating, air conditioning, or plumbing systems or to a water heater; or adding on a room or garage.

Can you finance the purchase of additional land, adjacent to your home, and deduct the interest as qualified residence interest? In Private Letter Ruling 8940061, the IRS said yes! In the ruling, a family built a home on 15 acres and later bought five more adjacent acres that will be cleared, landscaped, and incorporated into the family compound. The loan to finance the extra land is secured by both the new land and the original 15-acre tract. The family told the IRS it had no plans to separately develop the five acres.

The IRS said that the loan to buy the five acres was purchase debt, and since total purchase debt didn't exceed $1 million, all of the interest paid was deductible in full.

USING DEBT SECURED BY INVESTMENT PROPERTY

The major advantage of borrowing against a home rather than against property held for investment is that qualified residence interest is not subject to the investment interest expense limitation. When borrowing against property held for investment, care must be taken not to generate investment interest expense in excess of net investment income (plus excess amounts allowed under the phase-in rules for investment interest), or the interest deductions will be disallowed in the year paid or incurred. However, any excess may be carried forward indefinitely and deducted in later years when investment income exceeds investment interest expense paid or incurred in that year. Therefore, carryovers of investment interest will still generally be preferable to personal interest, which is no longer deductible.

Another disadvantage of using debt secured by investment property to finance consumer purchases is the margin limits set by the Federal Reserve. For example, debt secured by common stock may not exceed 50 percent of the value of the stock.

PASSIVE ACTIVITIES WITH PASSIVE INCOME

Individuals who own passive activities that are earning passive income may wish to increase borrowing against that activity even if they do not wish to finance consumer purchases. The proceeds could be used to acquire investment assets with appreciation potential that could as well be leveraged up to their respective margin limits, thereby creating investment interest deductions to offset the current income from the portfolio.

The interest on debt used to acquire or carry an interest in a passive activity is not subject to the investment interest expense limitation. Such interest is fully deductible against passive income from the passive activity. However, if the interest expense exceeds the passive income from the passive activity, the excess interest will be treated as a passive loss. That loss may be deducted only against passive income from other passive activities or, on disposition of that passive activity, against gains on the disposition, passive income from other passive activities, and any active income or gain of the taxpayer, in that order. There are exceptions provided under the phase-in rules for passive losses.

RENTAL REAL ESTATE ACTIVITIES WITH PASSIVE LOSSES

In general, passive losses that are allowable as a deduction under the phase-in of the passive loss rules reduce net investment income for purposes of determining the amount of investment interest expense that may be deducted under the investment interest limitation. However, this does not apply to passive losses that are allowable from rental real estate activities. Consequently, increasing debt secured by rental real estate, even when that activity is currently generating passive losses rather than passive income, may be advisable. During the phase-in period of the passive loss rules a certain percentage of the interest on that debt (65 percent in 1987, 40 percent in 1988, 20 percent in 1989, and 10 percent in 1990) was allowable as a deduction with no corresponding reduction in the amount of investment interest expense otherwise deductible.

PASSIVE ACTIVITIES WITH PASSIVE LOSSES

The same advice does not generally apply to debt secured by passive loss activities other than rental real estate. Any increase in passive losses due to the interest on the debt that is allowable as a deduction under the passive loss phase-in rules reduces the amount of investment interest expense otherwise deductible on a dollar-for-dollar basis (if investment interest expense already equals or exceeds the amount otherwise allowable for the year).

However, in some cases applying this strategy to passive activities other than rental real estate may still be beneficial.

Generally interest on debt to carry an interest in a passive activity is not deductible except against passive activity income. If an investor anticipates a large gain on the disposition of property held for investment in a subsequent year, the investor may create an "artificial" interest expense carryover. By increasing the allowable passive loss in a given year (by increasing debt and interest expense attributable to the passive activity), the investor may intentionally create an investment interest expense carryforward that may be used in the subsequent year to offset the anticipated gain on the disposition of the investment property. In effect the investor has circumvented the rule that disallows interest expense attributable to passive activities to offset income or gains from investment activities.

Example: In 1987 an investor had $20,000 of investment income and $26,500 of investment interest expense. He also owned an interest in a passive activity other than rental real estate that had $0 net passive income in 1987. In 1988 he has $15,000 of investment income and $19,000 of investment interest expense before taking into account the sale of common stock on which he has a $20,000 gain.

The investor was allowed to deduct all his investment interest expense in 1987 ($20,000 of net investment income plus $6,500 under the phase-in allowance). In 1988 the investor is allowed to deduct all his investment interest expense ($15,000 of net investment income plus $4,000 under the phase-in allowance) and has $20,000 of taxable gain.

If the investor secured additional debt on the passive activity in 1987 that generated $30,770 of interest each year, the passive loss from the activity would be $30,770. Under the phase-in of the passive loss rules, he could have deducted 65 percent of the $30,770, or $20,000, in 1987. In addition, the amount so allowed reduced his net investment income to $0 for purposes of determining the amount of investment interest he could deduct. Therefore, if he secured this debt, he would have created an investment interest expense carryover to 1988 of $20,000, which will exactly offset the gain in 1988.

What the investor does with the proceeds from the loan is important. If he uses it to purchase income-producing investment assets, the income earned on those assets will use up some or all of the carryover. However, if he purchases low-yielding investments such as growth stocks, the increase in investment income will be minimal and the artificial investment interest carryover will be preserved.

OTHER INTEREST PLANNING TIPS

To the extent that a loan finances an asset used partially for business and partially for personal purposes, it appears that interest would have to be prorated between the two uses.

Example 1: Ms. Agent, an insurance agent, finances a new automobile to be used 75 percent for business and 25 percent for personal purposes. She would treat 75 percent of the interest as deductible business interest and 25 percent as nondeductible consumer interest.

Example 2: In example 1, Ms. Agent was treated as a self-employed individual. If she was an outside salesperson and an employee, rather than a self-employed individual, apparently all the interest she would pay on her automobile loan would be treated as consumer interest and would not be deductible as interest, even if she used the automobile 75 percent of the time in her employer's business. It would, however, be deductible as an employee business expense under miscellaneous deductions

Under the 1986 law, it may be more advantageous to have a business-use vehicle owned by the employer rather than by the employee, even though the employee must include the value of any personal use as compensation income.

The term *residence* as used in the qualified residence interest exception includes, in addition to houses, condominium units and cooperative housing units and any other property that the taxpayer uses for personal purposes as a dwelling unit, which generally includes a mobile home, a motor home, or a boat with living accommodations. A taxpayer who owns a boat that is large enough to live aboard for short periods, a mobile home, or a motor home may be able to treat it as a second residence for purposes of the residential interest deduction.

Taxpayers who are planning to purchase a new home might consider having appliances and various options such as a deck, fencing, and landscaping installed by the builder and included in the sales price. The interest on these items would then qualify as fully deductible residential interest. Otherwise the interest will be treated as nondeductible consumer financing and will be deductible only to the extent permitted under the phase-in rule.

The use of interest-free and other below-market-rate loans is affected by the interest deduction limitation. An individual borrower's imputed interest deduction will no longer fully offset the imputed interest income. Both borrowers and lenders who are party to employment-related or gift-type interest-free loans should reconsider whether these types of arrangements are still suitable.

Taxpayers with excess investment interest expense should consider recognizing capital gains by selling property held for investment.

There are a number of tax strategies that you should employ in planning your interest deductions. First, you must consider the timing of your actual interest payments in relation to both exceeding your standard deduction amount and determining your subsequent year's income. This technique has been discussed in detail under medical expenses and taxes. Second, you must recognize that unlike many other forms of expenditure, interest expenses need not be reasonable to be deducted. If you borrow money at an exorbitant rate, that interest is deductible regardless of what it has been labeled in order to circumvent a state law on maximum percentages.

Interest is also deductible if paid to a related party for a bona fide indebtedness. This means that if you actually have a legal debtor-creditor relationship with your spouse, for example, you may deduct interest paid to that spouse. In fact, parents may legitimately deduct interest paid on money borrowed from their minor children as long as there is an effective debtor-creditor relationship. This means that you sign a note, arrange for a repayment schedule, and meet that repayment schedule. Substantial savings can be accrued by paying legitimate interest to a child in a lower tax bracket. For example, assume that you paid $1,500 in interest to your dependent child (who has no other income) and you are in the 31 percent bracket. The first $700 of that interest is not taxable to the child because of the standard deduction. Therefore, the child pays only $120 on the interest received ($800 × 15 percent). But if you are in the 31 percent bracket, you saved $465 in taxes—a net savings of $345!

STUDENT LOAN INTEREST DEDUCTION

The Tax Relief Act of 1997 provides a new *above the line* deduction of up to $1,000 for any interest on any qualified education loan in 1998, $1,500 in 1999, $2,000 in 2000, and up to $2,500 per year in 2001 and thereafter during the first 60 months in which interest payments are required. This deduction begins to phase out at a modified adjusted gross income level of $60,000 for joint filers and $40,000 for all others. These limits are also indexed for inflation.

A qualified education loan is a loan used to pay the costs of attendance at an eligible educational institution for a student enrolled at least half-time in a program leading to a degree, certificate, or other recognized educational credential. The student must be the taxpayer, the taxpayer's spouse, or the taxpayer's dependent at the time the loan was taken. A loan made by an individual who is related to the borrower is not a qualified education loan.

59 Charitable Contributions

A charitable contribution is a gift to a qualified charitable organization. (To be deemed as making a gift, the taxpayer must have "donative intent"—that is, a detached and disinterested generosity. There must be no *quid pro quo* expected or received.) The tax law allows charitable contributions to reduce taxable income, and therefore the actual cost of the donation will be reduced by your tax savings. As your income tax bracket increases, the real cost of your charitable gift will therefore decrease, making contributions more attractive for those in the higher brackets.

Regardless of the accounting method you use, contributions are usually deducted in the year in which they are paid. A contribution is paid when you unconditionally deliver or mail your gift to the recipient or to a designated agent or when you make a completed gift of property. A contribution made by a credit card is deductible immediately even if payment to the credit card company is made in a different year.

You can obtain an itemized deduction for your charitable contributions, but these deductions are limited to a maximum of 50 percent of your adjusted gross income for the year. These contributions may consist of gifts to public charities and certain private foundations.[1] If the 50 percent limit is not exhausted, you can deduct contributions to other entities subject to a more restrictive constraint of 20 percent of your adjusted gross income.[2]

Appreciated capital gain property generally is further subjected to an additional 30 percent limit. These limits will be detailed in the analysis under planning considerations.

Charitable contributions can take numerous forms. Though cash and property are the main ones, there are others that must be considered. Unreimbursed costs incurred for charity contributions, dues, admission charges, and other payments may be deductible, but not if they are made in exchange for benefits or property you receive. The amount deductible is usually the property's fair market value, yet for gifts of appreciated property this value may be reduced under special rules. Cancelled checks and receipts offer the best proof to the contributor. When a charitable deduction is taken you must be able to state the name of each charity and the amount and date of each gift. The *charitable mileage deduction* is 14¢/mile for 1999.

PLANNING CONSIDERATIONS

Qualified Donees

You can deduct charitable contributions only if they are made to or for the use of a "qualified donee." No charitable contribution deduction is allowed for gifts to other kinds of organizations, even if those organizations are exempt from U.S. income tax.

The gift must be made directly to an organization to qualify for the deduction. However, in the case of *Rockefeller,* 76 T.C. 178 (1981), the court held that unreimbursed expenses incurred in rendering services to a quali-

1. The following types of foundations qualify: 1. private operating foundations; 2. all other private foundations that distribute all their contributions to public charities within two and one half months after the year end; and 3. pooled community foundations.
2. The Tax Reform Act of 1984 increased the limits on contributions to tax exempt private *nonoperating* foundations from 20 percent to 30 percent of adjusted gross income, for gifts of cash or ordinary income property. It also provided that excess post-1984 contributions can be carried forward for five years. The Act, in addition, provided a deduction at full fair market value for contributions of up to 10 percent of the stock of a corporation to a private *nonoperating* foundation, provided the stock is publicly traded and is long-term capital gain property. These provisions are effective for contributions made after the enactment of the Act.

fied charitable organization constituted deductible contributions made "to" the charitable organization. The IRS has acquiesced in this decision (Rev. Rul. 84-61, I.R.B. 1984-17). No deduction to an individual or individuals is allowed by the IRS unless that individual or group is acting as an agent for a qualified organization. This rule is necessary because there is no guarantee that the money given to an individual will be forwarded to the charity. Payments to individual ministers have been disqualified as charitable contributions where there was no evidence that the money ever went to the minister's religious organization.

The Treasury Department publishes IRS Publication 78, which lists the organizations to which contributions are deductible, identifies each by type, and states their corresponding limit of deductibility. This list is updated annually. Three cumulative supplements listing only new additions are published every quarter. A list informing the public of organizations that no longer qualify as charitable organizations is published monthly.

Deductions are allowed for contributions given to or for the use of the following qualified organizations:

1. A state or possession of the United States, or the District of Columbia, if the contribution or gift is made for public purposes only.

2. A corporation, trust, or community chest, fund, or foundation if created in the United States and organized and operated exclusively for religious, charitable, scientific, literary, or educational purposes, or to foster national or international amateur sports competition (but not to help provide athletic equipment or facilities), or for the prevention of cruelty to children or animals. No part of the net earnings can benefit any private shareholder or individual. The organization must not be disqualified for tax exemption due to influencing legislation, and must not take part in any political campaign.

3. A post or organization of war veterans, if organized in the United States and if no part of the net earnings benefits any private shareholders or individual. Any dues, fees, or assessments paid by members of these organizations do not qualify for deductions.

4. A domestic or fraternal society, order, or association, operating under the lodge system, if the gift is to be used exclusively for religious, charitable, scientific, literary, or educational purposes, or to foster national or international amateur sports competition, or for the prevention of cruelty to children or animals. Dues to offset sickness or burial costs are deductible.

5. A nonprofit cemetery company whose funds are totally devoted to the continuous upkeep of the cemetery.

A contribution must be to an organization that has been created domestically. To help resolve the vagueness of the domestic creation requirement, the IRS has come out with a number of Revenue Rulings. In summary, they say that the domestic creation requirement won't be satisfied unless the recipient organization controls the final disposition of the funds. Control means that the recipient has the right to decide if the funds will be used abroad. If the recipient organization is required to transfer the funds abroad, the deduction will be denied.

A charitable contribution is also allowed if you maintain a student in your house under a written agreement with a charity. The student must be a full-time pupil in an elementary, junior high, or high school in the United States. The student must not be your dependent or relative but must be a member of your household. A deduction of up to $50 per month for each full month of residence during which the student is attending school is permitted by law. A total of 15 or more days of the month constitutes a full month. There is no deduction if you receive any compensation or reimbursement for maintaining the student.

If an organization qualifies as a church for tax purposes, it need not be required to seek exemption and has no filing requirements. Since Congress did not define the term "church," the common meaning and usage of the term have been applied. In making this decision, the IRS utilizes the following thirteen characteristics of a church:

A distinct legal existence
A recognized creed and form of worship
A definite and distinct ecclesiastical government
A formal code of doctrine and discipline
A distinct religious history
A membership not associated with any other church or denomination
A complete organization of ordained ministers chosen after completing prescribed courses of study
Literature of its own
Established places of worship
Regular congregations
Regular religious services
Sunday schools for religious education of the young
Schools to prepare their ministers

Not all of the above characteristics must be satisfied, and no single factor is given controlling weight. By listing these characteristics as a rough outline, the IRS gives guidelines for its determination as to whether an organization may qualify as a "church."

Contributions cannot be deducted if they are:

a) gifts to certain private foundations and nonexempt trusts that must pay tax on termination of their exempt status;

b) gifts to certain taxable private foundations and nonexempt trusts organized after 1969 whose charter does not include prohibitions against conduct that would subject them to excise taxes; *or*

c) gifts to charitable organizations after October 9, 1969, that do not notify the Internal Revenue Service that they are claiming exempt status.

Contributions to foreign governments, charities, and private foundations are disallowed. Gifts to Communist-ruled organizations are also disallowed. The Treasury Department does not allow tax-exempt status for private schools that practice racial discrimination, and any donations to them will not qualify as charitable contributions.

No charity can take part in any political activity. Charity status is lost by an organization if any substantial segment of its activities is devoted to formulating propaganda or otherwise trying to influence legislation. However, an organization (other than a church) may qualify as a charity and still perform some of these activities by keeping its political expenditures to an "insubstantial" part of its activities. Furthermore, donations to needy individuals are not deductible under the law.

ADDITIONAL PLANNING CONSIDERATIONS

Donation Limitations

Only if you contribute more than 20 percent of your adjusted gross income to a qualified charity is it necessary to be knowledgeable about donation limitations. Contributions up to this limit are automatically deductible if you itemize. For those who give more than 20 percent, certain rules apply.

If the contributions are all made to maximum deduction organizations (see the list that follows), the deduction ceiling is 50 percent of the contribution base (except that contributions of appreciated capital gain property are subject to a 30 percent ceiling, unless a special election is made). The contribution base is defined as adjusted gross income computed without regard to any net operating loss carryback to the taxable year.

To qualify for the 50 percent ceiling, the contribution must be made "to" one of the maximum deduction organizations (as opposed to "for the use of" an organization). If the contributions are not "to" 50 percent charities but rather are "for the use of" any charities, the deduction limit is 30 percent. Contributions of appreciated capital gain property to nonoperating foundations are limited to 20 percent. For contributions subject to the 20, 30, and 50 percent limits, the amount not deductible in the contribution year may be deductible in a future year as a carryover.

On a joint return, these limits apply to the aggregate contribution base.

You are allowed a 50 percent ceiling on contributions to any of the following maximum deduction organizations:

1. *Churches.*

2. *Tax-exempt educational organizations.* The educational organization should maintain a regular faculty and curriculum and have a regularly enrolled body of students in attendance at the place where its educational activities are regularly conducted.

   An organization set up for the benefit of certain state and municipal colleges and universities can also be included if it is organized and operated exclusively to receive, hold, invest, and administer property and to make expenditures to or for the benefit of an acceptable college or university.

   The educational organization must be engaged entirely in educational activities (although noneducational activity incidental to the educational activities is allowable). Tuition payments are not deductible, and contributions made under circumstances where you or those related to you benefit may be examined to see if personal benefit is the purpose of the payment.

3. *Tax-exempt hospitals and certain medical research organizations.* Hospitals, in this case, do not include homes for children or the aged or institutes that provide vocational training for the handicapped. The medical research organization must be engaged primarily and directly in the continuous active conduct of medical research. In addition, it must be committed to spending each contribution received on such active conduct of medical research before January 1 of the fifth calendar year after the date the contribution is made.

4. *A government unit* as referred to in the Internal Revenue Code Section 170(c)(1) (such as a state or a political subdivision of a state).

5. *A "publicly supported" organization* (such as a community chest). This type of organization normally receives a substantial part of its support (exclusive of operating income) from a governmental unit or from direct or indirect contributions from the general public.

6. *Certain private nonoperating foundations.* These distribute all contributions they receive to public charities within two and one-half months after the foundations' fiscal year end.

7. *A privately operating foundation.* This type of private foundation is one that pools all of its donations in a common fund. Any substantial contributor (or spouse) can annually direct the foundation as to which public charity shall receive the principal from his or her contribution and the interest from that principal.

8. *Certain membership organizations.* Only those in which more than one-third of their support comes from the general public are allowable.

The Public Support Test

To determine whether an organization is "publicly supported," you must apply the public support, or mechanical, test. An organization will be considered to be a "publicly supported" organization for its current taxable year and for the immediately succeeding taxable year if, for the four taxable years immediately preceding the current taxable year, the total amount of the support the organization received from governmental units, from donations made directly or indirectly by the public, or from a combination of the two equals 33.33 percent or more of the total support of the organization. In addition, contributions made by individuals, trusts, or corporations during the four taxable years may not exceed 2 percent of the organization's total support. The 2 percent limitation does not apply to support from governmental units or from other publicly supported organizations.

The Facts and Circumstances Test

A corporation, trust, or community chest, fund, or foundation that does not qualify as a "publicly supported" organization under the mechanical test may qualify on the basis of the facts and circumstances test. There are several requirements, but only requirements 1 and 2 below must be met on an aggregate basis. However, a substantial number of the remaining ones must also be met in the four taxable years preceding the current taxable year.

1. *10 percent of support limitations.* The percent of support "normally" received by an organization from governmental units, from the public, whether direct or indirect, or from a combination of these sources must be substantial. The amount of this support must equal at least 10 percent of the total support.

2. *Attraction of public support.* An organization must be so organized and operated as to attract new and additional public or governmental support on a continuous basis. It must maintain a continuous program for canvassing funds from the general public, community, or membership groups involved, or it must carry on other activities to attract support.

3. *Percent of financial support.* The percent of public support received will be considered. The higher the percent, the lesser will be the burden of establishing the publicly supported nature of the organization.

4. *Sources of support.* A large number of different contributors is preferred. In determining what a "representative number of persons" is, consideration will be given to the type of organization involved, the length of time it has been in existence, and any restrictions it practices.

5. *Representative governing body.* The fact that the organization has a governing body that represents the broad interest of the public will also be considered in determining whether an organization is publicly supported.

6. *Availability of public facilities for the benefit of the public.* Public participation in programs or policies will also be reviewed.

7. *Additional factors.* Pertinent to membership organizations are answers to the following questions:

   a) Is the organization designed to enroll a substantial number of persons in a particular field?

   b) Are dues set at fixed rates to be affordable by a broad cross section of the interested public?

   c) Are the activities of the organization likely to appeal to persons with a broad range of interests, or do they focus on a particular purpose?

Those factors relevant to each case and the weight given to each factor may change depending upon the nature and function of the organization.

Contributions shall be considered as support from the *general public* only if the total amount of all contributions, direct and indirect, does not exceed 2 percent of the organization's total support for a set period, except as provided by the *exclusion of unusual grants*. The 2 percent limit does not apply to support received from governmental units. (The donation is included in full in the denominator but will only be included in the numerator of such a fraction to the extent that it does not exceed 2 percent of the denominator. Any unusual grants may be excluded entirely from the fraction.) The unusual grant exclusion is generally intended to apply to substantial contributions or bequests from disinterested parties whose contributions or bequests:

a) are attracted by reason of the publicly supported nature of the organization;

b) are in unusual or unexpected amounts; *or*

c) would, by reason of size, adversely affect the status of the organization as normally being publicly supported.

Support does *not* include the following:

- Any amounts received by an organization from the exercise or performance of its functional purpose, which comprises the basis for its exemptions.
- Contributions of services for which there is no deduction.

Both of the above must be excluded from the numerator and the denominator.

An organization dependent on gross receipts from related activities will not satisfy either the mechanical test or the facts and circumstances test. The condition for public support will also not be met if an insignificant amount of the organization's support comes through governmental units from contributions made directly or indirectly by the general public. Support from a governmental unit includes any amount received from a governmental unit, which covers donations, contributions, and amounts received in connection with an agreement with a governmental unit for either the execution of services or for a governmental research grant. However, such amounts will not count as support from a governmental unit if they are for the performance of the organization's exempt activity, and if the reason for the payment is to enable the organization to offer a facility for the direct benefit of the public, rather than to serve only its members.

To summarize the tests involved in determining whether organizations qualify as publicly supported: The organization must normally receive in excess of 33.33 percent of its support from a governmental unit and from direct and indirect donations from the general public to qualify under the mechanical test; or, alternatively, at least 10 percent of its support must come from governmental units and public donations, and most, if not all, of points 3 through 7 of the facts and circumstances test must apply.

COMMUNITY TRUSTS

Community trusts have been established to invite large donations of a capital or endowment nature for the benefit of a certain community. Each has a governing body consisting of representatives of the community it serves. The contributions are often kept in the form of separate trusts or funds subject to changing degrees of control by the governing body.

A community trust must also meet the mechanical test or be able to attract sources on a continuous basis from the government and public in order to meet the facts and circumstances test. This test will usually be satisfied if the trust attracts a broad range of donors from the community served.

Another point concerning community trusts is the treatment of them as single entities. Any organization that meets the requirements described in points 2 through 5 below will be treated as a single entity; all funds linked with an organization that meets the requirements of point 1 will be considered as component parts of that organization.

1. The organization must be established by a gift, bequest, legacy, devise, or other transfer to a community trust that is considered a single entity, and it may not be subjected by the transferor to any restraints.
2. The organization must be recognized as a community trust, fund, or foundation to support charitable events in the community it serves.
3. All funds of the organization must be subject to common governing instruments.
4. The organization must have a common governing body that administers the fund.

5. Periodic financial reports must be prepared to show that all of the funds held by the community trust are funds of the organization.

A few final words on 50 percent limit contributions: Gifts made "for the use of" public charities or 50 percent limit private foundations do not qualify for the 50 percent limit. You must make the gift "to" a 50 percent charity to qualify for the donation. A charitable gift to a fraternal lodge that then contributes a gift to a 50 percent charity does not qualify for the 50 percent limit. A donation of an *income interest* is considered as made "for the use of" the recipient organization. Thus, you do not get the 50 percent limit. But a gift of a *remainder interest* is treated as made "to the donee charity," thus enabling you to reach the 50 percent ceiling.

LIMITS ON DEDUCTION

There is a 20 percent ceiling on deductions for any contributions of appreciated capital gain property to 30 percent charities—i.e., charitable organizations except those listed previously (e.g., a nonoperating foundation). For years beginning with 1987, the amount of your deduction is limited to your basis. Any excess over the ceiling can be carried over to the five succeeding tax years.

For example, assume you have a painting with a basis of $15,000 and a $20,000 fair market value. You have an adjusted gross income of $100,000. You want to contribute the painting to a veterans organization (a nonpublic charity). Your charitable deduction will be $15,000, because your basis does not exceed your ceiling of $20,000 (20 percent of $100,000). There is, however, a special rule for gifts of stock. If you contribute *qualified appreciated stock* to a *private nonoperating foundation,* you may take as a charitable deduction, subject to the above 20 percent ceiling limit, the full fair market value of the stock. Qualified appreciated stock is any stock of a corporation that (a) has price quotations readily available from an established securities market and (b) if sold would produce a long-term capital gain. This provision does not apply to the gift of any stock or portion of stock that exceeds 10 percent of the ownership interest in a corporation.

This special rule for stock was in effect through 1994 and was extended by the Small Business Job Protection Act of 1996 for gifts made July 1, 1996 through May 31, 1997, extended in 1997 to June 30, 1998, and made permanent in 1998.

If you give property that, if sold, would result in a long-term capital gain (appreciated capital assets or Section 1231 Property),[3] and the charity is a 50 percent donee, then you are subject to a 30 percent ceiling. If the contributions of capital gain property exceed 30 percent of your contribution base, the excess amount can qualify for a five-year carryover. Charitable contributions with 30 percent limitations paid during the taxable year are considered after all other charitable contributions.

Donation of a 30 percent capital gain property is defined as the charitable contribution of a capital asset that, if sold by the donor at its fair market value at the time of the contribution, would result in long-term gain; also, the amount of such a contribution must not be required to be reduced under Section 170(3)(1)(B) (this covers tangible personal property used by a donee in a function unrelated to the basis for its exemptions, and contributed "to" or "for the use of" certain private foundations).

You can make a special election to qualify for the 50 percent adjusted gross income limit on this property. In doing so, the deduction for the contribution is limited to your basis. If the election is made, it applies to all donations of capital gain property made during the year as well as to prior-year carryovers of appreciated capital gain property. The election must be made by the due date of the return and cannot be made on an amended return.

For example, assume that you have some stock that you would like to give to a public charity. You have held the stock for a number of years and your adjusted gross income is $100,000. The stock has a basis of $45,000 and a fair market value at the time of the donation of $50,000. If you do not make the 50 percent election, your charitable contribution deduction is limited to $30,000 (30 percent of $100,000) with the remaining $20,000 carried over. If you do make the election, you would get a deduction of the full $45,000 basis. Note that in exchange for getting the full $45,000 in the current year, you lose $5,000 of your deduction.

When making this special election, you are actually exchanging a reduced deduction on each separate contribution of appreciated capital gain property for the more generous 50 percent limit. The election of the 50 percent deduction ceiling is made by attaching to the original return for the election year a statement that the election is being taken. The following guidelines should be used in deciding whether the election should be taken:

3. Section 1231 Property is real or personal property used in a trade or business that would normally produce ordinary gains or losses upon sale or exchange. Gains on such property are capital gains and losses are ordinary losses.

1. If your long-term capital gain property contributions to 50 percent charities will not total more than 30 percent of your contribution base, do not make the election.

2. If you give long-term capital gain property in excess of the 30 percent ceiling to 50 percent charities, consider the following factors:

   a) any excess over the 30 percent limit, which can be carried over;

   b) your income for the current year, which should be compared with what you expect to earn in the following years; *and*

   c) the amount of unrealized long-term capital gain included in the value of the property.

Where long-term appreciated property consists of tangible personal property, such as works of art, the amount of the deduction *depends upon its use* by the charitable organization. If its use by the charity is unrelated to the charity's exempt function, then the amount of the deduction is limited to your basis.

For example, you own a work of art that you have held for more than one year and then you donate that work to a museum. If the donation is used by the museum for display, it is deemed related to the museum's exempt purpose. Therefore, if the work of art has a fair market value of $24,000 on the date of donation, that donation gives you a deduction of $24,000.

If the donation is made to a hospital, however, the amount of the deduction is limited to your basis. If the basis of the property is $4,000, then the deduction is limited to $4,000.

CARRYOVERS TO OTHER TAX YEARS

If the amount of contributions to 50 percent organizations made within a taxable year exceeds 50 percent of your contribution base for that year, the excess may be carried over for the next five succeeding taxable years. Current contributions must first be considered before any carryover is applied. Contributions that are carried over, plus the current year's contributions, must fall within the 50 percent limit. Five-year carryovers are also available for excess 20 percent and 30 percent contributions.

The amount of the carryover allowed is the lesser of:

a) the excess of 50 percent of adjusted gross income minus the sum of any actual contributions to public charities in that year plus any deducted carryovers (except carryovers of appreciated capital gain property) from a year before the contribution year of this carryover; *or*

b) the total carryovers available in the current year.

The charitable contribution deduction must be specially computed when taxpayers with carryovers change their filing status. Note that an unused carryover of a deceased spouse can be used on a return for the year the spouse dies; otherwise it is lost.

ORDER OF DEDUCTIBILITY

The amount that you should deduct in any year is determined in the following order:

1. gifts for the year to 50 percent charities
2. carryover of gifts to 50 percent charities from the preceding five years, from the earliest year first
3. gifts for the year to 30 percent charities
4. carryover of gifts to 30 percent charities from the preceding five years, from the earliest year first
5. gifts that are limited by the 20 percent ceiling

Your total deduction for any year cannot exceed 50 percent of your contribution base for that year and cannot exceed the amount actually contributed currently and in the past. Where 50 percent of your contribution base income exceeds the amount of your gifts, any carryovers from prior years are deductible, in order of time, to the extent of this excess. Any carryovers not used up may be carried forward to later years until exhausted or until the five-year period for each excess contribution runs out.

Contributions to which the 20 percent limitation would apply should be avoided when gifts are made of 30 percent limit property to 50 percent limit organizations that surpass your 30 percent limit. In this situation, you should consider the special election to reduce the 30 percent limit items and receive the 50 percent ceiling on them. This especially applies if a carryover of such a contribution exists from a prior year. Prior years' deductions are not influenced by this special election.

FORM OF THE GIFT

The deduction for a contribution of property is normally equal to the fair market value of the property at the time the donation is made. No gain is normally realized on a charitable contribution of appreciated property. You have an advantage when you contribute appreciated property because you get a deduction for the full fair market value of the property contributed, including both your basis and your unrealized paper profit. You are not taxed on this profit, so in effect you receive a deduction for an amount that you need not report as income.

If the fair market value of the property donated is below its basis, no loss is recognized on this donation. In such a case it would be better to sell the property first, realize the loss for tax purposes, and then make a gift of the proceeds. Using this approach, a deduction is allowed for the entire basis of the property.

The deduction of certain contributions for appreciated property must be reduced in some cases, depending on the type of appreciated property or the character of the donee. The amount of deduction for appreciated property must be reduced below its fair market value by the sum of ordinary income or short-term capital gain that would result if the property were sold at the time of the gift. Both a capital asset held for not more than 12 months and property subject to recapture of depreciation would result in ordinary income. Any appreciation in excess of the recapture amount is handled as a contribution of capital gain property. The above rule applies regardless of the type of donee. Other examples of property that would result in ordinary income are letters, memoranda, and works of art created by the donor.

For example, if an artist contributed a personal piece to a charity, there would be no charitable deduction. This portrait would generate ordinary income if it were sold by the artist at fair market value. Therefore, the deduction would be reduced to zero by the subtraction of this ordinary income component.

Except for "qualified appreciated stock" gifted to a private non-operating foundation, if appreciated long-term capital gain property is donated to a private foundation that is not a 50 percent limit donee, then its value must be

Ordering of Deductions to Charity*

	Deduct All:	Up to This % of Contribution Base
First—	Cash contributions to public charities	50%
Second—	Carryover of prior years' cash contributions to public charities	50%
Third—	Cash contributions to private foundations	30%
Fourth—	Carryover of prior years' cash contributions to private foundations	30%
Fifth—	Capital gain property contributions to public charities	30%
Sixth—	Carryover of prior years' capital gain property contributions to public charities	30%
Seventh—	Qualified appreciated stock contributions to private foundations	20%
Eighth—	Carryover of prior years' qualified appreciated stock contributions to private foundations	20%

*When contributions reach the indicated percentage, any excess must be carried over to the next year. If contributions in any tier are below the indicated percentage in any taxable year, contributions in the next lower tier may be deducted.

reduced by 100 percent of that long-term capital gain. Your deduction is limited to your basis. The deduction for contributed capital gain property that is tangible personal property is reduced in the same manner as when the use of the property is dissimilar to the donee's exempt status.

You will sometimes sell property to a charity for less than the property's fair market value, intending the "bargain" portion as a charitable contribution. Except in the case of ordinary income property sold for its adjusted basis, the seller may treat the amount of the bargain (fair market value minus purchase price) as a charitable donation for deduction reasons.

The donor usually also realizes taxable gain on the bargain sale; thus you must divide your basis (original cost) in the property between the part of the property sold and the part given. Your gain is determined only by that portion of your total cost that the bargain selling price (amount received) bears to the fair market value. The following formula can be used to calculate the adjusted basis of the property sold:

$$\frac{\text{Selling Price}}{\text{Fair Market Value}} \times \text{Property Basis} = \text{Adjusted Basis}$$

You must allocate this figure to the property sold and determine your taxable gain. For example, assume you have 100 shares of appreciated long-term capital gains stock with a tax basis of $4,000 and a fair market value of $10,000. You want to give $6,000 to the American College and you therefore sell this stock for your basis, or $4,000. Your realized gain is shown below:

Fair market value of stock			$10,000
Minus sale proceeds			–4,000
Charitable contribution			$ 6,000
Sale proceeds			$ 4,000
Tax basis in property sold:			
Sale price / Fair value	$ 4,000 / $10,000	× basis of $4,000	
			–1,600
Gain realized			$ 2,400

The rules for determining basis that apply to bargain sales also apply when mortgaged property is donated and the charity assumes the mortgage. The transfer is treated like a sale, with the purchase cost being the mortgage that the charity agrees to pay. In the case of both bargain sales and mortgaged property, the bargain sale rule does not apply unless the exchange produces a charitable deduction.

The courts have allowed owners of closely held corporations to withdraw funds from their firms tax-free by means of charitable contributions followed by a redemption: The owner gives stock to charity and at a later date the corporation redeems the stock. The donor is allowed a charitable contribution deduction, even though an understanding exists between the donor and donee that the stock will be redeemed shortly after contribution, where redemption is not required.

The valuation for the gift of stock is the average of the high and low sales price reported on the date of the gift.

ATHLETIC EVENT

In Rev. Rul. 86-63, 1986-1 C.B. 6, the IRS ruled that if you make a contribution to an educational institution where athletic games are regularly sold out in advance and in return receive the right to buy tickets to those games, you cannot take a charitable contribution deduction for the amount contributed. This has been congressionally overruled.

Retroactive to tax years beginning after December 31, 1983, 80 percent of the cost of the right to obtain preferred seating at athletic events of a college or university is deductible. No amount paid for the purchase of tickets, whether paid separately or as part of a lump-sum payment that includes the right to purchase tickets, is deductible as a charitable contribution. The statute of limitations for closed years was waived for years affected by this provision if you filed a refund claim before November 10, 1989.

CONTRIBUTION OF SERVICES

No deduction exists for the contribution of your services. However, unreimbursed expenses incurred during the rendering of free services for a qualified charity are deductible as charitable contributions.

Any cost incurred in traveling from your house to where you served is deductible. A standard mileage rate of 14¢ per mile is allowed if you use your car. Or you can choose to deduct your actual unreimbursed expenses for gas and oil. Parking fees and tolls are also deductible. No deduction is given for depreciation, insurance, or repairs on the car. Donating blood is considered the contribution of services and thus no deduction is allowed.

A deduction for reasonable outlays for meals and lodgings is also allowed if incurred while away from home. In addition, deductions have been allowed for the cost of baby-sitting services for children whose parents were performing services for charitable organizations.

LIFE INSURANCE POLICIES AND OTHER DONATIONS

If full rights of ownership are contributed, a gift of a life insurance policy is acceptable as a charitable gift. Any subsequent payments of premiums by the donor will also qualify as charitable contributions. The amount of the deduction for this type is its fair market value (Ltr. Rul. 9147040).

Dues, admission charges, etc., where you receive property or benefits can only be deducted if they exceed the value of the benefits received for them. Amounts paid for raffle tickets, bingo, or similar chance games and losses on games of chance are not deductible charitable contributions.

Where amounts are paid in connection with admission to fund-raising affairs for charity, you must show that a clearly identifiable segment of the payment is a gift, and only this amount will qualify. The same rule applies whether or not the tickets are actually used. If you have no intention of using the tickets, you should give them back and make a gift of the purchase price. Using this approach, you will get the full amount as a deduction.

Donations of less than your entire interest in property are not deductible, but there are certain exceptions to this rule. For example, the transfer of a remainder interest in a personal residence or a farm is deductible. Also, the contribution of an undivided portion of your entire interest in property will qualify for the deduction.

A charitable remainder gift made during your lifetime is also deductible, based upon the value of the remainder interest. The Internal Revenue Service tax code requires that a fixed percentage be paid to one or more persons for a specified term of years (not to exceed 20) or for the life or lives of the income beneficiaries, with an irrevocable remainder to be paid to the charitable organization. If the remainder interest to the charity is subject to a contingency, it is not deductible. In addition, the value of the gift must be readily determinable.

CHARITABLE REMAINDER TRUSTS

The ability to take a deduction today for a gift of a remainder interest to a charity has led to the creation of charitable remainder trusts. You would contribute appreciated property (stocks, real estate, etc.) to the trust in exchange for an income stream over your lifetime—either a fixed amount each year (an annuity trust) or a given percent of the value of the trust annually (a unitrust). The value of what is projected to go to the charity at your death (you can use multiple lives) is deductible today!

This value is a function of your age and life expectancy (based on IRS tables), the income stream you are receiving, and the assumed rate of return that the trust is expected to generate (the "applicable federal rate" which is published monthly by the IRS).

The advantages of the CRT are:

1. You and the trust pay no tax on the sale of the appreciated asset.
2. Therefore, you get a potentially much higher income stream during your life.
3. You get an immediate tax deduction even though you keep the income stream.
4. You can use the tax savings from the immediate tax deduction to purchase a life insurance policy to replace the value of the asset that goes to the charity at your death.
5. Structured correctly, life insurance can be removed from your estate. Your heirs after the estate tax may have more wealth go to them from a $500,000 life insurance policy not in your estate, than from $1,000,000 in assets had you not transferred them into the CRT.

PROOF

You are required to provide information in support of all of your deductions; therefore, you should be able to prove all charitable contributions through receipts, canceled checks, etc. If a contribution is made in property other than money, you should state the kind of property contributed, the method used in ascertaining the fair market value of the property at the time the contribution is made, and whether the amount of the contribution is reduced because the property is either ordinary income or capital gain property.

If you contribute property other than money valued in excess of $500, you must attach Form 8283 to the income tax return with the following information:

a) the name and address of the donee organization;

b) the date of the actual contribution;

c) a description of the property;

d) the manner of acquisition;

e) the fair market value of the property at the contribution time and the method utilized in determining the fair market value; *and*

f) the cost or other basis of the property.

Expert witnesses are frequently brought in during Tax Court cases to evaluate contributed property. The burden is on the individual to establish the value of the contribution.

An appraisal may be your best method to avoid an audit, especially if the property is difficult to value and a substantial contribution is involved. An added attraction is that the appraiser's fees are also deductible.

For other gifts, have the charity value the gift and send you a receipt. This will establish the proof necessary for a gift, and may avoid valuation difficulties. Taking out an insurance policy reflecting the property's value might also be a useful technique to establish the true value of the property.

Furthermore, for tax years beginning after 1982, IRS Proposed Regulation Section 1.170 A-13 (a) would require an individual taxpayer (or a corporation) making a charitable contribution of money to maintain a cancelled check, a receipt, or other reliable written evidence showing the amount of the charitable contribution, the date contributed, and the name of the donee. In the absence of a cancelled check or receipt, the reliability of the other written evidence will depend on the facts and circumstances of the particular case but, in all events, the burden would be on the taxpayer to establish reliability. Factors indicating that such other written evidence is reliable include, but are not limited to, the contemporaneous nature of the writing evidencing the contribution, the regularity of the taxpayer's recordkeeping procedures, and, in the case of the contribution of a small amount, any other written evidence from the donee charitable organization evidencing receipt of a donation that would not otherwise constitute a receipt.

For charitable contributions of property other than money for which the taxpayer claims a deduction in excess of $500, the taxpayer would be required to maintain additional records regarding the manner of acquisition of the property and the property's cost or other basis if it was held for less than one year prior to the date of contribution. For property held for one year or more preceding the date of contribution, cost or other basis information should be maintained by the taxpayer if it is available.

The Tax Reform Act of 1984 mandated the Internal Revenue Service to issue regulations, by December 31, 1984, which would impose appraisal and information reporting requirements on charitable contributions by individuals, closely held corporations, and personal service corporations. Appraisals will be required for each item with a claim value in excess of $5,000 ($10,000 for privately held stock). Similar items are to be added in determining the dollar threshold. This provision would not apply to publicly traded securities. When the rules apply, the donor must obtain a written appraisal of the property's fair market value from a qualified independent appraiser, and a summary of the appraisal must be attached to the donor's tax return.

If the donee charity sells, exchanges, or otherwise transfers donated property valued in excess of $5,000 within two years, the donee must furnish an information report to the IRS, with a copy to the donor. These provisions apply for contributions made after December 31, 1984.

Note that if a taxpayer contributes works of art with an aggregate value of at least $20,000, the taxpayer must attach a complete copy of the signed appraisal. In addition, an eight-by-eleven-inch color photograph, or a color transparency no smaller than four by five inches, must be submitted. For donations made after 1987, the submission of the appraisal is mandatory. It was optional for art donated before 1988.

For this purpose, the definition of art includes paintings, watercolors, prints, drawings, sculptures, ceramics, antique furniture, decorative arts, textiles, carpets, silver, rare manuscripts, historical memorabilia, and other similar objects. It does not include gems, jewelry, or books.

These requirements are intended to assist the IRS Art Advisory Panel, which is composed of art dealers, curators, museum directors, and other experts, in checking the valuation of artwork for tax purposes. An evaluation of $20,000 or more must be referred to the panel.

The Omnibus Budget Reconciliation Act of 1993 changed the substantiation and disclosure rules for charitable contributions. Effective for years after December 31, 1993, no deduction will be allowed for a separate contribution of $250 or more unless you have written confirmation from the charity. A cancelled check alone will not be enough. If the contribution is to a religious organization solely for an intangible religious benefit, written substantiation is still required but the charity need not value that benefit. All other contributions of cash must describe the estimated fair market value of any goods or services given in exchange for that contribution. Charities, however, are not required to value noncash contributions if you, as the taxpayer, are required to obtain from the charity a receipt that describes the donated property.

Moreover, any *quid pro quo* contributions of more than $75 solicited will require the charity to tell you in writing how much is deductible; e.g., a charitable dinner ticket costing $90 for a dinner worth $60 will give you a deduction of $30.

An interesting technique exists for obtaining a charitable deduction before a cash outlay. This can be done by establishing an irrevocable banker's letter of credit in favor of the charity. The full amount of the letter of credit will be deductible by you in the year in which it is established, even if the charity does not draw upon the credit until the next year. The charity, however, must have the absolute right to draw down the entire amount of the letter of credit immediately. This technique could present an important planning opportunity when you can reasonably expect that the charity would not draw down the funds immediately. For example, when the letter of credit will finance a construction project, it is reasonable to expect the charity to draw down those funds over the various phases of the construction, rather than immediately.

The tax saved from a charitable donation reduces the cost of donating. As the marginal tax rates increase, the actual cost of donating decreases. The actual cost to a person in the lowest tax bracket (15 percent) for a $1 charitable deduction is 85¢. For a person in the highest tax bracket (39.6 percent), the actual cost is only 60.4¢ on the dollar.

BEWARE

One final word on charitable contributions. Any contributions to a *non-exempt* organization will not be allowed. In *United Cancer Council v. Commissioner,* U.S. T.C., No. 2008-91X, 109 T.C. No. 17, 12/2/97, the court ruled that the charity's use of a professional fundraiser resulted in inurement of the organization's net earnings to the fundraiser and the IRS did not abuse its discretion in *retroactively revoking* the exempt status of the organization.

60 Casualty Losses

A *casualty* is the damage or destruction of property resulting from an identifiable event that is sudden, unexpected, or unusual in nature. Casualty losses can be used to lower your taxes.

Deductible casualty losses may result from a number of different causes, including but not limited to:

Automobile accidents
Civil disturbances
Drought
Earthquakes
Explosions
Fires
Flood
Freezing rain
Ice and snow
Hurricanes
Lightning
Mine cave-ins
Shipwrecks
Smog
Sonic booms
Storms
Vandalism
Winds and tornadoes

A reduction in your property's value because it is in or near an area that suffered a casualty or that might again suffer a casualty is usually not deductible. A neighbor of O.J. Simpson was denied a deduction for the reduction in value of his property due to its proximity to the murder. However, in *Finkbohner, Jr.*, 86-1 USTC para. 9393, 57 AFTRO 2d 86-1400 (CA-11, 1986), a permanent decline in market value due to buyer resistance was includable in the amount of a casualty loss deduction. There, the court refused to follow the prevailing view in two other circuits which limited the deduction to actual physical loss. In the *Finkbohner* case, the taxpayers' residence was unharmed, but seven of the twelve houses in the neighborhood had to be razed after a flood. The court ruled that the removal of most of the homes in the neighborhood was a permanent change. The diminished market value reflected more than a fear of future flooding, since the residence was above maximum flood levels. They concluded that the fair market value after the casualty would have to reflect such permanent loss of value. A loss is allowed only for the actual casualty damage to your property.

The partial or complete destruction of property must be the result of an identifiable event that is either sudden, unexpected, or unusual. For example, if your spouse, while washing the dishes, inadvertently knocks a diamond ring that you put in a glass next to the sink down the drain and activates the garbage disposal unit, thus destroying the ring, this unusual event will qualify as a deductible casualty. So, too, will the loss of a diamond ring if your spouse slams the car door on your hand. Both of the events were sudden and unusual, therefore allowing the casualty deduction. However, a loss due to the accidental breakage of articles such as glassware or china under normal conditions is not a casualty loss. Neither is a loss due to damage done by a family pet.

The event must be one that is sudden—that is, swift, not gradual or progressive. If a steadily operating cause from a normal process damages your property, it is not considered a casualty. So, for example, the steady weakening of a building due to normal wind and weather conditions will not qualify as a casualty. On the other hand, the rust and water damage to rugs and drapes caused by the bursting of a water heater will qualify—but not the deterioration and damage to the water heater itself.

If trees, shrubs, or other plants are damaged or destroyed by a fungus, disease, insects, worms, or similar pests, the loss is not deductible as a casualty loss. However, a sudden, unexpected, or unusual infestation by beetles or other insects may result in a casualty loss. If trees and shrubs are damaged by a storm, flood, or fire, the loss is also a deductible casualty loss.

Normally a loss from an accident to your car is deductible. This is not true, though, if your willful negligence or willful act causes the accident, or if it is caused by the willful act or willful negligence of someone acting for you.

If you do have an accident, you must file a claim with your insurance company. If you do not file the claim, you will not be entitled to a casualty loss deduction for the damage done to your car. Casualty loss deductions are allowed only for losses not compensated for by insurance or otherwise. But "not compensated for" doesn't just mean actual payment. When a collectible insurance claim *can* be filed, a deliberate election not to file will not give rise to a casualty loss deduction. Your loss can be "compensated for."

Yet in a 1981 case the Tax Court allowed a theft loss deduction despite a refusal to make an insurance claim predicated on a fear of increased premiums.[4] The court concluded that "compensated" did not mean "covered" and that since no "compensation" was received, a deduction could be allowed. This ruling was confirmed in the case of *Dixon F. Miller v. Commissioner* on May 2, 1984; the Sixth Circuit joined the Eleventh Circuit and the Tax Court in taking the above position. The Tax Reform Act of 1986, however, imposed a new pre-

4. *H.L. Hills.* 76 T.C. No. 42.

condition on the allowance of casualty losses. Any loss that is covered by insurance is taken into account only if the taxpayer files a timely insurance claim. This new limitation applies only to the extent that the insurance policy would have provided reimbursement if a claim had been filed (IRC § 165[a][4][i]).

For example, if you sustain $800 worth of damage for an insured loss with a $500 deductible, if no claim is made $300 of your loss will not be allowable as a deduction. The $500 balance will count as a loss, subject to the $100 and 10 percent adjusted gross income floors.

You should deduct your casualty loss in the year of occurrence. This timing rule is modified, though, when insurance enters the picture. In such a case, the loss deduction is limited to the part of the damage that is not reimbursed that year. If you deduct a casualty in the year of occurrence and receive insurance reimbursement in a later year, you should not amend the earlier return. Instead, the portion of the reimbursement that exceeds the original estimate of recovery should be taken back into income in the later year.

For example, you suffered a $6,000 deductible loss in 1999 and estimated an insurance recovery of $5,000, and you took a $1,000 casualty loss deduction in that year. In 2000, however, your insurance company pays the full $6,000. What you must do on your 2000 return is include the extra $1,000 as income. Note, though, that you must have received a tax benefit for the casualty loss in 1999. If you did not itemize your deductions in that year, you received no benefit and therefore have no additional taxable income when the insurance company repays the full $6,000 in 2000.

The amount of loss from a casualty that can be deducted is generally the lesser of the following two amounts:

a) the decrease in the fair market value of the property as a result of the casualty; *or*

b) your basis in the property before the casualty.

In the case of business property, if the fair market value of the property immediately before the casualty is less than the adjusted basis, the amount of the adjusted basis is deemed to be the amount of the loss. Alternatively, the loss may be measured by the cost of repairing the damage. In a case of nonbusiness (or personal use) property, the deduction is the amount by which the casualty loss exceeds 10 percent of your adjusted gross income plus $100.

The fair market value must be based on a valid judgment of the selling price of the property at the time of the casualty. An appraisal is the best way to do this.

The appraisal should be made by an experienced and reliable appraiser. Several factors are important in evaluating the accuracy of the appraisal:

- The appraiser's familiarity with your property before the casualty.
- Sales of comparable properties.
- Conditions in the area of the casualty.
- The method used in making the appraisal.

When available, photographs should be used in making the appraisal and in determining the extent of damage from a casualty. The costs of photographs obtained for this purpose are not a part of the loss but can be taken as a miscellaneous deduction. They are an expense of determining your tax liability. Furthermore, you may deduct as a miscellaneous deduction the amount you must pay for the appraisal itself, since it also is an expense of determining your tax liability.

The cost of cleaning up or making repairs after a casualty may be used as a measure of the decrease in fair market value if:

a) the repairs are necessary to restore the property to its condition before the casualty;

b) the amount spent for repairs is not excessive;

c) the repairs do no more than take care of the damage;

d) the value of the property after the repairs is not, as a result of the repairs, more than the value of the property before the casualty.

The cost of restoring landscaping to its original condition may also be taken as an indication of the decrease in fair market value. You may be able to measure your loss by what is spent on the following:

- Removing destroyed or damaged trees and shrubs, minus any salvage you receive.
- Pruning and other measures taken to preserve damaged trees and shrubs.
- Replanting that is necessary to restore the property to its approximate value before the casualty.

The incidental expenses you have due to a casualty, such as expenses for the treatment of personal injuries, for temporary housing, or for a rental car, are not deductible as casualty losses. Moreover, the cost of protecting your property against a potential casualty is not deductible. For example, you cannot deduct what you spend on insurance or to board up your house against a storm. Expenses like these are only deductible by businesses as business expenses. If you make a permanent improvement to your property to protect it against a casualty, the cost should be added to your basis in the property. An example would be the cost of a dike to prevent flooding.

61 Theft Losses

A *theft* is the unlawful and intentional removal of money or property from its rightful owner. It includes, but is not limited to, larceny, robbery, and embezzlement. If money or property is taken as the result of extortion, kidnapping for ransom, or blackmail, it may also be a theft. The simple disappearance of money or property does not constitute a theft. However, an accidental loss or disappearance of property may qualify as a casualty if it results from an identifiable event that is sudden, unexpected, or unusual in nature. The lost diamond ring in the example given in the previous section constitutes such a deductible casualty.

The amount of loss from a theft that can be deducted is generally the lesser of the following two amounts:

a) the decrease in the fair market value of the property as a result of the theft, *or*

b) your basis in the property before the theft.

The fair market value of property immediately after a theft is considered to be zero. That is, a theft loss deduction is either the full fair market value of the stolen property or its basis, whichever is less. If you get your stolen property back, however, your loss is measured like a casualty loss from vandalism. You must consider the actual fair market value of the property when you get it back in order to compute your loss.

The decrease in the fair market value must be based on a judgment of the actual price you could have asked if your property had been sold. Sentimental value is not a factor in determining the amount of the loss. Any loss from the theft of a family portrait, heirloom, or keepsake must be based on its actual market value apart from any sentiment. An appraisal is the best way to make this judgment. This appraisal must recognize the effect of any general market decline that may occur so that any deduction is limited to the actual loss resulting from deprivation of the property. See the preceding section on casualty losses for more information on appraisals.

The cost of any theft-preventive equipment, such as burglar alarm systems or theft insurance, is not deductible. If a protective device increases the value of your property, however, the cost may be added to your basis.

DEDUCTION LIMITS

The limits and computations for determining both casualty and theft loss deductions are very similar, so they are now grouped together for ease of discussion.

After you have figured the amount of your casualty or theft loss, you must figure how much of the loss you can deduct. There are three ways that you may adjust the casualty or theft loss before you can deduct it:

1. If you receive insurance or another type of reimbursement for your loss, you must subtract the reimbursement from the amount of the loss before you figure your deduction. As noted above, if you expect to get a reimbursement but have not yet received payment, you must still subtract the expected reimbursement from the loss. In a business situation, though, the cost of repairs made for business purposes *is* deductible, even if insurance recovery later is likely. The amount of the final recovery that is attributable to previously deductible items will be taxable in the later year.[5]
2. If the stolen, destroyed, or damaged property was for your own or your family's personal use, you must reduce each loss by an additional $100, because the first $100 of a casualty or theft loss on personal use property is not deductible. However, if you used the stolen, destroyed, or damaged property in your business or for investment purposes, this $100 limit does not apply.
3. For nonbusiness losses, you must reduce the *total* amount of the losses by 10 percent of your adjusted gross income. This is done after the $100 reduction in adjustment 2 above and after any reimbursement from insurance. Note that under the Tax Reform Act of 1984, for purposes of computing the 10 percent floor, the casualty loss deduction (adjusted gross income) is deter-

5. *R.R. Hensler, Inc. v. Commissioner* T.C. 317 (1979).

mined without regard to the application of Section 1231 to gains or losses from involuntary conversions arising from a casualty or theft. Gain and losses from these personal casualties (without regard to the period the property was held) will be netted. If the recognized gains exceed the recognized losses from these transactions, then all such gains and losses will be treated as gains and losses from the sale or exchange of a capital asset, and the losses will not be subject to the 10 percent floor. (The amount of any recognized loss will be subject to the $100 floor before netting.) If the recognized losses exceed the recognized gains, all gains and losses will be ordinary. Losses to the extent of gains will be allowed in full. Losses in excess of gains will be subject to the 10 percent adjusted gross income floor.

For example, assume you have $100,000 of adjusted gross income without regard to casualty gains and losses, $50,000 of such casualty gains, and $40,000 of such casualty losses (after applying the $100 floor) for a taxable year. All your personal casualty gains and losses for that year will be treated as capital gains and losses. The 10 percent floor will not be applicable. Assume, however, that your losses for the year are $70,000 rather than $40,000. The gains and losses will all be treated as ordinary. $60,000 of losses will be allowed as a deduction ($50,000 plus the $10,000 excess of the remaining $20,000 over the $10,000 [10 percent of $100,000] adjusted gross income floor).

If an insurance company reimburses you for any of your living expenses after you lose the use of your home because of a casualty, the insurance payments are not considered a reimbursement reducing your casualty loss. Any part of these payments that covers normal living expenses that you and your family would have during this period anyway must be reported as income on your tax return, but any insurance payments that cover a temporary increase in your living expenses should *not* be reported as income. The same rule applies if you are denied access to your home by government authorities due to the threat of a casualty. Generally, the amount you do not have to report is the amount of your extra expenses for renting suitable housing and for transportation, food, utilities, and miscellaneous services during the period you are unable to use your home because of the casualty.

For example, assume that as a result of a fire you vacated your apartment and moved to a motel. You normally pay $200 a month rent, but none was charged for the month the apartment was vacated. Your motel rent for this month was $275, but you received only $240 in reimbursement for rental expenses from your insurance company. Part of that reimbursement, $75, covers the difference between your actual rent and your normal rent. You do not have to report this amount as income, but the balance of the reimbursement, $165, must be reported as income.

As mentioned, the first $100 of a casualty or theft loss of personal use property is not deductible. This limit applies *after* all reimbursements have been subtracted. Furthermore, a single $100 limit applies to each individual casualty or theft, no matter how many pieces of property are involved. Generally, events closely related in origin are considered a single casualty or theft, as when your summer home suffers wind damage and flood damage caused by a hurricane. A single casualty may also damage two or more widely separate pieces of property.

Remember, though, that the $100 exclusion does not apply if the loss is on business property, property that earns you rent or royalty income, or other investment property. Furthermore, if a husband and wife each sustain a loss from the same casualty or theft and they file a joint return, only one $100 limit applies. It does not matter whether the property involved is jointly or separately owned. If they file separate returns, however, each is subject to a separate $100 limit for the loss, regardless of whether the property is jointly or separately owned. A husband and wife who file separate returns and have a casualty loss on property they own together may deduct one-half of the loss on each return, or either spouse may claim the entire deduction on a separate return.

COMPUTING THE DEDUCTION

The way to figure a deduction for a casualty or theft loss depends upon the kind of property involved. The rules for personal use property are different from those for business and investment property. The rules for real estate property, such as a house, differ from those for personal property, such as a car or furniture.

In figuring a loss to real estate property that you own for personal use, all improvements, such as buildings and ornamental trees, are considered together. A single loss is figured for the entire property. The amount of the loss is either the decrease in fair market value of the entire property or its adjusted basis, whichever is less. From this amount you must subtract any insurance or other reimbursement you receive or expect to receive. The amount remaining that is more than $100 is your personal casualty loss deduction.

As an example, assume that several years ago you bought a house that you then lived in as your home. You paid $5,000 for the land and $20,000 for the house itself; you also paid $1,000 for landscaping. This year, when your adjusted gross income was $10,000, your home was totally destroyed by fire. Competent appraisers said that before the fire the property as a whole had a fair market value of $36,000 but that its value after the fire was only $6,000. Shortly after the fire, the insurance company paid you $20,000 for the loss. Your casualty loss deduction is figured as follows:

Value of entire property before fire	$36,000
Minus value of entire property after fire	– 6,000
Decrease in value of entire property	$30,000
Basis (cost for entire property)	$26,000
Casualty loss (in this case basis)	$26,000
Minus insurance reimbursement	–20,000
Casualty loss before the $100 limit	6,000
Minus: $100 nondeductible amount	– 100
10% of adjusted gross income	– 1,000
Casualty Loss Deduction	$ 4,900

Personal property is generally any property that is not real estate. If your personal property is stolen or is damaged or destroyed by a casualty, you must figure your loss separately for each individual item of property.

For example, assume a fire in your home damaged an upholstered chair and completely destroyed a rug and an antique table. You do not have fire insurance to cover your loss. The chair cost you $150, and you establish that it had a fair market value of $75 just before the fire and $10 just after the fire. The rug cost you $200 and had a value of $50 just before the fire. You bought the table at an auction for $15 before discovering it was a valuable antique. It was appraised at $350 before the fire.

The loss on the chair is limited to the difference in fair market value before and after the fire, or $65, since that decrease is less than its basis ($150). The loss on the rug is limited to its value of $50 just before the fire, because this amount is also less than its basis ($200). The table, on the other hand, had a value just before the fire that was greater than your basis in it. Your loss on the table, therefore, is its basis, $15. Your total loss from the fire is $130, and after subtracting the $100 limit, your deductible is $30 before the reduction for 10 percent of your adjusted gross income.

When a casualty involves both real and personal property, a single $100 limit applies to the total loss, but you must figure the amount of the loss separately for each type of property, as discussed above. Remember, a loss on business property, property that earns you rent or royalty income, or other investment property is *not* subject to the $100 limit. For business and investment property, you must figure your loss separately for each item that is stolen, damaged, or destroyed. If casualty damage occurs to a building and to trees on the same piece of property, the loss is measured separately for each.

If you have business or investment property that is completely lost because of a casualty or theft, your deductible is your basis in the property minus any salvage value and minus any insurance or other reimbursement that you receive or expect to receive. For example, suppose you owned a building that you rented out and your basis in it, not including land, was $20,000 before it was completely destroyed by fire. Its fair market value just before the fire was only $15,000.

Since this was investment property and since it was completely destroyed, the deduction is your basis in the building, $20,000, decreased by salvage value and by any insurance or other reimbursement. Fair market value is not considered when figuring your loss, even though it is less than your basis in the building.

If business or investment property is damaged but not completely destroyed in a casualty, the loss is the decrease in value because of the casualty, or your basis in the property, whichever is less. From this amount you must subtract any insurance or other reimbursements you receive or expect to receive.

After you take a casualty or theft loss deduction, you must subtract from your basis in the damaged, destroyed, or stolen property the amount of your deduction and the amount of any reimbursement you receive. The result is a new, lower total for your basis in the property. In some cases, this lower basis will carry over to any property you get to replace the property that is stolen or destroyed.

PROOF OF LOSS

To take a deduction for casualty or theft loss, you must be able to show that there was actually a casualty or theft, and you must be able to support the amount you take as a deduction. For a casualty loss, you should be able to show:

a) the nature of the casualty and when it occurred;

b) that the loss was a direct result of the casualty; *and*

c) that you were the owner of the property; or, if you leased the property from someone else, that you were contractually liable to the owner for the damage.

For a theft, you should be able to show:

a) the date on which you found that the property was missing;

b) that your property *was* stolen; *and*

c) that you were the owner of the property.

To qualify for a theft loss deduction, the taking of your property must be illegal under the laws of the state where it occurred. If a theft loss is not reported promptly to the police, you must offer as a substitute the testimony of anyone who witnessed the event or its aftermath. If records were burglarized, steps must be taken to reconstruct the records by gathering substitutes.

Proof of the amount of a theft loss is difficult in the case of cash, where there is little likelihood that there is any documentation of how much you had on your person or in your home. Deductions will be allowed in full when you have evidence of why you had such a large amount of money with you. One theft loss deduction was allowed because the records showed that the victim was on his way to complete the closing on the acquisition of a house.

You do not have to be virgin-pure to qualify for a theft loss deduction. Even if you were naive or greedy and that naïveté or greed resulted in your being the victim of a theft, you may still receive a deduction for that theft. "Indeed," according to one court, "gullibility or cupidity of the victim is often a crucial factor that enables the swindler to succeed in his fraud."[6]

For both casualty losses and theft losses you must be able to give evidence supporting the amount you deduct. You should have supporting evidence in the following three areas:

1. *Basis.* The purchase contract or deed can show your original basis (its cost) in real estate. Improvements to the property that increase basis should be supported by checks, receipts, and similar items.

2. *Decrease in fair market value.* Appraisals should be used where possible. Photographs of your property before it was damaged or stolen will be helpful in showing its condition and value before the casualty or theft. Photographs taken after a casualty will be helpful in establishing the condition and value of the property after it was damaged. Photographs showing the condition of the property after it was repaired, restored, or replaced may also be helpful.

---

6. *Perry A. Nichols et al.,* T.C. 842 (1965).

3. *Insurance and other types of reimbursement.* Keep records of all you receive or expect to receive.

PLANNING CONSIDERATIONS

Ordinarily, a casualty loss is deductible in the year the event took place. However, the tax code permits a special election to take "disaster area" loss deductions in the year prior to occurrence. To qualify, the President must declare the region a "disaster area" eligible for federal relief under the Disaster Relief Act of 1964. Once this is done you can make an irrevocable election to treat the entire disaster loss as having occurred in the prior tax year. This allows you to get an immediate tax benefit for the loss rather than forcing you to wait until the subsequent year to claim it.

For example, assume you suffered a casualty loss in 1999. In order to get the tax benefit for that loss, it would have to be claimed as a deduction from your 1999 taxes, payable in April of 2000. But if you elected and qualified for the optional disaster relief provision, you could take the disaster loss deduction on your 1998 return, either before the return has been filed or by filing an amended 1998 return. Alternatively, if your income increased in 1998 and put you in a higher bracket, you could decline to make the election and take the higher valued deduction on your 1999 return.

As explained above, expenses to prevent a casualty are not normally deductible as casualty losses. Such expenditures are likely to involve the acquisition of property with an estimated useful life of more than one year. But a tax deduction *can* be claimed if the preventive measures do not add to the value of the property. In one case a plant had sustained cave-ins under its flooring, and further trouble of the same sort was anticipated. The drilling and grouting undertaken to forestall this was a deductible business expense. In another case, an individual used temporary dikes to protect his personal residence as well as his business property from flooding. The dikes were constructed of earth and sand bags and were removed immediately after the floodwater receded. While the cost of constructing and removing the temporary dikes was not allowed as a casualty loss with respect to either the business or the nonbusiness property, the cost of constructing and removing the dikes to protect business property was deductible as an ordinary and necessary business expense. In a third case, an expense that had been incurred to prevent an accident—and *was* held to be a different kind of deduction—was the cost of a vasectomy! The moral here is simple: What you may think of only in terms of a casualty loss expense may qualify as a deduction under a noncasualty classification—for example, as an ordinary and necessary business expense or as a medical expense.

62 Miscellaneous Trade and Business Deductions of Employees

Prior to the Tax Reform Act of 1986, if you were an employee who had travel, entertainment, or gift expenses in connection with your employment, you would be entitled to deduct the amounts you spent in those areas as "above the line" deductions. Note that under the Tax Reform Act of 1986, for years after December 31, 1986, all trade and business deductions of employees must be taken as miscellaneous itemized deductions. As of January 1, 1987, miscellaneous itemized deductions will be allowable only to the extent that they exceed 2 percent of your adjusted gross income.

Under the Tax Reform Act of 1986, this 2 percent floor will not apply to impairment-related work expenses for handicapped employees; to gambling losses to the extent of gambling winnings; and to certain actors who would be allowed to report their income and expenses from acting as if they were independent contractors, if they had two or more employers in the acting profession during the tax year, and if the expenses relating to their acting profession exceeded 10 percent of their gross income and their adjusted gross income (before deducting expenses related to acting) did not exceed $16,000. The 2 percent floor will also not apply to investment advisor fees for trusts in the 6th Circuit (C.A.6, *William J. O'Neill, Jr., Irrevocable Trust v. Comm.*, No. 92-1564, 6/2/93, but the IRS and the Tax Court still disagree with the 6th Circuit Court of Appeals, AOD 1994-006). Moreover, in private ruling 9316003, the IRS ruled that a partner may deduct in full (not subject to the 2 percent rule) any expenses that a partnership agreement requires him to pay.

63 Travel Expenses

If you are an employee, you may deduct as miscellaneous itemized deductions all the ordinary and necessary travel expenses, in excess of reimbursements, that you have in connection with your work.

"Ordinary and necessary" here again may be translated as "reasonable and customary." Travel expenses are those expenses incurred in traveling away from home for your business, profession, or job. Your tax home, for travel expense purposes, is your principal place of business or employment or your station or post of duty, regardless of where you maintain your family residence. The entire city or general area in which your business or work is located is your tax home.

For example, assume you live with your family in Chicago, but work in Milwaukee. You stay in a Milwaukee hotel and eat in a restaurant during the week and return to Chicago every weekend. You may not deduct any of your expenses for traveling back and forth, or for your meals and lodging in Milwaukee, because Milwaukee is your tax home and the travel over the weekends is not for a business reason.

If you regularly work in two or more separate areas, your principal tax home is the general area where your principal work or business is located. The main factors in determining your principal place of business or work are:

a) the total time ordinarily spent in performing your duties in each area;

b) the degree of your business activity in each area; *and*

c) the relative amount of your income from each area. (See *Bowles,* 85-1 USTC Para. 9244, 55 AFTR 2d, 85-1113 [DC Va. 1984], in which the place of the taxpayers' minor business in terms of income was held to be their tax home, since that was where they spent the majority of their time and effort.)

For example, assume you live in Miami where you have a seasonal job for eight months and earn $15,000, and you work the remaining four months in Cincinnati, also at a seasonal job, and earn $4,000. Miami is your principal place of work because you spend most of your time there and earn most of your income there.

You are considered "away from home" when you are on a *temporary* (rather than indefinite or permanent) job that takes you away from your regular or principal place of business. Temporary employment must be temporary in contemplation, and its termination must be foreseeable at the time of acceptance. (See Rev. Rul. 60-189, 1960-1 C.B. 60, Rev. Rul. 60-314, 1960-2 C.B. 48, and *Flowers,* 326 US 465 [S. Ct., 1946].)

In Rev. Rul. 83-82 the Internal Revenue Service stated that employment is temporary "only if its termination can be foreseen within a reasonably short period of time." Where a taxpayer anticipates employment to last for less than one year its status will be determined on the basis of the facts and circumstances. Where the taxpayer anticipates employment of one year or more, but less than two years, and it in fact falls within this range, there is a rebuttable presumption that the employment is "indefinite." An expected or actual stay of two years or longer is considered "indefinite" regardless of other facts and circumstances.

To rebut the one- to two-year presumption you must (1) clearly demonstrate by objective factors that you realistically expected that the employment in question would last less than two years and that you could then return to your claimed tax home, and (2) show that the claimed tax home is your regular place of abode in a real and substantial sense.

The following three factors may be used to determine if point (2) is met: (1) whether you have used the claimed abode as lodging while working in that vicinity immediately before the claimed temporary employment and you continue to maintain work contacts there; (2) whether your living expenses at the claimed abode are duplicated because of your work away from such abode; and (3) whether you (a) have a family member or members (marital or lineal only) currently residing at the claimed abode or (b) continue to currently use the claimed abode frequently for lodging.

If you satisfy the expectation test and all three of the abode tests the IRS will deem the work assignment "temporary." If only two of the three abode tests are met, then all the facts and circumstances will be subject to close scrutiny to determine if the assignment is temporary or indefinite. If only one of the abode tests is met the IRS will regard the assignment as indefinite.

In Notice 93-29, the IRS ruled that travel expenses paid or incurred in 1993 while away from home for a period or more than *one year* in pursuit of a trade or business will be *non*deductible even if such period began in 1992. This Notice, pursuant to the Energy Policy Act of 1992, now even more clearly defines the difference between temporary and indefinite. (See also Rev. Rul. 93-86.)

You may also be considered as *traveling* away from home when you work in the same city in which you and your family live. Suppose your family residence is in Pittsburgh, where you work for 12 weeks a year. The remainder of the time you work for the same employer in Baltimore, where you eat in restaurants and sleep at a rooming house. Your salary is the same whether you are in Pittsburgh or Baltimore. Since you spend most of your working time and earn most of your salary in Baltimore, that city is your tax home and you may not deduct any expenses incurred for meals and lodging there. However, when you go to work in Pittsburgh, you are away from your tax home even though you stay at your family home. Therefore, you may deduct the cost of your round trip between Baltimore and Pittsburgh, and that part of your family living expenses for meals due to your living in Pittsburgh while working there.

Deductible travel expenses include the following:

Air, rail, and bus fares
Operation and maintenance of your automobile
Taxi fares or other costs of transportation between the airport or station and your hotel, from one customer to another, or from one place of business to another
Transportation from the place where you eat and sleep to your temporary work assignment
Baggage charges and transportation costs for sample and display material
Meals (limited to 50 percent of cost) and lodging when you are away from home on business
Cleaning and laundry expenses
Telephone and telegraph expenses
Public stenographer's fees
Operation and maintenance of house trailers
Tips that are incidental to any of these expenses
Similar expenses incident to qualifying travel

You are considered traveling away from home if your duties require you to be away from the general area of your tax home for a period substantially longer than an ordinary day's work. It is not necessary, however, to work the full time. It is reasonable for you to need and to get some sleep or rest to meet the demands of your work or business. This does *not* mean napping in your car to make sure you qualify for the full period. You need not be away from your tax home for an entire 24 hours or from dusk to dawn so long as your relief from duty (rest period) while you are traveling constitutes a sufficient period of time in which to get necessary sleep or rest.

For example, assume you are a railroad conductor and you leave your home terminal on a regularly scheduled round trip between two cities, returning home 16 hours later. During the run you are released for six hours at your turnaround point, where you eat two meals and rent a hotel room to get necessary rest before starting the return trip. You are considered to be away from home for tax travel purposes and may deduct the expenses you incur.

Alternatively, assume you are a truck driver. You leave your terminal and return later the same day. You are released at your turnaround point for one hour in order to eat. Since you are not released to obtain necessary sleep and the brief interval of release does not constitute an adequate rest period, you are not away from home.

Here again the opportunity for sophisticated tax planning presents itself. You may deduct all those travel expenses you incur in attending a convention if you can show that your attendance benefits or advances the interest of your own work or business, as distinguished from the business or work of another. If the convention is for political, social, or other purposes unrelated to your business or work, the expenses are not deductible. But the agenda of the convention need not deal specifically with your official duties. It is sufficient if the agenda is related to your duties and responsibilities in such a way that attendance for a business purpose is indicated.

Regardless of whether the primary purpose of your trip is business or pleasure, all expenses incurred at your destination that are properly attributable to your trade or business are deductible. So if you make a trip primarily for business and, while there, you extend your stay for nonbusiness reasons, make a nonbusiness side trip, or engage in other nonbusiness activities, the travel expenses to and from your destination are still deductible. Furthermore, you may even deduct the expenses you paid or incurred in attending *foreign* conventions in a tax year. Here, however, the allowable expenses of attending the foreign convention must be extensively substantiated: You must make a schedule for the part of the total days of the trip devoted to business-related activities and even the number of hours of business activity you attend each day, which will limit the deduction.

No deductions are allowed for any travel expenses, including meals and lodging while away from home, for any expenses generally considered entertainment, amusement, or recreation expenses, including expenses for facilities used in connection with such activities, or for any gift expenses, unless you substantiate certain elements.

For *travel* you must prove *all* of the following elements:

- The amount of each separate expenditure for travel away from home, such as the cost of your transportation or lodging. The daily cost of your breakfast, lunch, and dinner and any incidental elements of such travel may be totaled if they are listed in reasonable categories, such as meals, gasoline and oil, and taxi fares.

- The dates of your departure and return for each trip, and the number of days spent on business away from home.

- The destination or locality of your travel, described by name of city, town, or similar designation.

- The business reason for your travel or the business benefit derived or expected from your travel.

Furthermore, an employee who receives reimbursement from an employer for travel expenses is excused from the normal record keeping and substantiation requirements if the standard reimbursement and allowance rules are satisfied. Under these rules, reimbursement for actual subsistence or travel away from home (exclusive of transportation to and from the destination) is limited to the greater of $115 for low-cost areas/$185 for high-cost areas per day or the maximum per diem rate for U.S. government employees in the locality in which travel is performed. If you elect to use the optional allowance, it must be used in computing the deduction for *all* meal expenses for the year (Rev. Proc. 83-71, 1983-39 I.R.B. 19). (See Rev. Proc. 93-21, Publication 1542, Rev. Proc. 93-50, Rev. Proc. 94-77, Rev. Proc. 96-28, Rev. Proc. 96-64, Rev. Proc. 97-59, and Rev. Proc. 98-64.)

The Tax Reform Act of 1986 further limited deductions for luxury water travel. (Luxury water travel consists of travel by ocean liner, cruise ship, or other form of luxury water transportation. This rule applies, for example, in the case of a taxpayer who has business reasons for traveling from New York City to London and who travels by ocean liner.) The deduction allowable in the case of luxury water travel cannot exceed twice the highest amount generally allowable with respect to a day of travel to employees of the executive branch of the federal government while away from home but serving the United States, multiplied by the number of days the taxpayer was engaged in luxury water travel. For example, if during a particular taxable year the applicable federal per diem amount is $75, a taxpayer's deduction for a 6-day trip cannot exceed $900 ($150 per day times 6 days). The applicable per diem amount generally is the highest travel amount applying for an area in the conterminous United States.

Moreover, under the Reform Act, no deduction is allowed for travel as a form of education. This rule applies when a travel deduction would be allowable only on the ground that the travel itself serves an educational purpose (for example, in the case of a teacher of French who travels to France in order to maintain general familiarity with the French language and culture). This disallowance does not apply, however, when a deduction is claimed with respect to travel that is a necessary adjunct to engaging in an activity that gives rise to a business deduction relating to education. (For example, when a scholar of French literature travels to Paris to do specific library research that cannot be done elsewhere or to take courses that are offered only at the

Sorbonne, in circumstances such that the nontravel research or course costs are deductible.)

The Tax Reform Act of 1986 also amended the rules on charitable travel. Under the Reform Act, as of January 1, 1987, no deduction will be allowed for transportation and other travel expenses incurred in performing services away from home for a charitable organization (whether paid directly by the individual or indirectly through a contribution to the organization) unless there is no significant element of personal pleasure, recreation, or vacation in the travel away from home.

Moreover, the Tax Reform Act of 1986 also provided that travel and other costs of attending a convention or seminar for investment purposes (i.e., not for trade or business purposes) are not deductible.

All of the foregoing provisions of the Tax Reform Act of 1986 are applicable for tax years beginning after December 31, 1986.

Note, in addition, that the IRS has ruled in Doc. 9237014 that a deduction would be allowed for Saturday travel expenses incurred to take advantage of reduced air fares.

64 Transportation Expenses

Transportation expenses, which must be differentiated from *travel* expenses, sometimes can be deducted. Transportation expenses include the cost of traveling by air, rail, bus, taxi, etc., and the cost of operating and maintaining your car, but *not* the cost of meals and lodging.

Commuting expenses, those expenses incurred between your principal or regular place of work and your home, are not part of deductible transportation expenses. This is true regardless of the distance between your home and your regular place of work or of whether you are employed at different locations on different days within the same city or general area. If you work at two places in a day, however, whether or not for the same employer, you may deduct the expense of getting from one to the other. These expenses are part of your allowable transportation deduction. Furthermore, if you have a temporary or minor assignment beyond the general area of your tax home and return home each evening, you can deduct the expenses of the daily round trip transportation.

If you use your car in your work, and you use it exclusively for that purpose, you may deduct the entire cost of its operation. Included among the deductible items are the cost of gas, oil, repairs, insurance, depreciation, interest to buy the car, taxes, licenses, garage rents, parking fees, tolls, etc.

If you use your car for both personal and business purposes, you must divide your expenses between business and personal use. For example, if you drive your car 20,000 miles during the year, 8,000 for business and 12,000 for personal use, only 40 percent (8,000 ÷ 20,000) of the cost of operating your car may be claimed as a work expense.

Furthermore, if you lease a car that you use in your business, you may deduct any lease payments that are for your business. You may not deduct any part of the lease payments for commuting or other personal use of the car, and any advance payments must be apportioned over the entire lease period. In addition, you may not deduct any payments you make toward the purchase of a car even if the payments are lease payments. They must be capitalized and recovered through a deduction for depreciation.

Instead of deducting your actual itemized automobile transportation costs, you may deduct a standard mileage rate. You must:

a) own the car;

b) not use the car for hire, for example, as a taxi;

c) not operate a fleet of cars, using two or more at the same time;

d) not have claimed depreciation using any method other than the straight-line method (equal depreciation over the life of the asset); *and*

e) not have claimed additional first-year depreciation on the car.

The 1999 standard mileage rate is 32.5¢ a mile for the first three months, and then, as of April 1, 1999, goes down to 31¢ a mile. In addition to the standard mileage rate, you can also deduct any tolls, interest, taxes, or parking fees paid. Of this 32.5¢/31.0¢ per mile, 12¢ a mile constitutes an allowance for depreciation, reducing your basis in the car (Rev. Proc. 98-63).

In *Wicker* (TCM 1986-1), a nurse-anesthetist maintained an automobile for travel between her office in the cellar of her home and the hospital where she performed anesthesia services. Although she served as head of the Department of Anesthesiology, no office space was provided to her at the hospital. She practiced exclusively at the hospital. The court found that her home office was her principal place of business and that her travel between her home office and the hospital was, therefore, business travel, rather than commuting. The expenses incurred in such travel were deductible.

If you are reimbursed or receive an allowance for your car expenses, you may use the standard mileage rate to determine the cost of operating your car. However, only the cost so figured that is more than your reimbursement or allowance may be deducted.

If you and your spouse have separate cars, *each* one of you can compute the deduction by claiming 32.5¢/31.0¢ per mile (Revenue Proclamation 89-66). You cannot use the optional mileage rate if you use two cars simultaneously in the same business (*Dillon,* T.C.M. 1989-14) but can even if you do not own the vehicle (Section 1.274(d) IT). It is allowable, however, if you use each car for a separate business.

Moreover, the Internal Revenue Service has stated that depreciation will be considered to have been allowed for standard mileage property "at the rate of $.07 per mile for 1980 and 1981, $.075 per mile in 1982, and $.08 per mile in 1983, 1984, and 1985, $.09 for 1986, $.10 for 1987, $.105 for 1988, $.11 for 1989, 1990, and 1991, $.115 for 1992 and 1993, and $.12 for 1994, 1995, 1996, 1997, 1998, and 1999" (Rev. Proc. 98-63). This per mile rate, according to the IRS, will be the "depreciation" used to adjust the basis of standard mileage property (see Rev. Rul. Proc. 85-49 and 87-49).

Most important, a car you acquire will qualify for the depreciation expense if it is used in your work or business. The deduction for transportation expenses may in effect reduce your net cash outlay for a new car to less than half its cost!

For example, assume you are in the 31 percent bracket and you bought a $6,000 car that you use 100 percent for business. You elect to expense the first $1,700 of the car's cost, reducing the basis for depreciation. You elect a five-year class recovery life for the car. If you run the car 30,000 miles in its first year, your net cost for the acquisition of the car can be reduced to less than half its cost as follows:

Cost of car	$6,000
Minus election to expense:	
$1,700 × .31	–527
Minus depreciation:	
([$6,000 – $1,700] × .20) × .31	–267
Net cost of car	$5,206

Minus expenses:	
30,000 miles @ 10 mpg =	
3,000 gallons @ $1.25/gal	$3,750
repairs, oil, and upkeep	900
insurance	1,210
garage rent, license, & registration	750
tolls, parking, interest on auto loan, etc. ($6/day)	2,190
Total expense	$8,800
Tax saving ($8,800 × .31)	–2,728
Final Net Cost	$2,478

If you drive the car more than 30,000 miles you actually can *make* money on the car purchase!

Let's assume that you are in the 31 percent bracket. Let's see what would happen if you run the car 60,000 miles over the first three years. Employing the appropriate tax-saving strategy above, not only would your net cost be zero, but you would have saved an *additional* $2,498 in taxes!

Cost of car	$6,000
Minus: election to expense ($1,700 × .31) and depreciation ($4,300 × .712 × .31)	–1,476
Net cost of car (end of third year)	$4,524
Minus expenses:	
60,000 miles @ 10 mpg =	
6,000 gallons @ $1.25/gal	$7,500
repairs, oil, and upkeep	2,700
insurance	3,630
garage rent, licenses, and registrations	2,250
tolls, parking, interest on auto loan etc. ($6/day)	+6,570
Total expenses	$22,650
Tax savings ($22,650 × .31)	–7,022
Final net cost	-0-
Incremental Tax Savings	$2,498

The numbers mentioned are just to give you a structure for analysis. For 1999, you could actually depreciate or expense as much as $3,060 in the first year alone!

65 Meals and Entertainment Expenses

Not only can you deduct the above travel and transportation expenses, but you can also take as additional miscellaneous deductions certain entertainment expenses. Entertainment expenses may be deducted if you can show that the entertainment of prospects has a direct effect on and can reasonably be expected to increase or maintain earnings or your commissions.

These entertainment expenses must be ordinary and necessary (reasonable and customary) and must be incurred in the course of your work. You may deduct entertainment expenses only if you can show that your employer required or expected you to have such entertainment expenses in connection with your work.

You must prove *all* the following elements for entertainment deductions:

- The amount of each separate expenditure for entertaining, except for incidental items such as taxi fares and telephone calls that may be totaled on a daily basis.
- The date the entertainment took place.
- The name, address or location, and type of entertainment, such as dinner or theatre, if the information is not apparent in the name or designation of the place.
- The reason for the entertainment or the business benefit derived or expected to be gained from entertaining and, except for certain business meals, any business discussion or activity that took place.
- The occupation or other information about the person or persons entertained, including the name, title, or other designation sufficient to establish the business relationship to you.

Under the Tax Reform Act of 1986, effective January 1, 1987, entertainment expenses were allowed only to the extent of 80 percent of what was spent. Exceptions allowing full deductibility include (a) expenses reimbursed by an employer (in which case the employer is subject to the 80 percent rule); (b) traditional employer-paid recreational expenses for employees (e.g., holiday parties); (c) items given as compensation to the recipient that are excludable from income as de minimis fringe benefits; (d) items made available to the general public (e.g., as promotional activities); and (e) tickets to certain charitable fund-raising sports events. Ticket costs in excess of face value are not deductible, except with regard to tickets for charitable fund-raising sports events. Moreover, deductions for the rental or other use of a sky box at a sports arena are disallowed, to the extent in excess of the cost of regular tickets, if the box is used by the taxpayer for more than one event. This sky box disallowal of deductibility was subject to a 3-year phaseout starting January 1, 1986.

In addition, the Tax Reform Act of 1986 also reduced to 80 percent the amount of deductions otherwise allowable for business meal expenses, including meals away from home and meals furnished on an employer's premises to its employees. Exceptions allowing full deductibility include (a) employee meal expenses reimbursed by the employer (in which case the employer is subject to the 80 percent rule); (b) employer-furnished meals that are excludable from the employee's income as de minimis fringes (including subsidized eating facilities); (c) meals taxed to employees as compensation; and (d) items sold to the public (such as the cost of food to restaurants) or furnished the public as samples or for promotion. Moreover, the meals, to be deductible at all, must be directly related to or associated with a business discussion—i.e., "quiet" business meals are no longer deductible.

The Omnibus Budget Reconciliation Act of 1993, effective for years beginning after December 31, 1993, reduced the 80 percent deduction to 50 percent. The Act also eliminated, after December 31, 1993, all deductions for club dues, including airline and hotel clubs (see page 431). Club meals may still be deducted if they satisfy the above standards for deductibility.

66 Gifts

You may deduct ordinary and necessary (reasonable and customary) expenses for business gifts made directly or indirectly to any individual. The total value of business gifts to any one individual during the tax year

> cannot be more than $25. If a gift is not intended for the eventual personal use or benefit of a particular individual or a limited class of individuals, the gift is not considered to be made to an individual.

A gift to the spouse or child of an individual with whom you are doing business is a gift to that individual. However, if one spouse has an independent bona fide business connection with you, such a gift generally will not be considered a gift to the other spouse unless it is intended for that spouse's eventual use or benefit.

An item costing $4 or less on which your name is clearly and permanently imprinted and which is one of a number of identical items distributed by you is not subject to the $25 rule. This includes such items as pens, desk sets, plastic bags, and cases. In addition, incidental costs, such as jewelry engraving or packaging, insuring, and mailing or other delivery costs, are not generally included in determining the cost of a gift for the $25 rule.

A related cost will be considered incidental only if it does not add substantial value to the gift. For example, although the cost of gift wrapping will be considered an incidental cost, the purchase of an ornamental basket for packaging fruit will not be considered an incidental cost of packaging if the basket has a value that is substantial in relation to the value of the fruit.

Furthermore, it must be remembered that we are dealing here with gift, entertainment, travel, and transportation expenses of *employees*. Any of these expenses incurred by employers may be deductible for adjusted gross income as trade or business deductions.

You must prove *all* the following to be allowed a deduction for business gifts:

- The cost.
- The date of the gift.
- A description of the gift.
- The reason for giving the gift or any business benefit derived or expected to be gained from giving it.
- The name, title, occupation, or other information about the person receiving the gift, or some other designation sufficient to establish the business relationship to you.

KEEP PROOF OF EXPENSES

Substantiation of travel, meals, entertainment, and business gift expenses should be kept in an account book, diary, statement of expense, or similar record, supported by adequate documentary evidence that together can support each element of an expenditure. For example, entries on a desk calendar, not supported by evidence, are not proper proof. The simple rule here, therefore, is to keep receipts and records. For example, if you take a business associate out to dinner, simply jot the associate's name and the general topic of discussion on the back of the receipt given to you by the restaurant.

Note that under DOC 9805007, faxed or e-mailed documents qualify as documentary evidence for meal and entertainment substantiation.

In the area of such deductions there is no such thing as too much documentation. If these deductions are questioned by the Internal Revenue Service, the only things an audit agent will look for are receipts. Therefore, *always* remember to get a receipt, note the cost of the expenditure, the person to whom it relates, and your business relationship. A total of 30 seconds of effort may guarantee you $100 of unquestioned deductions. If your 1999 taxable income is more than $62,450, that 30 seconds of effort would have saved you $31 in taxes—that's the equivalent of $3,720 an hour—even more than most tax attorneys make!

67 Reimbursable Employee Business Expenses

Normally, when reimbursement is available to an employee for a business expense incurred, if the employee does not obtain that reimbursement, no deduction is allowed [*Podems,* 24 T.C. 21 (1955)]. However, in *Kessler* (TCM 1985-254), the court ruled that if a taxpayer can establish that reimbursement, though nominally available, is unavailable as a practical matter, then out-of-pocket business expenses should be allowable as a deduction. (See also *Jetty,* TCM 1982-378.) The Tax Court's position was reinforced and supported by the Internal Revenue Service in Action on Decision 1986-011, on January 8, 1986, wherein a recommendation was made that the IRS acquiesce in *Kessler.*

68 Educational Expenses

Educational expenses incurred to maintain or improve your skills in your current position are deductible as a miscellaneous itemized expense. In a private letter ruling (PLR 8706048), the IRS held that a financial consultant may deduct the cost of obtaining a Master of Science degree in financial planning. The taxpayer was a financial consultant and the degree was sought in order to maintain and improve the taxpayer's financial planning skills. If the education will qualify you for a new trade or business or is a minimum requirement for your current job, that education expense is not deductible. In the private letter ruling the Internal Revenue Service held that a master's degree in financial planning was not a minimum requirement for the taxpayer's job as a financial consultant and did not qualify the taxpayer for a new trade or business. Therefore, the taxpayer's expenses for tuition and books incurred in obtaining the degree in financial planning were deductible as ordinary and necessary expenses.

As a general rule, however, if you earn a degree that makes you eligible for a new trade or business, there is no deduction for tuition. The real key is your intent at the time you take the course. For example, in one case, after 23 years in the accounting field, a CPA attended law school at night. He took all the tax courses he could at law school, intending to improve himself as an accountant. He did not intend to go into the practice of law and in fact did not. His purpose was not to obtain a new position or advancement in position. His only intent was to improve his skills as an accountant. The expense of going to law school in this case was deductible (*Berry,* T.C. Memo 1971-110).

69 Limit on Itemized Deductions

Under the Omnibus Reconciliation Act of 1990 (OBRA), a new limit was put on itemized deductions. For regular tax purposes, the new law establishes a floor that you must exceed before your itemized expenses are deductible. The 1999 floor for all taxpayers, regardless of filing status (except married filing separate, where it is 3% in excess of $63,300), is 3 percent of the amount of your adjusted gross income (AGI) exceeding $126,600 (indexed for inflation). Medical expenses, casualty and theft losses, and investment interest expenses are not subject to the floor, and the deduction cannot reduce by more than 80 percent your otherwise allowable deductions. This provision effectively raises the 31 percent marginal tax rate by 0.93 percent. It does not, however, affect the alternative minimum tax.

Example: If your AGI is $226,600, you must knock $3,000 ($100,000 × 3%) off the bottom line of your Schedule A. So each thousand dollars of excess income lops off $9.30 of tax benefits in the 31 percent bracket or $11.88 in the 39.6 percent bracket.

However, the slicer will not cut your itemized deductions by more than 80 percent (and does not apply at all when computing AMT). Better yet, the 80 percent stopper does not include deductions for medical expenses, investment interest, and casualty or gambling losses.

Note that this provision applies after the other deduction limits, e.g., 7.5 percent medical and 2 percent miscellaneous.

C Schedules of Deductions

70 Medical Deductions

Abortion
Acupuncture
Advances for lifetime care
Ambulance hire
Apartment rent
Artificial teeth or limbs
Autoette wheelchair
Automobile expenses
Birth control pills
Braille books and magazines
Capital expenditures in excess of property's increased value
Central air conditioning
Clarinet lessons
Commutation costs
Computer medical data bank
Contact lens insurance
Cosmetic surgery (limited)
Crutches
Dental care
Diagnostic services
Drug or alcohol therapy centers
Education aids
Elastic stockings
Employee medical plans
Eyeglasses
Guide dogs
Guide for blind individual
Handrails
Hearing aids and component parts
Hospital care
Invalid spouse
Iron lung
Kidney transplants
Laetrile
Last illness expenses
Lip reading
Massages
Mattresses and boards
Meals and lodging if part of hospital or treatment charge
Meat diet
Medical insurance premiums
Medical transportation
Medical travel
Medicare B

Medicinal liquors, if prescribed
Medicines and drugs
Nonlocal medical transportation costs
Nurse's transportation expenses
Nursing homes and homes for the aged
Nursing services
Operations affecting childbearing
Operations and treatments in general
Organic foods
Outdoor elevator
Oxygen and oxygen equipment
Paint removal
Patterning exercises
Physician's fees
Prepaid medical insurance
Prosthetic devices
Psychiatric or psychoanalytic care
Reclining chair
Remedial reading
Retirement homes
Salt-free diet
School for the physically or mentally handicapped
Sexual therapy
Smoke-ending program, if to cure specific disease
Special foods or beverages
Special home for mentally retarded
Special plumbing fixtures
Specially designed automobiles
Swimming pool
Telephone equipment
Throat treatment
Transporting patient's relative
Tutoring fees
Unlicensed practitioners
University medical plan, if charges separately stated
Vasectomy
Vitamins, if prescribed
Voluntary payments for Medicare A
Water fluoridation device
Wheelchair
X-ray treatment

71 Deductible Taxes

Taxes imposed by state, city, and possessions of the United States
Auto registration (to the extent that it is based on value)
Income (except where claimed as credit)
Personal property
Real property
Foreign taxes
Income, war profit, excess profit (unless claimed as credit)
Real estate

If paid or accrued in connection with business or for the production of income, you can also deduct these taxes:

Federal taxes
- Excise
- Import duties
- Liquor
- Railroad Retirement (employers)
- Social security (employers)

Tobacco
Unemployment (employers)
State and local taxes
Admission
Auto registration
Beverages
Cigarettes
Cosmetics
Driver's license fees
Excise
Stamp
Liquors
Mortgage
Occupancy
Stock transfer
Tobacco
Transfer (except estate, inheritance, legacy, succession, and gift taxes)
Unemployment

72 Charitable Deductions

Aid to evacuees
Artwork contributed by owner
Automobile expenses
Bargain sales to charity
Benefit performances
Book samples
Charitable travel
Church bonds, if donated after purchase
Church building funds
Church dues
Church repairs
Civil Defense volunteer's out-of-pocket expenses
Community chests
Credit card contributions
Delegate's expenses
Domestic fraternal societies
Essays
Excess rent
Eyeglass donations
Films and tape recordings
Foster parent's expenses
Future interest in tangible personal property
Government contributions
Home for elderly
Hospital fees
Installment notes
Insurance policies
Inventory donated
Legal expenses donated
Maintaining student in home
Medical equipment
Membership in art or fine arts association
Music manuscripts
Ordinary income property
Out-of-pocket charitable expenses
Partial interest in property
Patents donated
Promissory notes
Property donated
Rent in excess of fair rental value
Scenic easement
Tickets donated for resale
Uniforms
Unmarried pregnant women programs
Volunteer fire companies
Volunteer income tax assistance
War veterans' organizations

73 Casualty and Theft Loss Deductions

Accidents
Airplane, train, and other transport crashes
Appraisal fees
Automobile damage
Bomb damage
Casualty and theft losses of investment property
Cleanup and repair costs
Confiscation by foreign government
Disaster area losses
Driveway breakup
Earthquake or earth slide
Explosion
False representation or pretenses
Fire
Flood
Freeze
Hurricane
Insect and disease damage to trees and shrubs, if sudden
Lightning
Loss of property used partly for rental and partly for personal purposes
Mine cave-ins
Razing
Shipwrecks
Smog
Snow
Sonic boom
Storms
Swindles
Theft of business property
Theft of personal property
Thin ice
Tornado
Vandalism
Water damage (as from burst water heater)

74 Miscellaneous Deductions

Attorney fees paid by spouse to secure taxable alimony
Bad debts
Bar examination fee (amortizable)
Bond premium amortization
Gambling losses (to extent of gambling gains)
Job-hunting expenses
Labor union dues and assessments for noninsurance purposes
Physician's hospital privilege fee (amortizable)
Tax counseling costs
Tax litigation expenses
Tax return preparation
Uncollectible debts
Uncollectible loans

75 Employee Miscellaneous Deductions

- Automobile expenses (allocatable to business)
  - Depreciation
  - Garage rent
  - Gasoline and oil
  - Insurance
  - Parking fees
  - Repairs for business cars
  - State inspection and registration fees
  - Taxes
  - Tolls
  - Washing
  - Briefcase
  - Christmas gifts to customers (limited)
- Convention expenses
- Dues (except "Club Dues")
  - Business association
  - Labor unions
  - Professional societies
- Educational expenses (limited)
- Employment agency fees
- Entertainment expenses
- Fidelity bond costs
- Gifts to customers and prospects (limited)
- Insurance premiums
  - Automobile (to extent of business use)
  - Bonds (fidelity, etc.)
  - Malpractice
- Job-hunting expenses
- Labor unions, initiation fees, dues, fines, assessments for pension funds
- Laundry and cleaning while traveling away from home
- Meals or lodging while traveling away from home
- Office furnishings[7]
- Outside sales business expenses
- Passport fees for business travel
- Reimbursed expenses (if reimbursement included in income)
- Safety equipment
- Subscriptions to professional journals and magazines
- Tax return preparation
- Technical periodicals
- Telephone
- Tips
- Tools
- Transportation expenses
- Traveling expenses
  - Baggage charges
  - Fares
  - Laundry and cleaning while away from home
  - Meals and lodging while away from home
  - Passport fees, if for business
  - Sample rooms
  - Taxis
  - Telephone and telegraph messages
  - Tips
- Tuition fees
- Uniforms not adaptable to general wear
- Work clothes

7. For example, office furnishings bought by an executive with his own funds to maintain his image as a successful district sales manager (*Leroy Gillis,* T.C. Memo 1973-96).

76 Investor Deductions

Investors can deduct expenses incurred to produce or collect income and to conserve, manage, or maintain income-producing property. Anyone who owns securities, rents real estate, or owns other investments should not overlook the typical deductions listed below.

- Accounting fees
- Advertising expenses
- Alterations and repairs
- Attorneys' fees
- Auditing expenses
- Bad debts
- Bookkeeping expenses
- Collection of rent costs
- Custodian fees
- Damages paid for breach of contract or lease
- Depreciation
  - Buildings
  - Furniture and fixtures
- Exchange of asset losses
- Expenses of successfully resisting condemnation of property
- Fire insurance premiums
- Franchise taxes
- Heat and light
- Interest
- Investment counseling costs
- Leasehold improvements
- Leases
  - Amortization of improvements by lessee
  - Amortization of lease acquisition costs
  - Rentals paid
  - Repairs made by lessee
  - Taxes paid by lessee
- Legal expenses
- License taxes and fees (limited)
- Losses (to extent not covered by insurance)
  - Abandonment of worthless interest in real estate
  - Bad debts
  - Demolition of building
  - Forced sales
  - Foreclosure
  - Forfeitures
  - Property sales
  - Property seized by government
- Maintenance of property costs
- Management expenses
- Mortgage foreclosure losses
- Moving expenses of machinery and equipment
- Night protection services
- Office rent
- Porter and janitor services
- Recordkeeping costs
- Redecoration costs
- Refuse and waste removal expenses
- Repairs
- Safe-deposit boxes
- Salaries
- Sales of assets losses
- Stationery and supplies
- Tax counseling costs
- Tax return preparation
- Taxes (state)
  - General sales (add to basis)
  - Gross income

Income
License fees (limited)
Motor fuel
Personal property
Real estate
Stamp
Stock transfer (adjust basis)
Transfer of property (except estate, inheritance, legacy, gift, etc.) (adjust basis)

Traveling expenses

Worthless bonds and stock

CHAPTER 7

Traditional Tax Shelters

"As a citizen, you have an obligation to the country's tax system, but you also have an obligation to yourself to know your rights under the law and possible tax deductions. And to claim every one of them."

DONALD ALEXANDER,
former commissioner of the Internal
Revenue Service under three presidents

"The tax laws reflect a continuing struggle among contending interests for the privilege of paying the least."

LOUIS EISENSTEIN,
The Ideologies of Taxation

"When Congress talks of tax reform, grab your wallet and run for cover."

Senator STEVE SYMMS of Idaho

The art of sophisticated tax planning requires you to understand the elements of tax-sheltered investments. These investments allow you to offset certain "artificial losses"—noneconomic losses, but losses that are available as deductions under the present tax laws, and not only against the income from those investments but also against your other income from your regular business or professional activity.

Often, tax shelters have been described by the unsophisticated as gimmicks or "loopholes." Nothing could be further from the truth. These laws were adopted by Congress after careful deliberation, with the purpose of serving some major economic or social goal. Therefore, when you utilize these techniques you are not only improving your financial position, but you are also furthering a legitimate national economic goal. For example, the allowance of percentage depletion for oil and other tax provisions for mineral development have been effective incentives to investments in petroleum exploration and discovery. These attractive tax benefits have encouraged other taxpayers to provide the risk capital needed to bring into production many useful sources of oil that would otherwise go untapped. Special tax benefits for equipment leasing and life insurance also serve national economic and social goals.

The Internal Revenue Service, in a manner of speaking, sometimes finds itself involved in a shelter. For example, all of the staff at the regional IRS headquarters in New York are in a shelter. It seems the office building housing the Internal Revenue Service in New York was sold to a tax shelter syndicator.

Sales of publicly offered partnerships registered with the Securities and Exchange Commission exceeded $10.4 billion in 1988. Among those who have invested in tax shelters are former Attorney General William French Smith and former Internal Revenue Service Commissioner Rosco Egger, Jr. Clearly, tax shelters are investments that you should consider if appropriate.

THE TAX REFORM ACT OF 1986

The Tax Reform Act of 1986 significantly affected the attractiveness of traditional tax shelters. As of January 1, 1987, the long-term capital gains deduction is repealed. Moreover, the 1986 Reform Act effectively limits losses from passive trade or business activities (limited partnership tax shelters, etc.), generally to offset passive income. What this means is that, effectively, tax shelter losses can be used only to offset tax shelter gains. Passive income does not include portfolio income—e.g., dividends on stocks and interest on bonds—nor gain from the sale of stocks and bonds—nor does it include income from the rental or property to an entity in which you materially participate. You can't claim passive income from renting personally owned equipment to a partnership you manage. (But see Chapter 8 to learn how to use a trust for your kids to accomplish the same thing.) Although these limitations were phased in over a 5-year period, they must be considered in any evaluation of a tax shelter offering. The following discussion explains the Tax Reform Act and details the remaining potential alternative tax shelter vehicles.

The new passive loss rules are sweeping provisions that in general deny any individual, estate, trust, closely held C corporation, or personal service corporation the use of losses or credits generated in "passive activities" to offset other income such as salary, interest, dividends, and active business income. Deductions from passive activities may offset income from passive activities. Credits from passive activities generally are limited to the tax attributable to income from passive activities.

Disallowed losses and credits are carried forward and treated as deductions and credits from passive activities in the next taxable year. Suspended losses from an activity are allowed in full when the taxpayer disposes of his entire interest in the activity in a fully taxable transaction. Suspended credits may not be claimed in full in the year in which the taxpayer disposes of the interest in the passive activity. Rather, they are carried forward until used to offset tax liability from passive income. However, upon a fully taxable disposition of a passive activity, taxpayers may elect to increase the basis of property immediately before the transfer by an amount equal to the portion of any suspended credit that reduced the basis of the property for the taxable year in which the credit arose.

If a closely held C corporation (other than a personal service or S corporation) has "net active income" for any taxable year, the passive activity loss for the taxable year will be allowable as a deduction against net active income. A similar rule applies in the case of any passive activity credit of the taxpayer. The term *net active income* means the taxable income of the taxpayer for the taxable year determined without regard for any income or loss from a passive activity and any *net portfolio income.*

PASSIVE ACTIVITY DEFINED

In general, the term *passive activity* means any activity that involves the conduct of any trade or business and in which the taxpayer does not *materially participate.*

It also includes any rental activity of either real or tangible personal property regardless of whether the individual materially participates. With respect to equipment leasing, short-term rental to various users (where the lessor provides substantial services) is an active business rather than a passive activity.

In general, working interests in any oil or gas property that the taxpayer holds directly or through an entity that does not limit the taxpayer's liability with respect to such interests will be treated as an active trade or business and will not be subject to the passive loss rules.

MATERIAL PARTICIPATION DEFINED

In general, a taxpayer will be treated as materially participating in an activity only if the taxpayer is involved in the operations of the activity on a regular, continuous, and substantial basis.

All limited partnership interests are treated as not materially participating.

Management decision making by an individual may constitute material participation if such services are substantial and bona fide. For example, when management services are rendered on a full-time basis, and the success of the activity depends on the exercise of an individual's business judgment, such services constitute material participation. The test applies regardless of whether an individual owns an interest in the activity directly or through a pass-through entity such as a general partnership or an S corporation.

Taxpayers who own working interests in oil and gas properties through a limited partnership will be subject to the passive loss rules with respect to that interest. That is notwithstanding the special exclusion for working interests in oil and gas properties.

In 1988, the IRS attempted to clarify the definition of "material participation" and provided special standards for limited partners. A taxpayer who is not a limited partner is a material participant in an activity during the tax year if one of the following tests is met:

1. The taxpayer participates for more than 500 hours.
2. The taxpayer's participation represents substantially all participation in the activity by individuals (including nonowners).
3. The taxpayer participates for more than 100 hours, and no other individual's participation in the activity exceeds that of the taxpayer.
4. The activity is a significant participation activity for the tax year, and the taxpayer's total participation in all significant participation activities for the year exceeds 500 hours.
5. The taxpayer has materially participated in the activity for five of the ten preceding years.

6. The activity is a personal service activity in which the taxpayer has materially participated for any three preceding years.

7. In light of the facts and circumstances, the taxpayer participates in the activity on a regular, continuous, and substantial basis. To satisfy this facts-and-circumstances test, the taxpayer must have at least 100 hours of participation.

Limited partners materially participate in an activity only if they meet one of tests 1, 5, or 6, above.

A significant participation activity is a new concept created by the Internal Revenue Service's temporary regulations. It is any trade or business activity in which the taxpayer has more than 100 hours of participation during the tax year but fails to satisfy all the material participation tests (other than test 4, above, relating to significant participation activities).

This concept is important for taxpayers involved in several trades or businesses, because it allows them to satisfy the material participation test by aggregating hours of participation in different businesses. However, if the taxpayer enjoys *net income* from significant participation activities during the year, that income is considered *nonpassive* and cannot be used to offset losses from other passive activities. If the significant participation activities produce a net loss, the loss is considered *passive* and must be suspended unless there is sufficient income from other passive activities to offset the loss.

NET PORTFOLIO INCOME

In general, net portfolio income will not be included when determining the income or loss from any passive activity. Net portfolio income means gross income from interest, dividends, annuities, or royalties not derived in the ordinary course of a trade or business less expenses (other than interest) that are clearly and directly allocable to such gross income, less interest expense properly allocable to such gross income, plus gain or less loss attributable to the disposition of property held for investment or producing income such as interest, dividends, or royalties.

Any income, gain, or loss that is attributable to an investment of working capital will not be treated as income or loss from a passive activity.

This provision prevents taxpayers from placing property that would otherwise be producing active portfolio income into an entity that is subject to the passive loss rules, thereby using losses from passive activities to offset active portfolio income.

Income earned for personal services will not be taken into account in computing the income or loss from a passive activity for any taxable year. For example, if a limited partner is paid for performing services for the partnership (whether by way of salary, guaranteed payment, or allocation of partnership income), these payments cannot be sheltered by passive losses from the partnership or from any other passive activity.

TREATMENT OF FORMER PASSIVE ACTIVITIES

If an activity is a former passive activity for any taxable year and has suspended losses or credits from prior years when the activity was passive, the suspended losses may be offset against the income from the activity for the taxable year. Suspended credits allocable to such activity may be offset against the regular tax liability allocable to that activity for the taxable year. Any remaining suspended losses or credits continue to be treated as arising from a passive activity.

It appears that suspended losses and credits from a passive activity may be used to offset active income from the activity in the year in which the activity changes from passive to active and in later years. Any remaining suspended losses or credits will also be allowed as a deduction to income or credit against tax attributable to other passive activities.

If a taxpayer ceases for any taxable year to be a closely held C corporation or personal service corporation, suspended losses and credits will continue to be treated in the same manner as if the taxpayer continued to be a closely held C corporation or personal service corporation, whichever is applicable.

DISPOSITIONS OF ENTIRE INTERESTS IN PASSIVE ACTIVITY

If during the taxable year a taxpayer disposes of his entire interest in any passive activity (or former passive activity) and all gain or loss realized on such disposition is recognized, any suspended losses from the activity are no longer treated as passive activity losses and are allowable as a deduction against the taxpayer's income in the following order:

- income or gain from the passive activity for the taxable year (including any gain recognized on the disposition)
- net income or gain for the taxable year from all passive activities
- any other income or gain

However, if the person acquiring the interest is a related party to the taxpayer, then any suspended losses will not apply against the taxpayer's active income until the taxable year in which such interest is acquired by another person unrelated to the taxpayer. However, such suspended losses may be offset by income from other passive activities of the taxpayer.

To the extent that any loss recognized upon a disposition of an entire interest in a passive activity is a loss from the sale or exchange of a capital asset, the capital loss is limited to the amount of gains from the sale or exchange of capital assets plus $3,000 (in the case of individuals). The limitation on the deductibility of capital losses is applied before the determination of the amount of losses allowable upon the disposition under the passive loss rule.

For example, if a taxpayer has a capital loss of $10,000 upon the disposition of a passive activity that has $5,000 of suspended losses, the $5,000 of suspended losses are allowed, but the capital loss deduction is limited to $3,000 for the year (assuming the taxpayer has no other gains or losses from the sale of capital assets for the year). The remainder of the capital loss from the disposition is carried forward and allowed in accordance with the provisions determining the allowance of such capital losses.

PARTIAL DISPOSITION OF AN INTEREST IN A PASSIVE ACTIVITY

The 1986 law makes no provision for the allowance of part or all of the suspended losses and credits attributable to a passive activity when an individual makes a partial or incomplete disposition of an interest in that passive activity. All losses and credits apparently remain suspended until offset by income from the individual's remaining interest in that passive activity or other passive activities, or until the individual completes the disposition of his entire interest in that passive activity.

DISPOSITION AT DEATH

If an interest in an activity is transferred due to the taxpayer's death, suspended losses may be deducted against income to the extent such losses are greater than the excess (if any) of the basis of such property in the hands of the transferee, over the adjusted basis of such property immediately before the death of the taxpayer. Any unused suspended losses as a result of this limitation are not allowed as a deduction for any taxable year.

For example, assume Mother owns rental real estate with a market value of $70,000, an adjusted basis of $50,000, and $25,000 of suspended losses. Mother dies and leaves the property to Daughter. The basis is stepped up to $70,000 in the hands of Daughter. Only $5,000 of the suspended losses are deductible on the income tax return of the estate. The remaining $20,000 of suspended losses (equal to the step-up in basis) is lost forever.

DISPOSITION BY INSTALLMENT SALE

If an individual disposes of an entire interest in an activity in an installment sale, suspended losses are allowed each year based on the ratio of gain recognized each year to the total gain on the sale.

DISPOSITION BY GIFT

If an interest in a passive activity is disposed of by gift, the basis of the interest immediately before the transfer is increased by any suspended passive losses allocable to the interest. Suspended losses that are added to the basis because of the gift of an interest are not allowed as deductions for any taxable year.

Moreover, the specific language of the statute appears to imply that gain on the sale of an interest in a passive activity cannot be offset with passive losses and credits from other passive activities. Only suspended or current year losses and credits from the passive activity may be used to offset gains realized on the disposition of that activity.

For example, an individual has interests in two separate limited partnerships, A and B, which are separate passive activities. Assume the following facts apply:

	A	B
Current year loss	($30,000)	($10,000)
Prior suspended losses	($70,000)	($25,000)

Assume that the individual sells his interest in B for a gain of $40,000. The full amount of the losses from partnership B, $35,000, may offset this gain. However, it appears that none of the current or suspended losses from partnership A may offset the remaining $5,000 gain.

SPECIAL RULE FOR RENTAL REAL ESTATE ACTIVITIES

In the case of rental real estate activities in which an individual actively participates, up to $25,000 of losses (and credits in a deduction-equivalent sense) from all such activities are allowed each year against nonpassive income of the taxpayer. The $25,000 amount that is allowed under this special provision is reduced by 50 percent of the amount by which the taxpayer's adjusted gross income for the taxable year exceeds $100,000. Any losses that this provision disallows in the year incurred and that carry over as suspended passive losses to later years may not be used under the $25,000 allowance in later years.

For example, an individual has $30,000 of net losses from rental real estate activities in which she actively participates. Her adjusted gross income, without regard to the net losses from the rental real estate activity, is $120,000. First, only $25,000 of her net losses are eligible for the special allowance. Second, the amount of the net loss she may deduct against active income (her adjusted gross income before deductions for net losses from rental activities) must be reduced by $.50 for each dollar of adjusted gross income over $100,000, or by $10,000. Therefore, she may deduct $15,000 of these net losses from her adjusted gross income when computing her taxable income. The remaining $15,000 of net losses are carried forward.

The $25,000 allowance is applied by first netting income and loss from all of the taxpayer's rental real estate activities in which he actively participates. If there is net loss for the year from such activities, net passive income (if any) from other activities is then applied against it in determining the amount eligible for the $25,000 allowance.

For example, assume that a taxpayer has $45,000 of losses from a rental real estate activity in which he actively participates. If he also actively participates in another rental real estate activity from which he has $40,000 of passive income, resulting in a $5,000 net loss from rental real estate activities in which he actively participates, then only $5,000 is allowed under the $25,000 allowance for the year.

In the case of rehabilitation and low-income housing credits, the phase-out of the $25,000 allowance does not begin until the adjusted gross income of the taxpayer for the taxable year exceeds $200,000.

In the case of taxable years of an estate ending less than two years after the date of the decedent's death, the $25,000 allowance for rental real estate activities applies to all rental real estate activities with respect to which such decedent actively participated before his death.

Married individuals filing separate returns and living apart from their spouses at all times during the taxable year each qualify for half the $25,000 allowance. The phase-out begins for each at $50,000 rather than $100,000 for rental real estate activities other than low-income housing, and at $100,000 rather than $200,000 for low-income housing. If married taxpayers filing separate returns do not live apart from their spouses at *all* times during the taxable year, neither may use the $25,000 allowance for rental real estate activities.

RENTAL ACTIVITY

A rental activity is any activity from which gross income is derived primarily from payments for the use of tangible property. In addition, an activity may qualify as a rental activity if the property is held out for rent, even though no rental income is received in a tax year.

There are six exceptions to the general rule. An activity involving the use of tangible property is not a rental activity in any tax year if *any one* of the following situations exists:

1. If the average rental period is seven days or less, the activity is not considered a rental activity. This exception would exclude many resort properties from the rental category. However, the activity may remain passive if the owner does not materially participate, so the owner must be involved in the day-to-day management or operations of the activity—Treasury Reg. 1.469-5T(f)(2)(ii).

2. If the average rental period is 30 days or less and significant personal services are provided to the customers, the activity is not considered a rental activity.

3. The activity is not treated as a rental activity if extraordinary services are provided to the customers in connection with the use of the property. In order for the services to be "extraordinary," the use of the property by customers must be incidental to the receipt of such services. For example, providing a hospital room to patients would not be considered a rental activity, because the use of the room is incidental to the receipt of medical services.

4. The activity will not be treated as a rental activity if the rental is incidental to nonrental activity. For example:

   a) The property is held to realize gain for appreciation, and the gross rental income is less than 2 percent of the lesser of the unadjusted basis or fair market value of the property. This is the only situation in which rental property will be treated as property held for investment.

   b) The property is generally used in a trade or business owned by the individual, and the gross rental income is insubstantial. This exception applies to property that was predominantly used in the trade or business either in the current year or in at least two of the five preceding tax years. The 2 percent test described above is used to test the substantiality of the rental income.

c) If the property is held for sale to customers in the ordinary course of business, the rental of the property will not be rental activity if the property is sold during the year.

d) Lodging rented to an employee for the convenience of the employer is not rental property.

5. If property is customarily made available for nonexclusive use by various customers during specific business hours, the activity is not a rental activity. For example, a golf course where customers either pay daily fees or purchase passes for a longer period is not considered a rental activity regardless of the average period of customer use.

6. If an owner of an interest in a partnership or S corporation provides property to be used in a nonrental activity of the entity, the partner or shareholder is not treated as being engaged in a rental activity if the property is provided in the owner's capacity as a partner or shareholder and no rent is charged.

ACTIVE PARTICIPATION DEFINED

To qualify for the $25,000 allowance for rental real estate activities, an individual must actively participate in the rental activity. Individuals will not be treated as actively participating for any period if, at any time during such period, their ownership interest (including any interest of the individual's spouse) is less than 10 percent (by value) of all interests in such activity. The degree of participation that is required once this 10 percent or more ownership threshold is met is unclear. The Conference Report suggests that the degree of participation required to meet the active participation test is less than the material participation standard.

A limited partnership interest in rental real estate does not meet the active participation requirement (except as described below for rehabilitation and low-income housing credits).

What happens to the $25,000 deduction when you have several rental real estate properties? To the extent that the aggregate loss from several active participation rental real estate activities does not exceed $25,000, the entire loss is deductible. However, where the aggregate net loss exceeds $25,000, the loss must be allocated among activities on a pro rata basis with respect to the losses from each loss activity. For example, if a taxpayer who qualifies for the full $25,000 allowance has $10,000 of losses from one activity and $40,000 of losses from a second activity, then $5,000 is treated as allowed from the first activity and $20,000 is treated as allowed from the second activity.

This allocation is necessary in part because the suspended losses from a specific activity (those that are not deducted) are allowed in full when the taxpayer disposes of his or her interest in that activity.

Note that the IRS does not permit pro rata allocation between pre- and post-October 1986 investments. (See below for the phase-in of disallowance of losses and credits for interests held before October 23, 1986.) Where there were losses from both old (pre-October) activities and new (post-October) activities, the $25,000 allowance is applied to old activities first—that is, without proration. This generally results in a smaller amount of the loss being allowed.

For example, assume that you are an active participant in two rental real estate activities. In 1987, the loss from each was $50,000. One of the activities was acquired before October 23, 1986, and the other after. The following is a comparison of the Internal Revenue Service approach and the pro rata approach:

Note that the IRS method yielded an allowable loss for 1987 of $41,250

	IRS		**Pro Rata**	
	Pre-October 1986	*Post-October 1986*	*Pre-October 1986*	*Post-October 1986*
Loss	$50,000	$50,000	$50,000	$50,000
Allowed under $25,000 rule	$25,000	$ 0	$12,500	$12,500
Balance subject to 65% phase-in rule	$25,000		$37,500	
65% phase-in	$16,250		$24,375	
Total	$41,250		$49,375	

($25,000 plus $16,250). The pro rata method would permit $49,375 of the loss to be deducted in 1987 ($12,500 plus $12,500 plus $24,375).

The following example shows you how losses are carried forward. Assume that you have invested in three separate passive activities. Activity A is an interest acquired in 1985; Activity B is an interest in a rental activity acquired in 1987; and Activity C is an interest in rental realty acquired in 1987. Also assume that your gross income is under $100,000.

	Activity A	*Activity B*	*Activity C*
	$10,000	($50,000)	($100,000)
1987 results:			
Net passive activity loss			($140,000)
Net losses from B and C offset against A income:			
B = $10,000 × $50,000/$150,000 =			($3,333)
C = $10,000 × $100,000/$150,000 =			($6,667)
Net loss from B offset against active and portfolio income			($25,000)
Loss carryforward to 1988:			
B = $50,000 – $3,333 – $25,000 =			($21,667)
C = $100,000 – $6,667 =			($93,333)
			($115,000)

Assume the following activity in 1988:

	Activity A	*Activity B*	*Activity C*
	$110,000	($20,000)	($40,000)
1988 results:			
Net passive activity loss: ($60,000 + $115,000 NOL carryover – $110,000 income) =			($65,000)
Net losses from B and C offset against A income:*			
B = $110,000 × $41,667/175,000 =			$26,190
C = $110,000 × $133,333**/175,000 =			$83,810
			($110,000)
Net loss from B offset against A income: ($21,670 + $20,000 – $26,190) =			($15,480)
Loss carryforward to 1989:			

Activity A	*Activity B*	*Activity C*
-0-	-0-	($49,520)

*$21,667 + $20,000

**$93,333 + $40,000

REHABILITATION AND LOW-INCOME HOUSING CREDITS

In the case of the rehabilitation and low-income housing credits (but not losses), the $25,000 allowance applies on a credit-equivalent basis. This is so regardless of whether the individual claiming the credit actively participates in the rental real estate activity, including participation as a limited partner. After December 31, 1989, investors in low-income housing projects must actively participate to claim the low-income housing credit against the $25,000 allowance. However, if the property is placed in service after December 31, 1989, but before January 1, 1991, an investor will still not have to meet the active participation standard with respect to the low-income housing credit if at least 10 percent of the costs of such property are incurred before January 1, 1989.

The credit equivalent of the $25,000 allowance is $7,000 of passive credits for an individual in the 28 percent tax bracket. However, where a taxpayer has more than $250,000 of adjusted gross income, the taxpayer will generally receive no current benefit from the rehabilitation or low-income housing credit.

PHASE-IN OF DISALLOWANCE OF LOSSES AND CREDITS FOR INTERESTS HELD BEFORE OCTOBER 22, 1986

Interests in passive activities acquired by a taxpayer on or before October 22, 1986 are eligible for a phase-in under the passive loss rules. Interests in activities acquired after October 22, 1986 are not eligible for the phase-in but instead are fully subject to the passive loss rules. However, a taxpayer who had a binding contract to purchase an interest in a passive activity on October 22, 1986 would qualify under the phase-in rules.

Taxpayers who own interests in passive activities acquired both before and after October 22, 1986 will be permitted to apply the phase-in percentages (described below) only to the *lesser* of (1) their passive activity loss for the taxable year (including passive losses and passive income from *all* interests) or (2) the passive activity loss for the year attributable only to interests acquired before October 22, 1986.

Taxpayers who acquired interests after October 22, 1986 in passive activities that provide passive income for the year reduce the amount of passive losses that would otherwise be deductible under the phase-in rules for interests acquired before October 22, 1986. The passive losses from the preenactment interests must first be reduced by passive income from newly acquired interests before applying the phase-in percentages to determine the amount of losses that are deductible under the phase-in rule.

For example, in 1987 a taxpayer owns preenactment interests in passive activities that generate $25,000 of passive losses and acquires an interest in a passive activity that generates $10,000 of passive income. Only $15,000, the net passive loss from *all* passive activities, is eligible for deduction in 1987 (after applying the appropriate percentage as described below) and not the entire $25,000 of passive losses from preenactment interests only.

Passive activity losses or credits for any taxable year beginning in calendar years 1987 through 1990 that are attributable to interests in passive activities that qualify for the phase-in will be allowed as deductions against nonpassive income or credits against tax on nonpassive income to the extent of the percentages in the following table:

Taxable Years Beginning in:	Applicable Percentage Is:
1987	65%
1988	40
1989	20
1990	10
1991	0

Any passive loss that is disallowed for a taxable year during the phase-in period and carried forward as a suspended loss is allowable in subsequent years only to the extent that there is net passive income in the subsequent years or when there is a taxable disposition of the activity.

For example, assume that a taxpayer has a passive loss of $100 in 1987 that qualifies for the phase-in, $65 of which is allowed under the applicable phase-in percentage for the year and $35 of which is carried forward. The $35 is not allowed in a subsequent year under the phase-in percentage applying for that year. If the taxpayer has a passive loss of $35 in 1988, including the amount carried over from 1987, then no relief under the phase-in is provided. If the taxpayer has a passive loss of $50 in 1988 (consisting of the $35 of suspended losses from 1987 and $15 from 1988, all of which is attributable to preenactment interests), then $6 of losses (40 percent of the $15 loss arising in 1988) is allowed against active income under the phase-in rule. The $35 loss carryover from 1987 is disallowed in 1988 and is carried forward (along with the disallowed $9 from 1988) and allowed in any subsequent year in which the taxpayer has net passive income or in which the taxpayer makes a fully taxable disposition of his entire interest in the passive activity.

The overall effect of the passive activity loss limitation is not to *disallow* the tax benefits of a loss but to *defer* the timing of those benefits until the taxpayer recognizes income from passive activities, or until the taxpayer disposes of the entire interest in a fully taxable transaction. Consequently, the current value of any investment in a passive loss activity, relative to the value of the same investment made under the prior law, is diminished by the time value of the deferred losses.

You will have to plan carefully when evaluating any new tax-sheltered investment opportunity. The economics of the investment will be critical, as it always should have been. "Investment" planning will now be composed of two separate packages of investments: portfolio investments and passive activities. Managing the passive activity package of investments will for the next few years be a highly complicated procedure. Investors must take into account the phase-in of the passive loss rules for their existing passive activities when determining which new passive activity investments would provide the most benefits in the passive activity portfolio.

Prospective investments in rental real estate should be evaluated primarily on their potential economic return, especially by taxpayers whose adjusted gross income exceeds $100,000 (the level at which the $25,000 allowance begins to phase out). However, rental property that qualifies for rehabilitation credits or low-income housing credits may still offer some tax benefits to taxpayers with adjusted gross incomes between $100,000 and $200,000. Income-producing limited partnerships, such as nonleveraged rental real estate, will become a popular vehicle to offset passive losses from other activities. Individuals with passive activity losses and no offsetting passive activity income may find it advantageous to convert income from an active business into passive activity income by reducing the level of involvement in the business. Conversely, individuals with passive activity losses and little or no passive activity income could attempt to convert the passive activity into an activity in which they materially participate. The potential for this would be greatest for passive S corporation shareholders who have invested in a business but who have only marginally participated in its operation.

An alternative avenue of attack would be to attempt to generate passive income from a Passive Income Generator (PIG). One suggestion for creating a controllable passive activity income with which to absorb passive losses is to lease real estate or equipment to a closely held corporation. That rental income will be passive and will offset passive tax-shelter losses. However, if you lease real estate or equipment to a partnership or an S corporation, such rental income, unless paid under a binding lease in effect before February 19, 1988, is recharacterized to active income, which is ineligible to offset tax-sheltered losses.

The opportunity to create controllable passive activity income still exists, however, with a rental to a regular or C corporation.

Many taxpayers who actively participate in rental real estate activities may not realize that their effective marginal tax rate for income over $100,000 is considerably higher than 31 percent. The phase-out of the $25,000 allowance for income over $100,000 increases a taxpayer's effective marginal tax rate on income between $100,000 and $150,000 to 42.9 percent in 1988, 46.8 percent in 1989, 47.85 percent in 1990, and over 49 percent in 1991 and later years.

The following example computes the effective marginal tax rate resulting from the passive loss limitation by comparing two situations that are identical except for an additional income of $20,000 in 1988.

Example: In 1988, Mr. and Mrs. Couple have adjusted gross income of $120,000, not counting $25,000 of losses from rental real estate activities in which Mrs. Couple actively participates. Under the passive loss limitation rules, $19,000 of the real estate losses can be used to offset their other income. (The $120,000 of income phases out $10,000 of the loss that would be allowed under the rental real estate allowance. However, the amount disallowed under the $25,000 allowance phase-out is then subject to the more general passive loss rule under which only 60 percent is disallowed in 1988. Therefore, they are allowed $15,000 of losses under the $25,000 allowance rule and $4,000 under the general passive loss rule.) Consequently, their adjusted gross income is $101,000. After itemized deductions and personal exemptions, their taxable income is $90,000. Their tax liability is $22,237.

Mr. and Mrs. Family have an identical income pattern except for the fact that they have an additional $20,000 of capital gains. Under the $25,000 allowance phase-out rule, only $5,000 of their real estate losses are deductible (the $140,000 of income causes $20,000 to be phased out). Of the remaining $20,000 of loss, the general passive loss rule permits $8,000 to be deducted ($20,000 reduced by 60 percent). This produces $127,000 of adjusted gross income. With the same itemized deductions and personal exemptions, their taxable income is $116,000, and their tax liability is $30,817.

Summary:		
	Mr. and Mrs. Family's tax	$30,817
	Mr. and Mrs. Couple's tax	$22,237
	Tax on marginal income	$ 8,580

$$\text{Effective tax rate on marginal income} = \frac{\$\ 8{,}580}{\$20{,}000} = 42.9\%$$

A Deferral and Leverage

There normally are three elements that make up the typical tax shelter arrangement. One or more of these elements will be found in almost all tax shelters. The first is the *deferral concept,* in which deductions are accelerated in order to reduce the tax liability of an individual in the early years of the transaction instead of matching those deductions against the income that is eventually generated from the investment. This deferral of tax liability from the earlier years to the future years results, in effect, in an interest-free loan by the federal government, repayable when the investment either produces net taxable income, is sold, or is otherwise disposed of.

The other element of a typical tax shelter is *leverage,* in which borrowed funds are used in a taxpayer's investments to pay the expenses for which accelerated deductions are received. Your position is enhanced when the borrowing is on a nonrecourse basis, which means that you are not *personally* liable to repay loans and your personal investment risk is limited to your equity investment. Unfortunately, recent tax laws and Internal Revenue Service rulings have limited the availability of tax shelter investments with a nonrecourse-loan basis.

A third tax shelter element for many investments is the *conversion* of ordinary income to capital gains at the time of the sale or other disposition of the investment. Long-term capital gains are taxed at a *maximum* 20 percent rate. Conversion occurs when the portion of the gain reflecting the accelerated deductions taken against ordinary income is taxed as a capital gain. If you are in a lower income tax bracket in the later years, you effectively convert the tax rate as well.

The rest of this chapter will discuss several of the traditional tax shelters and examine and analyze their elements, advantages, and disadvantages. I will focus on traditional tax shelter investments—real estate, oil and gas, equipment leasing, etc. In the next chapter, I will unveil those super-sophisticated, nontraditional tax shelters that can bring your effective tax liability down to zero.

77 Real Estate

"It'd take a genius to invest in real estate and pay taxes": House Ways and Means Committee member Fortney H. (Pete) Stark, D-Calif., on the committee's decisions regarding the taxation of real estate, 1986. Of the various forms of investments available to you that involve possible tax incentives, the most

> widely used is real estate. Historically, real estate has been sold as an investment for income and long-term gain, as well as a hedge against inflation. Real estate can be purchased in the form of shopping centers, warehouse net leases, apartment buildings, residential housing, and even raw land.

In the decade before reform, one of the major reasons for the high degree of tax shelter investment in real estate was that the "at risk" rules introduced by the Tax Reform Act of 1976 did not apply to any partnership in which the principal activity was investing in real estate. The "at risk" rules limited your tax deductions to the amount you invested plus the amount of borrowed funds for which you were personally liable. Real estate tax shelters were exempt from this requirement until January 1, 1987 (Tax Reform Act of 1986).

Prior to 1987, the law provided an at-risk limitation on losses from business and income-producing activities other than real estate and certain active corporate business activities applicable to individuals and to certain closely held corporations. Taxpayers could deduct losses from an activity only to the extent of the amount they had at risk in the activity. The amount at risk is generally the sum of (1) the taxpayer's cash contributions to the activity; (2) the adjusted basis of other property contributed to the activity; and (3) recourse debt (amounts borrowed for use in the activity with respect to which the taxpayer has personal liability or has pledged property not used in the activity). Nonrecourse debt (amounts borrowed for use in the activity for which none of the participants assumes personal liability and which is secured only by the assets of the activity) is not considered an amount at risk in the activity. The amount at risk is generally increased (or decreased) each year by the taxpayer's share of income (or losses and withdrawals) from the activity.

The Tax Reform Act of 1986 applies the at-risk rules to the activity of holding real property, with an exception for *qualified nonrecourse financing*. In general, taxpayers will be considered at risk with respect to their share of any *qualified nonrecourse financing* that is secured by real property used in the activity. The term qualified nonrecourse financing means any financing that is borrowed by the taxpayer (1) with respect to the activity of holding real property; (2) from a *qualified person*, or represents a loan from a federal, state, or local government, or is guaranteed by any federal, state, or local government; (3) except to the extent provided in regulations, with respect to which no person is personally liable for repayment; and (4) which is not convertible debt.

In the case of a partnership, a partner's share of any qualified nonrecourse financing of the partnership will be determined on the basis of the partner's share of liabilities incurred in connection with the financing of the partnership.

Borrowing from a "qualified person" means (1) the loan is taken from an unrelated commercial lender, or is from or guaranteed by certain government entities; (2) the property is acquired from an unrelated person; (3) the lender is unrelated to the seller; (4) the lender or a related person does not receive a fee with respect to the taxpayer's investment in the property; (5) debt is not convertible; and (6) the nonrecourse debt does not exceed 80 percent of the credit base of the property. However, nonrecourse debt acquired from related persons may still be qualified nonrecourse financing if the financing from the related person is "commercially reasonable and on substantially the same terms as loans involving unrelated persons."

An analysis of the nontax advantages of real estate investments follows.

LEVERAGE

Leverage is the use of borrowed funds with the anticipation that the property will increase in value at a rate greater than the cost of borrowing, so that a profit will be realized not only on the investor's own money but also on the use of someone else's money. For example, if you make an investment of $100, putting up $10 in cash and borrowing $90 at an interest rate of 10 percent, at the end of the first year you will have a net cash outflow of $19 (your $10 initial investment plus $9 interest on the $90 borrowed). Assume your property increases in value 20 percent during that same period and then you sell it, paying off your $90 debt. You receive a total of $120; subtract the $99 ($90 in principal plus $9 in interest), and you have a net gain of $21. On your initial cash investment of $10, this represents a 210 percent return. You can often use borrowed capital in a real estate purchase to finance as much as 80 percent of the total cost of the property.

INFLATION HEDGE

The supply of real estate is clearly limited. For this reason, many people believe that investments in well-selected real estate can be expected to at least keep up with inflation, and perhaps even increase in value faster than inflation.

CASH FLOW

In many cases, good income-producing real property will generate a favorable cash flow. This cash flow can be augmented by increased income tax savings due to the shelter aspects of real estate investments.

EQUITY BUILDUP

Income-producing real estate may create increased liquidity. Debt reduction plus inflation may create equity that can be the source of new or additional financing.

ABILITY TO POOL CAPITAL

Syndicates or partnerships enable investors to pool their capital in order to acquire large, select properties they would not be able to buy individually.

DEDUCTIBLE EXPENSES

There are basically five different categories of expenses that are deductible on a real estate deal:

1. *Mortgage interest,* that portion of debt service payments represented by deductible interest costs.
2. *Depreciation,* an accounting adjustment that reflects the theoretical wear and tear and economic obsolescence of the property. Because of this, a portion of the income you receive is considered a return of your capital investment and not subject to tax.
3. *Operating expenses,* which include property management, maintenance, insurance, garbage removal, real estate taxes, common area utilities, etc.
4. *Construction period expenses,* deductible expenses incurred before the building is occupied, such as real estate taxes, interest on the construction loan, etc. These costs are not deductible when incurred, but must be amortized over a period of years.
5. *Fees,* a portion of the purchase price that, frequently, the seller of the property agrees to take as payment for services, resulting in an immediate deduction—for instance, guarantees for "rent up," completion, financing, etc.

Note that you can rent living space to a relative at below the fair market rate and still treat the activity as a business entitling you to deduct depreciation, utilities, insurance, and other business expenses. The Tax Court has validated this reduced rate despite a tax code requirement that relatives be charged a "fair" rent. This is because there is less risk involved in renting to a relative than to a stranger, so the relative is entitled to a discount. In one case, the court suggested that a discount of 20 percent would be reasonable (*Lee Bindseil,* T.C. Memo 1983-411).

The tax advantage of real estate results from the possibility that your deductible expenses for tax purposes may exceed your cash outflow. Only operating expenses and mortgage interest are paid in cash from property operations. As a result, your taxable income—for instance, your rental income from the property minus the expenses listed above—does not reflect the cash flow from property operations. Your true cash flow, therefore, is your taxable income or loss plus construction period expenses and fees and depreciation minus mortgage principal payments. Construction period expenses and fees are those costs normally paid when incurred from the limited partner capital contribution or from the mortgage proceeds (but not from property operations). Depreciation is, of course, not a cash expense but rather a bookkeeping entry. Mortgage principal payments are not deductible for tax purposes because they have been included in your basis of the property and are reflected for tax purposes in your depreciation deductions.

Although land itself cannot be depreciated, many land improvements may be. In Rev. Rul. 65-256, 1965-2 C.B. 52, the Internal Revenue Service ruled that the excavating, grading, and removal costs "directly associated" with the construction of buildings and paved roadways are depreciable. Such directly associated costs have included:

1. Grading and graveling of a private road to provide customers with access to a store and warehouse.
2. Plank road and filling in and grading of swampland on which a new lumberyard was constructed.
3. Expenditures for slag and for grading and building up swampland to make a level racetrack and to create roads and parking space for customers.
4. A tunnel constructed under a public road between two business buildings used by a taxpayer.
5. The cost of sidewalks, gutters, and drains constructed on a taxpayer's private property in a mill village.

Although real estate must now be depreciated over either 27.5 years (for residential) or 31.5 years (39 years for property placed in service after May 13, 1993 unless placed in service before January 1, 1994 and there was either a binding contract or construction started before May 13, 1993), taxpayers can write off *land improvements* over just 15 years, using 200 percent declining-balance depreciation.

The following computations show a hypothetical tax income statement loss and its conversion into a cash flow gain:

Tax Income Statement		
Rental Income		$500
Less:		
operating expenses	$150	
mortgage interest	250	
construction period expenses	80	
fees	25	
depreciation	+175	
	$680	
		−680
Tax Income (loss)		($180)

Cash Flow		
Tax Income (loss)		($180)
Add back:		
construction period expenses	$ 80	
fees	25	
depreciation	+175	
	$280	
		$100
Minus mortgage principal payments		− 25
Cash Flow from property operations		$ 75

At a 31 percent marginal tax bracket you would save $56 in taxes and have a positive total cash flow of $131 ($56 + $75).

Moreover, the normal real estate tax shelter is usually structured so that any actual cash losses in the first years will be provided, or paid for, by the limited partners' capital contribution or the proceeds of the mortgage itself. This item is referred to as "rent-up loss"—the operating deficit during the period before the property is fully rented.

SUMMARY OF BENEFITS

As the preceding statements indicate, there are a number of benefits achieved from real estate tax shelter investing. The bottom line of the tax income statement shows your taxable loss. Multiply this figure by your tax bracket to determine your tax savings.

The cash flow statement represents the cash distributions you will be paid from the property's operations. Add to this the cash in pocket from the above tax savings and that yields your net cash increase in wealth.

An additional benefit that investing in real estate tax shelters will yield is equity buildup. This is the amount of the mortgage principal that you are paying off each year. Even if the property value merely remains flat with no appreciation, your equity interest in that property will increase each year by the principal payoff.

The final benefit from such an investment is the potential appreciation in the property itself. Building costs are rising with inflation, so it is likely that in ten years the replacement cost of real estate will be much higher than construction costs today. If a property is well located and well maintained, its cash flow should expand over the years and its value should increase.

Before investing in a shelter you must recognize that real estate projects fall into three major categories:

Commercial
Residential
Government-supported housing

REHABILITATION—CERTIFIED HISTORICAL CREDITS

Each category of investment has its own rules and deduction limits for tax purposes. For example, rehabilitation costs on low-income housing and certified historic structures can still qualify for investment tax credits. For a building in service before 1936 (other than a certified historic structure), the credit is 10 percent; for a certified residential or commercial historic structure, the credit increases to 20 percent! This means that you get the equivalent of one-fifth off your rehabilitation expenses. If you use the rehabilitation credit, however, you must use straight-line depreciation, reduce the base by the full amount of its credit, and make a substantial rehabilitation of the building. This means that the qualifying expenditures of the tax year and the preceding tax year must exceed the adjusted basis of the property or $5,000, whichever is larger. For rehabilitations completed in phases, the 24-month measuring period is extended to 60 months. In addition, to qualify for the credit one of the following three tests must be met:

a) At least 50 percent of the external walls are retained as external walls;

b) at least 75 percent of the external walls are retained as either external or internal walls; and

c) at least 75 percent of the internal structural framework is retained in place.

Under government-sponsored housing, you can deduct construction loan interest and taxes immediately; with other real estate you must amortize them over four years. Furthermore, an owner of a subsidized housing project may defer any taxes due on the sale of the project if it is sold to a tenant cooperative and the proceeds reinvested in another subsidized housing project within one year.

The new rehabilitation credit may be used to offset tax on up to $25,000 of nonpassive income, regardless of whether the individual actively participates, subject to a phase out between $200,000 and $250,000 of adjusted gross income.

Parties interested in obtaining further information on historic preservation opportunities and procedures should contact the various agencies and organizations listed below.

Copies of historic preservation standards and guidelines set forth by the government for certifying historic structures and a current list of state historic preservation offices are available by writing to the following address:

Tax Reform Act
Office of Archaeology and Historic Preservation
Department of the Interior
Washington, DC 20240

The following is the address of the historic preservation agency that administers the Department of the Interior's preservation tax incentive program:

Historic Preservation Tax Incentives
Archaeology and Historic Preservation
National Park Service
Washington, DC 20240

The following regional offices of the National Park Service review certification applications:

Regional Office	*States Administered for Tax Certification Purposes*
Mid-Atlantic 143 South Third Street Philadelphia, PA 19106 (215)597-7013	Connecticut, Delaware, District of Columbia, Maine, Maryland, Massachusetts, New Hampshire, New Jersey, New York, Pennsylvania, Rhode Island, Vermont, Virginia, West Virginia
Southeast 75 Spring Street, NW Atlanta, GA 30303 (404)242-2635	Alabama, Florida, Georgia, Kentucky, Mississippi, North Carolina, Puerto Rico, South Carolina, Tennessee
Midwest Federal Building 200 East Liberty Street Ann Arbor, MI 48107 (313)378-2035	Illinois, Indiana, Iowa, Kansas, Michigan, Minnesota, Missouri, Nebraska, Ohio, Wisconsin
Rocky Mountain P.O. Box 25287 Denver Federal Center Denver, CO 80225 (303)234-2915	Colorado, Montana, North Dakota, South Dakota, Utah, Wyoming
Southwest 5000 Marble Street, NE Room 211 Albuquerque, NM 87110 (505)474-3514	Arkansas, Louisiana, New Mexico, Oklahoma, Texas
West 450 Golden Gate Avenue P.O. Box 36063 San Francisco, CA 94102 (415)556-7741 or 556-7090	Arizona, California, Hawaii, Nevada

Pacific Northwest Westin Building, Room 1920 2110 Sixth Avenue Seattle, WA 98121 (206) 399-0791	Idaho, Oregon, Washington
Alaska 1011 East Tudor Street Suite 297 Anchorage, AK 99503 (907) 277-1666	Alaska

The National Trust for Historic Preservation, a private, nonprofit membership organization, provides advice on preservation issues and techniques. For more information on membership, write:

National Trust for Historic Preservation
1785 Massachusetts Avenue, NW
Washington, DC 20036

The regional offices of the National Trust are as follows:

Regional Office	*States and Territories Administered*
Northeast 100 Franklin Street, 7th Floor Boston, MA 02110 (617) 223-7754	Connecticut, Maine, Massachusetts, New Hampshire, New York, Rhode Island, Vermont
Mid-Atlantic 1600 H Street, NW Washington, DC 20006 (202) 673-4203	Delaware, District of Columbia, Maryland, New Jersey, Pennsylvania, Puerto Rico, Virgin Islands, Virginia, West Virginia
South 456 King Street Charleston, SC 29403 (803) 724-4711	Alabama, Arkansas, Florida, Georgia, Kentucky, Louisiana, Mississippi, North Carolina, South Carolina, Tennessee

Regional Office	*States and Territories Administered*
Midwest 407 South Dearborn Street Number 710 Chicago, IL 60605 (312)353-3419 or 353-3424	Illinois, Indiana, Iowa, Michigan, Minnesota, Missouri, North Dakota, Ohio, South Dakota, Wisconsin
Southwest/Plains 210 Colcord Building Oklahoma City, OK 73102 (405)231-5126	Colorado, Kansas, Nebraska, New Mexico, Oklahoma, Texas
West 681 Market Street, Number 859 San Francisco, CA 94105 (415)556-2707	Alaska, Arizona, California, Guam, Hawaii, Idaho, Micronesia, Montana, Nevada, Oregon, Utah, Washington, Wyoming

The combination of first-year accelerated depreciation and heavy start-up costs may produce tax deductions exceeding the size of your initial cash investment when 80 percent of the cost of that investment is financed with borrowings. What that means is that if you are in the 31 percent bracket, your net initial cash outlay may be reduced to zero! However, with any tax shelter, as with any investment, *never* invest just on the basis of tax deductions alone. You must always consider the total expected cash flow from the property. The advantages of a real estate tax shelter are that the risks are normally minimal and the total cash flow is normally augmented in the early years by substantial tax savings. Furthermore, a good shelter should be structured to give you substantial cash rental income that is either minimally taxed or not taxed at all due to offsetting depreciation expense deductions even in the middle years. These depreciation deductions are pencil transactions that do not involve any real cash outflow, and they arise out of basis created by borrowed money. In effect, with a properly structured transaction you get to eat your cake and keep it too.

LOW-INCOME HOUSING CREDITS

Moreover, the Tax Reform Act of 1986 created a new low-income housing credit. This housing credit is claimed annually over a 10-year period with percentages set so that over that 10-year period, the credits will equal a present value of 70 percent of the basis of a new building which is not federally subsidized and 30 percent of the basis of an existing building or federally subsidized new building. The credit applies only to expenditures on the low-income units, and rehabilitation expenditures will qualify for the credit only if they exceed $2,000 per unit.

A building will qualify for the credit if either at least 20 percent of the units are occupied by individuals with incomes of 60 percent or less of area median income, or if at least 40 percent of the units are occupied by individuals with incomes of 50 percent or less of area median income. Furthermore, the rent charged to tenants may not exceed 30 percent of the applicable qualified income, which will vary depending on family size.

If a building is placed in service in 1987, the credit percentages are 9 percent annually over 10 years (that equates to the 70 percent present value credit), and/or 4 percent over 10 years (that equates to the 30 percent present value credit).

If a building is placed in service after 1987, the credit percentages will be adjusted monthly by the Treasury to reflect the present values of 70 percent and 30 percent at the time the building is placed in service. In a project consisting of two or more buildings placed in service in different months, a separate credit percentage may apply to each building.

One additional word on real estate tax shelters. The Senate Report on the Tax Reform Act of 1986 (S. Rep. at 742) states that hotel and motel properties are not considered to be rental activities, and thus are not per se designated as passive. Consequently, if a real estate investor holds hotel and motel property either through a general partnership interest or ownership in an S Corporation, and if that investor actively manages the property, it may be possible to have these properties designated as active businesses. In this case, the investor would be able to utilize losses from the property to offset other income. In order to qualify as an active manager, you must "materially participate" in the running of the hotel business. You should attempt to do each of the following:

1. Make frequent visits to the hotel for on-site inspections and consultations with the firm managing your condo.
2. Regularly establish room rental rates.
3. Set up and review hiring and other personnel policies.
4. Review and approve periodic financial reports.
5. Participate in budgeting operating costs and establishing capital expenditures.
6. Establish the need and level of financial resources.
7. Select the bank depository for rental proceeds and reserves.
8. Assist in off-site business promotion activities.

Alternatively, if the hotel or motel is producing taxable income, holding such property through a limited partnership interest would characterize the income generated therefrom as passive. By eliminating hotel or motel properties from the rental income classification, the Tax Reform Act presents a unique planning opportunity with respect to such properties. Such ownership gives you, the investor, the opportunity to classify the activities as either active or passive, depending upon which planning approach you choose to undertake.

Watch out for fees in many limited partnership deals. A typical limited partnership will pay 7 to 10 percent of equity in sales commissions; 1 to 3 percent or more of the equity raised for legal, accounting, and paperwork expenses; and up to 15 percent of the equity for organization and mortgage finding fees. Later, sponsors may take 5 to 6 percent of the cash flow in property management fees. After the property is sold, 3 to 6 percent of the sales price may go for commissions, and an additional 10 to 33 percent of any profit on the sale may go to the sponsors. Clearly, the greater the front-end fee, the less money is left to invest in property. According to Arnold G. Rudoff, who analyzes partnerships for the accounting firm of Price Waterhouse in San Francisco, real estate front-end fees should be under 20 percent.

According to a survey by the accounting firm of Coopers & Lybrand, privately offered real estate partnership transactions showed the following fees and structure:

	Typical	*Range*
Partnership participation		
Cash flow	10%	1–10%
Tax benefits	10%	1–10%
Refinancing/disposition (subordinated)	20%	15–30%
Initial fees (as % of equity raised)		
Sales commission	8%	6–10%
Acquisition and ancillary fees	30%	15–60%
Operating period (as % of revenues)		
Property management	4%	3–6%
Partnership management	Modest	Modest
Reimbursable expenses	Modest	Modest
Disposition fees		
Real estate commission	3%	Competitive
Participation in residual value	20%	15–30%

One measure of the fairness of offering terms is how the various fees relate to the North American Securities Administrators Association (NASAA) guidelines. These guidelines appear in the next section.

78 Fees in Public Real Estate Partnerships

Front-end fees include sales commissions for the broker/dealer, offering and organization costs, and property acquisition fees paid to the general partner and unaffiliated third parties. The NASAA front-end fee standard is 20 percent of limited partner capital contributions for unleveraged properties, 28.1 percent for 50 percent leveraged properties, and 33 percent for 80 percent leveraged properties.

Operational phase fees are typically paid to the general partner from cash flow (earnings) of the real estate as compensation for management of the day-to-day operation of the partnership and the properties. NASAA approves "property management fees" equal to 6 percent of gross revenues for residential properties and 3 percent of gross revenues for commercial properties, plus a "promotional" interest of 10 percent of annual cash flow (if the liquidation phase fee from net proceeds, explained below, is limited to 15 percent).

Liquidation phase fees are payable to the general partner upon resale or refinancing of the properties. These fees consist of a real estate commission and a percentage of the net proceeds from the sale or refinancing of the property. Normally, these fees are subordinated (not paid to the general partner) until the return of the limited partners' investment, plus a minimum return. NASAA approves a real estate commission to all parties, not to exceed 3 percent. The promotional or incentive fee is limited to 15 percent if the sponsor also received 10 percent of annual cash flow, or 25 percent otherwise. The real estate commission and the appreciation percentage are "subordinated" to the return of limited partner capital, plus a minimum return of 6 percent per annum on initial capital reduced by periodic cash distributions.

79 Oil and Gas

Petroleum and gas are important sources of energy throughout the world. Accordingly, Congress has determined that certain types of investments in oil and gas are deductible. Former Attorney General Smith invested in an oil and gas partnership. An investment in an oil and gas program is probably your most advantageous single-year tax-advantaged investment if the economics are viable.

The tax advantage in an oil and gas deal is the ability to deduct, as a current expense, the investments in capital expenditures known as intangible drilling and developing costs, or IDCs. The income tax regulations define *intangibles* as any cost incurred that has no salvage value and is "incident to and necessary for the drilling of wells and the preparation of wells for the production of oil and gas." This definition includes the hours worked by the drilling crew and the cost of the installation of tangible equipment placed *in the well,* although the cost of such equipment must be capitalized and recovered through depreciation. Expressly excluded from classification as *intangibles* are expenditures incurred in connection with equipment, facilities, or structures (including installation charges) that are not incident to or necessary for the drilling of oil or gas wells but are used in operations after the oil or gas is produced (for instance, structures for storing and treating oil or gas).

Essentially, then, nearly all costs of drilling and completing a well, except for the bare cost of the lease, the cost of tangible equipment and labor, and the geological and geophysical costs incurred prior to the selection of a drill site, are deductible in the year incurred. Without this special break accorded to intangible drilling and development costs, you would be unable to deduct them until drilling was either abandoned or the product was actually being extracted from the wells.

In the first year you are able immediately to deduct 70 percent to 80 percent of productive-well costs as intangible expenses, and 100 percent of dry well costs. In many public tax shelter programs, you pay for only intangible costs and can therefore immediately deduct up to 100 percent of the amount you invest.

There is a catch: with gas and oil deals the Internal Revenue Service will not permit deductions in excess of your personal cash investment, or "at risk" basis. In the past, however, it did permit the year-end deduction of all the intangible costs of wells even if those wells were not actually to be drilled until the following year. (Thus promoters of oil and gas shelters tried to "front load" deductions in the initial year of the shelter by prepayment of intangible costs.) In all other tax shelters, legislation has ruled out retroactive allocations of losses for year-end investments; it also no longer allows immediate deductions for many expenses that are incurred prior to actual operations—for example, cattle feeding programs—unless there is a clear business purpose. And on St.

Patrick's Day, 1980, the Internal Revenue Service asserted that prepaid intangible drilling costs *also* must be disallowed as a deduction in the year paid—unless the taxpayer can demonstrate the existence of some commercial exigency making it advisable to prepay the costs.[1]

In an Eighth Circuit 1984 Court of Appeals Case (*Keller,* 84-1 USTC Par. 9194, 53 AFTR2d 84-663), the Court found that prepayments for intangible costs served no business purpose and materially distorted the taxpayer's income. The taxpayer's deduction, therefore, was deferred until the subsequent year.

The Keller case, however, did not involve a "turnkey" contract. In fact, the Court found that with a "turnkey" contract, where the amounts expended could not be refunded, a prepayment would be deductible in the year paid. This was a validation of the general rule that intangible drilling and development costs under a "turnkey" agreement were deductible in the year paid (*Ruth,* T.C. Memo 1983-586).

Furthermore, the Tax Reform Act of 1984 provided that "tax shelters" (other than forming syndicates), whether on the cash or accrual method, will not be able to deduct prepaid expenses until both economic performance occurs and the expenses actually paid are incurred. A deduction, however, will be allowed for prepaid expenses where economic performance occurs after the end of the year under the following conditions:

1. economic performance occurs within 90 days after the end of the taxable year;
2. the deduction is limited to the cash investment made by the person (i.e., not paid for with any recourse or nonrecourse liabilities); *and*
3. the requirements of present laws are met.

For purposes of this exception in the case of intangible drilling expenses, economic performance occurs when the well is "spudded." If oil and gas prepayments do not meet the requirements of the 90-day exception, economic performance will occur as the drilling services are provided. If drilling is commenced in the year of prepayment (and the above exception is not met), only that portion of the intangible drilling cost attributable to drilling prior to the end of the year will be deductible in that year. This provision applies for pre-

1. Rev. Rul. 80-71, I.R.B. 1980-11, 7.

payments made after March 31, 1984, and enhances the potential significance of a “turnkey” contract.

Note, in addition, that working interest in any oil or gas property that you hold directly or through an entity that does not limit your liability with respect to such interest will be treated as an active trade or business and will not be subject to the passive loss rules.

TAX SHELTER STRATEGIES

A sophisticated shelter will sustain the current deductibility of an intangible drilling cost prepayment by the following techniques:

- The prepayment requirements should be set forth in the contract.
- The contract should set forth the particular well to be drilled and provide for a definite commencement date.
- If it is a co-owner situation, the same prepayment requirement should be imposed on other co-owners.
- The contract should be with the actual driller, if possible, and not with an intermediary.
- There should be a business benefit to be derived from the prepayment requirement (that is, the price might be lower if the driller is paid in advance).
- The contract should be binding on the driller.
- Prepayment should not be more than a reasonable estimate of the amount to come due to the driller.
- The payments should actually be made prior to the end of the year, and the driller’s access to the funds should not be restricted (that is, payment into an escrow account may not constitute a valid prepayment).

Additional tax shelter is still available through your ability to take 200 percent declining-balance depreciation on the remaining 20 to 30 percent of the costs of the wells (capitalized costs). A statutory depletion deduction (one that is provided by law), which is 15 percent of your gross income from the well before expenses, also is available.

After the development of the property and the drilling are completed, the program will begin to receive cash from oil or gas sales, if any successful wells are drilled. If receipts exceed operating and overhead costs as well as depletion and depreciation, you will have taxable income.

The depletion allowance you are allowed to claim is the *greater* of cost depletion or percentage depletion.

COST DEPLETION

Cost depletion is computed by dividing the estimated total units (barrels of oil or thousand cubic feet of gas) recoverable from the property into its adjusted tax basis in order to obtain the per-unit depletion allowance, and then multiplying the per-unit depletion allowance by the number of units sold during the year. Cost depletion is then compared to percentage depletion on a property-by-property basis to determine the amount to be deducted.

PERCENTAGE DEPLETION

Percentage depletion for up to 1,000 barrels of average daily production of oil or 6 million cubic feet of domestic natural gas is allowed to "independent producers and royalty owners" at the rate of 15 percent of gross revenue. This depletion allowance is limited to 50 percent of the net income from the property. The allowance calculated is further limited to 65 percent of your taxable income (prior to taking the depletion allowance). The 65 percent limitation and average daily production limitation are calculated at the individual investor or partner level.

Both cost and percentage depletion are computed separately for *each* property in which you have an interest. Percentage depletion at the applicable statutory rate is computed on *gross* income from the property before deductions of any kind, including production or windfall profit taxes, operating expenses, or depreciation. Accordingly, the benefit obtained is significantly more than the statutory rate as a percentage of net (taxable) income.

The Supreme Court has ruled, in *Commissioner v. Engle et ux.*, S. Ct. Docket 82-599, that lessors of interests in mineral deposits are entitled to percentage depreciation allowances on any bonus or advanced royalties whether or not there is actual production of the underlying mineral in the year of payment. Production, therefore, has been found not to be a prerequisite for claiming percentage depletion deductions on lease bonus and advanced royalty income.

Percentage depletion is almost always larger than cost depletion. For example, if a well is drilled on a lease that cost $2,000 and yields an estimated 100,000 barrels of recoverable reserves, the rate of cost depletion for that property would be 2¢ per barrel of oil produced. This is far less than percentage depletion at the applicable rate. Fifteen percent of the gross income of oil selling at $20 per barrel is $3.00. The net impact of the depreciation and depletion deductions is that with normal operating expenses, from about a quarter to a third of your income from the well is tax-free.

Oil and gas drilling tax shelter programs break down into three types:

1. *Wildcatting,* also known as exploratory drilling, which involves drilling operations in search of a yet-undiscovered pool of oil or gas, or with the hope of greatly extending the limits of a pool already developed. It is an attempt to find new fields where the probability of success for an individual well may be 10 percent and the chances of "proving," or discovering, a big field are about 1 percent to 2 percent.

2. *Development drilling,* which involves drilling an additional well to a reservoir that supports an already-producing well on a lease or on an offset lease that is usually close to or adjacent to the producing well. Development wells can have success rates of from 75 percent to 100 percent, but real fortunes are made only by "proving" a big field and selling or developing it.

3. *Balanced or combination programs,* which involve both exploratory and development drilling, therefore promising up-side potential with limited downside risk. Unfortunately, most balanced programs combine wildcatting's delayed significant cash flow (three years can be common) with a development program's low multiple cash return (on average, 2.5 × the cash investment).

Unlike most investments, investments in oil and gas exploration may result in a complete loss. Industry statistics reflect that about 1 out of 10 wildcat wells is productive and that many of the productive wells do not have sufficient reserves to cover the drilling, equipping, and operating costs of the wildcat venture. Approximately 1 out of 200 wildcat wells discovers a medium-size field, and only 1 out of 1,000 discovers a large field. As indicated by the statistics, investments in oil and gas exploration should be spread over a sufficient number of prospects to provide you with a reasonable expectation of a return on your investment.

If you are interested in entering the oil business, there are several ways to participate, including the following:

- Participation with an oil operator on a selective basis for fractional interest in a number of oil and gas prospects.
- Participation with several different oil operators for a fractional interest in selected oil and gas prospects.
- Investments in a limited partnership with one or more oil and gas prospects.
- Various combinations of these.

NONTAX CONSIDERATIONS

In addition to the tax considerations discussed above, you must examine the following nontax considerations if you want to get involved with oil and gas.

Management

Management in the oil business is of primary importance. The ability to operate an oil and gas investment program successfully consists basically of two skills: technical expertise and administrative competence. The organization must have the technical expertise to assemble prospects, select drilling sites, supervise the drilling and completion of wells, operate productive wells, and market the output. The competence of the technical staff is extremely difficult to evaluate on a short-run basis, since entirely new prospects are assembled and drilled each year.

Program Size

There is no optimum program size. However, the size of the technical and administrative staffs will dictate certain minimum and maximum projects that can be undertaken. The program should have enough capital to drill a sufficient number of prospects for a reasonable spread of the risks; also, a minimum amount of capital must be raised to be used for administrative costs associated with offering the program and other administrative matters.

The area in which operations will be conducted is also important. A $5 million program that will explore an area where the average well costs $400,000 could offer a satisfactory spread of risk. A $5 million program exploring in areas where the average well costs $1.5 million may *not* offer an adequate spread. The geographic area in which the technical staff has expertise should also be considered. A technical staff with operating experience in Colorado and Wyoming may not be qualified to conduct operations in Texas and Louisiana.

Past Performance

One of the most important nontax considerations that you must examine is the drilling company's past record of performance. You should measure and compare the net future revenues from proven oil and gas reserves in relation to limited partner capital contributions. Use only proven reserves, not what are called probable or possible reserves. Examine the price escalation figures and use only formulas provided by an independent reserve engineering firm.

Do not focus on past performance success ratios or cash distribution tables. The success ratio is the percent of all wells drilled that are completed as producing wells. A better success ratio does not necessarily mean a better economic result. For example, drilling in the Appalachian Basin (Ohio and West Virginia) should be successful 90 percent of the time, while drilling in Louisiana may be successful only perhaps 30 percent or 40 percent of the time. Why then should you invest in a project that drills in Louisiana? The answer is more abundant reserves and a potentially greater return on investment.

The cash distribution tables show the cash actually paid out to the investor. These can be deceiving in that some types of wells pay (or produce) over 50 percent of all that they will ever pay out in the first two years of their productive life; after the first four years, they do not produce any significant revenues. Other types of wells produce a lower percentage in their earlier life but continue to produce for as long as 20 to 30 years.

Management Costs

An additional nontax risk of oil and gas deals is the overpricing of the leases so that various parties in the promotional and marketing chain can realize this compensation from the initial capital invested. As compensation, the general partner and/or operator may receive up to 25 percent of the revenues earned by the limited partners after paying oil and gas royalties to the land owner and other promotional interests. In addition, there is usually a first-year management fee of about 5 percent of the amount of the investment.

Generally, you should expect to hold your interest in the well for its lifetime. Your investment is a capital asset and if sold should produce capital gains. But if the well is sold, then a portion of the intangible drilling costs deducted during the developmental phase of the shelter may be "recaptured" and treated as ordinary income, as may some of the depreciation taken. Many public programs offer buy-back provisions after two or three years of operation, but generally you will receive a better return if you wait five to seven years. With a successful shelter, you might well be advised to retain your interest in the shelter, collect the cash flow from the sale of the oil, and shelter this income with percentage depletion. It is not normally recommended that you buy the interest of an original investor as a tax shelter. This is because although percentage depletion is available to investors who are in a successful oil deal during the developmental phase, an investor who purchases the interest of the original investor in the deal is purchasing a "proven property" and therefore is not entitled to percentage depletion deductions.

Compensation

If you are interested in involving yourself as an active developer of oil and gas properties, you should note that compensation paid in oil rights potentially can be tax free. In Letter Ruling 813-7006, the Internal Revenue Service held that a consultant who contributed only services to the pool of capital, acquiring in return an interest in the minerals (oil) in place, is not required to include that interest in his income. The same reasoning has been extended to accountants, lawyers, geologists, petroleum engineers, and lease brokers who receive an interest in an oil or gas drilling venture in return for services rendered. The contributors are not viewed as performing services for compensation but are viewed as acquiring capital interests through making a contribution to the pool of capital that is necessary for development (see Rev. Rul. 77-176, 1977-1 C.B. 78, and G.C.M. 22730, 1941-1 C.B. 214, but see Rev. Rul. 83-46, where overriding royalty interest to a corporate promoter, an attorney, and an employee were found to be includable in gross income at fair market value immediately. See also Rev. Proc. 93-27, 6/9/93, where a partnership profit interest received for services was not a taxable event.)

STRUCTURING A SUCCESSFUL OIL OR GAS TAX SHELTER

Assume that you are in the 43 percent bracket, including not only federal taxes but state and local income taxes as well. You invest $50,000 in an oil program in which 80 percent of your investment is deductible as intangible drilling costs. The remaining 20 percent is depreciated and deducted on a ten-year straight-line basis. Assume in addition that the well produces a lifetime total income of only $50,000.

First Year

IDC deduction (80% of $50,000)	$40,000
Plus depreciation deduction (1/10 of 20% of $50,000)	+ 1,000
	41,000
First-year net cost [$50,000 – ($41,000 × .43)]	$32,370

Subsequent Years' Total

Total income		$50,000
Depletion sheltered (15% × $50,000)	$ 7,500	
Plus depreciation (9/10 of 20% of $50,000)	+ 9,000	
Nontaxable cash income	$16,500	
Plus after-tax cash from taxable income [$33,500 – (.43 × $33,500)]	+19,095	
After-tax return		$35,595
Minus first-year net cost		−32,370
Net Cash Return		$ 3,225

Note that while no allowance for discounting future income to present value is made in the above analysis, if your oil or gas investment returns a total income at least equal to your initial cash investment, it will be at least marginally successful. Any excess return over your initial investment will substantially multiply your yield on that investment, especially on an after-tax basis.

SELF-EMPLOYMENT TAX TECHNIQUES

The Tax Reform Act of 1986 has made purchasing a working interest in oil and gas wells a popular technique by allowing a working interest owner to escape the passive loss rules and claim drilling costs against other income, such as salaries, interest, or dividends. An interesting opportunity has recently been created with respect to self-employment tax on oil and gas income. The IRS has taken the position that a working interest constitutes a trade or business for purposes of the self-employment (social security) tax. It is irrelevant whether operations were conducted by the working interest owner or by a third party. In that case, the IRS viewed the third-party operator as acting as the agent for the owner (Rev. Rul. 58-166). The position of the Internal Revenue Service, therefore, was that any income from a working interest in a gas or oil well constituted self-employment income. Such income or such losses were therefore added or subtracted if the taxpayer was not over the social security maximum with compensation from other employment and the like. Such income, however, would qualify for a Keogh contribution.

In *Howard W. Hendrickson,* T.C. Memo 1987-566, November 12, 1987, the Tax Court ruled that a salesman who had no experience in the oil and gas industry and who purchased a 21.875 percent interest in a gas well, as well as similar interest in two other wells, was not in the trade or business of producing oil and gas and therefore was not subject to self-employment tax.

These conflicting opinions allow you the following choice. If you are under the social security maximum and have losses from a working interest in a gas or oil well, the IRS position should be adopted to further reduce your potential self-employment taxes. However, if you have gains from a working interest and are not at the social security maximum, and *if you fit within the parameters* of the *Hendrickson* case, you should adopt the position of the Tax Court and not increase your self-employment income for social security tax purposes. [Note that the Tax Court, in *Cokes,* 91 T.C. 222 (1988) and *Perry,* T.C. Memo 1994-215, came to a conclusion in opposition to *Hendrickson.* The facts in those cases, however, were different.]

80 Equipment Leasing

Leasing, as a method of financing capital assets for industry, has grown tremendously in recent years and can be a good tax shelter. According to the National Association of Securities Dealers, equipment leasing deals have been the fastest growing category of direct placement programs (tax shelters). Capital assets frequently financed by leasing include computers, airplanes, railroad rolling stock, ships, pollution control equipment, and industrial machinery.

A lease contract allows the lessee to use the equipment for a specified length of time in return for periodic rental payments. While a variety of lease contracts have been developed, such contracts will normally be classified either as finance (full-payout) leases or as operating (non-full-payout) leases.

Finance leases provide the lessor with recovery of the cost and a reasonable profit from rentals and tax benefits over the original noncancelable lease term. These leases may be leveraged or nonleveraged. A leveraged lease is one in which the lessor has financed a significant portion (typically up to 80 percent) of the equipment purchased from third-party lenders. In the case of a nonleveraged lease, the lessor provides 100 percent of the equipment cost, either entirely through equity or by a combination of equity and recourse debt (a debt on which you are personally liable). Finance leases are almost invariably net leases—that is, the lessee is obligated to pay for most of the expenses, such as maintenance and property taxes associated with the equipment and insurance.

Operating leases do not provide the lessor with a return of cost over the initial noncancelable lease term. In order to realize a profit, lessors rely on their ability to sell or re-lease the equipment profitably at the end of the initial lease term. An operating lease may or may not be a net lease. It is not unusual for lessors writing operating leases to provide other services, such as maintenance and repair, along with the equipment.

The typical format of an equipment leasing transaction includes the following:

- Purchase of the equipment by a limited partnership (or direct ownership by the investor) for a cash down payment plus financing (either recourse or nonrecourse) for the balance of the purchase price.
- The equipment is then typically leased as either a full-payout finance lease or an operating lease.
- The lease may grant an option to purchase the equipment at a specified price at its fair market value.
- The lease may contain renewal options.

NONTAX CONSIDERATIONS

As an investor-owner, you must be aware of several nontax considerations. First, with a normal financing lease, you are in effect making a loan to the lessee of the purchase price of the equipment. Under an equipment leasing deal, you normally will have a greater economic return than you could realize on a conventional loan transaction.

Alternatively, since you are the owner of the equipment, you must take the risk of technological improvements—for instance, the obsolescence of the equipment. This risk can be modified by leasing on what is known as a "hell and high water" basis. Under such an arrangement, the lessee is obligated to make lease payments whether or not continued use of the equipment is desired. In effect, you are shifting the risk of obsolescence to the lessee. But as a result of that shift, you will receive reduced lease payments.

In addition, you must face a credit risk. Will the lessee be financially able to meet the lease payments? If not, your cash flow will be terminated and you will have to find another lessee.

There is also an interest risk. You as a lessor are essentially extending credit throughout the lease term at a fixed rate, while at the same time you may obtain your funds at variable rates—usually from banks at the prime rate or higher. In addition, your total annual debt service cost can be quite a bit higher than the interest charge alone because of the repayment of principal. If the interest rates on your borrowing increase, they can completely eliminate your return. When the cost of debt service exceeds the cash flow from the property, you have what is known as "negative leverage." Under these circumstances, your only real alternative is to repay the debt.

Finally, the residual value risk must be considered. Will the property be worth the anticipated amount at the end of the lease term? If not, your return could be significantly reduced.

There are also some nontax considerations for the lessee. Normally, the lessee will be making lease rental payments in amounts less than the direct purchase price of the equipment, even if paid on an installment basis.

In many cases, the lessee is cash poor or has limited borrowing capacity, and an equipment leasing arrangement reduces short-term cash outlay. In some cases, equipment leasing tax shelters may be structured in a sale leaseback format: The lessee originally owns the equipment but sells it to meet an immediate cash need. Under the terms of sale, the lessee turns around and leases the equipment from the buyer-lessor. Such a transaction will immediately augment the lessee's short-term cash position.

TAX BENEFITS

The key tax benefit that results from equipment leasing is deferral, which is a means of postponing a tax liability until a later and more convenient time. In years when your tax liability is high, you can invest in an equipment leasing program. You deduct a large amount of depreciation in the first year, along with miscellaneous front-end expenses and interest on the borrowed capital. After the first three to five years, the lease will begin generating taxable income because depreciation and interest will have been reduced. Be aware, though, that there may not be any cash income paid to you because of the debt service payments due on the borrowed money. However, you should note that by the time you start receiving taxable income prior to sufficient tax-flow generation, you will have had the use and yield on the considerable tax savings for a significant period of time.

DEPRECIATION

The deferral advantage of equipment leasing discussed above comes mainly from depreciation. The accelerated depreciation rate is 200 percent of straight-line depreciation. Furthermore, what is known as "the half-year convention" is automatically imputed in the ACRS depreciation tables. The half-year convention allows a person who puts equipment into service anytime during the year to depreciate that equipment as though that person had had it for half the entire year. However, the Tax Reform Act of 1986 provides that a mid-quarter convention be applied to all property that is more than 40 percent of all property placed in service by a taxpayer during the last three months of the taxable year. This mid-quarter convention treats all property placed in service during any quarter of a taxable year as placed in service on the midpoint of such quarter. Moreover, if the leasing constitutes a trade or business, you now have the option of expensing up to $19,000 (in 1999) in personal property immediately rather than over time through depreciation deductions.

In addition, as an investor, you should recognize that you would normally need a long-term, full-recourse loan to help buy the equipment. Otherwise, the depreciation that you take will quickly exceed your cash basis, and you will not be able to take any further deductions. What this means is that you should be extremely careful in leasing the equipment. Your major risks are residual value and that the lessee will default, so a good equipment leasing program will involve major corporations with superior credit ratings. With such programs, your effective risk is minimal.

SUMMARY OF ADVANTAGES

By taking accelerated depreciation on the equipment over a life shorter than your loan repayment period, you can obtain substantial cash-flow benefits from federal income tax deferrals over the first few years of ownership. The total cash required to be put up is normally only about 20 percent of the cost of the equipment. These funds become available due to the tax deductions resulting from the purchase. Your tax deductions in each of the first few years of the transaction will be a significant multiple of the cash invested in that year. Substantial deductions will also normally be enjoyed for several more years.

You will enjoy an interest-free loan as a result of the transaction. If a reasonable value is attributed to the use of the funds produced by the interest-free loan, you will normally secure a return of your original investment in the equipment even if the equipment has less than the originally anticipated residual value at the end of the lease. An economic return over and above the profits earned on the interest-free loan is normally provided from re-lease revenues generated by the equipment at the end of the initial lease and by full payment of your bank debt.

81 Single-Premium Life Insurance

Prior to the Technical and Miscellaneous Revenue Act of 1988 (TAMRA), single-premium life insurance was one of the last remaining quality tax shelters. With single-premium life insurance, for a single lump sum, which may range from $1,000 to $5 million, a policyholder receives a little insurance protection and a big tax-deferred investment account. Single-premium life insurance offers a tax-free buildup of cash along with life insurance. Unlike universal life, the policy carries just enough insurance to qualify for tax-free status under the Internal Revenue Code. Therefore, more of the premium goes toward earning tax-deferred interest rather than buying insurance.

In fact, some experts have said that the insurance is a "free" bonus, since most single-premium policies quote a net rate of return. There are no fees or up-front commissions. That means that all of your cash immediately starts growing at the full rate quoted.

In the case of single-premium whole life, there is usually a 4 percent minimum guaranteed return. With an investment in single-premium variable life, like other variable products, there are no guaranteed rates of return, but the policyholder can pick his investments and move between alternative investments.

One suggested technique to avoid the limitations on Clifford trusts and the new kiddie tax on children under 14 years of age is to purchase a single-premium policy on the life of the parent with a young child as owner and beneficiary. The income can accumulate inside the policy until the child reaches 14 or college age. At that point the child has two options: he can take out the income and be taxed at his own, lower bracket, or he can simply borrow it. Prior to TAMRA, if he borrowed the money, there were no tax consequences. Policyholders can normally borrow against the amount of their initial deposit, in some cases at no interest, and in other cases with interest charges of 2 or 3 percent. They can borrow their accumulated interest typically at a rate equal to what the policy is then currently earning—i.e., at a net zero cost.

If the parent dies, the child receives the death benefit, and because the child is the owner of the policy, it does not go into the parent's estate. If the parent lives, the child is able to pay for his education with pre-tax dollars. The proceeds of the insurance policy are tax-free anyway, the parent has leveraged his investment, and the child's wealth has been magnified by compounding. If the loan is not repaid—it need never be—it is subtracted from the death benefit.

For example, a 35-year-old male pays $25,000 for a single-premium variable life insurance policy. He then can choose his own investment options and switch between different investments. For the $25,000, he would get a death benefit only of approximately $80,000 to $85,000 on a typical policy. While he could possibly buy the same protection for only $100 a year, the life insurance is not the real objective.

Assume the taxpayer is able, through a combination of stocks, bonds, and other investments, to achieve a return of 12 percent a year on the investment portion of his policy. At the end of 15 years, when he is 50 years old, the death benefit would be typically in excess of $230,000 and the policy would have a cash surrender value of $100,000.

If the taxpayer then cashes in the policy, he pays taxes at that time. Alternatively, he could have borrowed over $22,000 tax-free each year for four years to put his child through college. This would bring the death benefit down to between $160,000 and $170,000 with a cash surrender value of approximately $30,000.

If the taxpayer did not touch his policy until he retired at age 65, his 12 percent rate of return would give him a death benefit of approximately $650,000 with a cash surrender value in excess of $400,000. At that time he could cash in his policy and pay tax on the money. Alternatively, he could annuitize part of the policy when he retires by rolling over part of the cash surrender value into an annuity that would pay him income for life, leaving enough money in the policy to keep it in force and provide a tax-free benefit to his spouse. There would be no taxes due on the money rolled over into the annuity. This would allow the taxpayer to buy a cheaper annuity on his own life only, while he is providing insurance benefits for his spouse.

There are innumerable creative ways of using single-premium life insurance policies. For example, assume, prior to TAMRA, you have $1 million in bank certificates of deposit paying 10 percent and you are in the 33 percent tax bracket. After tax you get $67,000 in earnings. If you were to put the $1 million into a single-premium whole-life policy, also earning 10 percent, it would, in the past, throw off $100,000 in tax-free income through policy loans. Assume, to make the numbers simple, that you are also paying $100,000 in tax-deductible alimony. If you keep your $1 million in a taxable investment, remember you get to keep only $67,000 after tax. Alternatively, if you used your insurance policy $100,000 to pay the alimony, you would have, prior to TAMRA, reduced your tax bill by $33,000 (33 percent of $100,000).

Single-premium life insurance policies are not without their disadvantages. If you cash in your policy, every penny earned inside the policy over however many years you have held it is taxed as ordinary income. In addition, most insurance companies impose a surrender charge in the first few years of the policy, although the charge usually shrinks year by year.

Single-premium life insurance was too good to last in the above form. In order to discourage the purchase of life insurance as a tax shelter investment vehicle, TAMRA altered the federal tax treatment with respect to a class of life insurance contracts that are statutorily defined as "modified endowment contracts." If a contract is a modified endowment contract:

1. Amounts received under the contract are treated first as income, and then as recovered basis;

2. Loans under the contract (and loans secured by a modified endowment contract) are treated as amounts received under the contract; and

3. An additional 10 percent income tax is imposed on certain amounts that are includable in gross income.

Policies entered into before June 21, 1988, have been grandfathered and will not be affected by the TAMRA changes unless they undergo a material change. TAMRA changes the tax treatment of any policy entered into on or after June 21, 1988, in which the aggregate premiums paid during the first 7 years of the contract exceed 7 times the annual net level premium of a 7-paid policy. This is called the "7-pay test."

For example, if the annual net level premium for a $100,000 7-pay policy is $4,500, then any $100,000 policy for the same insured on which the aggregate premiums exceed $4,500 during the first year, $9,000 during the first 2 policy years, $13,500 during the first 3 policy years, $18,000 during the first 4 policy years, $22,500 during the first 5 policy years, $27,000 during the first 6 policy years, or $31,500 during the first 7 years of the policy will be considered and treated as a modified endowment contract.

If the aggregate premiums paid during the first 7 years are less than the aggregate premiums that would have been paid on a level annual premium basis using the net level premium amount ($4,500 a year in this example) for a 7-paid policy for the same insured, the policy will *not* be a modified endowment contract and will receive the same tax treatment previously applicable to all policies.

Under these new rules, single-premium policies have lost their potential for use as a strictly investment-oriented, tax-deferred vehicle. If a policyholder is forced to borrow from a modified endowment contract, he or she will have taxable income for the portion of the loan that represents internal gain on the policy. For example, a policy with a $50,000 single premium that has a $60,000 cash value would have a maximum of $10,000 gain that could be taxed. A policy loan of $15,000 ($10,000 of taxable income plus a $5,000 nontaxable portion) would generate $10,000 of taxable income plus a 10 percent penalty if the policy holder is under age 59fi. The penalty is applied only to the taxable portion of the loan. In this case the penalty will be 10 percent of $10,000, or $1,000. If you are in the 28 percent bracket, this loan would cost you a total of $3,800 ($10,000 × 28% plus $1,000 penalty).

Single-premium policies may still be viable and desirable for other reasons. They provide a mechanism to pass assets to others without subjecting them to the costs, delays, and uncertainties of probate. Attacks on or elections against an insured's will are avoided, as are any claims of potential creditors. Such policies also provide a way to fully prefund future debts or pledges with discounted tax-advantaged dollars. Moreover, at death they are still income tax-free and can be arranged to be both estate and inheritance tax-free.

In shopping for single-premium life insurance, the following considerations should be evaluated:

1. Does the life insurance company offering the policy have a rating of A or better from AM Best Corporation, the authoritative source on financial stability in the industry?
2. What is the current net interest being paid on the policy? Does this take into consideration the mortality charge—i.e., has that charge been taken out of the rate that is quoted?
3. Is the net rate guaranteed, and if so for what period of time?
4. Is there any minimum interest rate guaranteed over the life of the policy?
5. Is there a bailout provision under which you can get out of the policy if rates fall below a certain level?
6. What is the surrender charge if you cash in the policy?
7. Does the surrender charge decrease over a period of time?
8. What is the rate at which you can borrow the accumulated interest?
9. What is the rate at which you can borrow against your original premium?
10. Is there a minimum guaranteed death benefit?
11. Can you make additional payments, and if so what are the time and quantity limitations?

82 Cattle Feeding Programs

A cattle feeding program can enable you to spread income earned in one year over a number of years so that it can be taxed at lower rates. There are no capital gains or depreciation opportunities. You buy calves in the spring or early summer and deduct the cost of feeding them for the remainder of the year. When they reach commercial weight the following year, you will sell them and pay ordinary income taxes. You have, in effect, deferred income from one year to the next, unless beef prices have fallen in the interim.

Feeding programs seek to convert grain (or grass) into beef, at the same time offering a short-term tax deferral and an opportunity for substantial profit or loss. If the cost of converting feed to beef is less than the per-pound cost of the beef added, the cattle feeding program results in a profit to you. If the cost of feeding the cattle is more than the price of beef, you lose.

A 1979 IRS ruling made prepaid feed deductions difficult for tax shelter schemes.[2] Under the prior rule, a prepaid feed expense had to meet three criteria:

1. It could not be on "deposit"—you had to own the feed and bear the economic risk of price fluctuations.
2. The purchase of the feed had to be for a "valid" business purpose.
3. The deduction could not result in a "material distortion of income."

Under the new rule, these three criteria are retained, but in addition the Internal Revenue Service looks at the substantive purpose behind the transaction. According to the latest ruling, a motive based on the income tax advantages of prepayment is *not* a valid business purpose, and if you lack other motives, your deduction will be disallowed.

Moreover, the Tax Reform Act of 1984 included statutory language to include any arrangement with the principal purpose of tax avoidance within the definition of what constitutes a farm syndicate. According to the Conference Committee Report, "The prepaid expense provisions will apply to individual taxpayers engaged in farming activities with the principal purpose of

2. Rev. Rul. 79-229, 1979 C.B. 2.

tax avoidance. The conferees intend that marketed arrangements in which individuals carry on farming activities utilizing the assistance of a common managerial or administrative service may be presumed under certain circumstances to have the principal purpose of tax avoidance. If under such arrangements, taxpayers prepay a substantial portion of their farming expenses with borrowed funds, they should generally be presumed to have a principal purpose of tax avoidance."

The Internal Revenue Service could argue that all feed lot customers are tax shelters because they use the high leverage customary to the industry and feed cattle through a custom feed yard. If so, then the 1984 provisions would effectively limit all deductions for commercial cattle feeders to consumed feed. There would be no allowance of prepayments for feed, seed, fertilizer, or other farm supplies unless the taxpayer were "actively participating in the management." In addition, if the above provisions were to apply, they would preempt and eliminate the 90-day allowance rule on prepayments as contained in Section 461(i). Therefore, if you want to receive the benefits of a cattle feeding program, you must be able to document "active participation," establish a substantial business purpose, and prove that your principal purpose is not tax avoidance, in order to still be eligible to deduct valid prepayments for your farm expenditures.

A typical cattle feeding tax shelter will provide for the purchase of very young calves (or feeders) in the summer or fall. The animals are generally raised in feed yards for which you will be charged a fee in addition to the cost of the feed. The cattle are usually sold the following year, when they reach their commercial weight. If you meet the "valid business purpose" test just described by proper timing of feeder-cattle purchases and sales, you should be able to deduct your expenses in the first year and pick up this amount, plus or minus the profit or loss, in the following year. You should be able to meet the "valid business purpose" test if you can establish a legitimate expectation of higher feed costs in the future—that is, it is cheaper to buy the feed now than to wait—and a legitimate expectation of profit on the ultimate sale of the cattle.

Moreover, under the Tax Reform Act of 1986, farmers using the cash method of accounting will not be allowed to deduct any amount paid for feed, seed, fertilizer, or other supplies prior to the year in which such items are used or consumed to the extent that they exceed 50 percent of expenses for which economic performance has occurred. This provision is effective for prepayments made on or after March 1, 1986. Since most investors in cattle feeding will not have other farm expenses, they will not be entitled to deduct prepaid feed costs. Except for investors in other farming ventures who may have such expenses and who will therefore be entitled to the deduction within the specified limits, cattle feeding as a tax deferral for non-full-time farmers is no longer an effective tax shelter.

83 Cattle Breeding Programs

Cattle breeding programs seek to increase herd size. Prior to ultimate sale, the cattle breeding program offers substantial tax deductions of a long-range deferral nature.

In a cattle breeding program, you might purchase a herd of 50 to 100 cows, which should triple in three to four years. Over a five-year period your average annual outlay of cash on a 100-cow herd can be about $12,000. This outlay may be offset by tax deductions of $6,000 a year.

Expenses normally are deducted as incurred. This includes amounts paid for feed, seed, fertilizer, or other similar supplies. The provision that expenses are deducted as incurred normally prevents the allowance of current deductions for prepaid expenses. If use or consumption of the supplies during the taxable year is prevented on account of fire, storm, flood, or other casualty, however, the items may then be taken as an expense in the current period.

The cattle usually are bred in the summer or fall, so the calf crop will be born in warm weather. A calf crop of 75 percent to 95 percent can be expected. After the calves are weaned, the steers are sold and the heifers are retained to build up the breeding herd. The new crop of heifers is generally bred after two years. Each year, certain animals are culled from the breeding herd and sold.

After five to seven years, the entire herd is usually sold. You can take depreciation on your breeding cattle, but gain equal to the depreciation taken will be recaptured as ordinary income upon their sale. Depreciation can be taken over a five-year period using the 200 percent declining-balance method.

Prior to 1986, you were also entitled to the investment tax credit in a breeding operation. That was a credit against your tax bill of 10 percent of the purchase price, not just your investment. For example, if you bought a herd for $20,000 in 1985, putting in $2,000 in cash and borrowing the additional $18,000, you got an investment tax credit of 10 percent of the total $20,000, or $2,000. In effect, therefore, your initial net cash investment was zero. The Tax Reform Act of 1986 eliminated the investment tax credit as of January 1, 1986.

You can get into the breeding business with as little as 10 percent equity. With feeders, you can get in with as little as 5 percent equity. Up to 90 percent or 95 percent of the purchase price can be borrowed from the feedlot operator, the rancher, or a bank. You can therefore heavily leverage your investment, but this leverage must be based upon full-recourse financing.

The economics of breeding and feeding cattle can be seriously affected by the cyclical market price of cattle. Conditions such as increased costs (feed grains and supplies), price controls, reduced consumption due to high beef prices, and large supplies of available fat cattle have, at times, forced many one-way ventures into economic losses.

Diversification into combined feeding and breeding provides for a longer-lasting investment. The yearly cycle of feeding is extended to a period that provides for the building of herds in hope of a rising demand. In both feeding and breeding programs, management compensation is normally 5 percent to 10 percent of the herd value in the first year, and 5 percent to 10 percent of the operating expenses in subsequent years. Both activities are subject to the "at risk" limitation, and you will be personally liable for any loans if you finance your investment to obtain added tax leverage in order to take the full deductions available.

One very real advantage of cattle breeding is the flexibility that it extends to tax planning. Just as you can defer the recognition of income in a cattle feeding program by continuing to reinvest the proceeds of the sale of cattle, you can also pick the date on which you wish to realize the majority of the income from the sale of your breeding herd. Similarly, depreciation of the purchased cattle, the cost of their maintenance, and interest on any debt create additional deductions until the herd is sold. Remember, though, this flexibility, while useful in tax planning, does not insure that when the herd is eventually sold, it will be sold at a profit. Furthermore, cattle breeding is a long-term investment. You can expect little, if any, cash flow from the breeding venture for a substantial period of time. But the potential gains are there. Prior to 1987, all gain on the raised portion of the herd that had been held for more than 24 months and any gain on purchased animals in excess of prior depreciation would receive long-term capital gain treatment. And throughout the breeding and raising period, you would have been taking ordinary income deductions for your expenses. By eliminating the long-term capital gains deduction, however, the 1986 Reform Act significantly impaired the tax advantage of cattle breeding programs. However, the current tax on long-term capital gains is capped at 20 percent. In addition, cattle breeding programs still give you the advantage of tax deferral.

84 Tax Straddles

A commodity tax straddle is designed to defer short-term capital gain into your next year or to convert it into long-term capital gain. Straddling involves a simultaneous purchase and *short sale* (the sale of a security you do not currently own) of two futures contracts—that is, agreements first to buy and then to sell stated amounts of the same commodity at set prices and times in the future.

To offset the short-term capital gain, you straddle a very volatile commodity (such as copper, silver, or pork bellies) near year-end, hoping for significant price movement—up *or* down—before December 31. If prices rise, you cover your short position at a loss; if prices fall, you liquidate the long position. Either way, the short-term capital loss from commodities offsets your short-term capital gain from other sources. After year-end you liquidate the profitable position. This moves your short-term gain into the next year or (depending on how you hold the contract) converts it to a long-term capital gain. According to former IRS Commissioner Jerome Kurtz, the worst that can happen is that you "receive the equivalent of an interest-free loan from the government for the period of deferral." But if the price does not move, or if it turns around before you can liquidate the profitable position, you will have a loss.

Straddles can be used not only with commodities but with government securities, such as treasury bills, bonds, or "Ginnie Maes," or with options on those securities as well. The objective is the same—to create a loss that will reduce your taxable income for one year while you also set the stage to cover that loss with a capital gain in the next year. If the year works out right, you get a current tax benefit and come close to breaking even on the transaction itself.

Prior to 1987 it was possible through straddling to reduce your tax rate by as much as 30 percent. Ordinary income, which was taxed up to 50 percent, was converted into long-term capital gains, which were taxed at a maximum of 20 percent. Moreover, unlike other investments, commodity investments could qualify for long-term capital gain treatment after only six (rather than 12) months.

Treasury bills were a favorite vehicle for straddles because, unlike most securities, they are not classified as capital assets. Under tax rules, any gain or loss from the sale of Treasury bills was treated as ordinary income. These bills are sold at a discount of face value and appreciate to *par* (face value) at maturity. Because the bills are such safe collateral, margin requirements on these straddles are low, as little as 3 percent of the bills' face value. The following example shows you how a Treasury bill straddle might have worked.

Assume that on December 17 you sell short $1 million in Treasury bills due December 26, and you buy $1 million in Treasury bills due the following March 26, which you intend to sell on January 2. The March maturity date allows for what is generally considered a reasonable period of market risk. But for purposes of this example, assume that between December 26 and January 2 interest rates are high. The result is that you don't receive the full $1 million face value because the bills due December 26 have nine days to go until maturity. Assuming a discount of 16.83 percent, the purchase price is $995,793. On the maturity date, you have to cover the sale of borrowed securities. This will cost $1 million, giving you a loss on the transaction of $4,027 for the year.

The $1 million in bills due March 26 that you buy after making the short sale have 99 days to maturity. Assuming a discount of 16.30 percent, the purchase price is $955,175. When you sell those bills on January 2, you collect $962,419, for a gain of $7,244.

After commission costs of approximately $1,200, the net economic gain on the two transactions is $1,837. This gain is reduced by any interest charges on a margin account. In terms of the tax deduction, the straddles save an investor in the 50 percent bracket (including state, federal, and local taxes) $2,103.50 in taxes for the first year ($4,027 × .50).

Such commodity straddles appear to be no-lose situations. In fact, though, they may turn out to be no-win situations. The Internal Revenue Service views these transactions as "wholly tax motivated and without any real economic substance." Internal Revenue Service staff members who screen and classify returns are being trained to recognize "straddle" returns and are targeting them for audit. According to the IRS, "taxpayers claiming tax benefits from these transactions will face a substantial likelihood of having their return selected for audit and their claims of artificial losses disallowed on examination."

The bottom line on commodity tax straddles is that until they have been court approved as legitimate tax strategies, they should be avoided. The Economic Recovery Tax Act has made this shelter a dead issue by requiring you to "mark to market"—i.e., close all your positions even if they are not sold at year-end. Moreover, the Tax Reform Act of 1986 eliminated the capital gains deduction (long-term now capped at 20 percent). There is little reason, therefore, to use a tax straddle as a tax shelter. Stay away from straddles. There are too many *legal* tax shelters for you to buy into this kind of audit *dis*allowance.

85 Art Reproduction

Art reproduction is another tax shelter that you should forget. Almost all lithograph shelters are going to be disallowed by the Internal Revenue Service. Under a lithograph shelter, you will be asked to purchase a lithograph plate that the artist uses to make a limited number of prints (50 to 500). An estimate of revenues available from sales is used to value the plates, from which investment tax credits and depreciation could be obtained.

In a typical shelter, you would give an artist $30,000 cash, say, plus a promissory note for $170,000 and assume the entire responsibility for marketing the prints. Prior to 1986, you would then seek a 10 percent investment tax credit and a first-year depreciation of 25 percent. At a 50 percent tax rate, you would reduce your tax payments by $43,750 [(200,000 – 10,000) × .25 = $47,500 in depreciation, or a tax savings of $23,750 at a 50 percent rate, plus an additional $20,000 from the 10 percent investment tax credit]. You would therefore be $13,750 ahead. However, the Internal Revenue Service would view the personal promissory note as a sham unless there was a real compulsion to pay it and would argue that the actual investment was only $30,000. In fact, most of these deals are marketed with the assumption that the full risk of the personal promissory note will be paid only out of the proceeds from the sale of the prints. In effect, they are really nothing but shams.

Out of the $30,000 cash paid, $7,500 might go for printing, advertising, and sales; $7,500 to accountants and lawyers; $6,000 to the promoter; and $9,000 to the artist. You must either market the prints yourself or hire the promoter's "marketing" firm to do so for you. In one case, an investor sought to claim depreciation deductions and investment tax credit as a result of the purchase of a lithographic plate "master" and prints made from the "master."[3] According to the Internal Revenue Service, no depreciation could be claimed because the master was a nondepreciable work of art with a life of less than three years. The bottom line on this shelter is: Stay away.

3. Rev. Rul. 70-432, I.R.B. 1979-53, 20.

86 Noncash Gift Shelters

This is another that you should avoid unless you are anxious to be part of an audit. The noncash gift shelter works as follows: You are asked to buy property such as books, Bibles, gemstones, etc., that are supposed to appreciate in value. You hold these objects for a period longer than twelve months and then contribute these "investments" to a charity. In return, you will get a charitable contribution deduction equal to the fair market value of the property.

For example, assume that you purchase rare Bibles at a cost of $5,000, and one year later they "appreciate" to a value of $30,000. You then contribute those Bibles to a church, claiming a deduction of their alleged fair market value of $30,000. If you are in the 31 percent bracket, this saves you $9,300 in tax—a $4,300 profit over your cost.

This is another shelter that the Internal Revenue Service considers nothing more than a sham. In one case a taxpayer-investor purchased limited-edition art books at a volume discount and then donated them to charity. The Internal Revenue Service ruled that the investor's activity was tantamount to that of an art dealer and that the investor's charitable deduction had to be reduced by the amount of gain that would not have been long-term capital gain had the investor sold the books.[4] In other words, the deduction was limited to only the cost basis.

Internal Revenue Service auditors have been instructed to look for noncash gift deductions exceeding $5,000, particularly for deductions of well over the property's cost or basis, and especially if the property was held for less than two years. They will consistently challenge any determination of fair market value and try to disallow all of these shelters that they catch.

I question the validity of the Internal Revenue Service's position where it applies to true investments (for instance, gemstones) that may appreciate substantially over a year's period. However, in *Anselmo,* 80 T.C. No. 46, the Tax Court concluded that gems without settings would not be sold at retail, but rather sold to jewelers who would set the gems into rings or other jewelry. Since the jewelers are the consumers of gems, such stones should be valued on the basis of what the jeweler would pay to a *wholesaler* to obtain comparable gems.

---

4. Rev. Rul. 79-419, I.R.B. 1979-52, 9.

Nonetheless, even if your shelter were to be allowed as a matter of law, you would be buying an audit on the question of valuation. The courts have consistently ruled against the taxpayer in these situations. I therefore recommend avoiding these types of shelters.

87 Municipal Bond Swaps

A municipal bond swap is an intriguing tax idea that allows you to maintain your equivalent current investment and yet at the same time take a tax-deductible loss on it. The swap lets you write off current paper losses and keep the advantage of owning municipal bonds as a shelter from federal income taxes, and possibly from state and local taxes as well. When interest rates increase, municipal bonds will normally be traded at substantially less than their face value. To do a swap, you merely sell your devalued bonds. This gives you a tax deduction for the current year. Then you reinvest the proceeds in other municipals of comparable yield and quality.

If you are contemplating any kind of swap, you must be aware of—and *avoid*—the "wash sale": You can deduct the realized loss on your current federal income tax return by selling your devalued bonds any time right up through December 31. But the Internal Revenue Service will call it a wash sale—and disallow the loss deduction—if you turn around and buy the same bonds, or "substantially identical" ones, without waiting a full 30 days.

"Substantially identical" has never really been clearly defined. If the issuer is different, there should be absolutely no problem. But if the bonds you are selling and the bonds you are buying are from the same issuer, the farther apart they are in maturity or interest rate the safer you will be. At a minimum, you should look for a five-year difference in maturities, or a spread of at least 50 *basis points* (0.5 percent difference in yields to maturity).

If you hold the original bonds for a year or less, you have a short-term loss, which can be used to offset, dollar for dollar, gains from the sale of other assets. Likewise, long-term losses can be used to offset gains dollar for dollar.

Any loss up to $3,000 that isn't absorbed can be deducted from your ordinary income. Losses in excess of gains plus $3,000 can be carried over to future years.

B How to Analyze a Tax Shelter

The most important part of a tax shelter offering is the prospectus. It summarizes the deal, details the history of the participants, and gives you a lawyer's opinion as to the projected tax consequences. Read it carefully! The summary and introduction in the front of most prospectuses are a good starting point, but make sure that you go beyond them. Look at the section on sources and uses of the proceeds very carefully. This will indicate who gets what and how much of the proceeds are going to the promoters and their affiliates, as opposed to being invested in the main objective of the partnership. Read the tax risks and considerations section equally carefully, as this should explain in detail the various tax considerations that might affect you as an investor.

Choose carefully the lawyer or accountant who will evaluate the deal. An unfamiliar lawyer or accountant who brings a deal to your attention at a social gathering may simply be representing the promoters. Find out whether your lawyer or accountant will be receiving a commission from the promoters if the deal is sold. On the other hand, it could also be unwise to rely on your own lawyer or accountant in evaluating a deal. Lawyers and accountants are prejudiced in the other direction, since if the deal goes sour, they could lose you as a client. They therefore have very little incentive to recommend anything with any risk.

Make sure that the deal evidences an intent to make a profit. If a shelter is based on deductions of interest and depreciation, with only a remote possibility of the receipt of revenues, it stands a greater risk of being disallowed by the Internal Revenue Service. For example, a 1985 shelter that marked up a $10 product to $100, took a 10 percent investment tax credit to make the $10 initial contribution, and then took depreciation on the whole $100 was a high risk and unlikely to be approved if questioned in an audit.

Always invest in a tax shelter on the basis of economic returns. For example, the phaseout rule with respect to actively managed real estate could also produce a devastatingly high marginal tax rate as you approach the phaseout point. For example, assume you and your spouse have $102,000 of adjusted gross income. You can claim up to $24,000 of losses from actively managed real estate. If you have $104,000 of adjusted gross income, then you claim $23,000 of deductions from such real estate activities. Assume instead that you had $1,000 of such losses from actively managed real estate activities and adjusted gross income of $148,000. Clearly the $1,000 is fully deductible. But, if you get a $2,000 raise, your adjusted gross income would rise to $150,000 and the $1,000 deduction would be disallowed. As a result, an extra $2,000 of gross income would be taxed at an effective rate of 46.5 percent, the reasons being that there would be a tax of $930 (31 percent of $3,000 increase in taxable income based on the extra $2,000 salary plus the $1,000 loss deduction), when your adjusted gross income rose only $2,000. This $930 increase in taxes on a $2,000 increase in your tax base produces a marginal rate of 46.5 percent.

Many shelters appear to give high write-offs on the basis of interest expense accrued according to the Rule of 78's. The Rule of 78's computes interest in a manner analogous to the sum of the year's digits methods for depreciation. The interest is ascertained by applying a fraction to the total interest due, the numerator of which is the number of payment periods remaining and the denominator of which is the sum of the periods. In Rev. Rul. 83-84, I.R.B. 1983-23, 12, the IRS ruled that it would no longer recognize interest deductions computed under that rule which exceeded the "economic accrual of interest." An exception was made for short-term consumer loans in Rev. Proc. 83-40, I.R.B. 1983-23, 22.

Determine the actual profit potential—that means measure the potential *after-tax return* against the *after-tax cost.* This allows a comparison of the cost of the tax shelter investment with other alternatives, such as stocks and bonds acquired with after-tax dollars. Make sure that you take into consideration how long it will take to get the yield from the after-tax dollars. For example, a three-to-one return ($3 of cash received for each $1 invested) looks better than a two-to-one return at first, but it will not be better if it takes several years longer to realize the full profit.

Examine the promoter's past history. What kind of track record does the person have? Have past deals been successful? Examine the financial statements of the general partner and evaluate them to ascertain that person's strength and staying power in the face of adversity. What are the sharing arrangements and front-end fees of the general partner? That person's share of revenues should be reasonably related to the services he or she renders to the program. Fees, commissions, and other front-end-loaded charges should be reasonable, too.

Does the program provide for additional assessments? You must be told (a) the maximum amount of additional capital that the general partner can assess for unexpected expenses, (b) when the assessment can be made, (c) the tax consequences of meeting the assessment, and (d) the penalty if you fail to comply.

Carefully examine the forecast figures provided in the prospectus. Review even more carefully the footnotes accompanying the forecast, which explain the assumptions involved in putting that forecast together.

Review your state of mind. Probably the most important consideration that you must ponder before entering into a traditional tax shelter is your own personal tax-comfort level. Many people are not temperamentally suited to invest in projects that increase the possibility that they may be audited. It is important, therefore, for you to decide whether you can live comfortably with this added potential risk.

88 Getting Out of the Tax Shelter

Tax shelters, by definition, are long-term investments. However, there may come a time when you need to get out of the shelter immediately because of pressing cash requirements. There are four major firms that purchase partnership units:

- Liquidity Fund (1900 Powell Street, Emeryville, California 94608; 415-652-1462) buys public and private real estate programs, with the exception of government-subsidized housing partnerships.
- MacKenzie Securities (650 California Street, San Francisco, California 94108; 800-854-8357; in California, 800-821-4252) buys only public and private real estate deals that are at least three years old and have current cash flow. The firm won't buy private programs if the investor still owes payments to the sponsors.
- Equity Resources Group (1776 Massachusetts Avenue, Cambridge, Massachusetts 02140; 617-876-4800) deals only in private real estate programs. It turns down programs with more than half the investment unpaid.
- Livon Oil (220 Bush Street, San Francisco, California 94104; 415-781-6427) buys units in public and private oil and gas drilling and income programs. It also won't purchase partnerships from investors who still owe payments to the sponsors.

Other such firms include the following:

- Raymond James Limited Partnership
Trading Desk
140 66th Street North
St. Petersburg, FL 33710
1-800-237-7591

- National Partnership Exchange
  P.O. Box 578
  Tampa, FL 33601
  (813)222-0555

- Investors Advantage Corp.
  The Fountains Financial Center
  US 19 North
  Suite 302
  Palm Harbor, FL 33563
  1-800-282-5865

- Partnership Securities Exchange
  1814 Franklin Street
  Suite 820
  Oakland, CA 94612
  (415)763-5555

- Realty Repurchase, Inc.
  50 California Street
  Suite 1300
  San Francisco, CA 94111
  1-800-233-7357

- Oppenheimer & Bigelow
  489 Fifth Avenue
  New York, NY 10017
  1-800-431-7811

In addition, the Chicago Partnership Board, Inc. (800-272-6273) and the Partnership Exchange (10051 Fifth Street, North, Box 21438, St. Petersburg, Florida 33742; 800-356-2739; in Florida, 800-336-2739) match buyers and sellers of private and public real estate, oil and gas, equipment leasing, and cable TV partnerships.

89 Master Limited Partnerships

A master limited partnership is not a tax shelter. It is merely a vehicle or form in which an investment can be made. A master limited partnership is a large publicly registered limited partnership that is the principal or sole owner of multiple assets or partnerships that themselves may have been structured as tax shelters.

Master limited partnerships can pass through income and losses like traditional limited partnerships but provide investors greater liquidity. Units in numerous master limited partnerships are listed for trading on national securities exchanges, and master limited partnerships generally have the ability to issue additional units in the future.

There are two basic forms of master limited partnerships. The first is the roll-up, in which multiple assets or small limited partnerships are consolidated into a large single master limited partnership. The second is the roll-out, in which the apparent entity, like a corporation, spins off some of its assets into a separate master limited partnership. A third form is known as a roll-in. In this form new assets are put into a master limited partnership with the promise to add additional assets in the future.

Master limited partnerships may be attractive as passive income generators to shelter passive losses from other activities. For example, dividends distributed by real estate investment trusts (REITs) are classified as portfolio income, which cannot be sheltered by passive losses. However, income distributed by real estate master limited partnerships will be treated as passive income.

Another advantage of the master limited partnership is that it can pass through to investors a greater portion of each dollar of operating income than a corporation since the master limited partnership itself is not subject to taxation. Moreover, unlike REITs, a master limited partnership can actively engage in real estate activities, and they are entitled to more favorable depreciation. The master limited partnership structure, however, increases the difficulty of complying with the new partnership allocation rules because of the large number of investors and constant trading of partnership interests.

The Revenue Act of 1987 had a substantial impact on master limited partnerships. Such partnerships, falling under the classification of publicly traded partnerships (PTPs), will be treated as corporations for tax years after 1987. An exception is made, however, for those partnerships whose gross income is predominantly (90 percent or more) "qualifying income." Qualifying income consists of the following:

1. Interest: This category does not include interest derived in the conduct of a financial or insurance business, nor does it include amounts contingent on profits.

2. Dividends.

3. Real property rents: This category generally includes rents from interest in real property, charges for services customarily furnished in connection

with the rental of real property, and rental income attributable to personal property in connection with the lease of real property. Amounts contingent on income or profits are not generally treated as rents from real property.

4. Gain from the sale or other disposition of real property.

5. Income or gains from the exploration, development, mining or production, refining, transportation, or marketing of any mineral or natural resource.

6. Any gain from the sale or other disposition of a capital asset or Section 1231 asset held for the production of any type of income described in 1 through 5, above.

7. Income and gains from commodities (other than those held for sale to customers in the ordinary course of business) and futures, options, or forward contracts with respect to other commodities.

Moreover, although the general corporate treatment applies for tax years beginning after 1987, in the case of an "existing partnership" it applies to tax years beginning only after 1997. An existing partnership is any one of the following:

1. A partnership that was publicly traded on or before December 17, 1987.

2. A partnership for which a registration statement was filed with the Securities and Exchange Commission on or before December 17, 1987.

3. A partnership for which an application was filed with a state regulatory commission on or before December 17, 1987, seeking permission to restructure a portion of a corporation as a publicly traded partnership.

These "grandfathered" partnerships have been given the opportunity to remain partnerships by the Tax Relief Act of 1997. The price, however, is a 3.5 percent tax on gross income, or on gross receipts minus cost of goods sold. Those that choose not to pay will be taxed as corporations, and face the 35 percent corporate tax rate. In the case of publicly traded partnerships that are not treated as corporations, the passive loss rules are to be applied separately for the items attributable to each PTP. The net losses of a partner from each PTP are to be suspended at the partner level and carried forward and netted against the partner's share of the nonportfolio income of that PTP in a later year or years. Generally, these losses may not be applied against passive income from other activities. Similarly, a partner's share of the credits is to be suspended, carried forward, and applied against the tax liability of a subsequent year or years attributable to that PTP. Generally, these credits may not be applied against tax liability attributable to other activities. Moreover, a partner's share in the net income of a PTP (both portfolio and business income) will generally not be treated as income from a passive activity; that is, it will generally be treated as portfolio income. However, a partner's share of the net business (nonportfolio) income of a PTP will be treated as passive income for carryover purposes. This means that a partner's share of a PTP's net business income may be offset by any suspended business losses of that PTP carried forward from an earlier year, but a partner's share of portfolio income may not be offset by any other current or carryover losses from other passive activities.

Super Tax Shelters

"When more of the people's sustenance is exacted through the form of taxation than is necessary to meet the just obligations of government..., such exaction becomes ruthless extortion and a violation of the fundamental principles of a free government."

GROVER CLEVELAND
Second Annual Message
December 1886

As to the astuteness of taxpayers in ordering their affairs so as to minimize taxes, it has been said that "the very meaning of a line in the law is that you intentionally may go as close to it as you can if you do not pass it." *Superior Oil Co. v. Mississippi,* 280 U.S. 390, 395—96. This is so because "nobody owes any public duty to pay more than the law demands; taxes are enforced exactions, not voluntary contributions." Frankfurter, J., *Atlantic Coast Line v. Phillips,* 322 U.S. 168, 172—73 (1947).

This is the chapter that alone is worth more than a hundred times the cost of this book. Each of the following shelters is completely legal and has been sold to sophisticated taxpayers for thousands of dollars. These shelters have been worth the cost—they have saved those taxpayers many multiples of their acquisition price in taxes not paid. Each of these supershelters will be presented, explained, and structured in detail. Study them well. They will show you how legally and painlessly to reduce your own taxes to zero.

A Family Shifts

The first rule of income taxation is that a tax liability for personal service income may not be avoided by the earner of that income by assignment or other transfer before the income is realized. If you perform services that earn monetary reward, that income will be taxed to you. The second law of income taxation, however, is that income earned from *property* belongs to the owner of that property. Therefore, the first key to reducing your taxes is to transfer income-producing property to a family member in a lower bracket. If you make a bona fide transfer of income-producing property that you own, you have effectively shifted all future income from that property. After the transfer, the future income and all income tax due on that income will belong to the new owner in the lower tax bracket.

Part of your solution to the problem of reducing your tax, therefore, is to get your current income taxed to lower-bracketed family members. This strategy is based on the premise that a family is an economic and social unit and that it is immaterial to the welfare of the family as a whole which member derives income or owns property. From a tax perspective, however, it is extremely material.

For example, assume you are in the 31 percent bracket and transfer $700 of annual income to your son so that it is taxable to him instead of to you. Immediately you save $217 in taxes. Furthermore, the whole $700 will come tax-free to a child who has no other income, even if the $700 represents unearned income (for instance, interest, dividends, or rents). Moreover, not only can the savings be multiplied by the number of children involved, but if your son is under age 19 or is a full-time student under age 24, you can still claim the personal exemption for him on your tax return as long as you supply more than one-half of his total support.

The shift does not have to be made to a child. Suppose you are supporting a parent out of your current income. You might save an enormous amount of taxes if you could transfer some of that income so that the tax would be shifted from you directly to your lower-bracketed parent. For 1999, your parents, if over age 65, get personal exemptions of $2,750 × 2 and a standard deduction of $7,200 + ($850 × 2). Thus, if you are paying $14,400 a year of your after-tax income to your parents, you could save $4,464 a year in taxes if you are in the 31 percent bracket. Such a shift of income can be accomplished through a direct gift of income-producing property or by using one of a number of trusts that will be examined later in this chapter.

The standard deduction now permits the tax-free transfer of $700 of investment income to a child or other member of your family who has no other income. Alternatively, if the child is of sufficient age to work, that child can earn up to $6,300 ($4,300 standard deduction plus $2,000 IRA) a year in income and still pay zero taxes. Remember, however, that the objective is not necessarily that the family member pay zero taxes, but rather that the taxes paid be less than what you would pay if the income were taxed directly to you. For example, even if that family member is in the 15 percent bracket, a shift of $1,000 in income from you in the 31 percent would result in a net savings of $160.

There are a number of ways to effect an income shift within the family. Remember, when transactions among family members are genuine, they must be given full legal effect for tax purposes.

Note, however, that the Tax Reform Act of 1986 limits the availability of certain income-shifting techniques to children under age 14. Under the law, all net unearned income (as defined in computation B below) of a child who has not attained age 14 before the close of the taxable year and who has at least one parent alive at the close of the taxable year will be taxed to the child at special rates. This applies to all net unearned income; the source of the assets creating the income or the date the income-producing property was transferred is irrelevant.

The tax payable by the child on net unearned income is essentially the additional amount of tax that the parent would have had to pay if the net unearned income of the child were included in the parent's taxable income.

If parents have two or more children with unearned income to be taxed at the parent's marginal tax rate, all of the children's applicable unearned income will be added together and the tax calculated. The tax is then allocated to each child based on the child's pro rata share of unearned income.

The intent of the law is to create three stages:

1. There will be no tax on the first $700 of unearned income because of the child's standard deduction. The standard deduction for a dependent in 1999 is now the greater of $700 in *unearned* income or the sum of $250 plus any *earned* income.

2. The next $700 of unearned income will be taxed to the child at the child's bracket.

3. Unearned income in excess of the first $1,400 will be taxed to the child at the appropriate parent's rate.

The term *unearned income* means income from sources *other* than wages, salaries, professional fees, and other amounts received as compensation for personal services actually rendered.

The parent whose taxable income will be taken into account is the custodial parent of the child in the case of unmarried parents. In the case of parents who are married but filing separately, the individual with the greater taxable income will be the parent whose taxable income is used in these calculations.

The parent of a child under 14 receiving unearned income is required to provide that child with the parent's taxpayer identification number (TIN). That number (typically the parent's social security number) must be included in the child's tax return.

Upon written request a parent's return must be disclosed to the child or the child's legal representative to the extent necessary for the child's return to be properly filed.

PLANNING SUGGESTIONS

Note that the so-called *kiddie tax* rules discussed above apply regardless of who gave the children the income-producing property. They apply even if the cash or other property generating the income was transferred prior to 1987. So income from existing custodial accounts and income distributed from existing nongrantor trusts will be taxable to children under 14 at the parent's rates regardless of when the account or trust was created.

It may appear that the advantage of shifting income was eliminated by the reduction in bracket spreads (until 1987 the spread from the top bracket of 50 percent to the bottom bracket of 11 percent was 39 percentage points, but now the spread is from 39.6 percent to 15 percent, a 24.6 percentage point difference). But this is an oversimplification. Once a child becomes 14, all earned and unearned income is taxed at the child's rate. So dropping $10,000 a year of income from the 39.6 percent bracket to the 15 percent bracket will save 24.6 percent per year of the amount of income shifted. In 10 years that amounts to $24,600 in tax savings!

If a child can be claimed as a dependent on a parent's return, the child may not take a personal exemption. Furthermore, the child's standard deduction is limited to the greater of (a) the greater of $700 or the sum of $250 and the child's earned income, or (b) the child's earned income (both limited to a maximum of that year's standard deduction). This will force more parents than ever to file tax returns for their children (children with more than $700 of unearned income will have to file income tax returns), those returns will be more complicated than ever (and therefore the cost of filing the returns will be increased), and the taxes payable by children will rise precipitously.

90 Unearned Income of Minor Children

Under TAMRA, beginning in 1989, the parent whose marginal tax rate would be applied in calculating the tax on the new unearned income of a child under age 14 may elect to include the child's net unearned income on his or her own return. The election can only be made if:

1. the child has gross income only from interest dividends;
2. such gross income is more than $700 and less than $5,000; and
3. no estimated tax payments for such year are made in the name and taxpayer identification number of such child, and no amount of tax has been withheld.

If the election is made, the child will not have to file a tax return, and the parent's gross income will be increased by the amount of the child's net income over $1,400. Additionally, the parent's tax will be increased by the lesser of $75 or 15 percent of the child's gross income in excess of $700.

There may be two advantages to a parent in directly including a child's income on his or her own return. First, it avoids the filing of an additional return. Second, and perhaps even more important, if the parent is subject to a limit on the amount of investment interest that he or she can deduct, the inclusion of the child's investment income on the parent's return may obviate this interest expense limitation to the extent of additional investment income. However, to the extent that the parent's adjusted gross income is a factor in computing certain itemized deductions—such as the miscellaneous itemized, medical expense, and casualty loss deduction—such inclusion may actually reduce the deductions on the parent's return. You should weigh the administrative savings and the savings on tax preparation fees against any potential additional cost.

There are still many ways to shift both wealth and income and save taxes.

1. Give a Series EE U.S. Savings Bond that will not mature until after the donee-child is age 14. No tax will be payable until the bond is redeemed. At that time the gain will be taxed at the child's relatively lower tax bracket. Remember that this strategy will not work if the child already owns Series EE bonds and is already reporting each year's interest accrual as income. Once the election to report income currently is made, it is irrevocable.

2. Give growth stocks (or growth stock mutual funds) which pay little or no current dividends. The child will therefore pay no tax currently and can hold the stock until reaching age 14. Upon a sale the child will be taxed at the child's bracket.

3. Give *deep discount* tax-free municipal bonds that mature on or after the child's 14th birthday. The bond interest will be tax-free to the child and the discount (face less cost basis) will be taxed to the child at the child's bracket when the bond is redeemed at maturity.

4. Employ your children. Pay them a reasonable salary for work they actually perform. Remember that the standard deduction for children is the greater of (a) $700 or (b) earned income (up to a 1999 limit of $4,300 plus $2,000 more in a traditional IRA). Regardless of how much is paid to the child, the business will have a deduction at its tax bracket, and the amount will be taxable to the child at the child's bracket. Alternatively, the child could establish a Roth IRA to shelter income forever.

5. Sell all nonappreciated property (be sure to consider brokerage costs and time value of money) and purchase tax-free municipals for the child.

6. Consider the multiple advantages of a *term of years* charitable remainder trust for children over age 14—so the income will be taxed to the child, but the grantor will receive an immediate income tax deduction.

7. In making gifts to your children consider support obligation cases such as *Braun, Sutliff,* and *Miller.* Parents who can with ease meet the support needs of even an adult college-age child may be considered obligated to provide support. If UGMA (the Uniform Gifts to Minors Act) or 2503(c) trust funds are used to send a child to college, will the parent be taxed? Worse yet, do these cases mean the UGMA custodian (or 2503(c)) trustee violates a fiduciary duty by using such funds to pay for a college education when it's the parent's duty (thus making such funds unavailable for the very purpose for which they were intended)?

   Assuming the support problems addressed above are not applicable, judicious use of a 2503(c) trust (but not a UGMA account) will allow significant income shifting. The trust can accumulate income while the beneficiary is under age 14 and avoid the kiddie tax.

8. Life insurance and annuity policies that stay within statutory guidelines (ask for a written guarantee from the home office) for life insurance should be particularly attractive, assuming *loading* costs are relatively low and/or backended. This includes universal, variable, and traditional whole life of the single-, annual-, and limited-payment types. In the case of the SPWL (Single-Premium Whole Life) the entire single premium paid at purchase starts earning the declared interest rate immediately. The cost of insurance and expenses is recovered by the insurer from the difference between the declared interest rate and the rate the insurer actually earns. If surrendered, any unrecovered expenses are deducted from the policy's cash values. The owner can obtain cash values at any time by (1) surrender (gain over cost is taxable) or (2) loan (loan interest is probably nondeductible). But note the limitations and new penalties imposed by TAMRA in 1988. Interest is charged at about the same rate credited on borrowed sums and is free of current tax. Earnings compound free of current taxation. Unlike tax-free municipal bonds there is no market risk, and SPWL is highly liquid. A parent can purchase the product on his or her own life which makes college education for the children more likely, and the parent does not have to give up control or make a gift.

9. Concentrate on gift and estate tax savings devices such as the annual exclusion. Parents should consider gifting $10,000–$20,000 a year of non-income-producing assets to a minor's trust or custodial account, which could be converted into income-producing assets slowly after the child turns age 14. The fund can become self-liquidating and exhaust itself by the time the child finishes college/graduate school.

10. If the parent's return shows a loss, will the child's return be affected by it? The Code is silent.

11. The custodial parent is often the mother who may have less income (and therefore be in a lower tax bracket) than the father. But what about the logistics of tax-return disclosure where the father is filing returns and paying tax for the children? Suppose he doesn't want her to know how much he's put aside for the kids and she doesn't want to reveal her income or her new husband's income. Furthermore, the filing father cannot prepare the children's returns until the mother prepares her returns. What about multiple children from multiple marriages? Split custody?

12. The 1986 TRA still provides for limited shifting of income to children under the age of 14 with the $700 minimum standard deduction and the special rule taxing the first $700 of unearned income at the child's marginal tax rate. Assuming that the parent is in the highest marginal tax rate (39.6 percent), the first $700 of income shifted to the child would result in $277.20 of tax savings ($700 × .396), and the next $700 of transferred income would result in $172.20 of tax savings [$700 × (.396 – .15)].

    Over a period of years, the tax savings generated by shifting $1,400 of income to the child can be significant. For example, if the annual tax savings were invested at 8 percent for a 14-year period, the total tax savings and interest would be $10,882. Furthermore, the gifts necessary to generate the $1,400 of unearned income would closely approximate the $10,000 annual gift tax exclusion for the parent, so that little, if any, of his or her unified credit is used. (Parents electing to make a split gift would have a $20,000 exclusion to offset such gifts.)

The above limitations apply only to the shifting of unearned income—e.g., interest, dividends, rents, etc. For those shifts discussed later in this chapter, assume that whenever there is a reference to shifting unearned income to children, those children are not under age 14. The following techniques can be used to shift income to lower-income members of your family.

91 Outright Gifts

A gift of income-producing property to members of your family is perhaps the most common method of splitting income to gain a tax advantage. The simplest way to transfer money, tax-free, is by gifts in relatively small lumps. You can give an annual gift of $10,000 per person to any number of family members—$20,000 if the gift is made jointly with a spouse—without incurring any gift liability. In order to qualify for the $10,000 or the $20,000 exclusion in the year the gift is made, it must be a gift of a *present interest* (current value). A gift tax return is required for any gifts in excess of these amounts to any recipient in any year if the gift is one of a present interest. A gift tax return is required for a gift of any amount if it is of a future interest. A gift is a completed transfer of the entire legal and beneficial interest in the property given.

For a gift to your spouse, there is now an unlimited gift tax marital deduction. If the family members to whom you wish to give gifts are adults, then normally there are no problems. This is *not* true if the objects of your income shifting are minor children, who lack full legal capacity. In consequence, legal difficulties are often encountered in connection with their ability to manage and dispose of the property that they acquire. Furthermore, they normally lack full maturity and it is often less desirable from a practical standpoint to give them control over property.

Certain types of property are more suited than others to practical ownership by minors. Securities that require no management control can be put in the name of a minor when there is no desire to dispose of them before majority. If there is such a desire, the securities should be in bearer form or registered in the name of an adult nominee who may dispose of them at the direction of the minor. Under such circumstances you should file a Form 1087 putting the Internal Revenue Service on notice as to the true ownership of the stock. Alternatively, savings bonds may be purchased and registered in the sole name of a minor and may be redeemed at the option of the minor or a parent.

Cash is the simplest thing to give to a minor. It may be kept in a savings account by the parent in trust for the child. If you want to give cash to a family member but must sell appreciated stock to do so, it is normally cheaper to give your family member the securities and *then* have them sold. Any gain realized will be taxed at the lower marginal tax bracket rate of that person if he or she is 14 or older.

It is very important to note that under no circumstances should funds transferred to a minor be used to satisfy a parent's legal obligation of support (see *Sutliff v. Sutliff,* 489 A.2d 764 [Super. Ct. PA 1985], subsequently invalidated by a later ruling by the Pennsylvania Supreme Court, and *Braun v. Commissioner,* T.C. Memo 1984-285). If funds are so used, the income will be taxed to the parent!

GUARDIANS

Many of the practical and legal difficulties inherent in dealing with minors can be alleviated either by having a guardian appointed for the minor or by creating a trust for the benefit of the minor. A guardian must be appointed by the state court having jurisdiction over such matters. There is normally little difficulty in securing the appointment on the petition, with the consent of both parents. Once appointed, the guardian usually becomes responsible to the appointing court for the proper and faithful performance of any duties. The judiciary standards governing a guardian's investment powers are those set by state law. A guardian is not allowed a choice or discretion beyond standards that are usually quite conservative. There are, however, a number of problems in using a guardian. The guardian is usually required by state law to furnish a bond for the faithful performance of duties. If sureties are required on the bond, the guardian is further restricted by the supervision exercised by the sureties. Furthermore, the guardian may be required to get court approval and certification that any actions—for instance, a sale of securities—are in the best interest of the ward.

Each state has its own standards and requirements detailing the duties and responsibilities of a guardian. For example, some statutes require that annual or periodic accounts be presented for approval by the courts. On the other hand, many of these provisions are often disregarded in a parent-guardian situation where harmony prevails within the family. This is because, as a practical matter, the courts usually do not take any action except on a complaint of a party in interest.

TRUSTS

Many of the technical and legal difficulties of guardianship can be eliminated through the use of a trust for the benefit of the minor. The standards governing the investment and management powers of the trustee may be as broad or narrow as the creator of the trust desires. If the trust that is created comes into being during your lifetime (*inter vivos* trust), that trust usually is under no direct court supervision. Furthermore, if you should so provide, no bond will be required by the trustee for faithful performance of duties and no court approval will be necessary for the disposal of trust assets in the usual course of the trustee's administration of that trust. Furthermore, while it is usually preferable to have an independent trustee, it is legally permissible for you as a parent to act as trustee.

You should be aware, however, that there are certain limits and dangers in the use of the trust for income shifting:

1. The income must not be "applied or distributed for the support or maintenance of a beneficiary (other than the grantor's spouse) whom the grantor is legally obligated to support or maintain." You have the legal obligation to support your minor children. If the income or principal of a trust you create is used to discharge this obligation, it is regarded as your income and taxable to you. The solution here is to use the funds for nonsupport purposes. For example, in most states a college education would not constitute a legal obligation that would fall under the umbrella of "support." In the case of *Frederick C. Braun, Jr, et al. v. Commissioner* (T.C Memo 1984-285) however, the Tax Court found that under New Jersey law, financially able parents have the legal obligation to provide their children with a college education. The court therefore ruled that to the extent that income from two trusts was used to pay for tuition, room, and board for Braun's children, the income was taxable to Braun. The solution here would have been to distribute the income directly to the children and have them pay for their own college expenses. Structured that way, the income would not have been taxable to the parents. (See also the Pennsylvania case of *Sutliff v. Sutliff,* 489 A.2d 764, 1986, wherein the Appellate Court held that a parent may not use Uniform Gifts to Minors Act [UGMA] funds for a child's support. The import of this case, which arose out of a divorce situation, is that the court ruled that the parental duty of support may extend to providing a college education, even though the child has attained an age of majority under general state law but not under UGMA. This case was later invalidated by a subsequent ruling by the Pennsylvania Supreme Court. See also *Stone,* T.C. Memo 1987-454, wherein the Tax Court again ruled that trust payments for private school

tuition are within a parent's legal support obligation; thus, such payments are taxable to the grantor/parent instead of the minor trust beneficiary. *Stone* involved only the payment of private school tuition to minor beneficiaries, thus avoiding the more difficult question of the support obligation in regard to payments of college expenses for adult children. These cases follow the analysis in *Braun* with reference to a college education constituting parental support, and its solution should be approached in the same manner—i.e., distributing the income directly to the children and having them pay for their own education expenses.)

2. The trust must *not* be set up so that it could be considered to be carrying on a business or as having sufficient attributes of a corporation to make it taxable as a corporation by the federal government. An ordinary, valid, and legal trust is not an association taxed as a corporation.

3. The property contributed to the trust by gift must not be deemed a gift of a future interest. If it is, the gift will not be entitled to the benefits of the annual exclusion for gift tax purposes. A gift to a minor, in trust or otherwise, will *not* be considered a gift of a future interest (and the annual exclusion will be available) if:

   a) the property and income may be used for the benefit of the minor; *and*

   b) any amount not so used will pass to the minor at age 21, or to that person's estate, or to any testamentary appointee in the event of an early death. A gift of an income interest that meets this test is considered a present interest.

4. The trust must be irrevocable or, if the transfers to the trust were made prior to March 2, 1986, irrevocable for at least 10 years, and you as a grantor cannot retain powers that, in the eyes of the tax law, constitute a beneficial interest in the property.[1] I will examine these 10-year trusts in detail under the section on Clifford Trusts.

To simplify the procedures for making gifts to minors of securities and other specified property, all states have enacted what is known as the Uniform Gift to Minors Act. The effect of this act is to permit such gifts to be made through a custodian, and to permit a subsequent transfer without the appointment of a

1. Internal Revenue Code, Section 676.

guardian or the creation of a trust. Under the Act, securities can be transferred to minors by registering them in the donor's name, in the name of an adult member of the minor's family, or in the guardian's name, as *custodian* for the minor, and delivering the securities to the custodian. If the donor is the custodian, registration constitutes delivery. Securities in bearer form can be given by delivery to an adult member of the minor's family (other than the donor) or to the guardian as custodian for the minor, together with the deed in statutory form.

The custodian gets the managerial power a guardian would have, and the minor gets absolute legal title to the securities. The custodian can sell and reinvest, and can collect income and accumulate it or apply it for the minor's benefit. When the minor reaches the age of majority (21 or, in some states, 18), the custodian must turn over the securities and any accumulated income. If the minor dies before then, the securities and the income are part of the estate. Remember, however, that any income from the transfer that is used to discharge, in whole or in part, the legal obligation to support and maintain a minor is *pro tanto* taxable to the person who made the transfer. Furthermore, you should note that if you are the donor and name yourself as custodian of the securities or succeed to custodianship, your death before the minor reaches the age of majority will throw the securities into your estate.

92 Clifford Trusts

Prior to March 2, 1986, as an alternative to a completed gift, you could have considered the creation of a temporary trust commonly known as a Clifford Trust. Clifford or temporary trusts to shift taxable income from a high-bracket taxpayer to a low-bracket taxpayer were extensively used in the past.

The Tax Reform Act of 1986 effectively eliminated the use of Clifford Trusts. Except for transfers made prior to March 2, 1986—with another exception under which the 10-year rule of prior law would continue to apply to certain trusts created pursuant to certain binding property settlements entered into before March 1, 1986—Clifford Trusts were taxed as grantor trusts as of January 1, 1987. That means that the income of the trust is taxed at *your* higher marginal tax bracket.

93 Interest-Free Loans

Because of the limits imposed on the transfer of funds to a Clifford Trust free of gift tax, an alternative planning strategy was devised. As an alternative or a supplement to transferring funds to a Clifford Trust, you could have made an unlimited interest-free loan to your lower-bracketed family member.

Unfortunately, the use of interest-free loans as a method to allocate income to lower bracketed taxpayers was effectively eliminated by the Tax Reform Act of 1984. Under that Act, foregone interest on a loan is treated as a gift from the lender to the borrower and is subject to the gift tax. Moreover, the lender (parent) is deemed to have an interest expense. For loans from a corporation to a shareholder, the interest element is treated as if a dividend includable in income was paid by the corporation to the shareholder. A loan to a person providing services results in the foregone interest being treated as compensation.

94 The Schnepper Shelter: Gift Leasebacks

An alternative technique used to increase income-shifting potential is the gift-leaseback transaction. In the typical situation, the taxpayer, usually a professional such as a doctor, attorney, accountant, or even a shareholder in a closely held corporation, establishes a trust for any children. Then business property, such as an office building, furniture, equipment, autos, trucks, or machinery, is transferred to the trust, which agrees to lease it back to the taxpayer. The lease payments are then deductible by the high-bracketed taxpayer and reported as income by the low-bracketed trust beneficiary.

In effect, the taxpayer has relinquished title in exchange for significant income shifting. There is no depreciation recapture on such transfers,[2] nor should there be any investment credit recapture.[3] In addition, not only is the

2. See I.R.C. Section 1245(b)(1) and (3) and Section 1250(d)(1) and (3). Potential recapture is deferred until a subsequent disposition of the property—see *Rainier Companies, Inc. v. Comm.*, 61 T.C. 68 (1973), acq., 1974-1 C.B.2.
3. Reg. Section 1.47-3(g) provides that the recapture provisions will not apply where qualified property is disposed of and, as part of the same transaction, is leased back. The regulation is directed at sales but "disposed of" should incorporate and apply as well to gifts in trust situations.

first $700 of the shifted income to each child exempt from tax,[4] but the parent-taxpayer will also continue to be entitled to a personal exemption for each child until each is 19 or as long as each is a full-time student if more than half of each child's total support is received from the parent.[5]

The Tax Court has approved the gift-leaseback technique as a legitimate means of reducing your tax liability. It has developed four requirements that must be satisfied before it will permit a grantor to deduct the lease payments.[6] These requirements are as follows:

1. The grantor must not retain substantially the same control over the property that was held before making the gift. This requirement can be satisfied by appointing an independent trustee. The Tax Court has recognized both commercial banks[7] and personal attorneys[8] as independent trustees. In no case should the grantor-taxpayer become the trustee[9]; neither should the spouse.[10]

2. The leaseback should normally be in writing and must require payment of a reasonable lease rental. The trustee should have the trust property appraised[11] and find out the lease price of similar property to justify the reasonableness of the lease rental. A payment schedule should be established and adhered to.[12] Moreover, the trustee's powers detailed in the trust instrument should be broad enough to maintain independence. One suggested technique to assure the court's recognition of the trustee's independence is to make the initial term of the lease less than the term of the

4. I.R.C. Section 63(b)5.
5. See I.R.C. Section 152, Section 151(e)(1)(B) and Section 151(e)(4).
6. See *Mathews v. Comm.,* 61 T.C. 12 (1973), rev'd, 520 F.2d 323, 75-2 USTC Par. 9734, 36 AFTR2d 75-5965 (CA-5, 1975) *cert. den.* See also *Rosenfeld v. Comm.,* (CA-2, 1983), 51 AFTR 2d 83-1251 (May 2, 1983), and *May v. Comm.,* 76 T.C. 7 (1981) (CA-9, 1984), 53 AFTR 2d 84-626, where a gift leaseback was found valid despite an oral lease!
7. See *Serbousek,* TCM 1977-105.
8. See *Lerner,* 71 T.C. 290 (1978).
9. See *Penn,* 51 T.C. 144 (1968); *Van Zandt,* 40 T.C. 824 (1963), aff'd, 341 F.2d 440, 65-1 USTC Par. 9236, 15 AFTR2d 372 (CA-5, 1965) cert. den.
10. See *Larry Benson,* T.C. 86, for problems created with a spouse trustee. See also *Rosenfeld,* T.C. Memo 1982-263 re: control.
11. Supra, note 13.
12. Supra, note 14.

trust. In doing so the trustee is forced to exercise independent power to renegotiate renewal agreements.[13]

3. The leaseback (as distinguished from the gift) must have a bona fide business purpose. This requirement can be easily satisfied, since the trust property is business property intended to be used again in the taxpayer's business. Certain circuits of the U.S. district court, however, require a bona fide business purpose for *both* the leaseback *and the gift.* Merely to place trust property beyond the reach of creditors has been held to be insufficient as a business purpose for the gift.[14] One suggested business purpose would be to get managerial expertise in the control and operation of the property.[15] This would be especially effective, for example, if the taxpayer were a doctor, the property an office building, and the trustee an attorney expert in real estate.

4. The taxpayer must not possess a disqualifying "equity" in the property. Once the property is transferred, the taxpayer possesses only a reversionary interest in the trust property. The Tax Court holds that a reversionary interest is not a disqualifying equity, since its enjoyment is realized only after the trust expires.[16] Unfortunately, the Internal Revenue Service does not accept this position.[17] One way to avoid litigation on this matter would be to create a remainder interest that passes to the taxpayer's spouse or children, or to a corporation set up for the purpose, at the termination of the trust.[18]

Once the gift-leaseback trust is established, the benefits can be substantial. For example, assume a married taxpayer in the 31 percent tax bracket established a trust for three children by transferring business property valued at

13. See *Mathews,* supra, note 11, and *Quinlivan,* TCM 1978-70 aff'd 599 F.2d 269, 79-1 USTC Par. 9396, 44 AFTR2d 79-5059 (CA-8, 1979) cert. den.
14. See *Butler,* 65 T.C. 327 (1975).
15. See *Skemp,* 8 T.C. 415 (1947), rev'd, 168 F.2d 598, 48-1 USTC Par. 9300, 36 AFTR 1089 (CA-7, 1948).
16. See *Oaks,* 44 T.C. 524 (1965) and *Serbousek,* supra, note 12.
17. See Rev. Rul. 54-9, 1954-1 C.B. 20.
18. See supra, note 13 and supra, note 10.

$60,000 into the trust. No gift taxes are payable on such a transfer.[19] Assume further that this is property that has been fully depreciated and that therefore no further deductions are available to the taxpayer if the property is retained. The fair rental for such property, though, is $250 per month.

The higher-bracket taxpayer therefore pays lease rentals of $3,000 per year and takes that amount as a business deduction. This saves $930 in taxes.[20] The three children each include $1,000 in their income, less their share of the trustee's management fee. Ignoring that fee for illustrative purposes and assuming no other income, the three children may pay taxes as low as $45 × 3 and retain $2,865. As a result of a transfer of $3,000, total family wealth has increased by $3,795, for a net increase of $795.[21]

If the property were still subject to depreciation by the original taxpayer, the above benefits would be reduced by the tax savings from depreciation deductions foregone in the transfer. These deductions, though, would be available to the children-beneficiaries. Any maintenance or upkeep expenses incurred for the property can still be deducted by the lessee-taxpayer, if so provided in the lease agreement. Note that in this example the $955 retained by each child can be used to pay that child's college expenses.[22] If the trust were not used, to accumulate $2,865 for tuition would require the 31 percent taxpayer to earn an incremental $4,152 in pretax dollars.[23]

Furthermore, if the property that you're contemplating transferring into trusts for your children is subject to a mortgage, you should be aware that the Garn Act lists certain property transfers that should never trigger loan acceleration under a due on sale clause. These exceptions apply to all loans—to loans originated by state chartered institutions and by federal lending institutions, regardless of the date of their origination. Included in these safe harbor transfers is a transfer in which a spouse or *children* of the borrower receive ownership of the property.

Note that the Tax Reform Act of 1986 eliminated the viability of Clifford Trusts for tax savings. The above trust-leaseback technique, however, would still

19. Split gift ($10,000 × 2) × 3 = $60,000 exclusion.
20. The lease payments would be deductible as ordinary and necessary business expenses under I.R.C. Section 162—$3,000 × .31 = $930 reduction in taxes at that bracket level.
21. $2,865 retained plus $930 saved in taxes.
22. Or any other nonsupport expenses. See supra, note 8.
23. $4,152 at a marginal 31 percent rate leaves $2,865 after taxes.

be viable using an irrevocable trust. All of the other provisions, as discussed above, would apply.

Trust leasebacks have been specifically validated in the following 23 states: Alaska, Arizona, Arkansas, California, Delaware, Hawaii, Idaho, Illinois, Indiana, Missouri, Montana, Nebraska, Nevada, New Jersey, New York, North Dakota, Oregon, Pennsylvania, Rhode Island, South Dakota, Vermont, Washington, and Wisconsin.

The IRS will no longer litigate gift leaseback cases where the lessee is a taxable entity separate from the grantor. This position was announced in an Action on Decision on April 23, 1984. By separate taxable entity, the IRS means a regular corporation, rather than a partnership or a Subchapter S corporation. Two-party gift leaseback arrangements have been upheld not only by the Tax Court but by the following circuits: the Second (*Rosenfeld,* 706 F. 2d 1277, 83-1 USTC para. 9341 [CA-2, 1983], see *Use of gift-leaseback to shift income given substantial boost by new decision,* 12 TL 128 [Sep/Oct 1983]); the Third (*Brown,* 180 F. 2d 926, 50-1 USTC para. 9219; 39 AFTR 155 [CA-3, 1950]); the Seventh (*Skemp,* 168 F. 2d 598, 48-1 USTC para. 9300, 36 AFTR 1089 [CA-7, 1948]); the Eighth (*Quinlivan,* 599 F. 2d 269, 44-2 AFTR 2d 79-5059 [CA-7, 1979]), and the Ninth (*Brooke,* 468 F. 2d 1155, 72-2 USTC para. 9594, 30 AFTR 2d 72-5284 [CA-9, 1972]). However, they have been held invalid in the Fourth and Fifth Circuits (*Perry,* 520 F. 2d 235, 75-2 USTC para. 9629, 36 AFTR 2d 75-5500 [CA-4, 1975], and *Van Zandt,* 341 F. 2d 440, 65-1 USTC para. 9236, 15 AFTR 2d 372 [CA-5, 1965]). In the circuits where gift-leasebacks have been held invalid, however, the transactions only involved two parties; i.e., there was no corporation involved, but instead the lessee was the individual grantor.

An interesting twist on this technique has been developed by Schnepper Associates of Cherry Hill, New Jersey. Assume the children in the preceding example are too young for college and that the taxpayer has a current need for the funds being paid out in lease rentals. The Schnepper Shelter directs the taxpayer to make the lease payments and then to borrow back the money at a fair rate of interest.[24] The interest may be fully deductible, depending on what the money is used for.

---

24. Note that the interest expense need not be limited to the prime rate. In fact, "there is no requirement … that deductible interest be ordinary and necessary or even that it be reasonable." *Dorzback v. Collison,* 52-1 USTC Par. 9263, 195 F.2d 69, 72 (3d Cir. 1952). An interest payment as high as 60 percent to the taxpayer's *mother* has been upheld. *Raymond J. Barton,* 38 TCM 934 (1979).

To use the above example, the taxpayer would make payments of $3,000 and borrow back $3,000 for use in business, paying $300 in interest yearly (10 percent). Each child over age 14 would pay approximately an additional $15 in taxes on the interest payments, a total of an additional $45, but the taxpayer would save an additional $93 in taxes (31 percent of $300)—a difference of $48 per year or $240 over five years. Of course, as its lease rentals increase, so too do tax savings. For 1999, up to $25,750 in taxable income can be taxed to a child over age 14 at the 15 percent rate.

When the children begin college and tuition is due, the taxpayer would then repay the borrowed money, in effect getting a current income tax deduction for future cash payments for the children's tuition. If the taxpayer dies before repayment is made, any remainder value in the trust is included in the estate,[25] but that estate (and therefore any tax due on it) is reduced by any debts owed to the trust—further magnifying the benefits of the Schnepper shelter.[26]

While the Schnepper Shelter also appears to be contrary to congressional intent to eliminate assignment of income among family members, all of its components have been court tested and accepted. Here again, as long as the trustee is truly independent, the separate entity identity of the trust protects the legality and validity of a properly structured transaction. If such a shelter is to be eliminated, it too must be done through congressional action. Until such action, the Schnepper Shelter is a viable technique that should be considered in your planning to reduce your taxes to zero.

Moreover, the leaseback technique can provide substantial advantages to a taxpayer whose passive losses have been reduced or eliminated by the Tax Reform Act of 1986. For example, let's say a doctor operates out of a professional corporation and needs additional equipment, furniture, etc. Instead of buying that equipment through his or her corporation, the doctor will buy the equipment personally and lease it to the corporation. The lease rental payments made by the corporation would be extensively sheltered by the depreciation taken on this "leased business" equipment. Any net profits over and above the depreciation sheltered cash flow could be sheltered as passive income by the doctor's excess passive losses. By utilizing this technique, the doctor is able to take money out of the corporation at a zero tax cost. The cash flow is sheltered by previously unused passive losses and by the depreciation on the new

25. See I.R.C. Section 2033. The value of that reversionary interest is determined by actuarial tables. See *Comm.v. Henry's Estate (Biddle),* (3 Cir: 1947), 161 F2d 574, 35 AFTR 1252 aff'g 4T.C. 423.

26. See I.R.C. Section 2051; Section 2053 (a)(3) and Section 2053 (a)(4).

equipment. Moreover, the corporation is entitled to a tax deduction for the "nontaxable" lease rental payments made to the doctor!

Remember that the Tax Reform Act of 1986 effectively eliminates the use of Clifford Trusts as planning devices. Therefore, in order to effectively use the gift-leaseback technique, rather than a Clifford Trust, you should create an irrevocable trust. With an irrevocable trust, the property is transferred to the trust (beneficiaries) irrevocably. Unlike the Clifford Trust, you will not get it back after 10 years. However, if you are leasing back personal property—e.g., business furniture, equipment, etc.—that has been fully depreciated, that equipment would normally be over 15 years old when it would be returned using a Clifford Trust. The value of that equipment then would be minimal. Had you been gift-leasebacking an office building, however, the Tax Reform Act of 1986 forces you to relinquish present and future ownership of an asset with substantial value. If this is a strategy to be employed, the loss of that value is the price that must be paid.

95 The Schnepper Deep Shelter

Another alternative for shifting income to a lower-bracketed family member is to transfer rental property, excluding the building, to a trust for your children and rent the land back from the trust. The donor parent would still get all of the depreciation on the building, and the trust beneficiary children would be taxed on the lease rental income received. That lease rental income, however, would be a deductible investment expense by the parent. In effect, the parent would be paying lease rental income to the children, deducting that rent expense in the higher bracket, and having it taxed to the children at the lower bracket. Moreover, this transfer of family wealth could take place without any gift tax consequences. In *Stanley J. Wolfe,* T.C. Memo 1984-446, this arrangement was validated with a sale leaseback of land to an irrevocable 10-year trust. The leaseback had a bona fide business purpose, and the lease payments were determined to be reasonable rent. Here again, the Tax Reform Act of 1986 would require the use of an irrevocable trust if this technique were to be used effectively.

96 Family Partnerships

If you are an individual business owner, the use of a family partnership can play an important role in your income tax planning. By giving or selling an interest in your business to members of your family (particularly to your children), you can decrease your personal income tax payments and thereby increase your family unit's spendable income and capital.

For this arrangement to work however, the establishment of the partnership must be genuine. This has been simplified by an IRS tax code section that specifically allows you to set up a family partnership by gift or purchase even though the family partners render no services.[27] Therefore, in those cases where capital is a material income-producing factor for the partnership, significant income shifting to lower-bracketed family members can be accomplished through the establishment of family partnerships.

A family partnership can be established in any of the following ways:

- Take into the partnership any child or relative who can contribute capital.
- Make a gift of a partnership interest to children or other relatives.
- Sell a partnership interest to children or other relatives. This sale can be substantially on credit, to be paid out of subsequent partnership income.
- Accept into partnership any child or other relative who can be expected to perform important work in the business on a regular basis.

97 Family Trusts

A family trust should be very carefully differentiated from a family partnership. A family trust is a trust to which you transfer "the exclusive use of your lifetime services and all the currently earned remuneration therefrom."

27. Section 704(e) of the Internal Revenue Code.

The problem with family trusts is that they do not work. A basic rule of taxation is that income must be taxed to the person who earned it. The transfer of your lifetime services and the income earned through the performance of those services is simply an assignment of income, and therefore ineffective in shifting the tax burden from you to the trust. *You cannot shift income earned through personal service.* A family trust, therefore, is nothing more than a tax avoidance scheme.[28] Do not, however, confuse a family trust with a trust to which income-earning *property* is transferred. When property is transferred, the income from that property *can* be shifted.

98 Employing Members of the Family

If you are an individual business owner, a simple and effective method of splitting your income with a family member is to employ that family member in your business and pay compensation. The employment must be bona fide and the salary paid must be reasonable in relation to the services rendered. Even a young child can be compensated for the reasonable value of such services as cleaning your office, mailing your letters, or opening your mail. A 1982 tax court decision allowed a $1,200 deduction for a 7-year-old child who performed a variety of services—maintenance and office work—for a mobile-home-park operator.[29] Be aware, however, that wages actually used by your children for their own support can affect your claim for their dependency exemptions. When in doubt, have your children bank their wages, thereby saving the exemption and teaching them the virtue of thrift as well.

If your business is not incorporated, services performed by your child under the age of 18 are excluded from social security coverage. (Prior to the Revenue Act of 1987, the exclusion was for a child under the age of 21, and payments to your spouse were also exempt.) This means that you can deduct the value of the services that you pay to your children from your income tax without the added expense of paying social security taxes on that compensation. Services performed in the employ of a corporation, however, are not within this exclusion. But all is not lost if you are in a corporate firm. If your spouse is a

28. *Hailey, Jr.,* 73 T.C. No. 99 (1980).
29. See *Eller,* 77 T.C. No. 66. See also *James A. Moriarty,* T.C. Memo 1984-249, where a doctor was allowed to deduct salaries he paid his teenage children for handling business correspondence, insurance forms, etc., and for keeping patient files in order.

bona fide employee of your corporation, such tax breaks as social security, workmen's compensation, tax-free sick pay, pension or profit-sharing plan benefits, stock option plans, group life insurance, and many others are open to you. According to IRS regulations, services performed in the employ of a partnership are also not within the exclusion unless the requisite family relationship exists between the employee and each of the partners comprising the partnership. Although wages paid to a child under age 18 by an unincorporated business are exempt from social security and federal unemployment taxes, wages paid to a parent are exempt from federal unemployment taxes but not from social security taxes.

Furthermore, if your spouse works for you, you may be able to deduct all your medical expenses. (If you hire your spouse, make sure that you can substantiate the payments that are made. Keep records or a journal of hours worked, and make payments with a check. No record keeping means no substantiation. No substantiation means no deduction [L.T.R. 8753003].) Normally, the deduction for medical expenses is limited to expenses that exceed 7.5 percent of your adjusted gross income. If you have your own business, however, you can install a written medical reimbursement plan for your employees. As a sole proprietor, you would not be considered eligible because you do not qualify as a common-law employee. Your spouse, however, would qualify. *You* would qualify as well if the plan included all employees, the dependent children, and the employee's *spouse!* With such a plan, your cost for insurance coverage and for the medical reimbursement plan would be deductible in full as a business expense. Payments from the plan, of course, would be tax free to you and your spouse. To achieve the anticipated tax results, the plan must be a welfare plan for all employees (Rev. Rul. 71-588; see also Doc. 9409006).

The work need not be full-time and can even be done during your children's summer vacations. Furthermore, provided that you continue to furnish more than one-half of your child's support and your child is younger than 19 or is a full-time student under age 24 for part of each of five months during the year, you can continue to claim a personal exemption deduction for that child. Remember, a child with earned income in 1999 pays *zero* taxes on the first $4,300 worth of earned income. That means if you are in the 31 percent bracket and pay each of your three children $4,300 for services rendered, their tax is zero, the money remains within the family group, and your tax savings is $3,999! Note that another $2,000 could be paid tax-free to each child if placed in an IRA. That could produce a total tax saving of $5,859 ([$4,300 + $2,000] × 3 × .31).

99 Author's Delight

An interesting new income allocation technique has been made possible by an Internal Revenue Service ruling (Ltr. 8217037). A writer signed a contract with a publisher for royalties based on sales of a completed book. The contractual rights owned were then transferred to trusts for the benefit of minor children.

The IRS ruled that this was not a transfer of income, but rather of income-producing property. As long as the income was not used to meet the support obligations of the parents, such income would be taxed only to the trusts/children! In Letter Ruling 8444073, an author assigned to his child all royalties and interest in his publishing contract within 10 days after completing the book. The IRS again ruled that the author's child, not the author, would be taxed on the book royalties. Be careful, however: If an author assigns less than the entire contract, the IRS could assert the assignment of income doctrine to tax the income [see *Lewis,* 45-2 USTC Para. 9348, 34 AFTR 124 (CA-3, 1945)]. Both the contract and the royalties must be assigned: An assignment of the royalty income alone would not be a complete assignment of all of the author's property.

Note, however, that in IRS Letter Ruling 8444073, the IRS ruled that if the author was required in the contract to make revisions to the book, and no additional compensation were received for such revisions, the royalties would represent, in part, compensation for the author's services and would be taxable to that author. The measure of the compensation would presumably be what the publisher paid someone else to do the revisions. The solution to this problem is to have a separate contract or agreement specifying additional or different compensation for revisions. In addition, note that the rule that expenses incurred by an author in writing a book after 1986 must be capitalized and deducted over the life of the income stream of that book (Section 23[b] of the Tax Reform Act of 1986) has been repealed. The IRS had ruled that an author could deduct 50 percent of those expenses in the first year and 25 percent in each of the subsequent two years, in lieu of total income stream capitalization (Notice 88-62, 1988-22 I.R.B.). That ruling is now obsolete.

B Running Your Own Business

One of the important and effective techniques to reduce your taxes to zero is to convert your personal expenses to deductible *business* expenses. In order to do that you must own your own business. This is not complicated, expensive, or difficult to do, and incorporation is *not* needed. I will, however, detail the extensive tax benefits available if a corporate form of business is used.

To be in business, you merely declare yourself to be so. If you want to operate in a noncorporate form under a name different from your own, you can do that as well. In some states, however, if you are operating under an assumed name, you must file what is known as a "DBA" (Doing Business As) form with your local county clerk. Basically, this is merely a statement containing your name, address, and the assumed name under which you are doing business. For example, a form might merely say, "Jeff A. Schnepper is doing business under the name of 'Super Tax Savings Associates'."

Moreover, your business need not make a profit in order for your expenses to be allowable deductions. All you need to do is establish a "profit motive." Under the Internal Revenue Service tax code, a "profit motive" is presumed if you earn any net income in any three out of five business years. In the early loss years you can insist that the Internal Revenue Service defer challenge until the five-year period is up (Form 5213). Furthermore, in fact, you need *never* have to actually show a profit if you can show a *profit motive* (*Melvin Nickerson,* CA-7, No. 82-1323; see also *Paul Farrell,* T.C. Memo, 1983-542 where farming expenses were held deductible despite five straight years of losses. See also *Churchman,* 68 T.C. No. 59, where despite 20 years of losses, the court found a profit objective and allowed deductions of business losses in full, and *Frazier,* T.C. Memo 1985-61.)

The test for deductibility is whether you have an actual and honest profit *objective*—you need not even have a reasonable expectation of profit (Treasury Regulation Section 1.183-2(a); *Dreicer v. Commissioner,* 78 T.C. 642, 1982). While the Tax Court requires a primary or dominant profit motive (*Lemmen,* 77 T.C. 1326 [1981]), in *Johnson,* 86-2 U.S.T.C. Par. 9705, 58 AFTR 2d 86-5894, the U.S. Claims Court held that having a reasonable chance to make a reasonable profit, apart from tax considerations, would suffice. Although the ultimate question is whether or not you have an intent to make a profit, the determination of your motive is made by reference to objective standards, taking into account all of the facts and circumstances. The facts that will be taken into consideration include the following:

1. The manner in which you carry on the activity.
2. The expertise of yourself and your advisors.
3. The time and effort expended by you in carrying out this activity.
4. The expectation that assets used in your business may appreciate in value.
5. Your success in carrying on similar or dissimilar activities.
6. Your history of income or losses with respect to the activity.
7. The amount of occasional profits, if any, that are earned.
8. Your financial status.
9. The elements of personal pleasure or recreation. ("Suffering has never been made a prerequisite for deductibility."—*Jackson v. Commissioner,* 59 T.C. 312)

The fact that you are employed full-time elsewhere will not bar a finding of your being in a separate trade or business. (See *Watson,* T.C. Memo 1988-29. See also *Riddle,* 205 F.2d 357, 62-2 USTC para. 9261, 10 AFTR 2d 5042 [DC Colo., 1962], wherein a full-time government employee was held to be in the trade or business of a consultant, despite the fact that he couldn't deal with anyone who had a government contract; *Estes,* 69-1 USTC para. 9261, 23 AFTR 2d 69-903 [DC Ala., 1969], wherein another full-time government employee was held to be in the lapidary business, so that his expenses were deductible; and *Christensen,* T.C. Memo 1988-484.)

One effective tax planning strategy, therefore, is to convert your personal hobby into a business. For example, one of my clients raced stock cars as a hobby. When he came to me, I converted that hobby into a business. He had cards and stationery printed. He ran ads looking for a sponsor. He gave his "hobby" the image and appearance of a "business," and he demonstrated a real profit motive. This client had a salary income of $40,000. When his new "business" expenses were deducted, not only did he pay zero taxes, but because he qualified for the earned income credit, the Internal Revenue Service paid him money!

Two years later he was audited on that year's return. The law requires that you prove your business expenses, with receipts, checks, or a log book that is updated daily. Unfortunately, he had not kept a log or any receipts for his expenses for the first year. His expenses, though, were legitimate, and he had receipts for the subsequent two years. On the basis of the receipts for the two subsequent years not in question, this taxpayer with $40,000 in other income and *no* receipts, after an IRS audit, paid less than $100 in taxes, including interest and penalties! Had he kept receipts for the first year, he would have paid zero.

To be allowable, your business expenses must be:

a) ordinary and necessary;

b) paid or incurred during the taxable year; *and*

c) connected with the conduct of a trade or business.

"Ordinary and necessary" has been interpreted by the courts and the Internal Revenue Service as "reasonable and customary" and this really depends upon your specific business and the business customs in your locale. In fact, an "ordinary" expense is one that is customary or usual. It need not be customary or usual for you, provided that it is customary or usual for your particular trade, industry, or community. The Supreme Court has held that even a one-time outlay falls within the definition (*Welch v. Helvering,* 290 US 111, 1933). Similarly, the Second Circuit Court of Appeals defined "necessary" as "appropriate" and "helpful," rather than necessarily essential to a taxpayer's business (*Blackmer v. Commissioner,* 70 F.2d 255).

For example, in one case a husband and wife produced, exhibited, and sold their sculptured works. The expenses incurred by them in doing so were held to be ordinary and necessary business expenses.[30] In another case, a breeder and raiser of bird dogs tried to develop an outstanding dog so that he could reap profits from sales and stud fees. Some years were profitable and some showed losses, yet all of the business expenses were found to be deductible.[31] In a third, a coal miner operated a kennel for bird dogs. Despite the fact that he sustained eleven years of losses, there was sufficient evidence of an ever-present profit motive for all of his expenses to be allowed as deductible.[32] In fact, in *Donald C. Kimbrough,* T.C. Memo 1988-185, a high school teacher's golfing activity was engaged in "for profit," resulting in his losses being allowed as deductible expenses. In *Harrison,* T.C. Memo 1996-509, the Tax Court found a profit motive and allowed gold-hunting expenses as deductible.

30. *Road,* 184 F. Supp. 791.
31. *Sloan,* T.C. Memo 1956-36.
32. *Sasso,* T.C. Memo 1961-216.

Owning your own business, therefore, affords you the opportunity to convert a great many of your personal expenses into allowable business deductions. The rest of the section will detail some of the most important reservoirs of deductible expenses.

100 Your Home

Probably the most significant conversion of a personal expense into a business expense occurs when you use your home for your business. (This can apply to a primary *or* secondary business.) To be deductible, these home business expenses must be allowable under the Internal Revenue Service tax code.

The code states that no deduction for any business expenses attributable to an at-home office will be allowable unless these expenses are attributable to a portion of the home used "exclusively and on a regular basis" as:

a) the principal place of business; *or*

b) a place of business that is used by patients, clients, or customers in meeting or dealing with you in the normal course of your business.

Watch out for "exclusive." IRS auditors may question the amount you use your office computer for "business as opposed to investment." Is it 90%–10% or 50%–50%. The question is a trap! If you say anything less than 100%, you have failed the "exclusive" test and lose all your home office deductions. (Basic rule of thumb—never represent yourself at your own audit. You don't know what *not* to say and can never plead ignorance to a difficult question.)

While the code requires that any office at home constitutes your principal place of business, this does not mean that it must be your *single* principal place of business, where all of your businesses are considered together. The test according to the courts is "whether with respect to a particular business conducted by a taxpayer, the home office [is] his principal place for conducting that business." Also, your home office can qualify if it is the principal place of your first *or* second business. (See *Jones,* TCM 1984-544 and *Green,* TCM 1989-599.)

There have been many rulings on this important question. In *Drucker et al. v. Commissioner,* 52 AFTR 2d 83-5804, for example, the Second Circuit Court of Appeals allowed concert musicians home office deductions for the business use of their apartments because they spent most practice time at home and their employers did not provide the musicians with space for the essential task of private practice.

In *Weissman v. Commissioner,* 84-4031, December 20, 1984, the U.S. Court of Appeals for the Second Circuit ruled that a college professor may deduct the expenses of maintaining a home office used exclusively to do most of the research and writing expected of him as a condition of retaining his teaching position. The Court found that the college professor's principal place of business was not necessarily the college at which he teaches any more than a musician's principal place of business is necessarily the concert hall at which he performs. However, the Tax Court, in *Neville Bardsley Dudley et ux.*, T.C. Memo 1987-607, ruled that a full-time business professor at the downtown campus of Wayne County Community College in Detroit was provided office space at the college, was not required to maintain an office in his home, and had no substantial out-of-classroom responsibilities such as research and publication. The Court concluded that Dudley's deduction for home office expenses was legitimate only if his home office was indeed the principal place of business. It was not, so Dudley was denied his deduction.

In *John Meiers et ux. v. Commissioner,* No. 85-1209 (Seventh Cir., January 14, 1986), the Seventh Circuit found that the "principal place of business" must be determined by looking at both hours worked and functions performed. The Court found that the Meierses, who each day spent an hour in the laundromat and two hours at their home office devoted exclusively to administrative work on behalf of the laundry, were entitled to the claimed deductions for the home office. This was another reversal of the Tax Court's "focal point" test. Under that test, the principal place of business has been held to be that place where goods and services are provided to customers or clients or where income is produced.

The 9th Circuit Court of Appeals, in *Pomarantz v. Commissioner,* No. 87-7151, decided on November 7, 1988, that a physician's principal place of business was the hospital where he spent more of his time and treated patients, not his home where he studied medical journals and kept records of patients but treated no patients; therefore, no home office deduction was allowable. Here the court chose not to adopt a specific standard, but found that under any of these tests, the hospital, rather than the home, was the doctor's principal place of business. The doctor consistently spent more time on duty at the hospital than at home. The court found the essence of his profession to be the hands-on treatment of patients, which he did only at the hospital, never at home.

Finally, the court found that the doctor had generated income only by seeing patients at the hospital, not by studying or writing at home.

In another example, the taxpayer was a dermatologist, and the hospital was his principal place of business. But he also owned and managed six rental units, and he had set aside a room in his residence used exclusively for managing that activity. The court found that in this case the managing of rental property was a trade or business and that his home office expenses *were* deductible.[33] This decision was codified in PL 97-119 on December 28, 1981, when President Reagan signed into law an act specifically allowing a deduction for business use of a home for activities other than a taxpayer's primary occupation. (The Black Lung Benefits Revenue Act of 1981 [including other tax provisions adopted], Public Law No. 97-119, Section 113(c), 95 Stat. 1642 [1980].) Furthermore, these changes were made retroactive to years beginning after 1975. Moreover, on November 19, 1982, the Court of Claims ruled that investment activities can constitute a trade or business and therefore allowed home office deductions for taxpayers who managed large investment portfolios full-time (*Moller,* 82-2 USTC Par. 9694, 51 AFTR 2d 83-369). Unfortunately, on November 18, 1983 the Claims Court was overruled by the Federal Circuit Court of Appeals (721 F. 2d 810).

In *Anthony J. Ditunno* [80 T.C. No. 12 (February 7, 1983)], the Tax Court overruled prior precedent and provided a new definition and set of criteria for determining whether a taxpayer is engaged in a trade or business for tax purposes. The Court broadened the meaning of the phrase "trade or business" by replacing the previous "goods and services" test with a "facts and circumstances" test which requires a subjective determination to be made in each instance by "an examination of all the facts involved in each case." Despite a Second Circuit Court of Appeals decision to return to the "goods and services" test in *Gajewski,* 84-1 U.S.C. Par. 9116, 53, AFTR 2d 84-386 (CA-2, 1983), and the *Estate of Dan B. Cole,* No. 83-1601 (6th Circuit, October 23, 1984), where the Appeals Court ruled that one must hold oneself out to others as a provider of goods or services to be in a trade or business, the Tax Court has reaffirmed its "facts and circumstances" test in *Robert P. Groetzinger v. Commissioner,* 82 T.C. No. 61 (May 24, 1983) where it ruled that Groetzinger's trade or business under the Code was gambling. However, on May 23, 1985, the Tax Court revised its decision and deferred to the Second Circuit when it ruled that Gajewski was not in a trade or business (*Gajewski,* 84 T.C. No. 63). *Groetzinger,* however, *was* affirmed by the 7th Circuit Court of Appeals on August 21, 1985 (No. 84-2507). These

33. *Edwin R. Curphey,* T.C. 61.

conflicting decisions were resolved when the Supreme Court, on February 24, 1987, again affirmed *Groetzinger* (480 U.S. 23, 28 (1987)], ruling that the taxpayer, who made gambling his full-time livelihood "with continuity and regularity," was in a trade or business.

Furthermore, in *Morley v. Commissioner,* No. 40685-84, 87 T.C. No. 69, decided on November 19, 1986, the court ruled that a taxpayer's purchase, for the first time, of property that he intends to resell, followed promptly by bona fide efforts to resell the property, constituted a trade or business. Here, even the single purchase of a parcel of real estate, with the requisite intent, constituted a trade or business.

In 1982, the Tax Court ruled that an employee who was required by his employer to take frequent after-office-hours telephone calls from clients could deduct the cost of maintaining his at-home office used exclusively and regularly for that purpose. The Tax Court agreed with the Internal Revenue Service that the taxpayer had failed to prove it was "his principal place of business." But a majority of the Court, siding with the taxpayer, held that his office met the alternative test "as a place of business in which patients, clients, or customers meet or deal with the taxpayer in the normal course of the taxpayer's business." The significance of this decision is that the Court found no requirement "that such meetings or dealings are limited to physical encounters."[34] This decision, however, was reversed upon appeal to the Ninth Circuit on May 31, 1983, and the reversal was affirmed by the Tax Court in *Frankel,* 82 T.C. No. 26 on February 28, 1984. But in the case of *Feldman v. Commissioner,* 14126-82, 84 T.C. No. 1, on January 8, 1985, the Court allowed a taxpayer the costs of maintaining space in his home that he *leased* to his corporate employer for his use as a home office. Here Feldman maintained an office in his home that was rented to his employer for his own use. The employer, of which the taxpayer was a shareholder and director, paid $5,400 designated as rent to Feldman in 1979. The taxpayer reported the rental income and deducted his costs of maintaining the leased space, which he calculated as 15 percent of his home. The Court found, to the extent that the payments were reasonable, that they constituted rent and that the costs of producing that rental income may be deducted. By using the rental strategem, the taxpayer was able to create an allowable home office without "physical encounters." (But see below under depreciation for 1986 Tax Reform Act limits.) Moreover, in Rev. Rul. 86-148, the IRS allowed a deduction for a monthly fee to a security service for a home office used as a dental practice.

34. *John W. Green,* 78 T.C. No. 30.

In *Soliman,* 94 T.C. No. 3 (March 27, 1990), the Tax Court changed the rules again. An anesthesiologist spent approximately 30 percent of his work time at his home office. He kept office equipment there, as well as a telephone, insurance and patient records, and his medical library. He never saw patients at his home, however. For a deduction, Section 280A(c)(1)(A) requires a portion of the home to be used exclusively and regularly as the principal place of a trade or business. Under the "focal point" test previously used by the Tax Court, a home office is a principal place of business if that is where goods and services are provided to customers and revenues are generated. Noting that the test had been questioned by the Second, Seventh, and Ninth Circuits, the Tax Court now states that "where a taxpayer's occupation requires essential organizational and management activities that are distinct from those that generate income, the place where the business is managed can be the principal place of business." The court also concluded that such an administrative location of the business need not be where the taxpayer spends most of his work time. The time spent there need only be substantial and the activities conducted there must be essential to the business as a whole. The focal point test is now replaced by a "facts and circumstances" test—as per the wisdom of *Soliman.* This was affirmed in *Kahaku,* TCM 1990-34.

Unfortunately, *Soliman* was reversed by the U.S. Supreme Court No. 91-998 (January 12, 1993), which ruled that a home office must achieve preeminence in a comparative analysis of the various locations of your trade or business in order for that office to be your "principal place of business." Two primary factors must be examined:

1. The relative importance of the activities performed at each business location; and

2. the amount of time spent at each location.

In Rev. Rul. 94-24, the IRS ruled that a comparison of the relative importance of the activities performed at each location depends on characteristics of each business, and if the business requires a taxpayer to meet with clients or to deliver goods or services to clients, the place where the contact occurs must be given great weight in determining where the most important activities of the business are done.

The IRS also said in the ruling that a comparison of time spent on business at home must be compared to time spent on business at other locations and that the time test becomes more important if the relative importance test provides no definitive answer to the principal place of business.

The revenue ruling also holds that the relative importance test will be applied first to determine whether an office in the home is the taxpayer's principal place of business and if no definitive answer is reached, the IRS will apply the time test. In some cases, the application of both tests may result in a finding that there is no principal place of business.

The IRS provided four examples of how they would apply the ruling—a self-employed author who uses a home office to write, a self-employed retailer of costume jewelry, a self-employed plumber, and a teacher who grades papers at home.

In the example concerning the self-employed author, who spent approximately 30 to 35 hours per week in the home office to write, and 10 to 15 hours a week at other locations conducting research or meeting with publishers or attending promotional events, the IRS said that the essence of the author's home office is the principal place of business and the author can deduct expenses for the business use of the home, the IRS concluded.

The IRS said a self-employed plumber who works 40 hours at customer locations and spends 10 hours per week at a home office talking with customers on the telephone, deciding what supplies to order, and reviewing the books, cannot deduct expenses for the business use of the home.

Even though the plumber employs a nonrelated, part-time employee in the home office to schedule appointments, order supplies, and keep books, the essence of the plumber's business requires the plumber to work at the homes or offices of customers and the fact that the plumber has an employee working in the home office does not alter the result, the IRS said.

In the case of the jewelry retailer, the most important activity of the business—sales to customers—is conducted at a number of locations, including craft shows and consignment shops. In this case, the amount of time spent at each location assumes particular significance, the IRS said. Because the retailer spent more time per week in the home office, expenses for business use of the home are deductible.

In the case of the teacher, the IRS said the principal place of business is clearly the school, and although work done at home is essential and time-consuming, expenses cannot be deducted for business use of the home.

Purely administrative or billing activities alone would not normally be determinative. In *Crawford v. Commissioner,* No. 1380-90, T.C. Memo 1993-192, April 29, 1993, the Tax Court applied the *Soliman* test to deny a home office deduction to a doctor who did follow-up patient work at home and who worked as an independent contractor for several Dallas hospitals.

The Tax Relief Act of 1997 reversed *Soliman* for tax years beginning after December, 31, 1998. *Now* home offices will be allowed for purely administrative or management activities if you have no other fixed place of business for those activities.

Note that in *Lynn Crawford,* T.C. Memo 1993-192, the Tax Court ruled that the IRS could not add penalties to your tax bill when it disallows a home office deduction that was supported by the Tax Court's decision at the time it was taken.

Another option is available to qualify space for a home office deduction—if that space is used as a storage unit. The Small Business Job Protection Act of 1996 clarified that the special rule contained in prior law, Section 280A(c)(2), permits deductions for expenses relating to a storage unit in a taxpayer's home regularly used for inventory or product samples (or both) of the taxpayer's trade or business of selling products at retail or wholesale provided that the home is the sole fixed location of such trade or business. Such deductions will now be allowed for business expenses related to a space within a home that are used on a regular *(even if not exclusive)* basis as a storage unit.

Unfortunately, however, the Tax Reform Act of 1986 provided that when an employee leases a portion of his home to his employer, no net losses would be allowable. It is possible, nevertheless, to avoid this provision if the house were owned exclusively by the employee's spouse who was the only party to the lease with the corporation. In that situation the prohibition between an employee and his employer would not be violated.

The following expenses for your home office will be allowable:

1. *Depreciation on your office furniture and equipment.* This would include any desks, chairs, couches, lamps, etc., that you put into your office. In *Liddle,* No. 94-7733, 9/8/95, a professional musician was allowed depreciation on his violin. Moreover, in *Zeidler* T.C. Memo 1996-157, the court ruled that a computer used in a home office for business was deductible even without records of usage. Don't be a tax case—keep records.

2. *Depreciation on your "office building."* If your home is owned, you can depreciate the portion of the acquisition cost and improvements allocatable to your home office. Note that in *Weightman,* TCM 1981-301, the Tax Court held that a taxpayer need not have an entire room as an office but could set aside an area for exclusive business use. Therefore, one part of a room could be used for personal reasons without affecting the deduction for the business use of another part of the room.

3. *Rent.* If your home is rented, you can depreciate an allocatable portion of that rent for your home office.

4. *Homeowner's insurance.* If you own your home, an allocatable portion of your homeowner's insurance is deductible.

5. *Electric utilities.* An allocatable portion of your electric bill for providing current and light to your home office is also deductible.

6. *Heating and air conditioning.* An allocatable portion for heating your home office in winter or air conditioning your home office in summer would also be an allowable, ordinary and necessary business expense. In addition, if you put in an air conditioner that does not become a structural part of the building—a window or portable air conditioner—that air conditioner's cost can be recovered through depreciation.

7. *Phone.* The use of your home phone would also normally be an ordinary and necessary business expense. You can either deduct an allocatable portion of your regular phone bill or insert a separate line exclusively for the use of your "business." Even part of the basic charge for a home phone, when used for business, was deductible (*Robert H. Lee,* T.C. Memo 1960-58) until January 1, 1989. Thereafter, deductible costs for business use of a phone at home are still allowable for:

   a) Long-distance calls.

   b) Equipment rental.

   c) Call waiting.

   d) Call forwarding.

   e) Charges for a second phone line.

   Moreover, you should determine whether basic local service includes charges for local message units. If not, then a proportionate part of these would also be deductible.

The following example demonstrates the available tax advantage of having a home office: Assume that you have a five-room home costing $150,000, with $50,000 allocatable to land and $100,000 allocatable to the building. The home has a 39-year recovery life, because the "office space" is not *residential* rental space. You purchase $20,000 in furniture with a seven-year recovery life for your one-room home office and incur the following total costs over the year:

	Allowable Deductions
Heat and air conditioning ($2,400 × 1/5) =	$ 480
Electricity ($1,200 × 1/5) =	240
Phone (50 percent business) ($1,200 × 1/2) =	600
Depreciation on furniture:	
Election to expense	19,000
First year depreciation [($20,000 – $19,000) × .1428]	143
Depreciation on home (39 years) [(100,000 ÷ 5) × .02461]	492
Total Deductions	$20,955
Tax savings in the 31 percent bracket	$ 6,496

Under IRS regulations, these deductions are allowable only if they do not exceed the amount of gross income derived from the use of your home for your trade or business reduced by the deductions that are allowed without regard to their connection with your trade or business—that is, interest and taxes. Note that in addition to the expenses deducted above for your home office, you can also deduct an allocatable portion of the interest on your mortgage and your home taxes. These deductions are allowable as "above the line" business deductions even if you do not qualify to itemize your deductions.

The limitation on home office deductions can be shown by the following example. Assume the same deductions as in the previous case, but in addition, assume that you pay $3,000 in real estate taxes and $10,000 in mortgage interest. Furthermore assume that you have gross revenue of $5,000 from your "business." Your deductions are limited as follows:

Gross revenue (income)	$ 5,000
Minus allocatable portion of interest in taxes [1/5 × ($10,000 + $3,000)]	– 2,600
Limit on remaining expenses	$ 2,400
Remaining expenses (from above)	$20,955
Deductible expenses (lesser of actual expenses or limit)	$ 2,400

The $18,555 is carried forward as a deduction to offset income in the subsequent year.

Several additional factors should be noted. First, the Internal Revenue Service instructions talk about gross income, not gross revenue. They are equivalent. I am talking here about total inflow of dollars before *any* expenses. Second, with such high expenses in relation to income, you should elect straight-line depreciation over an extended life period. Third, note that even though your home office expenses are limited, there is no limitation on other expenses—for instance, travel, entertainment, supplies, etc.—for your business. Note that these examples do not contain *all* of the possible home office deductions. Anything that relates to your home office per se would be a potential deduction. For example, add any allocatable water charges, sewer charges, repairs, depreciation on such improvements as painting, aluminum siding, etc. In Rev. Rul. 86-148, the IRS allowed a deduction of a proportionate share of the monthly fee for a home security system, as well as depreciation deductions on that system, to a homeowner who used one-sixth of his house as office space. Your deductions are limited only by your imagination and your ability to relate your expenditures to your business.

Although the above limitations on home office deductions are contained in the Internal Revenue Service regulations, in the Tax Court case of *Scott v. Commissioner*, No. 18916-82, 84 T.C. No. 45, decided on April 15, 1985, Judge Simpson and the Court ruled that those regulations were invalid. According to the Judge, Section 280A(c) (5) limits the deductions allocable to the use of a home office to the gross income derived from such use. For purposes of this limitation, "gross income is not reduced by the other deductions attributable to the ... businesses carried on in the building." What this means is that in the above example, the deductions would be limited not to $2,400, but to the gross revenue of $5,000 (allowable, of course, to the actual remaining expenses incurred). While *Scott* was specifically overruled by the Tax Reform Act of 1986 for years after 1986, the Internal Revenue Service National Office has held that it will apply for open years prior to 1987 (TAM 8640001).

If you fear taxable recapture of depreciation upon sale of your house note that in Rev. Rul. 82-26 (February 8, 1982) the IRS ruled that the *prior* business use of a residence would not require the recognition of gain when the residence is sold. The IRS looked to the use of the residence at the time of the sale (Rev. Rul. 59-72). Thus, if the entire house was used as the principal residence in the year of sale, the entire gain on the sale would have been eligible for tax-deferral, regardless of prior use. [See IRC Sections 1234 and 1250(d) (7) (A).] Unfortunately, the Tax Reform Act of 1997 now requires the recapture of any depreciation taken upon sale, and this depreciation is taxed at a 25% rate. However, you still have the time value of the tax savings. Moreover, while any depreciation will be recaptured to the extent of the gain, real appreciation recognized on the sale can *now* be sheltered by the $250,000/$500,000 exclusion if you qualify.

To prove a home office, photograph it, have it on your business cards and stationery, and keep a log of whom you see, when you use the office, and what you work on.

In addition, travel expenses between your home office and job sites are deductible. For example, one taxpayer operated a home-repair business using his home as a business headquarters where he received inquiries for possible contracting services. He claimed a deduction for the expenses of traveling between his home and job sites. The deduction was allowable because his home was the sole fixed location of his business and was essential to his business operations (*Adams,* TCM 1982-223). In fact, in *Carl F. Worden,* T.C. Memo 1981-366, a home office had the effect of converting a personal residence into a job site. In that case, the Tax Court found that the insurance salesman's home was his place of business. Therefore, *all* his travel costs were allowable as business deductions. See also 76 T.C. No. 72, *Wisconsin Psychiatric Services, Limited,* where Wess R. Vogt, a psychiatrist, established that his home office was his principal office and therefore that trips to and from his home were business trips and not nondeductible commuting expenses; *Wicker,* TCM 1986-1, wherein the court ruled that a home office that was the principal place of business for a nurse-anesthesiologist enables her to deduct the costs of going from there to the hospital where she was associated and where she practiced exclusively, but without office space; and *Ronald Carey,* SD, OH, No. C-3-80-422, where a salesman who worked out of his home was able to deduct the cost of his daily sales trips because the salesman's home was his principal place of work.

In *Walker v. Comm.,* No. 20919-19, 101 T.C. No. 36, 12/13/93, the court applied Revenue Ruling 90-23 and held that a self-employed taxpayer could deduct truck expenses paid for traveling to various locations in a national forest where he worked as a logger. It found that his residence was a "regular place of business" and that transportation expenses between a "regular place of business" and a "temporary work location" were deductible. The advance in *Walker* was that the residence did *not* qualify as a home office—such as the principal place of business under *Soliman.*

In Revenue Ruling 94-37, the IRS ruled that *Walker* would be followed only if one of two other conditions apply.

Under the first condition, if the taxpayer has one or more regular work locations away from the taxpayer's residence, the taxpayer may deduct daily transportation expenses incurred in going between the taxpayer's residence and a *temporary* work location in the same trade or business, regardless of the distance.

Under the second condition, if the taxpayer's residence is the taxpayer's principal place of business, the taxpayer may deduct daily transportation expenses incurred in going between the residence and another work location in the same trade or business, regardless of whether the other work location is *regular or temporary* and regardless of the distance.

In 1999, the IRS modified the rule again. Issued January 15, 1999, Revenue Ruling 99-7 now provides three exceptions to the general rule that transportation expenses between a residence and a place of business or employment are not deductible. Now you *can* deduct:

1. Expenses incurred in going from your residence and a temporary work location outside the metropolitan area where you live and normally work;
2. Expenses incurred going between your residence and a temporary work location in the same trade or business in which you have one or more regular work locations away from this residence; and
3. Expenses incurred going between your home office (principal place of business) and another work location in the same trade or business, regardless of the distance or whether the work location is regular or temporary.

A work location is "temporary" if employment there is realistically expected to last—and does in fact last—for one year or less.

Note that if you file a separate income tax from your spouse, an additional income-shifting opportunity is available. In Rev. Rul. 74-209, the Internal Revenue Service ruled that rent paid by a husband to his wife for the use of the jointly owned Wisconsin real estate that the husband used in his business is deductible as a business expense on the husband's separate income tax return. For this strategy to be successful, you should compare the net results on a joint return to those on separate returns. It is a technique that should be considered where appropriate.

Moreover, additional tax savings can be found if you have a home office that requires a secretary or a receptionist to be present at all times during business hours and the only person available is a member of your family. In the previous section we discussed the advantages of employing members of your family in your business as an income-shifting device. In this case, any member of your family, including your spouse, can reap enormous tax-saving advantages. The tax code excludes from gross income the value of any meals furnished to an employee by the employer for the convenience of the employer if the meals are furnished on the business premises of the employer.[35] If your spouse, for example, is required as your employee to be on your business premises—that is, your home office—as a receptionist, telephone operator, etc., then any meals (for instance, lunch) provided are not compensation that your spouse would include in gross income, but they are a *deductible* business expense to you! By structuring your first or second business in this manner, you can effectively and *legally* deduct the cost of your spouse's or children's lunches. Your spouse must truly be employed and required to be on business premises during lunchtime or the deduction will not be allowed (*Weidmann,* 89-1 USTC ¶9197 [DC N.Y. 1989]). Given the price of food today, this is an enormous benefit that can result in substantial tax savings. Moreover, no social security payments are due on such lunches. At $5 per lunch, five times a week for 50 weeks, your total deductible expense would be $1,250. In the 31 percent bracket, this saves you $388 in taxes!

101 Your Car

Automobile expenses incurred in your business travel are deductible either as a travel expense (if away from home on business) or as a transportation expense (even if you are not away from home). Remember, transportation expenses are not normally deductible unless they are incurred in a business or investment situation. To get the deduction here, there must be a direct connection between the use of the car and your trade or business or some income-producing activity—for instance, to check on your investments. If you have one car that you use both for personal and for business use, only the portion of your car expenses directly attributable to business use is deductible.

In allocating your car expenses between business and personal use, there are a number of methods that you can use. One simple method is known as the mileage cost basis. Using this method, you multiply your business mileage by a standard mileage rate that the Internal Revenue Service allows in lieu of the operating and fixed costs of your car. The 1999 standard mileage rate is 32.5¢ per mile (31¢ per mile as of April 1, 1999) plus parking fees, interest, taxes, and tolls. So, for example, if you drive your car 24,000 business miles equally over the year, you will deduct $7,530 (6,000 @ .325 plus 18,000 @ .31). In addition to this $7,530

35. Section 119 of the Internal Revenue Code.

deduction, you will be allowed all of your expenses for parking fees, interest, taxes, and tolls.

As an alternative to the mileage cost basis, you can use either the mileage percentage basis or the weekly percentage basis. Under the mileage percentage method, you simply divide your business mileage by your total mileage and take that percentage of your total expenses as a deduction. Under the weekly percentage method, you take that percentage of the weekdays that you use your car for business use. So, for example, if you use your car two days a week on business, you will be able to deduct two-sevenths of your total auto expenses.

Included in such auto expenses, when using the mileage or weekly percentage method, are not only your parking fees and tolls but also depreciation on your car, interest, taxes, registration and license fees, and gas, oil, and repair expenses. Given the cost of gasoline, it would probably be to your advantage to keep receipts and records of your actual expenditures. Whereas the Internal Revenue Service allows you a deduction of 32.5¢/31.0¢ per mile under the mileage cost basis, studies by auto-renting firms have established that actual mileage costs may be two to three times greater than that allowance.

There is a special tax planning strategy that you can use if you have two cars in your family. Assume that you have been using one car exclusively for business and the other exclusively for personal family use and that you put 36,000 miles each year on your business car and only 12,000 miles a year on your family car. Normally you can deduct only the costs of using the business car. Now, suppose you switched the use of each car every six months. The combined mileage of both cars in the original example is 48,000 miles per year. By rotating your cars equally between business and family use, each car will be driven 24,000 miles a year, 75 percent of which will be business miles (36 ÷ 48). Therefore, 75 percent of your depreciation and other costs on *each* car will be deductible. This can be a lot more than simply deducting all of the costs on one car and nothing on the other.

A taxpayer cannot normally deduct commuting expenses. However, if you have a regular place of business, you *can* deduct daily transportation expenses from your *home* and a *temporary* work location (Rev. Rul. 90-23, 1990-11 I.R.B. Rev. Rul. 94-37, and Rev. Rul. 99-7).

What is a temporary place of business? For purposes of determining whether daily transportation expenses are deductible business expenses or nondeductible commuting expenses, a regular place of business is any location at which the taxpayer works or performs services on a regular basis, and a temporary place of business is any location at which the taxpayer performs services on an *irregular or short-term* (i.e., generally a matter of days or weeks) basis. A taxpayer may be considered as working or performing services at a particular location on a regular basis whether or not the taxpayer works or performs services at that location every week or on a set schedule. For example, daily transportation expenses incurred by a doctor in going between the doctor's residence and one or more offices, clinics, or hospitals at which the doctor works or performs services on a regular basis are nondeductible commuting expenses. However, daily transportation expenses incurred by the doctor in going between a clinic and a hospital or between the doctor's residence and a temporary work location are deductible business expenses.

Under this rule, a doctor's expense of travel from home to a patient's home for a house call is deductible.

An executive or salesperson may make calls on customers or clients. If these visits are on an infrequent basis, the client's office would be a temporary place of business. The cost of travel from home to client's office is deductible.

The rule is not limited to prospective application. Thus, it applies retroactively to open years (see also Rev. Rul. 99-7 discussed on page 349).

If the taxpayer is an employee, the deduction for these expenses can only be claimed as a miscellaneous itemized deduction. As such, it is subject to the 2 percent of adjusted gross income floor on such deductions.

The IRS warns that if an audit shows a clear pattern of abuse by the taxpayer in claiming a business expense deduction for daily transportation expenses paid or incurred in going between the taxpayer's residence and asserted temporary work locations without proof of a valid business purpose, the IRS will disallow any deduction for those expenses and impose appropriate penalties.

Employer reimbursement. In some cases, an employer may reimburse an employee for otherwise deductible daily transportation expenses. The IRS says that the employee doesn't have to include such reimbursement if it is paid under an accountable plan, i.e., one that (a) requires the employee to substantiate expenses covered by the arrangement to the person providing the reimbursement, and (b) requires the employee to return any amount above the substantiated expenses. Reimbursement that is paid under a nonaccountable plan must be included by the employee in gross income. In turn, the employee can deduct the deductible daily transportation expenses as a miscellaneous itemized deduction.

Employer reporting. An employer is not required to report on the employee's Form W-2, or to withhold payroll taxes on, amounts paid as a reimbursement or other expense allowance for daily transportation expenses that are paid under an accountable place. However, reporting and withholding are required for amounts paid as reimbursement or other expense allowance for daily transportation amounts that are paid under a nonaccountable plan.

102 Meals and Entertainment

Wouldn't it be great to have the Internal Revenue Service pay part of the cost of your meals and entertainment? When you have your own business, you can have the Internal Revenue Service split the bills for these expenses with you.

In order to deduct any expenses for travel, entertainment, gifts, or listed property, you must have a receipt or other documentary evidence for any lodging expenditure of $75 or more. For expenditures incurred prior to October 1, 1995, the $75 amount was $25. (Internal Revenue Service Notice 95-50, issued September 29, 1995.)

Any expenses for food and drink furnished under circumstances of a type generally considered conducive to a business discussion, and when a business discussion is held, are deductible business expenses. Therefore, the custom of entertaining business clients or potential business clients with food and drink in restaurants and hotels will be deductible if they meet the requirements of an ordinary and necessary expense. When you go out with friends or relatives for a meal or drink, do you ever pick up their check? If they are or *could be* potential clients or customers for your business, and if you discussed business with them, then that expense would be deductible. Alternatively, if they are in business and they pay your expenses for meals at a restaurant, those expenses would be deductible for them.

Note that under the Tax Reform Act of 1986, no deduction is allowed with respect to entertainment, amusement, or recreation unless the taxpayer establishes that the item was directly related to or, in the case of an item directly preceding or following a substantial and bona fide business discussion, that such item was associated with the active conduct of the taxpayer's trade or business and that meals are now included as entertainment expenses for this purpose. A meal expenditure is associated with the active conduct of a trade or business if the taxpayer establishes a clear business purpose in making the expenditure. The meal must directly follow or precede a substantial and bona fide business discussion. The directly follow or precede standard is satisfied if the meal occurs on the same day as the business discussion.

The directly related test is satisfied if any one of the following four tests is satisfied:

1. The taxpayer had more than a general expectation of deriving some business benefit; the taxpayer actively engaged in a business meeting, negotia-

tion, or other bona fide business transaction; the principal character or aspect of the meal was the active conduct of the taxpayer's business; and the expenditure was allocable to the taxpayer and persons with whom the taxpayer engaged in the active conduct of business.

2. The expenditure occurred in a clear business setting, directly in furtherance of the taxpayer's trade or business.
3. The expenditure was made directly or indirectly for the benefit of an individual (other than an employee), and if such expenditure was in the nature of compensation for services rendered or paid as a prize or award, that is required to be included in gross income.
4. The expenditure was made with respect to a facility used by the taxpayer for the furnishing of food or beverages in an atmosphere conducive to business discussion.

However, even if one of the four directly related tests is satisfied, expenditures will not be directly related to the active conduct of a trade or business if incurred under circumstances where there is little or no possibility of engaging in the active conduct of a trade or business.

You should have receipts specifying the name of the restaurant, the amount, and the date. The relationship of your guest to your business activity should also be noted. Recognize, however, that no actual business need come from the meeting so long as you discuss business at the restaurant. In this area be careful not to simply alternate days in which you and your friend pick up the check. Any "regular" exchange of meal checks, if caught by the Internal Revenue Service, will be disallowed as a sham in an audit and subject you to fraud penalties.

Moreover, not only can you deduct meals, but you can also deduct business entertainment expenses. Amounts spent for business entertainment, amusement, or recreation will be allowable if you can show that the expense was:

a) for entertainment directly preceding or following a substantial bona fide business discussion (including business meetings at a convention that was associated with your trade or business); *or*

b) directly related to the active conduct of your trade or business.

Examples of entertainment, amusement, or recreation include entertaining guests at nightclubs, theaters, football games, prizefights, and on hunting, fishing, and vacation trips. In *Detko v. Commissioner,* No. 14790-81, T.C. Memo 1987-99, February 18, 1987, an anesthesiologist was found to be entitled to deductions for entertainment expenses and depreciation in connection with a fishing boat on which he entertained doctors who were his referral source!

In applying the "directly related" or "associated with" tests, remember these points:

1. The entertaining must be to further your trade or business. So, for example, if you entertain at a time when you already have more business than you can possibly handle, your deduction will be disallowed.

2. Expenses that violate public policy or local law—for instance, providing "call girls" for clients or serving liquor where it is against local law—will not be deductible.

3. Entertainment, amusement, or recreation expenses that are considered lavish or extravagant under the circumstances will be deductible *only* up to a reasonable amount. What a "reasonable amount" is depends upon all of the facts and circumstances; given today's business and entertainment climate, it would be very difficult to exceed a "reasonable amount."

Remember that the Tax Reform Act of 1986 limited deductions for most meals and entertainment to 80 percent of cost. After December 31, 1993, the limit fell to 50 percent. Moreover, expenditures qualify as business meals or business entertainment only if business is actually discussed. Business transportation (airfare, taxis, etc.) remains fully deductible, but travel to *investment* seminars or *investment* conventions is not. The chart below summarizes these rules.

Type of Expense	Deductible
Lunch with customer/client; business before, during, or after the meal	50%
No business discussed	None
Cab fare to restaurant	100%
Air fare to Philadelphia to call on customer/client	100%
Lodging in Philadelphia	100%
Meals in Philadelphia (alone)	50%
Meals with customer/client; no business discussed:	
a. Your meal	50%
b. Customer's/client's meal	None
Air fare to New York for dentist to attend dental convention	100%
Meals in New York	50%
Air fare to Dallas for investment seminar	None
Lodging in Dallas	None
Tickets to ball game for taxpayer and customer/client; business discussed	50%
Taxi fare to game	100%
Food and drink at game	50%
Complimentary theater tickets for customer/client; taxpayer *not* present (note possible deduction as a gift)	None
Lunch at service organization as member	50%
Tickets to charity golf tournament run by volunteers	100%
Greens fees, carts, food and beverages consumed while hosting customer/client; business discussed	50%

Note that some meal and entertainment expenses remain fully deductible:

- Expenses treated by the employer as compensation to an employee (the 50 percent reduction applies at the employee level if the employee claims the deduction);
- Expenses reimbursed under an "accountable plan" (fully deductible to the person receiving the reimbursement, with the reduction applying to the person making the reimbursement);

- Expenses incurred for recreational or social activities provided by the employer for the benefit of its employees (e.g., holiday parties, summer outings, etc.);
- Expenses for goods, services, and facilities made available by the taxpayer to the general public, such as promotional tickets or customer samples;
- Food or beverage expenses excludable under the "de minimis fringe benefit" rules; and
- Expenses related to the ticket package costs for sporting events arranged primarily for the purpose of charitable fund-raising.

Note, in addition, that the percent disallowance did not apply to pre-1989 expenses for food or beverages furnished as an integral part of a convention, seminar, annual meeting, or similar program if: (a) the meal charge was not separately stated, (b) more than 50 percent of the participants were away from home, (c) at least 40 individuals attended, and (d) the meal event included a speaker.

For years after December, 31, 1997 the business meal deduction will be increased by 5% every other year to 80% *for persons subject to the federal hours of service limitation.*

With entertainment as well as with meals, your expenses must be substantiated. You should have a receipt detailing the amount paid, the client you entertained, the business relationship, the date, and the place. The deductions for meals and entertainment allow you substantial opportunities to convert your personal expenditures into allowable business deductions. Do not fail to claim them and do not fail to keep them because of lack of adequate substantiation. In the 31 percent tax bracket, $100 worth of football tickets costs you $84.50. No matter how much money you are making, it would be worth $15.50 in tax savings to spend thirty seconds noting the name of your business client on the back of the ticket stub.

103 Travel and Vacation

There is no law prohibiting you from combining a business trip and a vacation. The Internal Revenue Service concedes that you are entitled to a deduction for attending a business convention. While such attendance must benefit or advance your business to be a deductible expense, there is no reason why such a convention cannot coincide with your vacation. If a business purpose can be established, the expenses of your spouse may also be deductible (Rev. Rul. 56-168; see also *Bank of Stockton,* TCM 1977-24). Note, however, that such business conventions or seminars must relate to your specific business. For example, in IRS Letter Ruling 8451027 and Rev. Rul. 84-113, 1984-31 I.R.B. 5, the Internal Revenue Service ruled that investment seminars in resort locations and a financial planning seminar dealing with general planning strategies were not deductible because they did not relate specifically to the taxpayer's activities.

Moreover, the Omnibus Budget Reconciliation Act of 1993, effective after December 31, 1993, denies a deduction for travel expenses paid or incurred with respect to a spouse, dependent, or other individual accompanying a person on business travel, unless (1) the spouse, dependent, or other individual accompanying the person is a bona fide employee of the person paying or reimbursing the expenses, (2) the travel of the spouse, dependent, or other individual is for a bona fide business purpose, and (3) the expenses of the spouse, dependent, or other individual would otherwise be deductible. No inference is intended as to the deductibility of these expenses under present law. The denial of the deduction does not apply to expenses that would otherwise qualify as deductible moving expenses.

WITHIN THE UNITED STATES

If the business-vacation trip is within the United States, the transportation expenses will be deductible only if the trip is primarily for business. If the trip is primarily for pleasure, no transportation expenses can be taken as a deduction. This means that you have to establish a primary business motive for making the trip—for instance, a convention located in that city, or a client or potential client that you want to see at that location. It would be advisable under such a situation to write to this person and receive in return a letter requesting you to visit her or him to discuss business matters. The amount of time that you spend on business as opposed to pleasure will be a factor in answering the "primarily" question. For example, if you spend five days conducting business and three days sightseeing and seeing shows, the trip will be deemed primarily for business (five days vs. three days) and the transportation will be deductible. Alternatively, if you conducted business for two days and vacationed the remaining six, the trip will most likely be found primarily personal, and no transportation expenses will be allowed.

Even if the trip is found to be primarily personal, any expenses incurred at the destination that are properly allocatable to business—meals, lodging, and incidental expenses during your "business days"—will be deductible.

OUTSIDE THE UNITED STATES

If the business-vacation trip is outside the United States, Canada, certain other Caribbean countries,[36] Mexico, and the Pacific Islands Trust Territories, special rules apply. If you were out of the country for seven days or less, or if less than 25 percent of the time was for personal purposes, no allocation of transportation expenses need be made. Furthermore, no allocation is required if you had no substantial control over the trip arrangements and if the desire for a vacation was not a major factor in taking the trip. Alternatively, if the trip was primarily for pleasure, none of the transportation expenses will be deductible. In all other cases, all travel expenses must be allocated between business and personal expenses, and days devoted to travel are considered business days.

For example, assume that you took a trip from New York to London primarily for business purposes. You were away from home from July 20 through July 29 and spent three days vacationing and seven days conducting business (including two travel days). Your fare was $500 and your meals and lodging amounted to $75 per day. You can deduct 70 percent of your transportation expenses (seven days out of ten) and $75 per day for seven business days, as you were away from home for more than seven days and more than 25 percent of your time was devoted to personal purposes.

If you find your trip is subject to the allocation rule, there is a planning strategy to maximize your tax deductions. When booking your flight, arrange for a

36. The Caribbean Basin Initiative (CBI) was enacted on August 5, 1983, authorizing preferential tax measures for Caribbean Basin countries and territories. The Act allows deductions for business expenses incurred while attending conventions and meetings in a designated Caribbean Basin beneficiary country, if that country enters into an agreement with the United States to provide for the exchange of certain tax information. The provisions of the CBI expire September 30, 1995. Currently, the following countries are eligible and qualify for the benefits of the CBI: Antigua and Barbuda, the Bahamas, Barbados, Belize, Bermuda, the British Virgin Islands, Costa Rica, Dominica, the Dominican Republic, El Salvador, Grenada, Guatemala, Haiti, Honduras, Jamaica, Montserrat, the Netherlands Antilles, Panama, St. Christopher-Nevis, St. Lucia, St. Vincent, and Trinidad and Tobago. The countries that remain eligible but have not yet qualified for the benefits of the CBI are Anguilla, the Cayman Islands, Guyana, Nicaragua, Surinam, and the Turks and Caicos Islands (see Rev. Rul. 87-95). Updates to the list of qualifying countries can be obtained by calling (202)287-4851.

stopover within the United States at the point closest to your destination. That way, the portion of the trip between your home and the stopover point will be fully deductible. You will have to allocate only the cost of the remainder of the trip.

For example, assume that you live in New York and will be attending a three-day business convention in the Bahamas that will be followed by a six-day vacation. If you fly directly to the Bahamas from New York, only one-third of the cost of your round-trip flight is deductible (three business days out of nine days total). However, if you fly from New York to Miami, conduct business in Miami, then take another flight to the Bahamas, the entire cost of the trip from New York to Miami would be deductible—as well as one-third of the cost of the trip from Miami to the Bahamas and back.

FOREIGN CONVENTIONS

No deduction will be allowed for expenses attributable to a foreign convention/vacation unless it is "reasonable for the convention to be held outside North America." "North America" means the above countries including the Pacific Islands Trust Territories. Under Rev. Rul. 94-56, 1994-36 I.R.B. 10, for purposes of claiming deductions for expenses incurred in connection with a convention, seminar, or similar meeting, the following areas are included in the "North American Area":

1. The 50 states of the United States and the District of Columbia;
2. The possessions of the United States, which for this purpose are American Samoa, Baker Island, the Commonwealth of Puerto Rico, the Commonwealth of the Northern Mariana Islands, Guam, Howland Island, Jarvis Island, Johnston Island, Kingman Reef, the Midway Islands, Palmyra, the United States Virgin Islands, Wake Island, and other United States islands, cays, and reefs not part of any of the fifty states or the District of Columbia;
3. Canada;
4. Mexico;
5. The Trust Territory of the Pacific Islands (that is, Palau);
6. The Republic of the Marshall Islands;
7. The Federated States of Micronesia;

Country	For Expenses Incurred in Attending a Convention That Began After
8. Barbados	November 2, 1984
9. Bermuda	December 1, 1988
10. Costa Rica	February 11, 1991
11. Dominica	May 7, 1988
12. Dominican Republic	October 11, 1989
13. Grenada	July 12, 1987
14. Guyana	August 26, 1992
15. Honduras	October 10, 1991
16. Jamaica	December 17, 1986
17. St. Lucia	April 21, 1991
18. Trinidad and Tobago	February 8, 1990

In other words, there is no deduction if it is more reasonable to have the convention within rather than outside of North America. Three factors must be considered in determining the reasonableness of the convention location:

1. The purpose of the meeting and the activities taking place at the meeting.
2. The purpose and activities of the sponsoring organization or groups.
3. The residence of the active members of the sponsoring organization or groups and places where other meetings of the sponsors have been or will be held.

CRUISE CONVENTIONS

In addition, there is no limit on the number of foreign conventions/vacations that yield deductible expenses, but no deductions will be allowed for conventions, seminars, or other meetings held on cruise ships, except if:

a) the convention or meeting is directly related to your trade or business;

b) the cruise ship is U.S. registered; *and*

c) all ports of call are located in the U.S. or its possessions. Only the following ports qualify as possessions: The U.S. Virgin Islands (St. Thomas, St. John, St. Croix), American Samoa, Guam, the North Mariana Islands, and Puerto Rico.

Even under these circumstances, the maximum deduction is $2,000 for each taxpayer (Highway Revenue Act of 1982) and you must attach two written statements to your return. The first statement, signed by you, must include information as to the number of days that were devoted to scheduled business activities, a program of the scheduled business activities, and such other information as may be required by regulations. The other statement, signed by a representative of the sponsoring organization, must include a schedule of the business activities each day, the number of hours you attended such scheduled activities, and such other information as may be required by regulations. Business seminars on cruise ships that are U.S. registered are now being offered by American Hawaii Cruises (to Hawaii) and Delta Line Cruises (on the Ohio and Mississippi Rivers). In addition, American Cruise Lines and the new Clipper Cruise Line, which operates a variety of voyages in intercoastal waters from New England to Florida, are also operating under the seminar restrictions.

WATER TRANSPORTATION

Note that the Tax Reform Act of 1986 limits the deduction for expenses incurred for transportation by water to twice the highest federal government per diem allowance (for employees traveling away from home but serving in the United States) times the number of days in transit. These rates are changed annually and are found in Publication 1542 available free from the IRS. In addition, according to Notice 87-23, the now 50 percent limitation on meals and entertainment is applied prior to the above maximum per diem limitations. If meal expenses are not separately stated, the amount deductible under the luxury water or travel limitation is not subject to the 50 percent rule.

Ship travel, however, can be an asset on a combined business-vacation trip. Days spent in transit count as business days in the allocation formula. For example, assume a two-day business meeting in London followed by a two-week British vacation. If you fly (one day each way), only 22 percent of your travel excluding transportation is deductible—two business days plus two days of travel out of a total of eighteen days away. But if you sail (five days each way), 46 percent is deductible—two business days plus ten days of travel out of a total 26 days away.

Remember, the key to being able to deduct your vacation as a business expense is prior planning. Make sure that you can substantiate your business purpose for the trip and your expenses. Properly planned and substantiated expenses will allow you to deduct the cost of your transportation, food, meals, lodging, entertainment, cleaning, etc. I have found that perhaps the easiest way to maintain a substantiation record is to keep a diary or account book of such expenses. Combined with appropriate receipts, such a diary will help reduce your taxes to zero.

104 Gifts

Ordinary and necessary expenses for business gifts you make directly or indirectly to any individual will be allowed as deductible expenses. However, the total value of business gifts during the tax year to any one individual cannot be more than $25, and in addition, gifts from a husband and wife are treated as coming from one donor in applying this limitation. Incidental costs, such as packaging, mailing or other delivery, and insuring the gifts, are not included in this limitation. The giving of business gifts is big business. According to *Incentive Marketing Magazine,* in 1983 approximately 50 million business gifts were purchased in the United States at a total cost of over 1 billion dollars.

The following items are not subject to the $25 limitation:

1. Items of a clear advertising nature that cost $4 or less,
   - **a)** on which your name is permanently printed; *or*
   - **b)** which are among a number of identical items generally distributed by you.
2. Signs, display racks, or other promotional material given by you as a producer or wholesaler to a retailer for use on the business premises of the retailer.
3. Employee awards.

Here again you must provide substantiation for your expenses in order to make them allowable. While the price of allowance is increased record keeping, the benefit now is that gifts to friends, relatives, etc., who are or may become business clients or associates have been converted from nondeductible personal expenses to allowable income tax deductions. Every time you convert a personal expense to a deductible business expense you take one more step on the road to reducing your taxes to zero.

105 Advertising

The Tax Court allowed the sponsor of an amateur basketball team to deduct the costs of the team as an advertising expense. The taxpayer used the team sponsorship as the main form of advertising for his rental housing and commodity brokerage businesses. Before games, the taxpayer would meet with customers to discuss business. The Court said that, while there was an element of personal satisfaction, the team sponsorship promoted the taxpayer's business at low cost. *James C. Bower,* T.C. Memo 1990-16.

106 Deductible Clothes

The costs of buying and maintaining a uniform are deductible business expenses only if the uniform is (1) specifically required to be worn as a condition of employment and (2) is not adaptable for general or continued use. Uniforms that can be worn as ordinary clothing don't meet this second test and can't be considered ordinary and necessary business expenses.

Uniforms worn by police officers, fire fighters, nurses, bus drivers and railway workers have been held to meet this two-part test [Rev. Rul. 70-474, C.B. 1970-2, 34], as have commercial fishermen's protective clothing [Rev. Rul. 55-235, C.B. 1955-1, 274]. But work clothing worn by painters (white shirts, caps, bib overalls, and work shoes) did not qualify, even though the clothing was required by a union [Rev. Rul. 57-143, C.B. 1957-1,89].

Note, however, that ordering clothes imprinted with the name of your business may be deductible as *advertising.*

107 Creative Deductions—Busting the IRS

In Green Bay, Wisconsin, a stripper got a tax deduction for surgically enlarged breasts. Then she put her deductions on display and called it a victory for all exotic dancers.

"It is simply a stage prop we are carrying around to make money," Cynthia Hess said before appearing at the Bamboo Room.

Hess, otherwise known as "Chesty Love," and her husband, Reginald R. Hess of Fort Wayne, Ind., claimed a $2,088 deduction on the implants that enlarged her bust size to 56FF.

The Internal Revenue Service turned it down.

But Hess found an ally in Special Trial Judge Joan Seitz Pate, who ruled that the breasts did increase her income, and at 10 pounds each, were so cumbersome that she couldn't derive personal benefit from them.

108 Medical Premiums

Section 162(m), added by the Tax Reform Act of 1986, permits self-employed individuals to deduct a percentage of their health insurance premiums paid as a business expense. For 1998 and 1999, the percentage is 45 percent; it increases to 60 percent in 1999, to 70 percent in 2002, and to 100 percent in 2003. The amount of this deduction is limited to your self-employment income and is not available on a month-by-month basis, if you or your spouse is eligible to participate in any subsidized health plan maintained by any employer of either you or your spouse. The deduction is also not available unless the premium is paid under a nondiscriminatory health plan. The premium paid is an "above the line" deduction. That means that it is deductible even if you do not itemize your deductions.

109 Borrowing from Your Company

If your own business is in a corporate form, you have a special opportunity for tax savings. This opportunity is the supersophisticated technique of borrowing from your own corporation or from your corporate pension plan. This can be done as long as the loan bears a reasonable rate of interest—that is, the prime rate, give or take a percentage point.

This extraordinary technique allows you to borrow money, pay yourself interest, deduct the interest you pay (see Chapter 6 for limitations), and receive the same interest tax-free. It normally is done by having a qualified profit-sharing or pension plan make a loan to you as one of its participants. This technique was approved by the Internal Revenue Service for a qualified plan even with *single* participant.[37]

37. Letter Ruling 800-8059.

This technique will be approved by the Internal Revenue Service for a qualified plan that has a loan provision *if* the loan:

a) is available to all participants and beneficiaries on an equal basis;

b) is not made available to highly compensated office employees, officers, or shareholders in a percentage amount greater than that available to other employees;

c) is made in accordance with specific provisions regarding such loans set forth in the plan;

d) bears a reasonable rate of interest; *and*

e) is adequately secured.

The vested portion of your account (for a profit-sharing or money purchase plan) can be used as security for the loan. Moreover, loans from such plans can exceed the vested amount in your account without the plan's risking disqualification as long as:

- The loans are adequately secured by other than the nonvested portion of the plan.
- The loans bear a reasonable interest rate.
- The loans are repaid within a specified period of time.

Loan security for a defined benefit pension plan can be provided up to an amount equal to the actuarial equivalent, or present value, of your accrued benefit. Furthermore, the arrangement must be an actual loan. There must be evidence that a true debtor-creditor relationship exists; otherwise the "loan" will be labeled by the Internal Revenue Service as an "advance distribution," making such funds taxable income to you.

Note that the Tax Equity and Fiscal Responsibility Act of 1982 somewhat restricts borrowing against the vested benefits of your plan. Effective with respect to loans made after August 13, 1982, the law allows loans up to the lesser of $50,000 or 50 percent of the value of your vested employee benefit, but not less than $10,000. Additionally, the loan must be repaid within five years. But a loan used to acquire, construct, or rehabilitate your personal residence or the residence of a member of your family would not be subject to the five-year repayment rule.

The extraordinary savings from this technique can be demonstrated by the following example:

Your vested share in a profit-sharing plan	$100,000
Amount borrowed to purchase a home	$50,000
Interest rate	20%
Tax-free interest you pay into the plan	$10,000
Amount deducted	$10,000
Tax savings at 31% tax bracket	$3,100
New value of your profit-sharing plan	$60,000

In effect, you pay yourself $10,000 and, by virtue of your tax deduction, come out ahead by $3,100!

Note that the Tax Reform Act of 1986 eliminated this benefit for key employee loans made after December 31, 1986. Effective for loans made after that date, the top loan is limited to $50,000 less the outstanding loan balance of plan loans on the date of the loan *and* less the excess of the highest outstanding loan balance from the plan during the one-year period ending on the day before the date of the loan over the outstanding loan balance of plan loans on the date of the loan. For example, assume you have a balance of $150,000 in your profit-sharing plan and have never made any loans from the plan. On January 1, 1999, you borrow $35,000. On May 1, 1999, the loan balance is $30,000. On November 1, 1999, the loan balance is $25,000. At that time you would like to borrow an additional amount without having to include it in income. The maximum amount you may borrow on that date is $15,000 ($50,000 – $25,000 – [$35,000 – $25,000]).

Moreover, the former five-year repayment period has been tightened. Effective for loans made after December 31, 1986, the five-year period may be extended only in the case of a loan made to purchase the principal residence of the plan participant. The extension of the five-year period is not permitted in the case of refinancing a principal residence. In addition, the repayment of loans made after December 31, 1986, must be made in level payments. The use of balloon payment arrangements is no longer permitted. Such payments must be made no less frequently than quarterly.

Finally, no interest is deductible for any post-1986 loan to a key employee. This means that even if you use the funds to purchase a principal residence, if you are a key employee, no interest will be deductible, even though all interest would have been fully deductible had you secured normal financing of the home.

A key employee was defined as a plan participant who at any time during the plan year or the preceding four plan years was (1) an officer of the company, (2) an employee owning one of the 10 largest interests in the company, (3) a 5-percent owner of the company, or (4) a 1-percent owner of the company earning more than $150,000 per year (IRC § 416) (i) (1) (A).

110 Lending to Your Company

The previous technique demonstrated the tax saving opportunity in making loans *from* your corporation. But borrowing is a two-way street. You can make loans *to* your corporation and save taxes that way as well. If you have helped finance your corporation through loans over the years, there are some advantages in forgiving the principal and interest your corporation owes you. As far as the principal is concerned, the law provides that forgiveness of any principal due is a tax-free contribution to the capital of the corporation, and that you, as the stockholder, can increase the cost basis of your stock by the amount of the principal forgiven.

Interest unpaid to you by the corporation, however, is another matter. The Internal Revenue Service tax code allows your company to pay you interest, just as to any other lender, at a rate comparable to that charged by other lenders. If you are on the cash basis and wish to reduce your taxable income, simply do not collect the interest from your corporation. On the accrual basis, on the other hand, your company will accumulate the interest due on the loan and deduct it on its *own* tax return. Because of this tax benefit, the Internal Revenue Service has argued in the past that the unpaid interest should be treated as income to the company. This argument, however, was rejected by the Tax Court in 1976, when the court ruled that the unpaid interest was not income to the corporation, even though the company had accrued and deducted it in an earlier year.[38]

The net result of the case is that interest accrued and deducted by your corporation for a debt owed to you as one of its stockholders is not income either to the corporation or to you when you forgive that interest on that debt. This court-created tax loophole, however, will apply only if you do not own more than 50 percent of the corporate stock. Special rules in the Internal Revenue Code prohibit a corporation from deducting the interest in that case.

38. *Putoma,* 66 T.C. 652.

But if you own 50 percent or less of the stock, and you are in a similar stockholder-lender position, you may want to forgive the interest that your company owes you. While this rule is an anomaly in the law, it is the law. So long as it is a completely legal technique, you should have no compunction about using it to reduce your taxes.

111 Miscellaneous Corporate Advantages

There are a number of other miscellaneous tax saving strategies that owning your own company in a corporate form will allow you. They include the following:

1. The corporation can purchase for you \$50,000 of group term life insurance with tax-deductible dollars. Term life insurance in excess of \$50,000 is also available at a negligible after-tax cost to you. For example, assume that you are 39 years old and the corporation purchases \$100,000 in term life insurance for you in 2000. The premium would be 100 percent deductible to the corporation, and you would have to report only \$54 per year of additional income. In the 31 percent bracket, this would cost only an additional \$37.26.

2. The corporation can pay health insurance premiums for you with tax-deductible dollars and no additional tax to you.

3. Disability insurance premiums are also payable and deductible by the corporation with no tax to you.

4. The corporation can accumulate dividend income or other income at the low rate of 15 percent on the first \$50,000. Furthermore, the corporation can receive dividend income and exclude from taxation 80[39] percent of those dividends, reducing its effective tax rate to 3 percent (15% × 20% = 3%). Furthermore, such dividends can be placed tax-free into your retirement plan.

39. Seventy percent if the corporation does not own at least 20 percent of the dividend-paying corporation. In order to qualify for the dividends-received deduction, the stocks must have been held by the corporation for at least 46 days. The holding period is 91 days for cumulative preferred stock in arrears for more than 366 days. Borrowing to purchase equities by corporate investors will reduce the amount of the dividends-received deduction.

5. The corporation can pay you and/or your estate a $5,000 death benefit free of income and estate taxes for employees dying prior to August 20, 1996.

6. The corporation can utilize structured life insurance plans with deductible dollars at the same time that it is building up cash reserves.

7. Both Keogh and IRA plans absolutely prohibit owner-employees from borrowing money from the plan. But all plan participants *may* borrow their money from a corporate retirement plan. The advantages of such a provision have already been detailed.

Remember, the interest earned on such loans will not be taxed to either the corporation or the plan and may be deductible by you on your personal income tax return. In the process, it will increase the amount of money accumulating tax-free in the plan, as well as your total financial wealth.

8. Prior to the Tax Reform Act of 1984, a current deduction for future college costs could have been allowed. The corporation could have set up an educational benefit plan in which a trust was established to which the corporation contributed funds to provide a given amount per year for each employee's child enrolled in an accredited college or university, without regard for financial need or academic achievement. In the case of *Greensboro Pathology Associates,* Federal Circuit, December 15, 1982, the Court ruled that the contributions to the trust were deductible when made by the corporation and only taxable income to the employees when the money was withdrawn. This can be a significant deferral tax advantage if the children are relatively young. In such a situation, the company can receive its deductions several years before the employees must pick up the income.

In determining that this was a welfare plan rather than a plan of deferred compensation wherein the corporate deduction would have been deferred until the employee recognized the income, the court looked at the following questions:

a) Is the plan concerned with the employees' well-being?

b) Are the benefits based on the earnings of the employees?

c) Are benefits based on the length of service?

d) Are benefits available to all employees?

e) Are benefits really a substitute for salaries?

f) Does the plan serve its stated purpose, or is it a sham?

g) Does the employer lose control of the funds contributed?

h) Can the funds revert to the company or its shareholders?

i) Is the plan administered by someone independent of the company?

The court said that if items b and c were present, there was a strong presumption that the plan was a form of deferred compensation—no deduction allowed until funds were distributed. It also said that item d, availability to all employees, was essential if the plan was to qualify for current deductions.

The passage of the Tax Reform Act of 1984 appears, however, to effectively overrule the *Greensboro* case as to the immediate deductibility of plan contributions. The Tax Reform Act of 1984 provides that contributions to a funded welfare benefit plan will not be deductible under Section 162 but will now be governed by new Section 419. Section 419 provides that a contribution made to a funded welfare plan will be deductible in the year of contribution only to the extent that it would have been allowable as a deduction if the employer had paid the benefits directly and the employer used the cash-basis method of accounting. In essence, unless the plan is distributing benefits, no immediate deduction is allowable for fund contributions by the employer. Section 419, however, does provide for a carryover of contributions in excess of deductibility to the succeeding taxable year. Moreover, these new rules on plan contribution deductions apply not only to formal welfare benefit plans but to any method of employer contributions having the effect of a plan.

9. A final advantage of the corporate form of business is the elimination of the danger of vicarious liability that exists in a professional partnership. For example, assume that Dr. Smith and Dr. Jones operate as a partnership. Dr. Jones is on a vacation on the day that her partner, Dr. Smith, creates a potential malpractice problem in the operating room. Under the vicarious liability rules that apply to partnerships, Dr. Jones is just as responsible for the malpractice as is Dr. Smith, who is directly involved. In a corporate setting, Dr. Smith and the corporation are liable. Dr. Jones is personally off the hook.

CHAPTER 9

Investment Planning to Save Taxes

"If Patrick Henry thought that taxation without representation was bad, he should see how bad it is with representation."

OLD FARMER'S ALMANAC

"There's nothing more dangerous than the U.S. Congress with an idea."

E. PATRICK MCGUIRE of the Conference Board, *Opening a Conference Examining Tax Incentives*

The first key to investment planning for 1999 tax purposes is finding out the status of the capital gains tax on sales of capital assets. Capital assets include such things as stock, securities, real estate held as an investment, and most properties held for personal purposes. In fact, all property except the following is included under the umbrella of capital assets:

- Stock in trade, inventory, and other property held primarily for sale to customers in the ordinary course of business.
- Depreciable property used in a trade or business and real property used in a trade or business.
- Accounts and notes receivable acquired in the ordinary course of a trade or business for services rendered or from the sale of stock in trade, inventory, or other property held for sale to customers.
- A copyright or a literary, musical, or artistic composition held by a person whose personal efforts created it, or held by a taxpayer whose basis is determined by reference to the creator's basis (e.g., by gift).
- A letter or memorandum or similar property held by a person for whom the property was prepared or produced, or held by a taxpayer whose basis is determined by reference to the first person's basis (e.g., by gift).
- Obligations of the federal or a state government or one of its political subdivisions that are issued on a discount basis and payable without interest at a fixed maturity date not exceeding one year from the date of issue.
- Free U.S. Government publications.

Prior to 1987, an individual could deduct from gross income 60 percent of *net long-term capital gain* (the excess of net long-term capital gain over any net short-term capital loss), leaving only 40 percent taxable. Since the maximum regular income tax rate was 50 percent, the deduction meant that net capital gain was taxed at a maximum rate of 20 percent (50 percent × 40 percent).

Capital losses were allowed in full against capital gains. Capital losses were also allowed against up to $3,000 of ordinary income; however, only one-half of the excess of long-term capital loss over net short-term capital gain was allowed for this purpose. Unused capital losses could be carried forward indefinitely.

The Tax Reform Act of 1986 repealed the net long-term capital gain deduction. However, the maximum rate on long-term capital gains of individuals was made 28 percent.

The 1986 law did not change the character of gain as ordinary or capital, or as long- or short-term capital gain. Capital losses are allowed in full against capital gain, as under prior law.

Capital-loss treatment also was changed by the 1986 law. Capital losses will continue to be fully offset by capital gains. The overall deduction limit of $3,000 per year (against ordinary income) still applies. Losses over that amount can be carried over to future years. Short-term capital losses will continue to be fully deductible against ordinary income, up to this $3,000 limit. Long-term capital losses also will be fully deductible against up to $3,000 of ordinary income. Beginning in 1987, both short-term and long-term capital-loss carry-forwards can be used to offset ordinary income on a dollar-for-dollar basis up to a $3,000 limit.

Note that the difference between long-term and short-term capital gains and losses still exists under current law. A gain from the sale or exchange of an asset acquired after December 31, 1987, will not be treated as long-term capital gain unless you held it for more than one year. The holding period was more than six months for assets acquired after June 22, 1984, and before January 1, 1988. Recognize that the longer holding period still has an impact, beyond the maximum 28 percent rate, in that it affects charitable contributions of certain property. For example, a deduction normally cannot exceed 50 percent of your adjusted gross income. The equivalent limit for contributions to a private nonoperating foundation is 30 percent. For contributions of capital gain property, however, the limit is 30 percent of the contribution base, or 20 percent if the contribution is made to a private nonoperating foundation.

Capital-gain property includes only property that would have produced long-term capital gain if it had been sold at the time of the contribution. With the longer holding period, it would be that much longer before assets acquired after 1987 fall into that definition and within the lower percentage limits.

Moreover, the otherwise allowable deduction for a charitable contribution of property has to be reduced by the amount of gain that would not be long-term capital gain if the contributed property has been sold at the time of the contribution. That covers the amount of hypothetical gain that would have been recaptured in an actual sale (e.g., depreciation). However, it also covers all the hypothetical gain on an asset acquired after 1987 and not held for more than one year. Thus, the deduction for contributions of such post-1987 capital gain property is limited to the property's adjusted basis.

Moreover, in post-1986 tax years, if the sale of the property would have produced long-term gain, the difference between the allowable deduction for the contributed property and its adjusted basis is a preference item for alternative minimum tax purposes. The rule does not apply, however, to contributions of tangible personal property beginning in 1991 and all property, real, personal, and intangible, after December 31, 1992.

The Tax Relief Act of 1997 changed the above rules. Retroactive to May 7, 1997, the new law cuts the top capital gains tax rate from 28% to 20% for investments (excluding collectibles such as art, stamps, or coins which will retain a maximum 28% rate) held for at least 18 months (12 months if the investment was sold before July 29, 1997). The top rate would drop further to 18% for assets purchased after 2000 and held for 5 years or longer. Gains on real estate, to the extent of Section 1250 depreciation recapture, will be taxed at a maximum 25% rate. Capital assets held for more than 12 months but less than 18 months will retain the maximum 28% rate.

For those in the lower brackets, the rate would fall to as low as 10% on investments held more than 18 months by married couples with incomes less than $43,050 (in 1999). That rate would drop to 8% in 2001 for assets held for five years or longer regardless of when the asset was acquired.

Capital Gains Holding Period Changes

Holding Period	Maximum Rate
• Assets held less than one year (taxed at the same rate as ordinary income)	39.6%
• Assets held more than one year but less than 18 months (and sold after 7/28/97 but before January 1, 1998)	28.0%
• Assets held more than one year (and sold after 12/31/97) (10% for taxpayers in the 15% tax bracket)	20.0%
• Assets purchased after 2000 and held at least five years	18.0%
• For taxpayers in the 15% tax bracket with assets held at least five years (no matter when they were purchased) and sold after 2000	8.0%
• Assets purchased before 2000 and marked-to-market on 1/1/01 and held at least five years[1]	18.0%

[1]Taxpayers will have the option in 2001 of paying taxes at the 20% rate on accumulated profits with future profits being taxed at 18% provided the assets are held for five years or more.

The 1998 Reform Act changed the rules again. Now, as of January 1, 1998, the long-term holding period is again 12 months!

The impact of the change? Enormous! The difference between short-term and long-term gains is the difference between 39.6% and as low as 18% which is 21.6%. On a $100,000 gain, that's $21,600 in your pocket. The new law encourages investors, not traders. Net short-term gains are taxed like ordinary income. It hurts tax-deferred investments. All payments out of retirement plans (except for the new Roth IRA plans discussed in Chapter 13) are taxed at ordinary income rates. The advantage of tax deferral disappears when you could have paid an 18% capital gains tax and end up paying ordinary income tax at the 39.6% rate. If you are close to retirement and expect to remain in the higher brackets, tax deferral may even work against you.

As the lower rates apply only to net long-term capital gains, the following tax planning strategies and techniques are suggested to optimize the advantages of favored capital gains rates at the end of the year:

Planning Year-End Securities Transactions

Results to Date	Unrealized Portfolio Gains and Losses	Possible Action to Be Taken Before Year End
Short-term	Losses and gains	Cover short-term gain by taking losses. Take additional loss to offset ordinary income.
Short-term gain only	No losses	Taxwise, nothing need be done.
Short-term loss	Gains only	Generally no advantage to realizing additional gains, except gains can be realized tax-free to extent of losses.
Long-term gain	Losses and gains	Cover long-term gain by taking losses. Take additional losses to offset ordinary income.
Long-term gain	Gains only	Taxwise, nothing need be done.

Long-term loss	Gains only	Generally nothing further need be done. Long-term loss will offset ordinary income. Remainder will carry forward. Opportunity exists to realize gains at no tax cost to extent of losses.
Long-term loss	Losses only	Nothing need be done.
None	Losses and gains	Generally no advantage to realizing gains except to extent of losses. Consider taking loss to offset ordinary income.

The last year in which a tax choice was available when publicly traded securities were sold during the last five trading days of the year was 1986. Starting in 1987, taxes must be paid the year the sale is made.

112 Short Sales

In a short sale, you contract to sell stock that you do not own or intend to make available for delivery upon sale. The securities are borrowed for delivery to the buyer. The sale must eventually be covered by the purchase of the securities in the market or by the delivery of securities owned at the time of the short sale. The taxable event occurs when the securities are delivered to the lender (usually your brokerage firm), by the seller to close the short sale.

Whether capital gain or loss on a short sale is long- or short-term will generally be determined by how long the seller held the stock used to close the short sale. However, special rules exist regarding short sales where substantially identical property is held by the short seller at the time of the short sale. These rules prevent the conversion of a short-term gain into a long-term gain or the conversion of a long-term loss into a short-term loss.

The definition of substantially identical is a question of fact. Securities of different corporations are not substantially identical. However, a convertibility feature or an impending reorganization under which such securities will be exchanged for one another could lead to a different conclusion. Bonds of different issuers, or with a difference in maturity of at least 20 percent, or a difference in coupon of at least 30 percent would not be substantially identical.

A short sale could have been used to defer the recognition of a capital gain into the next taxable year. For example, an investor selling "short against the box," will lock in the selling price but can defer recognition of the gain until the position is closed, which can be in the next taxable year. Here you are selling short securities that you already own to lock in gain but defer recognition.

Unfortunately, the Tax Relief Act of 1997 closed this area of tax planning. Generally, for all short sales made after June 8, 1997, such sales are considered "constructive sales" and are taxable in the year made.

113 Broad-Based Index Options and Regulated Futures Contracts (RFCs)

Broad-based index options and RFCs are subject to special rules. Those open at year-end must be marked to market, and unrealized gains and losses are taxed as if the position had been closed at year-end. Under these special rules, 60 percent of the capital gain or loss is treated as long-term and 40 percent is treated as short-term, irrespective of the actual holding period.

114 Wash Sales

The wash sale rule applies only to losses. A wash sale occurs when an investor who sells a security at a loss purchases (or acquires an option to purchase) securities that are substantially identical to those sold within the 61-day period, beginning 30 days before the sale and ending 30 days after the sale.

A deduction is denied for losses realized under those circumstances. Instead, the disallowed loss is added to the basis of the substantially identical securities acquired. The holding period of the securities sold at a loss is added to the holding period of the newly acquired securities.

A wash sale may be avoided by purchasing an equivalent amount of the same security, holding both lots for 31 days, and then selling the original security at a loss. Alternatively, you could reinvest in securities that are not substantially identical, such as those of another company in the same industry.

115 Premiums on Taxable and Tax-Exempt Bonds

At your option, the premium on a taxable bond may be amortized and deducted each year (with a corresponding reduction in cost basis) over the remaining life of the bond.

Otherwise, upon sale or maturity, the premium may result in a capital loss that would be deductible at that time. For bonds acquired before October 23, 1986, the amortized amount of premium is considered a miscellaneous itemized deduction not subject to the 2 percent floor. For bonds acquired after October 22, 1986, and before 1988, the deduction for amortized bond premium is treated as interest expense, subject to the investment interest expense limitations.

However, effective for bonds acquired after 1987 or, if elected, for obligations acquired after October 22, 1986, amortizable bond premium is treated as an offset to interest income on the bond rather than as a separate interest deduction (and therefore not subject to investment interest expense limitations).

On tax-exempt bonds, the premium must be amortized over the life of the bond or to the earliest call date. The premium cannot be deducted because it is an expense of earning tax-exempt interest. The basis of the tax-exempt bond is reduced by the amount of premium attributable to the period for which the bond is held. If the bond is held to maturity, no capital loss will result from the purchase of a tax-exempt bond at a premium.

116 Original Issue Discount (OID)—Taxable Bonds

OID interest on government bonds issued after July 1, 1982, and corporate bonds issued after May 28, 1969, accrues and must be reported annually for tax purposes even though it is not payable until sale or maturity of the instrument. For corporate bonds issued before July 2, 1982, OID is computed on a straight-line monthly accrual basis. For corporate and government bonds issued after July 1, 1982, OID is computed on a constant-interest-rate method based on the original issue price and yield-to-maturity.

117 Original Issue Discount (OID)—Tax-Exempt Bonds

Tax-exempt OID is calculated under two different methods, depending on when the bond was issued. OID on a tax-free municipal bond is treated as tax-exempt interest income and is not included in taxable income. However, calculating OID on tax-exempt bonds is necessary for purposes of adjusting basis in order to determine whether there is a capital gain or loss on sale or redemption prior to maturity, and for determining whether Social Security benefits are taxable.

For tax-exempt OID securities issued prior to September 4, 1982, or acquired prior to March 2, 1984, OID is calculated on a straight-line basis. For tax-exempt OID securities issued after September 3, 1982, and acquired after March 1, 1984, OID is calculated under the constant-rate method.

118 Market Discount

A market discount occurs when you buy a bond in the secondary market for a price *below* a certain value. For most bonds, that value is par (usually $1,000). In the case of original issue discount (OID) bonds (e.g., zero coupon bonds), the measuring stick is the bond's current "accreted" value. This is the increased value of the bond due to the pro rata accretion of the discount while you hold the bond. If an old bond is bought for less than its accreted value, it becomes a market discount bond. The discount, therefore, is normally the difference between acquisition price and par or accreted value.

In the past, when market discount bonds were sold, called, or matured, the excess of the redemption or sales price over the purchase price was treated as capital gain rather than ordinary income. Market discount bonds *purchased after* April 30, 1993 will now have the difference taxed as ordinary income.

119 Municipal Bond Swaps

Municipal bond swaps are transactions in which municipal bonds in a given portfolio are sold and the proceeds of the sale are then used to purchase other municipal bonds of like quality, coupon, par value, and yield.

Traditionally, this "tax swap" is the favorite method among individual investors to reduce their tax liabilities. Municipal bond market prices characteristically move up or down uniformly. Therefore, in most cases, if your bonds have depreciated in value, all other issues have as well, because interest rates have risen. The result is that by effectuating a swap, you merely establish paper losses for tax purposes. Your capital loss is the difference between your adjusted cost (or book value) and the current selling price of the bonds. The proceeds of a sale can be used to purchase other bonds, which should differ from those sold in coupon, maturity, or issuer. In most cases, tax swapping can be accomplished with a small adjustment (extension) of maturity to overcome market spreads.

Correctly done, a timely tax swap can provide you with the following benefits:

- Equal or greater income from your investments.
- Equivalent quality and/or maturity in bond portfolios.
- Continued participation in a favored security, or realizing tax losses that reduce your tax.
- Meaningful tax savings to offset both capital gains taken in your current year and up to $3,000 of other income, by using capital losses realized through the tax swap.

The mechanics of a tax swap are relatively simple. If you want to establish a capital loss for tax purposes, sell a bond for less than you paid for it. If at the same time you want to maintain your portfolio, buy a similar bond. There is no actual loss. At maturity the bond pays its face amount. If you buy one bond at $900 and sell it at $850, and then buy another at $850 and hold it to $1,000 maturity, you still make the $100 difference between your original purchase price and maturity; the intermediate sale and purchase do not matter. If you have a portfolio of bonds, therefore, you should contact your broker at year-end to arrange for an appropriate tax saving swap. If structured correctly, whether you do it with municipal bonds or with regular bonds, you should be a tax winner.

120 Employee Options—Non-Qualified

Another investment tax saving strategy involves the handling of employee stock options. The grant of a nonqualified stock option results in no compensation to you as an employee. But exercising your option does result in compensation, measured by the difference between the option price and the fair market value at the time of the exercise.

For example, the *grant* of an option to buy 1,000 shares at $20 per share when the market value is $25 per share results in no income to you. If you *exercise* the option later when the market value is $40, you will recognize compensation income of $20,000 ($40,000 – $20,000). This taxable income plus the cash investment necessary to exercise the option are the major disadvantages of nonqualified stock options. In order to exercise the option in the above example, you must raise $26,200 in cash—$20,000 to buy the stock and as much as $6,200 to pay the tax in the 31 percent bracket.

The Internal Revenue Service has ruled that if full or partial payment for stock acquired upon exercise of a nonqualified stock option is made by transferring identical shares in the employer company, it will not result in any gain to you on the shares used to pay for the stock option.[2] The following example shows how you can take advantage of this ruling. Assume you own 1,000 shares of stock of your employer, acquired for $10 per share. You exercise a nonqualified option to acquire 2,000 shares of identical stock at an option price of $25 per share ($50,000 total). At the time of exercise, the market value of the stock is $50 per share ($100,000 total value).

If your employer agrees, you can pay for the 2,000 new shares by transferring to that employer the 1,000 shares of identical stock you already own. Since the value of the stock surrendered equals the option price, no cash is needed to buy the stock. In this way, you defer recognition of gain on the transfer of the 1,000 old shares, but you enjoy the full appreciated value by converting 1,000 shares of stock into 2,000 shares.

Using this technique, the cash required has been reduced to $15,500, the amount necessary to pay the tax on the $50,000 of compensation in the 31 percent bracket. Without this technique, you would also need $50,000 more to pay for the stock. Thus, the total cash outlay has been reduced from $65,500 to only $15,500. Of course, a proportionate reduction in the number of shares or the value of the shares would result in a proportionate reduction in the amount of cash that you actually would have to lay out.

121 Incentive Stock Options (Sec. 422A)

The Economic Recovery Tax Act of 1981 provides for a new type of stock option, called an "incentive stock option." No tax consequences result from the grant of an incentive stock option or from the exercise of an incentive stock option by an employee. You, the employee, will be taxed when you sell the stock. Furthermore, you must normally be an employee from the date of granting the option until three months before the date of exercise.

2. Revenue Ruling 80-244.

In its simplest form, a stock option is the right to buy a company's stock sometime in the future for a fixed priced. An option granted in 1988 to buy stock at $10 a share by 1998 yields a $5-a-share profit if the stock rises to $15 a share by then and the owner exercises the option and sells the stock.

Under pre-1987 law, an employee receiving an *incentive stock option* was not taxed on the exercise of the option and was entitled to capital gains treatment when the stock was sold. No deduction was taken by the employer when the option was granted or exercised. In order for options to qualify as incentive stock options, among other requirements, the options must have been exercisable in the order granted. Also the employer could not in any one year grant the employee such *options* to acquire stock with a value of (at the time the option was granted) more than $100,000 (increased by certain carry-over amounts).

The Tax Reform Act of 1986 repealed the requirement that the incentive stock options be exercisable in the order granted. It also modifies the $100,000 limitation. The 1986 law provides that an employer may not, in the aggregate, grant an employee incentive stock options that are first exercisable during any one calendar year to the extent the aggregate fair market *value of the stock* (determined at the time the options are granted) exceeds $100,000. For example, an employer cannot give an employee, in one year, qualifying incentive stock options to acquire 110 shares of stock currently selling at $1,000 per share. That would exceed the $100,000 value limitation.

The $100,000 limit was changed from the value of the *options* granted to the value of the *stock* covered by options that are exercisable. The availability of incentive stock options as an incentive is thereby reduced.

The tax-favored treatment of capital gains adds to the usefulness of incentive stock options for stock-based executive compensation. Moreover, incentive stock options still retain an advantage for an employee over *nonstatutory options* (those options that do not qualify under Sec. 422A—for example, an option that is exercisable 11 years after the date it is granted). The recipient of an incentive stock option will continue to avoid regular income tax on the exercise of such an option. However, the *open* spread by which the fair market value of the incentive stock option, at time of option exercise, exceeds the stock's option price is a tax preference under the alternative minimum tax rules.

In contrast, upon *exercise* of a nonstatutory option, the excess of the nonstatutory option stock's fair market value over the option price is treated as additional compensation and taxed at regular income tax rates. Thus, an employee who exercises a nonstatutory option must find the funds to pay tax as well as to pay for the stock.

Example: Assume an executive in the 50 percent tax bracket exercised an *incentive* stock option in 1986 to acquire stock worth $150 for $100. His total *costs* for the stock ranged from $100 (if he is not subject to the alternative minimum tax) to a maximum of $110 ($100 option price plus 20 percent minimum tax on the $50 spread). In contrast, if the stock was acquired through the exercise of a *nonstatutory* option, the cost to the executive to buy the stock would be $125 ($100 option price plus 50 percent tax on the $50 spread). In 1997 the cost would be $115.50 ($100 option price plus 31 percent on the $50 spread).

The employer is not entitled to a deduction for the benefit realized by the executive on an incentive stock option exercise. Since a deduction continues to be available when a nonstatutory option is exercised, nonstatutory options retain the employer's tax advantage over incentive stock options after 1986. However, the reduction in corporate tax rates will reduce this advantage.

Therefore, incentive stock options continue to provide better tax advantages to employees than nonstatutory options, and since the current corporate tax rates reduce the employer's tax benefits from nonstatutory options, incentive stock options will continue to offer advantages for executive compensation packages.

Under the 1998 Reform Act, when you sell your ISO shares, the entire profit (the spread at exercise plus subsequent appreciation) can qualify for the 20% maximum rate on long-term capital gains. This beneficial deal applies only when you sell the ISO shares more than two years after the option grant date (the date you received the option) and more than 12 months after you actually bought the shares by exercising your ISO.

Gains from ISO shares sold more than two years after the grant date and more than 12 months—but not more than 18 months—after the exercise date were taxed at a maximum 28% rate in 1997. Now the holding period is back to 12 months.

Example: On Jan. 2, 1996, you received an ISO giving you the right to purchase 100 shares of employer stock for $10 a share. You exercised on Feb. 1, 1997 when the market price was $16. Your per-share basis is $10 (exercise price). You sell on Feb. 2, 1998, for $25 a share. The sale date is more than two years after the Jan. 2, 1996 grant date and more than 12 months after the Feb. 1, 1997 exercise date. Therefore, your entire $1,500 profit is treated as a long-term capital gain qualifying for the 20% rate.

Now what if you meet the above rules but sell your ISO shares at a price that's either below the market value on the exercise date or (even worse) below the exercise price? In this case, your basis in the shares is the exercise price, so when the sale price exceeds that number, you have a gain that qualifies for either the 20 or 28 percent maximum rate. If your sale price is below the exercise price, you've got a long-term capital loss.

An interesting twist on the incentive stock option concept is the junior stock plan, which works as follows. The employer corporation issues special "junior" non-voting common stock, paying dividends. These shares can be exchanged by holders for regular common stock, share for share, at a specified date if the holders meet certain conditions. The junior shares are sold to employee executives at a bargain price—for example, $20 while the regular common is trading at $30. Each executive pays taxes on the original price differential—the $10 price spread. At the end of the term, with the employer common stock trading at, for example, $80, the executives swap the junior stock for the common in a tax-free exchange. On sale of the common stock, the executive has a tax basis of $30—the $20 paid for the junior shares plus the $10 on which he was taxed. Thus he has a gain of $50 per share—$80 less $30—taxed at a maximum 28 or 20 percent rate.

This technique adds several breaks not available under normal incentive stock option rules. For example, junior stock lets an executive effectively buy the company's shares at a price far below the market. This allows far easier financing of a purchase of a block of shares. Moreover, the plan escapes the $100,000-per-year limit on the value of incentive stock options shares bought by an executive.

122 Year-End Stock Sales

The Internal Revenue Service had ruled that gains from stocks sold in a year's last week come under the installment sales law. That allowed you to choose—at leisure—to incur the tax in either the current year or the next. Prior to 1982, a gain on stocks sold through a broker in one year for payment in the next was considered taxable in the payment year; to make it taxable in the year of sale, you had to allow five business days for settlement. Under the installment sales law, however, an installment sale is one where any payment is made in a later year. That makes gain taxable in the later year unless you elect not to use the installment method; in that case, the gain is taxable in the sale year. You do not have to make an election to choose the year in which to incur the tax until the due date for your sale-year return, including the automatic four-month extension. This means that if you expect your income to increase, it may be advisable for you to recognize the gain earlier, in the lower-bracketed year.

Under the Tax Reform Act of 1986, effective January 1, 1987, taxpayers who sell stock or securities *on an established securities market* are *not* permitted to use the installment method to account for such sales. The trade date is considered the date of tax recognition (see also Rev. Rul. 93-84).

123 Tax-Exempt Income

A final word should be said about tax-exempt income. In the investment context, tax-exempt income results primarily from nontaxable interest from municipal securities. The table shown here indicates the equivalent rate of return that fully taxable income, such as rents or taxable interest, would have to yield in order to produce net income equivalent to that produced by various tax-exempt returns at the same tax rates.

Based on federal income tax brackets (see page 40 for a more expansive chart):

A tax-exempt yield of:	**Income Tax Bracket**	**1%**	**4%**	**5%**	**6%**	**6.5%**	**7%**	**7.5%**
is equivalent to a taxable yield of:	15%	1.18	4.71	5.88	7.06	7.65	8.24	8.82
	28%	1.39	5.56	6.94	8.33	9.03	9.72	10.42
	31%	1.45	5.80	7.25	8.70	9.42	10.14	10.87

At a 31 percent marginal tax rate, you would need to earn 8.70 percent in taxable interest to have the same after-tax return as 6 percent tax-free.

To find the equivalent taxable income return for a tax-exempt return not given in the table, multiply the tax-exempt return rate by the figure in the 1 percent column next to the applicable tax rate. For example, at a 31 percent tax rate, a taxable investment would have to yield 8.70 percent to produce the same amount of after-tax income that is produced by a tax-exempt investment that yields a 6 percent return (6 percent × 1.45 = 8.70 percent).

To find the tax-free income equivalent to a given taxable income, divide that taxable income by the figure in the 1 percent column next to the given rate. For example, at a 31 percent tax rate, $2,000 in taxable income yields $1,379 ($2,000 ÷ 1.45).

Note, in addition, that state taxation of interest income should be taken into consideration in computing total yield. For example, most states do not tax interest on municipal bonds issued within their own state. Thus, a New Jersey tax-free municipal bond held by a New Jersey investor would be exempt both on the federal and on the New Jersey tax return. In many states there is no difference in the state tax treatment of in-state versus out-of-state bonds. The chart below summarizes state bond taxation as of 1993. If appropriate, check the current position of your own state.

States That Tax Their Own and Other States' Bonds

Illinois	Iowa
Oklahoma	Wisconsin

States That Tax Other States' Bonds but Not Their Own

Alabama	Mississippi
Arizona	Missouri
Arkansas	Montana
California	Nebraska
Colorado	New Hampshire
Connecticut	New Jersey
Delaware	New Mexico
Georgia†	New York
Hawaii	North Carolina†
Idaho	Ohio
Kansas	Oregon
Kentucky†	Pennsylvania
Louisiana	Rhode Island
Maine	South Carolina
Maryland	Tennessee
Massachusetts	Vermont
Michigan†	Virginia
Minnesota	West Virginia

States That Do Not Tax Their Own or Other States' Bonds

Alaska**	South Dakota**
District of Columbia	Texas**
Florida**†	Utah
Indiana	Washington**
Nevada**	Wyoming**
North Dakota***	

*Each of these states has specific issues that are exempt.

**Alaska, Florida, Nevada, South Dakota, Texas, Washington, and Wyoming do not currently levy an income tax.

***North Dakota does not tax its own or other states' bonds when the "piggyback" method is used to compute state income tax liability.

†These states also subject municipal interest income on out-of-state bonds to state intangibles taxes.

124 Special Report

As a result of the magnitude of the American Telephone and Telegraph divestiture, taxpayers selling shares of the new AT&T or any of the seven regional telephone companies have had difficulty in allocating their cost with respect to the value of the package they received. On November 21, 1983, the first day of when-issued trading in such stock, the value of the package was:

1.0 share American Telephone	@ 18¼	=	$18.25
0.1 share Ameritech	@ 63⅜	=	6.34
0.1 share Bell Atlantic	@ 67¾	=	6.77
0.1 share BellSouth	@ 88⅝	=	8.86
0.1 share NYNEX	@ 61⅛	=	6.11
0.1 share Pacific Telesis	@ 54	=	5.40
0.1 share Southwestern Bell	@ 61⅛	=	6.11
0.1 share USWest	@ 57⅛	=	5.71
Total Value		=	$63.55

Note that because of a three-for-one subsequent split in BellSouth, the stock's value now must be calculated on the basis of 0.3 shares of BellSouth for each share of AT&T prior to divestiture.

125 Alternative Minimum Tax for Individuals

Prior to 1987, individuals were subject to an alternative minimum tax (AMT), which was payable, in addition to all other tax liabilities, generally to the extent that it exceeded the individual's regular tax liability. The tax was imposed at a flat rate of 20 percent on alternative minimum taxable income (AMTI) in excess of an exemption amount.

In computing alternative minimum taxable income, adjusted gross income was reduced by AMT itemized deductions (which were a limited subset of the itemized deductions allowable for regular tax purposes).

The AMTI was computed by increasing the adjusted gross income (less allowable AMT itemized deductions) by the items of tax preference, which included the following:

- the dividend exclusion of $100 for a single return and $200 for a joint return
- for all real property and tangible personal property subject to a lease, the excess of accelerated depreciation over straight-line depreciation based upon the property's useful life
- an amount equal to the 60 percent net capital gain deduction for the year, other than gain from the sale of a personal residence
- for certified pollution-control facilities, the excess of 60-month amortization over the depreciation otherwise allowable
- for research and experimentation expenditures that were expensed rather than capitalized, the excess of the deduction claimed over the amount allowable if the expenditure were amortized over a 10-year period
- for mining exploration and development costs (other than intangible drilling costs [IDCs]), the excess of the amount expensed over that allowable if the expenses were amortized over a 10-year period
- for oil and gas IDCs, the amount by which the excess of the amount expensed exceeded the amount allowable if the IDCs were amortized over a 10-year period, and the amount of oil and gas income
- percentage depletion to the extent in excess of the adjusted basis of the property
- for circulation expenses relating to newspapers, magazines, and other periodicals, the excess of the amount expensed over the amount allowable if amortized ratably over a three-year period
- for incentive stock options, the excess of the fair market value received through the exercise of the option over the exercise price

For certain preferences, individuals could elect for regular tax purposes to take a deduction ratably over 10 years (three years in the case of circulation expenses) and thereby avoid an AMT preference.

In general, no refundable credits (such as investment tax credits) were allowed to offset the AMT except the foreign tax credit. Also, for years after 1982 net operating loss deductions were allowed in computing the AMT only to the extent not attributable to tax-preference items.

CURRENT LAW

The individual alternative minimum tax is retained under the current law, but with significant modifications. The AMT is computed starting with regular taxable income (rather than adjusted gross income, as under prior law), which is determined with certain adjustments. Preference items are then added back to regular taxable income in calculating the AMT. The minimum tax rate was increased by the Revenue Reconciliation Act of 1990 to 21 percent. The exemption amount ($40,000 for married persons filing jointly, $30,000 for singles, and $20,000 for married persons filing separately) was reduced by 25 percent of the amount by which AMTI exceeds $150,000. For married taxpayers filing separately the phase-out will begin at $75,000 and for single taxpayers at $112,500. More important, the AMT became a separate tax computation with its own accelerated cost recovery system, basis, gain or loss computations, etc. However, to remove an incentive for separate filing by married individuals,

	Exemption	Phaseout Begins At	Phaseout Ends At
Married filing jointly and surviving spouse	$40,000	$150,000	$310,000
Single and unmarried head of household	$30,000	$112,500	$232,500
Married filing separately	$20,000	$ 75,000	$155,000

Congress provided that the maximum exemption phaseout for married individuals filing separately will be the same as for married taxpayers filing jointly. It thus provides that the alternative minimum taxable income (AMTI) of married individuals filing separately is increased by the lesser of (1) 25 percent of AMTI over $155,000 or (2) $20,000. This provision is effective for taxable years ending after November 10, 1988.

Moreover, Congress retroactively provided that personal exemptions are not allowed for AMT purposes. Thus, taxpayers who were subjected to the AMT in 1987 and who did not add back the personal exemption owe additional taxes. The above rules were changed again by the Omnibus Reconciliation Act of 1993. Under the new law, effective January 1, 1993, a two-tiered graduated rate schedule has been established for the Alternative Minimum Tax. A 26 percent rate now applies to the first $175,000 of AMT income in excess of the exemption amount, and a 28 percent rate applies to AMT income more than

$175,000 in excess of the exemption amount. For married individuals filing separate returns, the 28 percent rate applies to AMT income more than $87,500 above the exemption.

The exemption amount has been increased to $45,000 for joint returns, $33,750 for single taxpayers, and to $22,500 for married individuals filing separate returns, estates, and trusts.

Preference Items and Adjustments

The current law retains most of the prior law preferences, although it modifies the computation of certain items. The items of preference adjustment include the following:

- Accelerated depreciation on real property placed in service after 1986 will be considered a preference item to the extent that it exceeds depreciation computed on a 40-year straight-line basis. For personal property the preference item will be the excess of accelerated depreciation over the depreciation computed using the 150 percent declining-balance method (switching to straight line in the year necessary to maximize the deduction). However, the preference does not apply to property that is expensed under Sec. 179.

- Depreciation with respect to property placed in service prior to 1987 is treated as a preference only to the extent that it constituted a preference under prior law. Also, for property placed in service after 1986 with respect to which the alternative depreciation system is used, no AMT preferences will arise.

  Under the revised AMT, the alternative depreciation system is substituted for the accelerated cost recovery system (ACRS). This system permits *netting*. If the AMT depreciation exceeds the ACRS with respect to real or personal property for that year, the amount of the preference is reduced. Since the AMT uses the alternative depreciation system, separate depreciation basis adjustments must be made for AMT purposes. Therefore, the amount of gain on disposition may differ for AMT and regular tax purposes.

- As under prior law, the rapid amortization for pollution-control facilities, the excess of allowable depletion over the adjusted basis of the property (determined without regard to the depletion deduction), mining exploration and development costs, circulation expenditures, research and development costs, the amount by which the fair market value of a share of stock at the time of exercise of an incentive stock option exceeds the option price, and intangible drilling costs (except that the net income offset is reduced from 100 percent to 65 percent) are all still tax preference items.

The 1986 law also added the following new preference items and adjustments:

- Tax-exempt interest on nongovernmental purpose bonds issued after August 7, 1986. Exceptions are provided for bonds issued on behalf of certain tax-exempt organizations and certain bonds issued before September 1, 1986. However, no exceptions are provided for industrial development bonds.
- For any long-term contract entered into by the taxpayer after March 1, 1986, use of the completed contract is not permitted for AMT purposes. Instead, the taxpayer is required to use the percentage-of-completion method for AMT purposes.
- For dispositions after March 1, 1986, the use of the installment-sale method is not permitted for AMT purposes by dealers and others subject to proportionate disallowance of the installment method (sales of trade or business or rental property when the purchase price exceeds $150,000).
- Charitable contributions of appreciated property. Prior to 1993, a tax preference existed to the extent of the unrealized appreciation of contributed capital gain property. Therefore, for minimum tax purposes, the charitable-contribution deduction was limited to the property's adjusted basis. In calculating the amount of the preference, unrealized gains on appreciated property were offset by unrealized losses. The amount of preference was determined by disregarding any amount that was carried forward to another taxable year for regular tax purposes. This preference was eliminated by the Omnibus Budget Reconciliation Act of 1993.
- Passive activity losses that are allowed under the passive loss phase-in rules must be added back to taxable income in computing the AMT with the following revisions: (1) the amount of losses that otherwise would be added back for the current taxable year is reduced by the amount of the taxpay-

er's insolvency; (2) in calculating passive losses, minimum tax measurements of items of income and deduction will be used rather than regular tax measurements; and (3) the amount added back is reduced by other items of tax preference to prevent double counting.

Because of these calculations the amount of suspended passive losses relating to a passive activity may differ for AMT and regular tax purposes. However, it appears that after the five-year phase-in of the regular tax passive loss rules, differences should be minimal.

- Passive farm losses from a tax-shelter farming activity are treated like passive activity losses with the revisions discussed immediately above (for passive activity losses) and with the following special provisions: (1) each farm is treated as a separate activity—no netting between farming activities is allowed; (2) the preference applies to personal service corporations; and (3) loss from a disposition of a tax-shelter farm activity shall be allowed for minimum tax purposes and not treated as a loss from a tax-shelter farm activity.
- The standard deduction must be added back to taxable income when computing the AMT.
- Non-AMT itemized deductions used in computing taxable income must be added back in computing the AMT.
- The $100 ($200 joint filing) exclusion for dividends and the net capital gain deduction have both been deleted as items of tax preference because they are no longer applicable for regular tax purposes.

AMT Itemized Deductions

In general, the AMT itemized deductions are the same as under prior law and include the following:

- theft, casualty, and wagering losses
- charitable contributions
- medical expenses, except the floor is 10 percent of adjusted gross income instead of 7.5 percent, as used for regular tax purposes
- qualified interest expenses (which include interest paid or incurred on debt to acquire, construct, or substantially rehabilitate the taxpayer's prin-

cipal or qualified dwelling and other investment interest to the extent it does not exceed the taxpayer's qualified net investment income for the taxable year)

- the deduction for estate taxes for recipients of income in respect of decedents

The definition of investment interest is the same as under the current law for regular tax purposes. No AMT deduction is allowed for consumer interest. Disallowed investment interest deductions may be carried forward. Interest paid on a refinanced loan is treated as qualified residence interest if it qualified under the original loan and the amount of the loan was not increased. Also refunds of state and local taxes are not included in alternative minimum taxable income.

Carry-over of Tax Credits

As under prior law, nonrefundable credits are not allowed against minimum tax liability. Refundable credits that do not benefit the taxpayer because of the minimum tax can be carried back or forward to other taxable years. The foreign income tax credit is allowed against AMT.

Minimum Tax Credit

Under prior law minimum tax incurred by a taxpayer in one year had no effect on regular tax liability in other years.

The current law creates a minimum tax credit for prior-year minimum tax liability that may offset regular tax in later years. The AMT tax credit is equal to the excess of the AMT tax liability attributable to *deferral preferences* over the regular tax liability for the year. Deferral preferences are essentially all tax preferences except those relating to percentage depletion, tax-exempt interest, the appreciated-property charitable deduction, and regular tax itemized deductions that are not allowed for AMT purposes. The AMT credit can be carried forward (but not back) indefinitely.

Example: Ms. Fortunate has a regular tax liability of $35,000 after taking into account $15,000 of passive losses attributable to accelerated depreciation deductions on leased equipment that were deductible under the phase-in of the passive loss limitation. Her AMT is $39,000. She must pay tax of $39,000 but has a minimum tax credit to the extent that her AMT was attributable to the accelerated depreciation deferral preferences. The minimum tax credit is $3,150 ($39,000 AMT – $35,850 adjusted net minimum tax).

If Ms. Fortunate has a regular tax liability of $28,000 and an AMT of $26,000 in the next year, $2,000 of the minimum tax credit may be applied in that year. The remaining $1,150 of credit carries forward to the following year and, if necessary, later years.

Net Operating Losses (NOLs)

For AMT purposes a separate computation of NOLs and NOL carry-overs will be required. In general, the AMT NOL, which cannot offset more than 90 percent of AMT income, is computed in the same manner as the regular tax NOL, except for two special rules. The items of tax preference arising during the taxable year are added back to taxable income, and only AMT itemized deductions are taken into account.

Example: In year 1 a taxpayer has $10,000 of income and $35,000 of losses, of which $10,000 are preference items. The AMT NOL for year 1 is $10,000.

Regular Tax Elections

Under the new law taxpayers may still elect for regular tax purposes to deduct ratably over 10 years (three years for circulation expenditures) certain expenditures (IDCs and mining exploration and development expenditures) that are otherwise currently deductible and thus avoid treatment of the items as minimum tax preferences.

PLANNING CONSIDERATIONS

In general, high-income individuals will have to pay even more attention to the alternative minimum tax. There are many changes. The AMT rate has been raised from 20 to 24 to as high as 28 percent, and the exemption amounts are phased out as AMT income increases. The passive loss rules apply for AMT purposes, except that the preference is reduced by the amount, if any, of the taxpayer's insolvency. In addition, passive losses are reduced to the extent attributable to tax preference, since those preferences are added in elsewhere.

Tax planning for the AMT will involve many of the techniques applicable under prior law. In years when the AMT is inevitable, a taxpayer's objective should be to *accelerate* income and *defer* deductions. A taxpayer's marginal tax rate while subject to the AMT is as high as 28 percent for all additional income realized until the AMT is used up. The taxpayer's tax rate jumps to the marginal rate for regular tax purposes as soon as the AMT is used. If a taxpayer is subject to the alternative minimum tax, non-AMT itemized deductions provide no tax benefit. Additional alternative minimum tax itemized deductions provide a tax deduction rate only equal to the AMT rate. Additional tax preferences, like non-AMT itemized deductions, provide no benefit when the taxpayer is subject to the AMT.

Methods taxpayers may wish to consider for accelerating income when subject to the AMT include:

- Take prepayments of salary and bonuses.
- Declare and pay corporate dividends from closely held corporations. This may also have a potentially positive effect on the corporation if it has a problem with the accumulated earnings tax.
- Consider redeeming Series EE U.S. savings bonds, or elect to report all the accrued interest on the bonds in the current year.
- Redeem certificates of deposit.
- Make early sales of U.S. T-bills.
- Make early sales of investment certificates.
- Recognize gains on portfolio securities.
- Elect out of the installment method for any installment sales (under Sec. 453(d)).
- Consider converting tax-free municipal investments into taxable investments.
- Sell stocks acquired by incentive stock options (ISOs) within a year after the ISOs are exercised. Under Sec. 422(a)(1) this is a disqualifying transaction that makes the gains taxable as ordinary income (even if the transaction takes place in a taxable year subsequent to the year the ISOs were exercised). In addition, this transaction eliminates the tax preference if the transaction takes place in the same taxable year as the exercise of the options. By so doing, you can possibly zero out the AMT (with no additional tax paid because the regular tax is increased while the AMT is reduced). You can immediately repurchase the stocks and effectively step up the basis in the stock and avoid the tax that would otherwise be realized sometime in the future.
- Withdraw funds from IRAs in some circumstances (if subsequent withdrawals are anticipated at tax rates greater than 36-38 percent—26-28 percent AMT plus 10 percent penalty).

Taxpayers may also benefit by deferring deductions, especially non-AMT itemized deductions.

Taxpayers subject to the AMT should also try to capitalize otherwise deductible expenses. For example, they should not expense any part of the cost of a depreciable business asset. They should consider electing 10-year write-offs on any portion of currently deductible expenses that constitute tax preferences (which also eliminates the preference). The items to which this applies are research and experimentation expenditures, mining exploration and development costs, and intangible drilling costs. In addition, magazine circulation expenses may be capitalized and written off over a three-year period. Taxpayers with research and experimentation expenditures for their own business should consider electing to amortize those expenditures over 60 months or longer. This will both shift deductions out of the current year and reduce AMTI. Taxpayers acquiring new depreciable property should consider electing depreciation under the alternative recovery system, which will defer deductions and reduce AMTI.

A 1999 IRS report showed 590,649 people hit by the AMT in 1997, up from only 132,103 in 1990. More than 9 million are expected to be subject to the tax by 2009. Note that you may be hit with the alternative minimum tax even if you don't have one single dollar of tax preferences. For example, assume that you had an adjusted gross income of $150,000. In 1987 you paid $25,000 in state and local income taxes (including your April 1987 payment for your 1986 taxes) and $22,000 in property taxes on raw land you own as an investment. You paid $6,000 in interest on home equity loans you took out to pay college expenses for your children and had $8,000 in other itemized deductions, including $2,000 for investment expenses in excess of 2 percent of your adjusted gross income. Assume further that you had absolutely no tax preferences.

Because your itemized deductions for purposes of the alternative minimum tax are not the same as your itemized deductions for your regular tax, your alternative minimum tax was $260 higher than your regular tax. Therefore, you paid an extra $260 in taxes for 1987. As the regular tax rates fell in 1988, however, the chance of being hit with the alternative minimum tax increased, and your potential alternative minimum tax bill got bigger. For example, on these same facts, you would have owed an alternative minimum tax of more than $2,400 in 1988! What this means is that you should watch your itemized deductions as they may, by themselves, subject you to the AMT.

Starting in 1998, nonrefundable personal credits (the dependent care credit, the credit for the elderly and disabled, the adoption credit, the child tax credit, the credit for interest on certain mortgages, and the Hope Scholarship and Lifetime Learning credits) are allowed to offset your regular tax in full. Now these credits can also reduce your alternative minimum tax.

Alternative Minimum Tax Preference Items under Prior Law and Current Law

	Individual		
Tax Preferences	**Prior Law**	**Current Law**	**Description of Tax Preference**
Long-term contracts	No	Yes	Income must be calculated on the percentage-of-completion method for new contracts
Certain tax-exempt interest	No	Yes	Interest income on certain private-activity tax-exempt bonds issued after August 7, 1986
Appreciated property charitable deduction	No	Yes prior to 1993	Unrealized appreciation on long-term capital gain property
Passive activity losses	N/A	Yes	Net losses from passive activities
Accelerated depreciation on new property	N/A	Yes	Depreciation for AMT is calculated using the Alternative Depreciation System except that the preference for personal property is based on the 150 percent DB method
Premodified ACRS and pre-ACRS depreciable leased personal property	Yes	Yes	Excess of accelerated over straight-line deductions
Mining exploration and development costs	Yes	Yes	Excess over amount allowable if amortized ratably over 10 years
Circulation expenditures	Yes	Yes	Excess over amount allowable if amortized ratably over three years

Alternative Minimum Tax Preference Items under Prior Law and Current Law *(Continued)*

	Individual		
Tax Preferences	**Prior Law**	**Current Law**	**Description of Tax Preference**
Research and experimental costs	Yes	Yes	Excess over amount allowable if amortized ratably over 10 years
Depletion	Yes	Yes	Excess of depletion over adjusted basis in property
Incentive stock options	Yes	Yes	Excess of fair market value over option price at date of exercise (basis of stock adjustment for AMT)
Dividend exclusion from income	Yes	N/A	Amount of dividends excluded
Capital gains	Yes	N/A	Under present law full LTCG deduction is no longer a preference
Intangible drilling costs	Yes	Yes	Excess over amount allowable if amortized ratably over 120 months over 65% of net income from oil and gas
Pollution-control facilities	Yes	Yes	Excess of amortization over allowable depreciation
Individual itemized deductions	Yes	Yes	Certain itemized deductions not allowed
Alternative tax net operating loss	Yes	Yes	NOLs with certain adjustments
Installment method accounting	No	Yes	Installment method generally not allowed for AMT purposes

126 U.S. Savings Bond Exclusion (Sec. 135)

To help finance qualified higher educational expenses, Congress has created a new incentive to purchase U.S. savings bonds. Under prior law, interest that accrues on certain U.S. savings bonds need not be reported until the bond is redeemed, unless you elect to report the increase in redemption value annually.

For years after 1989, you can potentially exclude all or a portion of the interest that accrues on the bond. In order to qualify for the exclusion, you must:

1. purchase a qualified U.S. savings bond;
2. pay qualified higher educational expenses in the year of redemption;
3. not be married and filing separately; and
4. not have income over a certain amount.

If your modified adjusted gross income exceeds $60,000 (indexed) in case of a joint return and $40,000 (indexed)[3,4] in all other cases, there is a phaseout of the benefit. For joint filers, the entire benefit was phased out once modified adjusted gross income exceeds $95,250. For all other taxpayers, the phaseout was completed at $58,500. There is a proportional phaseout of the benefit for income within the phaseout range. For example, if modified adjusted gross income on a joint return was $80,000, then approximately two-thirds of the total benefits would be phased out.

A qualified U.S. savings bond is any bond issued after 1989 at a discount to an individual who has attained age 24. Bonds acquired in the names of minor children will not qualify for the exclusion. Moreover, the exclusion is not available to the individual who is the owner of a Series EE bond that was purchased by another individual other than a spouse. The bond should therefore not be purchased by a parent and put in the name of a child or another dependent, even if such a child or dependent is 24 years of age at the time of the purchase. Nor should bonds be bought by a relative, such as a grandparent, and gifted to a parent or child if the exclusion is desired. If you bought "wrong," you can file a reissue form PDF 4000 with the Bureau of Public Debt, Parkersburg, WV 26106-1328 and plead your case.

Note that there is no direct tracing of the redeemed bond proceeds to the payment of tuition. However, the qualified higher education expense must equal or exceed the redeemed proceeds for the full exclusion to apply.

3. $79,650 and $109,650 for 1999.
4. $53,100 and $68,100 for 1999.

The Impact of Inflation on Yields

Rate of Inflation	Interest Rate Needed to Break Even in Following Tax Brackets: 15%	28%	31%
1%	1.18%	1.39%	
1.45%			
2%	2.35	2.78	2.90
3%	3.53	4.17	4.35
4%	4.71	5.56	5.80
5%	5.88	6.94	7.25
6%	7.06	8.33	8.70
7%	8.24	9.72	10.14
8%	9.41	11.11	11.59
9%	10.59	12.50	13.04
10%	11.76	13.89	14.49
11%	12.94	15.28	15.94
12%	14.12	16.67	17.39
13%	15.29	18.06	18.84
14%	16.47	19.44	20.29

The Value of Tax-Free Yields

Munis make the most sense for people whose tax-equivalent yield on a tax-free bond or bond fund would be greater than the yield from a similar taxable alternative. Here are two equations to determine whether tax-exempt yields are right for you.

For tax-equivalent yields:

$$\frac{\text{Tax-Free Yield}}{(1 - \text{Tax Rate})} = \text{Tax-Equivalent Yield}$$

For combined effective federal/state tax rates (if you're considering buying bonds or funds with bonds issued in your home state):

$$\text{State Rate} \times (1 - \text{Federal} = \text{Effective State Rate})$$

$$\frac{\text{Effective}}{\text{State Rate}} + \frac{\text{Federal}}{\text{Rate}} = \begin{array}{c}\text{Combined Effective}\\ \text{Federal/State Tax Rate}\end{array}$$

Tax-Free Yield (%)	Tax-Equivalent Yield if Free from Federal Taxes* (%)	Tax-Equivalent Yield if Free from State, Federal, and Local (if applicable) Taxes in the Following States* (%)											
		AZ	**CA**	**CT**	**FL**	**MA**	**MD**	**MI**	**MN**	**NJ**	**NY**	**OH**	**PA**
2.00	3.13	3.31	3.51	3.27	3.13	3.55	3.40	3.27	3.42	3.34	3.53	3.38	3.38
3.00	4.69	4.97	5.27	4.91	4.69	5.33	5.10	4.90	5.12	5.01	5.30	5.07	5.08
4.00	6.25	6.62	7.02	6.54	6.25	7.10	6.79	6.54	6.83	6.68	7.07	6.76	6.77
5.00	7.81	8.28	8.78	8.18	7.81	8.88	8.49	8.17	8.54	8.34	8.84	8.45	8.46
6.00	9.38	9.93	10.53	9.82	9.38	10.65	10.19	9.81	10.25	10.01	10.60	10.14	10.15
7.00	10.94	11.59	12.29	11.45	10.94	12.43	11.89	11.44	11.95	11.68	12.37	11.82	11.84

*Tax-equivalent yields in the table are based on the 1996 federal tax rate of 36%: all yields are hypothetical. There is no assurance that the bonds will attain any particular yields. A portion of income may be subject to the federal alternative minimum tax. Based on the following combined effective 1996 federal, state, and if noted, local tax rate: AZ-39.58%; CA-43.04%; CT-38.88%; MA-43.68%; MD-41.12% (includes county tax); MI-38.82%; MN-41.44%; NJ-40.08%; NY-43.41% (includes New York City rate); OH-40.80%; PA-40.90% (includes Philadelphia).

Source: Fidelity Focus, Summer 1996, p. 15.

CHAPTER 10

Last-Minute Tax Planning

"Potius sero quam numquam."
(Better late than never.)

TITUS LIVIUS, 59 B.C.–A.D. 17

"You cannot help the poor by destroying the rich. You cannot lift the wage earner by pulling down the wage payer."

ABRAHAM LINCOLN

While effective tax planning is basically a year-round proposition, certain techniques are still available even if you buy this book during the last week in December. This chapter will explain those last-minute tax strategies that can help you reduce your overall tax burden.

127 Defer Taxes

Certain kinds of investments allow you to postpone paying taxes from the year in which the income is earned to a later year. At that point, you may be in a lower tax bracket, or you will at least have had the use and yield on the tax savings in the interim.

Series EE savings bonds, which until April 30, 1997 paid interest at a rate that was adjusted periodically to keep it equal to 85 percent of six-month Treasuries for bonds held for five years or less and 85 percent of the average yield on 5-year Treasury securities for bonds held longer than five years, offer this feature, as do deferred annuity contracts. After April 30, 1997, they pay at a rate equal to 90% of the 5-year Treasury note rate. Interest on savings bonds is normally not taxed until the bonds are cashed. As with an annuity, you postpone taxes on the interest until the income is actually paid out. Note also that Series EE savings bonds sold after May 1, 1995 no longer have a *minimum* guaranteed yield of 4 percent (7.5 percent if purchased between November 1, 1982, and October 31, 1986) if the bonds are held for at least 5 years. When alternative investments are yielding amounts equal to or less than the Treasury rate, the investment attractiveness of Series EE bonds is magnified even more. The limit on Series EE bonds that can be purchased in the name of one person is $30,000 face amount (or $15,000 issue price) in any one calendar year.

The interest on Series EE bonds does not accrue daily, but only on two days every year. The interest accrual dates are:

1. the anniversary of the bond's issue date;
2. the midpoint between anniversary dates.

The interest rate earned now changes each May 1 and November 1. Thus, an owner who is considering an exchange or a cashing out of a bond would do well to do so on or shortly after an interest accrual date.

A current listing of redemption values for all savings bonds—Form PD 3600—is available free from the Bureau of the Public Debt. Values are shown for six months, so an investor who follows a bond across the six columns can figure out the two months of the year in which the value rises.

Meanwhile, two useful one-page listings are available by writing the public affairs office of the U.S. Savings Bonds Division, Department of the Treasury, Washington, D.C. 20226 (202-377-7715). One sheet shows the current guaranteed minimum interest rates for Series EE and E bonds and Savings Notes bought *prior* to May 1, 1995. Holders get the higher of those minimum rates, which range from 4 percent to 8.5 percent, or variable rates that are based on market conditions.

The second sheet, dubbed "Table of Interest Accrual Dates," shows the two months a year in which Series E and EE bonds rise in value.

Savings bond holders can also call their nearest Federal Reserve Bank for savings bond information. Another option is an information service offered by Mr. Pederson, the former Federal Bank of Chicago official. His Savings Bond Informer Inc. in Detroit (313-843-1910) sells computer printouts listing key dates, interest rates, and redemption values for an investor's bonds. The cost for between 26 and 75 bonds: $22.50. Alternatively, if you are on-line, you can get the value of a Series EE bond from www.execpc.com\nmmrsoft or from the Bureau of Public Debt at www.publicdebt.treas.gov/sav/sav.htm.

Taxes are also deferred on income that builds up in individual retirement account, corporate pension, and Keogh plans. Furthermore, as discussed earlier, if you qualify for these plans, you also can deduct from your current taxable income the amount you contribute to your plan each year.

A tax planning strategy for taxpayers close to retirement is to buy Series EE savings bonds today and, when they retire, exchange those bonds for HH bonds, which are available only through such an exchange. This would allow you to defer tax on the interest the EE bonds earned before the exchange until you redeem the HH bonds. In the meantime, you will get a check for interest on the HH bonds every six months. That interest rate is fixed, however, and is taxable. There is no limit to the dollar amount of HH bonds that may be acquired through the exchange process. It is important though that you compare the after tax cash flows from the bonds and alternative investments. It may be better to pay the tax and reinvest the net proceeds at a higher yield than the HH bonds for a higher net after tax cash return.

If you buy certain six-month bank certificates of deposit (CDs) now, you can defer paying part of the tax on the interest until you file your return in the subsequent year. The CD must be the type on which the interest is neither credited to your account nor made available to you without substantial penalty before the maturity date. In addition, an investment in U.S. Treasury bills provides a similar tax benefit. This is because interest on them is not recognized until the bills are redeemed. Note, furthermore, that Treasury bill (also called

T-bill) interest is not subject to state or local tax; however, taxable short-term CDs may yield a higher rate of interest.

You also can defer your taxes on fees and compensation. For example, a binding agreement to delay until January the grant of a bonus otherwise payable in December defers taxation on that bonus until the subsequent year. But this agreement must be entered into before the bonus is "constructively received." Deferring fees or service compensation is easy. All you need to do is delay billing until late December. You will not receive payment—therefore, no taxable income either—until the next year.

A final alternative strategy for delaying your tax payments is to delay your receipt of income with an installment sale. You should consider postponing part or all of the profit from a big gain to next year or later. Not only could an installment sale keep this year's tax cost down (you pay tax only on the share of the profit you receive during the year), but it could also allow you to avoid a big bulge in income that could force you into a higher bracket.

128 Accelerate Expenses

You may have a great deal of flexibility in the timing of a number of your expenses. For example, any of your medical expenses not reimbursed are deductible in the year they are paid. An effective tax reducing strategy, therefore, would be to concentrate as many expenses as possible in a year when it appears that the percent medical expense deduction limit will be exceeded. If, at year-end, it is apparent that no deduction will be available, defer payment of medical bills until the following year when the situation may be otherwise. In a year when the deduction is probable, make sure that all medical needs are satisfied and paid for in that year.

For example, eye examinations, new glasses, and dental work may be accelerated by a month or two to permit a deduction; the remaining balance on your children's orthodontic work may be paid immediately in full. Note, however, that a deduction *is* available in the current year for medical needs charged to your credit card before the year-end, even if payment is not actually made until the subsequent year.

Tax payments can also be accelerated. The principal categories here are real estate taxes, personal property taxes, and state and local income taxes. Amounts withheld for income taxes are deductible in the year withheld. If your state or city income tax exceeds your withholding, estimated tax payments are probably required. The last installments of these taxes should be paid before the end of the current year even though they may not be due until the next year.

This will accelerate your deduction into the current year. Moreover, prepayments of real estate taxes are deductible in the year paid—if they are not merely advance deposits paid before the tax becomes a liability. Each of these accelerated payments represents a current deduction from your income tax liability.

Charitable contributions are also susceptible to acceleration. Sometimes it is feasible to make a large contribution in a high-income year in order to satisfy a charitable commitment extending over a number of years. Never make a contribution on January 1 that you could have made on December 31. Remember, however, that contributions are deductible subject to certain limitations based upon your adjusted gross income. Contributions that exceed these limitations should *not* be made.

Moreover, contributions of appreciated capital gain property, such as securities held over 12 months, will allow you a tax deduction equal to their full market value. Therefore, a gift of appreciated securities has the advantage of a market value deduction without the payment of a tax. Conversely, you should never make charitable donations of securities that have depreciated in value below cost, since you would forfeit the tax loss. In those situations, it is better to sell the securities, take the tax loss, and contribute the cash proceeds.

129 Accelerate Special Deductions

The election to expense allowance is available for depreciable personal property used in your business and acquired after 1981. This is a deduction against your income. This accelerated expense is *in addition* to your regular depreciation (on the reduced basis) and is $19,000 for 1999. And, again, it does not matter how late in the year the property is put into service.

130 Dependents and Personal Exemptions

A dependent is someone related to you or a member of your household for whom you provide more than half the support. You may claim a 1999 dependency exemption of $2,750 for each person who meets *all* five exemption tests, with certain exceptions. For example, the gross income test does not apply if your child is a full-time student under age 24 or a nonstudent under age 19. Also, special support rules apply to children of divorced parents and to those dependents being claimed under multiple support agreements. Furthermore, whether the dependent is born or dies during the year is irrelevant. If you pass the five tests for the portion of the year during which the dependent was alive, you will receive the full $2,750 exemption.

The following five tests must be met with respect to the person in question in order to qualify you for a dependency exemption:

1. *Support.* You must furnish over one-half of the total support of the person in the calendar year in which your tax year begins. Support includes amounts spent for food, shelter, clothing, medical and dental care, education, church contributions, child care expenses, wedding apparel and receptions, capital items (a car or a TV set), and the like. It does *not* include the value of services performed for a dependent, or scholarships received by a dependent student. Also, support is what is spent, not what is available. This means that even if your child earns $10,000 and banks $5,000 of it, as long as you contribute $5,001 in support, you have contributed more than one-half.

   Several tax-saving strategies present themselves in this area. A year-end budgeting of support expenditures can produce substantial tax benefits and thus reduce the out-of-pocket cost of supporting a dependent. For example, assume that you are unmarried and live with your mother. By December 1, your mother has spent $4,000 of her nontaxable social security payments for her own support and you have contributed $2,000 for her support. During the rest of the year, you provide for all of your mother's support at a cost of $800 and give her a $1,400 television set for her exclusive use in her room. Consequently, you provide more than 50 percent of your mother's total support (that is, $4,200 of a total of $8,200) for this year. Thus, you can claim the $2,750 dependency deduction for your mother.

   When two or more persons furnish the support of a dependent, one of the contributing group is entitled to take the deduction for the dependent if:

   a) no one person contributes more than half of the dependent's support; *and*

   b) each member of the group, were it not for the support test, would be entitled to claim the individual as a dependent; *and*

   c) the one claiming the deduction gives more than 10 percent of the dependent's support; *and*

d) every other person who gives more than 10 percent of the dependent's support files a written relinquishment of the claim to the exemption in the same calendar year.

2. *Relationship of dependent.* The person supported must be your relative or a member of your household. Your relatives include your children, grandchildren, great-grandchildren, and step-children; brothers, sisters, half-brothers, half-sisters, step-brothers, and step-sisters; parents, grandparents, great-grandparents, step-mother, and step-father; nephews, nieces, uncles, and aunts; and sons-in-law, daughters-in-law, fathers-in-law, mothers-in-law, brothers-in-law, and sisters-in-law. A legally adopted child or one placed with you for adoption is considered a child by blood. Furthermore, on a joint return, this condition is satisfied if the qualifying relationship exists between the person claimed as a dependent and either you *or* your spouse.

   If a person is not one of your relatives, that person may qualify as a dependent if he or she is a member of your household. A member of your household is one who, during your entire tax year, or during part of it, uses your home as the principal dwelling.

3. *Dependent's gross income.* Your dependent's gross income for the calendar year in which your tax year begins must be less than $2,750. This does not apply to children who are students under age 24 or nonstudents under age 19. A child is a student if, during each of any five months of the calendar year in which your tax year begins, he or she (a) is in full-time attendance at an educational institution or (b) is taking a full-time course of institutional or farm training.

   In figuring your dependent's gross income, you exclude any type of exempt income. This includes social security benefits, tax-exempt interest, etc. Remember, though, that if your dependent has used these tax-exempt benefits for support, generally the benefits *will be* considered in determining whether the support test has been met.

4. *Joint return.* Generally, you will lose an exemption for a married dependent who files a joint return. This rule does not apply, however, if neither the dependent nor his or her spouse is required to file a return but they file a joint return solely to claim a refund of tax withheld. Here you should examine the advantage to your dependent in terms of tax savings

from filing a joint return as opposed to the tax cost to you from losing the $2,750 exemption. In many cases it would pay for you to compensate your dependent for a tax loss and claim the deduction for the exemption. For example, assume that you are in the 31 percent bracket and that the tax loss to your married dependent from filing a separate as opposed to a joint return is $200. The $2,750 personal exemption would save you $852.50 in taxes in your tax bracket. In this case, it would pay for you to give $200 to your dependent for this "loss." After taxes, you would still be ahead $652.50.

5. *Citizenship or residency.* A dependent, to qualify you for an exemption, must be a U.S. citizen or a resident of the United States, Canada, or Mexico at some time during the calendar year in which your tax year begins.

The above rules and tests are used to determine whether your dependent qualifies you for the $2,750 dependency deduction. If you fail the gross income test—that is, your dependent has a taxable income of $2,750 or more—but you pass the other four tests, you have what is known as a *nondeductible* dependent. This still affords several significant advantages. For example, a nondeductible dependent could qualify an unmarried taxpayer to use the more advantageous head of household rate schedule; likewise, a married but separated taxpayer with a nondeductible dependent child could also use the more advantageous single taxpayer or head of household rate schedule. Moreover, any payments made by you for a nondeductible dependent's medical expenses can qualify as a medical expense deduction on your return.

For example, assume that your mother and father, who have no tax liability, reside in a nursing home, primarily to obtain medical care. Therefore, the entire cost of their maintenance (including meals and lodging) at the home qualifies as a medical expense. You pay your parents' nursing home bills, totaling $12,400 yearly, and thereby provide over half of their support. Furthermore, assume that you are single, that you have an adjusted gross income of $80,000, and that, after all deductions except those relating to your parents, you are in the 31 percent bracket.

You can now claim a medical expense deduction of $6,400 ($12,400 – 7.5% of $80,000) and (if they pass the gross income test) a dependency deduction of $2,750 each for your mother and father. In the 31 percent bracket, this will save you $3,689 in taxes ($11,900 × .31). Moreover, you can probably reduce your taxes even further because you are now entitled to compute your tax as head of household instead of single taxpayer.

Note, however, that an individual who is eligible to be claimed as a dependent by another is not eligible for his or her own personal exemption. For that reason it becomes very important to examine the potential tax consequences to your parents. The loss of the dependency exemption may cause them to pay taxes in excess of your own tax savings. In all situations, therefore, a comparative analysis should be made to maximize the tax savings to all parties.

131 Phaseout of Exemptions

As part of the 1990 Tax Reform Act, Congress mandated a phaseout of personal exemptions for high income taxpayers. When adjusted gross income (AGI) exceeds the following thresholds, the new law begins to reclaim the tax savings from personal exemptions:

- $100,000 for singles (indexed) ($126,600 for 1999);
- $150,000 for joint returns (indexed) ($189,950 for 1999);
- $75,000 for marrieds filing separately (indexed) ($94,975 for 1999).

Every time AGI exceeds the threshold by another $2,500 ($1,250 for marrieds filing separately), 2 percent is cut off the dollar amount of personal exemptions. *Example:* If your AGI exceeds the threshold by $25,000, you will lose 20 percent of your personal exemptions ($25,000 ÷ $2,500 =10; 10 × 2% = 20%). At $122,500 ($61,275 for marrieds filing separately) above the threshold, all claimed exemptions are wiped out.

This translates into a marginal-rate increase of about one-half of 1 percent for each exemption claimed. Thus, parents of two children with sufficient taxable income might really be paying almost 41.6 percent. Add the effect of the itemized deduction cap and that marginal rate nears 42.6 percent.

132 Timing Strategies

We have already discussed timing strategies in terms of accelerating expenses and deferring income. Remember, you can take deductions on items paid for by check in the current year, even if you mail the check on New Year's Eve, as long as there is no impediment to cashing the check in the ordinary course of business in early January. If you mail a check covering a large deductible item in late December, use certified mail so that you will receive a date-stamped receipt as proof that you actually mailed the payment in the earlier year.

Furthermore, wherever possible you should charge deductible items on credit cards. Deductible items charged in the current year on credit cards can be deducted in that year, even if you do not actually pay (or receive) the credit card bill until next year. Credit card charges also provide excellent proof as to the amount and nature of expenses—especially travel and entertainment expenses. (In addition, credit card charges have been known to get lost. Lost credit card charges do not reduce your taxes but do provide you with free goods and services.)

133 Retirement Plans

If you participate in a qualified retirement plan of your employer, you receive a number of tax advantages—especially if you are your own employer. The employer is entitled to deduct payments to the plan immediately. As an employee, you do not have to recognize current income from the contributions; rather, you will be taxed only when you receive distributions from the plan. Since distributions are normally made after you retire and have less taxable income, these distributions may be taxed at lower rates. Moreover, the retirement plan itself is exempt from tax. This means that your earnings will accumulate tax-free at a faster rate.

If you are self-employed, you have the option of two basic forms of noncorporate qualified retirement plans, discussed in the next two sections.

134 Individual Retirement Plans (IRAs)

Even if you are covered by an employer retirement plan, and if you do not exceed the appropriate income limits, you may establish an IRA for your own retirement. You are eligible for an IRA deduction even if you have a Keogh, but cannot take both in the same year. The maximum allowable deduction is the lesser of $2,000 or earned income. In order to generate a deduction, the contribution must be made (and the plan established) by the due date (not including extensions) for filing your return. According to the IRS national office, you should make the contribution prior to filing the return—i.e., you cannot take the deduction and file on March 1 and make the contribution on April 15.

For married persons, the maximum deduction is computed separately for each individual who has compensation. An eligible individual with a non-employed spouse may make a deductible contribution to a special joint IRA account in an amount up to $4,000 ($2,000 each) in 1999 (but limited to total earned income).

Furthermore, in a 1983 Private Letter Ruling 832-9049 the IRS has held that a separate payment to an IRA for custodian fees does not constitute an excess contribution and such a payment is deductible as an itemized expense under Section 212. Moreover, according to IRS Letter Ruling 843-2109, the amount that you can contribute to an IRA is not diminished by the *separate payment* of brokerage commissions or other fees. Accordingly, the payment of brokerage commissions and other fees, such as administrative and service fees that are separately billed and paid, will not be considered additional contributions to your IRA.

135 H.R. 10 or Keogh Plans

In general, the maximum annual deduction for self-employed retirement plans is the lesser of 20 percent of earned income before the deduction or $30,000. (This equates to 25 percent of net earned income after the deduction.) Under certain circumstances, a defined benefit type of self-employed retirement plan may allow a contribution in excess of the usual limits.

Individuals who have part-time self-employment income, such as directors and consultants, are allowed to establish such a plan. Thus, even if you are covered by your employer's qualified retirement plan, you might also establish a Keogh plan with any outside fees or other income that you receive. If your self-employment income is from a business that has employees, they must also be included under the plan.

With a Keogh plan you may deduct contributions made *after* the end of the taxable year, if paid by the due date for filing your return. The plan must be established before the end of the tax year.

There are substantial tax advantages to either of these plans. You obtain an immediate tax deduction for the contribution; earnings accumulate on the contributions free of current taxes; and when distributed, the plan benefits may be taxed at a lower rate.

A number of considerations are involved in deciding whether to establish a retirement plan and selecting between IRAs and Keogh plans. For example, the amount that may be contributed under a Keogh plan is greater than the amount allowable under an IRA. Alternatively, using an IRA rather than a Keogh plan will allow you to restrict the retirement plan to cover only yourself, which can mean a substantial tax savings if you have a lot of employees. All of these factors must be considered and discussed with your tax advisor.

136 Marital Status

Whether you are single or married can have a substantial impact on your tax bill. Speeding or delaying the ceremony can yield you an enormous one-time tax savings.

In general, marriage will cut taxes only if one spouse works or earns almost all of the income. Alternatively, if both spouses work and earn relatively good salaries, marriage will substantially boost your taxes. This is because holy wedlock will push your combined income into a higher tax bracket.

If you are planning an end of the year/New Year's day wedding, it would be well worth your while to compute your taxes both singly and jointly. You may find that the savings from deferring (or accelerating) your wedding date could be enough to pay for your honeymoon vacation.

In conclusion, recognize that the focus of this chapter has been to reduce your current year's income tax. Due to inflation, any tax liability deferred to a later year will be paid with cheaper dollars. Moreover, a deferral of income to a later year is the equivalent of an interest-free loan because it enables you to use the funds that you would otherwise have to pay toward your tax liability. Be aware, however, that this might not always be the correct planning strategy. If you expect your income to go up substantially in later years, you do not want to bunch more income into those years, because the graduated rates could bring about a greater total aggregate tax liability over the years involved. Furthermore, you should *always* take into consideration the political climate for tax changes. If tax rates are expected to go down in the future, then income deferral and expense acceleration is the right strategy. Alternatively, if rates go in the other direction, you will want to recognize your income now and defer your expenses until later.

137 The Goldinger Deferral

An interesting tax deferral technique has been developed by Jay Goldinger in Beverly Hills. He suggests the acquisition of a one- or two-month bank certificate of deposit by putting up 1.5 percent of the purchase price and borrowing the rest from your broker. The deal is close to a wash. Assume the certificates would pay about 9.25 percent, and the loan would cost 9 percent, including the broker's markup. But by paying the interest on or before December 31, you could deduct the expense from your current year's income. If the certificate of deposit is from a sound bank, your risk is low.

To swing such a deal on a one-month $1 million certificate of deposit, the smallest negotiable denomination, you would need $24,000—a $15,000 down payment and about $9,000 for interest on the loan. In January of the next year, when the certificate matures, you would repay the loan and collect the income on the certificate of deposit. That income would be taxable in the new year, but you would have a $9,000 deduction allowable in the earlier year.

Be aware of the limits on personal and investment interest deductions here. You should have sufficient other investment income to cover the investment interest expense.

Also be aware that the courts have disallowed "straddle" transactions where the primary motivation was to generate tax benefits and not realize profits (*Ewing v. Com,* 91 T.C. 396, 1988). Be careful you document your motive here.

138 Educational Tax Incentives

Not that education should be last minute but the table below summarizes current educational tax incentives:

Provisions	Tax Benefit	Contribution/ Deduction Limits	Eligible Contributors (for Savings Incentives)/Eligible Claimants (for Deductions, Credits, and Exclusions)	Eligible Beneficiaries	Qualified Education Expenses	Coordination with Other Education Provisions
1. Education IRA (sec. 530)	Earnings are not subject to tax until distributed. Distributions are not subject to tax if the amount distributed does not exceed the qualified higher education expenses of the beneficiary during the year. Earnings portion of distributions in excess of qualified expenses is subject to an additional 10-percent tax.	Annual contributions may not exceed $500 per designated beneficiary. No contributions permitted after beneficiary attains age 18.	Contribution limit phased out for contributors with modified AGI of $95,000 to $110,000 ($150,000 to $160,000 for joint returns).	Eligible distributee (i.e., student) can be enrolled on full-time, half-time, or less than half-time basis.	Includes tuition, fees, books, supplies, and equipment required for attendance at an eligible educational institution (defined in sec. 481 of the Higher Education Act of 1965). Also includes certain room and board expenses if student enrolled on at least a half-time basis. Does not include expenses covered by certain scholarships or other tax-free educational benefits. Includes amounts contributed to a QSTP for the benefit of the beneficiary of the education IRA.	No exclusion from income for a particular student if either the HOPE credit or LLC is claimed for the same year with respect to the same student. Beneficiary will incur a penalty excise tax if a contribution is made by any person to an education IRA if, in the same year, a contribution is made to a QSTP on behalf of the same beneficiary.
2. Qualified State tuition program ("QSTP") (sec. 529)	Earnings are not subject to tax until distributed. Earnings not used for qualified higher education expenses are subject to an additional penalty.	QSTP must have adequate safeguards to prevent contributions in excess of amount needed for the beneficiary's higher education expenses.	No restrictions.	No restrictions.	Same as education IRA, although there is no restriction regarding expenses covered by tax-free educational assistance.	See education IRA discussion above. HOPE credit or LLC may be claimed in same year and with respect to same expenses for which a distribution from a QSTP is made.
3. HOPE credit (sec. 25A)	Credit against tax for qualified tuition and related expenses for first two years of post-secondary education.	Maximum credit is $1,500, computed on a per-student basis. Credit rate is 100% on first $1,000 of qualified expenses and 50% on next $1,000 of expenses.	Credit amount is phased out for taxpayers with modified AGI between $40,000 and $50,000 ($80,000 and $100,000 for joint returns). Credit may be claimed by student or by another taxpayer if the taxpayer claims the student as a dependent.	Eligible student must be enrolled on at least a half-time basis and must not have been convicted of Federal or State felony involving possession or distribution of a controlled substance.	Same as education IRA, except does not include charges or fees associated with room and board, athletics (unless part of student's degree program, and nonacademic fees (including insurance, transportation, and similar personal, living or family expenses).	HOPE credit not available with respect to a particular student if, the student elects an exclusion from income for a distribution from an education IRA in the same year. Also see QSTP discussion above.

Provisions	Tax Benefit	Contribution/ Deduction Limits	Eligible Contributors (for Savings Incentives)/Eligible Claimants (for Deductions, Credits, and Exclusions)	Eligible Beneficiaries	Qualified Education Expenses	Coordination with Other Education Provisions
4. Lifetime Learning credit ("LLC") (sec. 25A)	Credit against tax for qualified tuition and related expenses for undergraduate or graduate (and professional) courses. Unlike HOPE credit, LLC is available for an unlimited number of years.	For expenses paid between July 1, 1998 and December 31, 2002, maximum credit is $1,000. For expenses paid after December 31, 2002, maximum credit is $2,000. Credit rate is 20% of up to $5,000 ($10,000 beginning in 2003) of qualified expenses. Unlike HOPE credit, LLC is computed on family-wide basis, rather than per-student basis.	AGI phase-out ranges are same as HOPE credit. As with HOPE credit, LLC may be claimed by student or by another taxpayer if the taxpayer claims the student as a dependent.	Eligible students include: (1) those enrolled on at least a half-time basis as part of a degree or certificate program, and (2) those enrolled in any course of instruction at an eligible educational institution to acquire or improve the job skills on a full-time half-time, or less than half-time basis.	Same as HOPE credit.	Same as HOPE credit.
5. Student loan interest deduction (sec. 221)	Taxpayer may claim an above-the-line deduction for interest paid on qualified education loans, subject to an annual deduction limit.	Deduction allowed with respect to interest paid on qualified education loans during the first 60 months in which interest payments are required. Maximum deduction is $1,500 in 1999, $2,000 in 2000, and $2,500 in 2001 and thereafter.	Deduction is phased out for taxpayers with modified AGI of $40,000 to $55,000 ($60,000 to $75,000 for joint returns).	No restrictions.	Includes tuition, fees, room and board, and related expenses, reduced by (1) any interest on education savings bonds excluded from income, (2) any distribution from an education IRA excluded from income, and (3) any educational benefits (e.g., scholarships, employer-provided educational assistance) excluded from income.	No restrictions.
6. Education savings bonds (sec. 135)	Interest on certain savings bonds is not subject to tax if the proceeds of the bond upon redemption do not exceed qualified higher education expenses paid by the taxpayer during taxable year.	No limit on amount that may be excluded, but see income phase-out limitation.	For 1999, exclusion is phased out for taxpayers with modified AGI of $53,100 to $68,100 ($79, 650 to $109,650 for joint returns). To prevent avoidance of the income phase-out limitation, bonds must be issued to taxpayer who is at least 24 years old.	No restrictions.	Same as for HOPE credit and LLC, but without the restriction on nonacademic fees.	For purposes of computing excludable amount, taxpayer cannot include expenses taken into account in determining the HOPE credit or LLC claimed by the taxpayer, or the excludable amount of an education IRA distribution.

CHAPTER 11

The Attorneys' and Accountants' Relief Act of 1993

"In the last decade, taxes have been raised four times explicitly for deficit reduction. In the year following each hike, the deficit actually increased."

SENATOR DAN COATS

"Politicians tax the middle class for the same reason some people rob banks. That's where the money is."

Forbes Magazine
May 11, 1992

"If our current tax structure were a TV show, it would either be 'Foul-ups, Bleeps and Blunders,' or 'Gimme a Break.' If it were a record album, it would be 'Gimme Shelter.' If it were a movie, it would be 'Revenge of the Nerds' or maybe 'Take the Money and Run.' And if the IRS ever wants a theme song, maybe they'll get Sting to do 'Every breath you take, every move you make, I'll be watching you.'"

PRESIDENT REAGAN, in remarks to students at Northside High School, Atlanta, Georgia, June 6, 1985

"When Congress talks of tax reform, grab your wallet and run for cover."

SENATOR STEVE SYMMS of Idaho

An Internal Revenue Service commissioner, in response to a technical proposal sponsored by tax expert Stanley Surrey, once said: "You understand it, Stanley. I almost understand it. Now I must go out and teach it to 2,000 agents who have to apply it, and God help the millions of people who have to live with it."

After several weeks of debate in Conference Committee, Congress passed the Omnibus Budget Reconciliation Act of 1993 which was expected to increase revenues by $241 billion dollars and reduce spending by almost $254 billion dollars for a total of $496 billion dollars in deficit reduction over 5 years. The House passed the bill on August 5, 1993, with only a two-vote margin (218-216), and the Senate passed it on August 6, 1993, with Vice President Gore casting the deciding 51-50 vote. The Bill was signed by President Clinton on August 10, 1993.

Because of its complexity, its scope and its complications, the new law has been called The Attorneys' and Accountants' Relief Act of 1993. It contains a host of major tax provisions affecting both individuals and corporations. While public opinion polls indicate that most Americans feel that the middle class will be the group most affected by the new tax law, in fact it is the rich and the poor who will be affected, and the middle class will see little change in the taxes they pay. It is estimated that 98.5 percent of taxpayers will have no increase in their income taxes as a result of the new law. However, in its attempt to squeeze increased revenue from every possible source, the new law contains a plethora of changes that need to be reviewed. This chapter will review and detail the most significant parts of the new law, "OBRA '93," and will explain its potential impact on you. The next chapter, Stealth Tax Reform, will detail 1996 tax changes, some of which modify the 1993 amendment.

139 Training and Investment Provisions

EXTENSION OF EMPLOYER-PROVIDED EDUCATIONAL ASSISTANCE

Prior to July 1, 1992, an employee was generally allowed to exclude from gross income up to $5,250 paid by his or her employer for educational assistance. This educational assistance payment was also excluded from wages for employment tax purposes. The exclusion expired after June 30, 1992. The new law extends, for 30 months, the exclusion for employer-provided educational assistance, from July 1, 1992, through December 31, 1994.

EXTENSION OF TARGETED JOBS TAX CREDIT

Prior to July 1, 1992, a targeted jobs credit in a maximum amount of $2,400 per employee was available to employers who hired individuals from one of several, generally economically disadvantaged, groups. The credit expired after June 30, 1992. The new law extends the targeted jobs tax credit for 30 months, from July 1, 1992, through December 31, 1994.

140 Investment Incentives

EXTENSION OF RESEARCH TAX CREDIT

Prior to July 1, 1992, a taxpayer could claim a research and experimentation tax credit equal to 20 percent of the amount by which the taxpayer's qualified research expenditures for a taxable year exceeded its base amount for that year. The base amount was designed to approximate the research the taxpayer would have undertaken even if no credit were provided. In general, the base amount for a current year was calculated by multiplying the taxpayer's historical fixed-base ratio by its gross receipts in the most recent four years. Start-up firms were deemed to have a fixed-base ratio of three percent. The credit expired for expenses incurred after June 30, 1992. The new law extends the research tax credit for three years, from July 1, 1992, through June 30, 1995. It also provides a special rule for start-up firms, so that the fixed-base ratio for these firms eventually will be computed based upon actual research experience.

CAPITAL GAINS EXCLUSION FOR CERTAIN SMALL BUSINESS STOCK

The new law generally permits a noncorporate taxpayer who holds qualified small business stock for more than five years to exclude from income 50 percent of any gain on the sale or exchange of the stock. The amount of gain eligible for the 50 percent exclusion is limited to the greater of (1) 10 times the taxpayer's basis in the stock or (2) $10 million of gain from the stock in that corporation. One-half of any exclusion claimed is treated as an alternative minimum tax preference item. Various eligibility requirements must be satisfied for stock of a corporation to constitute qualified small business stock, including limitations regarding the size of a corporation ($50 million gross assets), the nature of the corporation's trade or business, and the manner in which the stock is acquired by the taxpayer (i.e., the stock must be acquired at original issuance in exchange for money or other property, or as compensation for services provided to the corporation). The provision applies to stock issued after the date of enactment (August 10, 1993).

INCREASED EXPENSING DEDUCTION FOR SMALL BUSINESS

Under prior law, a small business could elect to expense rather than depreciate up to $10,000 of the cost of tangible personal property purchased for use in the conduct of a trade or business. The new law increases the amount allowed to be expensed annually to $17,500 for property placed in service in taxable years beginning after December 31, 1992. As under prior law, the amount that can be expensed is phased out if a taxpayer places more than $200,000 of property in service during the year.

EXTENSION OF THE TAX CREDIT FOR ORPHAN DRUG CLINICAL TESTING EXPENSES

Prior to July 1, 1992, a taxpayer could claim a 50 percent tax credit on certain clinical testing expenses paid or incurred in the testing of certain drugs to treat rare diseases (so-called "orphan drugs"). The orphan drug tax credit expired after June 30, 1992. The new law extends the credit for orphan drug clinical testing expenses for 30 months, from July 1, 1992, through December 31, 1994.

141 Expansion and Simplification of Earned Income Tax Credit

Under the new law, the earned income tax credit (EITC) is expanded by (1) increasing the maximum credit available to taxpayers with one qualifying child; (2) increasing, over a three-year period, the maximum credit available to taxpayers with two or more qualifying children and lengthening the phaseout range; and (3) extending the credit to childless taxpayers over age 24 and under age 65 who are not claimed as an exemption on another taxpayer's return (a 7.65 percent credit on the first $4,000 of earned income). The new law repeals the supplemental tax credit for children under one year of age as well as the supplemental tax credit for health insurance expenses for qualifying children. In addition, the new law requires the IRS to provide notice to taxpayers who receive a refund attributable to the credit that they may be eligible to receive the credit on an advance-payment basis. The provision is effective for taxable years beginning after December 31, 1993.

142 Real Estate Provisions

EXTENSION AND MODIFICATION OF THE LOW-INCOME HOUSING TAX CREDIT

Prior to July 1, 1992, a tax credit was available for certain costs of acquiring and constructing or substantially rehabilitating low-income residential rental housing. The maximum value of the credit (70 or 30 percent present value) depended on the nature of the costs (i.e., acquisition, or construction or rehabilitation) and whether the project received other Federal subsidies. The low-income housing tax credit expired after June 30, 1992. The new law permanently extends the low-income housing tax credit, effective after June 30, 1992. It also makes certain modifications to the credit program, including allowing the 70 percent credit for certain housing receiving assistance under the HOME program of the National Affordable Housing Act of 1990, effective on the date of enactment (August 10, 1993).

MODIFICATION OF PASSIVE LOSS RULES FOR CERTAIN REAL ESTATE PERSONS

Under present and prior law, passive loss rules limit deductions and credits from passive trade or business activities. Passive activities generally include trade or business activities in which the taxpayer does not materially participate. Under prior law, passive activities also included all rental activities (regardless of the taxpayer's level of participation). The new law provides that deductions and credits from rental real estate activities in which an eligible taxpayer materially participates are not subject to limitation under the passive loss rules. An individual taxpayer is eligible if more than one-half of the taxpayer's business services for the taxable year, amounting to more than 750 hours of services, are performed in real property trades or businesses in which the taxpayer materially participates. A closely held C Corporation is also eligible if it meets a gross receipts test. The provision is effective for taxable years beginning after December 31, 1993.

RECOVERY PERIOD FOR DEPRECIATION OF NONRESIDENTIAL REAL PROPERTY

Under prior law, a taxpayer was allowed to recover over a period of 31.5 years, through annual depreciation allowances, the cost or other basis of nonresidential real property (other than land) used in a trade or business or held for the production of income. The new law lengthens the recovery period for determining the depreciation deduction with respect to nonresidential real property to 39 years. It generally applies to property placed in service on or after May 13, 1993. It does not apply to property placed in service before January 1, 1994, if the taxpayer or a qualified person entered into a binding contract to purchase or construct the property before May 13, 1993, or if construction of the property was commenced by or for the taxpayer or a qualified person before May 13, 1993.

143 Miscellaneous Provisions

REPEAL OF LUXURY EXCISE TAX ON BOATS, AIRCRAFT, JEWELRY, AND FURS; INDEX AND MODIFY LUXURY EXCISE TAX ON AUTOMOBILES

The new law repeals the 10 percent luxury excise tax imposed on boats, aircraft, jewelry, and furs, effective for sales on or after January 1, 1993. The luxury excise tax still applies to automobiles. However, the new law indexes the prior law's $30,000 threshold for post-1990 inflation. Indexation is in $2,000 increments, and is effective for sales on or after August 10, 1993. Thus, for 1993 sales on or after August 10, 1993, the applicable threshold will be $32,000. In addition, passenger vehicle dealers are not required to pay the luxury tax on vehicles used as demonstrators for potential customers, effective for vehicles used after December 31, 1992.

Moreover, the 10 percent luxury excise tax on any part or accessory installed on a passenger vehicle to enable or assist an individual with a disability to operate the vehicle, or to enter or exit the vehicle, is repealed, effective for purchases after December 31, 1990.

ALTERNATIVE MINIMUM TAX TREATMENT FOR CONTRIBUTIONS OF APPRECIATED PROPERTY

The new law provides that a contribution of appreciated property is not treated as a tax preference item for alternative minimum tax. Thus, you may claim the same charitable contribution deduction for both regular tax and alternative minimum tax purposes. This provision is effective for gifts of tangible personal property made after June 30, 1992, and contributions of other property made after December 31, 1992.

SUBSTANTIATION AND DISCLOSURE REQUIREMENTS FOR CHARITABLE CONTRIBUTIONS

The new law requires taxpayers who make a separate charitable contribution of $250 or more for which they claim a deduction to obtain written substantiation from the charity, rather than relying solely on a canceled check. In addition, any charity that receives a *quid pro quo* contribution exceeding $75 (meaning a payment in excess of $75 made partly as a gift and partly as consideration for goods or services furnished by the charity) is required to inform the contributor in writing of the value of the goods or services furnished by the charity; only the portion of the payment exceeding the value of the goods or services is deductible as a charitable contribution. The new law requires the written substantiation to include a general acknowledgment of intangible religious benefits not sold in commercial contexts, but such benefits need not be valued or described in detail. A charity is also not required to value contributions of non-cash property claimed by the donor to be worth $250 or more. These provisions are effective for contributions made after December 31, 1993.

EXTENSION OF HEALTH INSURANCE DEDUCTION FOR SELF-EMPLOYED INDIVIDUALS

Prior to July 1, 1992, self-employed individuals were allowed to deduct as a business expense up to 25 percent of amounts paid for health insurance coverage for the taxpayer and his or her spouse or dependents. The deduction was not available if the individual or his or her spouse was eligible to participate in an employer-paid health plan. This provision expired after June 30, 1992. The new law extends the 25 percent deduction for health insurance expenses of self-employed individuals from July 1, 1992, through December 31, 1993.[1]

In addition, the determination of whether a self-employed individual or his or her spouse is eligible for employer-paid health benefits (and is, thus, ineligible for the 25 percent deduction) is made on a monthly basis. This latter provision applies to taxable years beginning after December 31, 1992.

144 Revenue-Raising Provisions

INCREASED TAX RATES FOR HIGHER-INCOME INDIVIDUALS

The new law adds two new marginal tax rates that affect higher income individuals. A 36 percent rate applies to taxpayers with taxable incomes in excess of $140,000 (married individuals filing joint tax returns), $127,500 (unmarried individuals filing as head of household), and $115,000 (unmarried individuals filing as single). In addition, the new law imposes a 10 percent surtax on individuals with taxable income in excess of $250,000. This surtax is computed by applying a 39.6 percent rate to taxable income in excess of the threshold. The 36 percent and 39.6 percent rate also applies to estates and trust with taxable income in excess of $5,500.00 and $7,500.00, respectively. Net capital gains remain subject to a maximum 28 percent tax rate.

---

[1]A subsequent law made the deduction permanent and increased the rate to 30 percent as of 1/1/95.

The new law also establishes a two-tiered alternative minimum tax system for individuals, with a 26 percent rate applying to the first $175,000 of alternative minimum taxable income in excess of the exemption amount, and a 28 percent rate applying to alternative minimum taxable income more than $175,000 in excess of the exemption amount. The exemption amount is increased from $40,000 to $45,000 for married taxpayers filing joint returns and from $30,000 to $33,750 for unmarried taxpayers.

The increased rates are effective for taxable years beginning after December 31, 1992. The new law permits individuals who are subject to the new marginal regular income tax rates to elect to pay the increased tax liability attributable to the increased rates for taxable years beginning in 1993 over a three-year period (without payment of interest or penalties). Beginning in 1995, the income thresholds for the 36 and 39.6 percent rate brackets under the regular income tax are indexed for inflation.

OVERALL LIMITATIONS ON ITEMIZED DEDUCTIONS FOR HIGH-INCOME TAXPAYERS MADE PERMANENT

Under present and prior law, individuals who do not elect the standard deduction may claim itemized deductions for certain expenses, including unreimbursed medical expenses, unreimbursed casualty and theft losses, charitable contributions, home mortgage interest (subject to certain limitations), state and local income and property taxes, unreimbursed employee business expenses, and certain other miscellaneous expenses. Certain of these deductions are allowed only to the extent that the amount of the deduction exceeds a percentage of the taxpayer's adjusted gross income. In addition, the total amount of otherwise allowable itemized deductions is limited (but not reduced by more than 80 percent), if an individual taxpayer's adjusted gross income exceeds a certain amount indexed for inflation. Under prior law, this limitation was to expire after December 31, 1995. The new law permanently extends the limitation on itemized deductions.

PHASEOUT OF PERSONAL EXEMPTION OF HIGH-INCOME TAXPAYERS MADE PERMANENT

Under present and prior law, individuals are allowed to claim a personal exemption deduction for themselves, their spouse, and each dependent. However, the amount of exemptions that may be claimed is phased out to the extent a taxpayer's adjusted gross income exceeds certain threshold amounts. Under prior law, this phaseout provision was to expire after December 31, 1996. The new law permanently extends the phaseout of personal exemptions.

TREATMENT OF NET CAPITAL GAIN AS INVESTMENT INCOME

Under present and prior law, the amount of interest that a taxpayer (other than a corporation) can deduct on debt attributable to property held for investment is limited to the taxpayer's net investment income. Under prior law, investment income included gross income from investment property and any net capital gain attributable to the disposition of such property. The new law excludes net capital gain from the definition of investment income for purposes of computing the investment interest limitation. However, a taxpayer may elect to include net capital gain in investment income and forego the benefit of the 28 percent maximum capital gains rate on the included amount. This provision is effective for taxable years beginning after December 31, 1992.

REPEAL OF HEALTH INSURANCE WAGE BASE CAP

The new law repeals the dollar limit on wages and self-employment income subject to the Medicare hospital insurance (HI) tax. The limit is $135,000 for 1993. The provision is effective for wages and self-employment income received after December 31, 1993.

REINSTATE TOP ESTATE AND GIFT TAX RATES

The new law reinstates the two highest estate and gift tax rates that expired at the end of 1992. Thus, for taxable transfers over $2.5 million but not over $3 million, the marginal estate and gift tax rate is 53 percent. For taxable transfers over $3 million, the marginal estate and gift tax rate is 55 percent. Also, because the generation-skipping transfer tax is computed by reference to the maximum Federal estate tax rate, the rate of tax on generation-skipping transfers is 55 percent. The provision is effective for descendents dying, gifts made, and generation-skipping transfers occurring after December 31, 1992.

REDUCE DEDUCTIBLE PORTION OF BUSINESS MEALS AND ENTERTAINMENT EXPENSES

Under prior law, taxpayers were permitted to deduct 80 percent of meal and entertainment expenses incurred for business purposes, if certain legal and substantiation requirements were satisfied. The new law reduces the deductible portion of otherwise allowable business meals and entertainment expenses to 50 percent. This provision is effective for taxable years beginning after December 31, 1993.

DENY DEDUCTION FOR CLUB DUES

The new law prohibits any deduction for club dues. This rule applies to all types of clubs (including hotel and airline clubs). Specific expenses (e.g., meal expenses) incurred at a club are deductible to the extent they otherwise satisfy the standards for deductibility. The provision is effective for amounts paid or incurred after December 31, 1993.

In IA-30-94 issued August 11, 1994, the IRS proposed to define clubs to exclude professional organizations, such as bar associations and medical associations, as well as civic or public service organizations, such as Kiwanis, Lions, Rotary, Civitan, and similar organizations, from the definition of "club." They also excluded business leagues, trade associations, chambers of commerce, boards of trade, and real estate boards. Dues to airline and hotel clubs, as well as business luncheon clubs, pleasure, social, and athletic clubs, are disallowed.

DENY DEDUCTION FOR EXECUTIVE PAY OVER $1 MILLION

The new law limits, for purposes of the regular income tax and the alternative minimum tax, the deduction allowable to corporations for compensation paid or accrued with respect to the top five executives of a publicly held corporation to no more than $1 million per year. The top five executives are the chief executive officer of the corporation and the four other most highly paid officers, as determined under rules of the Securities and Exchange Commission. In general, this deduction limitation applies to all remuneration for services, including cash and the cash value of all noncash remuneration. However, the following types of compensation are not subject to the limitation: (1) remuneration payable on a commission basis; (2) remuneration payable solely on account of the attainment of one or more performance goals if certain outside director and shareholder approval requirements are met; (3) payments to a tax-qualified retirement plan including salary reduction contributions; (4) amounts that are excludable from the executive's gross income (such as employer-provided health benefits and miscellaneous fringe benefits); and (5) any remuneration payable under a written binding contract that was in effect on February 17, 1993, and remains in effect without material modification. In general, stock options and other stock appreciation rights meet the requirements for performance-based compensation because the amount of compensation that will be received depends solely on increases in the value of the corporation's stock. The limitation applies to compensation that is otherwise deductible by a corporation in a taxable year beginning after December 31, 1993.

REDUCE COMPENSATION TAKEN INTO ACCOUNT FOR QUALIFIED RETIREMENT PLAN PURPOSES

Present and prior law limits the amount of a participant's compensation that can be taken into account under a tax-qualified pension plan. The compensation limit applies for purposes of determining the amount of an employer's deduction for contributions to a tax-qualified pension plan and the amount of the participant's benefits. The limit for 1993 is $235,890. The new law reduces the amount of compensation that can be taken into account under a tax-qualified plan to $150,000 (indexed for inflation in $10,000 increments). The provision is effective for benefits accruing in plan years beginning after December 31, 1993. A delayed effective date applies to collectively bargained plans and a special grandfather rule applies to eligible participants in governmental plans.

MODIFY DEDUCTION FOR MOVING EXPENSES

Under present and prior law, an employee or self-employed individual may deduct from gross income certain expenses incurred as a result of moving to a new residence in connection with beginning work at a new location. For the taxpayer to claim the deduction under prior law, his or her new principal place of work must have been at least 35 miles farther from the former residence than was the taxpayer's former principal place of work. In general, the expenses deductible under prior law were the expenses of transporting a taxpayer's household goods and personal effects to a new residence, the cost of meals and lodging en route, the expenses for up to 30 days in the general location of the new residence, and certain expenses related to either the sale of the old residence or the acquisition of the new residence.

Under the new law, deductible moving expenses include only the expenses of moving household goods and personal effects and of traveling (including lodging, but excluding meals) from the former residence to the new place of residence. The new law also increases the mileage threshold from 35 to 50 miles. The new law provides that allowable moving expenses paid by an employer (whether directly or by reimbursement) are excludable from gross income and that unreimbursed allowable moving expenses are deductible in calculating adjusted gross income. This provision is generally effective for expenses incurred after December 31, 1993.

MODIFY ESTIMATED TAX REQUIREMENTS FOR INDIVIDUALS

Under present and prior law, individual taxpayers are subject to an addition to tax for underpayments of estimated tax. Under prior law, a taxpayer did not have underpayments of estimated tax if he or she made estimated tax payments equal to (1) 100 percent of last year's tax liability or (2) 90 percent of the current year's tax liability. Some individuals were denied the use of the 100 percent of last year's liability safe harbor.

The new law repeals a special rule that denies the use of the 100 percent of last year's liability safe harbor to certain individuals. In its place, the new law raises the 100 percent of last year's liability safe harbor contained in the provision to 110 percent of last year's liability for any individual with an adjusted gross income of more than $150,000, as shown on the individual's income tax return for the preceding taxable year. Under the provision, individuals with a preceding year adjusted gross income of $150,000 or less can still use the 100 percent of last year's liability safe harbor. All individuals may continue to pay estimated taxes based on 90 percent of the taxpayer's current year liability. The provision is effective for taxable years beginning after December 31, 1993.

INCREASE TAXABLE PORTION OF SOCIAL SECURITY

Under present and prior law, taxpayers are required to include in gross income a portion of their Social Security benefits when their provisional income exceeds a threshold amount. Under present and prior law, provisional income is defined for this purpose as adjusted gross income, plus one-half of Social Security benefits. Under prior law, the threshold amount was $32,000 for married taxpayers filing joint returns and $25,000 for unmarried taxpayers. For persons whose provisional income exceeded the applicable threshold amount, the amount of Social Security benefits includable in income was the lesser of 50 percent of Social Security benefits, or 50 percent of the amount by which provisional income exceeded the applicable threshold.

The new law creates a second tier of Social Security benefit inclusion in gross income. The second tier threshold applies to taxpayers with provisional income greater than $34,000 for unmarried taxpayers or $44,000 for married taxpayers filing joint returns. For these taxpayers, gross income includes the lesser of:

1. 85 percent of the taxpayer's Social Security benefit; or
2. the sum of:
    - **a)** the smaller of:
        - (i) the amount included under prior law; or
        - (ii) $4,500 (for unmarried taxpayers) or $6,000 (for married taxpayers filing joint returns); and
    - **b)** 85 percent of the excess of the taxpayer's provisional income over the applicable new threshold amounts.

For married taxpayers filing separate returns, gross income includes the lesser of 85 percent of the taxpayer's Social Security benefit or 85 percent of the taxpayer's provisional income. This provision is effective for taxable years beginning after December 31, 1993.

145 Business Provisions

INCREASE IN CORPORATE TAX RATE

The new law establishes a new 35 percent marginal tax rate on corporate taxable income (including net capital gains) in excess of $10 million, effective for taxable years beginning on or after January 1, 1993. A fiscal year corporation is required to use a "blended rate" that reflects the increased rate for its fiscal year that includes January 1, 1993.

A corporation with taxable income in excess of $15 million is required to increase its tax liability by the lesser of 3 percent of the excess or $100,000. This increase in tax phases out the benefits of the existing 34 percent marginal rate.

DISALLOWANCE OF DEDUCTION FOR CERTAIN LOBBYING EXPENSES

The new law provides that taxpayers may not deduct as a business expense amounts incurred in an attempt to influence federal or state (but not local) legislation through communication with members or employees of legislative bodies or other government officials who may participate in the formulation of legislation. It does provide, however, a $2,000 per taxpayer *de minimis* exception for in-house lobbying expenditures. The provision is effective for amounts paid after December 31, 1993.

AMORTIZATION OF GOODWILL AND CERTAIN OTHER INTANGIBLE ASSETS

The new law provides a uniform straight-line amortization method for certain acquired intangible assets, including goodwill, with an amortization period of 15 years. This provision generally applies to acquisitions after August 10, 1993, and, on an elective basis, to all property acquired after July 25, 1991.

DENY DEDUCTIONS RELATING TO TRAVEL EXPENSES PAID OR INCURRED IN CONNECTION WITH TRAVEL OF TAXPAYER'S SPOUSE OR DEPENDENTS

The new law denies a deduction for travel expenses paid or incurred with respect to a spouse, dependent, or other individual accompanying a taxpayer on business travel, unless that travel companion is a bona fide employee of the taxpayer paying or reimbursing the expenses, the companion's travel has a bona fide business purpose, and the companion's expenses would otherwise be deductible. The denial of the deduction does not apply to expenses that would otherwise qualify as deductible moving expenses. This provision is effective for amounts paid or incurred after December 31, 1993.

INCREASE WITHHOLDING RATE ON SUPPLEMENTAL WAGE PAYMENTS

The new law increases the applicable withholding rate on supplemental wage payments (such as bonuses, commissions, and overtime pay) from 20 to 28 percent. This provision is effective for payments made after December 31, 1993.

EMPLOYER TAX CREDIT FOR FICA TAXES PAID ON TIP INCOME

Under present and prior law, all employee tip income is treated as employer-provided wages for purposes of the Federal Unemployment Tax Act (FUTA) and the Federal Insurance Contributions Act (FICA). For purposes of the minimum wage provisions of the Fair Labor Standards Act, reported tips (up to one-half of the amount of the minimum wage) are treated as employer-provided wages. The new law provides food and beverage establishments with a business tax credit in an amount equal to the employer's FICA tax obligation attributable to reported tips in excess of those treated as wages for purposes of satisfying the minimum wage laws. A food and beverage establishment is any trade or business (or portion thereof) which provides food and beverages for consumption on the premises and with respect to which the tipping of employees serving food and beverages is customary. No credit is allowed with respect to FICA taxes paid on tips that are not received in connection with the provision of food or beverages. The provision is effective for FICA taxes paid with respect to services performed after December 31, 1993.

The objective of this chapter has been to focus on the specific tax changes created by the 1993 law. The impact of those changes, and the planning opportunities they present, have been reflected in the other relevant portions of this book. Note that some changes are retroactive to years prior to 1993. If those changes affect you, it may be dollars in your pocket to file an amended tax return for those years.

CHAPTER 12

Stealth Tax Reform

"Thousands of pages of pet rocks that have nothing to do with the national interest."

Senator Nunn of Georgia
On the tax code

On July 30, 1996, President Clinton signed the Taxpayer Bill of Rights 2, bringing about widespread changes in our tax laws. Forty-nine sections of the Internal Revenue Code were affected, including rules governing joint returns, liens and levies, attorney's fees, summonses, and mailing documents to the Internal Revenue Service.

On August 20, 1996, President Clinton signed HR 3448, the Small Business Protection Act of 1996; on August 21, 1996, he signed HR 3103, the Health Insurance Portability and Accountability Act of 1996; and on August 22, 1996, the President signed HR 3174, the Personal Responsibility and Work Opportunity Reconciliation Act of 1996. These three bills contain 655 additional tax code changes bringing the total to 704 tax changes in a "quiet" tax year. This chapter will examine some of the more pertinent changes and how they will affect your financial future.

146 The New Taxpayer Bill of Rights

On July 30, 1996, President Clinton signed into law legislation designed to make taxpayer dealings with the Internal Revenue Service easier and fairer. This new Taxpayer Bill of Rights No. 2 was contained in HR 2337 and according to the President, "With the Taxpayer Bill of Rights, we say to America's taxpayers, when you deal with the IRS, you also have privileges and we respect them. You have protection and we will help to provide it. You have rights and we will shield them."

The bill included provisions to ease taxpayer burdens in the areas of returns and examinations; interest and penalties; collections; taxpayer advocacy; and attorney's fees. Many of the provisions of the Taxpayer Bill of Rights No. 2 were administratively adopted by the Internal Revenue Service in Announcement 96-5 issued January 4, 1996. Below, I will detail the various provisions of the new Bill of Rights.

1. INCREASED TAXPAYER OMBUDSMAN AUTHORITY TO ADDRESS TAXPAYER CONCERNS

The Taxpayer Ombudsman was authorized by Congress in 1988 to issue Taxpayer Assistance Orders ("TAO") to resolve taxpayer problems. The Ombudsman has the authority to issue a TAO to direct IRS officials to stop certain actions to alleviate a hardship faced by a taxpayer. The Commissioner has delegated additional authority to the Ombudsman to issue TAO's to take *positive* action to relieve taxpayer hardship.

The new Bill of Rights expands the Ombudsman's authority to issue TAO's. For example, the Ombudsman has the authority to issue a TAO directing the IRS to pay a refund immediately to a taxpayer eligible for a refund to relieve severe hardship facing such a taxpayer. In addition, a TAO can stay temporarily an IRS collection action in order to allow the IRS to review the appropriateness of the action.

2. GREATER PROTECTION FOR TAXPAYER ASSISTANCE ORDERS

The Department of the Treasury and the IRS will now be required to publish proposed regulations to limit the authority to modify or rescind a TAO to only the Commissioner, Deputy Commissioner, or Ombudsman.

3. TAXPAYERS WILL NOW HAVE THE KNOWLEDGE TO APPEAL LIENS, LEVIES, AND SEIZURES PROPOSED BY THE IRS

Each taxpayer subject to a lien, levy, or seizure will receive Publication 1660, "Collection Appeal Rights for Liens, Levies and Seizures," which will explain the taxpayer's right to make such an appeal and the procedure for requesting an appeal.

4. NOTIFICATION OF COLLECTION ACTIVITY TO DIVORCED AND SEPARATED SPOUSES

The IRS will now be required to notify one spouse of collection activity against the other spouse to collect on a joint return liability. In addition, the IRS will begin a formal study of the unique tax issues facing divorced and separated spouses who file joint returns. The study's goal is to recommend specific legislative and administrative actions, where possible.

5. PROHIBITION ON COMPROMISING INFORMANT'S TAX LIABILITY

The IRS will issue procedures to formalize its long-standing practice of prohibiting special agents from compromising the tax liability of an informant in exchange for information about another taxpayer.

6. VOLUNTARY PAYER TELEPHONE NUMBERS ON FORM 1099

The IRS will request that payers include their telephone numbers on the taxpayers' copies of Forms 1099. Taxpayers may therefore find it easier to resolve their disputes with payers without IRS involvement. For tax years after December 31, 1996, they will be required.

7. STUDY OF INTEREST NETTING

Treasury and the IRS have begun a formal study of issues relating to the IRS's current and future interest netting procedures. Treasury and the IRS will issue a Notice that will ask for public comment on specific legal and administrative issues.

8. INCREASED IRS INVESTIGATION OF DISPUTED INFORMATION RETURNS

The IRS will increase current efforts to investigate tax information reported by payers where a taxpayer challenges the accuracy of the information, such as wage income reported to the IRS on Forms W-2 and other income payments reported on Forms 1099.

9. 30-DAY NOTICE BEFORE TERMINATING OR MODIFYING INSTALLMENT AGREEMENTS

The IRS procedures shall be modified to provide a taxpayer with 30 days' notice before the taxpayer's installment agreement with the IRS is either terminated or modified.

10. PENALTY FOR TRUST FUND TAXES

Taxpayers liable for trust fund taxes (such as social security and medicare) should be given 60 days' notice before being assessed a nonpayment penalty. A new IRS policy statement prevents the IRS from assessing this nonpayment penalty against honorary or volunteer trustees not involved in an organization's daily operation.

11. NOTICE OF OVERPAYMENTS

The IRS shall notify a taxpayer as soon as reasonably possible if the IRS receives a payment not apparently related to a taxpayer's liability when not identifiable to a proper taxpayer account.

12. APPEALS MEDIATION PROCEDURE

A one-year test of an Appeals Mediation Procedure has been instituted. The mediation procedure allows taxpayers with certain cases in Appeals, but not docketed in any court, to request a mediation of one or more issues.

13. OBTAINING ADVANCE VALUATION OF ART WORKS

Valuing art work is important for such tax purposes as estate and gift taxes and the charitable contribution deduction. In Revenue Procedure 96-15, taxpayers are told how to obtain an IRS review of a valuation of a work of art before filing a return.

14. The new Taxpayer Bill of Rights expands the authority of the IRS to abate interest and creates a procedure for the review of an IRS failure to abate interest.

15. The new law extends the interest-free period to pay tax from 10 to 21 calendar days.

16. AUTOMATIC EXTENSIONS WITH PAYMENT

Under past law, individuals were able to obtain an automatic four-month extension of time to file their tax returns if they paid any balance due. Under Notice 93-22, the requirement that the tax be fully paid upon application for the extension has been eliminated. Taxpayers may still be subject to failure to pay penalties and interest if they file a return with a balance due. However, they will no longer be subject to penalty and interest for failure to file.

17. BURDEN SHIFT

Under the new law, if you win a tax case in court, the IRS will have the burden of proof to establish that it was "substantially justified" in bringing the case or you will be eligible for attorney fees and costs.

18. TIMELY MAILING

Under prior law, only a U.S. postal receipt could be used to prove timely mailing. Under the new law, use of nonpostal delivery is now authorized. This means that services such as Federal Express or UPS can now be used to prove timely filing.

19. INCREASE IN DAMAGES

The new law will greatly increase the amount of money you can sue the IRS for in connection with "unauthorized collection actions." Under current law, you can sue for damages caused by an IRS worker who recklessly or intentionally disregards provisions of the Internal Revenue code or Treasury regulations. The new law lifts that amount to $1 million from $100,000. Lawyers predict this sharp increase will catch the attention of IRS officials and give them a much stronger incentive to play by the rules.

During the week of August 19 through August 23, 1996, President Clinton was very busy. During that week, he signed three additional new tax bills, HR 3734, aimed at reforming the welfare system; HR 3103, the Health Insurance Portability and Accountability Act of 1996; and HR 3448, the Small Business Job Protection Act of 1996. These three bills contained 655 new tax code changes. In this chapter, I will detail the most pertinent tax changes of these new laws.

147 Personal Responsibility and Work Opportunity Reconciliation Act of 1996, HR 3734

The primary tax changes with respect to this bill relate to the earned income credit. Individuals are not eligible for the credit if they do not include their taxpayer identification number and their spouse's taxpayer identification number on their tax return. If an individual fails to provide a correct taxpayer identification number, such an omission will be treated as a mathematical or clerical error under the new law and the taxpayer must be given an explanation of the asserted error and a period of 60 days to request that the IRS abate its assessment.

A second change relates to the disqualified income test for the earned income credit itself. Under prior law, an individual would not be eligible for the earned income credit if the aggregate amount of "disqualified income" of that taxpayer for the taxable year exceeded $2,350. This threshold was not indexed. Disqualified income was the sum of: (1) interest (taxable and tax exempt), (2) dividends, (3) net rent and royalty income. Under the new law, the following items are added to the definition of disqualified income: capital gain net income and net passive income that is not self-employment income.

Moreover, the threshold above which an individual is not eligible for the credit is reduced from $2,350 to $2,200 and that threshold is indexed for inflation after 1996.

In addition, the new law modifies the definition of adjusted gross income used for phasing out the earned income credit by disregarding certain losses. The losses disregarded are: (1) net capital losses, (2) net losses from trusts and estates, (3) net losses from nonbusiness rents and royalties and, (4) 50 percent of the net losses from businesses, computed separately with respect to sole proprietorships (other than in farming), sole proprietorships in farming, and other businesses.

For purposes of (4) above, amounts attributable to a business that consist of the performance of services by the taxpayer as an employee are not taken into account.

148 The Health Insurance Portability and Accountability Act of 1996, HR 3103

1. MEDICAL SAVINGS ACCOUNTS

Under prior law, self-employed individuals were entitled to deduct 30 percent of the amount paid for health insurance for the self-employed individual and his or her spouse or dependents. Any individual who itemizes tax deductions could deduct unreimbursed medical expenses (including expenses for medical insurance) paid during the year to the extent that the total of such expenses exceeds 7.5 percent of the individual's adjusted gross income. Prior law did not contain any special rules for medical savings accounts.

A Medical Savings Account (MSA) is a trust or custodial account created exclusively for the benefit of the account holder and is subject to rules similar to those applicable to individual retirement accounts. Within limits, contributions to a medical savings account are deductible if made by an eligible individual and are excludable if made by an employer of an eligible individual. Moreover, earnings on amounts in a medical savings account are not currently taxable and distributions from a medical savings account for medical expenses will also not be taxable.

Beginning in 1997, Medical Savings Accounts will be available to employees covered under an employer-sponsored high-deductible plan of a small employer and to self-employed individuals. An employer is a small employer if it employed on an average no more than 50 employees during either the preceding or second preceding year. In order for an employee of an eligible employer to be eligible to make medical savings account contributions (or to have the employer make contributions on his or her behalf), the employee must be covered under an employer-sponsored high-deductible health plan and must not be covered under any other health plan. In the case of an employee, contributions can be made to a medical savings account either by the individual or by the individual's employer. However, an individual is not eligible to make contributions to a medical savings account for a year if any employer contributions are made to a medical savings account on behalf of the individual for the year.

Similarly, in order to be eligible to make contributions to a medical savings account, a self-employed individual must be covered under a high-deductible health plan and no other health plan is allowed (except certain permitted coverage). With both self-employed individuals and employees, medical savings accounts are allowable if the taxpayer has another health plan that provides *only* certain limited permitted coverage for accidents, disability, dental care, vision care, or long-term care. This coverage may be by insurance or otherwise and permitted insurance includes: (1) Medicare supplemental insurance; (2) insurance if substantially all of the coverage provided under such insurance related to (a) liabilities incurred under Workers' Compensation Law, (b) tort liabilities, (c) liabilities relating to ownership and use of property (e.g., auto insurance), or (d) such other similar liabilities as the Secretary of the Treasury may prescribe by regulations; (3) insurance for a specified disease or illness; and (4) insurance that provides a fixed payment for hospitalization.

Individual contributions to a medical savings account are deductible (within limits) above the line. In addition, employee contributions are excludable within the same limits.

In the case of a self-employed individual, the deduction cannot exceed your earned income from the trade or business with respect to which the high-deductible plan is established. In the case of an employee, the deduction cannot exceed your compensation attributable to the employer sponsoring the high-deductible plan in which you are enrolled.

The maximum annual contribution that can be made to a medical savings account for a year is 65 percent of the deductible under the high-deductible plan in the case of individual coverage and 75 percent of the deductible in the case of family coverage. No other dollar limits on the maximum contribution apply. The annual contribution limit is the sum of the limits determined separately for each month, based upon the individual's status and health plan coverage as of the first day of the month.

A high-deductible plan is a health plan with an annual deductible of at least $1,500 and no more than $2,250 in the case of individual coverage and at least $3,000 and no more than $4,500 in the case of family coverage. In addition, the maximum out-of-pocket expenses with respect to allowed cost (including the deductible) must be no more than $3,000 in the case of individual coverage and no more than $5,500 in the case of family coverage. Beginning after 1998, these dollars amounts are indexed for inflation in $50 increments based on the Consumer Price Index.

Earnings on amounts in a medical savings account are not currently included in income and distributions from a medical savings account for the medical expenses of an individual and his or her spouse or dependents generally are excludable from income.

The medical savings account plan is a trial plan. The number of taxpayers benefiting annually from a medical savings account contribution is limited to a threshold level (generally, 750,000 taxpayers). If it is determined in a year that the threshold level has been exceeded then, in general, for succeeding years during the four-year pilot period, 1997–2000, only those individuals who (1) made a medical savings account contribution or had an employer medical savings account contribution for the year or a preceding year or (2) are employed by a participating employer, would be eligible for a medical savings account contribution.

During 1997–2000, the Department of the Treasury will evaluate Medical Savings Account participation and the reduction in federal revenues due to such participation and make reports of such evaluations to Congress.

2. INCREASE IN DEDUCTION FOR HEALTH INSURANCE EXPENSES OF A SELF-EMPLOYED INDIVIDUAL

Under prior law, self-employed individuals were entitled to deduct 30 percent of the amount paid for health insurance for that individual and his or her spouse and dependents. The deduction was not available for any month in which the taxpayer was eligible to participate in a subsidized health plan maintained by his or her employer. The new law increases the deduction for health insurance of self-employed individuals as follows: the deduction would be 40 percent in 1997; 45 percent in 1998 through 2002; 50 percent in 2003; 60 percent in 2004, 70 percent in 2005; and 80 percent in 2006 and thereafter. (See page 133 for current allowances.)

3. TREATMENT OF LONG-TERM CARE INSURANCE AND SERVICES

Prior law did not provide explicit rules relating to the tax treatment of long-term care insurance contracts or long-term care services. Beginning in 1997, the new law provides that long-term care insurance premiums will count toward itemized medical expenses and, to the extent that such expenses exceed 7.5 percent of adjusted gross income, a tax deduction will be available.

There is a cap on the amount of premium that can be applied to the medical expense deduction. The limit varies by attained age as follows:

Attained Age at the End of the Tax Year	Maximum Deduction
Not more than 40	$ 200
More than 40 but not more than 50	$ 375
More than 50 but not more than 60	$ 750
More than 60 but not more than 70	$2,000
More than 70	$2,500

For taxable years beginning after 1997, these dollar limits are indexed for increases in the medical care component of the Consumer Price Index. Moreover, long-term care insurance premiums will now qualify for the self-employed health insurance deduction.

4. TREATMENT OF ACCELERATED DEATH BENEFITS UNDER LIFE INSURANCE CONTRACTS

The new law generally excludes "qualified accelerated death benefits" from income. If a contract meets the definition of a life insurance contract, gross income does not include insurance proceeds that are paid pursuant to the contract by reason of the death of the insured. However, recently many chronically or terminally ill individuals with short life expectancies have sold or assigned their life insurance policies to qualified viatical-settlement providers. These companies typically buy policies from people with life-threatening illnesses for a percentage of the policy's face value. Under prior law, recipients of viatical payments would owe federal income taxes on those payments. The new law excludes these payments from income effective for amounts received after December 31, 1996.

5. PENALTY-FREE WITHDRAWALS FROM IRAs FOR MEDICAL EXPENSES

Amounts withdrawn from an individual retirement arrangement (IRA) are includable in income (except to the extent of any nondeductible contributions). In addition, a 10 percent additional tax applies to withdrawals from IRAs made before age 59fi unless the withdrawal is made on account of death or disability or is made in the form of annuity payments.

A similar additional tax applies to early withdrawals from employer-sponsored tax qualified pension plans. However, the 10 percent additional tax does not apply to withdrawals from such plans to the extent used for medical expenses that exceed 7.5 percent of adjusted gross income.

The new law extends the exception to the 10 percent tax for medical expenses in excess of 7.5 percent of adjusted gross income to withdrawals from IRAs. In addition, it provides that the 10 percent additional tax does not apply to withdrawals for medical insurance (without regard to the 7.5 percent of adjusted gross income) if the individual (including a self-employed individual) has received unemployment compensation under federal or state law for at least 12 weeks, and the withdrawal is made in the year such unemployment compensation is received or the following year. If a self-employed individual is not eligible for unemployment compensation under applicable law, he or she is treated as having received unemployment compensation for at least 12 weeks if the individual would have received unemployment compensation but for the fact that the individual was self-employed.

6. INTEREST DISALLOWED FOR CORPORATE-OWNED LIFE INSURANCE POLICY LOANS

Under the new law, no deduction will be allowed for interest paid or accrued on any indebtedness with respect to one or more life insurance policies or annuity or endowment contracts owned by a taxpayer covering any individual who is (1) an officer or employee of, or (2) financially interested in, any trade or business carried on by the taxpayer regardless of the aggregate amount of debt with respect to policies or contract covering the individual.

An exception is provided retaining present law for interest on indebtedness with respect to life insurance policies covering up to 20 key persons.

This provision is effective for interest paid or accrued after December 31, 1995 (subject to a phase-in rule).

149 The Small Business Job Protection Act of 1996, HR 3448

The Small Business Job Protection Act of 1996 was enacted to provide tax relief for small businesses, to protect jobs, to create opportunities, to increase the take-home pay of workers, and to increase the minimum wage rate. Below, I have summarized the more pertinent tax provisions of this act.

1. INCREASE IN EXPENSING FOR SMALL BUSINESSES

Under prior law, in lieu of depreciation, a taxpayer with a sufficiently small amount of annual investment may elect to deduct up to $17,500 of the cost of qualifying property placed in service for the taxable year (Section 179). In general, qualifying property is defined as depreciable taxable personal property that is purchased for use in the act of conduct of a trade or business. The $17,500 amount is reduced (but not below zero) by the amount by which the cost of qualifying property placed in service during the taxable year exceeds $200,000.

The new law increases the $17,500 amount allowed to be expensed to $25,000. The increased is phased in as follows:

Taxable Year Beginning In	Maximum Expensing
1997	$18,000
1998	$18,500
1999	$19,000
2000	$20,000
2001	$24,000
2002	$24,000
2003 and thereafter	$25,000

2. HOME OFFICE DEDUCTION: TREATMENT OF STORAGE OF PRODUCT SAMPLES

The new law clarifies that the special rule contained in prior law, Section 280A (c) (2), permits deductions for expenses relating to a storage unit in a taxpayer's home regularly used for inventory or product samples (or both) of the taxpayer's trade or business of selling products at retail or wholesale provided that the home is the sole fixed location of such trade or business. Such deductions will now be allowed for business expenses related to a space within a home that are used on a regular (even if not exclusive) basis as a storage unit.

3. APPLICATION OF INVOLUNTARY CONVERSION RULES TO PROPERTY DAMAGED AS A RESULT OF PRESIDENTIALLY DECLARED DISASTERS

A taxpayer may elect not to recognize gain with respect to property that is involuntarily converted if the taxpayer acquires, within an applicable period, property similar or related in service or use. If the taxpayer does not replace the converted property with property similar or related in service or use, then gain generally will be recognized. Under the new law, any tangible property acquired and held for productive use in a business is treated as similar or related in service or use to property that (1) was held for investment or productive use in a business and (2) was involuntarily converted as a result of a presidentially declared disaster. This provision is effective for disasters for which a presidential declaration is made after December 31, 1994 in taxable years ending after that date.

4. WORK OPPORTUNITY TAX CREDIT

Prior to January 1, 1995, the targeted jobs tax credit was available on an elective basis for employers hiring individuals from one or more of nine targeted groups. The credit generally was equal to 40 percent of qualified first-year wages (up to $6,000) for a maximum credit of $2,400.

The new law replaces the targeted jobs credit with a "work opportunity tax credit." The new credit is available on an elective basis for employers hiring individuals from one or more of eight targeted groups. The credit generally is equal to 35 percent of qualified first-year wages.

No credit is allowed for wages paid unless the eligible individual is employed by the employer for at least 180 days (20 in the case of a qualified summer youth employee) or 400 hours (120 hours in case of a qualified summer youth employee).

5. EMPLOYER-PROVIDED EDUCATIONAL ASSISTANCE

For taxable years beginning before January 1, 1995, an employee's gross income and wages did not include amounts paid or incurred by the employer for educational assistance provided to the employee if such amounts were paid or occurred pursuant to an educational assistance program that met certain requirements. This exclusion, which expired for taxable years after December 31, 1994, was limited to $5,250 of education assistance with respect to an individual during the calendar year. The exclusion applied whether or not the education was job related. Moreover, a 1996 IRS Revenue Ruling clarified that this tax relief applies to people who receive training help after being let go for any reason by their employers. In a period of downsizing, this is an important benefit. In the absence of this exclusion, education assistance is excludable from income only if it is related to the employee's current job.

The new law extends the exclusion for employer-provided educational assistance for taxable years beginning after December 31, 1994 and expires with respect to courses beginning after May 31, 1997. The exclusion for graduate courses applies in 1995. In 1996, the exclusion for graduate courses does not apply to courses beginning after June 30, 1996.

6. RESEARCH AND EXPERIMENTATION TAX CREDIT

Prior to July 1, 1995, a research tax credit equal to 20 percent of the amount by which a taxpayer's qualified research expenditures for taxable year exceeded its base amount for that year was allowed. The research tax credit expired and does not apply to amounts paid or incurred after June 30, 1995.

A 20 percent research tax credit also applied to the *excess* of (1) 100 percent of corporate cash expenditures (including grants or contributions) paid for basic research conducted by universities (and certain nonprofit scientific research organizations) *over* (2) the sum of (a) the greater of two minimum basic research floors, and (b) an amount reflecting any decrease in nonresearch giving to universities by the corporation as compared to such giving during a fixed base period, as adjusted for inflation. This separate credit computation was commonly referred to as "the university basic research credit."

The new law extends the research tax credit for eleven months—i.e., for the period July 1, 1996 through May 31, 1997.

7. ORPHAN DRUG TAX CREDIT

Prior to January 1, 1995, a 50 percent nonrefundable tax credit was allowed for qualified clinical testing expenses incurred in testing of certain drugs for rare diseases or conditions generally referred to as "orphan drugs." The new law extends the orphan drug tax credit for eleven months—i.e., for the period July 1, 1996 through May 31, 1997.

8. CONTRIBUTIONS OF STOCK TO PRIVATE FOUNDATIONS

In computing taxable income, a taxpayer who itemizes deductions generally is allowed to deduct the fair market value of property contributed to a charitable organization. However, in the case of a charitable contribution of short-term gain, inventory, or other ordinary income property, the amount of the deduction generally is limited to the taxpayer's basis in the property. In the case of charitable contribution of tangible personal property, the deduction is limited to the taxpayer's basis in such property if the use by the recipient charitable organization is unrelated to the organization's tax-exempt purpose.

In cases involving contributions to a private foundation (other than certain private operating foundations), the amount of the deduction is limited to the taxpayer's basis in the property. However, under a special rule, taxpayers were allowed a deduction equal to the fair market value of "qualified appreciated stock" contributed to a private foundation prior to January 1, 1995. Qualified appreciated stock was defined as publicly traded stock which is capital gain property. The fair market value deduction for qualified appreciated stock donations applied only to the extent that total donations made by the donor to private foundations of stock in a particular corporation did not exceed 10 percent of the outstanding stock of that corporation.

The new law extends the fair market value deduction for contributions of qualified appreciated stocks to private foundations made during the period July 1, 1996 through May 31, 1997.

9. S CORPORATIONS PERMITTED TO HAVE 75 SHAREHOLDERS

The taxable income or loss of an S corporation is taken into account by the corporation's shareholders, rather than by the entity, whether or not such income is distributed. A "small business corporation" is defined as a domestic corporation which is not an ineligible corporation, and one which does not have (1) more than 35 shareholders, (2) as a shareholder, a person (other than certain trusts or estates) who is not an individual, (3) a nonresident alien as a shareholder, and (4) more than one class of stock. For purposes of the 35 shareholder limitation, a husband and wife are treated as one shareholder.

The new law increases the maximum number of eligible shareholders from 35 to 75 effective for taxable years beginning after December 31, 1996.

10. ELECTING SMALL BUSINESS TRUST

Under prior law, trusts other than grantor trusts, voting trusts, certain testamentary trusts, and "qualified subchapter S trusts" may not be shareholders in an S corporation.

The new law creates a new kind of trust, "electing small business trust," which can now qualify to hold stock in an S corporation. In order to qualify for this treatment, all beneficiaries of the trust must be individuals or estates eligible to be S corporation shareholders, except that charitable organizations may now hold contingent remainder interests. Moreover, no interest in the trust may be acquired by purchase.

11. S CORPORATIONS PERMITTED TO HOLD SUBSIDIARIES

Under prior law, a small business corporation could not be a member of an affiliated group of corporations (other than by reason of ownership and certain inactive corporations). Thus, an S corporation may not own 80 percent or more of the stock of another corporation (whether an S corporation or a C corporation). In addition, a small business corporation may not have as a shareholder another corporation (whether an S corporation or a C corporation).

Applicable for taxable years beginning after December 31, 1996, an S corporation is now allowed to own 80 percent or more of the stock of a C corporation. In addition, an S corporation is now allowed to own a qualified Subchapter S subsidiary.

12. PENSION SIMPLIFIED DISTRIBUTION RULES

In general, a distribution of benefits from a tax-favored retirement arrangement is included in gross income in the year it is paid or distributed under the rules relating to the taxation of annuities. Lump sum distributions from qualified plans and qualified annuity plans are eligible for special five-year forwarding averaging. In general, a lump sum distribution is a distribution within one taxable year of the balance to the credit of an employee that becomes payable to the recipient first, on account of the death of the employee, second, after the employee attains age 59fi, third, on account of the employee's separation from service, or fourth, in the case of self-employed individuals, on account of disability. Lump sum treatment is not available for distributions from a tax-sheltered annuity.

Under the new law, the five-year averaging method for lump sum distributions from qualified plans is repealed effective for taxable years beginning after December 31, 1999.

Under prior law, the beneficiary or estate of a deceased employee could exclude up to $5,000 for employer-provided death benefit. Under the new law, this $5,000 exclusion for employer-provided death benefit is repealed with respect to decedents dying after the date of enactment of the law, Tuesday, August 20, 1996.

Amounts received as an annuity under a qualified plan generally are includable in income in the year received except to the extent that they represent the return of the recipient's investment in the contract (i.e., "recovery of basis"). Under prior law, a pro rata basis recovery rule generally applies to that portion of any annuity payment that represents nontaxable return of basis as determined by applying an exclusion ratio equal to the employee's total investment in the contract divided by the total expected payments over the term of the annuity.

Under a simplified alternative method provided by the IRS, the taxable portion of qualifying annuity payments is determined under a simplified exclusion ratio method. In no event can the total amount excluded from income as a nontaxable return of basis be greater than the recipient's total investment in the contract.

The new law provides that basis recovery on payments from qualified plans generally will be determined under a method similar to the prior law simplified alternative method provided by the IRS. The portion of each annuity payment that represents a return of basis is equal to the employee's total basis as of the annuity starting date, divided by the number of anticipated payments under the following table:

Age	**Number of Payments**
Not more than 55	360
56-60	310
61-65	260
66-70	210
More than 70	160

This provision is effective with respect to annuity starting dates beginning 90 days after the date of enactment (August 20, 1996). Under prior law, minimum distribution rules generally require a qualified plan to provide distributions beginning no later than April 1 of the calendar year following the calendar year in which the plan participant or IRA owner attains age 70fi. The new law modifies the rule that requires all participants in qualified plans to commence distributions by age 70fi without regard to whether the participant is still employed by the employer and generally replaces it with the rule in effect prior to the Tax Reform Act of 1986. Under the new law, distributions are generally required to begin by April 1 of the calendar year following the later of first, the calendar year in which the employee attains age 70fi or second, the calendar year in which the employee retires. However, in the case of a 5 percent owner of the employer, distributions are required to begin at no later than the April 1 of the calendar year following the year in which the 5 percent owner attains age 70fi.

In addition, in the case of an employee (other than a 5 percent owner) who retires in a calendar year after attaining age 70fi, the new law requires the employee's accrued benefit to be actuarially increased to take into account the period after age 70fi in which the employee was not receiving benefits under the plan. Thus, under the new law, the employee's accrued benefit is required to reflect the value of benefits that the employee would have received if the employee had retired at age 70fi and had begun receiving benefits at that time. However, this actuarial adjustment rule does not apply in the case of a defined contribution plan.

13. ESTABLISHMENT OF A SIMPLE RETIREMENT PLAN FOR EMPLOYEES OF SMALL EMPLOYERS

The new law creates a simplified retirement plan for small business called the Savings Incentive Match Plan for Employees (SIMPLE) Retirement Plan. A SIMPLE plan can be adopted by employers who employ 100 employees or fewer with at least $5,000 in compensation for any two preceding years and who reasonably expect to earn at least $5,000 for the current year ("eligible employees"). Union and nonresident alien employees may be excluded. Self-employed individuals may participate. Employers who no longer qualify are given a two-year grace period to continue to maintain the plan. A SIMPLE plan can be either an IRA for each employee or part of a qualified cash or deferred arrangement (401(k) plan). If established in IRA form, a SIMPLE plan is not subject to the nondiscrimination rules generally applicable to qualified plans (including the top-heavy rules) and simplified reporting requirements apply. Within limits, contributions to a SIMPLE plan are not taxable until withdrawn.

A SIMPLE plan can also be adopted as part of a 401(k) plan. In that case, the plan does not have to satisfy the special nondiscrimination test applicable to 401(k) plans and is not subjected to the top-heavy rules. The other qualified plan rules continue to apply.

A SIMPLE retirement plan allows employees to make elective contributions to an IRA. Employee contributions have to be expressed as a percentage of the employee's compensation, and cannot exceed $6,000 per year. The $6,000 limit is indexed for inflation in $500 increments.

All contributions to an employee's SIMPLE account have to be fully vested. Contributions to a SIMPLE account generally are deductible by the employer. Early withdrawals from a SIMPLE account generally are subject to the 10 percent early withdrawal tax applicable to IRAs. However, withdrawals of a contribution during the two-year period beginning on the date the employee first participated in the SIMPLE plan are subject to a 25 percent early withdrawal tax, rather than 10 percent. The provisions relating to SIMPLE plans are effective for years beginning after December 31, 1996.

Under prior law, contributions to an IRA could also be made by an employer at the election of an employee under a Salary Reduction Simplified Employee Pension (SARSEP). Under SARSEPs, which are not qualified plans, employees could elect to have contributions made to the SARSEP or to receive the contributions in cash. The amount that an employee elected to have contributed to the SARSEP was not currently included in income. Under the new law, SARSEPs are repealed for years beginning after December 31, 1996, unless the SARSEP was established before January 1, 1997. Consequently, an employee is not permitted to establish a SARSEP after December 31, 1996. SARSEPs established before January 1, 1997 can continue to receive contributions under prior law rules, and new employees of the employer who are hired after December 31, 1996 can participate in the SARSEP in accordance with such rules.

14. SPOUSAL IRAs

Under prior law, the maximum deductible contribution that could be made to an IRA generally is the lesser of $2,000 or 100 percent of an individual's compensation (earned income in the case of a self-employed individual). In the case of a married individual whose spouse has no compensation (or elects to be treated as having no compensation), the $2,000 maximum limit on IRA contributions is increased to $2,250.

The new law permits deductible IRA contributions of up to $2,000 to be made for each spouse (including, for example, a homemaker who does not work outside the home) if the combined compensation of both spouses is at least equal to the contributed amount. This provision is effective for taxable years beginning after December 31,1996.

15. EXCESS DISTRIBUTION TAX

Prior law imposed at 15 percent excise tax on excess distributions from qualified retirement plans, tax-sheltered annuities, and IRAs. An additional 15 percent estate tax was also imposed on an individual's excess retirement accumulation.

Under the new law, the additional estate tax on excess accumulations continues to apply. However, the excise tax on excess distributions is suspended with respect to distributions received in 1997, 1998, and 1999.

16. RETIREMENT BENEFITS OF MINISTERS NOT SUBJECT TO TAX ON NET EARNINGS FROM SELF-EMPLOYMENT

Effective for years beginning before, on, or after December 31, 1994, the new bill provides that retirement benefits received from a church plan after a minister retires, and the rental value or allowance of a parsonage (including utilities) furnished to a minister after retirement, are not subject to self-employment taxes.

17. TREATMENT OF QUALIFIED STATE TUITION PROGRAMS

The new law provides tax-exempt status to "qualified state tuition programs," meaning programs established and maintained by a State (or agency or instrumentality thereof) under which persons may (1) purchase tuition credits or certificates on behalf of a designated beneficiary that entitles the beneficiary to a waiver of payments of qualified higher education expenses of the beneficiary, or (2) make contributions to an account that is established for the sole purpose of meeting qualified higher education expenses of the designated beneficiary of the account. "Qualified higher education expenses" are defined as tuition, fees, books, and equipment required for the enrollment or attendance at a college or university (or certain vocational schools).

Contributions made to a qualified state tuition program will be treated as incomplete gifts for federal gift tax purposes. Moreover, no amount shall be included in the gross income of a contributor to, or beneficiary of, a qualified state tuition program with respect to any distribution from, or earnings under, such program except that (1) amounts distributed or educational benefits provided to a beneficiary (e.g., when the beneficiary attends college) will be included in the beneficiary's gross income (unless excludable under another code section) to the extent such amount or the value of the educational benefits exceeds contributions made on behalf of the beneficiary and (2) amounts distributed to a contributor (e.g., when a parent or other relative receives a refund) will be included in the contributor's gross income to the extent such amounts exceed contributions made by that person.

18. ADOPTION ASSISTANCE

Prior law did not provide a tax credit for adoption expenses nor did it provide an exclusion from gross income for employer-provided adoption assistance. The Federal Adoption Assistance Program provides financial assistance for the adoption of certain special needs children. Specifically, the program provides assistance for adoption expenses for those special needs children receiving federally assisted adoption assistance payments as well as special needs children in private and state-funded programs. The maximum federal reimbursement is $1,000 per special needs child. Reimbursable expenses include those nonrecurring costs directly associated with the adoption process such as legal costs, social services review, and transportation costs.

The new law provides taxpayers with a maximum nonrefundable credit against income tax liability of $5,000 per child ($6,000 in the case of special needs adoptions) paid or incurred by the taxpayer. Any unused adoption credit may be carried forward by the taxpayer for up to 5 years. Qualified adoption expenses are reasonable and necessary adoption fees, court costs, attorney's fees, and other expenses that are directly related to the legal adoption of an eligible child.

In the case of an international adoption, the credit is not available unless the adoption is finalized. An eligible child is an individual (1) who has not attained age 18 as of the time of the adoption, or (2) who is physically or mentally incapable of caring for himself or herself. No credit is allowed for expenses incurred (1) in violation of state or federal law, (2) in carrying out any surrogate parenting arrangement, or (3) in connection with the adoption of a child of the taxpayer's spouse. The credit is phased out ratably for taxpayers with modified adjusted gross income above $75,000, and is fully phased out at $115,000 of modified adjusted gross income.

Note that the credit for non-special-needs adoptions will not be available for expenses paid or incurred after December 31, 2001. Moreover, special needs foreign adoptions are limited to a maximum credit of $5,000 (rather than $6,000) for qualified adoption expenses until December 31, 2001, at which time the credit for special needs foreign adoptions is also repealed.

With respect to the exclusion from income, under the new law a maximum exclusion of $5,000 ($6,000 in the case of special needs adoptions) is available for specified certain adoption expenses by the employer. The limit is a per-child limit, not an annual limitation. The exclusion is phased out ratably for taxpayers with modified adjusted gross income above $75,000 and is fully phased out at $115,000 of modified adjusted gross income. No credit is allowed for adoption expenses paid or reimbursed under an adoption assistance program.

Note that the exclusion is not available for expenses paid or incurred after December 31, 2001 and that special needs foreign adoptions are limited to a maximum exclusion of $5,000 (rather than $6,000) for qualified adoption expenses until December 31, 2001 at which time the exclusion is repealed.

19. EXCLUSION OF DAMAGES RECEIVED ON ACCOUNT OF PERSONAL INJURY OR SICKNESS

Under prior law, gross income does not include any damages received (whether by suit or agreement and whether as lump sums or as periodic payments) on account of personal injury or sickness. The exclusion from gross income of damages received on account of personal injury or sickness specifically does not apply to punitive damages received in connection with a case not involving physical injury or sickness. Courts have differed as to whether the exclusion applies to punitive damages received in connection with a case involving a physical injury or physical sickness. Certain states provide that, in the case of claims under a wrongful death statute, only punitive damages may be awarded.

Courts have interpreted the exclusion from gross income of damages received on account of personal injury or sickness broadly in some cases to cover awards for personal injury that do not relate to a physical injury or sickness. For example, some courts have held that the exclusion applies to damages in cases involving certain forms of employment discrimination and injury to reputation where there is no physical injury or sickness. The damages received in these cases generally consist of back pay and other awards intended to compensate the claimant for lost wages or lost profits. The Supreme Court recently held that damages received based on a claim under the Age Discrimination in Employment Act could not be excluded from income.

The new law provides that the exclusion from gross income does not apply to any punitive damages received on account of personal injury or sickness whether or not related to a physical injury or physical sickness. Prior law continues to apply to punitive damages received in a wrongful death action if the applicable state law (as in effect on September 13, 1995 without regard to subsequent modification) provides, or has been construed to provide by a court decision issued on or before such date, that only punitive damages may be awarded in a wrongful death action.

The new law also provides that the exclusion from gross income only applies to damages received on account of personal physical injury or physical sickness. If an action has its origin in a physical injury or physical sickness, then all damages (other than punitive damages) that flow therefrom are treated as payments received on account of physical injury or physical sickness whether or not the recipient of the damage is the injured party. For example, damages (other than punitive damages) received by an individual on account of a claim for loss of consortium due to the physical injury or physical sickness of such individual's spouse are and will be excludable from gross income. In addition, damages (other than punitive damages) received on account of a wrongful death continue to be excludable from taxable income as under prior law.

The new law specifically provides that emotional distress is not considered a physical injury or physical sickness. Thus, the exclusion from gross income does not apply to any damages received (other than for medical expenses as discussed below) based on a claim of employment discrimination or injury to reputation accompanied by a claim of emotional distress. Because all damages received on account of physical injury or physical sickness are excludable from gross income, the exclusion from gross income applies to any damages received based on a claim of emotional distress that is attributable to a physical injury or physical sickness. However, the exclusion from gross income only applies to the amount of damages received that is not in excess of the amount paid for medical care attributable to emotional stress.

The above provisions generally are effective with respect to amounts received after the date of enactment. The provisions do not apply to amounts received under a written binding agreement, court decree, or mediation award in effect on or issued on or before September 13, 1995.

20. EXTENSION AND PHASEOUT OF EXCISE TAX ON LUXURY AUTOMOBILES

Prior law imposed an excise tax on the sale of an automobile whose price exceeded a designated threshold, $34,000 in 1996. The excise tax is imposed at a rate of 10 percent on the excess of the sales price above the designated threshold. The $34,000 threshold is indexed for inflation, and the tax applied to sales before January 1, 2000.

Under the new law, the luxury tax on automobiles is extended and phased out. The tax rate is reduced by 1 percentage point per year beginning in 1996. The sales rate for sales (on or after the date of enactment plus 7 days) in 1996 is 9 percent. The tax rate for sales in 1997 is 8 percent. The tax rate for sales in 1998 is 7 percent. The tax rate for sales in 1999 is 6 percent. The tax rate for sales in 2000 is 5 percent. The tax rate for sales in 2001 is 4 percent. The tax rate for sales in 2002 is 3 percent. The tax will expire after December 31, 2002.

21. CERTAIN PROPERTY NOT TREATED AS SECTION 179 PROPERTY

The new law includes a provision denying the Section 179 Expensing Allowance to (1) property described in Section 50(b)—i.e., generally property used outside the United States, property used in connection with furnishing lodging, property used by tax-exempt organizations, governments, and foreign persons and (2) air conditioning or heating units.

22. 401(k) EXPANSION

The new law now permits nongovernmental tax-exempt organizations and Indian Tribal Governments as eligible sponsors of 401(k) retirement plans. The prohibitions against state and local governments continue.

150 Tax Relief for Bosnian Effort

On March 20, 1996, Public Law 104-117 was signed into law giving special tax relief to U.S. military and support personnel involved in the peace-keeping efforts in the former Republic of Yugoslavia (Bosnia and Herzegovina, Croatia, and Macedonia). Formerly, these benefits were only available to our troops serving in "combat zones" designated by Presidential Order.

Before enactment of this legislation and based upon past policy, the IRS had granted administrative relief in the form of filing extensions until December 15, 1996, and suspensions of collection and examination activity.

This new legislation is generally effective on November 21, 1995—the date of the Dayton Accord—and has a two-pronged benefit for those serving in this endeavor—namely Internal Revenue Code (IRC) section 7508(a) extensions and IRC Section 112 income exclusions.

With this new tax law, members of the U.S. Armed Forces and civilian support personnel serving in these peacekeeping efforts get the benefits of IRC 7508(a), meaning they will not have to file their 1995 individual income tax returns until at least 180 days after they depart from that area. It also suspends all tax return examinations and actions to collect any back taxes owed by these taxpayers for any years prior to 1995 until at least 180 days after they leave the peacekeeping area. During this time no interest or penalty is added to any tax due for 1995 or prior years. This additional time for filing and paying taxes is also applicable to U.S. military personnel performing support services in areas outside the United States (such as Italy and Hungary) away from their permanent duty station as part of the peacekeeping efforts in Bosnia and Herzegovina and Croatia. All of the above relief provisions also apply to the spouses of these military and civilian personnel.

Also under this recent legislation, the income exclusion provisions of IRC Section 112 will apply to military pay received, but only for those serving in the former republic of Yugoslavia and only for military personnel. All military pay received by enlisted personnel while serving in these peacekeeping efforts is exempt from federal income tax. For commissioned officers, the new law excludes up to the "maximum enlisted amount" per month, currently $4,104.80 plus certain special pay. This had been only $500 per month under prior law.

Taxpayers, spouses, and others acting on behalf of a taxpayer involved in these peacekeeping efforts may call the IRS toll-free number, 1-800-829-1040, for additional information. The IRS offices in Rome and Bonn are also available for assistance. Contact the Rome office by calling [39] (6) 4674-2560, or via fax at [39] (6) 4674-2223, and the Bonn office by calling [49] (228) 339-2119, or via fax at [49] (228) 339-2810. Military members serving in these peacekeeping efforts who have access to E-mail may address questions to oje@ccmail.irs.gov. Those who receive correspondence about any collection or examination matter covered by these tax relief provisions should contact the IRS immediately so it can suspend the action.

CHAPTER 13

Tax Reform—Again!

"Our tax system is complicated and unfair, and it must be eliminated."

RICHARD K. ARMEY (R - Tex.)
Majority Leader of the House of Representatives
and
BILL ARCHER (R - Tex.)
Chairman of the House Ways & Means Committee

"Congress has a lot of respect for logic—they use it so sparingly."

JEFF SCHNEPPER

"Meow!"

SIMBA SCHNEPPER

151 The Mind-Numbing Complexity of the Tax Reconciliation Act of 1997, Also Known as the Taxpayer Relief Act of 1997

Given the opportunity to drive a stake through the heart of the deficit, Congress and the President chose instead to throw a party. On August 5, 1997, President Clinton signed into law a new tax package creating $94 billion in new net tax cuts. The first federal tax reduction in 16 years, this bundle of goodies provides relief to both the middle class and the rich, celebrates the value of the family, and encourages both having children and sending them to college.

Winners are investors, middle-class families with kids 16 or under or with kids going to college, poor children without health insurance, and heirs to large estates. Losers include the tobacco industry and the illusion of potential simplicity in the tax code. According to liberal organization Citizens for Tax Justice, 20% of our wealthiest citizens will reap 70% of the benefit. They failed to note, however, that the top 1% of our taxpayers alone also shoulder as much as 29% of our nation's total tax bill. This chapter will review the major tax provisions in the new tax agreement and try to translate the mind-numbing complexity into understandable language. Then it will detail the opportunities offered by these changes.

Retroactive to May 7, 1997, the new law cuts the top CAPITAL GAINS TAX RATE from 28% to 20% for investments (excluding collectibles such as art, stamps, or coins which will retain a maximum 28% rate) held for at least 18 months (12 months if the investment was sold before July 29, 1997). The top rate drops further to 18% for assets purchased after 2000 and held for 5 years or longer. Gains on real estate, to the extent of Section 1250 depreciation recapture, will be taxed at a maximum 25% rate. Capital assets held for more than 12 months but less than 18 months will retain the maximum 28% rate.

For those in the lower brackets, the rate falls to as low as 10% on investments held more than 18 months by married couples with incomes less than $41,200 (in 1998). That rate will drop to 8% in 2001 for assets held for five years or longer regardless of when the asset was acquired.

The impact of the change? Enormous! The difference between short-term and new long-term gains is the difference between 39.6% and as low as 18 to 21.6%. On a $100,000 gain, that's $21,600 in your pocket. The new law encourages investors, not traders. Net short-term gains are taxed like ordinary income. It hurts tax-deferred investments. All payments out of retirement plans (except for the new IRA plans discussed below) are taxed at ordinary income rates. The advantage of tax deferral disappears when you could have paid an

18% capital gains tax and end up paying ordinary income tax at the 39.6% rate. If you are close to retirement and expect to remain in the higher brackets, tax deferral may even work against you.

Stocks that reinvest their earnings, producing long-term capital gains, will be favored over dividend-paying stocks. Equity investments gain an edge over debt such as bonds. Losers would include high dividend yield stocks, such as telephone and utility issues. Investors who short against the box or who are involved in equity swapping also lose as these techniques have been eliminated as "constructive sales."

The new rules mean that long-term investing now has a substantial and meaningful advantage over short-term trading. Remember, to get these lower rates, you have to hold the investment for at least 18 months/five years. Mutual funds which actively trade will be at a tax disadvantage to those that buy and hold—such as index funds. According to fund researcher Morningstar Inc., some 29% of the capital gains distributed by diversified U.S. stock funds in 1996 comprised short-term gains. In the past, taxes were secondary to total return to mutual fund managers. I suspect that their goals, even in light of the new law, will not change.

However, you can change your investment strategy. Funds with a high turnover, creating primarily short-term gains, would be best for your IRAs and qualified plans. All income from these plans would be taxed at ordinary rates when distributed anyway. Your non-qualified money—the dollars in your taxable accounts—should be invested in either low turnover funds or in stocks directly. If you own the shares outright, you can hold for the 18 month/five year period and control both the timing of the income recognition, and the tax rate applied.

If you can shift some income from direct salary to stock options, you can potentially convert income taxable at 39.6% to income taxable as low as 18%. To qualify, you ask for tax favored Incentive Stock Options (ISOs) in lieu of cash compensation and hold the shares for at least two years after the grant of the ISO and at least one year after its exercise. Any gain from the time of the grant to the time of the sale would be taxed at the maximum 20% rate. If you hold for five years, you could qualify for the top 18% rate!

If you have non-qualified stock options (NSOs), any appreciation above the option grant price is taxed as ordinary income when the option is exercised. When you sell the stock, any subsequent appreciation is taxed as capital gains so long as you hold the stock for more than a year (or 18 months/five years if you want the even lower 20%/18% rate). The trick here is to exercise as quickly as possible, when the stock has a price close to the fair market value on the grant date. By doing this, you minimize the ordinary income component of your gain, and maximize the potential capital gain portion. Clearly, the better your company's stock performs, the more advantageous this strategy becomes.

What impact will these capital gains reductions have on the stock market? Clearly, by reducing transaction costs—i.e. the tax on gains—they have stimulated selling. Assets pregnant with capital gains can more easily be liquidated. Normally, an increase in supply would cut the price and therefore the value of these capital assets. However, our current stock market is fueled primarily by measures other than taxes alone. It is my opinion that the increases in the stock market in the past few years have been the result of baby boomers approaching fifty years of age and suddenly realizing that they have really not planned at all for their retirement. The bulk of the money coming into the market over the last few years has come from retirement vehicles such as pension, IRA, and 401(k) contributions. Each month we read about record amounts of dollars being invested in mutual funds in an attempt to catch up. I predict that this boomer generated demand will continue for the next decade (after which retirement distributions will potentially substantially destabilize the market). While there will be corrections, the reduction in capital gains rates will have no impact on these investors because, as noted above, distributions from these accounts will be totally taxed as ordinary income.

The impact of the reduction on non-qualified assets is to reduce the attraction of tax-free or tax-deferred investments. For those nearing retirement, deferral in a variable annuity or any other tax-deferred account where the distributions are taxed as ordinary income loses much of its advantage. Deferral is meaningful to the young and those who expect to be in a lower bracket when the income is recognized. The reduction in capital gains gives incentive to recognize gains today—who knows what the law will be like ten years from today?

In the meantime, sophisticated investors will be approached by creative tax planners with all kinds of strategies and techniques to convert ordinary income into capital gains. Real estate will become more attractive as an investment despite its higher rate for depreciation recapture. I really am not hurt by a 25% top rate on depreciation recapture when I have already deducted that depreciation in the 28%, 31%, or 36% brackets. In addition to the time value of the money, I will have enjoyed a spread of as much as 11% on the taxes saved compared to the taxes paid. Moreover, I still have the advantage of the 20% maximum rate on true appreciation.

Taxpayers with substantial gains on the **SALE OF A PRINCIPAL RESIDENCE** are really big winners. The new tax act will exclude $500,000 in gains on the sale of your principal residence ($250,000 for single filers) for sales after May 6, 1997. To qualify, you must have used the house as your principal residence for at least two out of the five years prior to the sale. However, the exclusion will be available once every two years, although there are exceptions to that rule too. Those close to retirement or whose children have moved out may be big winners here. They can now sell their old, big houses without the need to reinvest in new, more expensive homes to avoid taxation on the gains. They can now buy smaller residences, or even rent. The prior law provision under Section 1034 that deferred taxation upon a rollover of the sales proceeds into a new home has been repealed.

SELF-EMPLOYED taxpayers are also winners. The new law reverses the Supreme Court ruling limiting home offices and now they are available in cases where taxpayers use their home for administrative or management activities—and if there isn't any other fixed place where they conduct substantial administrative or management activities of their trade or business. Their use, however, must still be regular and exclusive. If you do your investments or play games on your computer in your new "office," you will not pass the "exclusive" test. This new rule is effective for years beginning after December 31, 1998.

The self-employed also win on their health insurance. Under the new law, if you pay your own health insurance premiums, 40% is deductible for 1997, 45% for 1998 and 1999, 50% for 2000 and 2001, 60% for 2002, 80% for 2003 to 2005, 90% for 2006, and 100% for 2007. The acceleration of the deductibility helps level the field with corporations, for whom 100% is currently deductible. Fewer individuals will now have to incorporate just to be able to deduct their health insurance premiums.

INDIVIDUAL RETIREMENT ACCOUNTS have been substantially modified and we now have three kinds of IRAs. The first is the current deductible IRA. The new law raises the phaseout income limits on these front-loaded IRAs for those covered by a qualified plan. Under current law, if your modified adjusted income (for a joint return) is between $40,000 and $50,000, your IRA deduction is reduced and then eliminated (the limits are $25,000–$35,000 for single filers). These phaseout amounts will be raised by $10,000 for couples and $5,000 for singles in 1998, and by $1,000 per year through 2002; in 2003 they increase to $40,000 for single filers and $60,000 for joint filers, and by $5,000 per year thereafter. At the end of that time the phaseout limits would have doubled. The phaseout will then be from $80,000–$100,000 for joint returns, and $50,000–$60,000 for single filers. Moreover, the new law allows a nonworking spouse to contribute a fully deductible $2,000, even if the other spouse participates in a qualified retirement plan, with a phaseout between $150,000 and $160,000. The following table summarizes the changes in phaseout rules:

	Joint (in thousands)	Single (in thousands)
1997	$40-50	$25-35
1998	50-60	30-40
1999	51-61	31-41
2000	52-62	32-42
2001	53-63	33-43

2002	54-64	34-44
2003	60-70	40-50
2004	65-75	45-55
2005	70-80	50-60
2006	75-85	
2007	80-100	

The new, second kind of IRA is the IRA PLUS. Here, contributions will not be deductible but, if the IRA is held for at least five years and the account holder is at least 59.5 years old, then all withdrawals will be tax free! Moreover, more people will be eligible for these accounts because the income limits phase out at from $95,000–$110,000 for single taxpayers and from $150,000–$160,000 for couples.

Holders of either of these two IRAs will be able to make penalty-free withdrawals to make a first-time home purchase, or for college expenses. However, the combined contributions to these two types of accounts is limited to $2,000 per year for each taxpayer, and you cannot withdraw the money for five years. You could roll savings over from a regular IRA into the IRA PLUS account but some taxes would be assessed upon the rollover. These taxes could be spread over several years to minimize the impact of the change. I think it is a reasonable toll charge to avoid all future taxes on the account.

The law also creates a new education IRA. Families are allowed to contribute up to $500 per child under age 18 into an education IRA, with an income limit of from between $95,000–$110,000 for singles and $150,000–$160,000 for couples. These IRAs will be nondeductible, but the earnings are tax free. There is no penalty if they are used for educational purposes, regardless of your age. The education IRA can be rolled over to another child but, if the children do not attend college, the amounts must be paid out when the last child turns 30.

The education IRA is not the only benefit for kids. The new law creates a **KIDDIE TAX CREDIT** for families earning $18,000 or more with children under age 17. The credit will be phased out for couples earning more than $110,000 and singles earning over $75,000. For every additional $1,000 or part thereof that a couple earns, the tax break is reduced by $50. For a joint return with income in excess of $119,000, it is eliminated completely (in 1999). The credit is effective as of January 1, 1998. The amount of the credit will be $400 in 1998 and $500 in 1999. If you have three or more children, you get an additional credit. These credits will be computed before any computation for the earned income tax credit, and will be payable even if no tax is due. However, taxpayers will not get any credit in excess of what they paid in payroll taxes minus any cash from the earned income credit. Partially in exchange for this credit, the new law requires the social security number of every child and parent to be recorded at birth to reduce fraud. In the past, people have been found to claim the child care credit for other people's children!

The tax bill also provides two new **EDUCATIONAL TAX CREDITS**. The first is the modified Hope Scholarship. Under these provisions, a credit is available for college tuition paid, in the amount of 100 percent of the first $1,000 in tuition and 50 percent of the second $1,000 (for a total of $1,500 in credits). The second credit, the Lifetime Learning Credit, will be 20 percent of up to $5,000 in tuition for graduate *or* undergraduate expenses. For years after 2002, eligible expenses are increased to $10,000. The effective date of the 20% credit is July 1, 1998. Payments made after December 31, 1997 qualify with an income phaseout at from $80,000–$100,000 for couples and $40,000–$50,000 for singles. Both eligible expenses and income limits are indexed in 2001. To qualify, the student must be carrying at least one-half the full-time workload and have never been convicted of a felony drug offense.

Congress really pushed for education. Under the new law, state prepaid tuition plans are tax free. A 10% penalty will be applied to amounts not used for tuition, books, room and board. Moreover, the exclusion for employer-provided education benefits is extended through May 31, 2000, and a new **EDUCATION INTEREST DEDUCTION** is created. Phased out at between $60,000 and $75,000 for couples and between $40,000 and $55,000 for individuals, it allows student loan interest deductions, even if you don't itemize, of $1,000 in 1998, $1,500 in 1999, $2,000 in 2000, and $2,500 in 2001 and after. The income limits are indexed beginning in 2003. Moreover, as of January 1, 1998, **PENALTY-FREE WITHDRAWALS** are allowed from all IRAs for undergraduate, post-secondary, vocational, and graduate education expenses for you, your spouse, child, or grandchildren.

CREDITS were also favored. Not only was the orphan drug credit extended permanently, but the research and development credit and the work opportunity credit were extended through June 30, 1998. **EXTENSIONS** were also legislated for employer-paid tuition (as noted above) and the fair market deduction for contributions of appreciated stock to private foundations (to June 30, 1998).

The **AIRLINE TICKET TAX** has been reduced from 10% to 7.5% over a three-year period. It falls to 9.5% in 1998, 8% in 1999, and 7.5% in 2000 and after. There will be a $1 per segment tax starting in 1998 which will increase to $3 in 2002. The new law also imposes a $12 arrival and departure fee for international flights.

TOBACCO TAXES will also fund the above cuts. There will be a 10-cent per pack increase in 2000, increasing the current tax to 34 cents per pack. A 15-cent per pack increase in 2002 will bring the total to 49 cents per pack.

ESTATE TAXES were also significantly modified. The credit equivalent amount that escapes taxation has been increased to $625,000 in 1998, $650,000 in 1999, $675,000 in 2000 and 2001, $700,000 in 2002 and 2003, $850,000 in 2004, $950,000 in 2005, and $1,000,000 in 2006. That means that in 2006, a married couple could avoid paying any estate taxes on an estate of as much as $2 million.

In addition, the new law creates a **FAMILY-OWNED BUSINESS** exclusion of $700,000 which means that as much as $1.3 million can be excluded by a single taxpayer

($600,000 in 1997 credit exclusion plus $700,000 family business exclusion). The combination of the credit equivalent and the family business exclusion is capped at $1.3 million—i.e., as the credit equivalent increases, the family business exclusion decreases to $675,000 in 1998, $650,000 in 1999, $625,000 in 2000 and 2001, $600,000 in 2002 and 2003, $450,000 in 2004, $350,000 in 2005, and $300,000 in 2006 and thereafter. To qualify, the family-owned business must account for at least half of the decedent's estate and surviving family members must "materially participate" in the running of the business for the next ten years.

FARMERS win not only as potential family business owners but also under new averaging provisions. Under the new law, they will be able to use a three-year income averaging method on their farm income for taxable years beginning after December 1, 1997 and before January 1, 2001.

The Tax Relief Act of 1997 contains a myriad of additional provisions. Designed to satisfy every need or desire, it is, as finance expert Mitchell Hymowitz of Seattle put it, "a nightmare of social engineering and pandering." If you have money or kids, you are a winner under the new law. If you are a tax attorney, a CPA, or are in any way involved in tax planning, it is both a minefield of tax change overload and a gold mine of potential new fees. If nothing else, it is conclusive proof that our Washington representatives clearly see the tax code as more than a mechanism to raise revenue, but as a blueprint for social and economic planning and restructuring in which the concepts of simplicity and understanding give way to the need to generate voting support.

The new law makes more than 800 changes to the massive Internal Revenue Code. Some changes become effective immediately, nearly seventy changes won't take effect until January, and a few others won't kick in until after 1998. There are changes that are phased in through 2007. Capital gains are now taxed at rates of 8%, 10%, 18%, 20%, 25%, 28%, or as much as 39.6% depending on what year you are in, what you are selling, and how long you held the property. You used to have one simple IRA. Now we have the regular IRA, the Roth IRA Plus, and the Education IRA. Each is taxed differently and each has different income limitations to qualify.

Having failed in his quest to get the Internal Revenue Service completely out of the lives of Americans, Rep. Bill Archer has given it new authority over everything from education to welfare policy. According to Yale University tax expert Michael Graetz. This bill could only have been written by a man who really hates the income tax.

Talk about social engineering. Our government's message to the American people is that Big Brother knows best. Do what he wants you to do, how he wants you to do it, and when he wants you to do it, and we will give you a tax break. The new law will benefit Generation X, but only if they have the discipline to make annual IRA deposits. Have kids, go to college, and invest—but only long term—and we will reward you. Please understand that kids, college, and long-term investing are not bad. I personally am very much in favor of all three. However, I just don't think that the federal income tax code should be the vehicle to encourage them.

Cutting taxes for social engineering is nothing more than a back door approach to tax spending. Rather than facing the hard choices of direct grants for specific constituencies, Congress and the President have hidden these expenditures by structuring them as tax deductions or credits. It is merely pork passed out as tax benefits. Our new tax law is a Christmas tree with presents for everyone. It is a pension reform law, a child welfare law, and an education spending law.

If you don't understand the myriad provisions in the new law, a tax preparation program can help—such programs prompt you with the right questions and the solution is often a mere mathematical computation. I am a tax expert with two law degrees, a MBA in finance, and am licensed by the New Jersey Board of Certified Public Accountants. I have spent two decades teaching taxation both on the undergraduate and the graduate level, have published twenty books and almost 400 articles on taxation and even I am overwhelmed! The new law is confusing for everyone, and so I suggest you not try to figure this out on your own. (As a matter of fact, I suggest you use a tax professional or a program, which prompts you with the proper questions.)

Let's look at an example. I have a client who sold stock on May 6, 1997, May 7, 1997, July 28, 1997 and July 29, 1997. The chart below details his potential tax nightmare.

Holding Period	**May 6, 1997**	**May 7, 1997**	**July 28, 1997**	**July 29, 1997**
Less than 12 months	39.6%	39.6%	39.6%	39.6%
More than 12 months*	28.0%	20.0%	20.0%	28.0%
More than 18 months	28.0%	20.0%	20.0%	20.0%

*But not more than 18 months.

If he sold real estate, there would be an additional 25% rate. If he sold stock after December 31, 2000, and held more than 18 months, there would be another maximum 18.0% rate.

Imagine what convoluted complications you would have if you owned appreciated property that you expected to decrease in value! How long could you hold to grab a lower rate in exchange for a smaller gain? Where would be the break-even and how much would you spend in time and money to figure it out?

Moreover, if you sold now, would the extra income deny you a deduction for the Roth IRA Plus, the normal IRA, the Education IRA, or the Education Tax Credits—all of which have different phaseout levels at different income levels? Talk about complexity!!

TABLE 1. What Is Your Maximum Capital Gains Rate for 1997?

IF the Sale* Took Place…	AND the Capital Asset Was Held…	AND your gain…	THEN Your Maximum Capital Gains Rate Is…
Before May 7, 1997	More than one year	Is from selling any type of capital asset	28%
After May 6, 1997, but **before** July 29, 1997	More than one year	1) Is a collectibles gain	28%
		2) Is an unrecaptured section 1250 gain	25%
		3) Is not a gain to which *(1), (2),* or *(4)* applies	20%
		4) Would be taxed, if there were no maximum capital gains rates, at the 15% regular tax rate—and *(1)* and *(2)* don't apply	10%
After July 28, 1997	More than one year but not more than 18 months	Is from selling any type of capital asset	28%
After July 28, 1997	More than 18 months	1) Is a collectibles gain	28%
		2) Is an unrecaptured section 1250 gain	25%
		3) Is not a gain to which *(1), (2),* or *(4)* applies	20%
		4) Would be taxed, if there were no maximum capital gains rates, at the 15% regular tax rate—and *(1)* and *(2)* don't apply	10%

* The term "sale" includes a trade, involuntary conversion, and installment payment received.

It's not like the tax code was simple before the new law was passed. Several years ago, Ralph Nader's Tax Reform Research Group prepared 22 identical tax reports based on the fictional economic plight of a married couple with one child, and these 22 identical copies were submitted to 22 different IRS offices around the country. Each office came up with an entirely different figure. The results varied from a refund of $811.96 recommended in Flushing, New York, to a tax due figure of $52.14 derived by the tax office in Portland, Oregon. The discrepancies were not just the result of IRS incompetency. Each tax season, *Money Magazine* gives identical tax data to fifty top tax preparers around the country and inevitability they get back fifty different answers.

The Tax relief Act of 1997 is a sacrifice of simplicity on the altar of greed. There will be a backlash, not now when everyone is uplifted by his or her own benefit, but later when the emotional and financial costs of the new law are really felt. I see the new law as a Trojan horse, a prelude to a complete overhaul of our tax system. Steve Forbes ran for President in 1996 on a Flat Tax platform. I predict the flat tax will be a major issue in the 2000 election.

If our tax experts in Congress had written the ten commandments, they would require 500 pages and have 2,000 special transaction rules. Maybe the arrival of the new millennium will bring with it true tax reform. Maybe the overwhelming complexity of the new law is the darkest moment before the light of simplicity. Clearly, this latest tax law change demonstrates the magnitude of respect Congress and the President have for logic and simplicity. They used it so sparingly!

CHAPTER 14

The Internal Revenue Service Restructuring and Reform Act of 1998

"Today we are creating an IRS where the American taxpayer comes first and customer service is second to none."

Treasury Secretary ROBERT RUBIN
and Commissioner of Internal Revenue CHARLES O. ROSSOTTI

It was passed overwhelmingly... 402-8 in the House of Representatives and 96-2 in the Senate, and signed by President Clinton on July 22, 1998. The Internal Revenue Service Restructuring and Reform Act of 1998 creates "a new day for the American taxpayer" according to Senate Finance Chairman William Roth of Delaware. The new law clears the way for the most comprehensive internal reorganization of the IRS in more than 40 years. This Chapter will review the most important changes created by the new law and explain how they affect you and your taxes.

152 IRS Reorganization

The Reform Act provides for the dismantling of the IRS's traditional geographic divisions and replaces them with operational divisions structured around four groups of taxpayers:

1. Wage & Income—for those with wages and investment income,
2. Small business/supplemental—for those who file Schedule C (self-employed), F (farm), E (rental, partnership, trust, estate, and S corporation income), 2106 (employee business expenses), partnerships, S corporations, and other corporations with income less than $5MM,
3. Large Corporate and Middle Market—for corporations with income $5MM or greater, and
4. Tax Exempt—for employee plans, exempt organizations, and state and local governmental entities.

It is now anticipated that the Chief Counsel's Office will retain a separate, independent structure that would address issues in each of the new divisions.

153 IRS Governance and Oversight Changes

Along with the structural changes above, the 1998 Reform Act seeks to change the character and group mindset of the IRS by creating a new nine-member, largely private sector oversight board, by strengthening the national taxpayer advocate, and by relocating most of the IRS Inspection Service to the Treasury Department, to be headed by a newly created treasury inspector general of tax administration.

The Commission of Internal Revenue would have a five-year term, including the current Commissioner. The Act also provides for annual joint hearings of the congressional committees with IRS jurisdiction.

These proposals are intended to provide greater oversight and accountability for the agency. However, as Representative Ben Cardin of Maryland pointed out, "The success of IRS reform will not be the passage of this bill but the implementation of the bill."

The object of the Act is to provide fair and equitable treatment of the American taxpayer under the law. Yet one day after the Senate passed the bill, the IRS released an internal report that found widespread overzealousness in the way property was seized from taxpayers.

The property seizures report, which reviewed 467 cases in which the IRS took cars, homes, cash and other assets from taxpayers, found that agents failed to follow proper procedures 130 times.

The problems, the report said, included failure to pursue alternatives to seizures, failing to notify taxpayers before seizures, taking assets worth little more than the costs of seizing them, and, by ignoring mitigating circumstances, creating special hardships for taxpayers.

In one case, a taxpayer's truck was seized, yielding a net $7 to the government. In another case, the collections division seized a man's car, and released it only after he had agreed to an installment plan with payments over 50 years. The man had a heart attack two years prior, was suffering from high blood pressure and bleeding ulcers, and had been cooperative in paying his tax bills, even charging his credit cards to the maximum to get cash for the IRS. At one point the IRS had recommended the case be classified as uncollectible, but the recommendation had been "nonprocessed" by cash-hungry collection agents.

The IRS also found widespread violations of its rules intended to bar production quotas or goals that would lead auditors to inflate tax liabilities or pressure taxpayers. The examination divisions' philosophy "focused primarily on enforcement statistics, which fostered improper use of enforcement statistics."

The following quotes from the report illustrate the problems:

> "When I received my Grade 12, the Branch Manager told me they expected at least $500,000 a year from a Grade 12."
>
> "Dollars per return and dollars per hour goals were circulated for signature."
>
> "Our group goals are 16 hours per return and $500 per hour..."

When evaluating the 1998 Reform Act, remember that the above actions were in direct violation of then IRS stated policy. It wasn't that the rules were wrong—they just were not followed.

The new law provides additional taxpayer protections and creates new procedural rules for the agency (both discussed below). However, what's really going on here is a change in attitude from the top more than anything else. Commissioner Charles O. Rossotti has mandated a climate of customer service for the IRS, and that climate is reflected in not only the new Reform Act but, even more importantly, in the way agents are treating taxpayers. While I have always maintained that the average IRS agent is a bureaucrat trying to do an impossible job—enforcing a law so complicated and convoluted that on occasion four of our nine top jurists on the Supreme Court get the answer wrong—there have been some really bad apples out there with too much power. This small minority has been allowed to flourish because there was little to no pressure from the top to eradicate the bad guys. It wasn't that the laws and rules supported them; they operated *outside* the normal rules and were allowed to get away with it.

The new Commissioner has changed that. I personally have found a significant difference in the attitude of auditors toward taxpayers over the past few months. I shudder to confess, but they have actually been reasonable! Let's look at some of the additional provisions of the 1998 Act which, hopefully, will help them retain this new fair and reasonable perspective.

154 Extension of Attorney-Client Privilege to Tax Advice

The 1998 Act extends the attorney-client privilege to tax advice given in noncriminal proceedings by practitioners authorized to practice before the IRS (CPAs and enrolled agents). However, this new privilege would not apply to written communications between a practitioner and any representative of a corporation in connection with the promotion of a tax shelter. A tax shelter is defined as any investment strategy that comes with the *significant purpose* of avoiding taxes. Because of the vagueness of the word "significant," it has been argued that the IRS could apply this to any corporate planning advice given by accountants. One of an accountant's functions is to help his client avoid taxes, when legal. A clarification of this issue should be imminent.

However, this provision now frees individual taxpayers to engage the professional who best supports their needs rather than forcing them to choose on the basis of whether the tax advice can be kept confidential. It's a big win for taxpayers and an even bigger win for the accounting profession.

155 Burden of Proof Shifted to IRS in Certain Civil Tax Cases

This provision is intended to help individuals and small businesses. (It is limited to those with net worth of $7 million or less.) It is also intended to promote taxpayer compliance with record keeping requirements and with reasonable requests for information.

The IRS now has the burden of proof in any court proceeding with respect to a factual issue relevant to determining his or her tax liability. Four conditions apply:

1. The taxpayer must comply with the requirements of the Internal Revenue Code and the regulations issued thereunder.
2. The taxpayer must maintain records required by the Code and regulations.
3. The taxpayer must cooperate with reasonable requests by the IRS for meetings, interviews, witnesses, information, and documents.
4. Taxpayers other than individuals, must meet the net worth limitations that apply for awarding attorney's fees.

This provision applies to income, estate gift, and generation skipping transfer taxes. While vehemently opposed by the administration when proposed, I see little change in the audit process. You still have the burden of proof during the administrative part of the audit; the change only applies in judicial proceedings. It doesn't apply unless you have provided all requested documentation, and, if you have, then you should have won on the administrative level. It is merely an added chip in the negotiating process before you go to court. What it really means is that if you can and do substantiate your deductions etc., it now becomes the burden of the IRS to explain why that substantiation was insufficient.

156 Taxpayer Rights

The Reform Act contains a host of taxpayer rights provisions, including penalty and interest reforms, innocent spouse relief, protection against

> abusive liens and levies, restrictions on IRS use of "financial reality" audit techniques, and expansion of the offer-in-compromise program. These provisions are intended to protect you from IRS abuses, smooth the process of working out tax problems, and ease your dealings with the agency.

With respect to interest, the Reform Act provides for a net interest rate of zero for periods of mutual indebtedness on tax overpayments and underpayments. This clarifies the issue created in 1996 when Congress had enacted a higher interest rate for underpayments. Now, if you owe the IRS, and they owe you, "interest netting" will produce a net interest of zero.

The Act now makes **innocent spouse** relief easier to obtain. It eliminates all prior thresholds and requires only that the understatement of the tax be attributable to an erroneous (and not just a grossly erroneous) item of the other spouse.

It also provides a separate liability election for a taxpayer who, at the time of the election, is no longer married to, or has been living apart for at least 12 months from the person with whom the taxpayer filed the original return. Such taxpayers may elect to have the liability for any deficiency limited to the portion of the deficiency that is attributable to items attributable to the taxpayer. This election is not available if assets were transferred between spouses as part of a fraudulent scheme or if both individuals had actual knowledge of the understatement of the tax.

The Act permits up to $100,000 in civil damages caused by an officer or employee of the IRS who negligently disregard provisions of the Code or Treasury regulations in connection with the collection of Federal taxes. It permits up to $1 million in civil damages caused by an officer or employee of the IRS who willfully violates provisions of the bankruptcy Code relating to automatic stays or discharge.

It also increases the cap for small case treatment in the Tax Court from $10,000 to $50,000, and it increases the value of personal effects exempt from levy to $6,250 and the value of books and tools exempt from levy to $3,125. Both these amounts are now indexed for inflation.

In addition, the Act prohibits the IRS from seizing any real property used as a residence and any other nonrental property owned by the taxpayer used by someone else as a residence to satisfy an unpaid liability of $5,000 or less, including penalties and interest. Moreover, the Act prohibits the IRS from collecting a tax liability by levy (1) during any period you have an offer in compromise being processed, (2) during the 30 days following a rejection of an offer in compromise, (3) during any period in which an appeal of the rejection of an offer is being considered, and (4) while an installment agreement is pending.

157 Roth IRA Conversion/Loophole

In order to convert a traditional IRA into a Roth IRA you must have an adjusted gross income of not more than $100,000. The 1998 Act makes qualifying easier by excluding any minimum distributions from IRAs from the definition of Adjusted Gross Income solely for determining eligibility for the conversion. This provision is effective for tax years beginning after December 31, 2004.

The 1998 Act also closes a loophole opened by the 1997 Reform Act. The old provision would have allowed eligible taxpayers to convert from a traditional IRA to a Roth IRA in 1998, close their Roth IRA, spread their tax payments over four years, and escape the 10% penalty. The 1998 Act slammed the door shut on this opportunity. Unless another exclusion applies, the 10% penalty will be assessed. However, the new law does make the four-year spread optional rather than mandatory for 1998. This will help those who expect to be in higher brackets in years to come and who would prefer to pay their tax bill in the year of conversion.

Moreover, for 1998 only, if you convert and then find out you didn't qualify because you earned too much income, you can "unconvert" prior to the due date of your tax return (including extensions) without any penalty.

158 Capital Gains

It has become very difficult to have a reform act without a capital gains provision. The 1998 Act is no different. It reduces the holding period to qualify for long-term capital gains from more than 18 months to more than 12 months and makes life a lot simpler for anyone who prepares a tax return. This provision is retroactive to January 1, 1998.

Reducing the holding period to 12 months could make stocks marginally more attractive. It also could encourage some investors to take profits sooner, thereby leading to more short-term trading.

Unfortunately, owners of mutual funds may still have paperwork nightmares for 1998. This is because mutual funds distribute the gains from sales of stocks in their portfolios based on their fiscal years, which for many funds ends in October or November. So, if a fund has a fiscal year that began last November, any gains that were generated in November/December of 1997 won't be distributed or taxable to you until December 1998. But those gains from 1997 won't qualify for the new rules.

159 Venture Capital

The 1998 Reform Act made venture capital partnerships a lot more enticing. Under prior law, individual investors potentially could defer capital gains taxes on small company investments sold at a profit if part or all of the gains were reinvested in another small company. Under the 1998 law, individuals who invest in venture capital funds will qualify for these same chances to defer taxes.

Investments must be made in "qualified small businesses," which have less than $50 million in assets and meet various other tests. To qualify for tax deferred status, you must reinvest proceeds of any sale within 60 days in another qualifying small business.

These provisions reward taxpayers who put their money back in the system. They should make investing in a venture capital fund substantially more attractive, and potentially more profitable.

160 Home Sales Clarification

The 1998 Reform Act clarified a provision from the prior year's Reform Act. Under the 1997 law, joint filers could exclude as much as $500,000 in gain from the sale of a principal residence if they owned and lived in it for at least two of the last five years. For singles, the limit is $250,000.

Unfortunately, the 1997 law was unclear if you owned the property for less than two years. The 1998 Act provides the answer. It provides partial relief based on a fraction of the *maximum exclusion*, rather than on the basis of your actual realized profit.

For example, assume you bought a house in 1997 for $250,000 and sell it in 1998 for a $25,000 profit. Because you are married, and lived there one year, you are eligible for half the $500,000 exclusion you would have been entitled to had you been there the full two years. Half the exclusion is $250,000, greater than the gain of $25,000, and therefore none of your gain is taxable. Had the alternative interpretation applied, you would have been able to exclude half your profit, and paid tax on the remaining $12,500.

Not everybody wins on this one. Miss Fortune bought her home in 1997 for $1.5 million and sold it one year later for a $400,000 profit. Since she is single and lived there only half the required two years, she gets to exclude $125,000, and pay tax on $275,000 of her gain. Had the alternative interpretation applied, she would have excluded half her $400,000 gain and only paid taxes on $200,000.

161 Conclusion

The Internal Revenue Service Restructuring and Tax Reform Act of 1998 is a major step in improving our system of taxation. It signals a significant shift in the attitude of those who run the IRS—an attempt to truly make the agency responsive to its customers. It expands taxpayer rights and actually *simplifies* capital gain computation. Perhaps, it will be the first step in the simplification of the Internal Revenue Code itself. While I am less than optimistic about that coming to fruit soon, others have put a more sunny glow on the matter. As Representative Rob Portman, Co-Chair of the National Commission on Restructuring the IRS exclaimed, "Taxpayers will get much better service than they're currently getting. This is truly an exciting day." I hope he is right.

CHAPTER 15

How to Avoid/Survive an IRS Audit

Where deductions are based on a number of small items not susceptible to complete documentary substantiation, reasonable determinations should be made at the district examination level. Consideration will always be given to the reasonableness of the taxpayer's claimed deductions.

Policy Statement P4-39

"If we don't change our system of collecting taxes, it will break down ... Our traditional approach cannot sustain an acceptable level of compliance."

IRS Commissioner SHIRLEY PETERSON
to the Annual Meeting of the
New York State Bar Association's Tax Section
(January 31, 1993)

Citing a survey showing that taxpayers annually spend more than 5 billion hours dealing with the tax system, former IRS Commissioner Fred Goldberg said, "American people have every right to demand a tax system they can live with."

October 10, 1991

The objective of the Internal Revenue Service is to "encourage and achieve the highest degree of voluntary compliance with the tax laws and regulations and to maintain the highest degree of public confidence in the integrity and efficiency of the IRS."

IRS statement of organization and functions, 39 Fed. Reg. 11,572, 1974

"A taxpaying public that does not understand the law is a taxpaying public that cannot comply with the law."

Former IRS Commissioner LAWRENCE B. GIBBS, March 2, 1987

Some agents "need more training in how to be courteous."

Former IRS Commissioner LAWRENCE B. GIBBS, April 14, 1987.

"The examiner has a responsibility to the taxpayer and to the government to determine the correct tax liability and to maintain a fair and impartial attitude in all matters relating to the examination … The fair and impartial attitude of an examiner aids in increasing voluntary compliance. An examiner must approach each examination with an objective point of view."

Internal Revenue Manual 4015.3(1)

"The IRS cannot do some of the basic accounting and recordkeeping tasks it expects American taxpayers to do."

GAO, March 1, 1999

Dear Taxpayer:

This is to inform you that we, at the Internal Revenue Service, have lost your file. Unless we find it within thirty (30) days, you will face a $10,000 fine and a jail sentence of not less than five (5) years. Please advise.

The letter on the preceding page is, of course, a phony. At least I thought it was a phony until an equivalent letter reached one of my clients. In fact, the Internal Revenue Service loses about 2 million tax returns or related documents from its files each year, according to an in-house study. “It’s very embarrassing to tell a taxpayer, ‘I am disallowing all of your losses,’ and then ask them to provide a copy of their return because we can’t find their original return,” said one IRS employee quoted in an agency study. The report drew on questionnaires, interviews, and a random sample of 15,000 requests for tax documents in 1987. “In most federal record centers, we found Forms W-2 scattered on the floor,” it stated. The report estimated that 21 percent of taxpayers who paid the fee for photocopies of tax returns got their money back because the document could not be found within 90 days.

It’s not surprising that to most American taxpayers, receiving correspondence from the Internal Revenue Service is on a par with spending three weeks in a dentist’s chair or two hours in a locked room with an encyclopedia salesperson. Greetings from the IRS means one thing: the ultimate curse of a civilized society—a tax audit.

The Internal Revenue Service defines an audit as “an impartial review of the taxpayer’s return to determine its completeness and accuracy.” Former Senator Edward V. Long of Missouri doesn’t agree. He has compared the Internal Revenue Service to a “Gestapo preying upon defenseless citizens.” His Senate committee found the audit and investigative techniques of the IRS to include defying court orders, picking locks, stealing records, illegally tapping telephones, intercepting and reading personal mail, using hidden microphones to eavesdrop on the private conversations of taxpayers with their lawyers, employing undercover agents with assumed identities, and using sexual entrapment.

In an April 26, 1982, hearing before the House Ways and Means Subcommittee on Oversight, Representative George Hansen of Idaho alleged the existence of “IRS Hit Lists, Snooping and Spying Operations, political retaliatory audits ... and arbitrary assessments and seizures for punitive rather than tax collection purposes....” The case against the Internal Revenue Service, however, was presented more strikingly by the alleged victims of Internal Revenue Service brutality, who methodically testified to individual confrontations with the service in great detail, including descriptions of forced detention, physical force, and the use of weapons for intimidation.

One taxpayer’s wife, stricken with polio, needed an iron lung to keep her alive. An IRS agent threatened to seize the iron lung unless taxes claimed to be due were immediately forthcoming. The panicked taxpayer paid the claimed deficiency immediately.

IRS terrorists show no fear. In Kansas City, police officer Paul Campbell stopped a speeder and started to write a ticket. The offending driver, after making the usual objections, identified himself as an agent for the Internal Revenue Service. When Officer Campbell continued to write, the agent sneered, "We'll just have to check out your taxes." Soon after Campbell filed his next tax return, he was ordered to report to the Internal Revenue Service for an audit. It took four months of agency interrogations, repeated phone calls, and constant letter writing before the IRS finally admitted that Campbell owed it nothing.

In *Richman*, 78-1 U.S.T.C. Par. 9331, 41 AFTR 2d 78-1072 (DC Ill., 1978), the court was outraged at the lengths to which the IRS went to collect and keep some $5,000 to which, it turned out, it was not entitled. The IRS agents had padlocked the door to the taxpayer's place of business and discussed with the taxpayer the various sources from which he might beg or borrow the money in a conversation "distressingly like those between 'juice loan' debtors and creditors." The court found that the "conduct of the IRS agents was almost beyond belief."

In a more recent case, senator Nancy Kassebaum of Kansas remarked, "They should not be hit with outlandish penalties for failing to memorize the Federal Tax Code." She was talking about a $50 penalty against an 84-year-old Kansas City woman who underpaid her income tax by $0.60! According to the *Washington Post*, on July 11, 1984, one couple was assessed $205 when they were found to be one cent shy after paying taxes of nearly $9,000!

In a 1977 incident, several IRS collection agents bashed in the side window of a Volkswagen owned by a woman in Alaska who owed some taxes, then dragged her from the car and seized it as a payment for the money she owed. A photographer caught the incident on film; otherwise, it would have gotten little national notice.

In March 1989, then Senator, now Vice President Albert Gore of Tennessee revealed that IRS tax examiners in the Memphis Service Center "have been instructed to remain silent" when they uncover legitimate deductions that taxpayers failed to take. "For example, retirees and those laid off from their jobs who failed to claim withholding on pensions in lump sum distributions are not given credit, even if tax examiners catch the mistakes." The IRS attributed the embarrassment to "procedures used in the information document matching program for tax year 1987." However, it was not explained where those procedures and the policy behind them originated. Moreover, one current IRS employee claimed that examiners had been *instructed* to let withholding errors in the IRS's favor go uncorrected.

According to Beryl Abbin, Director of Federal Tax Services for Arthur Andersen and Company, "On the local IRS level, you have some very bad apples out there—agents who try to push their way and intimidate."

In a recent study of the Internal Revenue Service, almost half the agents surveyed said they are hesitant to reveal their occupation to people they meet. Their general attitude is, "People don't trust us." Understandably so. As Internal Revenue Service agent Thomas Mennitt so succinctly put it in public testimony, "I violate laws at all times; it's part of my duties."[1] On June 28, 1987, the *Washington Post* reported three instances of the IRS intercepting first class mail and altering checks that were made out to third parties. These allegations followed an earlier report about a San Francisco man whose $1,300 mortgage check to a bank was intercepted by the IRS in July 1986. The words "Internal Revenue Service" were stamped over the bank's name, and the check was then cashed. According to Ronald Noll of the Pennsylvania Society of Public Accountants, testifying before a House subcommittee in Congress, "The IRS has sunk so low in public opinion that a responsible accountant honestly believes he needs a hood to protect himself from IRS retaliation." IRS agents have been authorized to pose as doctors, lawyers, journalists, and clergy to conduct undercover investigations.

As former senator from Kansas and former Chairman of the Senate Finance Committee, Bob Dole blasted the IRS as an "intrusive" and "oppressive" presence in American life. "We don't need the IRS, we can get rid of the IRS," he vowed. Dole suggested that we abandon what he called "the whole twisted wreck of federal tax law." He decried what he called "KGB-like" audits that allow the government to snoop into a citizen's style of life.

Moreover, despite Internal Revenue Service National Office policy against collection quotas, IRS regional managers continue to instruct their revenue agents to make collections at almost any cost. According to a June 22, 1987, hearing before the Senate Finance Subcommittee on IRS Oversight, there is considerable competition among revenue officers and almost a daily comparison of what they have collected. Management challenges employees to "go out and make seizures ... " and " ... intimidation, and [the] abusiveness and harshness ... is passed down to [the] taxpayers."

Things were no better in 1998. First, the IRS sent out apologies to 20,000 taxpayers for mistakes it made in handling their accounts. The the IRS sent 1 million taxpayers tax packages with the wrong bar code, making them unusable because of zip code errors.

1. Jeff A. Schnepper, *Inside IRS* (New York: Stein and Day, 1978), p. 187.

Things then got worse. Kenneth L. Steen of Chattanooga, TN expected a refund of $513. Instead, he received a letter from the IRS demanding the payment of $300,000,007.57! An IRS official reported 3,000 people around the nation got similar erroneous notices.

Then things got really bad with the Roth hearings discussed in Chapter 14. The IRS itself issued a detailed report of 12 of the agency's 33 districts.

It found that the IRS had increasingly relied in recent years on numerical goals—such as the dollars that each revenue officer collects or the number of properties seized by a certain office—in enforcing tax laws, and that an obsession with such goals has raised the possibility of overzealous collections.

Though Congress outlawed the use of numerical goals a decade ago, high-profile Senate hearings in 1997 and an IRS report released in December, 1997 showed that the practice remained common.

It was found that more than a third of the IRS front line collection managers were evaluated based on enforcement statistics and that a fourth of all collection officers "feel pressure to achieve enforcement goals and take enforcement actions."

Apparently, no one is immune from foul-ups by the Internal Revenue Service. In the summer of 1987, the Internal Revenue Service acknowledged that it had accidentally placed an erroneous $338.85 lien against then President and Mrs. Reagan. Although the lien was discovered and rescinded, it will remain a permanent entry in the County Court record system where it had been filed.

As the 1998 IRS report and Roth hearings demonstrate, IRS horror stories are not just in the far past. As a 1993 Tax Court decision noted, an IRS agent contacted Chicago businessman Vince Han and his wife to arrange an audit. At the second meeting—at Mr. Han's house—the agent's supervisor arrived on the premises and shouted: "You have to pay $70,000 now—if you don't pay it, you are going to jail!" Actually, Mr. Han owed the government nothing. The IRS auditor didn't bother reading key documents Mr. Han provided and instead merely asserted that Mr. Han "was not an honest taxpayer." It took a four-year legal struggle for Mr. Han to clear his name and recover some of the heavy legal costs he incurred.

Fear of the Internal Revenue Service *is* justified. All too often IRS agents are arbitrary, antagonistic, and capricious. According to a study commissioned by the Federal Administrative Conference, the Internal Revenue Service has been found to be "whimsical, inconsistent, unpredictable, and highly personal" in dealing with those caught in its machinery. The study concluded, among other things, that different IRS districts follow different rules and that the same district can be either easy or tough depending upon whether it is ahead or behind its acknowledged "quota" for recoveries.

For example, according to the conference, a New Yorker's chances of being audited averaged 1:39, compared to 1:78 in New Mexico. IRS audit negotiators in Brooklyn averaged 32¢ on the dollar in settling disputes, while those in Baltimore extracted 74¢. In Albany, New York, six of every ten delinquent accounts led to tax seizures, but only three of ten did in New Mexico. The Federal Administrative Conference also found that the higher the deficiency the Internal Revenue Service claimed, the lower the percentage it finally accepted in settlement. The conference suggested that this was due to the ability of rich taxpayers to hire lawyers to argue their cases while poorer taxpayers had no choice but to pay up.

Probability of an IRS Audit for Individuals (1987)

	Audit Rate (%)
United States	1.09
IRS Region	
West (W)	1.68
Southwest (SW)	1.55
North Atlantic (NA)	1.00
Midwest (MW)	0.90
Central (C)	0.86
Southeast (SE)	0.86
Mid-Atlantic (MA)	0.60
States and IRS Districts	
1. Alaska (W)	2.46
2. Nevada (W)	1.89
3. Wyoming (SW)	1.68
4. Utah (SW)	1.61
5. Oklahoma (SW)	1.45
6. North Dakota (MW)	1.40
7. Texas (all) (SW)	1.36
Austin District	1.23
Dallas District	1.21
Houston District	1.81
8. California (all) (W)	1.31
Laguna Niguel District	1.46
Los Angeles District	1.18
Sacramento District	1.00
San Francisco District	1.77
San Jose District	1.22

(continued)

Probability of an IRS Audit for Individuals 1987 ***(continued)***

	Audit Rate (%)
9. Washington (W)	1.20
10. Montana (MW)	1.11
11. Colorado (SW)	1.07
12. Arizona (SW)	1.03
International[a]	0.99
13. Kansas (SW)	0.95
14. Idaho (W)	0.94
15. Hawaii (W)	0.93
16. Georgia (SE)	0.93
17. Illinois (all) (MW)	0.93
Chicago District	1.01
Springfield District	0.71
18. Louisiana (SE)	0.71
19. New Mexico (SW)	0.93
20. Ohio (all) (C)	0.90
Cincinnati District	0.69
Cleveland District	1.06
21. Minnesota (MW)	0.89
22. New York (all) (NA)	0.89
Albany District	0.68
Brooklyn District	0.82
Buffalo District	0.72
Manhattan District	1.30
23. Delaware (MA)	0.86
24. Nebraska (MW)	0.85
25. Maryland[b] (MA)	0.81
26. Missouri (MW)	0.81
27. Alabama (SE)	0.80
28. Indiana (C)	0.77
29. Mississippi (SE)	0.77
30. Oregon (W)	0.77
31. Vermont (NA)	0.77
32. Tennessee (SE)	0.76
33. Florida (SE)	0.74
34. South Dakota (MW)	0.72

(continued)

Probability of an IRS Audit for Individuals 1987 ***(continued)***

	Audit Rate (%)
35. Connecticut (NA)	0.70
36. West Virginia (C)	0.70
37. Pennsylvania (all) (MA)	0.69
Philadelphia District	0.71
Pittsburgh District	0.64
38. Michigan (C)	0.67
39. Virginia (MA)	0.64
40. South Carolina (SE)	0.63
41. Arkansas (SE)	0.62
42. Kentucky (C)	0.62
43. New Jersey (MA)	0.62
44. Iowa (MW)	0.59
45. North Carolina (SE)	0.59
46. New Hampshire (NA)	0.58
47. Wisconsin (MW)	0.57
48. Massachusetts (NA)	0.57
49. Rhode Island (NA)	0.56
50. Maine (NA)	0.54

Source: Derived from statistics in the 1987 Commissioner's Annual Report.
[a]Returns filed in Puerto Rico and from abroad.
[b]Includes the District of Columbia.

Average Yield of an IRS Audit

United States	$5,330
IRS Region	
Southwest (SW)	$7,883
North Atlantic (NA)	$7,606
Mid-Atlantic (MA)	$5,013
West (W)	$4,441
Southeast (SE)	$4,401
Midwest (MW)	$3,665
Central (C)	$3,424

(continued)

Average Yield of an IRS Audit *(continued)*

States and IRS Districts	
1. Colorado (SW)	$17,614
2. Texas (all) (SW)	$9,780
Austin District	$4,002
Dallas District	$1,665
Houston District	$6,789
3. Alaska (W)	$8,973
4. Maryland[a] (MA)	$7,532
5. Oklahoma (SW)	$7,382
6. Arkansas (SE)	$7,218
7. Florida (all) (SE)	$7,136
Fort Lauderdale District	$8,980
Jacksonville District	$5,826
8. Nevada (W)	$6,566
9. New Jersey (MA)	$6,341
10. Idaho (W)	$6,295
11. New York (all) (NA)	$6,216
Albany District	$3,846
Brooklyn District	$6,216
Buffalo District	$3,846
Manhattan District	$8,414
12. Massachusetts (NA)	$5,642
13. California (all) (W)	$5,608
Laguna Niguel District	$4,735
Los Angeles District	$9,538
Sacramento District	$4,138
San Francisco District	$3,884
San Jose District	$3,884
14. Oregon (NW)	$5,561
International[b]	$5,391
15. Illinois (all) (MW)	$5,176
Chicago District	$5,590
Springfield District	$3,422
16. Kansas (SW)	$4,825
17. Pennsylvania (all) (MA)	$4,572
Philadelphia District	$5,089
Pittsburgh District	$3,550

(continued)

Average Yield of an IRS Audit ***(continued)***

18. Utah (SW)	$4,372
19. Michigan (C)	$4,315
20. Arizona (SW)	$4,290
21. Tennessee (SE)	$4,178
22. Wyoming (SW)	$4,154
23. Louisiana (SE)	$4,140
24. New Hampshire (NA)	$3,957
25. Connecticut (MA)	$3,889
26. Hawaii (W)	$3,882
27. Delaware (MA)	$3,756
28. Georgia (SE)	$3,727
29. Kentucky (C)	$3,713
30. Virginia (MA)	$3,640
31. New Mexico (SW)	$3,590
32. Ohio (all) (C)	$3,534
Cincinnati District	$3,057
Cleveland District	$3,765
33. Wisconsin (MW)	$3,382
34. North Carolina (SE)	$3,286
35. South Carolina (SE)	$3,209
36. Washington (NW)	$3,188
37. Indiana (C)	$3,180
38. Maine (NE)	$3,069
39. Iowa (MW)	$3,049
40. Rhode Island (NE)	$2,965
41. Minnesota (MW)	$2,949
42. Missouri (MW)	$2,922
43. Nebraska (MW)	$2,728
44. South Dakota (MW)	$2,629
45. Mississippi (SE)	$2,529
46. Alabama (SE)	$2,513
47. West Virginia (SE)	$2,375
48. Montana (MW)	$2,181
49. Vermont (NE)	$2,095
50. North Dakota (MW)	$1,825

Source: Derived from statistics in the 1987 Commissioner's Annual Report.

[a]Includes the District of Columbia.

[b]Returns filed in Puerto Rico and from abroad.

Percentage of Returns Examined Based on Geographic Location in 1996

	Individual	Corporation	Partnership
Manhattan, NY	0.74%	1.80%	0.85%
San Francisco, CA	1.42	1.57	0.29
Chicago, IL	0.52	1.42	0.21
New Orleans, LA	0.96	1.31	0.26
Anchorage, AK	0.85	1.27	0.13
Dallas, TX	0.93	1.25	0.15
Boston, MA	0.44	1.25	0.35
Atlanta, GA	0.76	0.93	0.35
Los Angeles, CA	1.57	2.23	0.29
Newark, NJ	0.42	0.95	0.37
Detroit, MI	0.43	1.15	0.32
Jacksonville, FL	0.51	0.76	0.41
Philadelphia, PA	0.41	1.36	0.18
Brooklyn, NY	0.58	0.69	0.23
Cincinnati, OH	0.37	1.02	0.27
San Jose, CA	1.14	1.84	0.17

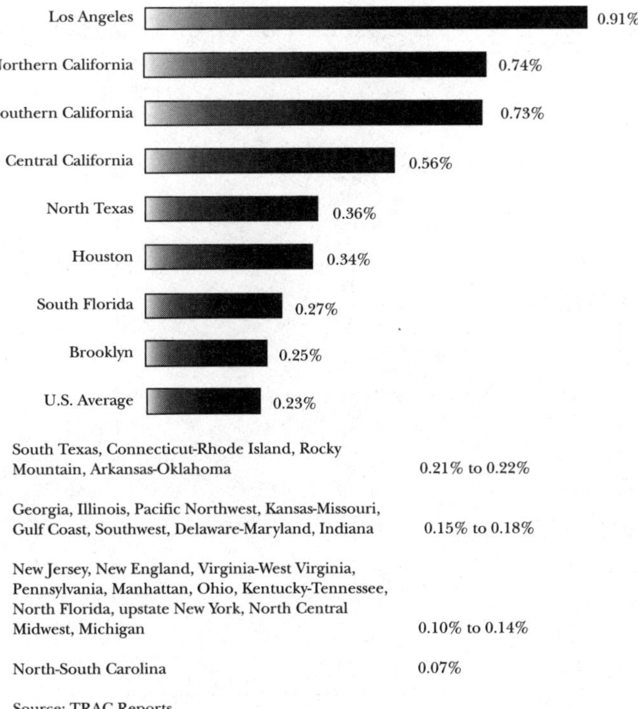

Percentage of Returns Examined Based on Geographic Location in 1995

	Individual	Corporation	Partnership
Manhattan, NY	1.06%	1.79%	0.54%
San Francisco, CA	1.36	1.86	0.46
Chicago, IL	0.55	1.21	0.15
New Orleans, LA	0.89	1.05	0.33
Anchorage, AK	1.05	1.01	0.29
Dallas, TX	1.02	0.86	0.18
Boston, MA	0.47	0.88	0.37
Atlanta, GA	1.11	0.90	0.45
Los Angeles, CA	1.37	1.28	0.46
Newark, NJ	0.39	0.87	0.45
Detroit, MI	0.46	1.18	0.22
Jacksonville, FL	0.56	0.59	0.28
Philadelphia, PA	0.41	1.20	0.16
Brooklyn, NY	0.59	0.51	0.18
Cincinnati, OH	0.32	1.49	0.25
San Jose, CA	0.93	1.26	0.27

Percentage of Returns Examined Based on Geographic Location in 1994

	Individual	Corporation	Partnership
Manhattan, NY	0.90%	1.25%	0.74%
San Francisco, CA	1.57	2.42	0.35
Chicago, IL	0.78	1.04	0.35
New Orleans, LA	1.02	1.87	0.34
Anchorage, AK	1.30	1.70	0.33
Dallas, TX	0.90	1.11	0.23
Boston, MA	0.51	0.75	0.24
Atlanta, GA	1.11	1.19	0.55
Los Angeles, CA	1.32	1.52	0.27
Newark, NJ	0.39	0.84	0.47
Detroit, MI	0.53	1.35	0.19
Jacksonville, FL	0.70	0.90	0.24
Philadelphia, PA	0.43	1.07	0.27
Brooklyn, NY	0.47	0.54	0.29
Cincinnati, OH	0.35	1.82	0.33
San Jose, CA	0.74	1.75	0.22

Percentage of Returns Examined Based on Geographic Location in 1993

	Individual	Corporation	Partnership
Manhattan, NY	0.63%	1.60%	1.16%
San Francisco, CA	1.63	2.86	0.58
Chicago, IL	0.39	1.27	0.38
New Orleans, LA	0.93	2.21	0.51
Anchorage, AK	1.11	3.20	0.60
Dallas, TX	0.82	1.69	0.38
Boston, MA	0.37	1.33	0.23
Atlanta, GA	1.06	2.06	0.40
Los Angeles, CA	1.43	2.26	0.39
Newark, NJ	0.43	1.31	0.32
Detroit, MI	0.41	1.99	0.21
Jacksonville, FL	0.68	1.22	0.46
Philadelphia, PA	0.34	1.26	0.38
Brooklyn, NY	0.43	1.18	0.27
Cincinnati, OH	0.36	2.38	0.31
San Jose, CA	0.86	3.30	0.37

Percentage of Returns Examined Based on Geographic Location in 1992

	Individual	Corporation	Partnership
Manhattan, NY	0.79%	1.64%	1.10%
San Francisco, CA	1.30	2.53	0.56
Chicago, IL	0.38	1.12	0.62
New Orleans, LA	1.05	2.46	0.64
Anchorage, AK	1.28	2.83	0.38
Dallas, TX	0.79	2.10	0.43
Boston, MA	0.43	1.39	0.43
Atlanta, GA	0.90	2.38	0.47
Los Angeles, CA	1.39	1.91	1.07
Newark, NJ	0.40	0.86	0.57
Detroit, MI	0.45	1.90	0.32
Jacksonville, FL	0.68	1.32	0.74
Philadelphia, PA	0.31	0.99	0.78
Brooklyn, NY	0.49	1.29	0.17
Cincinnati, OH	0.44	3.08	0.51
San Jose, CA	0.92	2.37	0.38

The last four charts show the variation in the percentage of returns examined in 1996, 1995, 1994, 1993, and 1992 in various IRS districts.

The variations between these districts may be, at least in part, due to differences in income categories—i.e., a greater or lesser proportion of "high-income" returns.

In response to these problems, Congress passed a Taxpayer's Bill of Rights in 1988. The creation of Senator David Pryor of Arkansas, it consists of procedural safeguards and penalties to help clarify and ensure the rights and obligations of a taxpayer and the IRS during an audit or appeal, as well as during the refund and collection processes. As then Finance Committee Chairman Lloyd Bentsen put it, the bill's provisions counter the "bully mentality" that many taxpayers perceive behind IRS tax law enforcement. The focus of the bill is to create a more balanced relationship between the tax agency and the citizenry. The details of the bill can be found on pages 537 and following. A second Taxpayer Bill of Rights was passed in 1996, and a third in 1998 as part of the Reform Act. The details of these laws can be found in Chapters 12 and 14.

In 1997, the IRS received two additional hits. Responding to reports of unauthorized inspection of tax return information by IRS employees, Congress passed the Taxpayers Browsing Protection Act, which imposes both civil and criminal penalties for the unauthorized inspection of tax returns and return information. Between late 1994 and April 1997, more than 700 IRS employees were punished for improperly accessing agency information.

Moreover, in March 1997, Rep. Bill Archer and Sen. William Roth, the Chairmen of the House Ways and Means and the Senate Finance Committees respectively, agreed to investigate allegations that the IRS is conducting politically targeted audits of exempt organizations.

Responding to serious IRS deficiencies, the National Commission on Restructuring the IRS, in a June 25, 1997 report, recommended sweeping changes for the agency.

The key recommendations in the commission's report call for:

- creating a seven-member board of directors for IRS, with five members from the private sector, appointed (and removable) by the president and confirmed by the Senate;
- consolidating congressional oversight of IRS by creating a joint committee of leaders of the multiple committees that now oversee IRS on Capitol Hill;

- stabilizing IRS' budget for the next three years so it can plan for modernization;
- giving IRS and Treasury more flexibility to hire the qualified personnel they need to implement modernization;
- giving IRS more input into the administrability of tax laws before they are enacted; and
- requiring IRS to provide taxpayers with compensation for damages incurred as a result of wrongful actions by IRS, among other taxpayer rights provisions.

Many of these issues were addressed again in the 1998 Reform Act. Things are changing. On August 5, 1999, the IRS issued T.D. 8830 to establish a balanced measurement system for employees. Specifically, the new rules measure employee performance and implement requirements that all employees be evaluated on the basis of "providing fair and equitable treatment to taxpayers." The use of records of tax enforcement results to evaluate or to impose or suggest goals for any employee of the IRS is barred.

But as IRS Commissioner Charles O. Rossotti stated in July 1999, "Frankly, we haven't yet succeeded in building an IRS that accomplishes, or is ever capable of accomplishing, our goals at an acceptable level."

Short of adopting a vow of poverty and hiding in a monastery or joining the ever-growing army of tax evaders, what can you do? The best defense is a good offense. If you know how the service works internally and where it is vulnerable, you can at least better your odds of winning when the tax man calleth.

Making your return indistinguishable from the "average" individual return can lessen your chances of facing an audit. Once you have prepared and signed your return, you mail it to the IRS Regional Service Center for your geographical area. The center checks some of the figures and transfers all information to magnetic tape, which then goes to the IRS computer center in Martinsburg, West Virginia. Here it becomes part of a master file for the Internal Revenue Service's complex automatic data processing system. With the master file, the Internal Revenue Service can locate people who fail to file returns and taxpayers who do not report such income as dividends or bank interest. Each tax return is assigned a document locator number (DLN) by the local Service Center. To better understand the document locator system, let us "decode" a hypothetical DLN: 3414133300134. Working from left to right, the digits indicate the following:

34 = the IRS district (viz., the Cleveland District)
1 = the tax class (viz., withholding tax)
41 = the document code (viz., Form 941)
333 = the control date (the numeric day of the year remittance was made)
001 = the block number
34 = the serial number of the specific DLN

An understanding of the document locator number system can help you better understand the communication process of the Internal Revenue Service.

In addition to printing out notices and letters to advise you of a tax refund due, to request information, or to report actions taken on returns already filed and the status of your account, the system is programmed to check returns for three basic mistakes.

First, all returns are examined for mathematical errors. Mistakes in arithmetic or in transferring figures from one schedule to another—for example, the total of excess itemized deductions to the Form 1040—result in an immediate correction notice. If the error leads to a tax deficiency, you automatically receive a bill for that amount. If you overpaid, the excess is applied to future taxes, credited, or refunded at your request. You cannot appeal such corrections, but you can ask in writing that they be reviewed. Errors in arithmetic alone rarely lead to a full audit.

The Internal Revenue Service's second computer check also provides for automatic adjustments to your return before any audit is made. This Unallowable Items Program is designed to catch clearly illegal deductions, such as claiming an exemption for a spouse who is filing separately. Under this program, the computer cross-checks reported income against the W-2 forms received from your employer. The dividends and interest reported by banks, brokerage houses, and other financial institutions are cross-checked in about 96 percent of the cases. The Internal Revenue Service attempts to match almost 100 percent of the information returns that they receive on computer tape and over 50 percent of those that are on paper. As a result of this cross-checking, the Internal Revenue Service sends out notices for taxes and interest on overdue taxes or for income or other payments that were not reported. Unfortunately, however, according to the General Accounting Office, about half of the ten million correction notices the IRS issues each year are "incorrect, unresponsive, unclear, or incomplete." If you get an incorrect notice, follow the appropriate procedures to contest it, or contact your local Problem Resolution office.

Another common mistake picked up by this program is a claim for a deduction that exceeds limits set by the Internal Revenue Service tax code. For example, not all medical expenses may be claimed. You may itemize and write off only those medical expenses that exceed 7.5 percent of adjusted gross income. The Unallowable Items Program is also likely to catch excessive deductions for charitable contributions or failure to reduce a "casualty loss" by $100, as required by the tax code. When an adjustment is made, you receive a letter allowing you to explain or protest. If you accept the change, you are asked to sign the "correction notice."

Unless the mistakes are extensive, these automatic adjustments do not usually lead to a full audit. However, basic errors like these should be avoided: Anytime your return is made to stand out, *for any reason*, it increases your chances for a full audit, with all the corresponding consequences.

Another IRS program for checking tax returns is the Questionable Items Program. Here, your whole return or a part of it is subjected to a detailed investigation. You are, in effect, being challenged rather than corrected. You must justify each deduction to the last penny, and to the satisfaction of the examining agent.

IRS computer programs use three techniques to decide which returns to review under this program: random selection, "discriminate function" selection, and special target selection.

Your income, claimed deductions, and profession are irrelevant when returns are selected at random. A student earning only $3,000 a year at part-time jobs may be invited to the local IRS office for a tax audit only to find a business executive making $300,000 in the same situation.

Once the return is in the computer, you are at the mercy of the second selection criterion—"discriminant function" *(Dif)* analysis. Based on previous experience, the Internal Revenue Service has created a number of composite hypothetical "taxpayers." These composite "norms" are determined by interviewing a random selection of taxpayers. Unfortunately, this can be a horror for the taxpayer selected as a "norm": The IRS agent asks questions about every single item on the return; the taxpayer has to produce a birth certificate, marriage certificate—the works. Each item is checked, and the results are fed into the computer. In a "discriminant function" analysis, the characteristics of these "average" taxpayers are given different weights and compared to a return selected for audit. Of the 1.1 million closed books and records audits received in 1992, 1993, and 1994, 59% were selected on the basis of "*DIF*" scores.

Average taxpayers are determined by the IRS Taxpayer Compliance Measurement Program (TCMP). The most recent research audits covered 54,000 personal returns for 1988. The IRS planned to TCMP audit about 153,000 returns of all types for 1994 to be picked randomly in 1995 to represent 25 business sectors, 5 personal income groups, and 30 geographic areas. Fortunately, budget constraints put these audits on hold.

First, the deductions on the selected returns are added up and weighed for what is called the "discriminant function" score. The computer then recommends audits for significantly differing returns. The computer is also programmed to notice special deviations. For example, it may recommend an audit if all your deductions turn out to be nicely rounded even numbers. It will also compare your deductions to your job. A person who works as a construction laborer will rarely have a need for a home office deduction. The computer model-match takes into account income level, profession, number of dependents claimed, whether your spouse works, and even your address: A Beverly Hills zip code with a ghetto-level reported income will immediately signal for an audit. According to former IRS Commissioner Roscoe L. Egger, Jr., two-thirds of the audited returns are selected on the basis of the IRS discriminate function formula. The rest are chosen on the basis of tax-avoiding trends, such as abusive tax shelters.

You should also understand the bar-coded envelopes and peel-off labels that come with your returns. Some taxpayers believe that the coding somehow triggers an audit. In fact, the coding simply allows the IRS to process the mail on their automatic sorting machine, which reads the bar codes and separates the mail by type of return (i.e., 1040A, 1040EZ, 1040), thus expediting processing. Uncoded mail must be sorted by hand, which is much more time-consuming and slows up processing, which slows up refunds.

The coded numbers on the preprinted address label affixed to your tax package also speed up processing of returns and expedite refunds. Again, the label coding has no relationship to audits. It assures the IRS that the name and social security number are valid and it includes, for each taxpayer, an assigned "check digit"—two characters based on the taxpayer's name. Data transcribers pick up the two-stroke check digit and the social security number from the label to input tax information to a taxpayer's account. If the label is not used, your full name, social security number, and complete address must be input—significantly extending processing time and adding the potential for common errors that delay the issuance of refunds. The illustration on the next page shows the preprinted label and explains the meaning of the various coded symbols.

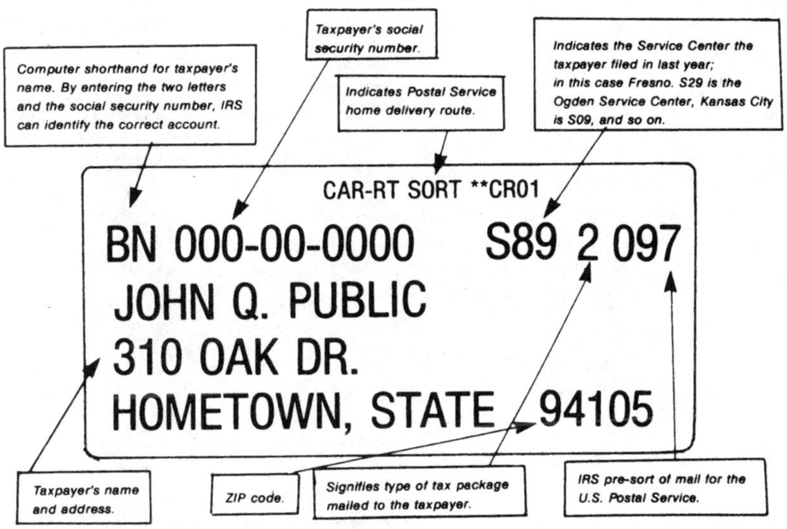

Actually, a single oversized deduction will probably not trigger an immediate audit. For you the name of the game is to match the computer's norm as closely as possible. The table on page 504 reveals average deductions claimed on returns filed in 1998 for 1997.

A dual expansion of IRS computer operations was substantially completed in 1985. First, the major equipment replacement program, with a new UNIVAC 1100 System, was made operational in all 10 Service Centers. This system tripled the capacity and speed of the old equipment. Second, administration of office examinations is now computerized and operates from the 10 Service Centers. As District appointments become available, the computer selects cases by priority and generates both appointments and taxpayer notification letters. These letters detail the time and place of the examination, the issues to be resolved, what to bring, etc. The new system also identifies whether the taxpayer has other years under examination and automatically routes the new examination to the same agent. In 1994, the IRS spent an additional $689 million to upgrade its computer system. Unfortunately, it still doesn't work properly. After spending $8 billion on new computer systems, even a top agency official, in 1997, admitted that the systems "do not work in the real world."

As of 1999, the computer system still does not work. A seven-year program to upgrade and modernize the agency's system at a cost of almost $4 billion received a scathing review from the General Accounting Office in 1995. Among the problems: cost overruns, failure to move toward a more efficient system, and contin-

Average Itemized Deductions for 1997 by Adjusted Gross Income in Thousands of Dollars

AGI Size	$20–30K	$30–50K	$50–75K	$75–100K	$100–200K	$200+K
Medical	$5,231	$4,475	$ 5,056	$ 6,957	$11,855	$32,982
% Itemizers	33.6%	18.4%	9.1%	5.3%	3.3%	1.2%
Taxes	$2,305	$3,049	$4,343	$5,986	$9,336	$36,555
% Itemizers	98.4%	99.4%	99.8%	99.8%	99.8%	99.8%
Interest	$5,733	$6,074	$6,925	$8,259	$11,118	$25,042
% Itemizers	77.1%	84.6%	88.6%	88.6%	85.9%	82.9%
Contributions	$1,454	$1,577	$1,881	$2,391	$3,526	$20,397
% Itemizers	81.7%	86.7%	91.4%	94.5%	95.6%	96.5%
Total Deductions	$10,702	$11,443	$13,639	$17,047	$23,664	$68,742
% Returns	18.2%	38.6%	65.4%	83.2%	91.1%	92.7%

Source: 1997 Statistics of Income, Internal Revenue Service, Pub. 1136, Spring, 1999.

ued inability of IRS employees to get current and accurate information on taxpayer returns.

The computer systems and processes do not interact with each other. The result is a problem that may be resolved by one IRS office, but another department shows the issue is still open. The taxpayer thinks the matter is closed ... but not every IRS office is necessarily in agreement. Steps are being taken to develop a centralized system that will allow all existing computers and systems to communicate with each other. The change won't happen overnight, however.

The new Commissioner of Internal Revenue, Charles D. Rossotti, is not an attorney nor an accountant—he is a computer systems expert. Rossotti has said that reforming the IRS could take the better part of a decade; the computer modernization program also is likely to extend into the next century.

After the computers have "graded" income tax returns to determine their "audit worthiness," the returns with the highest scores are screened by humans. The following characteristics are what these human screeners look for:

- Insufficient income to support claimed deductions.
- Refunds out of line with gross income and exemptions.
- Possibility of unreported income.
- Profit from business or profession below the "norm."
- Investment yield or profits below the interest income that would have been earned if the funds had been deposited in savings accounts.

Other Internal Revenue Service guidelines used in choosing returns to be audited include:

- Comparative size of the item—a questionable expense item of $5,000 when expenses total $25,000 would be significant; however, if total expenses were $250,000, the item ordinarily would not be significant.
- Absolute size of the item—despite the comparability factor, size itself may be significant. For example, a $60,000 item may be significant even though it represents a small percentage of taxable income.
- Inherent character of the item—although the amount of an item may be insignificant, the *nature* of the item may be significant. For example, airplane expenses claimed by a carpenter may be significant.
- Evidence of intent to mislead—this may include missing, misleading, or incomplete schedules, or showing an item incorrectly on the return.
- Beneficial effect of the manner in which an item is reported—expenses claimed on a business schedule rather than claimed as itemized deductions may be significant.
- Relationship to other items—the absence of a deduction for interest expense when real estate taxes are claimed may be significant. Similarly, the lack of dividends reported when the return shows sales of stock may also be significant.

According to a recently declassified handbook, the IRS looks for the following in selecting returns for an audit: exemptions claimed by noncustodial parents; losses claimed on rental property recently converted from a residence; and high receipt, low net profit business schedules for nonitemizers. The above deductions are listed as higher priority items than large medical expenses of large families or older taxpayers, home mortgage interest, auto expenses of users of the standard mileage rate, or transportation expenses of construction workers who work at more than one job site for more than one employer (*The Classification Handbook,* IRMO 41 (12) 0).

The Internal Revenue Service expects its management to use employee time productively. Therefore, each year, top administrators will "target" taxpayers in specific professions or with incomes from unusual sources where the highest potential monetary recovery may be found. For example, dentists, doctors, lawyers, and even accountants may receive much of their income in cash payments. The Internal Revenue Service believes that this permits them to "forget" to report all of their receipts. The Service also believes that the incentive to underreport would be greatly dulled if these professionals knew that, as a class, they were more likely to be audited. Therefore, as a class, they *are* more likely to be audited.

The IRS has increased the staff tracking nonfilers to 2,400 from 400. Elsewhere it's shifting auditors to focus more on personal returns with self-employment income and corporations with assets over $100 million.

The IRS audit manual, *The Policies of the Internal Revenue Service Handbook*, sets as the "primary objective" in selection of tax returns "*the highest possible revenue yield from the examination man hours expended*, and the examination of as many returns as is feasible for the maintenance of a high degree of voluntary taxpayer compliance" (author's italics).

Our federal income tax rates are imposed on a graduated progressive schedule. When you earn $1 more than the top of the previous bracket, a higher percentage of that *additional* dollar will be taken as taxes. Therefore, the more money you earn, the higher the potential return is likely to be on the time invested by the Internal Revenue Service in the case. If an agent denies a $100 deduction to a taxpayer in the 31 percent bracket, the United States Treasury receives $31, as opposed to only $15 from a taxpayer in the 15 percent bracket.

The Internal Revenue Service has also found that returns filed by people who make over $50,000 provide fertile grounds for audit reviews. Other groups watched closely include taxpayers with a second or sideline business, those who report hefty capital gain income, and all who might be involved in a partnership tax shelter.

The IRS has lately adopted a new, more efficient system for classifying individual taxpayers of similar economic circumstances in order to select returns for an audit. In the past, returns were selected on the basis of adjusted gross income. Under that old system, individuals were selected for audit by separating business and nonbusiness returns, grouping them into examination classes according to adjusted gross income, and running each class through the mathematical "discriminant function" formula to identify returns with high audit potential.

This system had definite drawbacks from the Internal Revenue Service's perspective, because adjusted gross income is determined *after* deductions and adjustments, which are of primary interest to auditors. A return showing a high gross income but large offsetting deductions (as from tax shelters) would present a relatively low adjusted gross income. Therefore, it would be assigned to a low adjusted gross income examination class, would generally receive light audit coverage, and would be scored under a "discriminant function" formula not geared to test its true audit potential.

The IRS's new classification system is based upon total positive income, relying on the total income of a taxpayer *before* adjustments or deductions. This is the sum of all positive items on your return. Any negative items—for instance, losses from tax shelters—are treated as zero. As a result of this reclassification, suspicious deductions and adjustments will not escape notice in, or distort the voluntary compliance level of, an examination class designed for lower-income taxpayers.

There is an additional reason why your return might be chosen for an audit. While the Internal Revenue Service does not publicly encourage tax informers, its representatives admit that many investigations could not be successfully conducted without the use of paid informants or the direct purchase of evidence. Most informers are former employees of a business that has been underreporting its income. A disgruntled employee who does not "rat" on the business itself may "rat" on its owner, or on a disliked manager.

But a neighbor who objects to your loud stereo at midnight or becomes jealous of your new car each year may just as quickly turn informer. These unofficial "agents" are used extensively in cases where the taxpayer under investigation is allegedly engaged in illegal activity. Tax informers are normally rewarded with up to 10 percent of the additional tax collected up to a $75,000, 5 percent of the next $25,000, and 1 percent of any additional amount. The maximum reward is $100,000. Informants fill out Form 211 which they can get by calling 1-800-TAX FORM. The Internal Revenue Service paid 650 rewards (out of 9,530 informants) totaling $3.5 million in the 1996 fiscal year ending September 30, 1996, to informants who provided it with information that enabled it to collect extra taxes from cheats. That figure was up from $1.8 million from the year before. The IRS does not divulge the identity of its informants, but such rewards are fully taxable. However, the grant of a reward is discretionary, not mandatory. (*Krug v. U.S. Fed Ct.*, No. 96-62IT, 5/27/98.)

Over the last several years, fewer than one out of every ten claims from tipsters has been judged worthy of a reward. However, as reported above, for the fiscal year ending September 30, 1996, the IRS paid out $3.5 million in rewards. The service collected an additional $102.7 million in taxes, fines, and penalties. To informers, though, the money is often secondary to revenge. You should, therefore, keep two rules in mind:

1. Never cheat on your income taxes.

2. If you do, never anger anyone who might know about it.

Despite its image as a bureaucracy of terror, in all fairness another side of the IRS story must be told. Staff turnover is one of the IRS's biggest problems, according to the internal study mentioned at the start of this chapter. More than 50 percent of the agency's file clerks have less than 12 months of experience in their present positions, and 36 percent of managers have been in their jobs less than one year. Moreover, many employees are in the lowest civil service pay grades, and, as one IRS employee quoted in the study put it, "We lose them to Hardee's," the fast-food franchise.

In 1999, the IRS reported losing more than 15,000 people over the last five years, and still losing about 450 tax examiners a year! In the last four years, the IRS has hired just 28 new revenue agents—total!

Even before the so-called Tax Simplification Act of 1978, the Service was responsible for interpreting and administrating codes, regulations, and revenue manuals that filled over 32 shelf-feet with an incredible 40,000 pages of the most arcane, unintelligible gobbledygook ever written. There have been many "tax reform" bills since 1978. The law is so complex, so convoluted, that it is incomprehensible. As former Citicorp Chairman Walter B. Wriston pointed out: "All the Congress, all the accountants and tax lawyers, all the judges and a convention of wizards cannot tell for sure what the income tax law says." Between 1985 and 1996 Congress has changed more than 3,000 sections of the tax code and created more than 100 new forms. Asked to perform an impossible function, it's not surprising that the IRS agent often fails. In December 1990, former IRS Commissioner Lawrence B. Gibbs noted that the numerous complex changes in the Internal Revenue Code in recent years have resulted in "confusion and frustration within the IRS and among taxpayers and their representatives."

Such failure was documented by Ralph Nader's Tax Reform Research Group. They prepared 22 identical tax reports based on the fictional economic plight of a married couple with one child, and these 22 identical copies were submitted to 22 different IRS offices around the country. Each office came up with an entirely different tax figure. The results varied from a refund of $811.96 recommended in Flushing, New York, to a tax-due figure of $52.14 derived by the tax office in Portland, Oregon.

In 1983, *USA Today* took an informal telephone survey of IRS tax-assistance offices in 15 major cities across the United States. Seven questions were picked that private tax consultants agreed were common and difficult but fair. For each question, interviewers called ten IRS telephone tax assistants—70 phone calls in all. In 20 cases—28.6 percent of the time—the Internal Revenue Service's answers were wrong. In five more cases, the Internal Revenue Service's answers were only partly correct, bringing the total of incorrect or incomplete answers to 35.7 percent.

Furthermore, getting through to the Internal Revenue Service by phone was close to impossible. In the *USA Today* study, it was found that the IRS telephone line was busy nine times out of ten in New York City. When it did ring, the phone often went unanswered. On one try it rang 48 times before being picked up, and twice it rang 25 times to no avail.

On February 12, 1985, the *Wall Street Journal* asked the same four tax law questions of 17 IRS offices. Two questions, involving the casualty loss deduction and one-time diesel credit, were answered correctly most of the time. The other two, involving the medical expense deduction and the wash sale rules, resulted in totally or partially wrong answers most of the time. Walter M. Alt, Director of the IRS Taxpayers' Services Division, told the *Journal* that he was "dismayed and unhappy" about the errors. IRS advice is not binding—whether oral or in print. In fact, the IRS is not bound by statements contained in its own publications, including *Your Federal Income Tax,* the IRS's free instruction booklet (*Thomas R. Underwood,* T.C. Memo 1983–99; *Harvey Richard Bennett,* T.C. Memo 1983–183; see also *Sundermeier,* T.C. Memo 1987–50, wherein taxpayers were not permitted to rely on an IRS publication, even though their local IRS office advised them that there was no other information available).

According to U.S. District Court Judge Michael M. Mihm, in his opinion in *Sinn Oil Company, et al. v. United States:* "The case law has girded the Internal Revenue Service with a nearly impregnable shield against the people it serves. Beginning with a Code which in its complexity is well nigh unfathomable to the average citizen...the judicial coup de grace is executed with the insistence that, if the taxpayer could find the relevant section and if he could be assured that there is not some supervening or nullifying regulation elsewhere and if he could then read and understand it, his reliance on the verbal representations of an agent [is] unreasonable."

The General Accounting Office did a study of its own: It checked out a sample of 2,543 tax returns in which the Internal Revenue Service had found 3,720 errors in arithmetic. Unfortunately, the General Accounting Office noted that the Internal Revenue Service itself had made nearly two-thirds of the errors. The General Accounting Office said that 33 million errors were found on the 94 million individual income tax returns processed in the fiscal year 1981, of which 37 percent were made by taxpayers and *63 percent* were made by employees of the IRS!

Another General Accounting Office survey in February and March of 1987 also faulted the accuracy of the IRS taxpayer telephone assistance program. The GAO found that taxpayers who called the Internal Revenue Service with tax law questions got inaccurate or incomplete answers more than one-third of the time. The survey showed that the IRS assisters provided correct answers to basic questions posed by callers from the General Accounting Office 63 percent of the time, correct but incomplete answers 15 percent of the time, and incorrect answers 22 percent of the time.

One year later things had not improved. A 1989 GAO report found that more than one-third of the answers that IRS telephone assisters provided were inaccurate. The GAO said that assisters provided the correct answer to a group of 20 questions only 64 percent of the time. According to House Ways and Means Committee Oversight Subcommittee Chairman J. J. Pickle of Texas, "Calling the IRS for tax advice is a real crap shoot."

Things are no better when the IRS takes the time to write. A GAO review dated May 24, 1988, found that IRS centers issued incorrect, incomplete, unresponsive, or unclear correspondence half the time. The GAO considered IRS errors in 30 percent of this correspondence critical; these letters each contained at least one instance in which the Adjustment/Correspondence Branch either provided incorrect information, failed to address all the taxpayer's questions, or acted incorrectly in adjusting or failing to adjust the taxpayer's account.

Things improved in 1990 when 77 percent of the telephone questions were answered correctly compared to 64 percent in 1989. However, while the questions asked by taxpayers were answered correctly more often than in 1989, fewer taxpayers were able to reach IRS personnel for assistance. IRS answered about 34 percent of the calls it received in 1990, while the balance either reached busy signals or hung up after being placed on hold, GAO said. In 1989, 58 percent of the incoming calls were answered.

The IRS's performance in handling calls from taxpayers deteriorated in 1992, according to the General Accounting Office. About seven out of every 10 calls to the IRS between January 1 and April 25 went unanswered, the congressional watchdog agency says. That was up from six out of 10 calls in 1991. On the bright side, IRS helpers correctly answered 85 percent of questions posed by anonymous IRS test callers, up from 84 percent the prior year.

The "most significant" decline was in the timeliness with which IRS filled GAO's test mail and phone orders, the report noted. For example, GAO received only 33 percent of the mail-ordered items within IRS' 14-day goal, as compared to 74 percent the previous year, the report said.

However, Internal Revenue Service data, as of April 8, 1992, showed that nine out of the 10 IRS service centers had met or exceeded IRS' 98 percent refund accuracy goal, and that all 10 service centers met IRS' goal of issuing taxpayers refunds in an average of 40 days or less, GAO said in the report *(Tax Administration: IRS' 1992 Filing Season Was Successful but Not without Problems,* GAO/GGD-92-132).

According to the GAO, taxpayers who called the IRS in 1993 had only a 1 in 4 chance of getting through—worse than in 1992. It found IRS efforts to communicate with taxpayers by mail littered with "delayed, inaccurate, incomplete, and confusing responses" to taxpayer questions.

In 1995, according to IRS data, telephone assistors answered 11 percent more calls than the IRS anticipated and provided accurate answers to 91 percent of the questions asked. However, the General Accounting Office reported that the IRS received many more calls than it was able to answer—only about 9 percent of the calls made during the study period were answered. In 1996, as a result of 119 million fewer calls, the IRS increased its rate of calls answered to 20%.

Moreover, the IRS, the auditor of us all, failed its own audit. The General Accounting Office in 1995 reported that it could not verify the reliability of the IRS's internal financial statements for 1993 and 1994 because of "poor accounting practices." They could not even verify either total revenue collected nor tax refunds paid!

In 1997, the GAO reported that at several facilities it inspected, the IRS could not account for about 6,400 missing tapes, cartridges, and other magnetic storage devices that could contain taxpayer data.

In a 1999 GAO audit, the IRS was found to continue to suffer from "serious financial management system deficiencies and internal control weaknesses … ."

The good news in 1998 was that the GAO found that the IRS "met or exceeded most" of its 1997 tax-filing season goals, such as making it easier for taxpayers to reach the agency by phone. Perhaps the tide is beginning to turn. Perhaps not—in 1999, the chances of a taxpayer actually getting through to the IRS were only 54%, lower than in 1998, and, according to Commissioner Rossotti, "May not improve in 2000." Why?—Budget limitations!

The law is so complicated that it is difficult to fault the IRS on their incorrect answers, even when the call goes through. In a 1988 study done by *Money* magazine, 50 tax professionals, including attorneys and CPAs, were asked to complete a tax return for a hypothetical family. The results were "unnerving"—no two preparers computed the same tax due and, worse, the answers varied by as much as 50 percent! In a second study by *Money*, done one year later, the answers were even more off the mark. Again, each participant computed a different tax for the family. And the bottom line ranged astonishingly from a low of $12,539 to a high of $35,813. The *Money* studies have continued each year with different bottom lines computed each year. The *minimum* spread was 50% in 1988; it was nearly 1,000% in 1991.

Thankfully, former IRS Commissioner Lawrence Gibbs, in a hearing of the Senate Finance Committee on Private Retirement Plans and IRS Oversight, stated that the IRS would not impose penalties on taxpayers who relied on incorrect information supplied by IRS telephone taxpayer assistance personnel. Nevertheless, the tax itself would not be forgiven, and the taxpayer would have the burden of maintaining a record of the name of the IRS employee who supplied the incorrect information as well as the date of the conversation.

Even though the Internal Revenue Service may not always be accurate, it strives always to be prepared. The IRS has revised IRM 1(16)00—Physical, Document, and Computer Systems Security—to include two former policy statements, P-1-165 and P-1-166. Both statements cover national emergency operations. The first statement discusses the function of the "IRS in the Event of a National Emergency—Especially Resulting from a Nuclear Attack." In case of an emergency, the primary duty of the IRS "is to support the Secretary of the Treasury." To this end, the duties of the IRS "will consist of analyzing and reporting on emergency tax legislation, prescribing regulations in forms, and issuing rulings and technical information of an emergency nature." The second statement specifies that, in the event of an emergency, the IRS will focus on operations that, given the circumstances, would yield the greatest revenue. "On the premise that the collection of delinquent accounts would be most adversely affected, and in many cases would be impossible in a disaster area, the Service will concentrate on the collection of current taxes," the manual said. Given the real possibility of a nuclear attack, I, for one, feel a lot more comfortable.

THE AUDIT

Internal Revenue Code Section 7605(a) gives the IRS the authority to fix the time and place of an audit as is reasonable under the circumstances. The Internal Revenue Manual states that IRS examiners should endeavor to make appointments at a time and place convenient for the taxpayer (IRM 4261.2). (See also Temp Reg. Section 301.7605-IT.)

Generally, the office that handles your audit will be determined by your domicile—where you live. However, the Internal Revenue Service will approve a request for a transfer of an audit if your domicile has changed before or during the examination or if you have died and your legal representative is in another district. The following rules for audit location generally apply:

1. A request for a transfer to a district closer to your residence will normally be approved.
2. If you live in one district, work in another, and are not represented by a Power of Attorney, you will be examined in the district where you reside.
3. If you are called for an audit in one district but live in another district that is within commuting distance (not defined) of the first, and are represented by a Power of Attorney within that distance, the audit will normally take place in the district where you reside.
4. If you live in one district and are represented by a Power of Attorney doing business in another district that is within commuting distance of the first, you will be audited in the district where you live.
5. If you live in another district outside commuting distance of the district where your return is scheduled for audit and are represented by a Power of Attorney in the other district, you will have a transfer request approved.
6. If you reside in the district where the audit is scheduled and are represented by a Power of Attorney in a district outside commuting distance of the first, you may obtain a transfer if the receiving district agrees.

Each IRS district office is made up of four divisions. Each division is subdivided into branches, the titles of which describe what is done in each branch. The four divisions are Administration, Collection, Audit, and Intelligence.

The Administration Division handles such matters as personnel, training, and facilities management of all types—from selection of the site of the office to ordering pens and paper.

The Collection Division is the bill-collecting arm of the Internal Revenue Service. It is represented in the field by Revenue Officers and in the Office Branch. The Collection Division also has a section known as the Taxpayer Service Section, which is a year-round information center manned by Taxpayer Service Representatives.

The Intelligence Division is the branch of the Internal Revenue Service that handles criminal investigations. It is staffed with Special Agents, who are enforcement officers and whose work is primarily technical. The main objective of an investigation by a Special Agent is to determine whether or not there should be criminal prosecution—as contrasted with an Internal Revenue Agent's objective, which is to determine the proper tax to be paid.

The Audit Division is charged with verifying the accuracy of tax returns filed, regarding both the substance of the law and the validity of the amounts reported. The major branches of the Audit Division are Field Audit, Office Audit, Review, and Audit Service. They have been renamed Examinations Branch. Field Audit employs Internal Revenue Agents and Estate Tax Examiners, and they are charged with auditing the more complex tax returns filed. Office Audit is staffed with Tax Auditors, who primarily audit individual returns. The Review staff is composed of former Field Agents and Tax Auditors, who check the accuracy of the audits made by the examining officers. Audit Service maintains the files on prior reports by examining officers and is a control center for cases under audit or cases that have been audited.

Victims of IRS errors now have a form on which to claim reimbursement. Such a claim is allowable under 31 U.S.C. Section 3732 but is limited to $1,000 and must be submitted within one year of its accrual. Filers of new Form 8489, Claim for Reimbursement for Expenses Incurred Due to Service Error, are instructed to submit substantiating documentation and are cautioned not to claim expenses for telephone calls, mileage or parking, lost wages, postage, or other nonreimbursable costs of the kind that are common to any disputed bill.

The scope of an audit will depend on various factors, but according to a recent addition to the IRS Manual, there are four items that *must* be reviewed by an agent:

1. Income probes, including bank statement analysis, bartering schemes, sale of assets, prizes, alimony, pensions, income tax refunds, etc.
2. Determination of the results of previous audits, including when the last took place, the results, and any recent correspondence the taxpayer may have had with the IRS.
3. Examination of subsequent and prior years' returns to make sure whether they were filed on time, where similar adjustments to the year under examination are necessary, and whether there are other issues that should be probed.
4. Determination of whether penalties have been previously assessed and whether they should be assessed as a result of the current examination.

The IRS Manual instructs the agents to comment on these items in their workpapers or to document the reasons why they were not examined.

According to IRS guidelines, unless specific recordkeeping requirements must be met, statements by the taxpayer, or others, may serve as adequate evidence in an audit. The IRS Manual notes that adequate evidence does not require complete documentation (IRM 4231, Audit Guidelines for Examiners, 330[2]).

Because the law is so vague in spots and so complicated, an intensive review and appeals procedure is available to you. Once your audit has been completed, the agent will present a Revenue Agent's Report stating recommendations and advising of any additional tax you owe. You will then be asked to sign a waiver indicating that you agree with the assessment. At this point you have three choices:

1. You can accept the adjustments, sign the waiver, and pay the tax.
2. You can pay the tax and file for a refund of the disputed amount.
3. You can request a conference with the IRS Appellate Division.

Prior to October 2, 1978, you could have taken a dispute with a revenue agent to a district conference. If an agreement was not reached there, a second hearing was available at the appellate division level. Alternatively, you could have elected to go directly to the appellate division. Under the present system the Internal Revenue Service maintains appeals offices at all locations where full-time district conferees and regional appellate offices were formerly located. The theory of eliminating the district conference is that, according to the Internal Revenue Service, the two-level system of administrative review was a costly duplication, for both the taxpayer and the Service.

The Internal Revenue Service believes that settlement results under the new single level of appeal are comparable to those under the old two-level appeal system. About 85 percent of the cases were agreed or defaulted in fiscal 1979. Of the remainder, about 5 percent claimed refunds and 10 percent filed tax court petitions.

It is almost universally agreed that it is best to settle at the agent level, if possible. If the tax deficiency involved is small, it may not justify the cost in time and dollars of pursuing your case to a higher level. Moreover, if the agent has missed items that you don't want questioned, your best approach may be to pay the deficiency and run. But *never* settle or concede any issue until the audit is completed. When the agent's cards are on the table, you have more leeway in planning your negotiation strategy.

For a psychological advantage, where appropriate, you may wish to tape record the audit proceedings. The Internal Revenue Service has revised the table of contents for, and added new text to, IRM 7600, Processing Determination Letter Applications. The new text, IRM 7610, Verbatim Recording of Conversations during Determination Proceedings, provides that verbatim recordings of Determination Proceedings will be permitted ordinarily with group manager approval (Manual Transmittal 7600-50 [11-18-83]; *Mott,* 214 F. Supp. 20 [N.D. Cal. 1963]; 1 Audit, CCH Internal Revenue Manual 4245). The absolute right to audiorecord a taxpayer interview was codified in Section 7520, enacted as part of the Omnibus Taxpayer Bill of Rights, but see *Huehne,* 83-2345 (October 23, 1983), wherein the Court ruled that the taxpayer did not have a right to videotape the audit.

If you disagree with the agent's assessment, you will receive a copy of the revenue agent's report with a preliminary note advising you that you have 30 days to appeal. If you ignore this letter, you will then receive a "90-day" letter advising you to pay or to petition the tax court for redetermination.

After receiving the 30-day letter, but before receiving the 90-day letter, you may request a hearing by notifying your IRS regional appeals office. If the original audit was conducted by a tax auditor at an IRS office or by correspondence, you do not have to file a written protest to begin the appeal process. Until recently, if the disputed amount was $2,500 or less, the same was true of a field examination conducted at your place of business; and if your field audit resulted in a disputed amount over $2,500, a written protest was necessary. These rules were changed by the IRS. Now, a written protest is required for field examinations only if the amount at issue for any tax year exceeds $25,000. (If the amount at issue does not exceed $25,000 but exceeds $2,500, a brief written statement of disputed issues is required [IA-85-91, 9/17/93]. As under prior law, no brief written statement or written protest is required to obtain an appeals office conference, in-office interview, or correspondence examination. An oral request will still suffice.) The protest should be filed in duplicate and should contain the following:

a) your name and address;

b) the date and case reference symbols on the letter from the Internal Revenue Service transmitting the findings that you are protesting;

c) the tax years or periods involved;

d) an itemized schedule of adjustments or findings with which you do not agree;

e) a statement that you want to appeal the findings of the revenue agent;

f) a statement of factual evidence supporting your position in the contested issues, which should be sworn to as true, under penalties of perjury;

g) a statement outlining the law or other authority upon which you are relying.

In response to your protest, an appellate conferee will meet with you at the regional office to discuss the disputed issues. While such a hearing is an informal procedure, you must remember that the burden of proof is still on you to provide clear and convincing evidence that the revenue agent's report should be amended. While oral statements and evidence will be considered, the best evidence is documentary—books, records, worksheets, journals, and so forth.

The informality of the conference hearing is designed to save time and trouble for all parties. You may represent yourself, or you may be represented by an attorney, CPA, or individual licensed to practice before the Internal Revenue Service. The aim of this stage of the appeals process is to resolve the issues with as little difficulty as possible. The objective here is to *settle!* In fiscal 1979 IRS agents at this level proposed to assess $1,900,124,000 in added tax and penalties. They *closed* these cases for $1,161,977,000—about 61 percent of the proposed assessments. In 1982, appeals officers heard more than 50,000 cases covering an estimated 150,000 separate tax returns in over 500 locations. According to Howard T. Martin, director of the Appeals Division, "Appeal officers have more flexibility, and we never give up the idea of resolving a case." A 1982 survey by the General Accounting Office found that extra taxes and penalties were reduced or eliminated in 84 percent of the cases in appeals. Unlike agents at the audit level, Appeals Officers can settle cases based on "hazards of litigation." Thus, in Appeals, it is possible to split or trade issues.

The Internal Revenue Service tells its Appellate personnel to negotiate settlements "on a basis which is fair to both the Government and the taxpayer. Strive to close on an agreed basis the highest possible number of cases." They are to maintain an overall agreement rate of at least 85 percent in cases not yet docketed for trial in the Tax Court except for certain tax shelter, protestor, and similar cases. In docketed cases, the Internal Revenue Service wants to "maximize" settlements, with the aim to maintain or improve the agreement rate achieved in the previous year.

If you want to stop the running of interest on any potential deficiency, you are entitled to make what is known as a "deficiency deposit." Such a deposit should be made before the mailing of a deficiency notice and designated in writing as a "deposit in the nature of a cash bond." If you request a part or all of your deficiency deposit to be returned before the assessment of any tax, the request will be granted—unless the Internal Revenue Service determines that the deposit should be applied against a jeopardy assessment or another tax liability. No interest will be paid or allowed with respect to an amount returned to you.

Outcome When Taxpayer Contests IRS Audit Results
Fiscal Year 1996

Level of Appeal	Original Dollars (billions)	Revised Dollars (billions)	Percent
Administrative (IRS Appeals-nondocketed)	$11.6	$3.9	33%
Settled after court filing (IRS Appeals-docketed)	2.0	0.4	21%

Source: Internal Revenue Service data.
Note: Includes all types of taxpayers—individuals, corporations, etc.

There's one additional avenue of administrative redress for taxpayer problems. In 1977, the IRS instituted "problem resolution offices" (PROs) (now under the National Taxpayer Advocate's Office) to handle problems that have not been resolved through normal channels. Such problems include not only complaints by disgruntled taxpayers but lost, stolen, or delayed refund checks, billing errors, and hardship situations. The following table lists the addresses and telephone numbers of the problem resolution offices. For each district, address correspondence to the Problem Resolution Officer, Internal Revenue Service.

Alabama
2121 Eighth Ave. N.
Room 1205
Birmingham, AL 35203
205/254-1177

Alaska
P.O. Box 101500
Anchorage, AK 99510
907/261-4230

Arizona
2120 N. Central Ave.
Stop 504
Phoenix, AZ 85004
602/261-3604

Arkansas
P.O. Box 3778, Stop 3
Little Rock, AR 72203
501/378-6260

California
P.O. Box 36136
Stop 13-0-04
450 Golden Gate Ave.
San Francisco, CA 94102
415/556-5046

P.O. Box 1791
Los Angeles, CA 90053
213/688-6111

Colorado
P.O. Box 1302
Denver, CO 80201
303/844-2305

Connecticut
P.O. Box 959
Hartford, CT 06101
203/722-3473

Delaware
P.O. Box 2415
Wilmington, DE 19899
302/573-6052

Florida
P.O. Box 35045
Stop 800
Jacksonville, FL 32202
904/791-3440

Georgia
4800 Buford Hwy.
Room 513A
Chamblee, GA 30341
404/455-5232

Hawaii
P.O. Box 50089
Honolulu, HI 96850
808/546-8932

Idaho
50 W. Fort St.
Box 041
Boise, ID 83724
204/334-1324

Illinois
230 S. Dearborn St.
Room 2869
Chicago, IL 60604
312/886-4394

P.O. Box 398
Springfield, IL 62705
217/492-4517

Indiana
P.O. Box 44687
Indianapolis, IN 46244
317/269-6332

Iowa
P.O. Box 1337
Room 345
Des Moines, IA 50305
515/284-6223

Kansas
P.O. Box 2907
Wichita, KS 67201
316/269-6223

Kentucky
P.O. Box 1735
Louisville, KY 40201
502/582-6030

Louisiana
P.O. Box 30806
New Orleans, LA 70190
504/589-3001

Maine
P.O. Box 787
Augusta, ME 04330
207/780-3310

Maryland
P.O. Box 1553
Baltimore, MD 21203
301/962-2082

Massachusetts
310 Lowell St.
Andover, MA 05501
617/681-5549

Michigan
P.O. Box 32514
Detroit, MI 48232
313/226-7899

Minnesota
P.O. Box 43599
St. Paul, MN 55164
612/725-7077

Mississippi
100 W. Capital St.
Stop 31A
Suite 504, Room 101A
Jackson, MS 39201
601/960-4800

Missouri
P.O. Box 1548
St. Louis, MO 63188
314/425-6770

Montana
Federal Bldg.
Drawer 10016
Helena, Mt 59626
406/449-5244

Nebraska
106 S. 15th St.
Stop 2
Omaha, NE 68102
402/221-4181

Nevada
P.O. Box 16045
Las Vegas, NV 89101
702/388-6281

New Hampshire
P.O. Box 720
Portsmouth, NH 03801
603/433-0571

New Jersey
970 Broad St.
Newark, NJ 07101
201/645-6263

New Mexico
P.O. Box 1040
Albuquerque, NM 87103
505/766-1197

New York
Leo O'Brien Federal Bldg.
Clinton Ave. & N. Pearl St.
Albany, NY 12207
518/472-4482

G.P.O. Box 380
Brooklyn, NY 11202
718/780-6511

P.O. Box 500
Niagara Square Station
Buffalo, NY 14201
716/846-4574

P.O. Box 408
Church Street Station
New York, NY 10008
212/264-2850

North Carolina
320 Federal Pl.
Room 214-B
Greensboro, NC 27401
919/378-5497

North Dakota
P.O. Box 8
Fargo, ND 58107
701/237-5771 Ext. 141

Ohio
P.O. Box 1818
Cincinnati, OH 45201
513/684-3094

P.O. Box 99709
Cleveland, OH 44199
800/424-1040

Oklahoma
P.O. Box 1040
Oklahoma City, OK 73101
405/272-9531

Oregon
P.O. Box 3341
Portland, OR 97208
503/221-2333

Pennsylvania
P.O. Box 12010
Philadelphia, PA 19106
215/597-3377

P.O. Box 705
Pittsburgh, PA 15230
412/644-5987

Rhode Island
P.O. Box 6528
Providence, RI 02940
401/528-4288

South Carolina
P.O. Box 386
Room 466
Columbia, SC 29202
803/253-3029

South Dakota
P.O. Box 370
Aberdeen, SD 57401
605/225-0250 Ext. 215

Tennessee
P.O. Box 1107
Stop 22
Nashville, TN 37202
615/251-5219

Texas
P.O. Box 1863
Stop 105
Austin, TX 78767
512/397-5875

P.O. Box 1040
Mail Code 171
Dallas, TX 75221
214/767-1289

3223 Briar Park Ave.
Stop 1005-BP
Houston, TX 77042
713/953-6436

Utah
P.O. Box 2069
Salt Lake City, UT 84110
801/524-6287

Vermont
11 Elmwood Ave.
Burlington, VT 05401
802/951-6354

Virginia
P.O. Box 10113
Richmond, VA 23240
804/771-2643

Washington
P.O. Box 2207
Mail Stop 405
Seattle, WA 98111
206/442-7393

West Virginia
P.O. Box 1388
Parkersburg, WV 26102
304/422-6616

Wisconsin
P.O. Box M-383
Room 118
Milwaukee, WI 53201
414/291-3046

Wyoming
308 W. 21st St.
Cheyenne, WY 82001
301/778-2162

877-777-4778
Toll-free

An Internal Revenue Manual Supplement (MT 1279-57, May 25, 1988) provides complete guidelines for the operation of the Problem Resolution Program at all levels of the agency. The IRS adopted 11 separate categories of rights to which taxpayers are entitled. Some of these categories include:

- The right to prompt, courteous, and impartial treatment that includes the assumption that "each taxpayer wants to comply" with the tax code;
- The right to a reasonable amount of time to produce requested documentation;
- The right to receive copies of their returns from IRS Service Centers and any other tax information, such as examination, criminal investigation, and collection division work papers; and
- Generally, the right to have a case transferred to a specific district office.

When the Internal Revenue Service determines that a deficiency exists, it must first send you a notice of the deficiency determination. You are then allowed a specific period—normally 90 days, beginning with the mailing of the notice—in which to file a petition for redetermination with the Tax Court. At that point the Internal Revenue Service is prohibited, with certain exceptions, from undertaking any assessment or collection activity until the deficiency notice has been mailed, the specified period has expired, and, if a Tax Court petition has been timely filed, the decision has become final [Section 6213(a)]. During the time this prohibition is in force, it is expressly provided that any assessment or collection activity by the IRS is subject to injunctive relief, notwithstanding the Anti-Injunction Act.

An *assessment* is, in essence, a bookkeeping notation that occurs when the IRS establishes an account against a taxpayer on the tax rolls. Technically, the assessment is made by an assessment officer for the district or regional service center by signing the summary record of assessment, which, through supporting records, provides the taxpayer's identification, the type of tax and taxable period, and the amount of the assessment. The date of the assessment is the date of the signing.

As soon as practical, and within 60 days after making the assessment, the IRS must give you notice of the unpaid amount and demand its payment by leaving the notice at your dwelling or usual place of business or by mailing it to your last known address. If you neglect or refuse to pay within 10 days after notice and demand, the IRS can proceed to collect the amount owed by levy. A *levy* includes the power of distraint and seizure by any means [IRC Section

6331(b)]. Ordinarily, a levy requires written notice of intent to levy at least 30 days prior to the day of levy, either in person or by leaving it at the dwelling or usual place of business or by certified or registered mailing to the last known address of the taxpayer [IRC Section 6331(d)(1), (2)]. In circumstances where you neglect or refuse to pay the tax after demand, a lien is created in favor of the United States on all property owned by you. The lien arises from the date of the assessment and is effective as against certain persons upon proper filing of a notice of lien. The Internal Revenue Service possesses additional power, subject to certain limitations, to sell property that it has seized (see IRC Sections 6335 and 6336). Remember, however, that a petition to the Tax Court, timely filed, will prevent the Internal Revenue Service from proceeding with any of these potential administrative actions.

If you are not satisfied at the administrative level, you must go to court. Even if the law is probably in favor of the Internal Revenue Service, it may pay for you to move a case into the judiciary if the dollar amount is large enough. This is because it provides an additional opportunity for you to compromise the case. When you go to court, the case is removed from the jurisdiction of the Internal Revenue Service district office, which started the investigation, and placed in the hands of the regional counsel. While agents in the district office are primarily concerned with the letter of the law, the regional counsel's staff is more concerned with disposing of cases. Remember, it costs the Internal Revenue Service time and money to litigate a case, just as it costs you. If there is no special reason, such as emphasizing an IRS stand on a particular issue for contesting a case, the regional counsel may offer a settlement just to save the trouble of going to court. Even if the offer is only 10 percent of an amount that the district office disallowed completely, you may still come out ahead.

The general rule is that a taxpayer will lose who attempts to sue an IRS agent for harrassment. In *Pope v. Organ*, 82-2 USTC Par. 9613, 50 AFTR 2d 82-5273 (DC Texas, 1982), the court held that an agent would be immune from prosecution if both of the following conditions were met: (1) the action was taken with the belief that it was lawful and without malicious intent to cause deprivation of constitutional rights, and (2) given the discretion of the official and the circumstances, it was reasonable to believe that there was a right to take the action.

However, on April 11, 1983, the U.S. Court of Appeals for the Fifth Circuit ruled that a taxpayer *could sue* an IRS agent as a federal official, acting under color of federal law when he allegedly violated taxpayers' constitutional rights to due process by willfully and maliciously assessing them for taxes they did not owe and harrassing them into paying those taxes. (*Rutherford* 83-1 USTC Par. 9289, 51 AFTR2d 83-1084.) The Court allowed suit for compensatory damages for mental anguish and for the legal fees incurred in resisting the government's claim as well as punitive damages in retribution for the agent's abuses of authority. (See also *Miklautsch v. Comm,* No. A89-291 Civil, 11/6/90 where it was held that the taxpayers have the right to bring action for unreasonable actions taken by IRS employees.) In 1998, Elvis E. "Johnny" Johnson was awarded $3.5 million when the IRS improperly publicized details of his tax situation.

The IRS has recognized the problem of employees' misconduct and has responded. IRS workers and the public may call 800-366-4484 to report IRS employee misconduct. Calls also may go to 800-826-0407 to reach the Treasury Inspector General's Office, which investigates senior IRS managers. In 1997, 172 IRS employees were fired or otherwise separated from the agency due to "administrative actions related to employee violations."

EMPLOYEE DISCIPLINARY ACTION

172 employees out of a total of 102,000 were disciplined because of complaints, misuse of position or authority or rude or discourteous conduct in 1997.

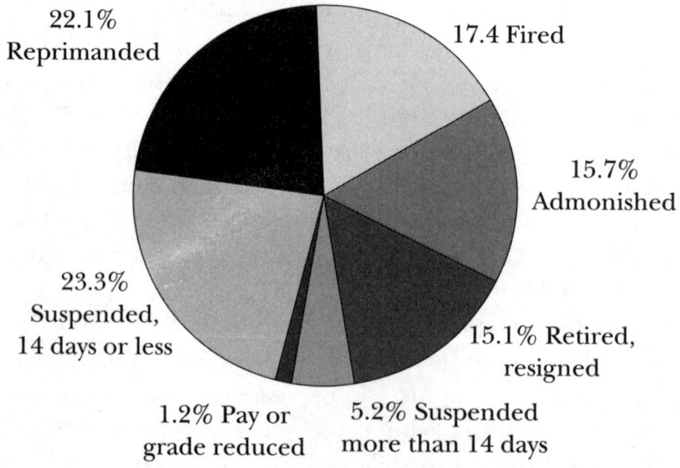

Moreover, before you go to court, you have one more alternative option. An offer in compromise is a contract (Form 656) with the Internal Revenue Service whereby you recognize your liability but offer to satisfy it for less than its full amount. Some indication of when an offer in compromise will be accepted was provided in the July 1984 issue of the Salt Lake City District Tax Practitioner Newsletter. Such offers are entertained only when there is doubt regarding either the taxpayer's liability or the collectibility of the amount assessed.

According to the IRS District Director's letter, before the IRS will accept an offer in compromise, it will almost always require the taxpayer to enter into a collateral agreement to make payments from future income. Where liability has been established by a valid court judgment, the IRS will not compromise the liability. An offer in compromise is made on Form 656 and must be accepted in writing by the Internal Revenue Service. For fiscal year 1995, the IRS accepted 26,668 offers out of the 99,078 filed.

The advantages of an offer in compromise are:

1. You may be able to satisfy the liability by paying less than the full amount.
2. You can defer payment over a number of years, thus reducing the immediate tax burden.
3. Making an offer will delay collection action, even if the offer is not accepted.
4. The compromise offer fixes your liability for the period once it is accepted.
5. If the offer is accepted, and you live up to it, there will be no surprise collection action by the IRS.
6. If you enter into a collateral agreement to make payments from future income, the IRS normally will release any tax liens that have been filed on your property.

Alternatively, the rejection of an offer can result in immediate collection action by the IRS. In addition, the offer requires the submission of detailed financial statements, which will aid the IRS Collection Division should the offer not be accepted; the offer requires a waiver of the statute of limitations; and when an offer is made, you will usually be required to make a cash deposit. This deposit will not draw interest, and it is subject to collection in case the offer is rejected.

An IRS official says a record 27,673 offers were accepted during the year ended September 30, 1996. That was up from 26,668 the prior year and 25,017 in 1995. In 1991, before IRS procedures were streamlined, the IRS accepted only 1,995. Roughly half the offers processed in recent years have been accepted, he says. In 1996, the IRS accepted about $287 million to settle debts totaling about $2.17 billion. The IRS recently released new forms and instructions that it says are designed to be easier for people to complete.

It is important to recognize that *oral* compromise agreements and unsigned settlements will not bind the Internal Revenue Service (see *Boulez,* 87-1 USTC Par. 9177, 59 AFTR 2d 87-608 (CA-D.C., 1987) and *Estate of Oman,* TCM 1987-71).

However, a negotiated agreement to pay in monthly installments over a lengthy period of time is now within the recognized policy guidelines of the IRS. IRS Policy Statement P-5-14 (approved on March 3, 1976) states: "Although there is no specific authority for allowing a taxpayer to liquidate a delinquent account by installment payments, installment agreements are to be considered, and may be entered into, when appropriate." IRM 5223: (4)(g) states that "the amount to be paid monthly on an installment agreement payment will be the difference between the taxpayer's net income and allowable expenses rounded down to the nearest $5.00 increment." The 1998 Tax Reform Act, however, made installment agreements mandatory under certain circumstances if the liability, with interest and penalties, is not more than $10,000.

When you are unable to pay all of your taxes on time, you should file Form 1127. It's called "Application for Extension of Time for Payment of Tax" and it will give you up to six months from the due date to pay the tax you owe. In order to qualify, you must be able to show that you cannot borrow money to pay your tax bill except under terms that would cause severe loss and hardship. If you are granted an extension, all late payment penalties will be excused. However, you will still owe the IRS interest on the late-paid tax. In addition, the IRS now charges a $43 user fee for entering into an installment agreement and a $24 user fee for restructuring or reinstating an installment agreement (IR 94-118).

In entering the judiciary, you have three basic options:

1. *The U.S. Tax Court.* The U.S. Tax Court was first established in 1923. It is made up of 19 judges who travel around the country and hear cases in major cities on a regular basis. It handles only tax litigation and consists exclusively of tax experts. The major advantage of choosing this court is that it will decide the case **before** you have to pay the tax. When you receive the 90-day letter, if you file a petition with the U.S. Tax Court within 90 days of the date of the letter, the Internal Revenue Service may not initiate any further tax collection mechanics until after the case is decided. Be careful: Your letter must be postmarked within 90 days after the *date* of the IRS letter, not after you receive it.

To get complete instructions on how to file a petition, write to the Clerk, United States Tax Court, 400 2nd Street, N.W., Washington, DC 20217, or call (202) 376-2754. Although you may represent yourself at the tax court, it is best to have an attorney specializing in taxation to handle the case.

If the disputed tax is $50,000 or less for any taxable year, a simplified alternative procedure is now available. Here you may want to represent yourself. Upon your request and with approval of the Tax Court, your case can be handled by the small claims division, under the small tax case rules, at little cost to you in time or dollars. Cases in the small claims division are heard by "special trial judges." If you want to use this procedure, write to the previously given address and ask that the clerk send you the small tax case division filing form, Petition, Form 2. You must file the original and two copies of the petition, a copy of the 90-day letter, and a fee of $60, along with your pick of one of the more than 100 cities in which the small claims division of the Tax Court sits. The fee for cases that are not small claims cases is also $60. The case is heard informally by a trial judge and the formal rules of evidence do not apply. One special caveat, however: If you lose your case before the small claims division you cannot appeal. Their decision is final and binding.

Several final comments must be made about the Tax Court. First, while the disputed tax is not paid until after the trial, or until the case is settled, any tax found due will be paid with interest. This interest, however, is no longer tax-deductible. Second, remember that the Tax Court consists exclusively of expert judges. There are no jury trials before the Tax Court. Therefore, if you have a case where the equities are strongly on your side, but the law itself is against you, you might be better advised to stay out of the Tax Court. Finally, don't expect quick action if you file a case in the Tax Court. The court is struggling to cope with a massive and ever-growing backlog of pending cases at a time when it also faces financial woes. Taxpayers in some large cities must now wait as long as a year and a half for their cases to come to trial. Furthermore, experts have predicted the problem will intensify, reflecting the complexity of new laws and confusing tax shelter controversies.

In Rev. Proc. 82-42, the Internal Revenue Service announced new procedures for processing Tax Court cases in an attempt to facilitate earlier disposition through trial or settlement. Docketed cases will be referred by district counsel to the appeals division for settlement unless counsel determines it unlikely that even a partial settlement will be reached there. Cases involving deficiencies of more than $10,000 (including tax and penalties for a period) will then be promptly returned to counsel when it appears that no progress toward a settlement has been made, unless counsel agrees to extend the period for the appeals division's consideration. Cases involving deficiencies of $10,000 or less (including small claims cases) will stay in the appeals division for six months or until receipt of notice of trial in regular cases, or 15 days before the trial calendar call in small claims tax cases if that is earlier. Again, counsel may extend the period in appeals division if it appears that a settlement may be reached.

Dispositions by Amount in Dispute
Tax Cases Filed by Individuals in U.S. Tax Court*
Fiscal Year 1996

Amount in Dispute	Percent of Original Dollars
less than $10,000	51%
$10,000 to $100,000	48%
$100,000 to $1 million	44%
$1 million to $10 million	35%
over $10 million	12%
Total	30%

Source: Internal Revenue Service data.
*Excludes tax shelter cases.

2. *The U.S. District Court.* The U.S. District Court, which is part of the federal judiciary system, is the only place where a jury trial is available. These courts hear all kinds of litigation involving federal laws and any kind of law, state or federal, if the litigants are citizens of different states. You can represent yourself in a district court, but the judges frown upon it. The advantages of going to the district court include the availability of a sympathetic jury and the fact that the judge may be more sympathetic to the equities of your case than to the letter of the tax law. To get into a U.S. District Court, however, you must first pay your tax deficiency and then file a claim for a refund with the Internal Revenue Service. Though the Internal Revenue Service has six months to act on your claim, chances are it will reject the claim promptly and you can then file suit for a refund in your district court. You can obtain information about the procedures for filing suit in a U.S. District Court by calling or writing the Clerk of the Court in the district in which you reside. See the following for the address of your area's office.

ALABAMA

Northern District
104 Federal Courthouse
Birmingham, AL 35203

Middle District
P.O. Box 711
Montgomery, AL 36101

Southern District
P.O. Box 2625
Mobile, AL 36652

ALASKA
Federal Building
701 C Street
Anchorage, AK 99513

ARIZONA
Room 1400
U.S. Courthouse
& Federal Building
230 N. 1st Avenue
Phoenix, AZ 85025

ARKANSAS

Eastern District
P.O. Box 869
Little Rock, AR 72203

Western District
P.O. Box 1523
Fort Smith, AR 72902

CALIFORNIA
Northern District
U.S. Courthouse
P.O. Box 36060
San Francisco, CA 94102

Eastern District
2546 U.S. Courthouse
650 Capitol Mall
Sacramento, CA 95814

Central District
U.S. Courthouse
312 N. Spring Street
Los Angeles, CA 90012

Southern District
940 Front Street
San Diego, CA 92189

COLORADO
Room C-145
U.S. Courthouse
1929 Stout Street
Denver, CO 80294

CONNECTICUT
141 Church Street
New Haven, CT 06510

DELAWARE
Lockbox 18
Federal Building
844 King Street
Wilmington, DE 19801

DISTRICT OF COLUMBIA
U.S. Courthouse
3rd & Constitution
Ave., N.W.
Washington, DC 20001

FLORIDA

Northern District
110 East Park Avenue
Tallahassee, FL 32301

Middle District
P.O. Box 53558
Jacksonville, FL 32201-3558

Southern District
301 N. Miami Avenue
Miami, FL 33128-7788

GEORGIA

Northern District
75 Spring Street, S.W.
2211 U.S. Courthouse
Atlanta, GA 30335

Middle District
P.O. Box 128
Macon, GA 31202

Southern District
P.O. Box 8286
Savannah, GA 31412

GUAM
6th Floor
Pacific News Building
238 O'Hara Street
Agana, Guam 96910

HAWAII
P.O. Box 50129
Honolulu, HI 96850

IDAHO
U.S. Courthouse
P.O. Box 039
550 West Fort Street
Boise, ID 83724

ILLINOIS
Northern District
U.S. Courthouse
219 South Dearborn St.
Chicago, IL 60604

Central District
P.O. Box 315
Springfield, IL 62705

Southern District
U.S. Courthouse &
P.O. Building
P.O. Box 677
Benton, IL 62812

INDIANA
Northern District
Federal Building
Rm 305, 204 S. Main St.
South Bend, IN 46601

Southern District
U.S. Courthouse
Room 105
46 East Ohio Street
Indianapolis, IN 46204

IOWA
Northern District
Federal Building
P.O. Box 4411
Cedar Rapids, IA 52407

Southern District
U.S. Courthouse
Room 200
E. 1st & Walnut Streets
Des Moines, IA 50309

KANSAS
204 U.S. Courthouse
401 N. Market
Wichita, KS 67202

KENTUCKY
Eastern District
P.O. Box 741
Lexington, KY 40586

Western District
230 U.S. Courthouse
601 West Broadway
Louisville, KY 40202

LOUISIANA
Eastern District
U.S. Courthouse
500 Camp Street
Chambers C-151
New Orleans, LA 70130

Middle District
Room 139, 707 Florida Ave.
Federal Building &
U.S. Courthouse
Baton Rouge, LA 70801

Western District
106 Joe D. Waggonner
Federal Building
500 Fannin Street
Shreveport, LA 71101

MAINE
P.O. Box 7505 DTS
Portland, ME 04112

MARYLAND
U.S. Courthouse
101 W. Lombard Street
Baltimore, MD 21201

MASSACHUSETTS
1525 Post Office &
Courthouse Building
Boston, MA 02109

MICHIGAN
Eastern District
U.S. Courthouse
Room 133
Detroit, MI 48226

Western District
458 Federal Building
110 Michigan Street, N.W.
Grand Rapids, MI 49503

MINNESOTA
708 Federal Building
316 N. Robert Street
St. Paul, MN 55101

MISSISSIPPI
Northern District
P.O. Box 727
Oxford, MS 38655

Southern District
P.O. Box 769
Jackson, MS 39205

MISSOURI

Eastern District
U.S. Court & Custom House
1114 Market Street
St. Louis, MO 63101

Western District
U.S. Courthouse
811 Grand Avenue
Room 201
Kansas City, MO 64106

MONTANA
Rm 5405, Federal Bldg.
316 N. 26th Street
Billings, MT 59101

NEBRASKA
P.O. Box 129
Downtown Station
Omaha, NE 68101

NEVADA
300 Las Vegas Blvd., S.
Las Vegas, NV 89101

NEW HAMPSHIRE
P.O. Box 1498
Concord, NH 03301

NEW JERSEY
U.S. Post Office &
Courthouse
P.O. Box 419
Newark, NJ 07102

NEW MEXICO
P.O. Box 689
Albuquerque, NM 87103

NEW YORK

Northern District
Box 950
Albany, NY 12201

Southern District
U.S. Courthouse
Foley Square
New York, NY 10007

Eastern District
U.S. Courthouse
225 Cadman Plaza East
Brooklyn, NY 11201

Western District
604 U.S. Courthouse
Buffalo, NY 14202

NORTH CAROLINA

Eastern District
P.O. Box 25670
Raleigh, NC 27611

Middle District
P.O. Box V-1
Greensboro, NC 27402

Western District
P.O. Box 92
Asheville, NC 28802

NORTH DAKOTA
P.O. Box 1193
Bismarck, ND 58501

NORTHERN MARIANA ISLANDS
P.O. Box 687
Saipan, 96950

OHIO

Northern District
102 U.S. Courthouse
201 Superior Avenue, NE
Cleveland, OH 44114

Southern District
328 U.S. Courthouse
85 Marconi Blvd
Columbus, OH 43215

OKLAHOMA

Northern District
411 U.S. Courthouse
333 W. 4th Street
Tulsa, OK 74120

Eastern District
P.O. Box 607
U.S. Courthouse
Muskogee, OK 74401

Western District
Room 3210
U.S. Courthouse
Oklahoma City, OK 73102

OREGON
516 U.S. Courthouse
620 S.W. Main Street
Portland, OR 97205

PENNSYLVANIA

Eastern District
2609 U.S. Courthouse
Independent Mall West
601 Market Street
Philadelphia, PA 19106

Middle District
P.O. Box 1148
Scranton, PA 18501

Western District
P.O. Box 1805
Pittsburgh, PA 15230

PUERTO RICO
P.O. Box 3671
San Juan, PR 00904

RHODE ISLAND
119 Federal Building
& U.S. Courthouse
Providence, RI 02903

SOUTH CAROLINA
P.O. Box 867
Columbia, SC 29202

SOUTH DAKOTA
Room 220
Federal Building &
U.S. Courthouse
400 South Phillips Ave.
Sioux Falls, SD 57102

TENNESSEE
Eastern District
P.O. Box 2348
Knoxville, TN 37901

Middle District
800 U.S. Courthouse
801 Broadway
Nashville, TN 37203

Western District
950 Federal Building
167 North Main Street
Memphis, TN 38103

TEXAS
Northern District
U.S. Courthouse
1100 Commerce Street
Room 15C22
Dallas, TX 75242

Southern District
P.O. Box 61010
Houston, TX 77208

Eastern District
309 Federal Building &
U.S. Courthouse
211 W. Ferguson Street
Tyler, TX 75702

Western District
Hemisfair Plaza
655 E. Durango Blvd.
San Antonio, TX 78206

UTAH
P.O. Box 45390
Salt Lake City, UT 84145

VERMONT
P.O. Box 945
Burlington, VT 05402

VIRGINIA
Eastern District
307 U.S. Courthouse
600 Granby St.
Norfolk, VA 23510

Western District
P.O. Box 1234
Roanoke, VA 24006

VIRGIN ISLANDS
P.O. Box 720
Charlotte Amalie
St. Thomas, VI 00801

WASHINGTON
Eastern District
P.O. Box 1493
Spokane, WA 99210

Western District
308 U.S. Courthouse
Seattle, WA 98104

WEST VIRGINIA
Northern District
P.O. Box 1518
Elkins, WV 26241

Southern District
P.O. Box 2546
Charleston, WV 25329

WISCONSIN
Eastern District
Room 362
U.S. Courthouse
517 East Wisconsin Ave.
Milwaukee, WI 53202

Western District
P.O. Box 432
Madison, WI 53701

WYOMING
P.O. Box 727
Cheyenne, WY 82001

3. *The U.S. Claims Court.* The U.S. Claims Court is a special court that hears all sorts of claims against the United States, including the claim of overpaying taxes and wanting the money back with interest. Here, too, the tax has to be paid in advance. The major advantage of the claims court is that it does not have to follow the same precedents as do the tax court and district courts. If the other courts appear unfavorable, this may be your best avenue of appeal.

   Currently, judges of the claims court usually hear case argument only in Washington, DC. However, before the argument, there is a fact-finding hearing before a trial judge of the claims court. This hearing will be conducted by the trial judge in a city near where you live. The trial judge will file the findings and the recommended decision. If either you or the Internal Revenue Service disagree, the case will come on for arguments before the full court in Washington. Legal briefs, which must be printed, are also required of both parties. Here the major disadvantage is the substantial expense of litigation. For information on filing suit here, contact the Clerk of the Court of Claims, 1717 Madison Place, N.W., Washington, DC 20005.

   Appeals from both the tax court and the U.S. district courts go to the U.S. courts of appeals. The United States is divided geographically into 12 judicial circuits, each with its own court of appeals. District and tax court decisions in each circuit must follow the precedents of that circuit's court of appeals. Note, however, that decisions of the claims court do not have to follow such precedents. Furthermore, the courts of appeals in different circuits do not have to agree with each other. And if one circuit's court of appeals has not ruled on an issue, the lower courts may disagree among themselves. This means that a supereffective tax planning strategy for tax appeals is to file your case, whenever possible, in a judicial circuit whose precedents support your position.

   Appeals from U.S. courts of appeals go directly to the Supreme Court. In addition, if you lose in the claims court, your appeal is directed first to the Federal Circuit Court of Appeals, then the Supreme Court, which may or may not accept such an appeal. As a practical matter, it accepts very few tax appeals from the claims court, or from appeals courts. Usually, it will only agree to do so where two U.S. courts of appeals have reached opposite results on a similar issue of fact and law.

   One final note about going to court: Under Internal Revenue Code Section 7430, enacted by Section 292(a) of the Tax Equity and Fiscal Responsibility Act of 1982, Public Law 97-248 (September 3, 1982), the Tax Court is enabled to award reasonable litigation costs to a prevailing party who establishes that the position of the IRS commissioner was unreasonable. That means if you exhaust administrative remedies, go to court, and win, and the position of the Internal Revenue Service was not "reasonable," your costs, including what you have to pay to your attorney, will be reimbursed by the Treasury. The Tax Reform Act of 1986 changed the "not reasonable" requirement to one where the taxpayer must establish that the government's position was "not substantially justified." The 1996 Taxpayer's Bill of Rights 2 reversed the burden. If you win in court, the IRS must now prove that *it* was "substantially justified." These awards are now being given—see *Ashburn,* D.C. Alabama, June 15, 1983 and *Marlar Inc. v. U.S.,* W.D. Wash., No. C95–0729L, 5/18/99. In the case of *David Kaufman v. Roscoe Egger,* on March 19, 1985, the First Circuit Court of Appeals ruled that "unreasonable" IRS conduct, even prior to a suit, can be considered. Examining the underlying congressional committee reports, the Court concluded "that Congress intended IRS' liability to be triggered by unreasonable IRS conduct regardless of which stage in the proceedings such conduct occurs." Moreover, the purpose of the provision would be frustrated if the Internal Revenue Service, "after causing the taxpayer all kinds of bureaucratic grief at the administrative level, could escape attorney's fee liability by merely changing its tune after the initiation of a suit by the taxpayer." These litigation costs can be awarded without limit at a rate of $110 per hour[2] (indexed for inflation after 1996) (unless the court finds justification for a higher rate)! Moreover, this provision applies to suits not only in the District Court but also in the Tax Court (suits in the U.S. Claims Courts are covered only between February 28, 1983, and December 31, 1985—see the Tax Reform Act of 1984, Section 714(c)).

Section 7430(a)(1) now permits the recovery of reasonable administrative costs incurred in an administrative proceeding with the IRS in connection with the determination, collection, or refund of any tax, interest, or penalty. Such costs, under Prop. Reg. 301.7430-4, include the following:

1. A representative's fee.
2. IRS administrative fees or similar charges.
3. Costs of studies, analyses, etc., incurred in preparing the taxpayer's case.

A taxpayer must meet the following conditions to be eligible for an award of administrative costs:

1. The underlying issues are not now, and were never, before a court.

---

[2]Now $125 per hour (indexed) under The 1998 Reform Act.

2. The taxpayer is the prevailing party.
3. The taxpayer did not unreasonably prolong the portion of the proceeding for which recovery of costs is sought.
4. The application procedures of the Proposed Regulations were followed.

To be a prevailing party, you must:

1. Establish that the Service's position was not justified.
2. Substantially prevail in the dispute.
3. Meet certain size and net worth limitations.

Administrative awards are available to estates and individuals only if their net worth is not over $2 million ($4 million for joint returns as per the Tax Relief Act of 1997) (based on cost, not fair market value, *Swanson v. Comm.*, No. 21203-92, 106 T.C. No. 3, 2/14/96) on the administrative proceeding date. Businesses, whether incorporated or not, and most other organizations cannot have a net worth of more than $7 million and 500 employees.

The procedures for claiming an award are detailed in Prop. Reg. 301.7430-2(c).

In general, a request must be made within 90 days of the mailing of the Service's final decision.

The claim must be filed with the Service employee who decided that issue, or the district office that considered the matter, if the employee's identity is unknown. The request must contain the following provisions:

1. A statement that neither the underlying issue or issues nor the claim for reasonable administrative costs is, or has been, before a court.
2. A clear and concise assertion as to why the Service's position was not substantially justified.
3. A declaration that the taxpayer prevailed with respect to the amount in controversy or the most significant issue or set of issues.
4. A statement that the taxpayer did not unreasonably prolong the proceeding.
5. An affidavit giving the nature and amount of each recovery item and a copy of the representative's billing records, if fees are requested.
6. Another affidavit stating that the taxpayer meets the net worth and size limitations.
7. An address where the taxpayer may be located.

If your request is denied, you can appeal to the Tax Court.

To survive an audit you must be able to document all deductions and you should demand the audit agent to document any claims of fact or law alleged. Alternatively, some tax practitioners have advised, "When in doubt, deduct." The rationale behind this perspective is that even if your deductions are disallowed, your maximum exposure is to pay the tax you would have paid originally plus about 9 percent interest (this rate will change every six months; the next change is scheduled for January 1, 1998). Remember, however, that your focus must be on tax avoidance rather than tax evasion. The focus of this book, as well, has been on avoidance—the completely legal objective of minimizing your taxes. You should *never* intentionally attempt to defraud the government with reference to your taxes. Such actions can bring about *criminal* penalties. In fact, a competitive writer, the author of *Pay No Income Taxes without Going to Jail*, is in jail. He also just lost a big Tax Court case in which it was found that he treated employees as independent contractors, wrote checks in nonphotocopiable ink, did not report all his income, and did not file returns for several years (Fry T.C. Memo 1991-51). However, the Internal Revenue Service has told its agents not to pursue criminal prosecution of most tax cheaters unless the underpayments average at least $2,500 a year for three straight years. Under these guidelines, a married person earning $20,000 a year and not itemizing deductions could file no return at all and not risk a felony prosecution, although civil penalties would probably be sought.

Further IRS internal guidelines with reference to criminal penalties include the following:

- Do not recommend felony prosecution in complex tax evasion schemes requiring difficult methods of proof unless the total amount of unpaid taxes is at least $10,000, including at least $3,000 for any single year.
- Do not recommend felony prosecution for willful failure to file or for filing a false return unless the average yearly unpaid tax involved is at least $2,500 over a three-year period.
- Do not recommend misdemeanor prosecution for delivery or disclosure of false returns or documents unless the unpaid tax involved is more than $500.

The preceding guidelines contain exceptions for "flagrant or repetitious conduct," which would allow IRS agents to ignore the minimum dollar amounts. These exceptions are more likely to be used against celebrities whose prosecution would be covered by the news media and therefore serve as a deterrent to others. If a doctor were to be prosecuted, for example, they would probably select one who had just written a popular diet book. Alternatively, if they were to look at an attorney, they would want someone well known, particularly a tax lawyer.

Taxpayers in some communities are ten times more likely to face criminal charges by the Internal Revenue Service than those living in others, but IRS recommends such action for only 17 per million taxpayers, according to an analysis of internal government records released April 13, 1996 by Syracuse University's Transactional Records Access Clearinghouse (TRAC).

TRAC said it found the chances of facing IRS criminal charges were higher in the federal judicial districts of Tulsa and Oklahoma City, Louisville, Wheeling, and Charleston, W.Va., New York's Manhattan and Bronx boroughs and northern suburbs, Pittsburgh, Miami, and Indianapolis. Among the least active, it added, were Madison, Wis., Montgomery, Ala., Topeka, Kan., Detroit, Boston, Milwaukee, St. Louis, Philadelphia, Houston, and Des Moines, Iowa.

TRAC, a data research organization connected with Syracuse University, said its findings emerged from an analysis of all 4,542 instances in fiscal 1994, the last year for which statistics are available on when IRS recommended that the Justice Department bring criminal charges.

IRS Criminal Referrals, Prosecutions, and Outcome
Fiscal Years 1980-1995

Fiscal Year	# Referrals	# Prosecutions	# Convictions	#Sentenced Prison
80	2,751	2,047	1,494	—
81	2,433	1,903	1,391	—
82	2,579	1,788	1,348	—
83	3,451	1,921	1,459	—
84	3,380	2,005	1,492	—
85	3,136	1,902	1,414	—
86	3,498	2,149	1,562	—
87	3,113	2,039	1,704	—
88	3,043	2,020	1,697	—
89	3,521	2,029	1,565	—
90	4,651	2,385	1,657	—
91	4,601	2,570	1,917	—
92	5,309	2,742	1,847	989
93	5,078	2,769	2,122	1,089
94	4,542	2,456	1,991	957
95	3,963	2,319	1,812	947

Source: TRAC analysis of Justice Department records.

WHAT ARE YOUR CHANCES?

The odds of facing criminal charges by the IRS depend on where you live. Of the 90 IRS offices, these are the top and bottom five by number of referrals to prosecutors in 1994 per million population.

IRS District Office	Per Capita Referrals
Washington, DC	71
Tulsa, Okla.	65
Louisville, Ky.	60
Oklahoma City	55
Charleston, W. Va.	45
Topeka, Kan.	5
Montgomery, Ala.	4
Madison, Wis.	4
Concord, N.H.	4
Burlington, Vt.	3

Source: Transactional Records Access Clearinghouse, Syracuse University.

According to Mark E. Matthews, Deputy Assistant Attorney General in the Tax Division, "...the certainty of prison time is generally faced only when the loss amount exceeds $40,000." This is not "...a realistic threat to many taxpayers." Do NOT, however, take this as a license to cheat up to $40,000!

REFUNDS

If you are due a refund and if you file by April 15, that refund must be paid by June 1 or else the IRS must pay you interest. Interest on your refund starts accruing 45 days after the return's due date or the date on which you actually filed, whichever is later, and ends accruing 30 days before the date on which the IRS makes out a check to you. The status of a refund may be checked by calling the IRS during regular business hours on a special number available in 27 cities. Under this system, 10 weeks after the return is filed, you may dial the special automated service, then dial your social security number and the amount of the expected refund. You will then be advised when to expect a check. The numbers to call are listed below:

New Jersey	1-800-554-4477	St. Louis, MO	314-241-4700
Phoenix, AZ	602-261-3560	Newark, NJ	201-624-1223
Los Angeles, CA	213-617-3177	Brooklyn, NY	212-858-4461
Oakland, CA	415-839-4245	Buffalo, NY	716-856-9320

Denver, CO	303-592-1118	Manhattan, NY	212-406-4080
Washington, DC	202-628-2929	Cincinnati, OH	513-684-3531
Jacksonville, FL	904-353-9579	Cleveland, OH	216-522-3037
Atlanta, GA	404-221-6572	Portland, OR	503-294-5363
Chicago, IL	312-886-9614	Philadelphia, PA	215-592-8946
Indianapolis, IN	317-634-1550	Nashville, TE	615-242-1541
Baltimore, MD	301-244-7306	Dallas, TX	214-767-1792
Boston, MA	617-523-8602	Houston, TX	713-850-8801
Detroit, MI	313-961-4282	Seattle, WA	206-343-7221
St. Paul, MN	612-224-4288	Milwaukee, WI	414-886-1615

If you have not read this book carefully, you may lose an audit and have to go into Collections. As of September 1, 1995, the IRS has implented new procedures which provide a consistent framework for evaluating a taxpayer's maximum ability to pay. The procedural changes center around allowable expenses—specifically, the types and amounts of expenses that are allowed.

BACKGROUND

The change in procedures came about as a result of concerns from tax practitioners and the General Accounting Office (GAO).

In order to address these concerns, a task force, consisting of National Office and district collection employees and NTEU, was organized to develop new Internal Revenue Manual (IRM) procedures. They received input and feedback from field focus groups as well as representatives from various tax practitioner organizations during the course of the development process.

PROCEDURES

The new procedures establish national standards for reasonable amounts for five necessary expenses: (1) food, (2) housekeeping supplies, (3) apparel and services, (4) personal care products and services, and (5) miscellaneous. All standards, except miscellaneous, are derived from the Bureau of Labor Statistics (BLS) Consumer Expenditure Survey. The miscellaneous standard has been established by the Service.

Local standards will be established for housing and transportation. Utilities are included under housing. "Other" expenses, not covered under the national or local standards (e.g., health care, job-related education), will be allowed if they meet the necessary expense test.

NECESSARY EXPENSE TEST

An expense is deemed to be necessary if it meets the test of:

- providing for a taxpayer's health and welfare and/or the production of income and
- being reasonable in amount.

ALLOWABLE NECESSARY EXPENSES

Necessary expenses will always be allowed when determining the amount of a taxpayer's disposable income. The national standards establish reasonable and allowable amounts for five types of necessary expenses.

CONDITIONAL EXPENSES

If an expense doesn't meet the necessary expense test, it is considered to be conditional. Conditional expenses will be allowed only if the taxpayer can pay the tax liability in full, including accruals, within three years. In addition, the expense amount must be reasonable and the taxpayer must be in compliance with all filing and paying requirements. If the liability cannot be paid within three years, taxpayers may have up to one year to modify or eliminate conditional expenses.

If expenses are determined to be excessive, e.g., luxury cars or extravagant housing, and the taxpayers cannot pay the liability within three years, they will have up to one year to adjust these expenses.

Installment agreements over three years

In general, if an installment agreement will last longer than three years, only necessary expenses will be allowed. However, the one-year rule will allow taxpayers time to adjust or eliminate their conditional expenses.

OFFERS IN COMPROMISE

Only necessary expenses will be allowed when Offers in Compromise are being evaluated. Conditional expenses will not be allowed.

Cases with an assessed balance under $10,000

The new procedures do not affect cases that have an assessed balance under $10,000 which can be processed under the Streamlined Installment Agreement procedures.

SUBSTANTIATION

Expenses may need to be substantiated by the taxpayer.

BENEFITS EXPECTED

The benefits expected from these new procedures include:

- consistency and fairness when evaluating a taxpayer's financial condition;
- improved relationships with taxpayers and practitioners since they know what to expect;
- additional revenue.

Moreover, the 1996 IRS appropriation bill (Public Law 104-52) includes the requirement that $13 million be used on a test program to use private counsel law firms and debt collection agencies in the collection activities of IRS.

- Of the cases involved in this program, 60 percent are in queue (cases currently awaiting assignment to field collection function), and 40 percent are specified as currently not collectible.
- The cases to be worked are for taxpayers currently or formerly located in Alaska, Arizona, California, Colorado, Hawaii, Idaho, Montana, Nevada, New Mexico, Oregon, Utah, Washington, and Wyoming.
- Contractors will not be engaged in work that is inherently governmental. They will locate taxpayers, and remind them of their tax liability and how to make payments. They will not have collection or enforcement authority.

All requests for proposals were to be submitted to IRS by April 12, 1996. Awards will be for one year, with an option for one additional year.

All requests for further information on this test program must be in writing. These requests can be faxed to (202) 283-1514, referencing "Collection Related Activity" in the fax.

In conclusion, it is important to reiterate that this book has not taught you how to evade taxes but rather how legally, within the full ambit of our tax code, to reduce your taxes to zero. According to a 1987 report issued by the American Bar Association's Commission on Taxpayer Compliance, one-third of all taxpayers deliberately fail to claim tax deductions to which they believe they are entitled. (Reasons for not taking these deductions include concern that they might not be correct, ignorance or forgetfulness, insufficient records, perceptions that the deduction was too trivial or too complicated, and fear of audits.) If you want to pay more in taxes than the law requires, you may. In 1983, 3,500 taxpayers voluntarily coughed up a total of $300,000 in voluntary donations to the Internal Revenue Service in an attempt to reduce the national debt. In fiscal 1984, the government received 2,513 gifts, totaling $405,007. Through July 27, 1985, the Internal Revenue Service counted an additional 2,205 voluntary—and deductible—gifts, totaling $350,394, to help Uncle Sam reduce the public debt. Americans donated $1,697,366 to the Bureau of the Public Debt in fiscal 1986 for the Debt Reduction Fund. Of this amount, $1.1 million came via the Internal Revenue Service, thanks to a note in tax return instructions. An additional $719,516 arrived in the six months ending March 31, 1987, bringing the then-to-date total since 1961 to $13,138,462. Through fiscal 1993, the total is $38.6 million. If you want to pay more taxes, you therefore have the opportunity to do so.

A great deal has been written and said on the question of the morality of tax saving in general, and on those who save taxes in particular. Perhaps the best statement on tax avoidance—the legal minimization of your tax liability—was written by Judge Learned Hand:

> If I understand the Commissioner, he wishes us to consider that these deeds may have been a preliminary step in a reprehensible scheme to lessen ... income taxes. There is not the faintest ground for imputing any such purpose to the parties at bar; and if there were, it ought not to count. Over and over again courts have said that there is nothing sinister in so arranging one's affairs as to keep taxes as low as possible. Everybody does so, rich or poor; and all do right, for nobody owes any public duty to pay more than the law demands; taxes are enforced exactions, not voluntary contributions. To demand more in the name of morals is mere Cant. (*Commissioner v. Neuman*, 159 F. 2d 848.)
>
> February 20, 1947

According to IRS figures, the 1998 overall audit rate for all returns declined from 1.28% in 1997 to 0.99% in 1998. Individual "face to face" exams for the year ending September 30, 1999 are expected to fall to only 0.38% of all individual returns filed. The percentage of individual income tax returns audited in 1996 was 1.67 percent, the same as 1995, up from 1.08 in 1994, 0.92 in 1993, and 1.00 percent in 1991. This is higher than the 1.12 percent audited in 1986, 1.31 percent in 1985, 1.27 percent in 1984, 1.49 percent in 1983, and 1.55

percent in 1982. The jump in the examination rate for individuals from 1.08% to 1.67% was due exclusively to a large increase in Service Center correspondence examinations.

IRS Audit Staff and Number of Individual Returns Audited

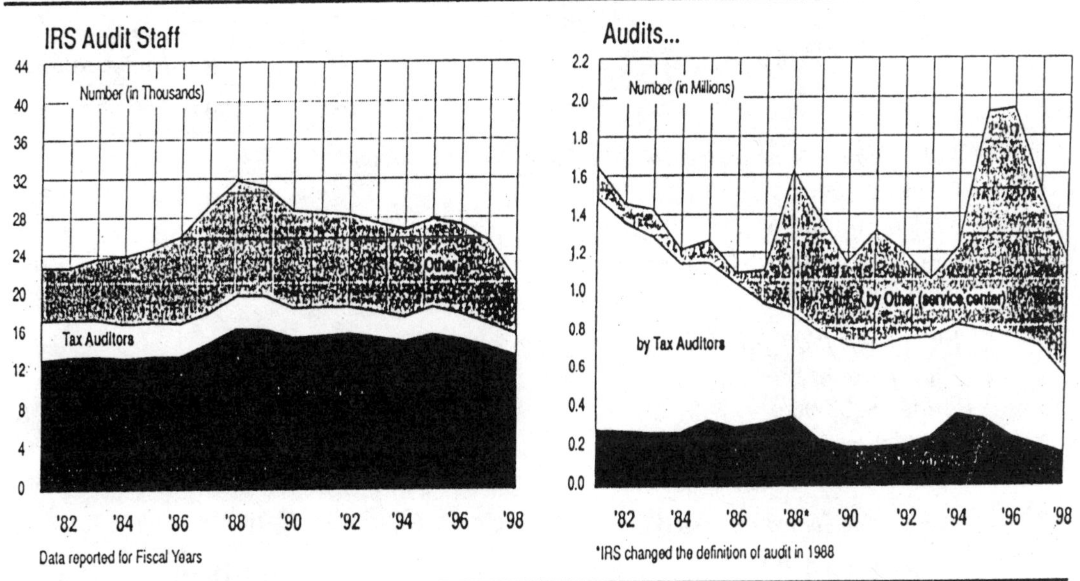

Source: IRS data from TRAC

Returns examined include examinations by correspondence by Service Centers, office examinations by tax auditors, and field examinations by revenue agents. Here's how the total *audit* coverage of individual returns breaks down:

	1994	1995	1996
Service Centers	31.1%	58.5%	
60.8%			
Office audit	37.2	23.9	26.2
Field audit	29.7	17.6	13.0

The number of office audits rose from 458,830 to 509,420 while field audits dropped from 338,605 to 252,430. Overall, only 0.22 percent of all individual returns were examined by field audit.

The following table shows the chances of being examined in fiscal 1997 as compared to 1996. The data is classified by types and amounts of income, type of returns, etc. The percentage of returns examined is shown separately for each category. For example, of individual returns filed with Schedule Cs showing total business gross receipts of from $25,000 to $100,000, the audit rate in 1996 was 285 per 10,000 such returns.

	Percentage of Returns Audited	
	1997	**1996**
Individuals—Nonbusiness (based on total positive income)		
Under 25,000	1.36%	1.62%
$25,000 to under $50,000	0.70	0.95
$50,000 to under $100,000	0.77	1.05
$100,000 and over	2.77	2.85
Individuals filing Schedule C showing gross receipts as indicated		
Under $25,000	3.19	4.21
$25,000 to under $100,000	2.57	3.08
$100,000 and over	4.13	4.09
Corporation (based on assets)		
Under $250,000	1.19	1.04
$250,000 to under $1,000,000	3.52	2.18
$1,000,000 to under $5,000,000	7.70	6.07
$5,000,000 to under $10,000,000	16.02	15.01
$10,000,000 to under $50,000,000	20.10	19.53
$50,000,000 to under $100,000,000	19.59	22.06
$100,000,000 to under $250,000,000	22.80	27.52
$250,000,000 and over	46.77	49.61
S Corporations	1.04	0.92
Partnerships	0.59	0.49

Estate tax (based on gross estate)		
Under $1,000,000	7.88	6.83
$1,000,000 to under $5,000,000	20.75	18.88
$5,000,000 and over	48.41	47.43
Gift tax	0.88	0.90

For 1996, the "no-change" rate for individual returns averaged 14 percent for office audits, 8 percent for field audits, and 35 percent for service center correspondence audits.

For 1996, in office audit, additional tax and penalty averaged $3,051 per individual return. In field audit, revenue agents recommended increases averaging $15,942 per individual return. Service Centers recommended an average of $1,714 per individual return. The corresponding figures for 1995 were $3,497, $13,403 and $1,404.

PENALTIES AND INTEREST

Late Filing of a Return: There is a penalty of 5 percent of the unpaid tax for each month or fraction thereof that the return is late, up to a maximum of 25 percent. For example, assume you owe $2,000 on your Form 1040, which you file on April 20 (five days late). The late filing penalty is $100. There is a minimum late *filing* penalty of the lesser of $100 or the tax due if the return is not filed within 60 days of the prescribed due date.

Understatement of Taxes: In IRS ruling 8802003, the Internal Revenue Service ruled that a taxpayer was liable for a 25 percent substantial understatement penalty even though his tax liability had been satisfied through withholding or estimated payments. In this case, the tax returns for more than three years were filed only after numerous contacts and inquiries by IRS personnel. The IRS ruled that the substantial underpayment penalty is imposed if an underpayment of taxes is attributable to an understatement that exceeds the greater of 10 percent of the tax required to be shown on the return or $5,000. An understatement is generally the excess of the amount of tax required to be shown on a tax return over the actual amount of tax shown on the return. The IRS concluded that for this purpose, the amount of tax shown on the return did not include any additional tax shown on a return filed *after* the Internal Revenue Service had contacted the taxpayer about the liability for the year. Moreover, the amount of tax required to be shown on the return is the tax *without* regard to any payments of tax or estimated tax by the taxpayer.

However, the Tax Court has held that the 25 percent penalty on a tax underpayment attributable to a substantial understatement of tax applies to the unpaid amount of tax after reduction by the amount of federal taxes withheld from a taxpayer's wages. (See *W.A. Woods, II,* C.C.H. Dec. 44903 91 T.C., No. 11.) The substantial understatement penalty is now 20 percent.

Negligence: There is a negligence penalty of 5 percent of the underpaid tax, plus 50 percent of the interest due on the portion of the underpayment attributable to negligence or intentional disregard. This 50 percent of the interest charge is a penalty and cannot be deducted from federal taxes.

Moreover, in Technical Advice Memorandum 8527012, the Internal Revenue Service ruled that a 5 percent negligence penalty may be imposed in the case of a taxpayer who was entitled to a refund on a late-filed return where the late filing was due to negligence or intentional disregard of the rules and regulations. According to the TAM, "the failure to file a timely tax return in itself can constitute the negligence or intentional disregard of rules and regulations." Whether this Technical Advice Memorandum can withstand the test of judicial scrutiny, however, is arguable.

Late Payment of Tax: There is a penalty of .5 percent (increasing to 1 percent on the tenth day after the date a notice of levy is given) of the tax due for each month or fraction thereof that the payment is late, up to a maximum of 25 percent. For example, assume you owe $2,000 on your Form 1040, which you filed timely, but did not pay the tax due until April 30. The late *payment* penalty is $10. In the event that the return is neither timely *filed* nor timely *paid,* both penalties will apply for the first five months, but the combined monthly penalty cannot exceed 5/(5.5) percent. After the five-month period, the late payment penalty continues at .5 percent per month until the maximum 25 percent is reached. Obviously, if you are short of cash and cannot pay the tax due at the filing date, you should still file the return. Remember that an extension of time avoids a penalty for failure to file but does not extend the time to pay the tax. These penalties apply to most types of returns, such as income, payroll, and fiduciary tax returns. They will be waived only if the failure to file or failure to pay is due to "reasonable cause," such as illness or incapacity.

Interest: In addition to the penalties, interest will compound daily on any taxes and penalties due until they are paid. The current interest rate, about 8 percent, will change on January 1, 2000. The rate is adjusted quarterly and calculated on the basis of the short-term federal rate plus 3 percent as of the first month of each quarter, effective as of the following calendar quarter.

For example, assume the short-term federal rate during January 2000 is 6 percent. Therefore, an underpayment rate of 9 percent will be established for the calendar quarter beginning April 1, 2000. Note that rates of interest paid by the IRS to corporate taxpayers for overpayments are always 1 percent lower than the rates paid to the Internal Revenue Service for underpayments. For non-corporations, the rates are the same. The personal interest paid and the penalties are both now not deductible.

Failure to File Information Returns: There is a $50 penalty for failure to file required information returns and statements with the IRS. There is an additional $50 penalty for failure to provide a copy to the payee. Thus, a failure *both* to file the information return with the IRS and to provide a copy to the payee results in a penalty of $100 per failure, with a total aggregate maximum penalty of $200,000. Every person engaged in a trade or business (including nonprofit organizations) must file an information return for payments of employees' salaries, rent and royalties, nonemployee compensation (independent contractors), interest, and dividends. Information returns are required if payments to a single individual total $600 or more, except for interest and dividends, where the limit is $10. Of course, all employee wages and salaries are reported on Form W-2 regardless of amount paid.

Stopping Interest: Interest on taxes owed is compounded daily, and charging interest on interest is allowed. In Revenue Proclamation 84-58, I.R.B. 1984-33, 9, the IRS detailed the steps that should be taken to stop the running of interest on a contested IRS determination. You may stop the running of interest by prepaying the amount contested, without jeopardizing your right to contest the issue, or by posting a cash bond. The prepayment would draw interest and the bond would not. However, the bond could be withdrawn at any time before assessment. Note, however, that a payment response to a proposed liability—e.g., as a result of a revenue agent's report—will be treated as a payment of tax, rather than a cash bond, unless you specifically designate the remittance as a "deposit in the nature of a cash bond." A remittance that is made before liability is proposed, however, will be treated as a cash bond. If the cash bond exceeds the amount of tax ultimately determined, you may have it applied against other liabilities, either assessed or unassessed. Furthermore, you may make a partial payment, but you must designate the part of the liability that is proposed to be satisfied. If the IRS cannot tell whether the payment is a partial payment of tax or a cash bond, it will treat it as being in the latter category. Moreover, the bond must include interest to date in order to stop the further running of interest on any interest accrued.

Partial Payments: If you do not pay the entire amount owed to the Internal Revenue Service, a partial payment generally will be applied first to tax, then to penalty, and finally to the interest that is owed.

Frivolous Tax Penalty: A frivolous tax penalty of up to $5,000 can be assessed on a taxpayer who institutes a Tax Court proceeding primarily to delay payment or for frivolous reasons. Moreover, a $5,000 penalty can be imposed upon any taxpayer who, in furtherance of a frivolous position or with a prima facie intent to delay or impede administration of the tax law, files a purported return that fails to contain information from which the correctness of a reported tax liability can be determined, or that clearly indicates that the tax liability shown must be substantially incorrect.

In fact, the IRS can assess a penalty against a taxpayer who files a return that it deems frivolous even when no taxes are owed and a return is not required to be filed. For example, in *Bradley v. U.S.* (No. 85-2445, May 22, 1987, CA9), the taxpayer wrote a statement to the IRS saying that he refused to pay taxes because of the government's intervention in Central America and filed that statement with his Form 1040. The taxpayer owed no tax and was not required to file a return. However, a notice was sent to Bradley informing him that he had filed a frivolous return and that a penalty was being assessed. The court upheld the penalty because the Form 1040 that Bradley returned purported to be a tax return but lacked the information on which the substantial correctness of the self-assessment could be judged and took a frivolous position.

Interest on Erroneous Refunds: Normally, if you receive an erroneous refund, the Internal Revenue Service will require that you pay it back with interest. However, in Delegation Order No. 231, published in *The Federal Register* on July 11, 1988, the IRS delegated authority to district service center directors to determine administratively that interest is not due on erroneous refunds under certain circumstances. These circumstances include the following:

1. Documentation is present that leaves no doubt that an IRS error caused the erroneous refund to be issued.

2. Documentation is present that substantiates that repayment of the refund has been made in full.

3. The official is satisfied—after considering the relative size of the erroneous refund, the amount of the interest involved, the circumstances surrounding any delay in the repayment of the refund, and the handling and collection cost that would be entailed—that a waiver would be fair and equitable to the government and the taxpayer.

Original Income Tax Return, 1913

Form 1040.

TO BE FILLED IN BY COLLECTOR.

List No. ....

.... *District of* ....

Date received ....

INCOME TAX.

THE PENALTY
FOR FAILURE TO HAVE THIS RETURN IN THE HANDS OF THE COLLECTOR OF INTERNAL REVENUE ON OR BEFORE MARCH 1 IS $20 TO $1000.

(SEE INSTRUCTIONS ON PAGE 4.)

TO BE FILLED IN BY INTERNAL REVENUE BUREAU.

File No. ....

Assessment List ....

Page ...... *Line* ......

UNITED STATES INTERNAL REVENUE.

RETURN OF ANNUAL NET INCOME OF INDIVIDUALS.

(As provided by Act of Congress, approved October 3, 1913.)

RETURN OF NET INCOME RECEIVED OR ACCRUED DURING THE YEAR ENDED DECEMBER 31, 191____

(FOR THE YEAR 1913, FROM MARCH 1 TO DECEMBER 31.)

Filed by (or for) .... *of* ....

(Full name of individual.) (Street and No.)

in the City, Town, or Post Office of .... *State of* ....

(Fill in pages 2 and 3 before making entries below.)

1. GROSS INCOME (see page 2, line 12)	$	......	......	....
2. GENERAL DEDUCTIONS (see page 3, line 7)	$	......	......	....
3. NET INCOME	$	......	......	....

Deductions and exemptions allowed in computing income subject to the normal tax of 1 per cent.

4. Dividends and net earnings received or accrued, of corporations, etc., subject to like tax. (See page 2, line 11) .... $ ....

5. Amount of income on which the normal tax has been deducted and withheld at the source. (See page 2, line 9, column A) ....

6. Specific exemption of $3,000 or $4,000, as the case may be. (See Instructions 3 and 19) ....

Total deductions and exemptions. (Items 4, 5, and 6)	$....	.....	.....	......
7. TAXABLE INCOME on which the normal tax of 1 per cent is to be calculated. (See Instruction 3).	$....	.....	.....	......

8. When the net income shown above on line 3 exceeds $20,000, the additional tax thereon must be calculated as per schedule below:

	INCOME				TAX			
1 per cent on amount over $20,000 and not exceeding $50,000	$ ...	......	......	....	$ ...	......	......	......
2 " " 50,000 " " 75,000	......	......	......	......	......	......	......	......
3 " " 75,000 " " 100,000	......	......	......	......	......	......	......	......
4 " " 100,000 " " 250,000	......	......	......	......	......	......	......	......
5 " " 250,000 " " 500,000	......	......	......	......	......	......	......	......
6 " " 500,000	......	......	......	......	......	......	......	......
Total additional or super tax					$ ...	......	......	......
Total normal tax (1 per cent of amount entered on line 7)					$ ...	......	......	......
Total tax liability					$ ...	......	......	......

STATE TAXES

To aid in the filing of state tax returns, the following is a list of telephone numbers and addresses for obtaining out-of-state income tax forms:

ALABAMA
(205) 262-1112
State Dept. of Rev
Income Tax Division
P.O. Box 327410
Montgomery, AL
36132-7410

ALASKA
(907) 465-2302
Dept. of Rev.
S.O.B. Box SA
Juneau, AK 99811

ARIZONA
(602) 542-4260
Dept. of Rev.
Attn: Forms
1600 W. Monroe
Phoenix, AZ 85007

ARKANSAS
(501) 682-7255
Dept. of Finance and
Administration
Rev. Division
P.O. Box 3628
Little Rock, AR 72203

CALIFORNIA
(916) 635-8023
Franchise Tax Board
Tax Forms Request
P.O. Box 942840
Sacramento, CA
94240-0070

COLORADO
(303) 534-1408
Dept. of Rev.
1375 Sherman Street
Denver, CO 80261

CONNECTICUT
(203) 566-8520
State Tax Dept.
Dept. of Rev. Services
92 Farmington Avenue
Hartford, CT 06105

DELAWARE
(302) 571-3300
Dept. of Finance
Division of Rev.
Delaware State Building
820 N. French St.
Wilmington, DE 19801

FLORIDA
(904) 487-3107
Dept. of Rev.
Supply Dept.
501 S. Calhoun St.
Tallahassee, FL
323/99-0100

GEORGIA
(404) 656-4293
Income Tax Unit
Dept. of Rev.
Trinity-Washington Bldg.
Atlanta, GA 30334

HAWAII
(808) 548-3270
First Taxation District
830 Punch Bowl St.
P.O. Box 259
Honolulu, HI 96809

IDAHO
(208) 334-7660
State Tax Commission
700 W. State St.
P.O. Box 36
Boise, ID 83722

ILLINOIS
(217) 782-3336
Dept. of Rev.
101 W. Jefferson
Springfield, IL 62708

INDIANA
(317) 232-2189
Dept. of Rev.
100 N. Senate Ave.
Room 113
Indianapolis, IN
46204-2253

IOWA
Dept. of Rev.
Hoover State Office
Building
Des Moines, IA 50319

KANSAS
(913) 296-305
Dept. of Rev.
Division of Taxation
Box 12001
Topeka, KS 66612-2001

KENTUCKY
(502) 564-3658
Rev. Cabinet
Property and Mail Service
Frankfort, KY 40620

LOUISIANA
(504) 925-7532
Dept. of Rev.
P.O. Box 201
Baton Rouge, LA 70821

MAINE
(207) 289-3695
Bureau of Taxation
Income Tax Section
Station 24
Augusta, ME 04333

MARYLAND
(301) 974-3117
Comp. of the Treasury
Income Tax Division
Annapolis, MD 21401

MASSACHUSETTS
(617) 727-4392
Income Tax Bureau
Services and Supplies Section
100 Cambridge Street
Boston, MA 02204

MICHIGAN
(517) 335-1144
Dept. of Treasury
Treasury Building
430 W. Allegan St.
Lansing, MI 48922

MINNESOTA
(612) 296-3781
Minnesota Dept. of Rev.
Tax Division
Mail Station 4451
St. Paul, MN 55145

MISSISSIPPI
(601) 359-1105
State Tax Commission
P.O. Box 960
Jackson, MS 39205

MISSOURI
(314) 751-4866
Dept. of Rev.
P.O. Box 3022
Jefferson City, MO 65102

MONTANA
(406) 444-2981
Income Tax Division
Sam Mitchell Building
Helena, MT 59620

NEBRASKA
(402) 471-2971
Dept. of Rev.
Box 94818
Lincoln, NE 68509-4818

NEVADA
(702) 885-4892
Dept. of Taxation
Capitol Complex
Carson City, NV 89710

NEW HAMPSHIRE
(603) 271-2191
Dept. of Rev.
61 S. Spring St.
P.O. Box 457
Concord, NH 03302

NEW JERSEY
(609) 292-6400
Division of Taxation
50 Barrack St.
Trenton, NJ 08646-0269

NEW MEXICO
(505) 827-0700
Rev. Division
P.O. Box 630
Santa Fe, NM 87509-0630

NEW YORK CITY
(718) 935-6000
Dept. of Finance
Forms Information
25 Elm Place, 3rd Floor
Brooklyn, NY

NEW YORK STATE
(518) 457-2772
Dept. of Taxation and Finance
Taxpayer Service
Harriman Campus
State Office Building
Albany, NY 12227

NORTH CAROLINA
(919) 733-3991
Dept. of Rev.
Box 25000
Raleigh, NC 27640

NORTH DAKOTA
(701) 224-3450
State Tax Commission
State Capitol
Bismarck, ND 58505

OHIO
(614) 433-7750
Dept. of Taxation
Forms Request
P.O. Box 2679
Columbus, OH 43270

OKLAHOMA
(405) 521-3108
Income Tax Division
2501 Lincoln Blvd
Oklahoma City, OK
73194-0020

OREGON
(503) 371-2244
Dept. of Rev.
955 Center St., N.E.
Salem, OR 97310

PENNSYLVANIA
(717) 986-4621
Dept. of Rev.
Bureau of Admin.
Services
Dept. 281200
Harrisburg, PA
17128-1200

RHODE ISLAND
(401) 277-3934
Division of Taxation
289 Promenade St.
Providence, RI 02908

SOUTH CAROLINA
(803) 737-5000
Tax Commission
Individual Income Tax
Division
P.O. Box 125
Columbia, SC 29214

SOUTH DAKOTA
(605) 773-3311
Dept. of Rev.
700 Governors Dr.
Pierre, SD 57501-2276

TENNESSEE
(615) 741-3133
Dept. of Rev.
Andrew Jackson
State Office Bldg.
Room 807
500 Deaderick St.
Nashville, TN 37242

TEXAS
(512) 463-4600
Comptroller's Office
Capitol Station
Austin, TX 78774

VERMONT
(802) 828-2545
Pavillion Office Bldg.
Dept. of Taxes
Montpelier, VT 05602

UTAH
(801) 530-6306
Heber Wells Building
160 East, 300 South
Salt Lake City, UT 84134

VIRGINIA
(804) 367-8055
Dept. of Taxation
P.O. Box 1317
Richmond, VA
23210-1317
Attn: Forms Request
Unit P.O. Box 3784

WASHINGTON
(206) 753-5540
Dept. of Rev.
AX-02
Olympia, WA 98504

WASHINGTON, D.C.
(202) 727-6104
District of Columbia
Finance Office Rev. Div.
Room 1046
300 Indiana Ave., N.W.
Washington, D.C. 20001

WEST VIRGINIA
(304) 348-3333
State Tax Dept.
Taxpayer Service Division
P.O. Box 3784
Charleston, WV 25337-3784

WISCONSIN
(608) 266-1961
Dept. of Rev.
P.O. Box 8903
Madison, WI 53708

WYOMING
(307) 777-7378
The State of Wyoming
Secretary of State
Capitol Building
Cheyenne, WY 82002-0020
Unit P.O. Box 3784
Charleston, WV

THE TAXPAYER'S BILL OF RIGHTS

The Technical and Miscellaneous Revenue Act of 1988 (TAMRA) created a consolidated statutory system that addressed a wide range of procedural subjects, including extensive changes in collection procedures. The intent of the Taxpayer's Bill of Rights is to provide a better balance between taxpayers' rights and the IRS's authority in administering the federal tax system. The Bill enhances many safeguards and remedies previously available to taxpayers and established several new restrictions on the procedures governing the assessment and collection of taxes by the Internal Revenue Service.

The provisions of the Bill include the following: The Internal Revenue Service must provide taxpayers with a written statement of taxpayer rights and the obligations of the Internal Revenue Service during audit, repeals, refund, and collection processes when taxpayers are contacted regarding determinations or collections of tax.

Within one year after November 10, 1988, the IRS must prescribe standards for selecting a reasonable time and place for taxpayer interviews. These regulations should provide that it is not reasonable to require an interview at a service office other than the one closest to the taxpayer's home. Moreover, it is unreasonable for the IRS to audit a taxpayer at his or her place of business if the business is so small that doing so effectively requires the taxpayer to close the business, except where facts, such as inventory, must be verified by a direct visit.

The Internal Revenue Service must prescribe procedures for a taxpayer to make an audio recording of an interview at his or her own expense. The IRS can also record an interview, provided that the taxpayer is given advance notice and a transcript or copy of the recording upon request and payment of costs. These changes largely codify existing practices.

The IRS must notify a taxpayer that an interview may be suspended at any time if the taxpayer clearly states the desire to consult with an authorized representative—that is, an attorney or accountant. Moreover, the IRS cannot require a taxpayer to accompany an authorized representative to an interview unless it issues an administrative summons.

The IRS must abate any portion of penalties on tax attributable to erroneous written advice provided by the IRS. However, the Bill does not require abatement of interest on deficiencies arising from such erroneous advice. The new provision applies (1) if the advice was given in response to a specific written request made after 1988, (2) if the advice was reasonably relied upon, and (3) if the penalty or addition did not result from the taxpayer's failure to provide full and accurate information to the IRS.

The Bill extends the time period within which levies can be issued by the IRS and within which banks must respond to a levy. The required minimum period of time between the IRS's issuance to a taxpayer of a notice of levy and the actual levy is increased from 10 to 30 days. Similarly, banks must now wait 21 days before surrendering deposits in response to a levy. The amount to be surrendered includes any interest that accrues during the escrow period.

Any notice of levy must contain a statement describing the statutory provisions and administrative procedures relating to the levy, sale and redemption of property, the administrative appeals available to contest the levy, and the alternatives available to the taxpayer (including an installment payment agreement) for preventing the use of a levy. This statement must be written in simple and nontechnical terms.

The Bill prohibits the use of a levy if the IRS estimates that the expenses that will be incurred for the levy and sale of the property will exceed the property's fair market value at the time of the levy.

Moreover, the Bill expanded the types and amounts of property exempt from levy. The exemption for wages and salary was increased from $75 plus $25 for each dependent, per week, to a weekly amount equal to the taxpayer's standard deduction and allowable personal exemptions, divided by 52. The exemption for fuel, provisions, furniture, and personal effects was also increased from $1,500 to $1,550 in 1989 and $1,600 thereafter. Similarly, the exemptions for books, tools, and personal effects was increased from $1,000 to $1,050 in 1989 and $1,100 thereafter. A new exemption was created for the principal residence of a taxpayer, except in jeopardy cases or where the district director or assistant district director personally approves the levy in writing. New exemptions were also created for certain public assistance and Job Training Partnerships payments.

The Bill directs that the IRS provide an accelerated appeals process to determine whether any seized personal property used in a trade or business should be released from levy on any appropriate statutory grounds. Such grounds would include the taxpayer's entering into an installment agreement with respect to the liability or an IRS determination that the levy "is creating an economic hardship due to the financial condition of the taxpayer."

The owner of seized property now has the right to request that that property be sold within 60 days after such a request.

The Bill requires the IRS to issue regulations under which taxpayers may obtain a review of a publicly filed notice of lien. The taxpayer will be able to correct erroneous filings—for example, when the underlying tax liability has been satisfied or the assessment was untimely or improperly made.

Regardless of whether a taxpayer challenges the lien, the IRS is required to issue a special certificate of release whenever a lien is found to be erroneously filed. The certificate must be filed expeditiously—"if practicable, within 14 days"—after the error is determined. It must also include a statement that the filing of the notice was erroneous.

The Bill codifies the current IRS practice of entering into installment agreements when taxpayers are unable to satisfy a tax delinquency in full. However, the IRS is given the authority to alter, modify, or terminate an agreement if it determines that the financial condition of the taxpayer has significantly changed. The IRS must give the taxpayer at least 30 days' notice prior to the action and must provide the reason for its determination.

The Bill allows the IRS's taxpayer ombudsman to issue taxpayer assistance orders (TAOs) that may include releasing taxpayers from levies of property and directing the IRS to cease collection attempts, though such orders can be modified or rescinded by certain other IRS officials. The issuance of a TAO will suspend any applicable period of limitation from the date of the taxpayer's application until the date of the ombudsman's decision on the application.

The Bill expands the jurisdiction of the Tax Court to intercede when the IRS decides to seize taxpayer property immediately if a taxpayer petition has been filed with the court. Effective November 10, 1988, the Tax Court has concurrent jurisdiction with the taxpayer's local district court to enjoin the assessment or collection of a tax that is the subject of a timely filed petition with the Tax Court. Note that taxpayers who are the subject of a premature assessment or collection activity but who have not yet filed a petition with the Tax Court must still pursue their injunctive remedy in a district court.

Moreover, the Tax Court now has jurisdiction, upon motion by a taxpayer, to order a refund if the IRS has failed to make a refund within 120 days after the court's decision becomes final. This provision is effective for overpayments not refunded by February 8, 1989.

In addition, the Tax Court is granted limited jurisdiction to consider disputes concerning the interest due on deficiencies that it has determined. The jurisdiction of both the Tax Court and the district courts to hear certain causes of action arising from jeopardy assessments and levies has also been expanded.

The Bill creates a new cause of action for damages against the United States in district courts for the reckless or intentional disregard of the Code or Regulations by an IRS employee in connection with the collection of any tax. However, to be eligible for a recovery, a taxpayer must exhaust all administrative remedies. This civil action must be commenced within 2 years after the date the right of action accrued, and the liability of the government under this provision is limited to the lesser of $100,000 or the sum of the "actual, direct economic damages, sustained as a proximate cause" of the reckless or intentional actions of the employee, plus the costs of the action.

Note that the court has the right to assess damages up to $10,000 against a taxpayer who the court determines to have instituted or maintained a frivolous or groundless action under this provision.

The Bill also creates a new cause of action for damages against the United States in a federal district court for an IRS failure to release a lien after 1988. Both the exhaustion of administrative remedies and the period of limitations are the same as the above newly created cause of action.

Reasonable litigation costs were available to prevailing taxpayers prior to the Bill. TAMRA creates an expanded remedy to permit taxpayers to recover reasonable administrative costs incurred for certain administrative proceedings. Such costs include costs incurred on or after the earlier of (1) the date the taxpayer receives a notice of deficiency or (2) the date the taxpayer received the decision notice from the IRS Office of Appeals. In order to collect, the taxpayer must be a "prevailing party," and the taxpayer retains the burden of proof that the position of the government was not substantially justified. "The position of the U.S." means the position taken by the IRS after the dates referred to above. If neither date is applicable, then the position of the United States is the position taken in litigation.

The Bill contains provisions that prevent temporary regulations from remaining in effect longer than three years.

The Bill contains provisions preventing the IRS from using tax enforcement results as a basis for evaluating its employees or for imposing or suggesting production goals or quotas for its employees to meet. Each district director must certify quarterly, in a letter to the commissioner, that tax enforcement records are not being used in a prohibited manner.

The Bill provides for a statutorily required position as second assistant commissioner responsible for Taxpayer Services.

The Bill creates a new civil penalty against tax return preparers who disclose any information obtained in preparing a return or who use such information for any purpose other than preparing a return. This new penalty is $250 for each such disclosure, up to a maximum of $10,000 per calendar year. The criminal penalty for such disclosures is modified to apply only when the prohibited disclosure is done knowingly or recklessly.

The creation of the Taxpayer's Bill of Rights represented a significant advance in the direction of tax equity and fairness. Further advances were achieved by the Taxpayer's Bill of Rights 2 passed in 1996, and 3, passed in 1998. The details of those laws can be found in Chapter 12, Stealth Tax Reform, and Chapter 14, The Internal Revenue Service Restructuring and Reform Act of 1998.

IRS PICKS UP SPEED ON INFORMATION SUPERHIGHWAY

With a computer and a modem, you can get federal tax forms and information online via FedWorld, a service that provides free public access to federal government information.

"This is another way the IRS is keeping its promise to serve our customers more efficiently and change the way we do business," said Bob Wenzel, IRS Chief of Strategic Planning and Communications.

Through FedWorld, you can access the IRS's Internal Revenue Information Services (IRIS) bulletin board to download and print forms, publications, and monthly newsletters. Once printed, online tax forms can be filled in and mailed off just like standard forms. This means instant access to forms and information that previously would have taken days or weeks to receive.

FedWorld can be dialed direct by setting modem parity to none, data bits to 8, stop bit to 1, terminal emulation to ANSI, duplex to full, and communication software to dial 703-321-8020. FedWorld is also available over the Internet by setting the telnet to fedworld.gov (192.239.93.3). For Internet File Transfer Protocol (FTP) services, connect to ftp.fedworld.gov (192.239.92.205). The address for the IRS homepage on the World Wide Web is http://www.irs.ustreas.gov. On it, you can get a list of qualified charitable organizations.

Technical questions regarding FedWorld and IRIS can be directed to the FedWorld help desk, 24 hours a day, at 703-487-4608.

To check the status of a refund, call 1-800-829-4477.

State Tax Department Internet Sites

Alaska Department of Revenue	http://www.revenue.state.ak.us/
Arizona Department of Revenue	http://aspin.asu.edu/aztax/
California Franchise Tax Board	http://www.ftb.ca.gov/
Colorado Department of Revenue	http://www.state.co.us/gov_dir/revenue_dir/home_rev.html
Delaware Division of Revenue	http://www.state.de.us/govern/agencies/revenue/revenue.htm
Florida Department of Revenue	http://fcn.state.fl.us/dor/revenue.html
Hawaii Department of Taxation	http://www.hawaii.gov/icsd/tax/tax.html
Idaho State Tax Commission	http://www.state.id.us/apa/idapa35/taxindex.htm
Illinois Department of Revenue	http://www.revenue.state.il.us/
Indiana Department of Revenue	http://www.state.in.us/sic//HTML/revenue.html
Iowa Department of Revenue and Finance	http://ww.state.ia.us/government/drf/index.html
Kansas Department of Revenue	http://www.ink.org.public/kdor/
Kentucky Revenue Cabinet	http://www.state.ky.us/agencies/revenue/rev.home.htm
Louisiana Department of Revenue Taxation	http://www.rev.state.la.us/
Maine Bureau of Taxation	http://www.state.me.us/taxation
Maryland Comptroller of the Treasury	http://www.inform.umd.edu:8080/UMS+State/MD_/Resources/COT/
Massachusetts Department of Revenue	http://www.magnet.state.ma.us/dor/
Michigan Department of Treasury	http://info.migov.state.mi.us/depts/treasury/treasury.html

Minnesota Department of Revenue	http://www.state.mn.us/ebranch/mdor/
Missouri Division of Taxation and Collection	http://www.state.mo.us/dor/tax
Nebraska Department of Revenue	http://www.nol.org/home/NDR/
Nevada Department of Taxation	http://www.state.nv.us/inprog.htm
New Hampshire Department of Revenue	http://www.state.nh.us/agency/drabbs.htm
New Jersey Division of Taxation	http://www.state.nj.us/treasury/taxation/
New Mexico Taxation and Revenue Department	http://www.state.nm.us/tax/
New York State Department of Taxation and Finance	gopher://unix2.nysed.gov:71/11/agencies/executive/tax
North Carolina Department of Revenue	http://www.dor.state.nc.us/DOR/
Ohio Department of Taxation	http://www.odh.ohio.gov/tax/
Oklahoma Tax Commission	http://www.state.ok.us/~tax/
Oregon Department of Revenue	http://www.dor.state.or.us/
Pennsylvania Department of Revenue	http://www.revenue.state.pa.us/
South Carolina Department of Revenue	http://www.state.sc.us:80/dor/
South Dakota Department of Revenue	http://www.state.sd.us/state/executive/revenue/revenue.html
Tennessee Department of Revenue	http://www.state.tn.us/revenue/
Texas Comptroller of Public Accounts	http://www.window.texas.gov/
Utah State Tax Commission	http://txdtm01.tax.ex.state.ut.us/
Virginia Department of Taxation	http://www.state.va.us/tax/tax.html
Washington Department of Revenue	http://www.wa.gov/DOR/wador.htm
Wisconsin Department of Revenue	http://badger.state.wi.us/agencies/dor/
Wyoming Department of Revenue	http://www.state.wy.us/state/government/state_agencies/text_revenue.html

Tax-Related Websites

www.aicpa.org—	The AICPA's Website, rated highly by professionals and non-CPAs alike. This site gives AICPA Tax Division members access to the online version of *The Tax Advisor.*
www.taxsites.com— or www.el.com/elinks/taxes	Probably the only other tax Website you'll really need, since either is a "metasite" (a site whose sole purpose is to provide links to other Websites of the same topic).
www.irs.ustreas.gov—	Homesite of the Internal Revenue Service, helpful for accessing and downloading Federal forms, instructions and other IRS materials.
www.ssa.gov—	The Social Security Administration's Website, which includes the text of totalization agreements the U.S. has with various foreign countries.
www.mtc.gov—	This site is a must for practitioners who service multistate clients. Here, the Multistate Tax Commission keeps you informed on the state uniformity of nexus issues.
www.ipl.org—	Even the Internet has a public library, and this is it. A great source for links to background information and numerous online publications.
The Big Six and national firms sites—	Although designed to market the firm's products and services, these sites offer useful information with their respective tax pages and links: www.arthurandersen.com www.bdo.com www.ey.com www.colybrand.com www.gt.com www.pw.com www.us.deloitte.com www.kpmg.com
Other sites—	The larger firms aren't the only ones in the game; some smaller practitioners are offering their own blend of creative and informative tax sites. Some to try: www.taxman.com; www.taxwizard.com

Governmental Sites

Internal Revenue Service: *http://www.irs.ustreas.gov*

Department of Treasury: *http://www.ustreas.gov*

Federal Register reflecting latest information on pending legislation: *http://www.access.gpo.gov/su_docs/aces/aces140.html*

Supreme Court and appellate court cases: *http://law.house.gov/6.htm*

IRS Bulletins: *http://www.fedworld.gov*

Highlights of latest revenue rulings, court opinions, legislation and other tax topics: *http://www.ppcinfo.com/5-min.htm*

Tax Code Online: *http://www.law.cornell.edu/uscode*

Federal Web Locator: *http://www.law.vill.edu/Fed-Agency/fedwebloc.html*

Library of Congress: *http://lcweb.loc.gov/homepage/lchp.html*

SEC database of corporate information: *http://www.sec.gov/edgarhp.html*

General Accounting Office: *http://www.gao.gov*

"The Internal Revenue Service has adopted a new mission statement:

Provide America's taxpayers top quality service by helping them understand and meet their tax responsibilities and by applying the tax law with integrity and fairness to all.

Taxpayers have the right to be treated fairly, professionally, promptly and courteously by Internal Revenue Service employees. Our goal at the IRS is to protect the rights of taxpayers and ensure the highest confidence in the integrity, efficiency and fairness of our tax system. To make sure that taxpayers always receive such treatment, you should know about the many rights you have at each step of the tax process.

1. Receive an explanation of the examination and collection processes and taxpayers' rights under these processes before or at the initial interview for the determination or collection of tax.

2. Have representation at any time during these processes by a person who may practice before the IRS, except in certain criminal investigations.

3. Make an audio recording or receive a copy of such a recording of an interview for the determination or collection of tax.

4. Reasonably rely on written advice of the IRS that was provided in response to a specific written request.

5. File an application for relief with the IRS National Taxpayer Advocate or Local Taxpayer Advocate in a situation in which the taxpayer is suffering or about to suffer a significant hardship as a result of the manner in which the IRS is administering the tax laws.

6. Receive a written notice of levy, no less than 30 days prior to enforcement, that explains in non-technical terms the levy procedures and the administrative appeals and alternatives to levy that are available."

April 19, 1999

"Activities engaged in by a citizen to prevent the Government from confiscating the fruits of his labor are the noblest endeavors of man."

BENJAMIN FRANKLIN

Appendix A

Cost Recovery/Depreciation

The Tax Reform Act of 1986 created a new accelerated depreciation system, which groups property in the following classes:

- 3-year class—asset depreciation range (ADR) midpoints of 4 years and less, except that automobiles and light trucks are excluded and present law for horses that are in the 3-year class is retained. The method is 200 percent declining balance, switching to straight line.
- 5-year class—ADR midpoints of more than 4 years and less than 10 years, adding automobiles, light trucks, qualified technological equipment, computer-based central office switching equipment, renewable energy and biomass properties that are small power production facilities, and research and experimentation property. The method is 200 percent declining balance.
- 7-year class—ADR midpoints of 10 years and more but less than 16 years, adding single-purpose agricultural and horticulture structures and property with an ADR midpoint that is not classified elsewhere. The method is 200 percent declining balance.
- 10-year class—ADR midpoints of 16 years and more but less than 20 years. The method is 200 percent declining balance.
- 15-year class—ADR midpoints of 20 years and more but less than 25 years, including sewerage treatment plants and telephone distribution plants and related equipment used for the two-way exchange of voice and data communications. The method is 150 percent declining balance.
- 20-year class—ADR midpoints of 25 years and more, other than real property with an ADR midpoint of 27.5 years and more, and including sewer pipes. The method is 150 percent declining balance.
- 27.5 years—residential real property. The method is straight line.
- 31.5 years—nonresidential real property (real property that is not residential rental property and does not have an ADR midpoint of less than 27.5 years). The method is straight line.

For personal property, both the first and last depreciation allowances for an asset reflect the one-half-year convention. The prior law mid-month convention applies to real property, and a midquarter convention applies to taxpayers who place more than 40 percent of their property in service during the last quarter of the taxable year.

Moreover, there is no recapture of previously allowed depreciation deductions in the case of residential rental property and nonresidential real property. Because of the elimination of capital gains, all gains will now be ordinary income.

Generally, the effective date for all depreciation provisions is for property placed in service on or after January 1, 1987. However, the Act allows taxpayers to start using the new system for property placed in service after July 31, 1986. In other words, buyers of 3- and 5-year property did not have to wait until January 1987 to get the benefit of the more rapid write-offs if property was placed in service between July 31, 1986, and December 31, 1986. The benefits here could be substantial. For example, the first-year deduction for a $100,000 tractor under the new law is $33,333, versus $25,000 under prior law. These benefits continued through 1987 as well. A tractor placed in service in the last five months of 1986 receives a $44,444 deduction under the new system, versus $38,000 under prior law. Therefore, the combined write-off in 1986 and 1987 would be $14,777 greater under the new option than under prior regulations.

Note that OBRA '93 changed nonresidential real estate from a 31.5-year basis to a 39-year basis for property placed in service on or after May 13, 1993 unless there was a binding contract or construction began prior to May 13, 1993.

The following tables list percentages for property in the 3-, 5-, 7-, 10-, 15-, and 20-year classes.

TABLE 1. General Depreciation System
Applicable Depreciation Method: 200 or 150 Percent
Declining Balance Switching to Straight Line
Applicable Recovery Periods: 3, 5, 7, 10, 15, 20 Years
Applicable Convention: Half-Year

If the Recovery Year Is:	and the Recovery Period Is: 3-Year	5-Year	7-Year	10-Year	15-Year	20-Year
	the Depreciation Rate Is:					
1	33.33	20.00	14.29	10.00	5.00	3.750
2	44.45	32.00	24.49	18.00	9.50	7.219
3	14.81	19.20	17.49	14.40	8.55	6.677
4	7.41	11.52	12.49	11.52	7.70	6.177
5		11.52	8.93	9.22	6.93	5.713
6		5.76	8.92	7.37	6.23	5.285
7			8.93	6.55	5.90	4.888
8			4.46	6.55	5.90	4.522
9				6.56	5.91	4.462
10				6.55	5.90	4.461
11				3.28	5.91	4.462
12					5.90	4.461
13					5.91	4.462
14					5.90	4.461
15					5.91	4.462
16					2.95	4.461
17						4.462
18						4.461
19						4.462
20						4.461
21						2.231

TABLE 2. General Depreciation System
Applicable Depreciation Method: 200 or 150 Percent Declining Balance Switching to Straight Line
Applicable Recovery Periods: 3, 5, 7, 10, 15, 20 Years
Applicable Convention: Mid-Quarter
(Property Placed in Service in First Quarter)

If the Recovery Year Is:	and the Recovery Period Is:					
	3-Year	5-Year	7-Year	10-Year	15-Year	20-Year
	the Depreciation Rate Is:					
1	58.33	35.00	25.00	17.50	8.75	6.563
2	27.78	26.00	21.43	16.50	9.13	7.000
3	12.35	15.60	15.31	13.20	8.21	6.482
4	1.54	11.01	10.93	10.56	7.39	5.996
5		11.01	8.75	8.45	6.65	5.546
6		1.38	8.74	6.76	5.99	5.130
7			8.75	6.55	5.90	4.746
8			1.09	6.55	5.91	4.459
9				6.56	5.90	4.459
10				6.55	5.91	4.459
11				0.82	5.90	4.459
12					5.91	4.460
13					5.90	4.459
14					5.91	4.460
15					5.90	4.459
16					0.74	4.460
17						4.459
18						4.460
19						4.459
20						4.460
21						0.557

TABLE 3. General Depreciation System
Applicable Depreciation Method: 200 or 150 Percent Declining Balance Switching to Straight Line
Applicable Recovery Periods: 3, 5, 7, 10, 15, 20 Years
Applicable Convention: Mid-Quarter
(Property Placed in Service in Second Quarter)

If the Recovery Year Is:	and the Recovery Period Is:					
	3-Year	5-Year	7-Year	10-Year	15-Year	20-Year
	the Depreciation Rate Is:					
1	41.67	25.00	17.85	12.50	6.25	4.688
2	38.89	30.00	23.47	17.50	9.38	7.148
3	14.14	18.00	16.76	14.00	8.44	6.612
4	5.30	11.37	11.97	11.20	7.59	6.116
5		11.37	8.87	8.96	6.83	5.658
6		4.26	8.87	7.17	6.15	5.233
7			8.87	6.55	5.91	4.841
8			3.33	6.55	5.90	4.478
9				6.56	5.91	4.463
10				6.55	5.90	4.463
11				2.46	5.91	4.463
12					5.90	4.463
13					5.91	4.463
14					5.90	4.463
15					5.91	4.462
16					2.21	4.463
17						4.462
18						4.463
19						4.462
20						4.463
21						1.673

**TABLE 4. General Depreciation System
Applicable Depreciation Method: 200 or 150 Percent
Declining Balance Switching to Straight Line
Applicable Recovery Periods: 3, 5, 7, 10, 15, 20 Years
Applicable Convention: Mid-Quarter
(Property Placed in Service in Third Quarter)**

If the Recovery Year Is:	and the Recovery Period Is:					
	3-Year	5-Year	7-Year	10-Year	15-Year	20-Year
	the Depreciation Rate Is:					
1	25.00	15.00	10.71	7.50	3.75	2.813
2	50.00	34.00	25.51	18.50	9.63	7.289
3	16.67	20.40	18.22	14.80	8.66	6.742
4	8.33	12.24	13.02	11.84	7.80	6.237
5		11.30	9.30	9.47	7.02	5.769
6		7.06	8.85	7.58	6.31	5.336
7			8.86	6.55	5.90	4.936
8			5.53	6.55	5.90	4.566
9				6.56	5.91	4.460
10				6.55	5.90	4.460
11				4.10	5.91	4.460
12					5.90	4.460
13					5.91	4.461
14					5.90	4.460
15					5.91	4.461
16					3.69	4.460
17						4.461
18						4.460
19						4.461
20						4.460
21						2.788

TABLE 5. General Depreciation System
Applicable Depreciation Method: 200 or 150 Percent Declining Balance Switching to Straight Line
Applicable Recovery Periods: 3, 5, 7, 10, 15, 20 Years
Applicable Convention: Mid-Quarter
(Property Placed in Service in Fourth Quarter)

If the Recovery Year Is:	and the Recovery Period Is:					
	3-Year	5-Year	7-Year	10-Year	15-Year	20-Year
	the Depreciation Rate Is:					
1	8.33	5.00	3.57	2.50	1.25	0.938
2	61.11	38.00	27.55	19.50	9.88	7.430
3	20.37	22.80	19.68	15.60	8.89	6.872
4	10.19	13.68	14.06	12.48	8.00	6.357
5		10.94	10.04	9.98	7.20	5.880
6		9.58	8.73	7.99	6.48	5.439
7			8.73	6.55	5.90	5.031
8			7.64	6.55	5.90	4.654
9				6.56	5.90	4.458
10				6.55	5.91	4.458
11				5.74	5.90	4.458
12					5.91	4.458
13					5.90	4.458
14					5.91	4.458
15					5.90	4.458
16					5.17	4.458
17						4.458
18						4.459
19						4.458
20						4.459
21						3.901

The following tables show recovery percentages for residential and nonresidential real property.

TABLE 6. General Depreciation System
Applicable Depreciation Method: Straight Line
Applicable Recovery Period: 27.5 Years
Applicable Convention: Mid-Month

Recovery Year Is:	and the Month in the First Recovery Year the Property Is Placed in Service Is:											
	1	2	3	4	5	6	7	8	9	10	11	12
	the Depreciation Rate Is:											
1	3.485	3.182	2.879	2.576	2.273	1.970	1.667	1.364	1.061	0.758	0.455	0.152
2	3.636	3.636	3.636	3.636	3.636	3.636	3.636	3.636	3.636	3.636	3.636	3.636
3	3.636	3.636	3.636	3.636	3.636	3.636	3.636	3.636	3.636	3.636	3.636	3.636
4	3.636	3.636	3.636	3.636	3.636	3.636	3.636	3.636	3.636	3.636	3.636	3.636
5	3.636	3.636	3.636	3.636	3.636	3.636	3.636	3.636	3.636	3.636	3.636	3.636
6	3.636	3.636	3.636	3.636	3.636	3.636	3.636	3.636	3.636	3.636	3.636	3.636
7	3.636	3.636	3.636	3.636	3.636	3.636	3.636	3.636	3.636	3.636	3.636	3.636
8	3.636	3.636	3.636	3.636	3.636	3.636	3.636	3.636	3.636	3.636	3.636	3.636
9	3.636	3.636	3.636	3.636	3.636	3.636	3.636	3.636	3.636	3.636	3.636	3.636
10	3.637	3.637	3.637	3.637	3.637	3.637	3.636	3.636	3.636	3.636	3.636	3.636
11	3.636	3.636	3.636	3.636	3.636	3.636	3.637	3.637	3.637	3.637	3.637	3.637
12	3.637	3.637	3.637	3.637	3.637	3.637	3.636	3.636	3.636	3.636	3.636	3.636
13	3.636	3.636	3.636	3.636	3.636	3.636	3.637	3.637	3.637	3.637	3.637	3.637

14	3.637	3.637	3.637	3.637	3.637	3.637	3.636	3.636	3.636	3.636	3.636	3.636
15	3.636	3.636	3.636	3.636	3.636	3.636	3.637	3.637	3.637	3.637	3.637	3.637
16	3.637	3.637	3.637	3.637	3.637	3.637	3.636	3.636	3.636	3.636	3.636	3.636
17	3.636	3.636	3.636	3.636	3.636	3.636	3.637	3.637	3.637	3.637	3.637	3.637
18	3.637	3.637	3.637	3.637	3.637	3.637	3.636	3.636	3.636	3.636	3.636	3.636
19	3.636	3.636	3.636	3.636	3.636	3.636	3.637	3.637	3.637	3.637	3.637	3.637
20	3.637	3.637	3.637	3.637	3.637	3.637	3.636	3.636	3.636	3.636	3.636	3.636
21	3.636	3.636	3.636	3.636	3.636	3.636	3.637	3.637	3.637	3.637	3.637	3.637
22	3.637	3.637	3.637	3.637	3.637	3.637	3.636	3.636	3.636	3.636	3.636	3.636
23	3.636	3.636	3.636	3.636	3.636	3.636	3.637	3.637	3.637	3.637	3.637	3.637
24	3.637	3.637	3.637	3.637	3.637	3.637	3.636	3.636	3.636	3.636	3.636	3.636
25	3.636	3.636	3.636	3.636	3.636	3.636	3.637	3.637	3.637	3.637	3.637	3.637
26	3.637	3.637	3.637	3.637	3.637	3.637	3.636	3.636	3.636	3.636	3.636	3.636
27	3.636	3.636	3.636	3.636	3.636	3.636	3.637	3.637	3.637	3.637	3.637	3.637
28	1.970	2.273	2.576	2.879	3.182	3.485	3.636	3.636	3.636	3.636	3.636	3.636
29	0.000	0.000	0.000	0.000	0.000	0.000	0.152	0.455	0.758	1.061	1.364	1.667

TABLE 7. General Depreciation System
Applicable Depreciation Method: Straight Line
Applicable Recovery Period: 31.5 Years
Applicable Convention: Mid-Month

Recovery Year Is:	and the Month in the First Recovery Year the Property Is Placed in Service Is: 1	2	3	4	5	6	7	8	9	10	11	12
	the Depreciation Rate Is:											
1	3.042	2.778	2.513	2.249	1.984	1.720	1.455	1.190	0.926	0.661	0.397	0.132
2	3.175	3.175	3.175	3.175	3.175	3.175	3.175	3.175	3.175	3.175	3.175	3.175
3	3.175	3.175	3.175	3.175	3.175	3.175	3.175	3.175	3.175	3.175	3.175	3.175
4	3.175	3.175	3.175	3.175	3.175	3.175	3.175	3.175	3.175	3.175	3.175	3.175
5	3.175	3.175	3.175	3.175	3.175	3.175	3.175	3.175	3.175	3.175	3.175	3.175
6	3.175	3.175	3.175	3.175	3.175	3.175	3.175	3.175	3.175	3.175	3.175	3.175
7	3.175	3.175	3.175	3.175	3.175	3.175	3.175	3.175	3.175	3.175	3.175	3.175
8	3.175	3.174	3.175	3.174	3.175	3.174	3.175	3.175	3.175	3.175	3.175	3.175
9	3.174	3.175	3.174	3.175	3.174	3.175	3.174	3.175	3.174	3.175	3.174	3.175
10	3.175	3.174	3.175	3.174	3.175	3.174	3.175	3.174	3.175	3.174	3.175	3.174
11	3.174	3.175	3.174	3.175	3.174	3.175	3.174	3.175	3.174	3.175	3.174	3.175
12	3.175	3.174	3.175	3.174	3.175	3.174	3.175	3.174	3.175	3.174	3.175	3.174
13	3.174	3.175	3.174	3.175	3.174	3.175	3.174	3.175	3.174	3.175	3.174	3.175

14	3.175	3.174	3.175	3.174	3.175	3.174	3.175	3.174	3.175	3.174	3.175	3.174
15	3.174	3.175	3.174	3.175	3.174	3.175	3.174	3.175	3.174	3.175	3.174	3.175
16	3.175	3.174	3.175	3.174	3.175	3.174	3.175	3.174	3.175	3.174	3.175	3.174
17	3.174	3.175	3.174	3.175	3.174	3.175	3.174	3.175	3.174	3.175	3.174	3.175
18	3.175	3.174	3.175	3.174	3.175	3.174	3.175	3.174	3.175	3.174	3.175	3.174
19	3.174	3.175	3.174	3.175	3.174	3.175	3.174	3.175	3.174	3.175	3.174	3.175
20	3.175	3.174	3.175	3.174	3.175	3.174	3.175	3.174	3.175	3.174	3.175	3.174
21	3.174	3.175	3.174	3.175	3.174	3.175	3.174	3.175	3.174	3.175	3.174	3.175
22	3.175	3.174	3.175	3.174	3.175	3.174	3.175	3.174	3.175	3.174	3.175	3.174
23	3.174	3.175	3.174	3.175	3.174	3.175	3.174	3.175	3.174	3.175	3.174	3.175
24	3.175	3.174	3.175	3.174	3.175	3.174	3.175	3.174	3.175	3.174	3.175	3.174
25	3.174	3.175	3.174	3.175	3.174	3.175	3.174	3.175	3.174	3.175	3.174	3.175
26	3.175	3.174	3.175	3.174	3.175	3.174	3.175	3.174	3.175	3.174	3.175	3.174
27	3.174	3.175	3.174	3.175	3.174	3.175	3.174	3.175	3.174	3.175	3.174	3.175
28	3.175	3.174	3.175	3.174	3.175	3.174	3.175	3.174	3.175	3.174	3.175	3.174
29	3.174	3.175	3.174	3.175	3.174	3.175	3.174	3.175	3.174	3.175	3.174	3.175
30	3.175	3.174	3.175	3.174	3.175	3.174	3.175	3.174	3.175	3.174	3.175	3.174
31	3.174	3.175	3.174	3.175	3.174	3.175	3.174	3.175	3.174	3.175	3.174	3.175
32	1.720	1.984	2.249	2.513	2.778	3.042	3.175	3.174	3.175	3.174	3.175	3.174
33	0.000	0.000	0.000	0.000	0.000	0.000	0.132	0.397	0.661	0.926	1.190	1.455

Example: Assume American Corporation bought a residential apartment building in January 1986 and a second residential apartment building in January 1987. Both buildings cost $100,000 (exclusive of land).

The 1986 apartment building has a 19-year ACRS recovery period. The depreciation deduction for the first year is $8,800 and for the second year, $8,400—a total of $17,200.

The 1987 apartment building has a 27.5-year recovery period and must be depreciated on a straight-line basis. Based on percentages under the new law, the first-year depreciation deduction is $3,485 and the second-year deduction is $3,636—a total of $7,121.

Placing property in service in 1987 rather than 1986 caused a reduction in depreciation deductions over the first two years of $10,079, a 58.6 percent decrease. If the building were a department store, the first two years' depreciation deductions would be $3,042 and 3,175 under the 1986 law. This $6,217 total is $10,983 less than under prior law—a 63.9 percent reduction.

Table 8 lists depreciation rates for nonresidential real property placed in service after 5/13/93, unless there was a binding contract prior to that date.

TABLE 8. Depreciation Rates for Nonresidential Real Property Placed in Service After May 13, 1993, Unless There Was a Binding Contract Prior to May 13, 1993
Mid-Month Convention
Straight Line—39 Years

Year	Month Property Placed in Service											
	1	2	3	4	5	6	7	8	9	10	11	12
1	2.461%	2.247%	2.033%	1.819%	1.605%	1.391%	1.177%	0.963%	0.749%	0.535%	0.321%	0.107%
2-39	2.564	2.564	2.564	2.564	2.564	2.564	2.564	2.564	2.564	2.564	2.564	2.564
40	0.107	0.321	0.535	0.749	0.963	1.177	1.391	1.605	1.819	2.033	2.247	2.461

Appendix B

Law Prior to the Tax Reform Act of 1986

The following table is provided for tangible personal property depreciation. It uses the 150 percent declining-balance method changing to straight line with the half-year convention.

Property Placed in Service after December 31, 1980 and Prior to January 1, 1987

	Class of Investment			
Ownership Year	**3-Year**	**5-Year**	**10-Year**	**15-Year Utility Property**
	%	%	%	%
1	25	15	8	5
2	38	22	14	10
3	37	21	12	9
4		21	10	8
5		21	10	7
6			10	7
7			9	6
8			9	6
9			9	6
10			9	6
11				6
12				6
13				6
14				6
15				6
	100	100	100	100

The following tables were issued by the Treasury Department on September 10, 1981, for depreciating real estate under the ACRS system from 1/1/81 until 3/15/84.

1. All Real Estate (Except Low-Income Housing)

If the Recovery Year Is:	The Applicable Percentage Is: (Use the column for the month in the first year the property is placed in service)											
	1	2	3	4	5	6	7	8	9	10	11	12
1	12	11	10	9	8	7	6	5	4	3	2	1
2	10	10	11	11	11	11	11	11	11	11	11	12
3	9	9	9	9	10	10	10	10	10	10	10	10
4	8	8	8	8	8	8	9	9	9	9	9	9
5	7	7	7	7	7	7	8	8	8	8	8	8
6	6	6	6	6	7	7	7	7	7	7	7	7
7	6	6	6	6	6	6	6	6	6	6	6	6
8	6	6	6	6	6	6	5	6	6	6	6	6
9	6	6	6	6	5	6	5	5	5	6	6	6
10	5	6	5	5	5	5	5	5	5	5	6	5
11	5	5	5	5	5	5	5	5	5	5	5	5
12	5	5	5	5	5	5	5	5	5	5	5	5
13	5	5	5	5	5	5	5	5	5	5	5	5
14	5	5	5	5	5	5	5	5	5	5	5	5
15	5	5	5	5	5	5	5	5	5	5	5	5
16	—	—	1	1	2	2	3	3	4	4	4	5

2. Low-Income Housing

If the Recovery Year Is:	The Applicable Percentage Is: (Use the column for the month in the first year the property is placed in service) 1	2	3	4	5	6	7	8	9	10	11	12
1	13	12	11	10	9	8	7	6	4	3	2	1
2	12	12	12	12	12	12	12	13	13	13	13	13
3	10	10	10	10	11	11	11	11	11	11	11	11
4	9	9	9	9	9	9	9	9	10	10	10	10
5	8	8	8	8	8	8	8	8	8	8	8	9
6	7	7	7	7	7	7	7	7	7	7	7	7
7	6	6	6	6	6	6	6	6	6	6	6	6
8	5	5	5	5	5	5	5	5	5	5	6	6
9	5	5	5	5	5	5	5	5	5	5	5	5
10	5	5	5	5	5	5	5	5	5	5	5	5
11	4	5	5	5	5	5	5	5	5	5	5	5
12	4	4	4	5	4	5	5	5	5	5	5	5
13	4	4	4	4	4	4	5	4	5	5	5	5
14	4	4	4	4	4	4	4	4	4	5	4	4
15	4	4	4	4	4	4	4	4	4	4	4	4
16	—	—	1	1	2	2	2	3	3	3	4	4

Appendix C

Law After March 14, 1984 (Real Estate)

The following are the cost recovery tables for real estate created by the Tax Reform Act of 1984.

1. 18-Year Real Property (No Mid-Month Convention)—For property placed in service after 3/15/84 and before 6/23/84

The Applicable Percentage Is:

If the Recovery Year Is:	(Use the column for the month in the first recovery year the property is placed in service)										
	1	**2**	**3**	**4**	**5**	**6**	**7**	**8**	**9**	**10-11**	**12**
1	10	9	8	7	6	6	5	4	3	2	1
2	9	9	9	9	9	9	9	9	9	10	10
3	8	8	8	8	8	8	8	8	9	9	9
4	7	7	7	7	7	7	8	8	8	8	8
5	6	7	7	7	7	7	7	7	7	7	7
6	6	6	6	6	6	6	6	6	6	6	6
7	5	5	5	5	6	6	6	6	6	6	6
8	5	5	5	5	5	5	5	5	5	5	5
9	5	5	5	5	5	5	5	5	5	5	5
10	5	5	5	5	5	5	5	5	5	5	5
11	5	5	5	5	5	5	5	5	5	5	5
12	5	5	5	5	5	5	5	5	5	5	5
13	4	4	4	5	5	4	4	5	4	4	4
14	4	4	4	4	4	4	4	4	4	4	4
15	4	4	4	4	4	4	4	4	4	4	4
16	4	4	4	4	4	4	4	4	4	4	4
17	4	4	4	4	4	4	4	4	4	4	4
18	4	4	4	4	4	4	4	4	4	4	4
19			1	1	1	2	2	2	3	3	4

2. 18-Year Property (Mid-Month Convention)—For property placed in service 6/23/84 until 5/8/85

If the Recovery Year Is:	The Applicable Percentage Is: (Use the column for the month in the first recovery year the property is placed in service)											
	1	**2**	**3**	**4**	**5**	**6**	**7**	**8**	**9**	**10**	**11**	**12**
1	9	9	8	7	6	5	4	4	3	2	1	0.4
2	9	9	9	9	9	9	9	9	9	10	10	10.0
3	8	8	8	8	8	8	8	8	9	9	9	9.0
4	7	7	7	7	7	8	8	8	8	8	8	8.0
5	7	7	7	7	7	7	7	7	7	7	7	7.0
6	6	6	6	6	6	6	6	6	6	6	6	6.0
7	5	5	5	5	6	6	6	6	6	6	6	6.0
8	5	5	5	5	5	5	5	5	5	5	5	5.0
9	5	5	5	5	5	5	5	5	5	5	5	5.0
10	5	5	5	5	5	5	5	5	5	5	5	5.0
11	5	5	5	5	5	5	5	5	5	5	5	5.0
12	5	5	5	5	5	5	5	5	5	5	5	5.0
13	4	4	4	5	4	4	5	4	4	4	5	5.0
14	4	4	4	4	4	4	4	4	4	4	4	4.0
15	4	4	4	4	4	4	4	4	4	4	4	4.0
16	4	4	4	4	4	4	4	4	4	4	4	4.0
17	4	4	4	4	4	4	4	4	4	4	4	4.0
18	4	3	4	4	4	4	4	4	4	4	4	4.0
19		1	1	1	2	2	2	3	3	3	3	3.6

3. 18-Year Real Property (No Mid-Month Convention)—For property placed in service after 3/15/84 and before 6/23/84

The Applicable Percentage Is:

(Use the column for the month in the first recovery year the property is placed in service)

If the Recovery Year Is:	1	2	3	4	5	6	7	8	9	10-11	12
1	10	9	8	7	6	6	5	4	3	2	1
2	9	9	9	9	9	9	9	9	9	10	10
3	8	8	8	8	8	8	8	8	9	9	9
4	7	7	7	7	7	7	8	8	8	8	8
5	6	7	7	7	7	7	7	7	7	7	7
6	6	6	6	6	6	6	6	6	6	6	6
7	5	5	5	5	6	6	6	6	6	6	6
8	5	5	5	5	5	5	5	5	5	5	5
9	5	5	5	5	5	5	5	5	5	5	5
10	5	5	5	5	5	5	5	5	5	5	5
11	5	5	5	5	5	5	5	5	5	5	5
12	5	5	5	5	5	5	5	5	5	5	5
13	4	4	4	5	5	4	4	5	4	4	4
14	4	4	4	4	4	4	4	4	4	4	4
15	4	4	4	4	4	4	4	4	4	4	4
16	4	4	4	4	4	4	4	4	4	4	4
17	4	4	4	4	4	4	4	4	4	4	4
18	4	4	4	4	4	4	4	4	4	4	4
19			1	1	1	2	2	2	3	3	4

4. Optional Straight-Line Method for 18-Year Property (Mid-Month Convention)—For property placed in service 6/23/84 until 5/8/85

If the Recovery Year Is:	The Applicable Percentage Is: (Use the column for the month in the first recovery year the property is placed in service)					
	1-2	3-4	5-7	8-9	10-11	12
1	5	4	3	2	1	0.2
2	6	6	6	6	6	6.0
3	6	6	6	6	6	6.0
4	6	6	6	6	6	6.0
5	6	6	6	6	6	6.0
6	6	6	6	6	6	6.0
7	6	6	6	6	6	6.0
8	6	6	6	6	6	6.0
9	6	6	6	6	6	6.0
10	6	6	6	6	6	6.0
11	5	5	5	5	5	5.8
12	5	5	5	5	5	5.0
13	5	5	5	5	5	5.0
14	5	5	5	5	5	5.0
15	5	5	5	5	5	5.0
16	5	5	5	5	5	5.0
17	5	5	5	5	5	5.0
18	5	5	5	5	5	5.0
19	1	2	3	4	5	5.0

5. Optional Straight-Line Method for 18-Year Property (No Mid-Month Convention)—For property placed in service after 3/15/84 and before 6/23/84

The Applicable Percentage Is:

(Use the column for the month in the first recovery year the property is placed in service)

If the Recovery Year Is:	1	2-3	4-5	6-7	8-9	10-11	12
1	6	5	4	3	2	1	0.5
2	6	6	6	6	6	6	6.0
3	6	6	6	6	6	6	6.0
4	6	6	6	6	6	6	6.0
5	6	6	6	6	6	6	6.0
6	6	6	6	6	6	6	6.0
7	6	6	6	6	6	6	6.0
8	6	6	6	6	6	6	6.0
9	6	6	6	6	6	6	6.0
10	6	6	6	6	6	6	6.0
11	5	5	5	5	5	5	5.5
12	5	5	5	5	5	5	5.0
13	5	5	5	5	5	5	5.0
14	5	5	5	5	5	5	5.0
15	5	5	5	5	5	5	5.0
16	5	5	5	5	5	5	5.0
17	5	5	5	5	5	5	5.0
18	5	5	5	5	5	5	5.0
19		1	2	3	4	5	5.0

6. Optional 35-Year Straight-Line Method for 18-Year Real Property (Mid-Month Convention)—For property placed in service 6/23/84 until 5/8/85

If the Recovery Year Is:	The Applicable Percentage Is: (Use the column for the month in the first recovery year the property is placed in service)				
	1-2	3-6	7-10	11	12
1	3	2	1	0.4	0.1
2	3	3	3	3.0	3.0
3	3	3	3	3.0	3.0
4	3	3	3	3.0	3.0
5	3	3	3	3.0	3.0
6	3	3	3	3.0	3.0
7	3	3	3	3.0	3.0
8	3	3	3	3.0	3.0
9	3	3	3	3.0	3.0
10	3	3	3	3.0	3.0
11	3	3	3	3.0	3.0
12	3	3	3	3.0	3.0
13	3	3	3	3.0	3.0
14	3	3	3	3.0	3.0
15	3	3	3	3.0	3.0
16	3	3	3	3.0	3.0
17	3	3	3	3.0	3.0
18	3	3	3	3.0	3.0
19	3	3	3	3.0	3.0
20	3	3	3	3.0	3.0
21	3	3	3	3.0	3.0
22	3	3	3	3.0	3.0
23	3	3	3	3.0	3.0
24	3	3	3	3.0	3.0
25	3	3	3	3.0	3.0
26	3	3	3	3.0	3.0
27	3	3	3	3.0	3.0
28	3	3	3	3.0	3.0
29	3	3	3	3.0	3.0

If the Recovery Year Is:	The Applicable Percentage Is: (Use the column for the month in the first recovery year the property is placed in service) 1-2	3-6	7-10	11	12
30	3	3	3	3.0	3.0
31	2	2	2	2.6	2.9
32	2	2	2	2.0	2.0
33	2	2	2	2.0	2.0
34	2	2	2	2.0	2.0
35	2	2	2	2.0	2.0
36		1	2	2.0	2.0

7. Optional 45-Year Straight-Line Method for 18-Year Real Property (Mid-Month Convention)—For property placed in service 6/23/84 until 5/8/85

If the Recovery Year Is:	The Applicable Percentage Is: (Use the column for the month in the first recovery year the property is placed in service) 1	2	3	4	5	6	7	8	9	10	11	12
1	2.1	1.9	1.8	1.6	1.4	1.2	1.0	0.8	0.6	0.5	0.3	0.1
2	2.3	2.3	2.3	2.3	2.3	2.3	2.3	2.3	2.3	2.3	2.3	2.3
3	2.3	2.3	2.3	2.3	2.3	2.3	2.3	2.3	2.3	2.3	2.3	2.3
4	2.3	2.3	2.3	2.3	2.3	2.3	2.3	2.3	2.3	2.3	2.3	2.3
5	2.3	2.3	2.3	2.3	2.3	2.3	2.3	2.3	2.3	2.3	2.3	2.3
6	2.3	2.3	2.3	2.3	2.3	2.3	2.3	2.3	2.3	2.3	2.3	2.3
7	2.3	2.3	2.3	2.3	2.3	2.3	2.3	2.3	2.3	2.3	2.3	2.3
8	2.3	2.3	2.3	2.3	2.3	2.3	2.3	2.3	2.3	2.3	2.3	2.3
9	2.3	2.3	2.3	2.3	2.3	2.3	2.3	2.3	2.3	2.3	2.3	2.3
10	2.3	2.3	2.3	2.3	2.3	2.3	2.3	2.3	2.3	2.3	2.3	2.3
11	2.3	2.3	2.3	2.3	2.3	2.3	2.3	2.3	2.3	2.3	2.3	2.3
12	2.2	2.2	2.2	2.2	2.2	2.2	2.2	2.2	2.2	2.2	2.2	2.2
13	2.2	2.2	2.2	2.2	2.2	2.2	2.2	2.2	2.2	2.2	2.2	2.2

(continued on next page)

If the Recovery Year Is:	The Applicable Percentage Is: (Use the column for the month in the first recovery year the property is placed in service)											
	1	2	3	4	5	6	7	8	9	10	11	12
14	2.2	2.2	2.2	2.2	2.2	2.2	2.2	2.2	2.2	2.2	2.2	2.2
15	2.2	2.2	2.2	2.2	2.2	2.2	2.2	2.2	2.2	2.2	2.2	2.2
16	2.2	2.2	2.2	2.2	2.2	2.2	2.2	2.2	2.2	2.2	2.2	2.2
17	2.2	2.2	2.2	2.2	2.2	2.2	2.2	2.2	2.2	2.2	2.2	2.2
18	2.2	2.2	2.2	2.2	2.2	2.2	2.2	2.2	2.2	2.2	2.2	2.2
19	2.2	2.2	2.2	2.2	2.2	2.2	2.2	2.2	2.2	2.2	2.2	2.2
20	2.2	2.2	2.2	2.2	2.2	2.2	2.2	2.2	2.2	2.2	2.2	2.2
21	2.2	2.2	2.2	2.2	2.2	2.2	2.2	2.2	2.2	2.2	2.2	2.2
22	2.2	2.2	2.2	2.2	2.2	2.2	2.2	2.2	2.2	2.2	2.2	2.2
23	2.2	2.2	2.2	2.2	2.2	2.2	2.2	2.2	2.2	2.2	2.2	2.2
24	2.2	2.2	2.2	2.2	2.2	2.2	2.2	2.2	2.2	2.2	2.2	2.2
25	2.2	2.2	2.2	2.2	2.2	2.2	2.2	2.2	2.2	2.2	2.2	2.2
26	2.2	2.2	2.2	2.2	2.2	2.2	2.2	2.2	2.2	2.2	2.2	2.2
27	2.2	2.2	2.2	2.2	2.2	2.2	2.2	2.2	2.2	2.2	2.2	2.2
28	2.2	2.2	2.2	2.2	2.2	2.2	2.2	2.2	2.2	2.2	2.2	2.2
29	2.2	2.2	2.2	2.2	2.2	2.2	2.2	2.2	2.2	2.2	2.2	2.2
30	2.2	2.2	2.2	2.2	2.2	2.2	2.2	2.2	2.2	2.2	2.2	2.2
31	2.2	2.2	2.2	2.2	2.2	2.2	2.2	2.2	2.2	2.2	2.2	2.2
32	2.2	2.2	2.2	2.2	2.2	2.2	2.2	2.2	2.2	2.2	2.2	2.2
33	2.2	2.2	2.2	2.2	2.2	2.2	2.2	2.2	2.2	2.2	2.2	2.2
34	2.2	2.2	2.2	2.2	2.2	2.2	2.2	2.2	2.2	2.2	2.2	2.2
35	2.2	2.2	2.2	2.2	2.2	2.2	2.2	2.2	2.2	2.2	2.2	2.2
36	2.2	2.2	2.2	2.2	2.2	2.2	2.2	2.2	2.2	2.2	2.2	2.2
37	2.2	2.2	2.2	2.2	2.2	2.2	2.2	2.2	2.2	2.2	2.2	2.2
38	2.2	2.2	2.2	2.2	2.2	2.2	2.2	2.2	2.2	2.2	2.2	2.2
39	2.2	2.2	2.2	2.2	2.2	2.2	2.2	2.2	2.2	2.2	2.2	2.2
40	2.2	2.2	2.2	2.2	2.2	2.2	2.2	2.2	2.2	2.2	2.2	2.2
41	2.2	2.2	2.2	2.2	2.2	2.2	2.2	2.2	2.2	2.2	2.2	2.2
42	2.2	2.2	2.2	2.2	2.2	2.2	2.2	2.2	2.2	2.2	2.2	2.2
43	2.2	2.2	2.2	2.2	2.2	2.2	2.2	2.2	2.2	2.2	2.2	2.2
44	2.2	2.2	2.2	2.2	2.2	2.2	2.2	2.2	2.2	2.2	2.2	2.2
45	2.2	2.2	2.2	2.2	2.2	2.2	2.2	2.2	2.2	2.2	2.2	2.2
46	0.1	0.3	0.4	0.6	0.8	1.0	1.2	1.4	1.6	1.7	1.9	2.1

8. Optional 35-Year Straight-Line for 18-Year Real Property Used Predominantly Outside the U.S. (Mid-Month Convention)—For property placed in service 6/23/84 until 5/8/85

The Applicable Percentage Is:

If the Recovery Year Is:	(Use the column for the month in the first recovery year the property is placed in service) 1	2	3	4-5	6-8	9-11	12
1	4	4	3	3	2	1	0.2
2	4	4	4	4	4	4	4.0
3	4	4	4	4	4	4	4.0
4	4	4	4	4	4	4	4.0
5	4	4	4	4	4	4	4.0
6	3	3	3	3	4	4	4.0
7	3	3	3	3	3	3	3.8
8	3	3	3	3	3	3	3.0
9	3	3	3	3	3	3	3.0
10	3	3	3	3	3	3	3.0
11	3	3	3	3	3	3	3.0
12	3	3	3	3	3	3	3.0
13	3	3	3	3	3	3	3.0
14	3	3	3	3	3	3	3.0
15	3	3	3	3	3	3	3.0
16	3	3	3	3	3	3	3.0
17	3	3	3	3	3	3	3.0
18	3	3	3	3	3	3	3.0
19	3	3	3	3	3	3	3.0
20	3	3	3	3	3	3	3.0
21	3	3	3	3	3	3	3.0
22	3	3	3	3	3	3	3.0
23	3	3	3	3	3	3	3.0
24	3	3	3	3	3	3	3.0
25	3	2	3	2	2	3	3.0
26	2	2	2	2	2	2	2.0
27	2	2	2	2	2	2	2.0
28	2	2	2	2	2	2	2.0

(continued on next page)

If the Recovery Year Is:	The Applicable Percentage Is: (Use the column for the month in the first recovery year the property is placed in service)						
	1	**2**	**3**	**4-5**	**6-8**	**9-11**	**12**
29	2	2	2	2	2	2	2.0
30	2	2	2	2	2	2	2.0
31	2	2	2	2	2	2	2.0
32	2	2	2	2	2	2	2.0
33	2	2	2	2	2	2	2.0
34	2	2	2	2	2	2	2.0
35	2	2	2	2	2	2	2.0
36		1	1	2	2	2	2.0

9. 19-Year Property (Mid-Month Convention)—For property placed in service after 5/8/85

If the Recovery Year Is:	The Applicable Percentage Is: (Use the column for the month in the first recovery year the property is placed in service)											
	1	**2**	**3**	**4**	**5**	**6**	**7**	**8**	**9**	**10**	**11**	**12**
1	8.8	8.1	7.3	6.5	5.8	5.0	4.2	3.5	2.7	1.9	1.1	.4
2	8.4	8.5	8.5	8.6	8.7	8.8	8.8	8.9	9.0	9.0	9.1	9.2
3	7.6	7.7	7.7	7.8	7.9	7.9	8.0	8.1	8.1	8.2	8.3	8.3
4	6.9	7.0	7.0	7.1	7.1	7.2	7.3	7.3	7.4	7.4	7.5	7.6
5	6.3	6.3	6.4	6.4	6.5	6.5	6.6	6.6	6.7	6.8	6.8	6.9
6	5.7	5.7	5.8	5.9	5.9	5.9	6.0	6.0	6.1	6.1	6.2	6.2
7	5.2	5.2	5.3	5.3	5.3	5.4	5.4	5.5	5.5	5.6	5.6	5.6
8	4.7	4.7	4.8	4.8	4.8	4.9	4.9	5.0	5.0	5.1	5.1	5.1
9	4.2	4.3	4.3	4.4	4.4	4.5	4.5	4.5	4.5	4.6	4.6	4.7
10	4.2	4.2	4.2	4.2	4.2	4.2	4.2	4.2	4.2	4.2	4.2	4.2
11	4.2	4.2	4.2	4.2	4.2	4.2	4.2	4.2	4.2	4.2	4.2	4.2
12	4.2	4.2	4.2	4.2	4.2	4.2	4.2	4.2	4.2	4.2	4.2	4.2
13	4.2	4.2	4.2	4.2	4.2	4.2	4.2	4.2	4.2	4.2	4.2	4.2

If the Recovery Year Is:	The Applicable Percentage Is: (Use the column for the month in the first recovery year the property is placed in service)											
	1	2	3	4	5	6	7	8	9	10	11	12
14	4.2	4.2	4.2	4.2	4.2	4.2	4.2	4.2	4.2	4.2	4.2	4.2
15	4.2	4.2	4.2	4.2	4.2	4.2	4.2	4.2	4.2	4.2	4.2	4.2
16	4.2	4.2	4.2	4.2	4.2	4.2	4.2	4.2	4.2	4.2	4.2	4.2
17	4.2	4.2	4.2	4.2	4.2	4.2	4.2	4.2	4.2	4.2	4.2	4.2
18	4.2	4.2	4.2	4.2	4.2	4.2	4.2	4.2	4.2	4.2	4.2	4.2
19	4.2	4.2	4.2	4.2	4.2	4.2	4.2	4.2	4.2	4.2	4.2	4.2
20	0.2	0.5	0.9	1.2	1.6	1.9	2.3	2.6	3.0	3.3	3.7	4.0

Appendix D

Business Use of "Listed Property"

Prior to 1984, computers, automobiles, and other types of personal property were eligible for annual depreciation deductions with accelerated rates and recovery periods. Where such property was partly used for business purposes and partly used for personal purposes, the allowable amount of the otherwise available depreciation deduction was determined on the basis of the proportion of business use.

In 1984, Congress drew a sharp distinction between property used more than 50 percent for business purposes as compared to property having business use of 50 percent or less. Furthermore, for automobiles, additional restrictions have been imposed upon the maximum amount of yearly depreciation deductions.

The property covered by the stricter rules is referred to as "listed property" and includes the following:

1. passenger automobiles weighing 6,000 pounds or less,
2. other transportation property,
3. entertainment, recreation, or amusement facilities,
4. computers and peripheral equipment, *and*
5. "other" property to be specified by regulations.

For *all* categories of the above listed property used 50 percent or less for business purposes, depreciation is to be determined on the straight-line method over a period of years that is longer than the minimum period otherwise provided.

In addition, satisfaction of the 50 percent test will be determined solely with reference to the use of the property in a *trade or business.* Use of the property in connection with the production of investment income is not taken into account for this purpose. Once it is determined, however, on the basis of business use, whether the property is to be treated under the more than 50 percent or the 50 percent or less rule, the use of the property in investment activities will be taken into account in determining the proportion of the tax benefits that are allowable.

For example, assume a computer is used 40 percent in the conduct of a trade or business and 30 percent for investment activities. The more than 50 percent business use test is *not* satisfied. Depreciation will be determined on the straight-line method. However, *70* percent of that depreciation so determined will be allowable.

Except for *automobiles,* the depreciation deductions for listed property used *more* than 50 percent in a trade or business will be determined under prior law. The accelerated rates and periods under 1987 modified ACRS may be used to determine depreciation and then the percentage of business use will be combined with the percentage of use in investment activities to determine the portion of the total amount of depreciation that will be allowable.

For automobiles, however, including those with more than 50 percent business use, there are additional restrictions and limitations. Depreciation deductions are limited for each year. These fixed limitations apply to all depreciation deductions, not just depreciation under the accelerated method.

If business use is less than 100 percent, you are entitled to claim the portion of the depreciation deduction allowable which corresponds to your business use percentage.

Moreover, leasing an automobile will not avoid the limitations. Lessees of property will be subject to restrictions on lease payments. These restrictions are comparable to the limitations on depreciation that would apply if the automobile were owned instead of leased. The percentage of lease payments allowable will be calculated pursuant to tables published by the Treasury. These restrictions, however, do not apply to the tax benefits available under prior law to the lessors of property regularly engaged in the business of leasing property.

Employees

If you are an employee, the rules are even more stringent. *No* depreciation will be allowable for listed property owned by employees unless the property is:

1. required for the convenience of the employer, *and*
2. required as a condition of employment.

These requirements will *not* be satisfied merely by an employer's statement that the property is required as a condition of employment. It is intended that the property must be required in order for an employee to properly perform the duties of his/her employment.

Furthermore, if in years subsequent to the year of purchase, there is a reduction of the percentage of business use, that reduction can trigger an investment credit recapture. If the business use declines to 50 percent or less of the use of the property in the subsequent year, the *entire* amount of the investment credit will be recaptured. However, the Treasury can provide a rule that a *de minimus* reduction in the business use of the property will not trigger any recapture.

In addition to the existing rules governing the recapture of depreciation, the law requires recapture in the event property used more than 50 percent for business in the year it is placed in service declines to 50 percent or less of business use in a subsequent year. The amount of the recapture will be based upon the difference between the depreciation allowed in prior years and the amount that would have been allowed if the applicable accelerated rate and period of ACRS had not been available in such years. The Treasury has been instructed to provide for comparable recapture requirements applicable to lessees whose business use declines in subsequent years.

In IRS Letter Ruling 8615024, the IRS ruled that an employee's use of a personal computer did *not* meet the convenience of the employer and condition of employment tests. In denying any deduction or credit, the Internal Revenue Service said that to meet the convenience of the employer test, the employee must be *required* to purchase the computer to properly perform the duties of her employment. In that case, the taxpayer was not "required" to purchase the computer to properly perform her duties. Although the benefits of the taxpayer's use of the computer may inure to her employer, the purchase of a computer was clearly not required as a condition of employment. The facts of the case suggested that computer use, although work-related, was not inextricably related to proper performance of the taxpayer's job. Moreover, there appeared no evidence in the facts that those employees who did not purchase a computer were professionally disadvantaged.

In IRS Letter Ruling 871009, this position was reiterated. Here the Internal Revenue Service held that an insurance agent's use of a portable computer as an aid in selling financial products did not meet the convenience of the employer test. They concluded that the taxpayer, who used the computer exclusively for business purposes, must be required to purchase the computer to properly perform the duties of his employment in order to take the deduction. The computer purchase was optional rather than mandatory. "The facts indicate that computer use, although work-related, is not inextricably related to the proper performance of 'the taxpayer's' job. Further, there appears no evidence that those employees who do not purchase computers are professionally disadvantaged." (See also Rev. Rul. 86-129, 1986-45 IRB 4 and Letter Rul. 8725067.)

Luxury Cars

The Tax Reform Act of 1986 defined a passenger automobile as any four-wheeled vehicle that is manufactured primarily for use on public streets, roads, and highways and is rated at 6,000 pounds unloaded gross vehicle weight or less. The Act requires that fixed limitations on automobile deductions be conformed to the new recovery period, so that the price range of affected cars is unaffected. Depreciation deductions are limited for each year. These fixed limitations apply to all depreciation deductions, not just depreciation under the accelerated method.

Limitations on Luxury Auto Depreciation Deductions

	Yearly Maximum			
Date of Purchase	**1**	**2**	**3**	**4 and After**
6/19/84 to 4/2/85[a]	$4,000 (25%)	$6,000[b] (38%)	$6,000[b] (37%)	$6,000[b]
4/3/85 to 12/31/86[a]	3,200 (25%)	4,800 (38%)	4,800 (37%)	4,800
1987 to 12/31/88[c]	2,560 (20%)	4,100 (32%)	2,450 (19.2%)	1,475 (11.52%)
1989 to 12/31/90[c]	2,660 (20%)	4,200 (32%)	2,550 (19.2%)	1,475 (11.52%)
1991[c]	2,660 (20%)	4,300 (32%)	2,550 (19.2%)	1,575 (11.52%)
1992[c]	2,760 (20%)	4,400 (32%)	2,650 (19.2%)	1,575 (11.52%)
1993	2,860 (20%)	4,600 (32%)	2,750 (19.2%)	1,675 (11.52%)
1994	2,960 (20%)	4,700 (32%)	2,850 (19.2%)	1,675 (11.52%)
1995	3,060 (20%)	4,900 (32%)	2,950 (19.2%)	1,775 (11.52%)
1996	3,060 (20%)	4,900 (33%)	2,950 (19.2%)	1,775 (11.52%)
1997	3,160 (20%)	5,000 (33%)	3,050 (19.2%)	1,775 (11.52%)
1998	3,160 (20%)	5,000 (33%)	2,950 (19.2%)	1,775 (11.52%)
1999	3,060 (20%)	5,000 (33%)	2,950 (19.2%)	1,775 (11.52%)

[a]Year of disposition: zero.

[b]The limit is $6,200 if placed in service after 12/31/84 and before 4/3/85.

[c]Year of disposition: half-year.

The following is a worksheet to determine the expense deduction for a $10,000 automobile placed in service on January 1, 1992, and used 100 percent for business:

Determination of the Sec. 179 Expense Deduction to Achieve a Targeted Total ACRS Deduction for an Asset (or Total Assets)

(1)	Enter targeted total ACRS deduction (include the Sec. 179 expense deduction in line 1)	$2,760
(2)	Percentage of business use: 100% or 1.000	100%
(3)	Basis of asset	10,000
(4)	Business percentage of basis (multiply the amount on line 3 by the percentage on line 2)	10,000
(5)	Enter the first-year ACRS percentage: 20% or 0.20	.20
(6)	Multiply the amount on line 4 by the percentage on line 5	2,000
(7)	Subtract line 6 from line 1	760
(8)	Total asset value as a percent: 100.0% or 1.00	1.00
(9)	Enter first-year ACRS percentage: 20% or 0.20	.20
(10)	Subtract line 9 from line 8	.80
(11)	Divide line 7 by line 10. This is the exact Sec. 179 expense deduction to achieve the targeted total ACRS deduction for the year	950

Total deduction:

(a) ($10,000 – 950) × .20 =	1,810
(b) Sec. 179 expense	950
	$2,760

Alternatively, the following rules can be used to determine the optimal amount to be expensed:

1. If the auto cost $2,760 or less, the full amount should be expensed.
2. If the auto cost $13,800 or more, none of the basis should be expensed.
3. If the auto cost more than $2,760 but less than $13,800, then the amount to be expensed is equal to ($13,800 minus the adjusted basis) ÷ 4.

For example, assume that the auto's adjusted basis is $10,000. The optimal expense amount is:

$$\frac{\$13{,}800 - \$10{,}000}{4} = \frac{\$3{,}800}{4} = \$950$$

Note that the 1986 law put automobiles in the 5-year class. However, if the amount limitation prevents full use of the percentage depreciation in any year, the recovery period will be extended. Any unrecovered cost will be treated as an automobile expense subject to the annual limitation in taxable years after the end of the ordinary recovery period. The annual depreciation deduction, assuming the 200 percent declining-balance method, therefore, will be the lesser of the expense deduction or the percentage depreciation, as follows:

Year	Depreciation Deduction	Percentage of Basis
1	$2,760	20
2	4,400	32
3	2,650	19.2
4	1,575	11.52
5	1,575	11.52
6	1,575	5.76

Example: Assume two cars were purchased after December 31, 1986, to be used 100 percent for business at a cost of $12,900 and $15,000, respectively. The depreciation deductions allowed would be as follows:

Year	$12,900 Car	$15,000 Car
1992	$ 2,760	$ 2,760
1993	4,400	4,400
1994	2,650	2,650
1995	1,575	1,575
1996	1,515	1,575
1997	0	1,575
1998	0	465
	$12,900	$15,000

Note that in 1996, the percentage limitation prevents expensing up to the amount of the annual limitation.

The dollar caps must be proportionately reduced if the business or investment use is less than 100 percent.

Example: A taxpayer bought a $20,000 car in 1987 to be used 60 percent for business and 40 percent for personal driving. The depreciation deduction for 1987 was $1,536 [the lesser of $2,560 × 60 percent business use ($1,536), or 20 percent of $20,000 × 60 percent ($2,400)].

If qualified business use in the year the automobile is placed in service does not exceed 50 percent, then the basis must be recovered over 5 years using the straight-line method and the half-year convention. If qualified business use falls to 50 percent or less of total use during any part of the recovery period, part of the depreciation claimed in prior years must be included in the taxpayer's income, and a switch must be made to straight-line depreciation.

Appropriate limitations with respect to comparable dollar caps will be applicable to leased automobiles. Lessees of luxury automobiles used in business will be required to have income included to reflect the reduction in their deduction for lease payments. This income inclusion will be based on special tables provided by the Treasury after netting out the repeal of the investment tax credit. See Appendix E for inclusions required.

Appendix E

Auto Leases

Lessors of automobiles having a cost of more than $11,250 had to include in their 1986 income an amount based on tables in Announcement 85-127 that was equal to the value of the limitations imposed by the 1985 law change. For example, a lessee(s) (including an employer or self-employed individual) who leased a car worth $14,300 that was first used on September 1, 1985, and was used 90 percent for business, included approximately $61 in income ($204 times 122/365 of a year times 90 percent business use).

For any passenger automobile leased after April 2, 1985, but before January 1, 1987, the inclusion amount for each of the first three taxable years during which the automobile was leased was based on the fair market value of the automobile, the lessee's amount of business use, and the quarter of the taxable year during which the automobile was first used under the lease.

The inclusion amount is based upon the following tables and is computed as follows:

1. For the appropriate range of fair market values, find the dollar amount from the column for the quarter of the taxable year in which the automobile is first used under the lease.
2. Prorate the dollar amount for the number of days of the lease term included in the taxable year.
3. Multiply the prorated dollar amount by the percentage of business use for the taxable year.

Priced-Based Inclusion Table for Cars Leased after April 2, 1985, but before 1987

Fair Market Value		Taxable Year			
Greater than	But not greater than	First	Second	Third	Fourth
$11,250	$11,500	$ 6	$ 6	$ 7	$ 8
11,500	11,750	17	19	21	24
11,750	12,000	29	32	35	40
12,000	12,250	40	44	49	56
12,250	12,500	52	57	64	72
12,500	12,750	63	70	78	88
12,750	13,000	75	83	92	104
13,000	13,250	86	95	106	120
13,250	13,500	104	115	128	144
13,500	13,750	124	137	153	172
13,750	14,000	145	159	177	200
14,000	14,250	165	182	202	228
14,250	14,500	185	204	227	256
14,500	14,750	206	226	252	284
14,750	15,000	226	249	277	312
15,000	15,250	246	271	302	340
15,250	15,500	266	293	327	369
15,500	15,750	287	316	352	397
15,750	16,000	307	338	377	425
16,000	16,250	327	360	402	453
16,250	16,500	348	383	426	481
16,500	16,750	368	405	451	509
16,750	17,000	388	428	476	537
17,000	17,500	419	461	514	579
17,500	18,000	459	506	563	635
18,000	18,500	500	550	613	691
18,500	19,000	541	595	663	748
19,000	19,500	581	640	713	804
19,500	20,000	622	685	763	860
20,000	20,500	662	729	812	916
20,500	21,000	703	774	862	972

Priced-Based Inclusion Table for Cars Leased after April 2, 1985, but before 1987 *(continued)*

Fair Market Value		Taxable Year			
Greater than	But not greater than	First	Second	Third	Fourth
$21,000	$21,500	$ 744	$ 819	$ 912	$1,028
21,500	22,000	784	863	962	1,084
22,000	23,000	845	930	1,036	1,169
23,000	24,000	926	1,020	1,136	1,281
24,000	25,000	1,007	1,109	1,236	1,393
25,000	26,000	1,089	1,199	1,335	1,506
26,000	27,000	1,170	1,288	1,435	1,618
27,000	28,000	1,251	1,377	1,534	1,730
28,000	29,000	1,332	1,467	1,634	1,842
29,000	30,000	1,413	1,556	1,734	1,955
30,000	31,000	1,495	1,646	1,833	2,067
31,000	32,000	1,576	1,735	1,933	2,179
32,000	33,000	1,657	1,824	2,032	2,292
33,000	34,000	1,738	1,914	2,132	2,404
34,000	35,000	1,819	2,003	2,232	2,516
35,000	36,000	1,901	2,093	2,331	2,629
36,000	37,000	1,982	2,182	2,431	2,741
37,000	38,000	2,063	2,271	2,530	2,853
38,000	39,000	2,144	2,361	2,630	2,965
39,000	40,000	2,225	2,450	2,730	3,078
40,000	41,000	2,307	2,540	2,829	3,190
41,000	42,000	2,388	2,629	2,929	3,302
42,000	43,000	2,469	2,718	3,028	3,415
43,000	44,000	2,550	2,808	3,128	3,527
44,000	45,000	2,631	2,897	3,228	3,639
45,000	46,000	2,713	2,987	3,327	3,752
46,000	47,000	2,794	3,076	3,427	3,864
47,000	48,000	2,875	3,165	3,526	3,876
48,000	49,000	2,956	3,255	3,626	4,088
49,000	50,000	3,037	3,344	3,726	4,201

For any passenger automobile that has a fair market value greater than $18,000, but not greater than $50,000, the inclusion amount for the fourth, fifth, and sixth taxable years during which the automobile is leased is determined by using the table below instead of the formulas provided in Section 1.280F-5T(d)(1)(i) through (iv) of the temporary regulations. The inclusion amount is computed as follows: (1) For the appropriate range of fair market values, select the dollar amount from the column for the taxable year in which the automobile is used under the lease; (2) prorate the dollar amount for the number of days of the lease term included in the taxable year; and (3) multiply this dollar amount by the percentage of business use for the taxable year.

Inclusion Amounts: Years 4-6

Fair Market Value				
Greater than	But not greater than	Year 4	Year 5	Year 6
$18,000	$18,500	$ 15	—	—
18,500	19,000	45	—	—
19,000	19,500	75	—	—
19,500	20,000	105	—	—
20,000	20,500	135	—	—
20,500	21,000	165	—	—
21,000	21,500	195	—	—
21,500	22,000	225	—	—
22,000	23,000	270	—	—
23,000	24,000	330	$ 42	—
24,000	25,000	390	102	—
25,000	26,000	450	162	—
26,000	27,000	510	222	—
27,000	28,000	570	282	—
28,000	29,000	630	342	$ 54
29,000	30,000	690	402	114
30,000	31,000	750	462	174
31,000	32,000	810	522	234
32,000	33,000	870	582	294
33,000	34,000	930	642	354

Inclusion Amounts: Years 4-6 *(continued)*

Fair Market Value				
Greater than	But not greater than	Year 4	Year 5	Year 6
$34,000	$35,000	$ 990	$ 702	$ 414
35,000	36,000	1,050	762	474
36,000	37,000	1,110	822	534
37,000	38,000	1,170	882	594
38,000	39,000	1,230	942	654
39,000	40,000	1,290	1,002	714
40,000	41,000	1,350	1,062	774
41,000	42,000	1,410	1,122	834
42,000	43,000	1,470	1,182	894
43,000	44,000	1,530	1,242	954
44,000	45,000	1,590	1,302	1,014
45,000	46,000	1,650	1,362	1,074
46,000	47,000	1,710	1,422	1,134
47,000	48,000	1,770	1,482	1,194
48,000	49,000	1,830	1,542	1,254
49,000	50,000	1,890	1,602	1,314

For any passenger automobile that has a fair market value greater than $50,000, the inclusion amount for the first six taxable years during which the automobile is leased is determined according to special rules. *(Source:* See Internal Revenue Service Announcement 85-127.) *For cars leased after 1986,* see the following tables.

Price-Based Inclusion Table for Cars First Leased in 1987 or 1988

Fair Market Value		Year of Lease*				
Greater than	But not greater than	First	Second	Third	Fourth	Fifth and later
$12,800	$13,100	$ 2	$ 5	$ 7	$ 8	$ 9
13,100	13,400	6	14	20	24	28
13,400	13,700	10	23	34	41	47
13,700	14,000	15	32	47	57	65
14,000	14,300	19	41	61	73	84
14,300	14,600	23	50	74	89	103
14,600	14,900	27	59	88	105	122
14,900	15,200	31	68	101	122	140
15,200	15,500	35	77	115	138	159
15,500	15,800	40	87	128	154	178
15,800	16,100	44	96	142	170	196
16,100	16,400	48	105	155	186	215
16,400	16,700	52	114	169	203	234
16,700	17,000	56	123	182	219	253
17,000	17,500	62	135	200	240	277
17,500	18,000	69	150	223	267	309
18,000	18,500	76	166	246	294	340
18,500	19,000	83	181	268	321	371
19,000	19,500	90	196	291	348	402
19,500	20,000	97	211	313	375	433
20,000	20,500	104	226	336	402	465
20,500	21,000	111	424	358	429	496
21,000	21,500	117	257	381	456	527
21,500	22,000	124	272	403	483	558
22,000	23,000	135	295	437	524	605
23,000	24,000	149	325	482	578	667
24,000	45,000	163	356	527	632	729
25,000	26,000	177	386	572	686	792
26,000	27,000	190	416	617	740	854
27,000	28,000	204	447	662	794	917
28,000	29,000	218	477	707	848	979
29,000	30,000	232	507	752	902	1,041

Price-Based Inclusion Table for Cars First Leased in 1987 or 1988

Fair Market Value		Year of Lease*				
Greater than	But not greater than	First	Second	Third	Fourth	Fifth and later
$30,000	$31,000	$246	$538	$797	$ 956	$1,104
31,000	32,000	260	568	842	1,010	1,166
32,000	33,000	274	599	887	1,064	1,228
33,000	34,000	288	629	933	1,118	1,291
34,000	35,000	302	659	978	1,172	1,353
35,000	36,000	316	690	1,023	1,226	1,415
36,000	37,000	329	720	1,068	1,280	1,478
37,000	38,000	343	751	1,113	1,334	1,540
38,000	39,000	357	781	1,158	1,388	1,602
39,000	40,000	371	811	1,203	1,442	1,665
40,000	41,000	385	842	1,248	1,496	1,727
41,000	42,000	399	872	1,293	1,550	1,789
42,000	43,000	413	902	1,338	1,604	1,852
43,000	44,000	427	933	1,383	1,658	1,914
44,000	45,000	441	963	1,428	1,712	1,976
45,000	46,000	455	994	1,473	1,766	2,039
46,000	47,000	468	1,024	1,518	1,820	2,101
47,000	48,000	482	1,054	1,563	1,874	2,164
48,000	49,000	496	1,085	1,608	1,928	2,226
49,000	50,000	510	1,115	1,653	1,982	2,288
50,000	51,000	524	1,146	1,698	2,036	2,351
51,000	52,000	538	1,176	1,743	2,090	2,413
52,000	53,000	552	1,206	1,788	2,144	2,475
53,000	54,000	566	1,237	1,834	2,198	2,538
54,000	55,000	580	1,267	1,879	2,252	2,600
55,000	56,000	594	1,297	1,924	2,306	2,662
56,000	57,000	607	1,328	1,969	2,360	2,725
57,000	58,000	621	1,358	2,014	2,414	2,787
58,000	59,000	635	1,389	2,059	2,468	2,849
59,000	60,000	649	1,419	2,104	2,522	2,912

*For the last tax year of the lease, use the dollar amount for the preceding year.

Dollar Amounts for Cars First Leased in 1989 or 1990

Fair Market Value		Tax Year of Lease*				
		1st	2nd	3rd	4th	5th and Later
Over	Not Over					
$ 12,800	$ 13,100	$ 0	$ 0	$ 0	$ 1	$ 2
13,100	13,400	0	2	3	5	9
13,400	13,700	3	11	15	21	26
13,700	14,000	8	19	29	37	45
14,000	14,300	12	29	42	53	64
14,300	14,600	16	38	55	70	83
14,600	14,900	20	47	69	86	101
14,900	15,200	24	56	83	102	120
15,200	15,500	28	65	97	118	139
15,500	15,800	33	74	110	134	158
15,800	16,100	37	83	123	151	176
16,100	16,400	41	93	136	167	195
16,400	16,700	45	102	150	183	213
16,700	17,000	49	111	164	199	232
17,000	17,500	55	123	182	220	258
17,500	18,000	62	138	204	248	289
18,000	18,500	69	153	227	275	319
18,500	19,000	76	168	250	301	351
19,000	19,500	83	184	271	329	382
19,500	20,000	90	199	294	356	413
20,000	20,500	97	214	317	382	445
20,500	21,000	104	229	339	410	476
21,000	21,500	111	244	362	437	507
21,500	22,000	117	260	384	464	538
22,000	23,000	128	282	419	504	585
23,000	24,000	142	313	463	558	647
24,000	25,000	156	343	508	613	709
25,000	26,000	170	373	554	666	772
26,000	27,000	183	404	599	720	834
27,000	28,000	197	435	643	774	897
28,000	29,000	211	465	688	829	959
29,000	30,000	225	495	734	882	1,021
30,000	31,000	239	526	778	936	1,084
31,000	32,000	253	556	824	990	1,146
32,000	33,000	267	586	869	1,044	1,209
33,000	34,000	281	617	913	1,099	1,270
34,000	35,000	295	647	959	1,152	1,333
35,000	36,000	309	677	1,004	1,206	1,396
36,000	37,000	322	708	1,049	1,260	1,458
37,000	38,000	336	738	1,094	1,315	1,520
38,000	39,000	350	769	1,139	1,368	1,583
39,000	40,000	364	799	1,184	1,423	1,664
40,000	41,000	378	829	1,230	1,476	1,707
41,000	42,000	392	860	1,274	1,530	1,770
42,000	43,000	406	890	1,319	1,585	1,832
43,000	44,000	420	920	1,365	1,638	1,894
44,000	45,000	434	951	1,409	1,693	1,956
45,000	46,000	448	981	1,454	1,747	2,019
46,000	47,000	461	1,012	1,499	1,801	2,081
47,000	48,000	475	1,042	1,545	1,854	2,144
48,000	49,000	489	1,073	1,589	1,909	2,205
49,000	50,000	503	1,103	1,634	1,963	2,268
50,000	51,000	517	1,133	1,680	2,016	2,331
51,000	52,000	531	1,164	1,724	2,071	2,393
52,000	53,000	545	1,194	1,770	2,124	2,455
53,000	54,000	559	1,224	1,815	2,179	2,517
54,000	55,000	573	1,255	1,859	2,233	2,580
55,000	56,000	587	1,285	1,905	2,286	2,643
56,000	57,000	600	1,316	1,950	2,340	2,705
57,000	58,000	614	1,346	1,995	2,395	2,767
58,000	59,000	628	1,376	2,041	2,448	2,829
59,000	60,000	642	1,407	2,085	2,502	2,892
60,000	62,000	663	1,452	2,153	2,584	2,985
62,000	64,000	691	1,513	2,243	2,691	3,110
64,000	66,000	719	1,574	2,332	2,800	3,235
66,000	68,000	746	1,635	2,423	2,907	3,360
68,000	70,000	774	1,695	2,514	3,015	3,484
70,000	72,000	802	1,756	2,603	3,124	3,609
72,000	74,000	830	1,817	2,693	3,232	3,733
74,000	76,000	858	1,877	2,784	3,340	3,858
76,000	78,000	885	1,939	2,873	3,448	3,983
78,000	80,000	913	1,999	2,964	3,556	4,107
80,000	85,000	962	2,106	3,121	3,745	4,325
85,000	90,000	1,031	2,258	3,346	4,015	4,638
90,000	95,000	1,101	2,409	3,572	4,285	4,949
95,000	100,000	1,170	2,562	3,796	4,556	5,261

*For the last tax year of the lease, use the dollar amount for the preceding year.

Dollar Amounts For Cars First Leased in 1991

Fair Market Value		Tax Year of Lease*				
Over	Not Over	1st	2nd	3rd	4th	5th and Later
$ 13,400	$ 13,700	$ 2	$ 4	$ 6	$ 6	$ 6
13,700	14,000	5	10	16	18	18
14,000	14,300	8	17	25	29	32
14,300	14,600	11	23	35	41	45
14,600	14,900	14	30	44	52	58
14,900	15,200	17	36	54	64	71
15,200	15,500	20	43	63	75	85
15,500	15,800	23	49	73	87	98
15,800	16,100	26	55	83	98	112
16,100	16,400	29	62	92	110	124
16,400	16,700	32	68	102	121	138
16,700	17,000	35	75	111	133	151
17,000	17,500	39	83	125	147	169
17,500	18,000	44	94	140	167	191
18,000	18,500	49	105	156	186	213
18,500	19,000	54	116	172	205	235
19,000	19,500	59	126	189	224	257
19,500	20,000	63	138	204	243	279
20,000	20,500	68	148	220	263	301
20,500	21,000	73	159	236	282	323
21,000	21,500	78	170	252	301	345
21,500	22,000	83	180	269	319	368
22,000	23,000	90	197	292	348	401
23,000	24,000	100	218	324	387	445
24,000	25,000	110	240	356	425	489
25,000	26,000	120	261	388	463	534
26,000	27,000	130	283	419	502	578
27,000	28,000	140	304	452	540	622
28,000	29,000	149	326	484	578	666
29,000	30,000	159	347	516	617	710
30,000	31,000	169	369	547	655	755
31,000	32,000	179	390	580	693	799
32,000	33,000	189	412	611	732	843
33,000	34,000	199	433	644	769	888
34,000	35,000	208	455	676	808	931
35,000	36,000	218	477	707	846	976
36,000	37,000	228	498	739	885	1,020
37,000	38,000	238	519	772	923	1,064
38,000	39,000	248	541	803	961	1,109
39,000	40,000	258	562	835	1,000	1,153
40,000	41,000	267	584	867	1,038	1,197
41,000	42,000	277	606	899	1,076	1,241
42,000	43,000	287	627	931	1,115	1,285
43,000	44,000	297	649	962	1,153	1,330
44,000	45,000	307	670	995	1,191	1,374
45,000	46,000	317	692	1,026	1,230	1,418
46,000	47,000	326	714	1,058	1,268	1,462
47,000	48,000	336	735	1,091	1,306	1,506
48,000	49,000	346	756	1,123	1,344	1,551
49,000	50,000	356	778	1,154	1,383	1,595
50,000	51,000	366	799	1,187	1,421	1,639
51,000	52,000	376	821	1,218	1,459	1,684
52,000	53,000	385	843	1,250	1,498	1,727
53,000	54,000	395	864	1,282	1,536	1,772
54,000	55,000	405	886	1,314	1,574	1,816
55,000	56,000	415	907	1,346	1,613	1,860
56,000	57,000	425	929	1,378	1,650	1,905
57,000	58,000	435	950	1,410	1,689	1,949
58,000	59,000	444	972	1,442	1,727	1,993
59,000	60,000	454	993	1,474	1,766	2,037
60,000	62,000	469	1,026	1,521	1,824	2,103
62,000	64,000	489	1,068	1,586	1,900	2,192
64,000	66,000	508	1,112	1,649	1,977	2,280
66,000	68,000	528	1,155	1,713	2,053	2,369
68,000	70,000	548	1,198	1,777	2,130	2,457
70,000	72,000	567	1,241	1,841	2,206	2,546
72,000	74,000	587	1,284	1,905	2,283	2,634
74,000	76,000	607	1,327	1,969	2,359	2,723
76,000	78,000	626	1,370	2,033	2,436	2,811
78,000	80,000	646	1,413	2,097	2,512	2,900
80,000	85,000	680	1,489	2,208	2,647	3,054
85,000	90,000	730	1,596	2,368	2,838	3,276
90,000	95,000	779	1,704	2,528	3,029	3,497
95,000	100,000	828	1,812	2,687	3,221	3,718

*For the last tax year of the lease, use the dollar amount for the preceding year.

Dollar Amounts for Cars First Leased in 1992

Fair Market Value		Tax Year of Lease*				
		1st	2nd	3rd	4th	5th and Later
Over	Not Over					
$ 13,700	$ 14,000	$ 0	$ 2	$ 2	$ 2	$ 4
14,000	14,300	3	7	10	13	15
14,300	14,600	5	13	18	23	26
14,600	14,900	8	18	27	32	38
14,900	15,200	11	23	35	43	49
15,200	15,500	13	29	44	52	61
15,500	15,800	16	35	51	62	72
15,800	16,100	18	40	60	72	84
16,100	16,400	21	46	68	82	95
16,400	16,700	23	52	76	92	106
16,700	17,000	26	57	84	102	118
17,000	17,500	29	65	95	115	133
17,500	18,000	33	74	109	132	152
18,000	18,500	38	83	123	148	171
18,500	19,000	42	92	137	164	190
19,000	19,500	46	102	150	181	209
19,500	20,000	50	111	164	198	228
20,000	20,500	55	120	178	214	247
20,500	21,000	59	129	192	230	267
21,000	21,500	63	139	205	247	285
21,500	22,000	67	148	219	263	305
22,000	23,000	74	162	239	288	333
23,000	24,000	82	180	268	321	371
24,000	25,000	90	199	295	354	409
25,000	26,000	99	217	323	387	447
26,000	27,000	107	236	350	420	485
27,000	28,000	116	254	378	453	523
28,000	29,000	124	273	405	486	561
29,000	30,000	133	291	433	518	600
30,000	31,000	141	310	460	552	637
31,000	32,000	150	328	488	584	676
32,000	33,000	158	347	515	618	713
33,000	34,000	167	365	543	650	752
34,000	35,000	175	384	570	684	789
35,000	36,000	184	402	598	716	828
36,000	37,000	192	421	625	750	865
37,000	38,000	200	440	652	783	904
38,000	39,000	209	458	680	816	942
39,000	40,000	217	477	707	849	980
40,000	41,000	226	495	735	882	1,018
41,000	42,000	234	514	762	915	1,056
42,000	43,000	243	532	790	948	1,094
43,000	44,000	251	551	817	981	1,132
44,000	45,000	260	569	845	1,013	1,171
45,000	46,000	268	588	872	1,047	1,208
46,000	47,000	277	606	900	1,079	1,247
47,000	48,000	285	625	927	1,113	1,284
48,000	49,000	293	644	955	1,145	1,323
49,000	50,000	302	662	982	1,179	1,360
50,000	51,000	310	681	1,010	1,211	1,399
51,000	52,000	319	699	1,037	1,245	1,436
52,000	53,000	327	718	1,065	1,277	1,475
53,000	54,000	336	736	1,092	1,311	1,513
54,000	55,000	344	755	1,120	1,343	1,551
55,000	56,000	353	773	1,147	1,377	1,589
56,000	57,000	361	792	1,175	1,409	1,627
57,000	58,000	370	810	1,202	1,442	1,666
58,000	59,000	378	829	1,230	1,475	1,703
59,000	60,000	386	848	1,257	1,508	1,741
60,000	62,000	399	875	1,299	1,557	1,799

Fair Market Value		Tax Year of Lease*				
Over	Not Over	1st	2nd	3rd	4th	5th and Later
$ 62,000	$ 64,000	$ 416	$ 912	$ 1,354	$ 1,623	$ 1,875
64,000	66,000	433	949	1,409	1,689	1,951
66,000	68,000	450	987	1,463	1,755	2,027
68,000	70,000	467	1,024	1,518	1,821	2,103
70,000	72,000	484	1,061	1,573	1,887	2,179
72,000	74,000	501	1,098	1,628	1,953	2,255
74,000	76,000	518	1,135	1,683	2,019	2,331
76,000	78,000	535	1,172	1,738	2,085	2,407
78,000	80,000	551	1,209	1,794	2,150	2,484
80,000	85,000	581	1,274	1,889	2,267	2,617
85,000	90,000	623	1,367	2,027	2,431	2,807
90,000	95,000	666	1,459	2,165	2,595	2,998
95,000	100,000	708	1,552	2,302	2,761	3,188

REV. PROC. 93—35
Dollar Amounts for Automobiles with a Lease Term Beginning in Calendar Year 1993

Fair Market Value of Automobile		Tax Year During Lease				
Over	Not Over	1st	2nd	3rd	4th	5th and Later
$ 14,300	$ 14,600	1	1	2	2	3
14,600	14,900	3	5	7	9	9
14,900	15,200	4	9	13	15	17
15,200	15,500	6	13	18	22	25
15,500	15,800	8	16	24	29	32
15,800	16,100	9	20	30	35	40
16,100	16,400	11	24	35	42	48
16,400	16,700	13	27	41	49	55
16,700	17,000	14	32	46	55	63
17,000	17,500	17	36	54	64	73
17,500	18,000	20	42	63	75	87
18,000	18,500	22	49	72	86	99
18,500	19,000	25	55	82	97	112
19,000	19,500	28	61	91	108	125
19,500	20,000	31	67	100	120	137
20,000	20,500	34	74	109	130	150
20,500	21,000	37	80	118	142	163
21,000	21,500	39	86	128	153	175
21,500	22,000	42	92	138	163	189
22,000	23,000	47	101	151	181	207

REV. PROC. 93—35
Dollar Amounts for Automobiles with a Lease Term Beginning in Calendar Year 1993 *(continued)*

Fair Market Value of Automobile		Tax Year During Lease				
Over	Not Over	1st	2nd	3rd	4th	5th and Later
$ 23,000	$ 24,000	52	114	170	202	233
24,000	25,000	58	127	187	225	259
25,000	26,000	64	139	206	247	285
26,000	27,000	69	152	224	270	310
27,000	28,000	75	164	243	292	335
28,000	29,000	81	176	262	313	362
29,000	30,000	86	189	280	336	387
30,000	31,000	92	201	299	358	412
31,000	32,000	98	214	317	380	438
32,000	33,000	103	226	336	402	464
33,000	34,000	109	239	354	424	490
34,000	35,000	115	251	373	446	515
35,000	36,000	120	264	391	469	540
36,000	37,000	126	276	410	491	566
37,000	38,000	132	288	429	513	591
38,000	39,000	137	301	447	535	617
39,000	40,000	143	314	465	557	643
40,000	41,000	149	326	484	579	669
41,000	42,000	154	339	502	601	695
42,000	43,000	160	351	521	623	720
43,000	44,000	166	363	539	646	746
44,000	45,000	171	376	558	668	771
45,000	46,000	177	388	577	690	796
46,000	47,000	183	401	594	713	822
47,000	48,000	189	413	613	735	847
48,000	49,000	194	426	631	757	874
49,000	50,000	200	438	650	779	899
50,000	51,000	206	450	669	801	925
51,000	52,000	211	463	687	824	950
52,000	53,000	217	475	706	846	975
53,000	54,000	223	488	724	867	1,002
54,000	55,000	228	501	742	890	1,027
55,000	56,000	234	513	761	912	1,052

REV. PROC. 93—35
Dollar Amounts for Automobiles with a Lease Term Beginning in Calendar Year 1993 *(continued)*

Fair Market Value of Automobile		Tax Year During Lease				
Over	**Not Over**	**1st**	**2nd**	**3rd**	**4th**	**5th and Later**
$ 56,000	$ 57,000	240	525	780	934	1,078
57,000	58,000	245	538	798	956	1,104
58,000	59,000	251	550	817	978	1,130
59,000	60,000	257	563	835	1,000	1,155
60,000	62,000	265	581	863	1,034	1,194
62,000	64,000	277	606	900	1,078	1,245
64,000	66,000	288	631	937	1,123	1,295
66,000	68,000	299	656	974	1,167	1,347
68,000	70,000	311	681	1,011	1,211	1,398
70,000	72,000	322	706	1,048	1,255	1,450
72,000	74,000	333	731	1,085	1,300	1,500
74,000	76,000	345	756	1,121	1,345	1,551
76,000	78,000	356	781	1,158	1,389	1,603
78,000	80,000	367	806	1,195	1,434	1,654
80,000	85,000	387	849	1,261	1,510	1,744
85,000	90,000	416	911	1,353	1,622	1,871
90,000	95,000	444	974	1,445	1,733	1,999
95,000	100,000	472	1,036	1,538	1,843	2,128
100,000	110,000	515	1,130	1,676	2,010	2,319
110,000	120,000	572	1,254	1,861	2,232	2,575
120,000	130,000	629	1,379	2,046	2,453	2,831
130,000	140,000	685	1,504	2,231	2,674	3,088
140,000	150,000	742	1,628	2,416	2,896	3,344
150,000	160,000	799	1,753	2,600	3,119	3,599
160,000	170,000	856	1,877	2,786	3,340	3,855
170,000	180,000	912	2,002	2,971	3,561	4,112
180,000	190,000	969	2,127	3,155	3,783	4,368
190,000	200,000	1,026	2,251	3,340	4,006	4,623
200,000	210,000	1,083	2,376	3,525	4,227	4,879
210,000	220,000	1,140	2,500	3,710	4,449	5,135
220,000	230,000	1,196	2,625	3,895	4,670	5,392
230,000	240,000	1,253	2,749	4,081	4,892	5,647
240,000	250,000	1,310	2,874	4,265	5,114	5,903

REV. PROC. 94—53
Dollar Amounts for Automobiles with a Lease Term Beginning in Calendar Year 1994

Fair Market Value of Automobile		Tax Year During Lease				
Over	Not Over	1st	2nd	3rd	4th	5th and Later
$14,600	$ 14,900	0	1	1	2	2
14,900	15,200	2	5	6	9	11
15,200	15,500	4	9	14	17	20
15,500	15,800	6	14	21	25	30
15,800	16,100	8	19	27	34	39
16,100	16,400	10	24	34	42	49
16,400	16,700	12	28	41	51	58
16,700	17,000	14	33	48	59	68
17,000	17,500	17	39	57	70	81
17,500	18,000	21	47	68	84	97
18,000	18,500	24	55	80	97	113
18,500	19,000	28	62	92	111	129
19,000	19,500	31	70	104	124	145
19,500	20,000	35	78	115	138	161
20,000	20,500	39	85	127	152	176
20,500	21,000	42	93	138	166	193
21,000	21,500	46	101	149	180	208
21,500	22,000	49	109	161	193	225
22,000	23,000	54	121	178	214	248
23,000	24,000	62	136	201	242	280
24,000	25,000	69	151	224	270	312
25,000	26,000	76	167	247	297	344
26,000	27,000	83	182	270	325	376
27,000	28,000	90	198	293	352	408
28,000	29,000	97	213	317	379	440
29,000	30,000	104	229	339	408	471
30,000	31,000	111	244	363	435	503
31,000	32,000	118	260	385	463	535
32,000	33,000	125	276	408	490	567
33,000	34,000	132	291	431	518	599
34,000	35,000	139	307	454	545	631

REV. PROC. 94—53
Dollar Amounts for Automobiles with a Lease Term Beginning in Calendar Year 1994 *(continued)*

Fair Market Value of Automobile		Tax Year During Lease				
Over	Not Over	1st	2nd	3rd	4th	5th and Later
$ 35,000	$ 36,000	146	322	478	573	662
36,000	37,000	153	338	500	601	694
37,000	38,000	161	353	523	628	726
38,000	39,000	168	368	547	656	757
39,000	40,000	175	384	569	684	790
40,000	41,000	182	399	593	711	822
41,000	42,000	189	415	615	739	854
42,000	43,000	196	431	638	766	886
43,000	44,000	203	446	661	794	918
44,000	45,000	210	462	684	821	950
45,000	46,000	217	477	708	849	981
46,000	47,000	224	493	730	877	1,013
47,000	48,000	231	508	754	904	1,045
48,000	49,000	238	524	776	932	1,077
49,000	50,000	245	539	800	959	1,109
50,000	51,000	252	555	822	987	1,141
51,000	52,000	260	570	845	1,015	1,172
52,000	53,000	267	585	869	1,042	1,204
53,000	54,000	274	601	892	1,069	1,236
54,000	55,000	281	617	914	1,097	1,268
55,000	56,000	288	632	938	1,125	1,299
56,000	57,000	295	648	960	1,153	1,331
57,000	58,000	302	663	984	1,180	1,363
58,000	59,000	309	679	1,006	1,208	1,395
59,000	60,000	316	694	1,030	1,235	1,427
60,000	62,000	327	717	1,065	1,276	1,475
62,000	64,000	341	748	1,111	1,332	1,538
64,000	66,000	355	780	1,156	1,387	1,602
66,000	68,000	369	811	1,202	1,442	1,666
68,000	70,000	383	842	1,248	1,497	1,730
70,000	72,000	397	873	1,294	1,553	1,793

REV. PROC. 94—53
Dollar Amounts for Automobiles with a Lease Term Beginning in Calendar Year 1994 *(continued)*

Fair Market Value of Automobile		Tax Year During Lease				
Over	**Not Over**	**1st**	**2nd**	**3rd**	**4th**	**5th and Later**
$ 72,000	$ 74,000	412	903	1,341	1,608	1,857
74,000	76,000	426	935	1,386	1,663	1,921
76,000	78,000	440	966	1,432	1,718	1,985
78,000	80,000	454	997	1,478	1,774	2,048
80,000	85,000	479	1,051	1,559	1,870	2,160
85,000	90,000	514	1,129	1,674	2,008	2,319
90,000	95,000	550	1,206	1,789	2,146	2,478
95,000	100,000	585	1,284	1,904	2,284	2,637
100,000	110,000	638	1,400	2,077	2,491	2,876
110,000	120,000	709	1,555	2,307	2,767	3,195
120,000	130,000	779	1,710	2,537	3,043	3,514
130,000	140,000	850	1,865	2,767	3,319	3,833
140,000	150,000	921	2,020	2,997	3,595	4,151
150,000	160,000	992	2,175	3,228	3,870	4,470
160,000	170,000	1,062	2,331	3,457	4,147	4,788
170,000	180,000	1,133	2,486	3,687	4,423	5,107
180,000	190,000	1,204	2,641	3,917	4,699	5,425
190,000	200,000	1,274	2,796	4,148	4,974	5,745
200,000	210,000	1,345	2,951	4,378	5,250	6,063
210,000	220,000	1,416	3,106	4,608	5,527	6,381
220,000	230,000	1,487	3,261	4,838	5,803	8,699
230,000	240,000	1,557	3,416	5,069	6,078	7,019
240,000	250,000	1,628	3,571	5,299	6,354	7,337

REV. PROC. 95—09
Dollar Amounts for Automobiles with a Lease Term Beginning in Calendar Year 1995

Fair Market Value of Automobile		Tax Year During Lease				
Over	Not Over	1st	2nd	3rd	4th	5th and Later
$ 15,500	$ 15,800	4	8	11	13	14
15,800	16,100	7	15	21	25	28
16,100	16,400	10	22	31	37	43
16,400	16,700	13	28	42	50	56
16,700	17,000	16	35	52	62	71
17,000	17,500	20	45	65	78	89
17,500	18,000	26	56	82	98	113
18,000	18,500	31	67	99	119	136
18,500	19,000	36	79	116	139	159
19,000	19,500	41	90	133	159	184
19,500	20,000	46	102	150	179	207
20,000	20,500	52	113	167	200	230
20,500	21,000	57	124	184	220	254
21,000	21,500	62	136	201	240	277
21,500	22,000	67	147	218	261	301
22,000	23,000	75	164	244	291	336
23,000	24,000	86	187	277	332	383
24,000	25,000	96	210	311	373	429
25,000	26,000	106	233	345	413	477
26,000	27,000	117	256	378	454	524
27,000	28,000	127	279	412	495	570
28,000	29,000	138	301	447	535	617
29,000	30,000	148	324	481	575	665
30,000	31,000	159	347	514	616	711
31,000	32,000	169	370	548	657	758
32,000	33,000	179	393	582	698	804
33,000	34,000	190	416	616	738	851
34,000	35,000	200	439	650	778	899
35,000	36,000	211	461	684	819	946
36,000	37,000	221	484	718	860	992
37,000	38,000	232	507	751	901	1,039

REV. PROC. 95—09
Dollar Amounts for Automobiles with a Lease Term Beginning in Calendar Year 1995 *(continued)*

Fair Market Value of Automobile		Tax Year During Lease				
Over	**Not Over**	**1st**	**2nd**	**3rd**	**4th**	**5th and Later**
$ 38,000	$ 39,000	242	530	785	942	1,086
39,000	40,000	253	552	820	982	1,133
40,000	41,000	263	576	853	1,022	1,180
41,000	42,000	273	599	887	1,063	1,227
42,000	43,000	284	621	921	1,104	1,274
43,000	44,000	294	644	955	1,145	1,320
44,000	45,000	305	667	989	1,185	1,367
45,000	46,000	315	690	1,022	1,226	1,415
46,000	47,000	326	712	1,057	1,266	1,462
47,000	48,000	336	735	1,091	1,307	1,058
48,000	49,000	346	759	1,124	1,347	1,556
49,000	50,000	357	781	1,158	1,388	1,603
50,000	51,000	367	804	1,192	1,429	1,649
51,000	52,000	378	827	1,226	1,469	1,696
52,000	53,000	388	850	1,260	1,510	1,743
53,000	54,000	399	872	1,294	1,551	1,790
54,000	55,000	409	895	1,328	1,591	1,837
55,000	56,000	419	919	1,361	1,632	1,884
56,000	57,000	430	941	1,395	1,673	1,931
57,000	58,000	440	964	1,429	1,714	1,977
58,000	59,000	451	987	1,463	1,754	2,024
59,000	60,000	461	1,010	1,497	1,794	2,072
60,000	62,000	477	1,044	1,548	1,855	2,142
62,000	64,000	498	1,089	1,616	1,937	2,235
64,000	66,000	519	1,135	1,683	2,018	2,330
66,000	68,000	539	1,181	1,751	2,100	2,423
68,000	70,000	560	1,227	1,819	2,180	2,517
70,000	72,000	581	1,272	1,887	2,262	2,611
72,000	74,000	602	1,318	1,955	2,343	2,704
74,000	76,000	623	1,364	2,022	2,424	2,799
76,000	78,000	644	1,409	2,090	2,506	2,892

REV. PROC. 95—09
Dollar Amounts for Automobiles with a Lease Term Beginning in Calendar Year 1995 ***(continued)***

Fair Market Value of Automobile		Tax Year During Lease				
Over	**Not Over**	**1st**	**2nd**	**3rd**	**4th**	**5th and Later**
$ 78,000	$ 80,000	655	1,455	2,158	2,586	2,986
80,000	85,000	701	1,535	2,277	2,729	3,150
85,000	90,000	753	1,650	2,445	2,932	3,385
90,000	95,000	806	1,763	2,616	3,135	3,619
95,000	100,000	858	1,878	2,784	3,339	3,853
100,000	110,000	936	2,049	3,039	3,643	4,206
110,000	120,000	1,040	2,278	3,377	4,050	4,674
120,000	130,000	1,145	2,506	3,716	4,456	5,144
130,000	140,000	1,249	2,735	4,055	4,862	5,613
140,000	150,000	1,353	2,963	4,394	5,269	6,082
150,000	160,000	1,458	3,191	4,733	5,675	6,551
160,000	170,000	1,562	3,420	5,072	6,081	7,020
170,000	180,000	1,666	3,649	5,410	6,488	7,489
180,000	190,000	1,771	3,877	5,749	6,894	7,958
190,000	200,000	1,875	4,105	6,089	7,300	8,427
200,000	210,000	1,979	4,334	6,427	7,706	8,897
210,000	220,000	2,084	4,562	6,766	8,113	9,365
220,000	230,000	2,188	4,791	7,105	8,518	9,835
230,000	240,000	2,292	5.019	7,444	8,925	10,304
240,000	250,000	2,397	5,247	7,783	9,332	10,772

DRAFTING INFORMATION: The principal author of this revenue procedure is Bernard P. Harvey of the Office of Assistant Chief Counsel (Pass-throughs and Special Industries). For further information regarding this revenue procedure contact Mr. Harvey on (202) 622-3110 (not a toll-free call).

REV. PROC. 96—25 Table 2
Dollar Amounts for Automobiles with a Lease Term Beginning in Calendar Year 1996

Fair Market Value of Automobile		Tax Year During Lease				
Over	Not Over	1st	2nd	3rd	4th	5th and Later
$ 15,500	$ 15,800	3	6	8	10	10
15,800	16,100	5	11	16	19	21
16,100	16,400	7	16	24	27	32
16,400	16,700	10	21	31	37	42
16,700	17,000	12	26	39	46	53
17,000	17,500	15	33	49	58	67
17,500	18,000	19	42	61	73	84
18,000	18,500	23	50	74	88	102
18,500	19,000	27	59	86	104	119
19,000	19,500	31	67	99	119	136
19,500	20,000	35	75	112	134	154
20,000	20,500	38	84	125	149	171
20,500	21,000	42	93	137	164	189
21,000	21,500	46	101	150	179	207
21,500	22,000	50	110	162	194	225
22,000	23,000	56	122	182	217	250
23,000	24,000	64	139	207	247	286
24,000	25,000	71	157	232	277	320
25,000	26,000	79	174	257	308	355
26,000	27,000	87	191	282	338	390
27,000	28,000	95	207	308	369	425
28,000	29,000	103	224	333	399	460
29,000	30,000	110	242	358	429	495
30,000	31,000	118	259	383	459	531
31,000	32,000	126	276	408	490	565
32,000	33,000	134	293	433	520	600
33,000	34,000	141	310	459	550	635
34,000	35,000	149	327	484	581	670
35,000	36,000	157	344	509	611	705
36,000	37,000	165	361	535	641	740
37,000	38,000	172	378	560	672	775

REV. PROC. 96—25 Table 2
Dollar Amounts for Automobiles with a Lease Term Beginning in Calendar Year 1996 *(continued)*

Fair Market Value of Automobile		Tax Year During Lease				
Over	Not Over	1st	2nd	3rd	4th	5th and Later
$ 38,000	$ 39,000	180	395	585	702	810
39,000	40,000	188	412	611	732	844
40,000	41,000	196	429	636	762	880
41,000	42,000	203	446	661	793	915
42,000	43,000	211	463	687	822	950
43,000	44,000	219	480	712	853	985
44,000	45,000	227	497	737	883	1,020
45,000	46,000	235	514	762	914	1,054
46,000	47,000	242	531	788	944	1,089
47,000	48,000	250	548	813	974	1,125
48,000	49,000	258	565	838	1,005	1,159
49,000	50,000	266	582	863	1,035	1,195
50,000	51,000	273	599	889	1,065	1,230
51,000	52,000	281	616	914	1,096	1,264
52,000	53,000	289	633	939	1,126	1,299
53,000	54,000	297	650	964	1,157	1,334
54,000	55,000	304	668	989	1,186	1,370
55,000	56,000	312	684	1,015	1,217	1,404
56,000	57,000	320	701	1,040	1,247	1,440
57,000	58,000	328	718	1,066	1,277	1,474
58,000	59,000	336	735	1,091	1,307	1,509
59,000	60,000	343	753	1,115	1,338	1,544
60,000	62,000	355	778	1,154	1,383	1,597
62,000	64,000	370	812	1,205	1,443	1,667
64,000	66,000	386	846	1,255	1,504	1,737
66,000	68,000	402	880	1,305	1,565	1,807
68,000	70,000	417	914	1,356	1,626	1,876
70,000	72,000	433	948	1,406	1,686	1,947
72,000	74,000	448	982	1,457	1,747	2,016
74,000	76,000	464	1,016	1,508	1,807	2,086
76,000	78,000	479	1,050	1,558	1,868	2,156

REV. PROC. 96—25 Table 2
Dollar Amounts for Automobiles with a Lease Term Beginning in Calendar Year 1996 *(continued)*

Fair Market Value of Automobile		Tax Year During Lease				
Over	Not Over	1st	2nd	3rd	4th	5th and Later
$ 78,000	$ 80,000	495	1,084	1,609	1,928	2,226
80,000	85,000	522	1,144	1,697	2,034	2,349
85,000	90,000	561	1,229	1,823	2,186	2,523
90,000	95,000	600	1,314	1,950	2,337	2,698
95,000	100,000	638	1,400	2,075	2,489	2,873
100,000	110,000	697	1,527	2,265	2,716	3,135
110,000	120,000	774	1,697	2,518	3,019	3,485
120,000	130,000	852	1,868	2,770	3,322	3,834
130,000	140,000	930	2,038	3,023	3,624	4,185
140,000	150,000	1,007	2,208	3,276	3,927	4,534
150,000	160,000	1,085	2,378	3,529	4,230	4,884
160,000	170,000	1,163	2,548	3,781	4,533	5,234
170,000	180,000	1,240	2,719	4,033	4,837	5,583
180,000	190,000	1,318	2,889	4,286	5,139	5,993
190,000	200,000	1,396	3,059	4,539	5,442	6,282
200,000	210,000	1,473	3,230	4,791	5,745	6,632
210,000	220,000	1,551	3,400	5,044	6,047	6,982
220,000	230,000	1,629	3,570	5,296	6,351	7,332
230,000	240,000	1,706	3,740	5,550	6,653	7,681
240,000	250,000	1,784	3,911	5,801	6,956	8,032

REV. PROC. 97—20 Table 2
Dollar Amounts for Automobiles with a Lease Term Beginning in Calendar Year 1997

Fair Market Value of Automobile		Tax Year During Lease				
Over	Not Over	1st	2nd	3rd	4th	5th and Later
$ 15,800	$ 16,100	1	5	5	8	10
16,100	16,400	4	10	13	18	21
16,400	16,700	6	15	22	27	32
16,700	17,000	9	20	30	36	44
17,000	17,500	12	28	40	49	58
17,500	18,000	16	37	53	65	77
18,000	18,500	20	46	66	82	95
18,500	19,000	24	55	80	97	114
19,000	19,500	28	64	93	113	132
19,500	20,000	32	73	106	129	151
20,000	20,500	36	82	120	145	169
20,500	21,000	40	91	133	161	187
21,000	21,500	45	99	147	177	205
21,500	22,000	49	108	160	193	224
22,000	23,000	55	122	180	216	252
23,000	24,000	63	140	206	249	288
24,000	25,000	71	158	233	280	326
25,000	26,000	79	176	259	313	362
26,000	27,000	88	193	287	344	399
27,000	28,000	96	211	313	377	435
28,000	29,000	104	229	340	408	473
29,000	30,000	112	247	366	441	509
30,000	31,000	120	265	393	472	546
31,000	32,000	128	283	420	504	583
32,000	33,000	137	301	446	536	620
33,000	34,000	145	319	472	568	657
34,000	35,000	153	337	499	600	693
35,000	36,000	161	355	526	631	731
36,000	37,000	169	373	552	664	767
37,000	38,000	178	391	578	696	804

REV. PROC. 97—20 Table 2
Dollar Amounts for Automobiles with a Lease Term Beginning in Calendar Year 1997 ***(continued)***

Fair Market Value of Automobile		Tax Year During Lease				
Over	Not Over	1st	2nd	3rd	4th	5th and Later
$ 38,000	$ 39,000	186	409	605	727	841
39,000	40,000	194	427	632	759	878
40,000	41,000	202	445	658	791	915
41,000	42,000	210	463	685	823	951
42,000	43,000	218	481	712	854	989
43,000	44,000	227	498	739	886	1,026
44,000	45,000	235	516	765	919	1,062
45,000	46,000	243	534	792	951	1,098
46,000	47,000	251	552	819	982	1,136
47,000	48,000	259	570	845	1,015	1,172
48,000	49,000	268	588	871	1,047	1,209
49,000	50,000	276	606	898	1,078	1,246
50,000	51,000	284	624	925	1,110	1,282
51,000	52,000	292	642	951	1,142	1,320
52,000	53,000	300	660	978	1,174	1,356
53,000	54,000	308	678	1,004	1,206	1,394
54,000	55,000	317	695	1,032	1,237	1,430
55,000	56,000	325	713	1,058	1,270	1,467
56,000	57,000	333	732	1,084	1,301	1,504
57,000	58,000	341	750	1,110	1,334	1,540
58,000	59,000	349	768	1,137	1,365	1,578
59,000	60,000	358	785	1,164	1,397	1,615
60,000	62,000	370	812	1,204	1,445	1,670
62,000	64,000	386	848	1,257	1,509	1,743
64,000	66,000	403	884	1,310	1,573	1,817
66,000	68,000	419	920	1,363	1,637	1,890
68,000	70,000	435	956	1,417	1,700	1,964
70,000	72,000	452	991	1,470	1,764	2,038
72,000	74,000	468	1,027	1,524	1,827	2,112
74,000	76,000	484	1,063	1,577	1,891	2,186
76,000	78,000	501	1,099	1,630	1,955	2,259

REV. PROC. 97—20 Table 2
Dollar Amounts for Automobiles with a Lease Term Beginning in Calendar Year 1997 *(continued)*

Fair Market Value of Automobile		Tax Year During Lease				
Over	Not Over	1st	2nd	3rd	4th	5th and Later
$ 78,000	$ 80,000	517	1,135	1,683	2,019	2,333
80,000	85,000	546	1,198	1,776	2,130	2,462
85,000	90,000	587	1,287	1,909	2,291	2,645
90,000	95,000	627	1,377	2,042	2,450	2,830
95,000	100,000	668	1,467	2,175	2,609	3,014
100,000	110,000	730	1,601	2,375	2,848	3,290
110,000	120,000	812	1,780	2,641	3,167	3,659
120,000	130,000	893	1,960	2,907	3,486	4,027
130,000	140,000	975	2,139	3,173	3,805	4,395
140,000	150,000	1,057	2,318	3,439	4,125	4,763
150,000	160,000	1,139	2,498	3,704	4,444	5,131
160,000	170,000	1,221	2,677	3,971	4,762	5,500
170,000	180,000	1,302	2,857	4,236	5,082	5,868
180,000	190,000	1,384	3,036	4,053	5,400	6,237
190,000	200,000	1,466	3,215	4,769	5,719	6,605
200,000	210,000	1,548	3,394	5,035	6,039	6,973
210,000	220,000	1,630	3,574	5,300	6,358	7,341
220,000	230,000	1,712	3,753	5,567	6,676	7,710
230,000	240,000	1,793	3,932	5,833	6,996	8,078
240,000	250,000	1,875	4,112	6,099	7,314	8,446

REV. PROC. 98—30
Dollar Amounts for Automobiles (Other than Electric Automobiles) with a Lease Term Beginning in Calendar Year 1998

Fair Market Value of Automobile		Tax Year During Lease				
Over	Not Over	1st	2nd	3rd	4th	5th and Later
$ 15,800	$ 16,100	1	5	8	12	14
16,100	16,400	4	10	16	22	25
16,400	16,700	6	15	25	31	36
16,700	17,000	9	20	33	41	47
17,000	17,500	12	28	43	53	62
17,500	18,000	16	37	56	70	80
18,000	18,500	20	46	70	85	99
18,500	19,000	24	55	83	101	117
19,000	19,500	28	64	96	117	136
19,500	20,000	32	73	110	133	154
20,000	20,500	36	82	123	149	173
20,500	21,000	40	91	136	165	191
21,000	21,500	45	99	150	181	209
21,500	22,000	49	108	163	197	228
22,000	23,000	55	122	183	221	255
23,000	24,000	63	140	210	252	292
24,000	25,000	71	158	236	285	329
25,000	26,000	79	176	263	316	366
26,000	27,000	88	193	290	348	403
27,000	28,000	96	211	317	380	439
28,000	29,000	104	229	343	412	477
29,000	30,000	112	247	370	444	513
30,000	31,000	120	265	396	476	550
31,000	32,000	128	283	423	508	587
32,000	33,000	137	301	449	540	624
33,000	34,000	145	319	476	571	661
34,000	35,000	153	337	502	604	697
35,000	36,000	161	355	529	635	735
36,000	37,000	169	373	556	667	771
37,000	38,000	178	391	582	699	808

REV. PROC. 98—30
Dollar Amounts for Automobiles (Other than Electric Automobiles) with a Lease Term Beginning in Calendar Year 1998 *(continued)*

Fair Market Value of Automobile		Tax Year During Lease				
Over	Not Over	1st	2nd	3rd	4th	5th and Later
$ 38,000	$ 39,000	186	409	608	731	845
39,000	40,000	194	427	635	763	882
40,000	41,000	202	445	662	794	919
41,000	42,000	210	463	688	827	955
42,000	43,000	218	481	715	859	992
43,000	44,000	227	498	742	891	1,028
44,000	45,000	235	516	769	922	1,066
45,000	46,000	243	534	795	955	1,102
46,000	47,000	251	552	822	986	1,140
47,000	48,000	259	570	849	1,018	1,176
48,000	49,000	268	588	875	1,050	1,213
49,000	50,000	276	606	901	1,082	1,250
50,000	51,000	284	624	928	1,114	1,286
51,000	52,000	292	642	955	1,145	1,324
52,000	53,000	300	660	981	1,178	1,360
53,000	54,000	308	678	1,008	1,209	1,398
54,000	55,000	317	695	1,035	1,241	1,434
55,000	56,000	325	713	1,062	1,273	1,471
56,000	57,000	333	732	1,087	1,305	1,508
57,000	58,000	341	750	1,114	1,337	1,544
58,000	59,000	349	768	1,140	1,369	1,582
59,000	60,000	358	785	1,168	1,400	1,619
60,000	62,000	370	812	1,207	1,449	1,674
62,000	64,000	386	848	1,261	1,512	1,747
64,000	66,000	403	884	1,313	1,577	1,821
66,000	68,000	419	920	1,367	1,640	1,894
68,000	70,000	435	956	1,420	1,704	1,968
70,000	72,000	452	991	1,474	1,767	2,042
72,000	74,000	468	1,027	1,527	1,832	2,115
74,000	76,000	484	1,063	1,580	1,896	2,189
76,000	78,000	501	1,099	1,633	1,959	2,263

REV. PROC. 98—30
Dollar Amounts for Automobiles (Other than Electric Automobiles) with a Lease Term Beginning in Calendar Year 1998 *(continued)*

Fair Market Value of Automobile		Tax Year During Lease				
Over	Not Over	1st	2nd	3rd	4th	5th and Later
$ 78,000	$ 80,000	517	1,135	1,686	2,023	2,337
80,000	85,000	546	1,198	1,779	2,134	2,466
85,000	90,000	587	1,287	1,913	2,294	2,649
90,000	95,000	627	1,377	2,046	2,453	2,834
95,000	100,000	668	1,467	2,178	2,613	3,018
100,000	110,000	730	1,601	2,378	2,852	3,294
110,000	120,000	812	1,780	2,644	3,172	3,662
120,000	130,000	893	1,960	2,910	3,490	4,031
130,000	140,000	975	2,139	3,176	3,810	4,398
140,000	150,000	1,057	2,318	3,443	4,128	4,767
150,000	160,000	1,139	2,498	3,708	4,447	5,135
160,000	170,000	1,221	2,677	3,974	4,766	5,504
170,000	180,000	1,302	2,857	4,240	5,085	5,872
180,000	190,000	1,384	3,036	4,506	5,404	6,241
190,000	200,000	1,466	3,215	4,772	5,724	6,608
200,000	210,000	1,548	3,394	5,039	6,042	6,977
210,000	220,000	1,630	3,574	5,304	6,361	7,345
220,000	230,000	1,712	3,753	5,570	6,680	7,714
230,000	240,000	1,793	3,932	5,837	6,999	8,082
240,000	250,000	1,875	4,112	6,102	7,318	8,450

REV. PROC. 98—30
Dollar Amounts for Electric Automobiles)
with a Lease Term Beginning in Calendar Year 1998

Fair Market Value of Automobile		Tax Year During Lease				
Over	Not Over	1st	2nd	3rd	4th	5th and Later
$ 47,000	$ 48,000	5	11	18	21	23
48,000	49,000	13	29	45	52	60
49,000	50,000	21	47	71	85	96
50,000	51,000	29	65	98	116	134
51,000	52,000	38	83	124	148	171
52,000	53,000	46	101	151	180	207
53,000	54,000	54	119	177	212	244
54,000	55,000	62	137	204	244	281
55,000	56,000	70	155	231	275	318
56,000	57,000	79	172	258	307	355
57,000	58,000	87	190	284	340	391
58,000	59,000	95	208	311	372	428
59,000	60,000	103	226	338	403	465
60,000	62,000	115	253	378	451	520
62,000	64,000	132	289	430	515	594
64,000	66,000	148	325	484	578	668
66,000	68,000	164	361	537	643	741
68,000	70,000	181	396	591	706	815
70,000	72,000	197	432	644	770	888
72,000	74,000	214	468	697	834	962
74,000	76,000	230	504	750	898	1,035
76,000	78,000	246	540	803	962	1,109
78,000	80,000	263	576	856	1,025	1,183
80,000	85,000	291	639	949	1,137	1,312
85,000	90,000	332	728	1,803	1,296	1,496
90,000	95,000	373	818	1,215	1,456	1,681
95,000	100,000	414	908	1,348	1,615	1,865
100,000	110,000	475	1,042	1,548	1,855	1,141
110,000	120,000	557	1,221	1,814	2,174	2,509
120,000	130,000	639	1,401	2,080	2,492	2,878
130,000	140,000	721	1,580	2,346	2,812	3,245

Dollar Amounts for Electric Automobiles)
with a Lease Term Beginning in Calendar Year 1998 *(continued)*

Fair Market Value of Automobile		Tax Year During Lease				
Over	**Not Over**	**1st**	**2nd**	**3rd**	**4th**	**5th and Later**
$140,000	150,000	803	1,759	2,612	3,131	3,614
150,000	160,000	884	1,939	2,878	3,450	3,982
160,000	170,000	996	2,118	3,144	3,769	4,350
170,000	180,000	1,048	2,297	3,410	4,088	4,719
180,000	190,000	1,130	2,477	3,676	4,406	5,087
190,000	200,000	1,212	2,656	3,942	4,726	5,455
200,000	210,000	1,293	2,835	4,209	5,044	5,824
210,000	220,000	1,375	3,015	4,474	5,364	6,191
220,000	230,000	1,457	3,194	4,740	5,683	6,560
230,000	240,000	1,539	3,373	5,006	6,002	6,928
240,000	250,000	1,621	3,552	5,273	6,320	7,297

Rev. Proc. 99-14
Dollar Amounts for Automobiles (Other Than Electric Automobiles) with a Lease Term Beginning in Calendar Year 1999

Fair Market Value of Automobile		Tax Year During Lease				
Over	Not Over	1st	2nd	3rd	4th	5th and Later
$ 15,500	$ 15,800	2	3	4	4	6
15,800	16,100	4	7	10	13	14
16,100	16,400	6	11	17	20	23
16,400	16,700	8	15	23	28	32
16,700	17,000	10	20	29	35	41
17,000	17,500	13	25	38	45	53
17,500	18,000	16	32	48	58	68
18,000	18,500	19	39	59	71	82
18,500	19,000	22	47	69	83	96
19,000	19,500	26	53	80	96	111
19,500	20,000	29	61	90	108	126
20,000	20,500	32	68	101	121	140
20,500	21,000	35	75	111	134	155
21,000	21,500	39	82	122	146	169
21,500	22,000	42	89	132	160	183
22,000	23,000	47	100	148	178	206
23,000	24,000	53	114	169	204	235
24,000	23,000	60	128	190	229	264
25,000	26,000	66	142	212	254	293
26,000	27,000	73	156	233	279	322
27,000	28,000	79	171	253	305	351
28,000	29,000	85	185	275	330	380
29,000	30,000	92	199	296	355	410
30,000	31,000	98	214	316	381	439
31,000	32,000	105	227	338	406	468
32,300	33,000	111	242	359	431	497
33,000	34,000	118	256	380	456	527
34,000	35,000	124	270	402	481	556
35,000	36,000	131	284	423	506	585
36,000	37,000	137	299	443	532	614
37,000	38,000	144	313	464	557	643
38,000	39,000	150	327	486	582	672

Rev. Proc. 99-14
Dollar Amounts for Automobiles (Other Than Electric Automobiles) with a Lease Term Beginning in Calendar Year 1999 *(continued)*

Fair Market Value of Automobile		Tax Year During Lease				
Over	Not Over	1st	2nd	3rd	4th	5th and Later
$ 39,000	$ 40,000	157	341	507	607	702
40,000	41,000	163	355	528	633	731
41,000	42,000	170	369	549	658	760
42,000	43,000	176	384	570	683	789
43,000	44,000	183	398	591	708	819
44,000	45,000	189	412	612	734	848
45,000	46,000	196	426	633	759	877
46,000	47,000	202	441	654	784	906
47,000	48,000	208	455	675	810	935
48,000	49,000	215	469	696	835	964
49,000	50,000	221	483	718	860	993
50,000	51,000	228	497	739	885	1,023
51,000	52,000	234	512	759	911	1,052
52,000	53,000	241	526	780	936	1,081
53,000	54,000	247	540	802	961	1,110
54,000	55,000	254	554	823	986	1,140
55,000	56,000	260	569	843	1,012	1,169
56,000	57,000	267	582	865	1,037	1,198
57,000	58,000	273	597	886	1,062	1,227
58,000	59,000	280	611	907	1,087	1,256
59,000	60,000	286	625	928	1,113	1,285
60,000	62,000	296	646	960	1,151	1,329
62,000	64,000	309	675	1,002	1,201	1,387
64,000	66,000	322	703	1,044	1,252	1,446
66,000	68,000	335	732	1,086	1,302	1,504
68,000	70,000	348	760	1,128	1,353	1,563
70,000	72,000	361	788	1,171	1,403	1,621
72,000	74,000	374	817	1,212	1,454	1,679
74,000	76,000	387	845	1,225	1,504	1,738
76,000	78,000	399	874	1,297	1,555	1,796
78,000	80,000	412	902	1,339	1,606	1,854

Rev. Proc. 99-14
Dollar Amounts for Automobiles (Other Than Electric Automobiles) with a Lease Term Beginning in Calendar Year 1999 *(continued)*

Fair Market Value of Automobile		Tax Year During Lease				
Over	Not Over	1st	2nd	3rd	4th	5th and Later
$ 80,000	$ 85,000	435	952	1,413	1,694	1,956
85,000	90,000	467	1,023	1,518	1,821	2,102
90,000	95,000	500	1,094	1,623	1,947	2,248
95,000	100,000	532	1,165	1,729	2,073	2,394
100,000	110,000	581	1,271	1,887	2,263	2,612
110,000	120,000	645	1,414	2,097	9,516	2,904
120,000	130,000	710	1,556	2,308	2,768	3,196
130,000	140,000	775	1,697	2,519	3,021	3,488
140,000	150,000	840	1,839	2,730	3,274	3,779
150,000	160,000	904	1,982	2,940	3,526	4,072
160,000	170,000	969	2,124	3,151	3,779	4,363
170,000	180,000	1,034	2,265	3,362	4,032	4,655
180,000	190,000	1,099	2,407	3,573	4,284	4,947
190,000	200,000	1,163	2,550	3,783	4,537	5,238
200,000	210,000	1,228	2,692	3,994	4,789	5,530
210,000	220,000	1,293	2,833	4,205	5,043	5,822
220,000	230,000	1,358	2,975	4,416	5,295	6,114
230,000	240,000	1,422	3,118	4,626	5,548	6,405
240,000	250,000	1,487	3,260	4,837	5,800	6,697

Rev. Proc. 99-14
Dollar Amounts for Electric Automobiles with a Lease Term Beginning in Calendar Year 1999

Fair Market Value of Automobile		Tax Year During Lease				
Over	Not Over	1st	2nd	3rd	4th	5th and Later
$ 47,000	$ 48,000	7	14	21	26	30
48,000	49,000	14	28	42	51	59
49,000	50,000	20	43	62	77	88
50,000	51,000	27	57	83	102	118
51,000	52,000	33	71	105	127	147
52,000	53,000	39	86	126	151	177
53,000	54,000	46	100	147	177	205
54,000	55,000	52	114	168	202	235
55,000	56,000	59	128	189	228	264
56,000	57,000	65	142	211	253	292
57,000	58,000	72	156	232	278	322
58,000	59,000	78	171	252	304	351
59,000	60,000	85	185	273	329	380
60,000	62,000	95	206	305	367	424
62,000	64,000	107	235	347	417	483
64,000	66,000	120	263	389	468	541
66,000	68,000	133	291	432	518	600
68,000	70,000	146	320	473	569	658
70,000	72,000	159	348	516	619	716
72,000	74,000	172	377	558	669	775
74,000	76,000	185	405	600	720	833
76,000	78,000	198	433	643	771	891
78,000	80,000	211	462	684	822	949
80,000	85,000	234	511	758	910	1,052
85,000	90,000	266	582	864	1,036	1,198
90,000	95,000	298	654	968	1,163	1,343
95,000	100,000	331	724	1,075	1,289	1,489
100,000	110,000	379	831	1,232	1,479	1,708
110,000	120,000	444	973	1,443	1,731	2,000
120,000	130,000	509	1,115	1,654	1,984	2,291
130,000	140,000	574	1,257	1,864	2,237	2,583

Rev. Proc. 99-14
Dollar Amounts for Electric Automobiles with a Lease Term Beginning in Calendar Year 1999 *(continued)*

Fair Market Value of Automobile		Tax Year During Lease				
Over	Not Over	1st	2nd	3rd	4th	5th and Later
$140,000	$150,000	638	1,399	2,075	2,490	2,875
150,000	160,000	703	1,541	2,286	2,742	3,167
160,000	170,000	768	1,683	2,497	2,994	3,459
170,000	180,000	833	1,825	2,707	3,248	3,750
180,000	190,000	897	1,967	2,918	3,500	4,042
190,000	200,000	962	2,109	3,129	3,753	4,333
200,000	210,000	1,027	2,251	3,340	4,005	4,625
210,000	220,000	1,092	2,393	3,550	4,258	4,917
220,000	230,000	1,156	2,535	3,761	4,511	5,209
230,000	240,000	1,221	2,677	3,972	4,763	5,501
240,000	250,000	1,286	2,819	4,183	5,016	5,792

Index